To Jo
Daniel

The first day of the rest of your lives as Okie's

Paul & Jane Daughtry
1-4-01

MW01620360

HISTORIC OKLAHOMA

An Illustrated History

by Paul F. Lambert, Kenny A. Franks & Bob Burke

Editor Gini Moore Campbell

Contributing writers Eric Dabney & Clyda Reeves Franks

Published for the Oklahoma Heritage Association

Oklahoma Horizons Series

Historical Publishing Network
A division of Lammert Publications, Inc.
San Antonio, Texas

The Oklahoma Hall of Fame Galleries feature the portraits, busts, and biographies of its members. The galleries are located on the third floor of the Oklahoma Heritage Center in Oklahoma City.

COURTESY JUDY DAWSON.

First Edition

Copyright © 2000 Historical Publishing Network

All rights reserved. No part of this book may be reproduced in any form or by any means, electronic or mechanical, including photocopying, without permission in writing from the publisher. All inquiries should be addressed to Historical Publishing Network, 8491 Leslie Road, San Antonio, Texas, 78254. Phone (210) 688-9008.

ISBN: 1-893619-04-4

Library of Congress Card Catalog Number: 99 80130

Historic Oklahoma: An Illustrated History

authors:	Paul F. Lambert
	Kenny A. Franks
	Bob Burke
editor:	Gini Moore Campbell
cover artist:	Charles Banks Wilson
cover photography:	David Fitzgerald
	Fred Marvel
contributing writers for "sharing the heritage":	Eric Dabney
	Clyda Reeves Franks

Historical Publishing Network

president:	Ron Lammert
vice president:	Barry Black
project managers:	Lou Ann Murphy
	Lindell Bridges
director of operations:	Charles A. Newton, III
administration:	Angela Lake
	Donna Mata
	Dee Steidle
graphic production:	Colin Hart
	John Barr

CONTENTS

Foreword

If you want to better understand what it means to be an American, read the history of Oklahoma. In many ways, it provides a unique insight into the essence of the American Spirit and the ways in which our nation's founding principles were put into action. It is about Indians and cowboys, pioneer women, religious revivalism, populism, rugged industrialism, and a strong bond of community. Oklahoma history is like a rich tapestry, which includes threads from the histories of both western and eastern Indian tribes who came to live together after the forced migration of the eastern tribes in the 19th century. Other threads include those of the westward movement of the pioneers, cowboys, farmers, merchants, and professionals, circuit riding preachers and teachers and, later, wildcatters who participated in one of the greatest oil booms in American history. Still others were woven by African Americans who struck out for "The Territory" as they called it, to establish all black towns where they could control their own destiny. Their story has been chronicled by the great Oklahoma born novelist, Ralph Ellison. Jews from Russia and Eastern Europe, Lebanese from the same town in Lebanon coming as peddlers with their goods on their backs, Asians and Hispanics and many others would follow.

For all of them what would become the State of Oklahoma, represented opportunity and a chance to live out their dreams. For Native Americans, it was a chance to preserve their heritage and values. For newcomers, it was a chance for a fresh start in a place where there were unlimited possibilities.

Howard Lamar, one of the most respected historians of the American West, has described the great land runs, which opened parts of Oklahoma to permanent settlement, as uniquely American. He pointed out that the men and women who participated in the run were conscious of the fact that they were making history. In other parts of the world, the great figures in history were kings and queens, emperors, generals, and chiefs. But, in Oklahoma, rank and file citizens made history. They knew that they were not only staking out land for themselves, but, in addition, they were building a new state, new communities, and important institutions like churches, synagogues, schools, and colleges.

From the beginning, there was little social stratification. Family genealogy did not matter. What mattered was character, ability, and hard work. Schools were built early and there was an understanding that equal opportunity could not exist without equal access to education. It is not surprising that those who came seeking opportunity would be committed to providing it for those who would follow them.

While there was a strong current of rugged individualism in Oklahoma's history, there was also a strong sense of community. The spirit of community had always been strong among Native American nations and tribes. It also grew among pioneers who realized that they had to help each other in adversity if any of them were to survive and prosper. That spirit of volunteerism and the ethic of helping a neighbor in need remained strong as the 20th century came to a close. Through coverage by the national news media, the entire nation was inspired by the help fellow Oklahomans gave to the victims of the terrorist bombing of the Murrah Federal Building in Oklahoma City and to the victims of devastating tornadoes which struck the state in the last year of the century. It was often said that the spirit of America was alive and well in Oklahoma. National television commentators began to refer to Oklahoma as "the heartland."

If there is one thread that ties Oklahoma's history together it is a shared sense of possibility. Students of comparative history have often commented that the creativity and vitality of a nation rests upon the belief of its people that each succeeding generation will achieve even more than those who have come before.

There is a story told about David Ross Boyd, the first president of the University of Oklahoma. He accepted the position by mail. He had never been to Oklahoma. When he arrived on the train in Norman, early in the 1890s, he found a small dusty town of 600, no campus, and only a handful of students studying in a small rock building on the unpaved main street. He was taken by a community leader to an open stretch of prairie with hard clay soil and not a single tree for miles. He was told that we would build the campus of the university at that barren location. Undiscouraged and undaunted, he is said to have exclaimed, "What possibilities!" Perhaps that is the phrase that should have been placed on the state seal though "work conquers all," which was selected, in many ways expresses the same thought.

Oklahoma is young enough that many of the state's current leaders either personally knew those who now loom large in the state's history, or they knew those who could speak of them from first hand experience. As Oklahomans begin a new century and a new millennium, their reaction remains "What possibilities!" Hopefully, the study and understanding of this rich and fascinating history will help keep that spirit alive for years to come.

David L. Boren, President
University of Oklahoma

David L. Boren is president of The University of Oklahoma. He served previously as Governor of Oklahoma and United States Senator from Oklahoma.

PREFACE & ACKNOWLEDGMENTS

The purpose of this book was to provide the citizens of Oklahoma an overview of the unique history and heritage of the Sooner State by examining Oklahoma's geography, Native American background, formation, settlement, politics, cultural and ethnic identity, and role in national politics from pre-history to present. It is not a definitive history, for limitations of space precludes detailed investigation of many facets of state history. Nonetheless, we hope to provide insights into what made Oklahoma what it is today, the contribution of individuals and institutions to the ethnic diversity of the state, and to capture the essence and spirit of our heritage.

Without the encouragement of the board of directors of the Oklahoma Heritage Association, the Association's chairman of the board, Lee Allan Smith, the Publications Committee, the Committee on the Teaching of Oklahoma History, and Ron Lammert, of Historical Publishing Network, and his staff this work would not have been possible.

A multitude of individuals cooperated in making *Historic Oklahoma* a reality. Chief among them were Clyda Reeves Franks, Eric Dabney, and Gini Moore Campbell. Both Clyda and Eric spent many hours researching and writing the numerous business profiles contained in the book. All of these businesses contributed to the growth and development of the state and the telling of their stories is a fundamental part of Oklahoma's history. In addition, Gini spent untold hours editing, organizing, proofreading, indexing, gathering illustrations, and performing the countless other tasks that go into completing a book of this magnitude.

Among those individuals and organizations which provided the numerous illustrations for the book are John Lovett, Western History Collections, University of Oklahoma Libraries, Norman; Fred Marvel, Oklahoma Department of Tourism and Recreation in Oklahoma City; Richard Welch, executive director, Deborah Baroff and Brian L. Smith of the Museum of the Great Plains, Lawton; Stuart Howard, Air Space Museum, Oklahoma City; J. Brooks Joyner, director, and Ken Busby, assistant to the director, Gilcrease Museum, Tulsa; Minisa Crumbo Halsey, Mounds; Carol Campbell, Melissa Hayer, Mary Phillips, and Robin Davison, *The Daily Oklahoman*, Oklahoma City; Brummett Echohawk, Tulsa; Albert Harjo, Okemah; David Fitzgerald, Oklahoma City; Ken Townsend, executive director, National Cowboy Hall of Fame and Western Heritage Center, Oklahoma City; Anita Arnold, BLAC, Inc.; Everett and Jean Berry, Stillwater; Judy Dawson, Oklahoma City; Edgar E. Weston, Dewey; Royce Peterson, Edmond; Wayne Spears, Pawnee; Cindi Cartmell, Pawnee; OK Events, Oklahoma City; Cities Service Oil Company, Tulsa; Ardmore Public Library; the Bartlesville Public Library; and Cecilie Henning, *Cleveland American*, Cleveland.

One of the principal sources for Oklahoma history is the Oklahoma Department of Libraries under the direction of Robert Clark. Among its staff who helped make *Historic Oklahoma* possible are Adrienne Abrams, Steve Beleu, William Boone, Chris Bittle, Mike Cameron, Melecia Caruthers, Annette Coppenbarger, Karen Fite, Carol Guilliams, Mary Hardin, Marilyn Miller, Kitty Pittman, and Tanya Wiggins.

Blake Wade, the director of the Oklahoma Centennial Celebration, has worked for years to preserve the state's history, as has Bob L. Blackburn, the director of the Oklahoma Historical Society. Other members of the Historical Society who have helped are Connie Shoemaker, Fred Standley, Brian Basore, Mary Logsdon, Nancy Laub, Laura Martin, Kristina Southwell, Bill Welge, Phyllis Adams, Judith Michener, Scott Dowell, Delbert Amen, and Barbara Pierce.

Kathy Triebel, the corporate archivist for Phillips Petroleum Company, and her assistant, Kathy Leeper, also were invaluable in their help.

Finally, the authors wish to acknowledge the many Oklahoma historians and scholars who have labored over the decades to preserve the history of the Sooner State. Without their work, much of Oklahoma's heritage would have disappeared.

Kenny A. Franks
Paul F. Lambert
Bob Burke

CHAPTER I

CROSSROAD OF EMPIRES

Oklahoma is old. The sedimentary rocks of the state formed by the ancient seas that once covered the region date from one billion years ago. In the intervening eons the state's topography was altered by drastic upthrusts that formed the state's three major mountain systems—the Ouachitas, Arbuckles, and the Wichitas—and corresponding sinking that allowed shallow seas to cover the region and lay down thick layers of mud, sand, the remains of swamp plants, and calcium skeletons of sea animals that were buried, compressed, and cemented together to form deposits of shale, sandstone, limestone, and coal. The Wichitas, in southwest Oklahoma, and the Arbuckles, in the south-central portion of the state, date from the Pennsylvania Period, 320 million years ago, and are among the oldest mountains in the world. Once the size of the Alps, the forces of nature have reduced them to eroded stumps and exposed outcrops. Unlike the older mountains, the Ouachitas, which are a mountain chain that includes the San Bois, Winding Stair, Kiamichi, Jackfork, Rich Buffalo, and Blue Bouncer Mountains, are covered with thick vegetation. Four large basins, the Anadarko, Arkoma, Hollis, and Ardmore, border these mountains and were formed when the adjoining lands were thrust up.

Trilobites, sea urchins, sea lilies, clams, snails, oysters, squids, nautiloids, scallops and other sea animals thrived in the ancient seas between 600 million and 400 million years ago. Their fossils can be found throughout the state, along with fossilized coral reefs. Huge carboniferous ferns and palm-like trees lined the edges of the seas. Their fossilized remains can be seen in petrified logs in the Panhandle. When the last of the ancient seas that covered Oklahoma dried up about 270 million years ago, it left behind huge deposits of gypsum and salt that are known as the Gypsum Hills and the Great Salt Plains of northwestern Oklahoma.

About seventy million years ago, Oklahoma's topography stabilized, giving it a gentle northwest to southeast slope in which the land drops from 5,000 feet above sea level near Black Mesa in the Panhandle to 300 feet above sea level near Idabel in southeastern Oklahoma. Volcanic activity increased during this period, leaving behind deposits of ash. Black Mesa, the highest point in Oklahoma, is the eroded lava flow of an extinct volcano in southeastern Colorado.

About 220 million years ago, Oklahoma's climate became subtropical, and the state entered the Age of the Reptile. Large, palm-like trees topped with fern-like leaves and ornamental bark covered the landscape. Rich, moisture-filled soil supported lush carpets of ferns and primitive flowering plants, and hardwood forests appeared in the highlands. Volcanoes filled the skies with ash, which allowed less heat to escape the atmosphere, thereby warming the climate. Such an environment helped give rise to the dinosaurs.

Some of these prehistoric beasts were large and often slow-moving herbivores, feeding off the rich plant life. Others were carnivores who devoured other dinosaurs. The Oklahoma Panhandle is rich in dinosaur fossils and footprints. Among the fossilized remains found in Oklahoma are those of the Apatosaurus (deceptive lizard), Ceratosaurus (horned lizard), Camposaurus (bent lizard), stegosaurus (plated lizard), Acrocantosaurus (high-spined lizard), and Tenontosaurus (tendon lizard). These creatures ranged in size from that of a turkey to a weight of three tons.

Some seventy million years ago the dinosaurs began to disappear to be replaced by mammals such as ancient horses, primitive buffaloes, armadillos, llamas, camels, hyenas, sabre-tooth tigers, tapirs, and mastodons. The bones of these and other prehistoric mammals have been unearthed throughout Oklahoma. Although the state avoided the ice sheets of the Ice Age, losses formed by the glaciers farther north drifted over Oklahoma as wind-blown silt.

Along with the ancient mammals came prehistoric humans known as the Clovis Mammoth Hunters who followed the animals into the state in search of food. The Mammoth Hunters killed with shafts tipped with distinctive fluted projectile points, called Clovis Points, that were left behind along waterways as far east as Tulsa County. One of their kills, a 17,000+ year old

When the last of the prehistoric shallow seas that once covered Oklahoma dried up, huge deposits of gypsum remained. As these eroded, they formed the large mesas of the Glass Mountains, which are a part of the Blaine Escarpment of gypsum extending across west-central and northwest Oklahoma.

COURTESY DAVID FITZGERALD.

Columbian Mammoth, was unearthed near Cooperton in Kiowa County. Another group of wandering hunters were called Folsom Bison Hunters.

These early hunters were followed by others known as the Ozark Bluff Dwellers in eastern Oklahoma and the Basket Makers in the western parts of the state. Flourishing between 9,500 and 2,000 years ago, they hunted with throw sticks and cane-shafted darts, tipped with flint points; utilized flint knives, scrapers, hammers, and choppers; and practiced rudimentary agriculture. Surplus food was stored in bark or fabric containers lined with pitch. The Ozark Top Layer Culture occupied ledges and caves in northeastern Oklahoma and hunted with bows and arrows and tended fields of corn. The Kenton Cave Dwellers were their counterpart in the caves of western Oklahoma and flourished between 300 and 1500 AD.

About 2,000 years ago, Oklahoma's primitive people abandoned their cave and ledge dwellings and began constructing more permanent structures. These people were called Mound Builders. They constructed huge mounds, some forty feet in height, which supported mud and wattle homes or served as religious shrines. Some were solid. Others were built over cedar frames and were hollow. The Mound Builders were farmers who cultivated corn, beans, squash, pumpkins, and sunflowers, and developed a complex society of workers, craftsmen, priests, and warriors.

Above: An enduring place of beauty, Turner Falls is located in the Arbuckle Mountains. Formed more than 320 million years ago, the Arbuckles are among the oldest mountains in North America and cover almost 1,000 square miles in south-central Oklahoma. Only the eroded stumps, cut by numerous streams, remain of the mountain range that once rivaled the Alps of Europe.

COURTESY OKLAHOMA DEPARTMENT OF TOURISM AND RECREATION; PHOTOGRAPH BY FRED MARVEL.

Right: The highest point in the Wichita Mountains, Mount Scott dominates the topography for miles around. The large granite boulders are strewn near the summit, from which one can see for miles in all directions.

COURTESY DAVID FITZGERALD.

✧

Left: The Talimena Scenic Drive from Talihina, in LeFlore County, through the Ouachita National Forest to Mena, Arkansas, passes through the heart of the Ouachita Mountain Chain, which greatly influenced settlement in southeastern Oklahoma. The ridge and valley topography of the Ouachitas greatly restricted travel in the region and created a number of isolated settlements in the area.

COURTESY OKLAHOMA DEPARTMENT OF TOURISM AND RECREATION; PHOTOGRAPH BY FRED MARVEL.

Below: Seventy million years ago Oklahoma's topography took on today's northwest to southeast slope from a height of 4,973 feet above sea level in the extreme northwestern Panhandle to 287 feet above sea level in southeastern Oklahoma. The cypress-lined shore of the Mountain Fork River near Beaver's Bend State Park, just north of Broken Bow, is one of the lowest points in the state.

COURTESY DAVID FITZGERALD.

In western Oklahoma, Slab House People dug pits, lined them with flat stones, emplaced a central post, and used rafters to support a reed and earth roof. They also were primitive agriculturists and had developed pottery. For weapons, they depended on the lance and bow and arrow.

Just before the arrival of non-Indians, these primitive societies disappeared and were replaced by the Caddo and Wichita confederations. The Caddoes lived in the southeastern part of the state along the Kiamichi River and supported themselves by hunting and tending patches of muskmelons, plums, cherries, white grapes, and mulberries. Salt also was gathered for trading with neighboring tribes. Upriver from the Caddo, along the Arkansas River, was the Wichita Confederation, which included the Taouaya, Tawakoni, Yscani, Waco, and Kichai. They also lived in permanent settlements and supported an economy based on hunting and farming.

The northern part of Oklahoma was claimed by the Osage, Quapaw, Kansa, and Ponca Indians, who supplemented their crops of corn and squash with spring and fall buffalo hunts on the Great Plains. This annual trek provided dried meat for the winter months and buffalo hides for clothing, shelter, and trade. On the plains of western Oklahoma were the Lipan Apaches, who had migrated into the region between 900 and 1200 AD. They were nomadic, warlike Plains Indians who followed the buffalo herds from the Arkansas River south to central Texas.

◇

Above: The Wedding Party is one of a number of unusual sandstone rock deposits found in Cimarron County. The only county in the United States bordered by four states—Colorado, Kansas, Texas, and New Mexico—the topography of the county is more akin to New Mexico and eastern Colorado than the remainder of the state. The Panhandle is the driest part of Oklahoma, receiving an annual rainfall of only 15.2 inches.

COURTESY OKLAHOMA DEPARTMENT OF TOURISM AND RECREATION; PHOTOGRAPH BY FRED MARVEL.

It was the quest for the Gran Quivira or the Seven Cities of Gold that brought the first non-Indians to Oklahoma. The story of seven Christian bishops that had fled the Moorish conquest of Spain had given rise to the myth of rich cities awaiting Spanish conquest. Fuel was added to the rumor by the wealth of the Aztec and Inca empires discovered in Mexico and South America. When Cabeza de Vaca reported hearing stories of wealthy cities in the American Southwest to Viceroy Antonio de Mendoza, an expedition under the command of Francisco Vásquez de Coronado was organized. Marching northward from Culiacán on April 22, 1540, Coronado traveled throughout Arizona and New Mexico and across the

Right: Dr. C. E. Decker, right, and Ralph Sneed of the University of Oklahoma's School of Geology are shown examining the tusk of an imperator elephant discovered in Cleveland County in 1936. Two tusks, approximately ten feet long, as well as other bones, were found at this site. Oklahoma proved to be one of the most prolific sites of prehistoric fossils during the early twentieth century. The imperator elephant roamed the region during the Great Ice Age.

COURTESY *THE DAILY OKLAHOMAN*.

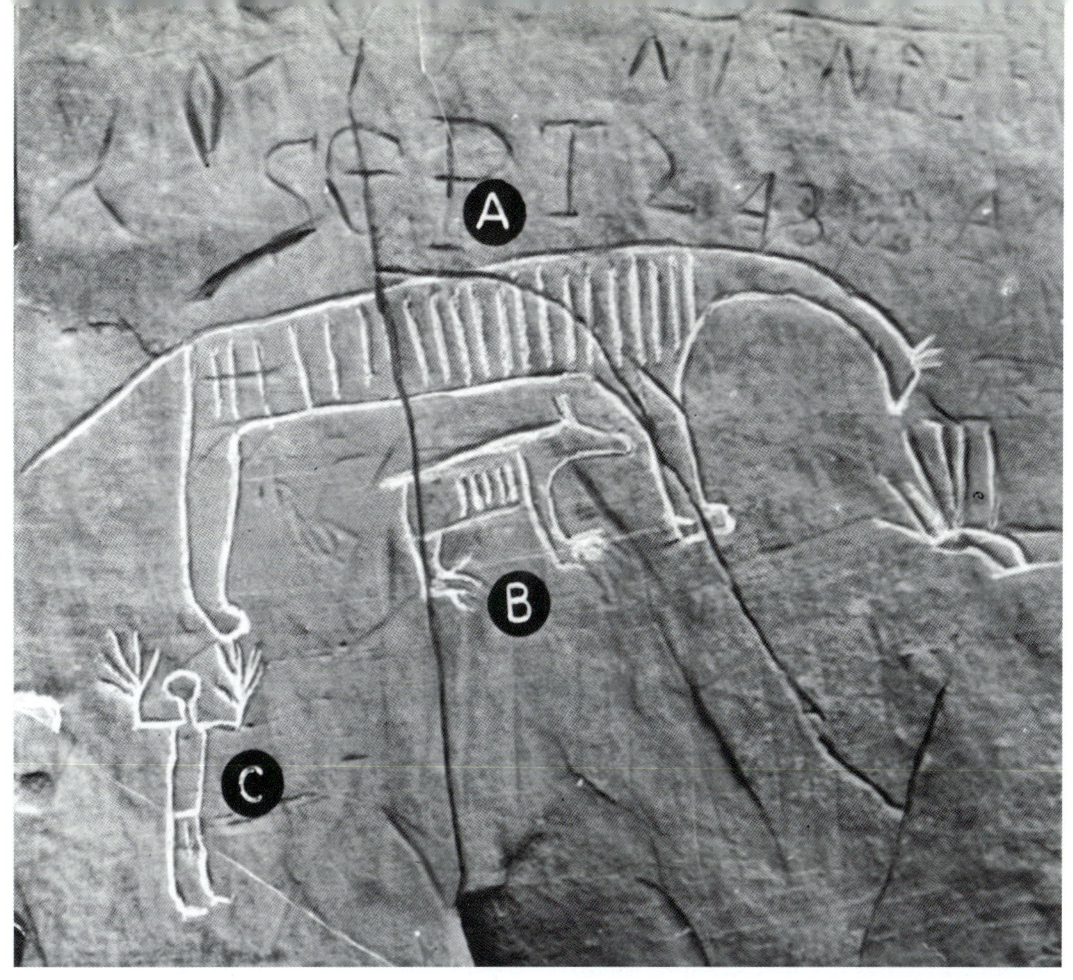

✧

Left: Among the several groups of peoples in prehistoric Oklahoma were the Slab House People, who occupied the Oklahoma Panhandle and left carvings such as these near the banks of Beaver Creek in Beaver County.

COURTESY THE DAILY OKLAHOMAN.

Below, left: The Kenton Cave Dwellers flourished in a series of caves in northwestern Cimarron County between 300 and 1500 AD. These caves were first examined in 1929. On May 13, 1933, archaeologists were astounded to find the naturally mummified remains of a two- to three-year-old male in one of the caves.

COURTESY THE DAILY OKLAHOMAN.

Below, right: Black Mesa in Cimarron County in the Panhandle, the highest point in Oklahoma, was formed by an ancient volcano flow from southeastern Colorado. Volcanoes dominated Oklahoma about seventy million years ago. Okfuskee County in east-central Oklahoma contains several deposits of volcanic dust from these eruptions.

COURTESY DAVID FITZGERALD.

panhandles of Texas and Oklahoma searching for the Seven Cities of Gold before ending his quest at a poor Wichita Indian village north of present-day Ford, Kansas. Having failed to find any riches, Coronado returned to Mexico; however, Fray Juan de Padilla, a Franciscan priest, and two Mexican Indians, Lucas and Sebastian who were lay brothers, asked to remain to Christianize the local Indians. Coronado granted Padilla's request

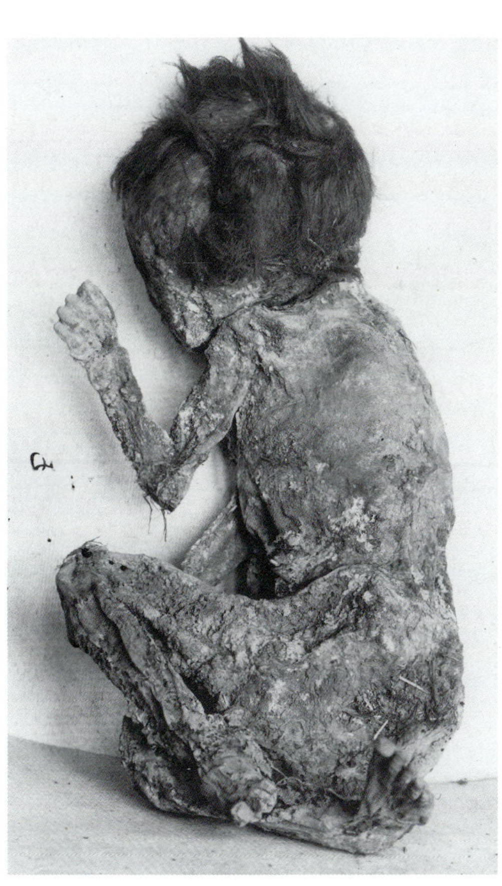

✧

Right: Visitors pause before Craig Mound in the Spiro Mound complex of the Mound Builder Culture. The Mound Builders, who occupied eastern Oklahoma, constructed huge mounds both as religious shrines and to support mud and wattle homes above the flood waters of nearby rivers. Some were solid. Others were built over cedar frames and were hollow.

COURTESY *THE DAILY OKLAHOMAN.*

Below: The Mound Builders position along the Arkansas River between the Ouachita Mountains to the south and the Ozark Plateau to the north allowed them to control prehistoric trade between the southeastern tribes and the Great Plains Indians. The Mound Builders maintained a complex society and high forms of art. This disk from LeFlore County was made by cutting incisions and then filling them with red oxide of iron to give them color.

COURTESY *THE DAILY OKLAHOMAN.*

and left a soldier, Andrés de Campo, to protect the missionaries.

The missionaries and the soldier spent the summer of 1542 ministering to the Wichita with little success. Hearing of another tribe to the east, the Kansa, Fray Padilla, Campo,

Lucas, and Sebastian set out for their village. On the way they were ambushed. Fray Padilla was killed, and the others were made slaves by the Kansa. It was almost a year before Campo, Lucas, and Sebastian escaped and marched south across central Oklahoma. In 1548, almost five years after they escaped, they reached the safety of Spanish settlements in Mexico.

At the same time that Coronado entered Oklahoma from the west, another Spanish conquistador, Hernando de Soto, was spending the winter of 1541-1542 near the junction of the Arkansas and Canadian Rivers in eastern Oklahoma. As governor of Florida, de Soto led a 622-man Spanish army ashore at Tampa Bay, Florida, on May 30, 1539, in search of riches. Instead of finding gold or silver, his expedition spent the next two years wandering throughout much of Florida, Georgia, North and South Carolina, Tennessee, and Alabama before crossing the Mississippi River and Arkansas into present-day Oklahoma. Camping at the junction of the Arkansas and Canadian Rivers, de Soto ordered an impregnable stockade built while his men explored the area.

Unable to find the anticipated riches and facing the inhospitable Great Plains, de Soto abandoned his quest and turned back

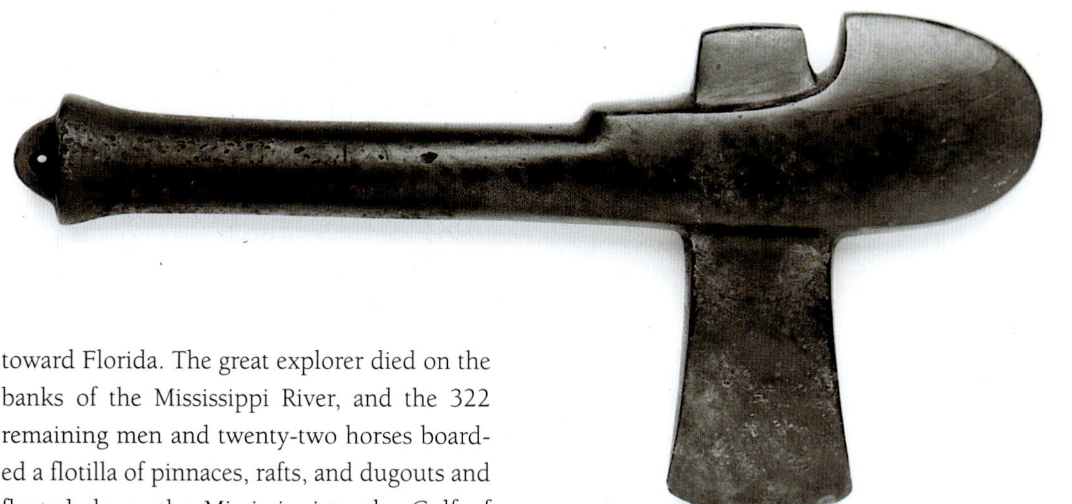

toward Florida. The great explorer died on the banks of the Mississippi River, and the 322 remaining men and twenty-two horses boarded a flotilla of pinnaces, rafts, and dugouts and floated down the Mississippi to the Gulf of Mexico and Spanish settlements, which they reached on September 10, 1543. Like Coronado, they had found nothing of substantial value in the hinterland of North America. Subsequent expeditions led by Francisco Leyva de Bonilla and Antonio Gutiérrez de Humana also failed in the search for riches.

Because of the failures of Coronado, de Soto, and other explorers it was not until 1601 that the Spanish returned to Oklahoma. In that year, Juan de Oñate led a party from New Mexico, across the Pecos River, and along the Canadian River to the Antelope Hills in western Oklahoma. Like the others, he found little of value. With the exception of Spanish miners who penetrated the Wichita Mountains in search of gold, the Spanish exploration of Oklahoma was over. They left little record of their passing except the remains of their primitive mines which can still be seen in the vastness of the Wichitas today.

Replacing the Spanish were the French *coureurs du bois*, or runners of the woods, who used the inland waterways to gain access to the rich fur territory of Oklahoma. As early as 1719, Claude de Tisne ascended the Mississippi River to the Osage lands along the Missouri River and then turned southwest into Oklahoma, where he visited the Wichita villages along the Arkansas River near present-day Newkirk. That same year Bernard de la Harpe moved upstream from New Orleans, Louisiana, to the Indian villages along the Canadian River in eastern Oklahoma and from there to the Wichita village on the Arkansas River near Haskell in present-day Muskogee County. One of his men, Sieur de Rivage, was sent west to the Wichita, Apache, and Comanche villages along the Red River. In 1725, Etienne Venieard Sieur du Bourgmont allied the French with the Comanches in western Oklahoma against the Spanish and their allies,

✧

Above, left: A stone-edge axe from the Mound Builder era in Oklahoma. Note the hole at the base of the handle, which allowed its owner to carry it by a leather thong.

COURTESY GILCREASE MUSEUM.

Below: Shell gorget from Spiro Mound culture dating from about 1400. Carved from a seashell, the gorget was suspended from the neck by a leather thong that passed through the two holes in its top.

COURTESY GILCREASE MUSEUM.

✧

Francisco Vásquez de Coronado led one of the first Spanish expeditions of conquistadors through Oklahoma, marching across the Panhandle in the summer of 1541. Shown in the background of this Charles Banks Wilson mural, on display in the State Capitol, are the grass huts of the Wichita and Caddo tribes that occupied much of the state at that time. Also in the background is a representative of the French coureurs du bois, *or runners of the woods, as the early French fur traders were called.*

COURTESY OKLAHOMA DEPARTMENT OF TOURISM AND RECREATION; PHOTOGRAPH BY FRED MARVEL.

the Apaches. Fernandina, near present-day Newkirk, became the principal French trading post in Oklahoma.

Hoping to open trading relations with the Spanish Southwest, de la Harpe visited Santa Fe in 1724. Seventeen years later, in 1741, Fabry de la Bruyere was dispatched to map an overland route from Louisiana to Santa Fe. Bruyere ascended the Mississippi and Arkansas Rivers to the Canadian and then followed it west to near Calvin in Hughes County. Stopped by shallow water and sand bars, Bruyere built Fort Fabry, where the expedition spent the winter of 1741-1742.

As a result of the French penetration of the Spanish Southwest, Oklahoma became a battleground between the two imperial powers. Fort Fabry was never permanently occupied and Fernandina was destroyed by the Osage in 1757. At that time, the French and their Wichita and Comanche allies established two new trading posts along the Red River—San Bernardo in Jefferson County, Oklahoma, and, across the river, San Teodore in Montague County, Texas. In 1759, Colonel Diego Ortiz de Parilla was ordered to destroy these bastions of French dominance and end their trading with the Comanches. With a force of 380 soldiers and more than 100 Apache warriors, Parilla attacked San Teodore on October 7, 1759, in what became known as the Battle of Spanish Fort. Although Parilla was accompanied by artillery, he could not force his way into the split log stockade. As night fell his Apache allies stole his horses and abandoned the battle. Afterward Parilla was forced to withdraw, leaving his cannon behind.

With the Peace of Paris of 1763, France surrendered its claim to Louisiana to Spain. With Spain controlling both New Orleans and Santa Fe, Pedro Vial was ordered by Governor Domingo Cabello y Robles to open a trade route between Louisiana and New Mexico. In 1786, Vial and Cristobal de los Santos pioneered a road between San Antonio and Santa Fe. In 1788, Vial and Francisco Xavier Fragoso, three Indians, Captain Santiago Fernández, and three soldiers marched from Santa Fe to the Wichita Mountains in southwestern Oklahoma. While Captain Fernández and the troops returned to Santa Fe, Vial and Fragoso followed the Red River east to Natchitoches, Louisiana. In 1792, Vial pioneered a 1,185-mile route between Santa Fe and St. Louis.

Vial's route between Santa Fe and Natchitoches became known as the Great Spanish Road to the Red River, and for decades traders plodded along the trail in huge oversized carts on cottonwood wheels. The road

✧

Left: This detail from the Charles Banks Wilson mural portrays Juan de Padilla and Andrés de Campo, members of Coronado's expedition, and two lay Indian converts, Lucas and Sebastian, who remained among the Wichita and Kaw Indians in an effort to Christianize them. In the summer of 1543, the four, along with a dog, marched across central Oklahoma in an effort to return to Spanish Mexico. The dog managed to catch rabbits and other small animals to keep them from starving during the journey.

COURTESY OKLAHOMA DEPARTMENT OF TOURISM AND RECREATION; PHOTOGRAPH BY FRED MARVEL.

Right: George Catlin's 1836 painting Cler-Mont, Chief of the Osages. *Clermont was a friend of the early American explorers in Oklahoma and welcomed First Lieutenant James B. Wilkinson, the first official American representative to enter Oklahoma, to his village in the fall of 1806. Like most Osage, Clermont's ears had been pierced to support huge earrings that distended his ear lobes with their weight.*

COURTESY GILCREASE MUSEUM.

Below: A map of early Oklahoma.

followed the Canadian River from New Mexico to Oklahoma and then southeast to the Red River and along the waterway to Louisiana. It was the major east-west route through the area until the end of the Mexican War.

France regained Oklahoma in the Treaty of San Ildefonso in 1800 only to transfer it to the United States by the Louisiana Purchase in 1803. American authorities quickly dispatched a series of expeditions to the area. In April of 1804, Congress appropriated $3,000 for an expedition led by Sir William Dunbar and Dr. George Hunter. Blocked by Spanish troops from following the Red River westward, the two scientists spent four months exploring the Ouachita River Valley in southeastern Oklahoma and southwestern Arkansas.

They were followed by First Lieutenant James B. Wilkinson, a member of the Zebulon Pike expedition dispatched by his father, Brigadier General James Wilkinson, westward from St. Louis, Missouri, in July of 1806. When the younger Wilkinson became ill near Great Bend, Kansas, Pike ordered him and six men to descend the Arkansas River to the Mississippi and follow it upstream to St. Louis. Wilkinson started down the Arkansas on October 28, 1806, and took two weeks to reach present-day Wichita, Kansas. There the party paused for ten days to build canoes before resuming the journey. Plagued by sand bars and ice, they lost much of their supplies and were fortunate to meet an Osage who killed game for them. Learning of an Osage camp near present-day Ponca City, Oklahoma, Wilkinson decided to visit the camp, and in so

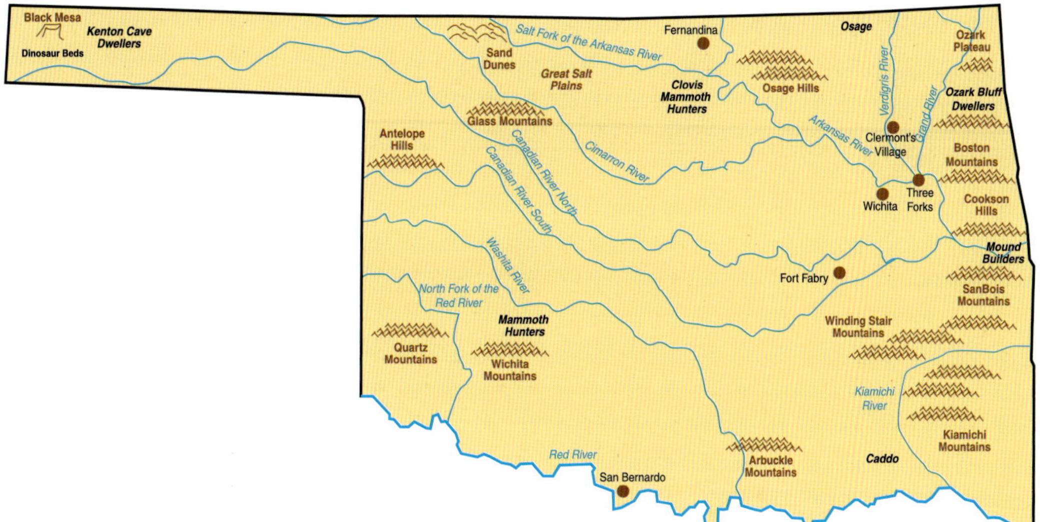

doing became the first official American representative to enter Oklahoma.

On December 1, Wilkinson's party resumed their trip down the Arkansas. Wilkinson paused at the site of Sand Springs and made a side journey up the Cimarron River and then continued down the Arkansas to the Verdigris. Here they traveled sixty miles up the Verdigris to Osage Chief Clermont's village, present-day Claremore, before returning to the Arkansas. On December 29, 1806, they were at the seven-foot tall Falls of the Arkansas at Webbers Falls, and on January 7, 1807, they arrived at Arkansas Post, where the Arkansas and Mississippi rivers join.

In 1806, Thomas Freeman, Richard Sparks, and Peter Custis pushed up the Red River to the Great Raft. Cutting their way through the seventy miles of waterlogged logs, they continued upstream until they were turned back by Spanish troops when they reached the Great Bend of the Red River. Five years later, in 1811, Major George C. Sibley led an overland expedition to the Great Salt Plains in northwestern Oklahoma. Impressed with the huge salt deposit, Sibley proposed that the government build a wagon road from the salt plains to the Arkansas River so the salt could be exploited for sale. In 1819, Thomas Nuttall, an English botanist, conducted a scientific examination of the Winding Stair Mountains and eastern Oklahoma while accompanying a military expedition commanded by Major William Bradford.

The information gained by government explorers was bolstered by a number of private trading expeditions. In 1807, James Bogy moved up the Arkansas River and opened a trading post on the banks of the Verdigris River, a short distance upstream from the Three Forks—the junction of the Arkansas, Grand, and Verdigris Rivers. Auguste and Pierre Chouteau followed the Osage into northeastern Oklahoma as early as 1802. Samuel Rutherford, Hugh Glenn, Nathaniel

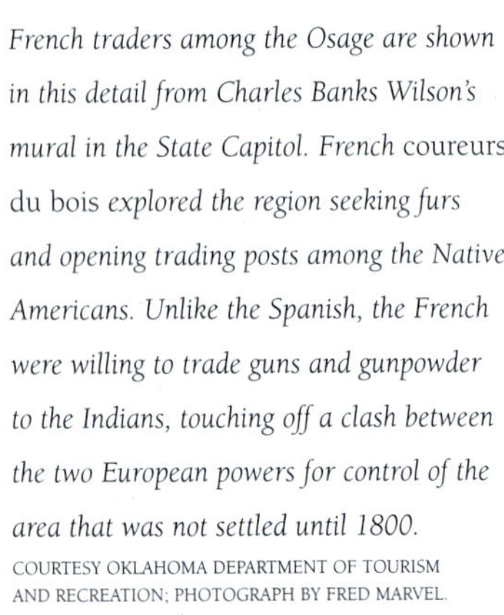

French traders among the Osage are shown in this detail from Charles Banks Wilson's mural in the State Capitol. French coureurs du bois *explored the region seeking furs and opening trading posts among the Native Americans. Unlike the Spanish, the French were willing to trade guns and gunpowder to the Indians, touching off a clash between the two European powers for control of the area that was not settled until 1800.*

COURTESY OKLAHOMA DEPARTMENT OF TOURISM AND RECREATION; PHOTOGRAPH BY FRED MARVEL.

Pryor, and Jacob Fowler also penetrated northeastern Oklahoma seeking to trade with the Indians. Lured by rumors of gold in the Wichita Mountains, William C. Alexander, Joseph Lucas, Anthony Glass, John Manley, and others made their way up the Red River, seeking the old Spanish mines.

In 1819, the Adams-Onis Treaty specified the boundary between the Spanish Southwest and the United States as beginning three leagues out in the Gulf of Mexico, up the south or west bank of the Sabine River to the Thirty-second Parallel, north to the Red River, and along the south bank of the river to the 100th Meridian. The boundary then ran north to the Arkansas River, which it followed to its source. From there the boundary ran north to the Forty-second Parallel and then west along the parallel to the Pacific Ocean. Major Stephen H. Long and Captain J. R. Bell were sent in 1820 to mark the boundary.

After reaching the Rocky Mountains, Long and Bell separated. Bell and half the expedition were to follow the Arkansas River downstream and chart its course. Long was to do the same for the Red River. Long, however, mistook the Canadian River for the Red and surveyed the wrong river. Both commands suffered during the trip through Oklahoma, running short of water and food and plagued by the heat. When they submitted their report, they included a description by Edwin James, a botanist, who characterized the region as the Great American Desert, unfit for American settlement and "forever...the unmolested haunt of the native hunter, the bison, and the jackal."

Thus, by the close of the first quarter of the nineteenth century, Oklahoma, especially the western part of the state, had been labeled as uninhabitable. The treeless plains west of the Cross Timbers were incompatible with the settlement patterns of the Eastern frontier. There were no trees to build log cabins or split rail fences, the heat and dryness of the summer made it difficult to grow familiar crops, huge herds of buffalo roamed across the plains, and nomadic and warlike Indians disputed ownership of the region. Studying the reports of the early American explorers, government officials determined that such a region, undesirable to American settlers, would be an opportune place for the resettlement of the Eastern Indians.

✧

George Catlin's Comanche Indians Throwing the Lasso. *Catlin, who toured the western part of Oklahoma with the ill-fated Dragoon Expedition of 1834, discovered that the region was the domain of the Comanche. A part of the horse culture that dominated the Great Plains, the Comanche were dependent on the wild horses introduced onto the Great Plains by the early Spanish expeditions. The acquisition of the horse transformed the Comanche into a feared nomadic tribe that followed the migration of the buffalo herds across vast hunting grounds.*

COURTESY GILCREASE MUSEUM.

CHAPTER II

TRAILS OF TEARS

The concept of an Indian homeland in Oklahoma took root in 1803, when President Thomas Jefferson contemplated voluntary removal as a means to protect the Indians from non-Indian domination and as a method to satisfy the land hunger of frontiersmen. Although some tribes developed lifestyles and governments similar to their non-Indian neighbors, the desire for Indian land, and a tragic "clash of cultures" conspired to cause conflict. For example, Native American tradition did not provide for individual ownership of land; instead, land belonged to all members of the tribe. Any tribal member could make productive use of as much land as he was capable, but could not dispose of the land because its ownership rested in the tribe. However, individual ownership of land was the norm in Anglo-American society. Once a frontiersman acquired ownership of land, it was his to do with as he wished. It was this concept that made the transfer of land between Indians and non-Indians so difficult.

The War of 1812 stimulated demand for Indian removal. Those tribes that followed Tecumseh in his frontier uprising gave the Americans the excuse needed to demand withdrawal of most of the tribes from the Old Northwest to a country "beyond the Mississippi River." In 1825, Congress withdrew a strip of land west of Missouri and Arkansas between the Platte and Red Rivers and westward to the 100th Meridian and named it Indian Territory. This was to be a new homeland for the Eastern tribes. Many were resettled in what became Kansas. Others fled to Texas. Eventually these tribes were concentrated in Oklahoma when Texas expelled its tribes in 1859 and Kansas did likewise in 1867.

In the South, the Five Tribes—the Choctaws, Chickasaws, Creeks, Seminoles, and Cherokees—had seen their ancient homelands eroded by non-Indian encroachment. Governed by a mixed-blood elite, the Choctaws, Chickasaws, and Cherokees established tribal governments based on the American model, accepted Christian missionaries among their people, and incorporated other elements of Anglo-American culture into their societies in an effort to co-exist with their non-Indian neighbors. For example, aided by the creation of the *Cherokee Syllabary* by Sequoyah, the Cherokees printed the *Laws of the Cherokee Nation* in 1821, and in 1828 began publication of a tribal newspaper, the *Cherokee Phoenix*. Southern politicians, however, were more influenced by local voters, who wanted the Indians removed and the land opened to settlement.

The Choctaws were the first to accept removal to Oklahoma under the provisions of the Treaty of Doak's Stand in 1820. However, this agreement gave the Choctaws land that partially was in Arkansas and claimed by non-Indians. Consequently, a new treaty was negotiated in 1825 which placed the Choctaws west of Arkansas if the tribe found the region suitable. For five years tribal leaders and federal officials quibbled over actual removal; however, the passage of the Indian Removal Act of 1830 and the extension of the laws of the State of Mississippi over the Choctaw Nation persuaded tribal leaders to sign the Treaty of Dancing Rabbit Creek in 1830 and start the migration westward. Choctaw removal was completed by 1833 and the tribe reestablished in their new homeland.

The Muscogee, or Creeks, were divided into the Upper, or conservative, faction of full-bloods and Lower, or progressive, faction of mixed-bloods and lived mainly in Georgia, Mississippi, and Alabama. Determined to push the Creeks out, the Americans negotiated a series of land cessions until 1805, when a Creek Blood Law was passed punishing by death additional sales of land. During the War of 1812, the Red Stick faction of the Creeks joined Tecumseh, and the resulting Creek War of 1812-1813 led to their defeat at the Battle of Horseshoe Bend. Although most of the Creeks had sided with the Americans and had helped defeat the Red Sticks, the Treaty of Fort Jackson in 1814 forced the tribe to surrender most of its lands in Alabama and southern Georgia. In 1825, the Lower Creeks, led by William McIntosh, signed the Treaty of Indian Springs, ceding even more territory and agreeing to remove to Indian Territory. Although McIntosh was executed according to the Creek Blood Law, many of his followers moved west to the region around Fort

Renowned Oklahoma artist Charles Banks Wilson's portrait of Sequoyah is displayed in the Oklahoma State Capitol.

COURTESY OKLAHOMA DEPARTMENT OF TOURISM AND RECREATION; PHOTOGRAPH BY FRED MARVEL.

✧

Right: Pushmataha, Apushamatahubib or Warrior's Seat *by Charles Bird King. Choctaw Chief Pushmataha raised Native American troops to serve with Andrew Jackson during the Red Stick uprising of 1813-1814, hoping to preserve the tribe's ancestral homeland. His efforts did not placate land-hungry Americans. In 1820, Pushmataha signed the Treaty of Doak's Stand, trading Choctaw land in Mississippi for a new homeland in the West.*

COURTESY EVERETT AND JEAN BERRY; PHOTOGRAPH BY JUDY DAWSON.

Below: George Catlin's portrait of Ha-tchoo-tuck-nee or the Snapping Turtle, *better known as Peter Pitchlynn. He led the 1828 Choctaw expedition into southeastern Oklahoma to examine the tribe's proposed new homeland. Although he reported that the area was unsuitable, federal officials insisted on compliance with the removal treaties. By 1833 most of the Choctaw were resettled.*

COURTESY GILCREASE MUSEUM.

Gibson; however, the full-blood faction refused to leave their ancient homeland.

In 1832, the leaders of the Upper Creeks signed the Creek Treaty of 1832, which ceded all tribal lands east of the Mississippi River. Nonetheless, for three years most tribal members refused to emigrate. Non-Indian settlers swarmed over their lands in the East, igniting the Creek War of 1836-1840. The federal government dispatched troops commanded by Brigadier General Winfield Scott to remove those who refused to move westward. Scott entrapped more than 14,500 Creeks who then were herded west during the winter of 1836-1837. No count was made of those who died on the trip, but after their arrival in Oklahoma 3,500 Creeks died of exposure or disease.

In a series of acts between 1828 and 1830, Mississippi extended its laws over the Chickasaw Nation and abolished the tribe's government. Realizing that removal was inevitable, tribal leaders signed a series of agreements ceding the tribe's eastern lands for a new home in

Indian Territory if a suitable location could be agreed upon. For half a decade, government officials and tribal leaders debated over a new homeland, but could not agree. To solve the dilemma, in 1837, the Chickasaws accepted an area to be known as the Chickasaw District of the Choctaw Nation. Removal started in the fall of 1837, with most of the Chickasaws settling in the western part of the Choctaw Nation. The Choctaw-Chickasaw union proved unsatisfactory, and an independent Chickasaw Nation was established in 1855.

As early as 1785, Cherokees had started moving west. This faction of the tribe became known as the Old Settlers. In a long war with the Osage, the Old Settlers gained control over northeastern Oklahoma and established the Cherokee Nation, West. Those Cherokee remaining in the East were organized as the Cherokee Nation, East, and to counter demands to open their land to non-Indian settlers, established a tribal government along American lines, with executive, judicial, and legislative branches. However, the discovery of gold in the Cherokee Nation, East, prompted Georgia officials to extend state laws over tribal lands and to strip the Indians of any redress in state courts.

In response, Cherokee officials hired William Wirt as the tribe's attorney, and in a series of cases—the George Tassel case, and *Cherokee Nation vs. Georgia*, both in 1830, and *Worchester vs. Georgia*, in 1831—secured

✧

Located near Swink, in eastern Choctaw County four miles east of Fort Towson, the home of Choctaw Chief Thomas LeFlore still stands. It is one of the oldest houses in Oklahoma.

COURTESY DAVID FITZGERALD.

decisions from the United States Supreme Court prohibiting Georgia's actions. However, President Andrew Jackson refused to enforce the court's decision. Tribal members split over the question, with most full-bloods, led by Principal Chief John Ross, opposing removal, and a powerful mixed-blood minority, led by Major Ridge, John Ridge, Elias Boudinot, and Stand Watie, favoring removal. In 1835, the mixed-blood element signed the Treaty of New Echota, committing the entire tribe to accept a new homeland in Oklahoma. The Ridge-Watie-Boudinot faction quickly moved west and settled among the Old Settlers by 1837. However, Ross maintained that the Treaty of New Echota had not been signed by representatives of the majority of the tribe and refused to submit to its provisions.

✧

Right: Following their removal, the Choctaws established their national capital west of Tuskahoma at Nunih Waya, named after the tribe's sacred mound in Mississippi. In 1850 the Choctaw capital was moved to Doaksville, next to Fort Towson, and in 1858 to Boggy Depot in Atoka County. In 1861, the capital was established at Chahta Tamaha, Choctaw Town or Armstrong, just east of Bokchito. It remained there until 1883, when it was moved to Tuskahoma, until the abolition of tribal governments in 1906. Today the tribe's government is centered at Durant.

COURTESY DAVID FITZGERALD.

Below: Menawa by Charles Bird King. William McIntosh proposed the 1811 Creek Blood Law, which called for the death of any tribal member ceding tribal land but later signed the 1825 Treaty of Medicine Springs surrendering Creek lands in Georgia and Alabama. For their part in the negotiations, McIntosh, Etomme Tustunnuggee, and Samuel and Benjamin Hawkins, McIntosh's sons-in-law, were sentenced to death. Menawa was assigned the task of carrying out the sentence by the Creek National Council. Under his direction, a band of Creeks surrounded Lockchau Talofau—McIntosh's plantation on the Chattahoochee River—in the predawn of April 29, 1825. McIntosh and Tustunnuggee were in the house when Menawa ordered an outbuilding set on fire to illuminate the main building. As they rushed to the front door, Tustunnuggee was shot dead and McIntosh was wounded. Seeking shelter upstairs, McIntosh traded gunfire with the executioners until the main house was set afire and the flames drove him outside, where he was killed. Accounts of the execution are conflicting. One story maintains that his daughter was allowed to bury McIntosh. The other story maintains that his body was hacked into pieces and thrown into the nearby river. Menawa's men killed Sam Hawkins the next day. As a result of the killings McIntosh's faction of Creeks began moving west to Oklahoma in 1828.

COURTESY EVERETT AND JEAN BERRY; PHOTOGRAPH BY JUDY DAWSON

State officials ordered the Georgia Guard into the Cherokee Nation, East, on the pretense of maintaining order. Instead they joined those seizing Cherokee property and added to the confusion. Chaos ruled the region until President Martin Van Buren ordered General Winfield Scott and regular troops into the area to reestablish order in May of 1838. Scott established a series of camps into which the Cherokees were herded. Suffering terribly from disease and hunger, with families separated and little chance of being reunited, the Cherokees were forced along the infamous Trail of Tears during the winter of 1838-1839. Of the estimated 16,000 Cherokees rounded up by Scott, approximately 4,000 died during the movement westward.

The Seminoles, like the Creeks, forcefully resisted removal. Originally living along the coast of Georgia, they had been forced to relocate

Left: Vinson Lackey's painting of the Chickasaw Female Seminary *at Stonewall. Stonewall was the seat of Pontotoc County of the Chickasaw Nation. Other Chickasaw counties and their seats were: Pickens County and Oakland; Tishomingo County and Tishomingo; and Panola County and Rock Creek.*

COURTESY GILCREASE MUSEUM.

Below: William McIntosh *by Charles Bird King.*

COURTESY EVERETT AND JEAN BERRY; PHOTOGRAPH BY JUDY DAWSON.

along the Spanish-American border in the Florida panhandle because of the general disruption of tribes caused by English colonies on the East Coast. Runaway slaves fleeing their owners in the South found a ready refuge among the Seminoles and prompted Andrew Jackson to invade Spanish Florida in 1817 to end the problem. Often called the First Seminole War, this invasion prompted the Spanish to sell Florida to the United States in 1819, and, four years later, in 1823, the Seminoles signed the Treaty of Camp Moultrie, in which they accepted a new home in the Everglades.

Runaway slaves continued to be a problem, and the federal government decided to relocate the Seminoles to Oklahoma. In the Treaty of Payne's Landing in 1832, the Seminoles agreed to remove to the Creek Nation in the West if they found the new homeland agreeable and dispatched an exploring party westward to examine the area. At Fort Gibson, in 1832, the exploring party signed an agreement which they believed stated that they had rejected their proposed new homeland, but which actually indicated that they had looked and found it suitable for removal.

When the Seminoles learned of the duplicity, they rejected the agreement. Nonetheless, the federal government refused to negotiate a new agreement and told the Seminoles they were bound to remove westward. The result was the Great Seminole War of 1835-1842. The conflict was the longest, most costly Indian war in American history, covering seven years, costing between $30,000,000 and $40,000,000, and involving more than 40,000 troops to subdue between 1,500 and 1,800 Seminole warriors, led by Osceola, Wildcat, and Billy Bowlegs. A third Seminole war broke out in 1849, and it was not until 1858 that the last Seminoles were removed to Indian Territory.

Left: Trail of Tears *by prominent Creek artist Albert Harjo. Clinging to their ancient homeland in Georgia and Alabama the majority of Creeks opposed removal. Following the Creek War of 1836-1840, approximately 14,500 were herded west to their new home in Oklahoma by federal troops during the winter of 1836-1837. No one knows how many died on the Creek Trail of Tears, but 3,500 died of exposure or disease after arriving in their new homeland. The two factions of Creeks were reunited in 1839.*

COURTESY ALBERT HARJO.

Right: Major Ridge *by Charles Bird King. Originally known as The Ridge, Major Ridge was commissioned a Major and raised Cherokee troops to serve with Andrew Jackson during the Red Stick War of 1813-1814. Afterward he adopted his rank as his first name. Major Ridge and his son John Ridge, along with their cousins Elias Boudinot, originally called Buck Watie, and Stand Watie, were the leaders of the Ridge-Watie-Boudinot faction of Cherokees who opposed Cherokee Principal Chief John Ross. They signed the Treaty of New Echota in 1835, providing for the removal of the Cherokees to a new homeland in Oklahoma. Both of the Ridges and Boudinot were killed in 1839 for signing the treaty. Watie escaped and the Watie-Ross feud dominated tribal politics until the close of the Civil War.*

COURTESY EVERETT AND JEAN BERRY;
PHOTOGRAPH BY JUDY DAWSON.

Bottom: The division of land among the relocated Indian tribes between 1825 and 1855.

Many of the Seminoles originally settled in the Cherokee Nation. The Creek-Seminole Treaty of 1845, however, allowed the Seminoles to settle in the Creek Nation, either individually or collectively, and to enforce their own tribal laws. However, Seminoles wanted their own homeland and government and, in 1856, were separated from the Creeks, and a new Seminole Nation was established.

The separation of the Chickasaws from the Choctaws and the Seminoles from the Creeks helped those tribes adjust to their new homelands. However, the Creeks remained divided into the Upper and Lower elements, and it was not until 1839 that the tribe was reunited. Even so, the hatred generated over removal and the tribe's blood law continued to smolder. It burst into flames once again when the tribe split over the question of aligning with the Confederacy, and a tribal civil war erupted.

The Cherokees also continued to be divided after removal. In June of 1839, Major Ridge, John Ridge, and Elias Boudinot were executed for signing the Treaty of New Echota. Stand Watie also was to be killed, but managed to escape. The result was open warfare between the two factions that continued until the federal government threatened to divide the tribe into separate political units. This resulted in the Cherokee Treaty of 1846, which reunited the factions under the leadership of John Ross.

Left: John Ridge *by Charles Bird King.*

COURTESY EVERETT AND JEAN BERRY; PHOTOGRAPH BY JUDY DAWSON.

Right: Sequoyah's cabin near Sallisaw. Although best known as Sequoyah, the inventor of the Cherokee Alphabet, he often was called George Guess after his white father Nathaniel George Gist. The difference in spelling resulted from Charles Hicks spelling Gist phonetically as Guess when he taught Sequoyah how to write his name. Sequoyah never learned to read or write English, but as early as 1812 began thinking about reducing the Cherokee language to written form. By 1820 he had produced an eighty-six-letter Cherokee Syllabary, *which he called "Talking Leaves," and taught it to his six-year-old daughter, Ahsokah. Within a short time, its use had spread among the Cherokee Nation, East. In 1821 he took his innovation to the Cherokee Nation, West, and eventually settled in a log cabin near Sallisaw. Sequoyah died between 1843 and 1845 near San Fernando in Tamaulipas, Mexico, while searching for a missing band of Cherokee that he believed had migrated to the region prior to the American Revolution.*

COURTESY OKLAHOMA DEPARTMENT OF TOURISM AND RECREATION; PHOTOGRAPH BY FRED MARVEL.

The feud did not end, however. Both sides continued to bide their time, plotting revenge. The opportunity came with the American Civil War. Ross wanted to remain neutral, and Watie saw the opportunity to seize control of the tribe. Watie joined the Confederacy, raised troops for the South, and forced the tribe into the Cherokee-Confederate alliance. Although Ross reluctantly signed the alliance, he fled north shortly thereafter to wait out the war in Philadelphia, Pennsylvania, leaving Watie to be chosen principal chief.

A second round of Indian removals to Oklahoma took place in 1859 with the expulsion of the Caddoes, Anadarakoes, Keechis, Wacoes, Tawakonis, Tonkawas, Absentee Shawnee, some Delaware, and the Penateka Comanches from the Brazos Reservation in Texas. Some of these tribes willingly removed to the Leased District in southwestern Oklahoma. Others continued their warlike ways until they were defeated by Texas Rangers during a campaign in the Wichita Mountains in 1858. That same year regular troops commanded by Captain Earl Van Dorn established Camp Radziminski on Otter

Bottom: Tsa-la-gi or the Cherokee Heritage Center south of Tahlequah. This unique tribal undertaking recreates the ancient Cherokee way of life through a living village and an interpretive center. Seen here are traditional Cherokee dwellings as they appeared prior to the arrival of the Europeans.

COURTESY OKLAHOMA DEPARTMENT OF TOURISM AND RECREATION; PHOTOGRAPH BY FRED MARVEL.

Right: Traditional Seminole artist Fred Beaver's painting Seminoles Making Sofkey. *Sofkey is a traditional Seminole and Creek food staple made by pounding corn into corn meal and then boiling it. After cooling, the meal was dripped through wood ashes and then ground nuts, such as hickory, and bone marrow, were added to form the finished food product. The Seminoles were the last of the Five Tribes to be removed to Oklahoma, with the final band making the journey in 1858. The war fought over their removal was the longest and most costly Indian war in American history. Spread over seven years, the Great Seminole War involved 40,000 American troops and cost between $30 million and $40 million.*

COURTESY GILCREASE MUSEUM.

Bottom: Because of their close trading relations with the French, the Osage were exposed to early Catholic missionaries. A part of this cultural heritage is preserved in the stained glass Osage Window of Immaculate Conception Parish in Pawhuska. Paid for by Osage oil money, the window, which was installed in 1920, portrays the Osages' relationship with the early Catholic missionaries. Many of the figures pictured in the window were actual Osage tribal members. A special dispensation was necessary to allow the portrayal of living individuals in the window.

COURTESY DAVID FITZGERALD.

Creek in Tillman County and defeated the Comanches at the Battle of Rush Springs.

The concentration of Eastern Indians in Oklahoma prompted the federal government to construct a line of north-south military posts across Oklahoma. Prior to 1824, Fort Smith in Arkansas had been the center of military activity in Indian Territory; however, in April of that year Fort Gibson was established on the east side of Grand River, about three miles upstream from its junction with the Arkansas River. A month later, in May of 1824, Fort Towson was established in southeastern Oklahoma. Fort Gibson was garrisoned until 1890 and Fort Towson was deactivated in 1854.

As the Eastern Indians spread westward, another post was needed to separate them from the Plains Tribes. Fort Washita was established in Bryan County in April of 1842 and was occupied by Union troops until May of 1861, when it was seized by Confederate forces for the remainder of the Civil War. Farther west, Fort Arbuckle was located on the banks of Wild Horse Creek in Garvin County in June of 1852. It also was abandoned by Union troops and then seized by the Confederates in May of 1861. Several other less important posts also were built.

Service at the frontier posts was both boring and dangerous. Most of the troops' time was spent building a network of military roads. The first of these was between Fort Gibson and Fort Smith in 1825 and was the first real road ever built in the state. So many men died of disease at Fort Gibson that it became known as the "graveyard of the army." At the first Fort Wayne, a minor post located on the site of present Watts High School in Adair County, men lived in tents and crude log huts until the post was abandoned. Desertions were such a problem that two deserters were branded with a "D" on their thighs as a warning to others.

✧

Left: Osage Boarding School, Pawhuska by Vinson Lackey. Government boarding schools were established throughout Indian Territory to educate Native American youth. Unfortunately, these schools did much to destroy traditional Indian culture. Children entering such boarding schools were stripped of tribal identity, forced to wear uniforms, speak only English, and abandon their heritage.

COURTESY GILCREASE MUSEUM.

Below: A traditional Osage medicine house of the Native American Church near Big Heart in Osage County. The Native American Church has undergone a rebirth among Oklahoma tribes, helping to restore traditional Native American beliefs. Generally eight-sided and facing the east, the churches are the sites of tribal peyote ceremonies.

COURTESY OKLAHOMA HERITAGE ASSOCIATION.

In addition to the military roads, there were several well-known trails opened across Oklahoma prior to the Civil War. For many years the Great Spanish Road to the Red River, which was pioneered by Pedro Vial in 1788, ran from Santa Fe to western Oklahoma and then along the North Fork of the Red River and down the river to Natchitoches, Louisiana. There were two other Santa Fe Trails across Oklahoma. One, the Cimarron Cutoff, ran from Dodge City, Kansas, across the Oklahoma Panhandle to the Mora River crossing, where it rejoined the Mountain Route of the Santa Fe Trail southward to Santa Fe. The other was pioneered by Josiah Greg in 1839 and ran from Fort Smith to North Fork Town, Camp Mason, and on to the Antelope Hills, or Boundary Mounds, before crossing the Texas Panhandle and continuing on to Santa Fe. Greg popularized the route in his book *Commerce on the Prairie*. This route became known as the California Road, and was one of the major routes to the California gold fields following its marking in 1849 by Major Randolph B. Marcy.

The main north-south road in Oklahoma was the Texas Road, which later became the Shawnee Cattle Trail. It ran from southwestern Missouri through eastern Oklahoma along what today is US-69, to American settlements in Texas. In 1858, John Butterfield and his partners received a government contract to provide semi-weekly mail service between Fort Smith and California. Basically the Butterfield Overland Stage route through Oklahoma followed the Texas Road, and was developed by the Choctaws and Chickasaws as a turnpike, with individual contracts let to maintain it.

✧

The remains of the West Barracks of Fort Washita in Bryan County. The post was one of several constructed by federal authorities to separate the Five Tribes from the Plains Indians. Garrisoned by federal troops from 1843 until 1861, when it was occupied by the Confederacy, the post was abandoned following the Civil War. The site was selected by Zachary Taylor, who later became President of the United States. In addition to Taylor, the president of two other republics lived in Oklahoma. Sam Houston, President of the Republic of Texas, operated the Wigwam Neosho Trading Post, and Jefferson Davis, President of the Confederate States of America, served at Fort Gibson.

COURTESY THE DAILY OKLAHOMAN.

Statutory fees were established: fifty cents for each four-wheeled vehicle pulled by four horses; twenty-five cents for each four-wheeled vehicle pulled by two horses; ten cents for a man and horse; and one cent per head for livestock. It cost $1.50 to cross the Red River on B. F. Colbert's ferry.

River traffic also expanded. Many of the early traders used the state's rivers, hauling supplies by canoe or pirogues. Larger cargo was hauled on flatboats. Auguste P. Chouteau maintained a boatyard at his trading post at the Falls of the Verdigris, two miles northwest of Wigwam Neosho, where Sam Houston opened his trading post in 1830. The first keel boat in Oklahoma was used by Thomas James in an attempt to push up the Cimarron River in 1821. River traffic was revolutionized in 1820 when the steamboat *Comet* reached Fort Smith. Eight years later, in 1828, the steamboat *Facility* opened steamboat traffic on to Fort Gibson. Steamboating on the Red River was limited by the Great Raft. Between 1830 and 1838, under the direction of Captain Henry M. Shreve, workers removed the Great Raft and opened the river to navigation. Hundreds of steamboats operated on the Red River, and in 1843 Captain J. B. Earhart pushed his steamboat up the Washita River to Fort Washita.

Missionaries of various denominations followed the Eastern tribes to Indian Territory. As early as 1808, the American Board of Commissioners of Foreign Missions was formed at Andover Theological Seminary. Nine years later, in 1817, the United Foreign Mission Society was organized in New York City. Both were dedicated to missionary work among the Indians and were subsidized by the federal government. In 1821, the United Foreign Mission Society organized Union Mission among the Osages along the banks of the Verdigris River, and a branch mission,

called Hopewell, was established in 1823. The American Board of Commissioners formed Dwight Mission among the Cherokees in Arkansas in 1822 and moved with the Indians to a new site on Sallisaw Creek, just upstream from its junction with the Arkansas River in 1828, where it was known as New Dwight. A branch, Mulberry Mission, was organized near Stilwell in 1828. In 1829 it was renamed Fairfield Mission. In 1830 another mission, Forks of the Illinois, was established.

Other missionaries such as Cyrus Kingsbury, Cyrus Byington, Alfred Wright, and Loring S. Williams were active among the Choctaws. Wheelock Mission was established in 1832; Pine Ridge Mission in 1835; Greenfield Mission, also called Lukfata, or White Clay Mission, in 1837; Mountain Fork Mission in 1837; and Goodwater Mission in 1837. Four schools, the Chuahla Female Seminary, Iyahnobi Female Seminary, Kunsha Female Seminary, and Norwalk Boys School were operating in 1844. Much of the funding for these mission schools was provided by the Choctaw Nation.

In the Cherokee Nation, Samuel A. Worchester established a printing plant, first at Union Mission and then at Park Hill, which soon became the leading center for secular and religious training among the tribe, and published portions of the Bible in Cherokee. The *Cherokee Phoenix* and the *Cherokee Almanac* regularly were issued from there. New Spring Place, north of Tahlequah, was operated by the Moravians, and the Baptists published the *Cherokee Messenger* at the Cherokee Baptist Mission at Westville.

By the onset of the American Civil War, the tribes in Indian Territory had recovered from the physical effects of removal. However, the Creeks and Cherokees, and to a lesser degree the Seminoles, continued to be split between full-blood and mixed-blood factions. The old hatreds over forced removal were aggravated by the question of slavery.

Above, left: Built by Mathias Splitlog, a Wyandotte born in Canada, the Catholic Cayuga Mission Church, more commonly known as Splitlog Church, at Cayuga in Delaware County was dedicated on November 25, 1896, in the name of St. Mathias.

COURTESY DAVID FITZGERALD.

Above, right: Established in 1824, Fort Gibson remained in service until 1871. During its early history it was the most important military post in Indian Territory. Today it has been restored and operates as the Fort Gibson Military Park.

COURTESY OKLAHOMA DEPARTMENT OF TOURISM AND RECREATION; PHOTOGRAPH BY FRED MARVEL.

Left: The fur trade-era rendezvous is held annually at Fort Washita near Durant in Bryan County. Many early American traders pushed up the Red River from Natchitoches, Louisiana, in the first two decades of the nineteenth century. Their goal was to reach the Wichita Mountains, where they hoped to find furs and the remains of Spanish mines.

COURTESY OKLAHOMA DEPARTMENT OF TOURISM AND RECREATION; PHOTOGRAPH BY FRED MARVEL.

CHAPTER III

THE CIVIL WAR AND RECONSTRUCTION

Being Southern in culture, some members of the Five Tribes were slave owners. This was especially true among the Choctaws and Chickasaws, who developed a profitable cotton culture along the Red River. Among the prominent slave owners was Robert M. Jones, who operated four plantations in the Choctaw Nation. Many of the mixed-blood Cherokees, the Creeks, and Seminoles also owned slaves.

Slavery was not as harsh among the Five Tribes as it was in the South. Slaves from the Five Tribes, therefore, were considered "undesirable" by slave traders and were difficult to sell outside of Indian Territory. Slaves were excluded from most tribal rights, as were free blacks. Free blacks were not allowed to enter the Choctaw Nation. Abolitionism also was not tolerated, and abolitionists were expelled. The education of slaves was limited by tribal law, and any slave freed by a Choctaw was ordered to leave the nation. The Cherokees prohibited any individual of mixed black and Indian blood from holding office, and marriage between Cherokees and blacks was prohibited.

Nonetheless, the American Board of Commissioners of Foreign Missions was active in the abolitionist movement in Indian Territory prior to the Civil War. In 1847, its secretary toured the region to inspect its missionaries and appraise their attitude toward slavery. To pressure the Indians to abandon slavery, missionaries were ordered to withhold church ordinances from slave owners. This prompted several missionaries, including Elizur Butler, to resign. To increase the pressure, the commissioners withheld financial support for tribal missions, and finally in 1859 and 1860 the missionaries were ordered to abandon their missions in the Choctaw and Cherokee Nations.

The tribes split over slavery. In the Cherokee Nation, the Kee-too-wah Society supported abolition, while the Knights of the Golden Circle were pro-slavery. As the secession movement grew, the Indians found themselves caught between pro-Union Kansas and secessionist Arkansas and Texas. This strategic position was apparent to Confederate leaders, and both states sent delegations to the tribes, urging them to side with the South. Also, most tribal agents were pro-Southern.

While the South courted the Indians, the North abandoned the area. In the spring of 1861, Lieutenant Colonel William H. Emory withdrew all federal forces from Indian Territory. They were replaced by state troops from Arkansas and Texas. On March 4, 1861, Albert Pike was appointed Confederate commissioner to the tribes of Indian Territory. Accompanied by Benjamin McCulloch, he first visited the Cherokees, but John Ross declared that he was determined to keep the tribe neutral. Meeting with the Creeks at North Fork Town, Pike secured a treaty of alliance signed by mixed-blood leaders on July 10, 1861. The full-blood element, holding a council with the Plains Indians at the time, took no part in the deliberations and repudiated the agreement when they returned home. The Confederate-Choctaw-Chickasaw Treaty was signed on July 14, 1861, and the Seminole Treaty was finalized on August 11, 1861. Pike then marched to the Wichita Agency, where he secured an alliance with the Wichita, Comanche, Tonkawa, Shawnee, Delaware, and other tribes on August 12.

In the meantime, Stand Watie had accepted a commission as a colonel in the Confederate Army and had organized a regiment of Cherokees. Riding into Tahlequah, he raised the Confederate flag above the Cherokee capitol. The fear of a Southern-backed coup against him, combined with the Confederate victory at the Battle of Wilson's Creek in Missouri, prompted Chief Ross to abandon his policy of neutrality and sign a treaty with the Confederacy on October 7, 1861. Portions of the Osage, Seneca, Shawnee, and Quapaw also joined the Southern alliance.

The Confederate treaties with the Five Tribes gave the Indians more independence than they had experienced with the federal government. For example, the new treaties offered the possibility of Indian statehood, representation in the Confederate Congress, and Indian courts on the same level as state courts. In return, the Five Tribes agreed to raise troops for the South; however, these troops would not serve outside of Indian Territory. Although the Confederacy attempted to fulfill its treaty

Murrell Home, Park Hill
by Vinson Lackey. On a per capita basis more people were killed in Indian Territory than any other state or territory during the Civil War. Inasmuch as it was the culmination of years of bitterness over the tribal divisions resulting from removal, the Civil War in Indian Territory was a civil war within a civil war. The hatred spilled over into a frenzy of destruction that left very little standing as first the pro-Northern Indians were driven into exile in Kansas and then the pro-Southern Indians were forced into exile along the Red River. Looters from Arkansas and Missouri added to the devastation. One of the few surviving antebellum homes is the Murrell Home at Park Hill, just south of Tahlequah.

COURTESY GILCREASE MUSEUM.

✧

Top, left: Established in 1842 as a buffer between the Five Tribes and the Plains Indians, Fort Washita was seized by Southern forces in 1861 and served as the headquarters for Confederate Brigadier General Douglas Cooper and was a major supply point and hospital facility.

COURTESY OKLAHOMA DEPARTMENT OF TOURISM AND RECREATION; PHOTOGRAPH BY FRED MARVEL.

Top, right: John Ross, Principal Chief of the Cherokees, *by* Charles Bird King. *Ross bitterly opposed removal during the 1830s and became the political enemy of Stand Watie in Cherokee politics. Ross opposed slavery and any Cherokee alliance with the Confederacy. After Watie accepted a commission in the Confederate Army and raised troops for the South, Ross reluctantly signed the Cherokee-Confederate Treaty of 1861. In 1862, Ross fled to Philadelphia, Pennsylvania, for the remainder of the war.*

COURTESY EVERETT AND JEAN BERRY; PHOTOGRAPH BY JUDY DAWSON.

Right: Distinguished in the fighting at the Battle of Honey Springs were members of the First Kansas Colored Infantry, depicted here by reenactors, who launched a vicious assault on the Confederate line. Plagued by wet powder, the Southern troops broke and fled, leaving the field to the Union forces.

COURTESY OKLAHOMA DEPARTMENT OF TOURISM AND RECREATION; PHOTOGRAPH BY FRED MARVEL.

obligations, the distance of Indian Territory from the Eastern battlefields, the indifference of many non-Indian commanders to Native American troops, and the declining fortunes of the South combined to prevent their full implementation. However, Robert M. Jones, E. C. Boudinot, and S. B. Callahan were elected Choctaw-Chickasaw, Cherokee, and Creek-Seminole delegates respectively to the Confederate Congress.

A sizable minority of Creeks, Seminoles, and Cherokees were opposed to the treaties with the Confederacy. Numbering about 2,000 men and their families, the pro-Northern Creeks and Seminoles gathered near Northfork Town under the leadership of Opothleyahola. In a campaign involving three battles—Round Mountain on November 19, 1861; Chusto-Talasah on December 9, 1861; and Chusteuahlah on December 26, 1861—they were defeated. During the battles, many of Ross' supporters among the Cherokee troops refused to fight the

✧

Left: Fort Gibson was the most important military post in Oklahoma prior to the Civil War and the westernmost fort at the time of its establishment in 1824. Abandoned by the army in 1857, it stood neglected until occupied by Confederate forces in 1861. In 1863 it was recaptured by Union troops commanded by Colonel William Phillips.

COURTESY THE DAILY OKLAHOMAN.

Below: The Peter Conser home near Heavener in LeFlore County. A pro-Southern refugee from the Choctaw Nation, Conser fled to the Red River in 1862 where he was given refuge by Robert M. Jones, who opened his plantation to Confederate refugees fleeing the Union occupation of northern Indian Territory. Following the Civil War, Conser returned home and became deputy sheriff of Sugar Loaf County of the Choctaw Nation. He later was appointed a captain in the Choctaw Lighthorse, the tribe's law enforcement arm. As a lighthorseman, Conser served as lawman, judge, and jury. He also was charged with carrying out any sentence he prescribed.

COURTESY OKLAHOMA DEPARTMENT OF TOURISM AND RECREATION; PHOTOGRAPH BY FRED MARVEL.

pro-Union Indians and deserted to the Northern side. Following their defeat, these pro-Northern Indians were forced to flee to Kansas, where they were herded into squalid refugee camps. The Union military command soon realized the potential of using the men as troops to regain control of Indian Territory, and they were organized into the three regiments of the Union Indian Home Guard and formed into the Indian Brigade. During the remainder of the war, they fought to regain control of Indian Territory.

Early in March of 1861, the pro-Confederate Indians participated in the Battle of Pea Ridge, Arkansas. Following this defeat, they withdrew to Indian Territory to counter an expected Union attack. The anticipated first Northern invasion of Indian Territory, under the command of Colonel William Weer, began in June of 1862. The Union troops easily pushed aside Confederate opposition and captured Tahlequah and Chief Ross, who had refused to flee. Arrested without incident, Ross placed himself under the protection of the Union troops and was released on parole.

Although the campaign had been a success, the extended supply lines of the Northern troops caused some apprehension, and, in a case of mutiny, Colonel Frederick Salomon, second in command of the expedition, arrested Weer. Salomon then marched back to Kansas. Ross fled Indian Territory with him and remained in Philadelphia, Pennsylvania, for the remainder of the war. To fill the political void, the pro-Southern Cherokees elected Stand Watie principal chief.

In the fall of 1862, the second Northern invasion of Indian Territory was launched under the command of Brigadier General James G. Blunt, who defeated Watie at the Battle of Fort Wayne on October 22 and then occupied Fort Gibson. During the fighting,

Right: *Confederate cannon opening fire on advancing Union troops during a reenactment of the Battle of Honey Springs. It was when Confederate Brigadier Douglas H. Cooper ordered the withdrawal of his artillery across the only bridge over Honey Creek that the Southern retreat almost became a rout. Only the timely intervention of Cooper's cavalry in a rear guard action held the Union troops in check to allow a rapid Southern retreat.*

COURTESY OKLAHOMA DEPARTMENT OF TOURISM AND RECREATION; PHOTOGRAPH BY FRED MARVEL.

Below: *Union reenactors form a line and begin their advance toward Confederate forces deployed along Honey Creek in this reenactment of the July, 1863, Battle of Honey Springs.*

COURTESY OKLAHOMA DEPARTMENT OF TOURISM AND RECREATION; PHOTOGRAPH BY FRED MARVEL.

more pro-Northern Cherokees deserted to the Union forces. With the Union in control of the Cherokee Nation, the pro-Northern Cherokees enacted the Cherokee Emancipation Proclamation in February of 1863.

Watie was forced to resort to guerrilla warfare to offset Northern superiority in arms. On July 1-2, 1863, he ambushed a Union wagon supply train at the First Battle of Cabin Creek; however, Northern troops forced his withdrawal. As the

Union wagon train continued southward, Blunt followed and on July 17, 1863, defeated the Union forces at the Battle of Honey Springs. This was the largest engagement fought in Indian Territory during the war and marked the high water mark for the South. After Honey Springs, the North won another victory at the Battle of Perryville on August 23, 1863, and then burned Fort Coffee and Scullyville before capturing Fort Smith.

Although Watie was promoted to brigadier general on May 6, 1863, it was impossible to stem the Union offensive. Watie did win a major victory with the capture of the steamboat *J. R. Williams* on June 15, 1864, and $1.5 million worth of Union supplies at the Second Battle of Cabin Creek on September 18-19, 1864. However, Indian Territory became a backwater for the fighting.

On May 24, 1865, the pro-Southern Indians met at Camp Napoleon on the Washita River to discuss surrender. Two days later, Confederate Lieutenant General Edmond Kirby-Smith surrendered the Trans-Mississippi Department. Peter Pitchlynn and the Choctaws surrendered on June 19, 1865. Watie became the final Confederate general officer to lay down his arms when he surrendered at the home of R. M. Jones on June 23, 1865.

Indian Territory had been ravaged by the fighting. Many civilians had been dislocated and forced to seek refuge in overcrowded camps in either Kansas or Texas. Civilians from Arkansas and Missouri took advantage of the situation to loot the farms, homes, and businesses of the Indians. Proportionally, more people were killed in Indian Territory during the Civil War than any other state or territory. Much of the destruction was due to the nature of the fighting, which had rekindled the hatred first generated by forced removal three decades earlier. It was a civil war within the larger American Civil War. Among the Cherokees, 10,500 tribal members supported the Union and 6,000 favored the Confederacy. The Creeks and Seminoles both favored the North with respective majorities of 6,000 versus 1,500 and 6,500 to 950. Only among the Choctaws and Chickasaws was there a predominately Southern sympathy, with only 225 Chickasaws and twelve Choctaws fighting for the Union. During Reconstruction, however, all the tribes were treated as rebels.

Left: The Confederate battle line erupts in flames as it opens fire on federal troops in the reenactment of the Battles of Cabin Creek. There were two Civil War battles fought at Cabin Creek. In the 1863 engagement, Confederate Brigadier General Stand Watie was defeated in an attempt to capture a Union wagon supply train escorted by troops commanded by Colonel James M. Williams as it attempted to ford Cabin Creek on the Texas Road. In the 1864 Battle of Cabin Creek, Watie and Confederate Brigadier General Richard M. Gano captured a Northern wagon supply train and $1.5 million worth of supplies. After the battle the Southerners burned any disabled wagons and returned southward with 130 captured wagons filled with food, clothing, and ammunition. The second Battle of Cabin Creek was the last major Civil War engagement in Indian Territory. The flag carried by the Confederate troop, with the inscription Cherokee Braves, is a replica of the one actually carried by Cherokee troops in the fighting.

COURTESY OKLAHOMA DEPARTMENT OF TOURISM AND RECREATION; PHOTOGRAPH BY FRED MARVEL.

Bottom: Confederate and Union troops maneuver in the reenactment of the Battle of Middle Boggy, originally fought on February 14, 1864, on the north side of Middle Boggy Creek, one mile north of Atoka in Atoka County. Confederate Colonel John Jumper, commanding the Seminole Battalion, Captain Adam Nail's detachment of the First Choctaw and Chickasaw Confederate Cavalry, and a portion of the Twentieth Texas Cavalry were surprised and defeated by a Union force composed of elements of the Fourteenth Kansas Cavalry and a section of artillery.

COURTESY OKLAHOMA DEPARTMENT OF TOURISM AND RECREATION; PHOTOGRAPH BY FRED MARVEL.

✧

Right: The Battle of Honey Springs as depicted in this Civil War-era newspaper illustration was the largest engagement in Indian Territory. Fought on July 17, 1863, along Elk Creek in McIntosh and Muskogee Counties, 3,000 Union troops under Major General James G. Blunt assaulted 5,000 Confederates deployed along the creek. The Northern victory destroyed Confederate power in Indian Territory.

COURTESY OKLAHOMA HERITAGE ASSOCIATION.

Below: Confederate cavalry prepare to engage Union troops at the reenactment of the Battles of Cabin Creek. The mobility offered his mounted troops, which originally were designated the Cherokee Mounted Rifles, allowed Confederate Brigadier General Stand Watie to wage a successful guerrilla campaign in Indian Territory throughout the fighting.

COURTESY OKLAHOMA DEPARTMENT OF TOURISM AND RECREATION; PHOTOGRAPH BY FRED MARVEL.

Northern officials convened the Fort Smith Council on September 8, 1865, to negotiate a series of Reconstruction Treaties. At first, only the pro-Northern Indians appeared and protested their treatment, pointing out they had enlisted in the Union Army. When the pro-Southern delegates arrived on September 13, negotiations stalemated and the council was adjourned to reconvene at Washington, D.C., in December of 1865. When the meeting reconvened, all but the Cherokees presented united delegations.

The Seminoles were the first to sign a Reconstruction treaty on March 11, 1866. In the agreement their land was reduced from two million acres to 200,000 acres. The surplus land was sold to the government for fifteen cents per acre, while the tribe paid thirty cents per acre for a new homeland in the Creek Nation. Slavery was abolished and the freedmen were admitted to the Seminole Nation and given a pro rata share of tribal annuities.

When the Choctaws and Chickasaws signed their treaty on April 28, 1866, they sold the Leased District in western Oklahoma to the government as a new homeland for Plains Tribes. Freedmen were not given tribal citizenship. It was not until the Choctaw Freedmen Bill of 1883 that the ex-slaves were made Choctaw citizens. The Chickasaws never granted their freedmen citizenship; however, Chickasaw freedmen were enrolled by the Dawes Commission in 1902, and each was given forty acres of land.

The Creek Reconstruction Treaty, signed on June 14, 1866, ceded 3,250,560 acres to the federal government. The Seminoles were sold their new homeland, and Creek freedmen were made tribal members. A sum of $200,000 was set aside from the sale of Creek land to be divided among the pro-Northern faction of the tribe.

The Cherokee Reconstruction Treaty, signed on July 19, 1866, was the last to be negotiated. Under its provisions the tribe sold all its land in Kansas and allowed the settlement of other tribes within the Cherokee Nation. The Canadian District, south and west of the Arkansas River, was set aside for the settlement of the pro-Southern Cherokees and Cherokee freedmen. Slavery was abolished and full tribal rights for the freedmen were recognized with certain restrictions.

Most of the Reconstruction Treaties also provided for the formation of a territorial government and an intertribal territorial council. The Choctaw-Chickasaw Treaty called for the formation of the Territory of Oklahoma. The name for the new territory was suggested by the Reverend Allen Wright and was taken from the Choctaw words *Okla* meaning people and *Homma* meaning red.

The close of the Civil War was the beginning of the end for the domination of Oklahoma by the Eastern tribes. The federal government quickly expanded its policy of Indian removal to include those tribes in Kansas and other Plains Indians. The creation of reservations for the Plains Indians ignited a long series of Indian Wars that began in 1867 and culminated in the Ghost Dance movement in 1890. During this time, a myriad of additional tribes, some from as far away as the Pacific Northwest, were removed to Oklahoma.

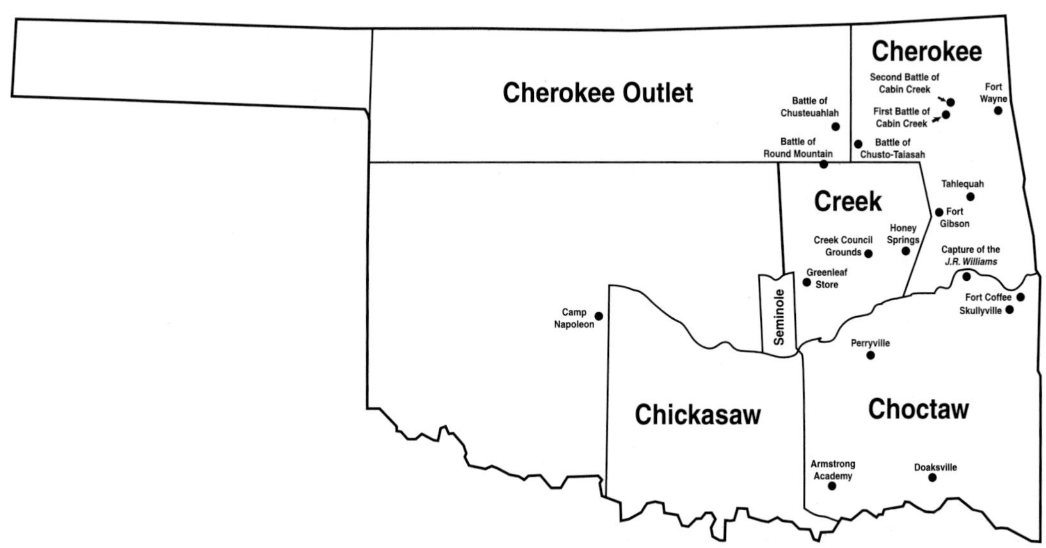

Top, left: Standing on the courthouse square in Tahlequah is a memorial dedicated in 1913 by the United Daughters of the Confederacy to those Confederate troops killed in Oklahoma during the Civil War. It also marks the location where Confederate Brigadier General Stand Watie rode into the Cherokee Capital with his First Cherokee Regiment of Southern troops and raised the Confederate flag over the Cherokee National Capital. This action forced Cherokee Principal Chief John Ross to abandon his role of neutrality in the Civil War and sign a military alliance with the South.

COURTESY *THE DAILY OKLAHOMAN.*

Top, right: Built in 1910, the Oklahoma Confederate Veterans Home in Ardmore reflects the Southern heritage of the state and was constructed to provide for aged veterans who fought for the South in the Civil War. Likewise, the State Capitol faces south in recognition of Oklahoma's ties to the South.

COURTESY *THE DAILY OKLAHOMAN.*

Bottom: Lands designated for certain Indian tribes changed or were resized between 1860 and 1866.

CHAPTER IV
INDIAN WARS

After the Civil War, there was a series of Indian removals to Oklahoma following the expulsion of tribes from Kansas beginning in 1867. First to be resettled were the Potawatomi and the Shawnee, who were given a reservation between the Canadian and the North Fork of the Canadian Rivers west of the Seminole, and the Iowa and Sac and Fox who were settled between the North Fork of the Canadian and Cimarron Rivers west of the Creek Nation. These three removals took place in 1867.

A number of tribes from the Old Northwest had settled in the extreme northeast corner of the Cherokee Nation in present Delaware and Ottawa Counties. The Seneca-Cayuga Confederation, that included the Mingoes, Conestoga, Cayuga, Mohawk, Erie, Oneida, Tuscarora, Onondaga, Seneca of Sandusky, and the Shawnee of Ohio moved there in 1831. Following the Civil War, they were joined by the Wyandotte in 1865 and the Eastern Shawnee, Ottawa, Ojibway, the Confederated Peoria—which included the Peoria, Kaskaskia, Wea, Piankshaw, Cahokia, Moingwena, Michigamea, and Tamaroa—and the Miami, the Eel River, and the Quapaw in 1867.

In 1871, the Osage sold their reservation in Kansas and purchased a new one from the Cherokees west of the Ninety-sixth Meridian and north and east of the Arkansas River. By 1872 that tribe had completed removal to Indian Territory. That same year, the Kansa Indians moved from Kansas to a reservation along the Arkansas River in the northwest corner of the Osage Reservation, and the Pawnee were resettled in a reservation along Black Bear Creek between the Arkansas and Cimarron Rivers. The Poncas were removed from their reservation in Nebraska to a new land along the Arkansas River west of the Pawnee Reservation in 1877. The Otoe and Missouria were resettled in the Cherokee Outlet in 1881.

Western Oklahoma was the domain of the Plains Indians—warlike, nomadic tribes that vigorously resisted resettlement in the post-Civil War era. Dependent on the buffalo and the horse, these tribes maintained a lifestyle and culture that was incompatible with non-Indian settlers.

The Plains Indian War of 1867 started when Major General Winfield Scott Hancock marched to Fort Larned, Kansas, to put an end to Indian "depredations." Hancock dispatched Major Edward W. Wynkoop to order the Cheyenne and Arapaho, led by Roman Nose, to present themselves at Fort Larned for a council. Many of the Indians ignored the summons, and in response Hancock burned Roman Nose's village, touching off a frontier war that raged through the summer and into the fall of 1867.

Unable to keep in the field on their grass-fed ponies during the colder months, approximately 7,000 Cheyenne, Arapaho, Comanche, Kiowa, and Plains Apache, although undefeated, agreed to a peace council at Medicine Lodge, Kansas, as the winter of 1867-1868 approached. Three treaties were signed—the Kiowa-Comanche Treaty on October 18, 1867, the Apache Treaty on October 21, 1867, and the Cheyenne-Arapaho Treaty on October 28, 1867. These treaties, the first in which the Plains Indians accepted reservations, assigned the Kiowa, Comanche, and Apache a reservation in the Leased District between the Canadian and Arkansas Rivers west of the Ninety-eighth Meridian and the Cheyenne and Arapaho a reservation north of the Kiowa, Comanche, and Apache.

The tribes remained on their reservations through the winter of 1867-1868 but returned to the warpath with the coming of spring. In response, the army decided to crush the hostile Indians with a campaign of converging columns to push the tribes back onto their reservations.

Lieutenant Colonel George Armstrong Custer had participated in the 1867 campaign but had been court-martialed and suspended from duty for leaving his regiment without orders, abandoning stragglers, ordering the shooting of deserters, and marching his men beyond endurance. However, Custer persuaded Major General Philip Sheridan to intervene and return his command. Custer led the column advancing south from Fort Supply.

✧

Charles C. Schreyvogel's Attack at Dawn. *Marching his men through an early-winter snow storm, Brevet Brigadier General George Armstrong Custer discovered Cheyenne Chief Black Kettle's camp on the Washita River in western Oklahoma. Black Kettle was not hostile and had a letter from federal officials stating that fact. To make sure that the army did not mistakenly attack his village, Indian officials had given him an American flag to fly over his village. Black Kettle also hoisted a white flag of peace over his camp. Nonetheless, at dawn on November 28, 1868, Custer ordered his men to charge. As his men regrouped after killing mostly women and children, Custer noticed that the Cheyenne and Arapaho from nearby villages were massing on a nearby hill. Content with his "victory" he ordered his men back to Fort Supply, abandoning Major Joel Elliott and twenty men to be killed by the Indians.*

COURTESY GILCREASE MUSEUM.

✧

Above: An Osage buffalo hunt. The Osage were prairie Indians who occupied the eastern border of the Great Plains. This photograph of an Osage buffalo hunt was taken in 1874, just as the once huge herds of buffalo began to disappear under the onslaught of non-Indian hunters. The man in the right center, next to the man cleaning his rifle, is holding one of the large caliber buffalo guns used to decimate the herds.

COURTESY PHILLIPS PETROLEUM COMPANY.

The weather was bitter. Many of Custer's officers wanted to return to Fort Supply because of freezing temperatures and heavy snow, but Custer pressed on until his scouts, led by California Joe, discovered Black Kettle's band of Cheyenne camped on the Washita River in western Oklahoma. Black Kettle's band had remained on the reservation, was not hostile, and had been assured that they were safe from attack. To indicate his peaceful intentions, Black Kettle had been given an American flag to fly over his camp along with a white flag of peace.

However, when Custer approached the camp, he quickly decided to attack. To prevent any Indians from escaping, Custer ordered Major Joel H. Elliott and twenty men to circle the village. Black Kettle unsuccessfully rushed toward the troops, hoping to stop the fighting. It took Custer only ten minutes to capture the Cheyenne village, but, as a large party of Indians from farther downstream began to gather on the nearby hills, Custer ordered a withdrawal, abandoning Elliot and his men to be killed. Most of the Indians killed in the attack were women and children.

Right: Fort Sill *by Vinson Lackey. Following the Plains Indian War of 1867-1868, the army established Fort Sill along Cache Creek north of Lawton. Much of the work on the post was done by troops of the Tenth Cavalry, an all-black unit better known as Buffalo Soldiers. They also helped rebuild Fort Arbuckle in 1867-1868. One of the Tenth Cavalry's troopers, Private Filmore Roberts, was detailed to carry dispatches from Fort Arbuckle to Fort Gibson in the bitter cold of winter. He never reported to Fort Gibson. His remains were found lodged in some willow trees on the banks of the Canadian River. He had drowned while trying to ford the river.*

COURTESY *THE DAILY OKLAHOMAN.*

The Battle of the Washita, followed by two other army victories, at Soldier Springs on the North Fork of the Red River near Lugart in Kiowa County, and Sweetwater Creek in the Texas Panhandle, convinced the Cheyenne, Arapaho, and Kiowa to return to their reservation. Fort Sill, originally called Camp at Medicine Bluff or Wichita Camp, was established on January 7, 1869, to keep watch over the Indians. In 1902, Fort Sill was transformed into the army's main artillery training center.

Much of the garrison duty in Indian Territory was assigned to members of the Ninth and Tenth Cavalry, better known on the frontier as Buffalo Soldiers. At the beginning of the Plains Indian War of 1867, portions of the Tenth Cavalry were ordered to garrison Fort Gibson and rebuild Fort Arbuckle. Afterward, they were transferred to Fort Sill, where they built much of that post, as well as the Fort Arbuckle to Fort Sill road. They also served in the Red River War of 1874. The Ninth Cavalry was transferred to Indian Territory in 1870 to keep settlers out of the Indian reservations. And, between 1879 and 1885, the unit was assigned the task of removing boomers from the Unassigned Lands.

The Cheyenne-Arapaho Agency was moved from Pond Creek to Darlington, north of El Reno, in 1870. Four years later, in 1874, Fort Reno was established just to the southwest to protect the agency. Made a permanent post in 1874, it remained in service until 1949. In 1879, Cantonment, in present-day Blaine County, was established as a link between Fort Supply and Fort Reno to keep watch on the Cheyenne and Arapaho. Three stone buildings were built and occupied until 1882, when it was transferred to the Mennonites for use as an Indian school.

Left: Geronimo, who was called Goyakla or "He Who Yawns" as a youth, terrorized the Southwest between 1881 and 1886, frustrating the 5,000 American soldiers who searched for him. After being promised to be allowed to return to Arizona after two years imprisonment in Florida, Geronimo, his followers, and the Apache Scouts who hunted him down were exiled first to Florida and then to Alabama. The group was imprisoned as prisoners of war at Fort Sill from 1894 until 1913. Shown here as an old man, Geronimo became quite a showman, touring with Wild West Shows, and was featured at the St. Louis World's Fair in 1904, as well as several other major expositions.

COURTESY SAM DEVENNE COLLECTION, MUSEUM OF THE GREAT PLAINS.

Bottom: Winter on the Reservation *by Woodrow Wilson Crumbo. The concentration of the plains tribes onto the reservations of western Oklahoma stopped their nomadic lifestyle of following the buffalo herds north in the summer and south in the winter and forced the Indian to become dependent on the government for issues of beef for food.*

COURTESY MINISA CRUMBO HALSEY.

Top: William J. Hayes' A Herd of Buffaloes on the Bed of the River Missouri. *The huge herds of buffalo that wandered across western Oklahoma and the remainder of the Great Plains gave rise to the powerful horse-buffalo culture of Indians. However, once the buffalo were destroyed, their way of life quickly came to an end.*

Right: A Plains Indian bag, called a strike-a-light. Made of colorful beads and a leather and metal cone jingle, the bag was used to carry the materials necessary to start a fire.

Bottom: Kiowa Family Moving Camp *by George Silverhorn. With the acquisition of the horse following the arrival of the Europeans, the Kiowas became true Plains Indians. Because they followed the buffalo migrations, the Plains Indians had no permanent villages. In addition, their weapons were superior to those of the army during the early Indian wars. The long buffalo lance, carried by the warrior in front, far outreached anything issued by the military except firearms, and muzzle-loading firearms took so much time to reload that the Indians could close and kill with their lances before a second shot could be fired. The buffalo hide shield carried by the same warrior sometimes was made of three layers of buffalo hide and could turn a musket ball. When riding toward the enemy, the shield was held in front. When retreating it was thrown over a warrior's back to provide protection.*

COURTESY GILCREASE MUSEUM.

It was during this time that federal officials turned over the administration of the reservations to religious denominations in the hope that Native Americans would be Christianized. The best known agent charged with carrying out the Quaker Peace Policy was Lawrie Tatum at the Kiowa-Comanche-Apache Reservation. Under his control, the Kiowas, led by Satanta, Big Tree, Lone Wolf, and Satank pledged to stop their raiding. Unfortunately their pledges meant little, and, when Tatum provided the Indians arms and ammunition to hunt buffalo, they used the weapons to raid into Texas.

Finally, Tatum grew weary of the treachery, and, with Sherman and Colonel Benjamin H. Grierson, arrested Satank, Satanta, and Lone Tree at Fort Sill. On June 7, 1871, the Indians were loaded into wagons for the trip to Jacksboro, Texas, for trial. Satank was killed on the way as he tried to escape. Found guilty, the others were sentenced to hang, but Texas Governor Edmund Davis commuted their sentences to life in prison. In August of 1873, Satanta and Lone Tree were freed and allowed to return to the reservation. Disgusted, Tatum resigned.

✧

Left: An elaborate Plains Indian warbonnet, possibly Cheyenne.

COURTESY GILCREASE MUSEUM.

Below: Brevet Brigadier General George Armstrong Custer, shown here in a detail from Charles C. Schreyvogel's painting, Custer's Demand, *was a key figure in the Plains Indian War of 1867-1868. During the campaign of 1867, he was court-martialed for leaving his regiment without orders, abandoning stragglers, shooting deserters, and pushing his men beyond endurance when he marched his command 150 miles in sixty hours, with only six hours of rest, so he could join his wife. Removed from command of the Seventh Cavalry, he was reinstated just before the beginning of the 1868 winter campaign against the Cheyenne, and he was determined to regain his reputation.*

COURTESY GILCREASE MUSEUM.

◆

Right: The famous Geronimo Guardhouse at Fort Sill. Geronimo died, still a prisoner of war, at Fort Sill in 1909. The guardhouse is at the west end of the fort's famous "Cannon Walk," a collection of artillery pieces from around the world.

COURTESY OKLAHOMA DEPARTMENT OF TOURISM AND RECREATION; PHOTOGRAPH BY FRED MARVEL.

Below: A group of Apache Mountain Spirits or Fire Dancers in southwestern Oklahoma. Brought to Fort Sill as prisoners of war in 1894, Geronimo's followers remained there until 1913, when they were given the option of taking eighty-acre homesteads in the Kiowa- Apache-Comanche Reservation or returning to Arizona. Eighty-seven opted to remain in Oklahoma and most settled in southern Caddo and northern Comanche Counties. Ironically, the Apaches organized one of the early baseball teams in Oklahoma and regularly competed against teams from Fort Sill.

COURTESY WESTERN HISTORIES COLLECTION, UNIVERSITY OF OKLAHOMA LIBRARIES.

Even more successful than the army's efforts to force the Plains Indians onto reservations was the destruction of the buffalo. Following the Civil War, a market was created for buffalo tongues, hides, and skins. Armed with .50 caliber Sharps buffalo rifles, hunters virtually exterminated the animals. Because their nomadic lifestyle depended on the buffalo, the Southern Plains Tribes rose in revolt when the hunters moved into the Texas Panhandle in the early 1870s. The result was the Red River War of 1874.

Fighting actually started in the fall of 1871, when some Kiowa and the Comanches, led by Quanah Parker, began raids into Texas. For the following two years, sporadic fighting took place between the Kiowa and Comanche and the army, led by Colonel Ranald Mackenzie.

Following a sun dance in the spring of 1874, open warfare broke out. The Indians caught a group of buffalo hunters at Adobe Walls in the Texas Panhandle in June of 1874, but they were driven off. The final battle was fought at Palo Duro Canyon on September 28, 1874, when Mackenzie destroyed the Indians' hidden camp, burned their supplies, and seized their horse herd. Horses not used to remount his troops were killed, thereby virtually dismounting the Kiowa and Comanche. By February of 1875, most of the Indians had returned to their reservation.

At the same time, 1872-1873, the Modoc War broke out in southwestern Oregon and northwestern California. The Modoc had been forced onto a reservation in Oregon in 1864, but, led by Captain Jack, they abandoned their reservation and returned to their homeland in 1870. The army was ordered to round up the Indians and return them to their reservation. Fighting from the lava beds south of Tule Lake, the Modoc proved difficult to defeat. It took more than 1,000 troops and seventy-eight Indian scouts to defeat Captain Jack and eighty Modoc warriors. Captain Jack was hanged and the surviving Modoc were herded onto a 4,040-acre reservation purchased from the Eastern Shawnee on the Quapaw Agency in northeastern Oklahoma. In 1909, federal officials allowed the Modoc to return to the Klamath Reservation. The tribe split, with some returning to the Pacific Northwest and others remaining in Oklahoma.

✧

Top, left: The army employed many of the Plains Indians on reservations in western Oklahoma as scouts. This photograph shows Corporal of Scouts Flacko, who was stationed at Fort Reno on the Cheyenne-Arapaho Reservation. With him are his two daughters. Fort Reno, now the Oklahoma State University Agriculture and Applied Science Experimental Station, was established in 1874 to provide protection for the Cheyenne-Arapaho Agency at Darlington. During the 1880s, members of the Ninth Cavalry garrisoned the fort, and the Buffalo Soldiers spent much of their time patrolling the Unassigned Lands and removing Boomers.

COURTESY OKLAHOMA HERITAGE ASSOCIATION.

Top, right: A group of Comanches gathered near Cache to witness the return of buffalo to the Wichita National Wildlife Refuge on the morning of October 18, 1907. Having been hunted almost to extinction, buffalo were a rare sight by the onset of the twentieth century. The reintroduction of the buffalo onto the plains of southwestern Oklahoma was a major conservation project by federal officials. Note the papoose in the cradleboard propped against the tree on the right and the man with the pistol in a holster on the left.

COURTESY ARTHUR HALLORAN COLLECTION, MUSEUM OF THE GREAT PLAINS.

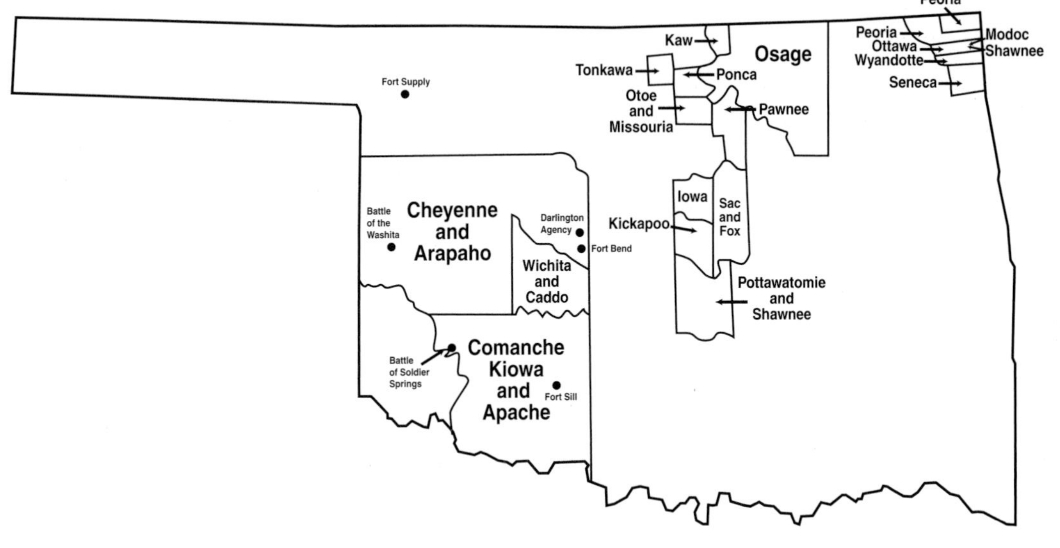

Bottom: The Oklahoma Plains and Prairie Tribes that were relocated to the state during the nineteenth century.

◆

Right: Buffalo Dance *by Woodrow Wilson Crumbo. Some of the participants, those with buffalo headdresses, are portraying buffalo, while others, wearing wolf or coyote headdresses, are portraying the hunters, who would cover themselves with wolf or coyote skins in order to approach the buffalo herds without causing the animals to stampede, before they made their kills. The symbols and arrows on the buffalo hides and skulls were to foretell a successful hunt.*

COURTESY GILCREASE MUSEUM.

Bottom: A Plains Indian peyote ceremony depicted by renowned Native American artist, Woodrow Wilson Crumbo. The revival of traditional tribal religion foreshadowed the establishment and recognition of the Native American Church in Oklahoma.

COURTESY MINISA CRUMBO HALSEY.

Another Pacific Coast tribe, the Nez Perce, was brought to Oklahoma in 1873. Under their leader, Chief Joseph, the Nez Perce refused to move from their homeland in Oregon's Wallowa Valley and along the Salmon River in Idaho to a new reservation in northwest Idaho. Instead he decided to take them to Canada. What followed was a 1,700-mile chase in which the Nez Perce either outfought or outsmarted the military. When the Nez Perce reached Bear Paw Mountain in Montana, only twenty miles short of the American-Canadian border, Joseph was persuaded to pause to allow his people to rest. Trapped there by the army, the Nez Perce were besieged for five days before Joseph surrendered by saying "I am tired of fighting…It is cold and we have no blankets. The little children are freezing to death. Hear me my chiefs, my heart is sick and sad. From where the sun now stands, I will fight no more forever."

After first being sent to Kansas, the Nez Perce were removed in 1879 to a reservation along the Chikaskia River in southwestern Kay County. They remained there until 1885, when they were allowed to return to the Colville Reservation in Washington. The Tonkawa, who had fled Wichita Agency after most were killed by an attack on their village by Delaware and Shawnee in October of 1862, had sought refuge first at Fort Arbuckle and then Fort Griffin, Texas, and were moved onto the old Nez Perce Reservation in 1885.

The final tribe to be removed to Oklahoma in the post-Civil War era was the Chiricahuas Apache. In 1875, they were forced onto the San Carlos Reservation in Arizona, where they were settled with the Warm Springs and other Apache bands. Led first by Victorio and then by Nana, portions of the Chiricahuas and Warm Spring bands broke out between 1877 and 1880. The final outbreak was led by

Geronimo in 1881. For five years the army hunted Geronimo and his band back and forth across the American-Mexican border before he surrendered in September of 1886.

As part of his surrender, Geronimo was promised that his band would be imprisoned in Florida for two years and then returned to Arizona; however, federal officials refused to honor the agreement. Geronimo's band was imprisoned at Fort Pickens in Florida until 1888, when it was moved to Mount Vernon Barracks, Alabama. In 1894, Geronimo and his followers were transferred to Fort Sill, where they remained as prisoners of war until 1913, when they were given the choice of remaining in Oklahoma or returning to the Southwest. Eighty-seven remained near Fort Sill and became known as the Fort Sill Apaches. They eventually were granted eighty-acre homesteads in southern Caddo and northern Comanche Counties. During Geronimo's imprisonment at Fort Sill, he became a celebrity, signing autographs at county and regional fairs and festivals.

Adjustment to life on the reservations was difficult for the plains tribes. With the destruction of the buffalo, they became dependent on the distribution of beef from federal Indian agents, many of whom were corrupt, providing inferior or even spoiled beef. Conditions were so bad that army officers frequently wrote that they understood why the Indians periodically bolted the reservations and they found the task of forcing "renegades" back on the reservations to be distasteful. In addition, the men of the tribes were expected to be farmers, performing tasks that for generations had been considered the work of women. Many of the men, traditionally revered as hunters and warriors, were devastated by the situation and turned to alcohol, which multiplied cultural problems.

✧

One of the nation's largest and most attended Native American events is Oklahoma City's annual Red Earth Festival, where hundreds of dance contestants compete for national honors.

COURTESY OKLAHOMA DEPARTMENT OF TOURISM AND RECREATION; PHOTOGRAPH BY FRED MARVEL.

CHAPTER V

Cattle Drives & Cowboys

The result of forcing the Plains Indians onto reservations and the destruction of the buffalo, was the opening of the rich grasslands of Oklahoma to cattlemen and the creation of a market for beef to feed the reservation Indians. The rapidly growing industrial states of the Northeast soon became the most important market for beef, and the growing demand caused beef prices to rise. The staple of the range cattle industry was longhorn cattle—a cross between Moorish and Mexican breeds. They were wild; required little, if any, human care; came in a wide variety of colors; possessed keen senses of smell, sight, and hearing; had huge horns; had no natural predators; could survive extreme climate shifts; required little food or water; and could walk thousands of miles.

By the early 1770s, Texas cattlemen were driving herds from south Texas to markets in Louisiana; however, in 1846, Edward Piper drove 1,000 longhorns from Texas to Ohio, and by the 1850s the Shawnee Trail had developed into the nation's first major north-south cattle trail. There were three Shawnee Trails through Oklahoma. The East Shawnee Trail ran from Colbert's Ferry northeast through Boggy Depot and Fort Gibson into Missouri. The Arkansas River branch split from the East Shawnee Trail at Fort Gibson and angled northeast along the Arkansas River to Kansas. The West Shawnee Trail left the East Shawnee Trail at Boggy Depot and ran northward to Kansas. In 1853, an epidemic of Texas fever decimated the domestic cattle herds in Kansas and Missouri. The disease was spread by tick-infested longhorns as they were driven north. Although the longhorns had developed a natural immunity to Texas fever, ninety percent of the infected Kansas and Missouri cattle died. To combat the disease, the Missouri legislature in 1855 banned the importation of Texas cattle in certain counties, and the Kansas legislature followed with similar legislation in 1859. The outbreak of the Civil War soon interrupted the north-south cattle trade.

With the close of the fighting in 1865, Texans returned home to find millions of cattle roaming free and a beef-starved north willing to purchase all that could be driven to market. However, the Shawnee Trails were still closed because of the importation prohibition enacted by Kansas and Missouri.

Another trail was needed farther west, beyond the line of settlement. Such a trail had been pioneered by Colonel William H. Emory and his column of Union troops as they abandoned Indian Territory at the outbreak of the Civil War and ran from Silver City on the Canadian River to Fort Leavenworth, Kansas. After the war, Jesse Chisholm had used the route to trade with the Indians. Popularized by Joseph G. McCoy, who convinced the railroads to construct sidings and loading racks in central Kansas and spread the word among Texas cattlemen about the new route, cattle were driven north along the Chisholm Trail in 1867.

The route ran from south Texas to Red River Station on the Oklahoma-Texas border near Terral in Jefferson County and then almost due north across the Chickasaw Nation past Monument Hill, Duncan's Store, and the Cooke Brothers' Store. It forded the Washita River at Rock Crossing and the Canadian River at Silver City, where it entered the Unassigned Lands. Here it split with the west branch, following the stage route to Fort Reno. The east branch continued northward. The branches rejoined to ford the Cimarron River and entered the Cherokee Outlet, where it again split, with the main branch following Turkey Creek past Buffalo Springs and into Kansas just south of Arkansas City. The other branch followed the Cimarron River into Kansas.

The third cattle route through Oklahoma was the Great Western Trail, which became necessary as the line of settlement reached the Chisholm Trail. Another reason to move west was to avoid fees demanded by the Five Tribes to drive herds across their land. The Great Western Trail originally was "pioneered" by buffalo. For centuries the vast herds had migrated annually from the Missouri River to the Rio Grande between the Ninetieth and the 100th Meridians, thereby establishing a route that took advantage of the best water sources, grazing areas, and river fords.

✧

Years after the cattle frontier vanished, former cowboys who worked in the Cherokee Outlet formed the Cherokee Strip Cowpunchers' Association. In September of 1951, only six of the hundreds who once rode the range in the Outlet remained. They gathered before a memorial to the Chisholm Trail for a final photograph. Left to right: Chas. E. Sexton, C. E. Lemmert, B. G. Woodruff, Tom Gilbert, Rolla Goodnight, and Frank Eaton, better known as Pistol Pete.

COURTESY NATIONAL COWBOY HALL OF FAME & WESTERN HERITAGE CENTER, OKLAHOMA CITY.

◇

Right: The Tall Grass Prairie Preserve in Osage County preserves the rich grasslands of the prairie which gave rise first to the huge herds of buffalo that roamed the region and later the range cattle industry that thrived in central and western Oklahoma. The region still is a major cattle-producing area.

COURTESY DAVID FITZGERALD.

Below: Return of the Last War Party *by Woodrow Wilson Crumbo. The subjugation of the Plains Indians, their concentration on reservations in western Oklahoma, and the destruction of the buffalo herds opened the region to cattlemen. Not only were the buffalo removed from the rich grasslands, but the Indian reservations provided a market for cattle, which were purchased by the agents to feed the tribes.*

COURTESY MINISA CRUMBO HALSEY.

✧

Left: Frederic Remington's The Stampede. *Cowboying was not the glamorous profession depicted in the movies. The hours were long and hard, and the work was dangerous. A hard fall, especially during a stampede, or "stompedes" as the cowboys called them, usually resulted in serious injury or death. Many stampedes were caused by the spring storms that periodically swept over the plains; however, according to old-time drovers, lightning killed more cowboys. During electrical storms many cowboys would throw away their knives, spurs, or anything else made of metal in the belief that the items attracted lightning. Others put beeswax inside their hats in the belief that the beeswax would not conduct electricity.*

COURTESY GILCREASE MUSEUM.

Below: The major cattle trails that ran through Oklahoma.

Like the others, the Great Western Trail started in south Texas before crossing the Red River at Doan's Store. It then continued north along the North Fork of the Red River past Gyp and Soldier Springs before fording the Washita River at Edward Rock Crossing and the Canadian River at Trail Post Office. Then it went north to Cedar Spring and into the Cherokee Outlet where it turned northwest to Fort Supply and across the North Fork of the Canadian River into Kansas.

There were several other cattle routes, including the Osage Trail, which took cattle to the Osage Reservation from Texas, and the Jones and Plummer Trail in the Panhandle. C. E. Jones and Joe Plummer pioneered the Panhandle route in 1874. It ran from Dodge City, across the Panhandle, to cattle ranches in the northern part of the Texas Panhandle.

Trail driving was a well-organized affair by the mid-1860s, with the number of cattle and cowboys standardized at 2,500 and twelve, respectively, and the duties of each drover well-established. The trail boss oversaw the eight cowboys on the drive. The cowboys were divided into pairs: the "point" was stationed at the head of the herd and maintained the correct route of march; the "swing," about

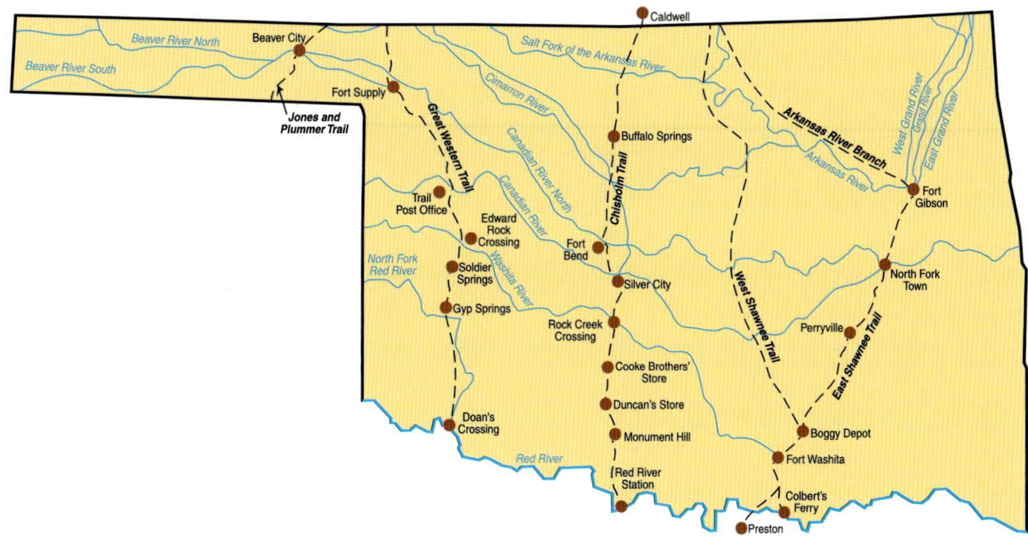

◇ *Right: Frederic Remington's* Drifting Before A Storm. *Longhorns were notorious for straying before a weather front. Whenever they started to drift, there was little the cowboys could do but wait for the weather to pass and then reform the herd. Longhorns made the cattle drives possible. Requiring little food—it was not uncommon for them to eat prickly pears if pasturage was in short supply—or water, they could walk thousands of miles and had no natural predators.*

COURTESY *CENTURY MAGAZINE*, FEBRUARY, 1888.

Below: Pulling a Cow Out of the Mud *by Frederic Remington. One of a cowboy's most used possessions was his lariat. It was indispensable on a cattle drive. Among its functions was roping the animals for branding, herding them along the drive, and freeing them from bogs. To free a cow trapped in mud, a cowboy would get as close as possible and throw his lariat around its neck and then pull it out.*

COURTESY *CENTURY MAGAZINE*, FEBRUARY, 1888.

a quarter of the way down the herd, was responsible for turning the cattle; the "flank," who rode along the side of the herd to prevent straying; and the "drag," who was positioned at the rear to prevent straggling. The cook and his helper moved ahead of the herd to select a site to prepare either the noon or evening meal. The horse wrangler kept watch over the *remuda* to the side of the herd. A calf wagon later was added to the drives. Its task was to haul newborn calves until they could manage for themselves.

It cost about $1 a mile for a cattle drive. Cowboys usually were paid between $25 and $40 per month; the trail boss received $250 per month; and the cook between $30 and $40 per month. Each cowboy furnished his own saddle and bedding, while the horses were provided by the herd's owner at a ratio of seven horses for each cowboy. With cattle bringing $2 to $4 a head in Texas and selling for as much as $40 per head in Kansas, and the average drive being about 1,500 miles, an investment of $11,500 could return as much as $88,500 profit.

The drives started slowly to allow the cattle to become accustomed to the trail. A grown steer easily could walk more than three miles per hour, but a day's drive normally was between ten and fifteen miles. The day started at dawn, when the drovers were fed and the cattle allowed to graze for a few hours. As the march started, the cowboys spaced the herd into a line that was about a mile in length and fifty feet wide. A two-hour halt was called at noon to allow the cattle to graze while the drovers ate. The drive then continued until late afternoon, when the herd was bedded down for the night. The grazing periods were important to prevent the cattle from walking off their weight. The night watch was divided into three two-men shifts. The first lasted until 11:00 p.m., the second from 11:00 p.m. until 2:00 a.m., and the third from 2:00 a.m. until dawn.

Twenty percent of cowboys were black, and ten percent were Native American. Most were young, and the average working life of a cowboy was only seven years. The typical cowboy wore heavy woolen trousers and shirts, a neckerchief knotted around his neck to be pulled up to protect his face from the weather and trail dust. A wide-brimmed hat offered protection from the sun and rain. Coats were worn in the winter, but vests always were present. Seated on his horse, a cowboy could not reach his pockets, so essentials such as tobacco, a watch, and money were kept in the vest's pockets. Gloves covered his hands, and chaps were strapped on to protect his legs when going through thick brush. The saddle was a cowboy's most prized possession and sometimes was decorated with pounds of silver.

Few cowboys had sufficient money to purchase guns or ammunition. Moreover, trail bosses were hesitant to allow them to be carried. An accidental discharge could start a "stompede," as the cattlemen called stampedes. Stampedes could be caused by almost anything, including birds flying up at the cattles' feet. "Agitators," or nervous cattle, however, were the most dangerous, for at any moment their sudden movements could start a stampede. Many trail bosses searched out agitators and shot them before

Above: Much of Oklahoma's western heritage was borrowed from the Mexican cowboys who made their way north over the cattle trails to railheads in Kansas. For example, the large wide brimmed hat that was used to shade them from the sun and protect them from the weather was patterned after the sombrero. *José "Mexican Joe" Barrera, who toured with the Pawnee Bill Wild West Show, was famous for roping six running horses at once. Making the feat even more difficult was the fact that he threw the loop with his foot.*

FROM PAWNEE BILL MONTAGE; COURTESY BRUMMETT ECHOHAWK.

Left: With the Horse Herd *by Frederic Remington. Although his saddle was the most prized possession of a cowboy, the owner of the herd was obligated to provide each of the drovers sufficient horses to make a cattle drive. The usual ratio was seven horses for each drover. The horse herd was kept in a* remuda, *which maintained pace with the drive to one side of the cattle under the care of a horse wrangler. Because the horses belonged to the herd owner, once the drive was completed the drovers were left afoot. Some would purchase horses from the owner to ride back to Texas, but most had little money to spare after visiting the wild cattle towns filled with saloons, brothels, and gambling dens at the end of the drives. Therefore, many accepted the railroad's offer of a free ride on top of the cattle cars to the Mississippi River in exchange for help loading and unloading the cattle. From the river the cowboys would make their way south by working on riverboats.*

COURTESY *CENTURY MAGAZINE*, FEBRUARY, 1888.

the drive started. Cowboys also faced drowning when the herds balked at river crossings. Dick Withers once reported that 116 head of cattle drowned while milling in a river before the drovers could get them up the bank. Many cowboys lost fingers in roping accidents. Most suffered from arthritis from sleeping on the ground.

By the beginning of the 1880s, the range cattle industry had overgrazed most of the pasture land in Texas. Texas cattlemen thus began to look upon Indian Territory as a source for new pasture. No Man's Land, as the Oklahoma Panhandle was known, was adjacent to the vast ranches of the Texas Panhandle. Not attached to any state or territory, the region had no courts or land offices. The cattlemen who moved into the area simply claimed a watershed, and all land drained by that watershed was considered to be their grazing territory. Within a short time as many as 30,000 head of cattle were grazing there.

Old Greer County, between the Prairie Dog Fork and the North Fork of the Red River, also was invaded by Texas cattlemen. Prior to 1896, it was claimed by Texas and, in 1879, the Texas legislature began granting 640-acre homesteads to state veterans of the Mexican War. Beginning in 1881, Texas cattlemen started permanently pasturing cattle in the region, and, within a year, there were 60,000 head of cattle in Old Greer County.

No Man's Land and Old Greer County were insufficient to offset the loss of rangeland in Texas and additional pasturage was needed. In 1882, Texas cattlemen moved 50,000 head of cattle onto the Kiowa-Comanche-Apache Reservation in southwestern Oklahoma. Although the secretary of war ordered troops to remove the cattle, the soldiers found it impossible to do so

Above: Wayne Spears of Pawnee is known nationwide for his depiction of Pawnee Bill. He is shown here on his horse, Y, on the grounds of the Pawnee Bill Museum and State Park on Blue Hawk Peak, west of Pawnee. Gordon W. Lillie, the original Pawnee Bill, and his wife May toured the world with his Pawnee Bill Wild West Show. A true cowboy, Pawnee Bill once worked for the Zimmerman Ranch along Skeleton Creek in the Cherokee Outlet and was wounded in a gunfight with a band of three rustlers. Lillie later recalled that two of the outlaws were killed in the gun battle and the third was hanged at "the first tree we found."

COURTESY WAYNE SPEARS; PHOTOGRAPH BY CINDY CARTMELL.

Right: The Dewey Hotel in Dewey, Oklahoma. Dewey was the end of the Osage Cattle Trail over which cattle were herded north to the Osage Reservation. The octagonal turret room on the right was the site of the famous poker games played by the herd owners after they had sold their cattle. It was not uncommon for thousands of dollars to be gambled away each night during the trail-driving season.

COURTESY DAVID FITZGERALD.

because the cattlemen returned as soon as the troopers left.

Texas cattlemen were so firmly established that when the region was opened to homesteaders in 1891, 480,000 acres were reserved for use as a common grazing area. Of this, 401,000 acres were set aside in one contiguous area known as the Big Pasture, which later composed western Cotton, southeastern Tillman, and a small portion of southern Comanche Counties. It was not until 1901 that the pastures were closed, the cattlemen removed, and the area opened to settlers by sealed bid.

Texas cattlemen also invaded the Cheyenne-Arapaho Reservation. Once again federal troops were ordered to remove them, and once again they found this impossible. Finally, in January of 1883, tribal leaders asked that their agent be empowered to lease grazing rights on the reservation. Seven ranchers quickly agreed to lease 3,117,880 acres for ten years at two cents an acre per year, payable semi-annually in advance. The agreement also transferred any permanent facilities, such as buildings and fences, to tribal ownership when the lease expired.

The first payment of $30,000 was made in silver dollars, and Lewis M. Briggs, Edward Fenlon, William E. Malaley, Hampton B. Denman, Albert G. Evans, Robert D. Hunter, and Jesse Morrison assumed control of individual leases varying from 140,000 to 570,000 acres. More than 300,000 head of cattle were herded onto the reservation and remained until 1885, when President Grover Cleveland canceled the leases. However, cattlemen continued to graze cattle on the reservation until the area was opened to homesteaders in 1892.

✧

Left: The Camp Cook's Troubles *by Charles M. Russell. The horses in the remuda were supposed to be broken and trained, but this was not always the case. In this scene a frightened horse disrupts the morning meal of coffee and eggs. Although Russell portrays the cowboys on the left carrying revolvers, such was not generally the case. Few cowboys owned pistols. They simply could not afford them on their wages of $25 to $40 per month. Those who did usually left them in the chuck wagon. They were too easily lost, and an accidental shot could start a stampede or wound a cowboy, and medical aid was non-existent on most drives. In the event of a serious injury, the trail boss would send for a doctor from the nearest settlement while the cook did what he could. When one cowboy was killed after falling from a horse in the Cherokee Outlet, his foreman had five other cowboys dig the grave. Afterward, the foreman asked "Does anybody know the right words to say?" When no one answered, the foreman continued, "Well, throw some dirt on the son of a gun, and let's get back to work."*

COURTESY GILCREASE MUSEUM.

Bottom: Bull Riding competition at the International Finals Youth Rodeo held annually in Shawnee. Rodeos originated with competition between ranches during the cattle frontier and were made popular with such Wild West shows as Pawnee Bill's and that of the 101 Ranch.

COURTESY OKLAHOMA DEPARTMENT OF TOURISM AND RECREATION; PHOTOGRAPH BY FRED MARVEL.

Right: The chuck wagon was an important part of a cattle drive. However, unlike most Hollywood movies, the chuck wagon did not march alongside the herd, but instead moved ahead to select a site for the noon break and evening halt. Once there, the cook, who was usually paid between $30 and $40 per month, and his helper, prepared meals.

COURTESY JACK HALEY COLLECTION, MUSEUM OF THE GREAT PLAINS.

Below: Crossing Cottonwood Creek with a herd of horses near Guthrie in Logan County. Most of the river crossings in Oklahoma were like this one—shallow. However, others were steep-sided, deep and swift, and presented great dangers for the cowboys, most of whom could not swim. One hundred and sixteen longhorns once drowned while attempting to cross the North Fork of the Canadian River in Oklahoma. The leaders made it across, but as they climbed out the bank caved in, throwing them back into the water. After that, none of the cattle would attempt the climb, and the herd jammed against one another and drowned before the drovers could force the animals out of the water.

COURTESY OKLAHOMA HERITAGE ASSOCIATION.

The largest of the Indian lease agreements involved the Cherokee Strip Live Stock Association, which controlled the Cherokee Outlet. Initially, the cattlemen had negotiated individual leases, but, beginning in 1880, a series of meetings were held by the cattlemen to discuss common problems, and the Cherokee Strip Live Stock Association was formed. Governed by a constitution and bylaws providing for a board of directors and a separate board of arbitration, it became one of the largest organizations in the world dedicated to the promotion of the cattle industry.

In 1883, the association leased the entire six million-acre Cherokee Outlet for five years in exchange for $500,000 to be paid in five annual $100,000 payments. The first payment, made on October 1, 1883, was made in silver dollars. Afterward the Cherokee Outlet was divided between members of the association, special cattle trails were reserved, and quarantine areas were established.

In 1885 negotiations for renewal of the lease started. The Cherokee Strip Live Stock Association found itself bidding against a New York syndicate, and the lease became an issue in the disputed tribal elections. Charges of bribery were levied against several tribal officials, and Chief Joel B. Mayes called the Cherokee National Council into session to settle the issue. The first bill to lease the Cherokee Outlet raised the rent to $125,000 per year, but Mayes vetoed the agreement. Successive bills calling for $150,000, $165,000, and $175,000 also were vetoed, until a price of $200,000 per year for five years was agreed to.

Unfortunately for the cattlemen, federal officials, who were under pressure to open the Cherokee Outlet to homesteaders, maintained that the Cherokees had no right to lease the area, and the 1889 Springer Amendment created the Cherokee Commission to negotiate

Left: Headquarters of the 150,000-acre U Ranch, founded by Major Andrew Drumm in the Cherokee Outlet in 1870. For years the Cherokee Outlet in north-central Oklahoma had been used by cowboys to fatten cattle before driving them to markets in Kansas; however, beginning in 1883, the Cherokee Strip Live Stock Association leased the Outlet's six million acres from the Cherokees for an annual fee of $100,000 for five years. In 1885, during a bidding war over the lease, the price was doubled to $200,000 per year. Unfortunately, the federal government ruled that the Cherokees had no right to lease the Outlet and, in 1889, ordered the cattlemen out. The ranchers countered by offering to buy the Outlet for $3.00 per acre, but federal officials blocked the sale. Instead, the government paid the Cherokees about $1.40 per acre in 1893 and opened the region to homesteaders.

COURTESY NATIONAL COWBOY HALL OF FAME & WESTERN HERITAGE CENTER, OKLAHOMA CITY.

the purchase of the Outlet for $1.25 per acre. The cattlemen countered with an offer of $3.00 per acre. Federal officials then ordered the removal of all cattle from the Cherokee Outlet by October 1, 1890, thus making the land worthless to the Cherokees. Three years later the Cherokees agreed to sell the land to the federal government for $1.40 per acre—$1.60 per acre less than the Cherokee Strip Live Stock Association had offered.

One of the lasting results of the range cattle industry was the rodeo and Wild West Show. Two of these—the Pawnee Bill Wild West Show and the 101 Ranch Wild West Show—originated in Oklahoma. In addition, the 101 Ranch was one of the state's earliest agribusinesses. Organized by George Washington Miller and his three sons—Joseph, or Joe; Zack; and George—it was founded in 1879 on land leased from the Ponca Indians and eventually expanded to 110,000 acres. By 1905, it was the showplace of Oklahoma Territory, producing an income in excess of $1 million annually from livestock, fruit, wheat, and poultry. It also was the home of the 101 Ranch Round-up Show, which often played to crowds as large as 30,000 people and was host to one of the first dude ranches in the nation.

Ranching operations developed on the leased rangelands differed from the glamour of the trail drives. It was hard, difficult work filled with monotony. Cattle had to be tended and treated and fences had to be strung and maintained. Cowboys found themselves digging post holes, stretching barbed wire, building corrals, working like common laborers. Free air, free land, and free water on which the range cattle industry depended ended with the opening of the reservations to homesteaders as farmers fenced and plowed their fields. Likewise, selected cattle breeding resulted in the fencing of much of the open range. By the time the Big Pasture opened in 1901, the era of the range cattle industry had passed, but the lore of the cowboy had become woven into the fabric of American culture.

Below: The renowned Cain's Ballroom in Tulsa featured live music by Bob Wills and His Texas Playboys and other bands. Wills combined cowboy music and jazz to create western swing. His innovative music was broadcast live throughout much of the nation on Tulsa's KVOO Radio.

COURTESY DAVID FITZGERALD.

CHAPTER VI

PUBLIC LAND TO PRIVATE PROPERTY

The last quarter of the nineteenth century was the great era of railroad building in the United States. Oklahoma, which occupied a strategic position between the upper Midwest and the Southwest, as well as being the starting point for the southern route to the Pacific Coast, was the location of much railroad construction. All the Reconstruction Treaties with the Five Tribes contained provisions for the construction of railroads across their domain. As early as 1853, federal officials had plotted a transcontinental route through Oklahoma; however, it was not until 1866 that Congress passed legislation for land grant subsidies for the construction of one north-south railroad through the region.

Three railroads—the Kansas & Neosho Valley; the Leavenworth, Lawrence & Fort Gibson; and the Missouri, Kansas, & Texas, also known as the M-K-T or "Katy,"—competed for the route. Federal officials finally granted the right-of-way to the M-K-T, whose construction crews crossed the northern border of the Cherokee Nation on June 6, 1870. Building south along the Texas Road through the Creek and Choctaw Nations, Katy construction crews bridged the Red River at Colbert's Ferry, allowing the first train to cross into Texas on Christmas Day of 1872.

The 1866 legislation did not prohibit the construction of an east-west railroad across Indian Territory, and in late 1870 the Atlantic & Pacific Railroad started work on a line that would build west from Missouri along the Canadian River to New Mexico. By late 1870, workers reached Vinita in the Cherokee Nation where the line intersected with the M-K-T line and touched off what was known as the "Battle of Vinita." Katy officials had built their station at Big Cabin, south of Vinita, and refused to allow their trains to stop at the Atlantic & Pacific's station at Vinita. Thus anyone wishing to make connections with the Atlantic & Pacific trains had to find transportation from Big Cabin to Vinita. This feud eventually developed into a price war on freight and passenger rates on both lines.

It was not until 1886 that the Atlantic & Pacific line reached Sapulpa. Unfortunately, shortly afterward the railroad was forced into receivership and was purchased by the St. Louis & San Francisco Railroad. Initially, the St. Louis & San Francisco had been chartered to build from Fort Smith across the Choctaw Nation to Paris, Texas. This portion of their line was completed in 1887. Work then started to complete the east-west route; however, it was not until 1902 that the line from Sapulpa was completed across Oklahoma to Lawton and from there to Quanah, Texas.

Another north-south railroad was built across central Oklahoma by the Atchison, Topeka & Santa Fe, commonly known as the Santa Fe, which wanted to extend its line from Caldwell, Kansas, across Indian Territory to Galveston, Texas. Congress granted a charter to the railroad in 1884 but refused to provide a land grant, forcing the Santa Fe to purchase a 100-foot right-of-way across the region. Two crews, one working south from Kansas and the other north from the Red River, were put to work on the route through Guthrie, Oklahoma City, Pauls Valley, and Ardmore. They met at Purcell on April 6, 1887. Another Santa Fe route was built through the Cherokee Outlet southwest across the Cheyenne-Arapaho reservation to Panhandle City, Texas, between 1884 and 1887.

In May of 1888, the Chicago, Rock Island & Pacific Railroad, known as the Rock Island, started building through Indian Territory along the Chisholm Trail from Kansas to Texas. It took four years to complete the work from Caldwell, through Enid, El Reno, Chickasha, to Terral on the Red River. From there the line continued south to Fort Worth, Texas.

The Choctaw Coal & Railway Company was organized to develop the coal fields of southeastern Oklahoma. By 1891, rail had been laid from Wister, where it connected with the Santa Fe line, to McAlester. That same year, work started on a line from El Reno to McAlester. Later reorganized as the Choctaw, Oklahoma & Gulf Railroad in 1895, it provided a direct link between El Reno and Arkansas.

✧

Frontier Woman *by Jay O'Meilia in the Pioneer Gardens of Gilcrease Museum in Tulsa. The statue was commissioned in memory of Fred D. Marvel and represents the role of pioneer women in settling Oklahoma. Shown here churning butter while keeping a watchful eye out for her family, the frontier women's belief in the future helped turn the Sooner State into modern Oklahoma. Life for women on the frontier was one of hardship. It was reported that some had nothing but mush made from Kaffer corn and milk to feed their families following the opening of the Cherokee Outlet. Another wrote that she would walk down to the nearby railroad tracks to watch the trains pass, just so she could enjoy the company of people outside of her isolated homestead.*

COURTESY GILCREASE MUSEUM.

✧

Above: Building the Atchison, Topeka, and Santa Fe Railroad across the Oklahoma Panhandle near Boise City. After the rail bed was prepared and the crossties were laid, the rail car was pushed to the head of the tracks by an engine. The rails were then lowered from the car with the aid of rollers and a crane, laid on the crossties, and held in place by spikes. The Santa Fe, as the line commonly was called, was the third major railroad built across Oklahoma.

COURTESY *THE DAILY OKLAHOMAN*.

Right: The Atchison, Topeka, and Santa Fe Depot at Edmond. Originally named Summit by railroad officials, the Santa Fe's tracks reached Edmond in 1887—two years prior to the opening of the Unassigned Lands to homesteaders. The arrival of the railroads and the lack of suitable land elsewhere focused the attention of the nation on the Unassigned Lands and increased the demand for its opening to homesteaders.

COURTESY NADINE PENDLETON COLLECTION, OKLAHOMA HERITAGE ASSOCIATION.

One other main line route was built in eastern Oklahoma. The Missouri, Oklahoma & Gulf Railroad constructed a rail line from Muskogee to Durant and south into Texas between 1904 and 1913 to tap into the coal fields of the region. It proved unprofitable, however, and the M.O. & G. filed for receivership in 1919.

The last of the major railroad construction projects across Oklahoma was the Fort Smith & Western, which was to link Fort Smith to Pueblo, Colorado. Work started in 1900 from Fort Smith west across the Choctaw and Creek Nations to the territorial capital at Guthrie in 1906. Purchasing the St. Louis, El Reno & Western Railroad gave trackage to El Reno. However, in 1923 the company was forced into receivership.

Closely related to railroad construction was the building of the state's electric traction railroads, or interurbans. The first interurban was organized in 1900 as the Oklahoma City Electric, Gas & Power Company. The initial operational line was opened in 1903 by the Choctaw Railway & Lighting Company, which built the Pittsburg County Railway between South McAlester and Alderson. The largest was the Oklahoma Railway Company's lines that radiated from Oklahoma City north to Britton, Edmond, and Guthrie; west to Putnam City, Bethany, Yukon, Banner, and El Reno; and south to Moore and Norman.

The railroads were among the leaders of the "boomers," as those who "boomed" or promoted the opening of Oklahoma to homesteaders were called, because such an action

would bring in more settlers, thereby generating more business for the railroads. They were supported by businessmen in border communities in Kansas and Texas who saw an opportunity to increase their market radius. Elias C. Boudinot, a Cherokee, became the spokesman for these groups and lobbied in Congress in 1878 for an Oklahoma Territory Bill that would open the Unassigned Lands, almost two million acres of land in the center of Indian Territory that had not been assigned as a reservation for any tribe, to homesteaders.

In 1879, Charles C. Carpenter began organizing homesteaders to move into Indian Territory, but abandoned his effort when President Rutherford B. Hayes threatened to use troops to block the move. David L. Payne then took over leadership of the boomer movement. Born in Indiana, Payne had served as a guide in Indian Territory and in the Union Army during the Civil War. After serving in the Kansas legislature, he was named a doorkeeper for the United States House of Representatives before returning to Kansas where he became president of the Oklahoma Colony. For a fee of $2, Payne promised members of the colony a claim of 160 acres of land in Indian Territory, for another $2 the claim would be surveyed, and for an additional fifty cents the settler could receive a seal for their claim certificate. He also was elected vice president of the Oklahoma Town Company, or Southwestern Colonization Society. Membership in the Oklahoma Town Company cost $25 and entitled the member to a town lot in the capital city of the new settlement. Colonel Edward Hatch, who was in charge of removing boomers from Indian Territory, estimated that Payne collected more than $100,000 in dues and fees.

Payne issued his first proclamation in 1879, and thousands rushed to join. Each family or individual had to have sufficient money to support themselves for one year, a wagon, one team, agricultural implements, and seeds worth $500. Single men not meeting these requirements could participate if they were employed by members of the colony and contracted for at least six months of work. No "hangers-on or idlers" were allowed. Payne set March 25, 1880, as the date of his invasion. However, when troops were ordered to patrol the Indian Territory-Kansas border, only ten

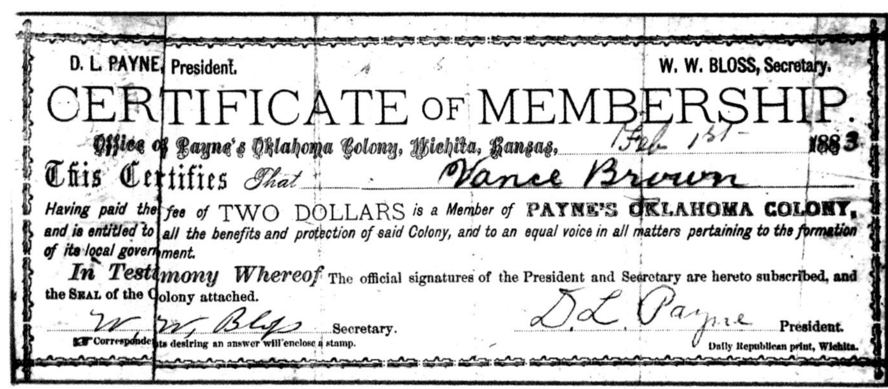
D. L. PAYNE, President. W. W. BLOSS, Secretary.

CERTIFICATE OF MEMBERSHIP.

Office of Payne's Oklahoma Colony, Wichita, Kansas, Feb 1st 1883

This Certifies That Vance Brown

Having paid the fee of TWO DOLLARS is a Member of PAYNE'S OKLAHOMA COLONY, and is entitled to all the benefits and protection of said Colony, and to an equal voice in all matters pertaining to the formation of its local government.

In Testimony Whereof The official signatures of the President and Secretary are hereto subscribed, and the SEAL of the Colony attached.

W. W. Bloss Secretary. D. L. Payne President.

Correspondents desiring an answer will enclose a stamp.

Daily Republican print, Wichita.

Above: Vance Brown's certificate of membership in David L. Payne's Oklahoma Colony. For a $2.00 fee members of the colony were entitled to a 160-acre homestead in the Unassigned Lands of Indian Territory. For another $2.00 the claim would be surveyed and for an additional fifty cents an official seal would be attached to the claim certificate. Of course, the membership was worthless to homesteaders when filing their claim with the federal land office. Nonetheless, it was estimated that Payne raised as much as $100,000 in dues and fees to support his Boomer movement.

COURTESY GORDON AND MARY SUE BROWN.

Left: A typical Boomer family. Most of the people making the Run of 1889 into the Unassigned Lands were poor. Wealthy farmers did not abandon proven farms to risk all on an unproven homestead. What is shown in the photograph is probably all this family of eight owned. The oldest son is holding a puppy and the younger children in the center are without shoes, as were most frontier children during the warmer months. A stove, a few chairs, some bedding, two horses, and two mules are all that are visible. The spring seat of their wagon has been removed to be used as seating.

COURTESY GILCREASE MUSEUM.

✧

Above: The railroads led the movement for the opening of the Unassigned Lands for homesteaders in the post-Civil War era. By pressuring the federal government to open that part of Oklahoma not occupied by Indian tribes, the railroad hoped to expand their business in the area. The railroads employed such lobbyists as E. C. Boudinot, a Cherokee, and helped fund such Boomers as David L. Payne to pressure congress to open what became known as "The Promised Land." The actual opening of the Unassigned Lands in 1889 is depicted in this detail from a Charles Banks Wilson mural in the state capitol.

COURTESY OKLAHOMA DEPARTMENT OF TOURISM AND RECREATION; PHOTOGRAPH BY FRED MARVEL.

or twelve wagons actually crossed the line on April 26, 1880.

Evading the patrols, Payne and his followers made their way to what became present-day Oklahoma City and established a camp about one-mile west of the present Santa Fe Railroad depot. New Philadelphia was the name given to their city, a pole stockade was built, and a water well dug. From the center of a knoll, eight major avenues radiated outward. Each was a mile in length and had a park at its end. Seven hundred and twenty squares made up the townsite, with each square being 300 feet by 600 feet. Streets were eighty feet wide.

Troops arrived at New Philadelphia on May 15, 1880, arrested members of the colony, transported them to Fort Reno, and then marched toward the Kansas border. Just short of the line, the troopers escorting Payne and the others stopped until June 6 to avoid being served a writ ordering the military to appear before the federal Thirteenth Judicial District to show cause for the boomers detention. On June 7 the boomers were thrown out of Indian Territory.

Payne led another invasion in July of 1880 from Kansas in the hope of being arrested and getting the issue before the federal courts. Taken before Judge Isaac Parker, he was disappointed when Parker released him without a trial. Payne then sued the army in the federal court in Wichita, Kansas, in May of 1881, but little came of the legal case. Payne led a third invasion in November of 1881, this time from Texas, but was intercepted by troops and escorted out of Indian Territory. Payne then visited Washington, D.C., to ask the U.S. secretary of the interior to intervene on behalf of the boomer movement. Receiving no support, he returned to Kansas and led a fourth invasion in September of 1882. Arrested and taken first to Fort Reno and then to the federal court at Fort Smith, the boomers were bound over for trial, but the case was continued at the request of the federal prosecutor.

Payne's fifth invasion, in February of 1883, was made from Kansas, Arkansas, Missouri, and Texas. Approximately 900 boomers flooded Indian Territory. Payne was arrested and then ejected from the region. In August of 1883 another invasion, this time without

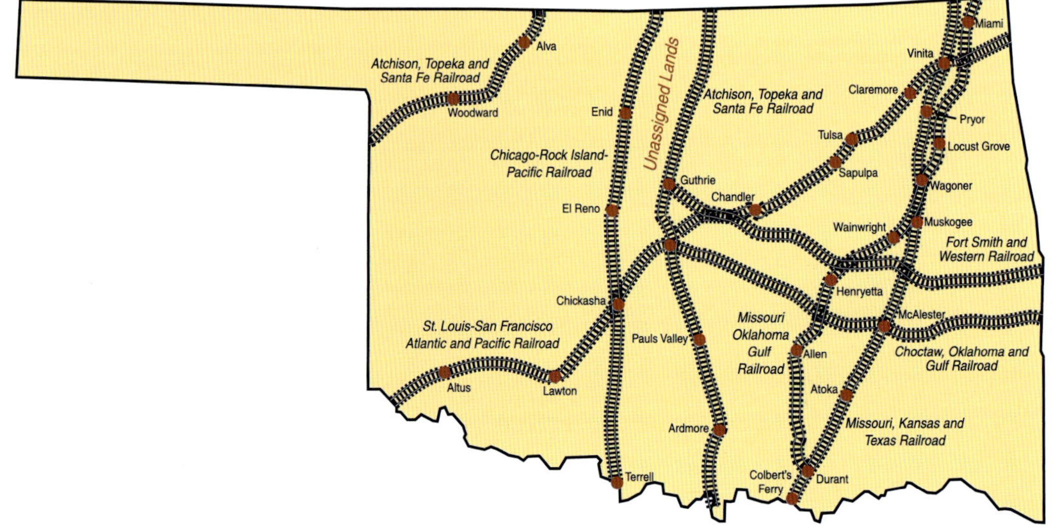

Right: Railroads crisscrossed the state in the late nineteenth century.

Payne, took place from Kansas. Although Payne was not with them, he was arrested and charged with conspiring to violate federal law. Formally indicted, Payne was elated when Federal Judge Cassius G. Foster ruled that the Unassigned Lands were part of the public domain and open to homesteaders.

Afterward, boomers rushed into Indian Territory, only to discover that President Chester A. Arthur had forbidden settlement in the region. Payne again was arrested inside Indian Territory in August of 1884, was charged with conspiring against the United States and indicted. Unfortunately, he died suddenly on the morning of November 27, 1884, before the issue was settled.

Payne's replacements were W. L. Couch and Samuel Crocker, who led an invasion of boomers to present-day Stillwater in December of 1884. They were discovered by soldiers on January 25, 1885, and escorted back to Kansas. At the same time, the boomer movement received some unexpected support from Milton W. Reynolds, who wrote under the name Kickingbird. He published *The Land of the Fair God*, which publicized the boomer effort and described the fertility of the Unassigned Lands.

Surrendering to the demands of the boomers, Secretary of the Interior Henry M. Teller recommended that the Unassigned Lands be opened to homesteaders, and Congress approved an Indian Appropriations Bill authorizing the purchase of the area from the Creeks and Seminoles who received $2,280,000 and $1,912,942, respectively, for their unoccupied land. Authorized to settle the area in the manner he thought best, President Benjamin Harrison ordered the Unassigned Lands to be opened by a run at noon on April 22, 1889.

As a part of the Reconstruction Treaties of 1866, most of the land previously had been surveyed. All of Indian Territory east of the 100th Meridian was surveyed from Initial Point, which was located about one mile south of Fort Arbuckle. From there a base line ran east and west, and the Indian Meridian was marked north and south. These lines divided the region into thirty-eight townships—twenty-nine north of Initial Point and nine to the south—and fifty-three ranges—twenty-seven east of Initial Point and twenty-six to the west. Each township and range was six miles square and contained thirty-six square miles or sections. Each section

✧

Above: The location of a railroad depot in most frontier towns was the difference between survival and disappearance, and many Oklahoma communities provided land or cash to lure railroads. While many depots were nothing more than utilitarian shacks, others were architecturally significant. The Santa Fe's Depot in Shawnee, built in 1903 and in use until 1973, featured Romanesque Revival architecture and is one of the few of this design remaining.

COURTESY DAVID FITZGERALD.

Left: Oklahoma Station on the Atchison, Topeka, and Santa Fe Railroad on April 22, 1889, the day of the Run of 1889. There was little in what became Oklahoma City prior to the opening of the area to homesteaders—just a railroad depot, a soldiers camp, and several buildings. Notice the cabin built of logs set upright in the ground on the right of the photograph. Today, the restored Santa Fe Depot is the gateway to Bricktown, one of the Southwest's premier tourist attractions.

COURTESY NADINE PENDLETON COLLECTION, OKLAHOMA HERITAGE ASSOCIATION.

✧

Above: To prevent the confusion caused by Sooners, who crossed into the Unassigned Lands early, hid, and then came out on April 22 to stake their claims, federal officials, at first, required those making the Cherokee Outlet Run to register. The requirement proved difficult to enforce, however, and later was abolished. These men are waiting in line three miles north of Stillwater on the southern border of the Cherokee Outlet to register. Notice the armed guards patrolling the line to keep order and the men in the right foreground eating watermelon as they wait.

COURTESY WILL HAWKS COLLECTION, MUSEUM OF THE GREAT PLAINS.

Right: Guthrie on April 24, 1889, two days after the Unassigned Lands were opened. Guthrie was one of seven cities that were "born grown" when an estimated 60,000 individuals participated in the Run of 1889. Streets and town lots already have been claimed and tents housing stores, banks, and newspapers were open for business. In the background some wooden buildings already are under construction. In 1890 Guthrie was named the territorial capital of Oklahoma Territory.

COURTESY NADINE PENDLETON COLLECTION, OKLAHOMA HERITAGE ASSOCIATION.

was subdivided into quarter sections of 160 acres each. The Panhandle also was divided into townships and ranges, with the Cimarron Meridian, the western border of the Panhandle, and the southern boundary of the Panhandle serving as the guidelines. There were twenty-eight ranges measured from the Cimarron Meridian eastward and six townships from the southern border north. Each homesteader was entitled to 160 acres. Sections 16 and 36 were reserved for the benefit of public schools. Townsites measuring 320 acres were provided for.

As estimated 60,000 people took part in the Run of '89. As many as thirty percent were Sooners who had ventured into the Unassigned Lands ahead of time to stake a claim before the official opening. By nightfall on April 22, six cities had been "born grown"—Oklahoma City, Norman, Guthrie, Edmond, Kingfisher, and Stillwater.

A year later, on May 2, 1890, the region was organized as Oklahoma Territory. The Organic Act divided the area into seven counties—Logan, Oklahoma, Cleveland, Payne, Kingfisher, and Canadian, in what once was the Unassigned Lands, and Beaver County from No Man's Land in the Oklahoma Panhandle. The president appointed the territorial governor and three federal district judges. These judges, when sitting together, made up the territorial supreme court. The territorial legislature was divided into two houses—an upper house of thirteen members called the council and a lower house of representatives with twenty-six members. In addition, the Organic Act provided that, as other areas of Indian Territory were opened, they would be added to Oklahoma Territory.

As early as 1887, Congress had started the process of the allotment of tribal lands and the assimilation of the Indians into the dominant white society. Under the provisions of the Dawes Act, tribal lands were to be allotted to individual members and the surplus lands opened to homesteaders. Those Indians accepting allotments would get title to their land in twenty-five years. In the meantime, tribal cultures were to be eliminated by a system of Indian schools that would stress the values and traditions of the white society while punishing Indian children for speaking their native languages and playing traditional games. The Choctaw, Chickasaws, Creeks, Seminoles, and Cherokees were exempted

from the provisions of the Dawes Act until 1893, when the Five Civilized Tribes Act provided for the allotment of their lands. In an effort to speed the assimilation of the Indians, the Curtis Act of 1898 eliminated tribal governments as of March 4, 1906.

To negotiate the opening of the reservations, Congress created the Cherokee Commission, headed by David H. Jerome. Almost immediately, the commissioners began meeting with tribal authorities to negotiate the allotment of land. On September 22, 1891, the Sac and Fox and Pottawatomi and Shawnee reservations were opened. After tribal members received their allotments, there were 868,414 surplus acres. Twenty thousand people competed for the 7,000 160-acre homesteads in a land run. Originally called

✧

Top: Mound Valley east of Weatherford filled with spring wheat. It was the arrival of the homesteader that resulted in the permanent settlement of western Oklahoma. The fertile grasslands once covered with buffalo and cattle gave way to drought resistant strains of wheat, such as Turkey Red, which was introduced by Mennonite immigrants that transformed the region into "America's Breadbasket."

COURTESY DAVID FITZGERALD.

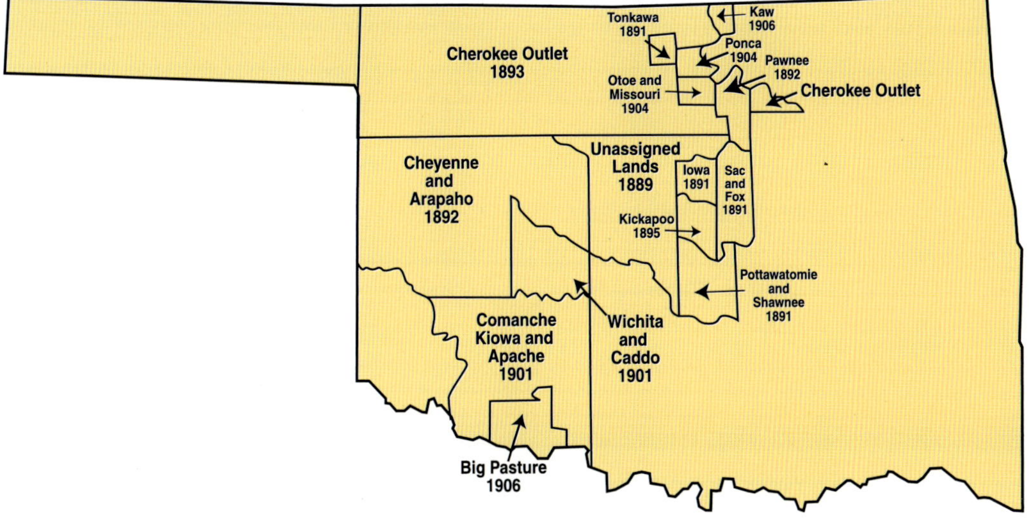

Middle: Land openings in the late nineteenth and early twentieth centuries.

Bottom: The famous Round Barn at Arcadia. William H. Odor, who settled in the region in 1892, built the two-story barn of burr oak in 1898. Odor chose the round shape because he believed it would survive a tornado, which, he believed, would slide around the curved sides. Odor convinced his brother-in-law, J. H. Keely, to build another round barn nearby. Keely's round barn was destroyed by a tornado in 1912, thus disproving Odor's theory. The restored round barn is a familiar site on US-66.

COURTESY OKLAHOMA DEPARTMENT OF TOURISM AND RECREATION; PHOTOGRAPH BY FRED MARVEL.

Above: The Mattie Beal home in Lawton. Lawton was named the county seat of Comanche County following the opening of the Kiowa-Comanche-Apache Reservation by lottery in 1901. More than 100,000 people registered for the 13,000 homesteads. Drawings were held at a rate of 125 a day in Lawton and El Reno to determine who received the 160-acre homesteads. At both sites 6,500 winners were selected. Town lots were sold on August 6, 1893, in Lawton, Hobart, and Anadarko. Beal, who registered on July 17, was known as "lucky number 2" in the El Reno lottery on July 29, 1901.

COURTESY MATTIE BEAL COLLECTION, MUSEUM OF THE GREAT PLAINS.

counties A and B, they became Lincoln and Pottawatomie Counties.

The Cheyenne-Arapaho Reservation was next. The 3,329 tribal members received 160-acre allotments and were paid $1,500,000 for the remaining surplus lands. The money was paid in hard cash, with each Cheyenne and Arapaho receiving seventy-five silver dollars, weighing six pounds, at the first payment in July of 1891. The surplus land was opened to homesteaders by run at noon on April 19, 1892, and was organized into Blaine, Dewey, Day, Roger Mills, Custer, and Washita Counties. Much of the western portion of the reservation went unclaimed because of its poor soil, and it was not until the twentieth century that all of the region was settled.

On April 3, 1893, the Cherokees agreed to sell the Cherokee Outlet, which opened 6,122,754 acres to homesteaders by run on September 16, 1893. At the same time, the Pawnee and Tonkawa Reservations were allotted and opened by run. Kay, Grant, Woods, Woodward, Garfield, Noble, and Pawnee Counties were added to Oklahoma Territory from these lands. The last of the great land runs took place in 1895, when the Kickapoo Reservation was opened to settlement on May 23. Because the region was added to existing counties, no new counties were created from this land.

When the Kiowa-Comanche-Apache and Wichita-Caddo Reservations were opened on August 6, 1901, a lottery system was used. Once the tribal members had been granted their allotments, potential homesteaders registered either at the Lawton or El Reno land offices. Approximately 150,000 people filed for the 13,000 quarter sections. Six thousand five hundred winners were drawn in Lawton and a like number were selected in El Reno. The lucky winners were given the opportunity to select their homesteads in the order in which their names were drawn. Caddo, Comanche, and Kiowa Counties were created from these lands.

Initially, 480,000 acres of the newly opened Kiowa-Comanche-Apache and Wichita-Caddo Reservations were reserved for cattle grazing. Four hundred and one thousand acres were set aside as the Big Pasture, and the remaining 79,000 acres became the Little Pasture. These lands were opened by sealed bids on September 19, 1906, and sold for an average of $10.50 per acre.

Right: Downtown Perry, Oklahoma, on October 1, 1893. Perry was in the Cherokee Outlet that was opened to homesteaders by run on September 16, 1893. Already many businesses have moved out of tents and into wooden buildings—note the physician and surgeon's office in the lower left. Most of its residents maintained contact with loved ones by mail, and the line at the local post office when the mail came in became long. Some postal customers brought logs to sit on, like the man on the left, while others carried umbrellas for shade. The young boy on the right took the opportunity to sell newspapers to the crowd.

COURTESY NADINE PENDLETON COLLECTION, OKLAHOMA HERITAGE ASSOCIATION.

✧

Left: A homesteader's sod house. Timber was scarce in western Oklahoma. Therefore most homesteaders lived in "soddies." They would cut the prairie sod into bricks, which were stacked to form the sides of the home. A ridge pole was placed across the top and rafters of branches were laid. The rafters were covered with brush that was often waterproofed by a layer of tar paper. A final layer of sod bricks was placed on the tar paper to form the roof. Unfortunately, the space between the rafters and the sod roof was a common place for snakes to spend the colder months, and many winter meals were interrupted when cooking heat woke the snakes, which would fall down into the house.

COURTESY OKLAHOMA DEPARTMENT OF TOURISM AND RECREATION; PHOTOGRAPH BY FRED MARVEL.

Below: Waiting for the Cherokee Outlet Run to start on September 16, 1893. The land was organized into K, L, M, N, O, P, and Q counties of Oklahoma Territory. Later the counties were renamed Kay, with Newkirk as its seat; Grant, with Pond Creek as its seat; Woods, with Alva as its seat; Woodward, with Woodward as its seat; Garfield, with Enid as its seat; Noble, with Perry as its seat; and Pawnee, with Pawnee as its seat.

COURTESY NADINE PENDLETON COLLECTION, OKLAHOMA HERITAGE ASSOCIATION.

The final land opening took place in 1904. On April 21 of that year, Congress ordered the arbitrary allotment of the Ponca, Otoe-Missouria, and Kaw Reservations. These lands were added to existing counties.

Many of those making openings left their families behind to join them later if they were successful in getting a claim. Most were not wealthy and had spent much of the money they had to prepare for the run. Many lived in dugouts or half dugouts which were merely holes in the ground, covered with a roof of straw or sod. Later some constructed sod houses, or "soddies," made of stacked blocks of tough prairie sod. Holes were left for windows and doors, and the roof was covered with straw, tar paper, and then a layer of sod. Inside walls were plastered with mud and whitewashed. Windows were made from paper rubbed with grease.

The prairies of western Oklahoma offered little firewood, so the settlers used buffalo chips for fuel. Often the ground water was "gyp" and unpalatable, so cisterns were dug to collect rainwater. Sometimes it was too late to plant crops after the land openings, and food was in short supply. Following the opening of the Cherokee Outlet, many of the homesteaders lived on a diet of kefir corn mush and milk the first winter.

By the beginning of the twentieth century, Oklahoma was occupied by the Twin Territories—Oklahoma Territory in the west and Indian Territory in the east. The question facing the citizens of the region was that of future statehood. Compounding the issue was the issue of whether there should be two states or one created?

CHAPTER VII

THE TWIN TERRITORIES

While Oklahoma Territory continued to grow with the addition of the various Indian reservations as well as Cimarron Territory and Old Greer County, the leaders of the various tribes in Indian Territory could not agree on the formation of a territorial government. Although the Reconstruction Treaties of 1866 provided for an intertribal council that met periodically between 1867 and 1876, the only substantial result was the Okmulgee Constitution of 1870, which called for the unification of all the tribes. The individual tribes refused, however, fearing that it would lead to the abolishment of the tribal authorities. The unwillingness of the separate tribes to surrender their autonomy eventually resulted in the region being joined with Oklahoma Territory to create the State of Oklahoma on November 16, 1907.

Old Greer County was the name given to that region between the Prairie Dog Fork and the North Fork of the Red River, which was claimed by both Oklahoma and Texas. The confusion over ownership resulted from the inaccurate maps used to establish the southern boundary of the Louisiana Purchase in the Treaty of 1819. The one by John Melish, upon which the treaty makers relied, showed only one channel for the Red River east of the 100th Meridian. In addition, the early American explorers could not accurately locate where the 100th Meridian intersected the Red River.

Mexico accepted the 1819 line in its treaty of independence with Spain in 1828. Texas did likewise when it became independent of Mexico. The Missouri Compromise of 1850 also left the mislocated boundary intact. It was not until 1852 that an accurate survey was attempted by Captain Randolph B. Marcy, and his survey put the intersection of the 100th Meridian at the North Fork instead of the Prairie Dog Fork of the Red River. This mistake was discovered when the Choctaw-Chickasaw Agreement was ratified in 1855, but nothing was done to correct the error. Greer County, Texas was created in 1860, and, in 1879, Texas began granting homesteads in the region for Texas veterans of the Mexican War.

There was a mounting concern that the boundary was not as it should be, however, and in 1883 Texas Governor John Ireland proposed to President Chester A. Arthur that a Joint Boundary Commission be created to permanently affix the line between Texas and Oklahoma Territory. Federal officials responded and the Boundary Commission of 1886 was established, first meeting in February of that year. Nothing was accomplished because the Texas commissioners refused to consider any boundary other than the North Fork of the Red River, while the federal commissioners insisted it was the Prairie Dog Fork. With no agreement in sight, the commissioners ceased meeting in June of 1886.

On December 30, 1887, President Grover Cleveland affirmed the report of the federal boundary commissioners that the Prairie Dog Fork was the main channel of the Red River under the provisions of the Treaty of 1819. On May 2, 1890, federal officials decided to take the case to the Supreme Court of the United States. The case, *United States v. Texas*, lasted until March 16, 1896, when the court ruled that the main channel of the Red River was the Prairie Dog Fork and that the true 100th Meridian must be used as the boundary line, not the mistakenly located one. On May 4, 1896, Greer County, Texas, was reorganized as Greer County, Oklahoma Territory, with the county seat at Mangum.

Under the Greer County Homestead Act of 1897, original settlers who had been granted land by Texas officials were allowed to keep 160 acres and purchase an additional 160 acres at $1 per acre. The remainder was opened to homesteaders. At statehood, in 1907, the area was divided into Greer and Jackson counties. Two years later, in 1909, a third county, Harmon County, was created out of a portion of Greer County, and the remainder of the county was made a part of Beckham County. A second United States Supreme Court case in 1930 readjusted the 100th Meridian and returned 28,500 acres to Texas.

✧

Lake Altus deep in the granite hills of the Quartz Mountains. Stretching along the North Fork of the Red River in southwestern Oklahoma, the Quartz Mountains in reality are the westward extension of the Wichita Mountain Chain. Prior to the Unites States Supreme Court ruling in United States v. Texas *in 1896, Texas claimed that that part of present-day Oklahoma south of the North Fork of the Red River belonged to that state. Greer County, Texas was organized in 1860.*

COURTESY DAVID FITZGERALD.

✧

Right: Al Spencer was a cowboy on Sherman Moore's ranch in Washington County before he turned to outlawry. On the ranch he was in charge of the hounds that were used by the ranch hands to chase wolves and coyotes. A noted train robber, Spencer was killed in a gun battle with lawmen in Osage County on September 20, 1923. The rugged Osage Hills were a favorite hideout for outlaws.

COURTESY EDGAR E. WESTON.

Below: The Twin Territories were a haven for outlaws in the last decades of the nineteenth century. One of the region's most infamous bandits was Henry Starr, shown here on the right with his friend Ed Newcom. A notorious bank robber, Starr was captured after being wounded while attempting to rob two banks at the same time in Stroud on March 27, 1915. Starr's life of crime began in 1890 and covered three decades. After his capture in Stroud, he was sentenced to twenty-five years in prison but was paroled after serving four years. He was killed in Arkansas in 1921, while robbing another bank. Starr's nephew, Pat Fields, was a lawman who served as the night marshal at Dewey.

COURTESY OKLAHOMA HERITAGE ASSOCIATION.

Cimarron Territory was also known as "No Man's Land" because of the saying that it was God's land, but no man's, resulting from its exclusion from the surrounding states. The Compromise of 1850 had excluded slavery from all territory north of thirty-six degrees, thirty minutes. Texas thus ceded that portion of its panhandle north of that line. The compromise also established the eastern border of New Mexico as the 103rd Meridian and the southern border of Kansas at the Thirty-seventh Parallel. The western border of Indian Territory was the 100th Meridian. These circumstances caused the area that ultimately would become the Oklahoma Panhandle to be unclaimed by any state or territory.

Left: Outlaw Elmer J. McCurdy was killed by a posse near Pawhuska on October 7, 1911. Lawmen had tracked him to a barn and called on him to surrender; however, McCurdy, who was drunk, began firing at the officers. After the shootout, McCurdy's body was taken to an undertaker in Pawhuska, embalmed, and held until it could be claimed by a relative. Five years passed before a man claiming to be a relative appeared and offered to pay for the undertaker's services. Glad to be rid of the body, the undertaker took the money. Soon thereafter the former outlaw was put on display in a carnival. Later the body appeared in a wax museum. In 1976, while filming a television show in a Los Angeles, California funhouse, a technician knocked off one of McCurdy's arms and noticed a bone protruding from the "wax dummy." Turned over to the Los Angeles County coroner's office, the body subsequently was returned to Oklahoma and buried in the Guthrie cemetery in 1977.

COURTESY *THE DAILY OKLAHOMAN.*

Below: Gambling and liquor flourished in Oklahoma Territory prior to statehood in 1907. Here Walter Steciak, Anton Scybak, John Klimkowski, Pat Senkowski, and Andrew Jarski enjoy a card game and a friendly drink. After statehood liquor was prohibited and gambling joints were closed.

COURTESY ELENORA WYSKUP COLLECTION, WESTERN HISTORY COLLECTIONS, UNIVERSITY OF OKLAHOMA LIBRARIES.

✧

Above: The Three Sisters are a well-known landmark near Black Mesa in what once was known as No Man's Land, now the Oklahoma Panhandle. Excluded from Texas, New Mexico, Kansas, and the Cherokee Outlet by the Compromise of 1850 and other historical developments, the region, bounded by the 103rd Meridian on the west, the 100th Meridian on the east, the Thirty-seventh Parallel on the north, and thirty-six degrees, thirty minutes on the south, was called "God's Land, but no man's." It was added to the newly created Territory of Oklahoma by Congress in 1890 as County Number 7.

COURTESY DAVID FITZGERALD.

Few non-Indians had entered the region prior to the 1880s, with the exception of those traveling along the Cimarron Cutoff of the Santa Fe Trail. Between June and August of 1865, Camp Nicholas was garrisoned to stop Indian depredations along the Santa Fe Trail; however, the army mistakenly believed the post was in New Mexico. In 1882, the secretary of the interior ruled that the region was not a part of the Cherokee Outlet, and, in 1885, the general land office declared it was available to homesteaders.

Numerous settlers moved into what was called the Public Land Strip. In 1885, the Beaver City Town Company was organized and Beaver City became the unofficial capital. By 1887 an estimated 6,000 people had settled in No Man's Land; however, they had no title to their holdings. In an attempt to settle rival land claims, about fifty men met in the Beaver City school house in 1886 and organized a claimant's board. This was followed by a petition calling for the election of a territorial council, which was set for February 22, 1887. Meanwhile, the claimant's board acted as a steering committee. Each community in No Man's Land elected three representatives to meet at Beaver City on March 4, 1887. Although the voting mostly was limited to the eastern part of the region, the Beaver City Convention convened on time with seven of the nine elected officials present.

The delegates declared themselves the Territorial Council of Cimarron Territory and divided the region into seven counties—Benton, Beaver, Shade, Springer, Turner, Kilgore, and Sunset. Each county contained four vertical townships. Laws covering property, marriage, taxes, and corporations were adopted and the laws of the State of Colorado were to be enforced until additional statutes could be approved. An election for a nine-member senate and fourteen-member house of representatives was set for the first Monday in November of 1887. Those elected were to

Right: Cimarron Territory was added to Oklahoma Territory in 1890. Old Greer County was added to Oklahoma Territory in 1896.

convene the first Monday in December as a Territorial Council. On April 5, 1888, the council members chose Dr. Orville G. Chase as Cimarron Territory's congressional delegate.

There was much opposition to the Beaver City Convention, and in July of 1887 a rival convention convened at Rothwell. It chose a different delegate to Congress, J. E. Dale. Both appeared before Congress seeking recognition. The confusion in Congress as to who was the actual representative and the inability of the Beaver City Convention to enforce its laws, resulted in the failure of a bill to create the Territory of Cimarron. Separate bills to attach No Man's Land to either Kansas or New Mexico also failed. Eventually No Man's Land was placed under the jurisdiction of the United States Court at Muskogee, and then, with the organization of Oklahoma Territory on May 2, 1890, No Man's Land became County Number Seven of Oklahoma Territory, with Beaver City as its seat. The Oklahoma Territorial Council renamed it Beaver County. At statehood, Old Beaver County was divided into Beaver, Cimarron, and Texas Counties.

Unlike Oklahoma Territory, which had an organized territorial government, Indian Territory often was referred to as "west of hell's fringe" meaning that it was beyond most federal, state, or local lawmen. As independent-dependent governments, tribal courts ruled in each Indian nation, with tribal lighthorsemen enforcing tribal law. There were few tribal prisons and most lawbreakers were punished by whipping or other forms of corporal punishment. Those convicted of capital punishments usually were shot.

It was not uncommon for tribal and federal authorities to disagree over jurisdiction. In 1872, when Ezekial Proctor was being tried by Cherokee officials for killing an Indian, a group of federal deputy marshals burst into the courtroom to arrest him for killing a white man. A gunfight ensued between tribal and federal lawmen that left seven marshals and four Cherokees dead.

Above: When law and order failed, self-appointed vigilantes often took justice into their hands. On April 19, 1909, Jim Miller, Joe Allen, B.B. Burrell, and Jesse West, left to right, were hanged from the rafters of a barn in Ada. They had been accused of murdering a local resident, A. A. Bobbitt.

COURTESY ADA PUBLIC LIBRARY COLLECTION, WESTERN HISTORY COLLECTIONS, UNIVERSITY OF OKLAHOMA LIBRARIES.

Left: The Yeller Dog Saloon in Red Rock, Oklahoma Territory. In the Twin Territories, liquor was legal in Oklahoma Territory and banned in Indian Territory and the Osage Nation. Because of its proximity to the Osage Nation, which was dry, Red Rock was a frequent destination for Indians wanting to purchase liquor legally. At midnight on November 16, 1907, all saloons in the new State of Oklahoma were closed. Although much of the remaining liquor was corked and shipped to other states, much of the beer, which was in barrels, was poured into gutters. So stringent was the new state's ban on liquor that local officials tried to prosecute Catholic priests for importing sacramental wine.

COURTESY HELEN HOLMES COLLECTION, WESTERN HISTORY COLLECTION, UNIVERSITY OF OKLAHOMA LIBRARIES.

✧

Top, left: In Indian Territory and on the reservations in western Oklahoma, Indian officials were responsible for maintaining law and order prior to statehood. Harry Hall, on the right, is shown with a friend, Bill Komsah, Sr. Both were Kiowa. Hall was a member of the Indian police who patrolled the Kiowa-Comanche-Apache Reservation.

COURTESY SAM DEVENNEY COLLECTION, MUSEUM OF THE GREAT PLAINS.

Top, right: Chris Madsen at age ninety, posing with his revolver, automatic pistol, and shotgun that he used while serving as a United States Deputy Marshal in Oklahoma. Madsen remained in law enforcement until 1933.

COURTESY *THE DAILY OKLAHOMAN.*

Non-Indians escaping from justice in surrounding states transformed Indian Territory into a haven for bandits, bootleggers, swindlers, and other undesirables. Younger's Bend, near Eufaula in the Choctaw Nation, was maintained by Sam and Belle Starr and was a well-known outlaw hideout. Another was a fortified cabin maintained by Ned Cristie, just east of Tahlequah. Cristie, who had killed a deputy marshal, was tracked to his hideout and cornered on November 2, 1892. The posse eventually used a Civil War cannon and dynamite to drive Cristie out of the cabin before shooting him down.

The Doolin and Dalton gangs featured many of the most notorious outlaws. Gratton, or Grat; Franklin, or Frank; Robert, or Bob; Emmett; and William, or Bill, Dalton were the core of the Dalton Gang. At times, other members included Dick Broadwell, George "Bitter Creek" Newcomb, Charlie "Black Face Charlie" Bryant, Tim Evans, and Charlie Pierce. At one time, the M-K-T Railroad offered a $5,000 reward for the capture of any member of the Dalton Gang, and the aggregate reward for the various members totaled $33,600, the largest sum up to that time ever offered for the capture of an outlaw gang.

Their demise took place on October 5, 1895, when Emmett, Bob, Grat, Dick Broadwell, and Tim Evans tried to rob two banks in Coffeyville, Kansas, at the same time. Bill Doolin, who was to join in the robbery, did not because his horse went lame. The robbery failed. Four of the five outlaws were killed, and Emmett Dalton was captured when he stopped to help his brother. After confessing his crimes, Emmett was sentenced to prison. When released, he became a law-abiding citizen.

Following the ill-fated bank raid at Coffeyville, Bill Doolin formed his own outlaw band, which at one time or another included Bill Dalton; George Waights, alias Red Buck; George "Bitter Creek" Newcomb; Ol Yantis; Bill Raidler, alias "Little Bill"; Dick West, alias "Little Dick"; Dan Clifton, alias "Dynamite Dick"; Bud Smith; Tom Daugherty, alias "Arkansas Tom"; and "Tulsa" Jack Blake. With Doolin as their

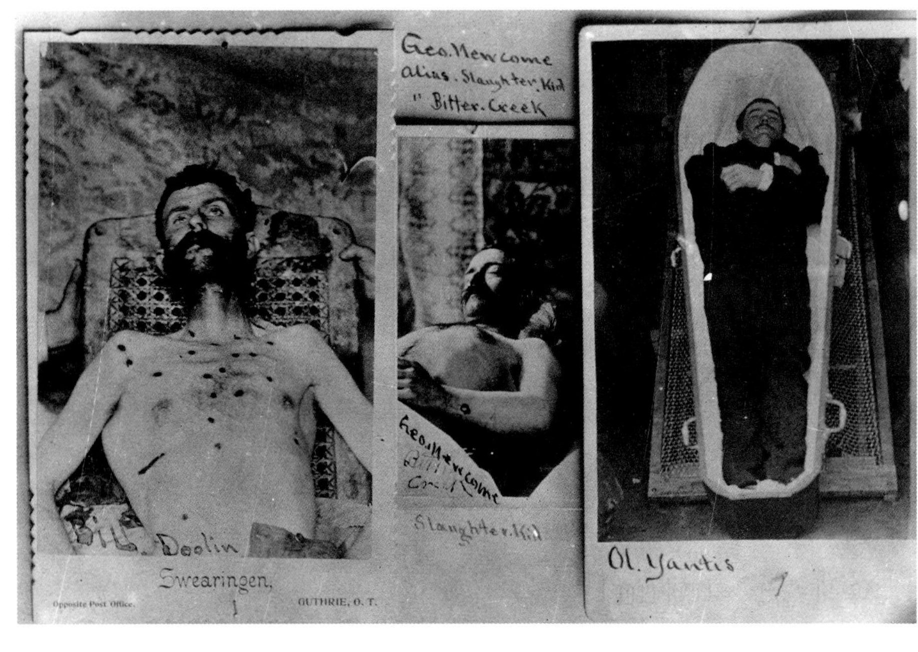

Below: Three members of the Doolin Gang, formed after the ill-fated raid on the banks in Coffeyville, Kansas, in October of 1892. Left to right, Bill Doolin, who was killed by a shotgun blast on August 25, 1896, near Lawson in Pawnee County; George "Bitter Creek" Newcomb, who died in a gun fight at the Dunn Ranch on Council Creek near Ingalls in Payne County on May 2, 1895; and Ol Yantis, who was killed near Orlando, in Logan County, on November 30, 1892.

COURTESY *THE DAILY OKLAHOMAN.*

leader, they robbed trains and banks throughout the Twin Territories, Kansas, Missouri, and Texas. The gang was almost captured at the Battle of Ingalls on September 8, 1893, when they were ambushed by a party of twenty-seven lawmen while they were staying in the Ramsom and Murray Saloon and the nearby hotel operated by Mary Pierce.

In the shootout that followed, lawmen Dick Speed, Tom Houston, and Lafe Shadley were killed, and Frank Briggs was seriously wounded. Bitter Creek Newcomb also was wounded, but managed to escape with the help of Rose Dunn, who was known as the "Rose of the Cimarron."

Within three years, however, most of the Doolin Gang either were killed or jailed. Bill Dalton was shot and killed by Deputy United States Marshals near Ardmore on June 8, 1894. Bud Smith was killed by lawmen at Watonga a few weeks later. Bitter Creek Newcomb and Charlie Pierce were shot and killed on May 2, 1894, near the Dunn Ranch northeast of Ingalls. Bill Doolin was captured by Deputy Marshall William Tilghman at Eureka Springs, Arkansas, in January of 1896 and taken to Guthrie, where he joined Dynamite Dick in awaiting trial. The two outlaws escaped on July 5, 1896, and in the following manhunt Doolin was shot and killed by Deputy Marshal Heck Thomas on August 25. Dynamite Dick was shot to death by a posse as he hid in a ravine west of Newkirk on December 4, 1896.

The last of the great outlaw gangs was the Jennings Gang, led initially by Little Dick West; however, when West proved inept, he was replaced by Al Jennings and his brother, Frank. Both were captured on December 1, 1897, and sent to prison. Released in 1902, Jennings returned to Oklahoma Territory where he starred in the movie *Beating Back*, and ran for governor of Oklahoma in 1914. Defeated in his election bid, he moved to California and became a chicken rancher.

Marshall Evett D. Nix was the most famous of the United States Marshals in Oklahoma Territory. Under his supervision were "The Three Guardsmen"—William Tilghman, Heck Thomas, and Chris Madsen—who became

Top, left: A whipping tree next to a Choctaw Nation courthouse. Unlike Oklahoma Territory, the various Indian nations in Indian Territory did not imprison most criminals. Instead they received corporal punishment, such as whipping. The punishment was carried out by tribal lighthorsemen.

COURTESY PUSHMATAHA COLLECTION, WESTERN HISTORY COLLECTIONS, UNIVERSITY OF OKLAHOMA LIBRARIES.

Top, right: Two of the famous United States Deputy Marshals known as the Three Guardsmen—Chris Madsen (left) and William "Bill" Tilghman (right). Tilghman captured the outlaw Bill Doolin in a bathhouse in Eureka Springs, Arkansas, without firing a shot. In 1924, Tilghman came out of retirement to become marshal of Cromwell, an oil boom town in Seminole County known as "Wicked Cromwell." On November 1, 1924, he was killed while trying to disarm Wiley Lynn, a drunken federal prohibition agent. Tilghman recorded his feats in a movie he produced titled Passing of the Oklahoma Outlaws.

COURTESY THE OKLAHOMA HISTORICAL SOCIETY.

Bottom: Tom Mix, the famous movie star of the 1920s, once served as the night marshal of Dewey, in Washington County. He also held a commission as a Washington County Deputy Sheriff. Often called "Pussyfoot Mix" because of his ability to sneak up on criminals, Mix later documented his exploits as a lawmen in Dewey in a story titled Fe-Fi-Fo-Fum! I Smell Smuggled Rum.

COURTESY *THE DAILY OKLAHOMAN.*

✧

Right: Top, left to right: Bill Powers, sometimes identified as Tim Evans, and Dick Broadwell. Bottom, left to right: Bob Dalton, Emmett Dalton, and Grat Dalton. The Dalton brothers, Powers, and Broadwell were shot on October 5, 1892, when they attempted to rob two banks at the same time in Coffeyville, Kansas. Bob and Grat Dalton, as well as Broadwell and Powers, were killed. Emmett Dalton survived his wounds and was sent to prison. Bill Doolin, who was supposed to join the gang's Coffeyville raid, was delayed by a lame horse and did not participate. He later warned the citizens of Coffeyville that "all of the gang ain't dead yet by a damn site…and we shall come and see you."

COURTESY *THE DAILY OKLAHOMAN.*

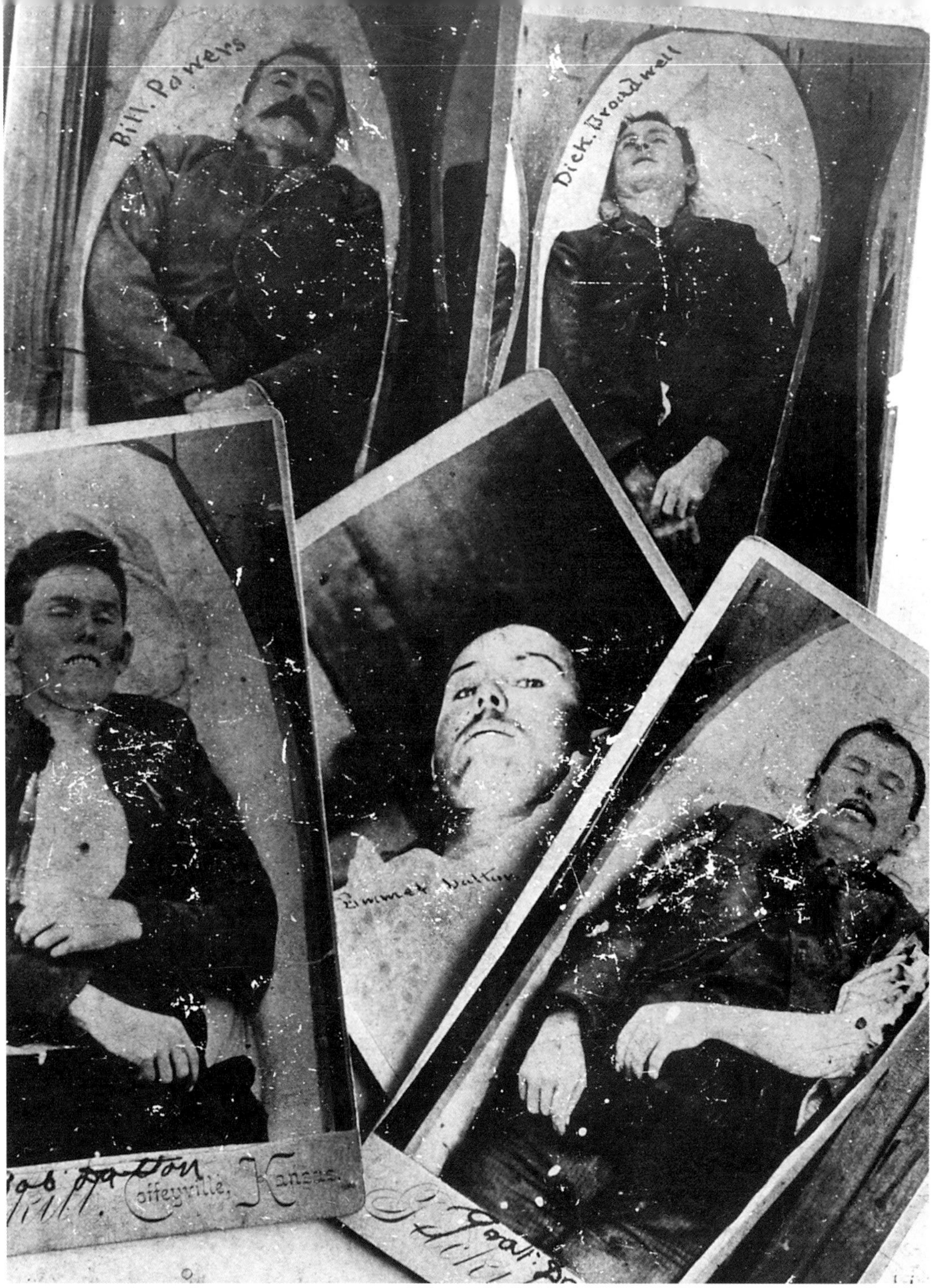

Below: President Theodore Roosevelt, standing second from the right, visited Frederick in May of 1905 to accept John "Jack" Abernathy's, center holding a coyote, invitation for a cowboy wolf hunt, in which the cowboys chased the coyotes on horseback and roped them. Roosevelt was particularly fond of Oklahoma because of his relationship with many of its citizens who served with him in the Rough Riders during the Spanish-American War. Abernathy served as a United States Deputy Marshal in western Oklahoma from 1906 until 1910.

COURTESY SAM DEVENNEY COLLECTION, MUSEUM OF THE GREAT PLAINS.

famous Western lawmen. They were among the 200 United States deputy marshals appointed by Judge Isaac Parker. Of the 200, sixty-five were killed in the line of duty.

Known as the "hanging judge," Parker had jurisdiction over crimes committed in Indian Territory when he took the bench of the United States District Court for Western Arkansas. He first assumed the bench on May 10, 1875, and by the end of June had tried ninety-one criminal cases. Eighteen were murder cases. Fifteen of the accused were convicted. Eight were sentenced to be hanged. One escaped, and one had his sentence commuted to life in prison. The remaining six were hanged simultaneously on September 3, 1875. They were the first of eighty-eight men hanged by Judge Parker.

There also were self-appointed vigilante organizations stalking criminals in the Twin Territories, the best known of which was the White Caps. Formed after the opening of the Cherokee Outlet in 1893, the White Caps wore white paper fool's caps, masks, and coats of coffee sacking. They spread terror among Sooners and claim jumpers. At first they simply ordered them to leave the Outlet; later several homes and barns were burned. Other bands of vigilantes dispensed a more violent brand of "justice," which sometimes was intended to "send a message" to Indians or blacks. For example, near Earlsboro two Indians were burned alive while chained to a brush arbor after being accused of raping a white woman. On the bridge over the North Fork of the Canadian near Bearden a black man was hanged and his body burned after being accused of taking part in the killing of a deputy sheriff. At Ada, four accused murderers were hanged in a barn by vigilantes.

It was little wonder that the Twin Territories were a mecca for those seeking to escape justice. The region truly was one of the last frontiers of the Wild West. However, with the movement for statehood came the demand for law and order.

Top: The remains of the Cherokee Female Seminary at the Cherokee Heritage Center, south of Tahlequah. Higher education in the Indian Territory was equal to that of any surrounding state. Located at Park Hill, the Cherokee Female Seminary was authorized by the Cherokee National Council in 1847 and was one of 106 public schools in the Cherokee Nation in 1880. It burned in 1887.

COURTESY OKLAHOMA DEPARTMENT OF TOURISM AND RECREATION; PHOTOGRAPH BY FRED MARVEL.

Bottom: Churches in the Twin Territories offered not only spiritual solace but entertainment that competed with the more rowdy saloons, gambling dens, and brothels. This is the Catholic Friar's Musical Band. Seated, left to right, Joachim Dougherty, Marcus Fuerstenberg, John Laracy, Raphael de Fives, Blaise Haritchabelet. Standing, left to right, Gregory Gerrer, Hildebrand Zoeller, Sylvester Castera, Stansilaus Testavin, Timothy Murphy, Emil Labat, Lawrence Carrico, and Vincent Montalibet.

COURTESY SOONER CATHOLIC MAGAZINE COLLECTION, WESTERN HISTORY COLLECTIONS, UNIVERSITY OF OKLAHOMA LIBRARIES.

TERRITORIAL GOVERNORS OF OKLAHOMA

George W. Steele, 1890-1891
Robert Martin, 1891-1892
Abraham J. Seay, 1892-1893
William C. Renfrow, 1893-1897
Cassius M. Barnes, 1897-1901
William M. Jenkins, 1901
William C. Grimes, 1901
Thomas B. Ferguson, 1901-1906
Frank Frantz, 1906-1907

CHAPTER VIII

The State of Sequoyah

The Twin Territories presented a problem for national political leaders. Both regions had sufficient population and economic base for statehood; however, the citizens of the territories and the politicians in Washington, D.C., debated how the process should proceed. The options included admitting the two territories separately as two states, combining them into one new state, allowing Oklahoma Territory to become a state immediately and admitting Indian Territory to statehood later, or letting both regions remain territories.

The decision was greatly influenced by national politics. The Republicans, who controlled the federal government during the final decades of the nineteenth century, did not want to expand Democratic power by increasing the number of Democratic senators. Admitting Oklahoma Territory by itself likely would result in the election of one Democratic and one Republican senator. If the Twin Territories were joined, the more populous Indian Territory, controlled by the Democrats, probably would result in the election of two Democratic senators. If nothing was done, there would be no Democratic senators chosen, and the Republicans would remain in control of the territorial government. Thus, while politicians debated, the development of the region continued.

Oklahoma Territory politics was dominated by "carpetbag" Republican governors. Of the nine men who held the office of territorial governor, all were northern Republicans, except for William C. Renfrow, who was a Democrat from North Carolina. Most were undistinguished politicians appointed in recognition of their political connections instead of their administrative abilities. Most political fights in the territory resulted from a split among local Republicans. Democrats controlled the governor's office for four years between 1893 and 1897, the territorial house of representatives between 1900 and 1902, the territorial council between 1902 and 1904, and both houses of the Territorial Legislature between 1896 and 1900.

Perhaps the most significant action of the Territorial Legislature was the creation of a system of secondary and higher education. However, several scandals associated with the operation of territorial facilities, such as the Oklahoma Sanitarium Company's contract to care for the insane, marred territorial politics. Territorial Governor Cassius M. Barnes and congressional representative Dennis T. Flynn played a major role in the Free Homes Bill enacted by Congress in 1900. It allowed the free settlement of unoccupied lands in Oklahoma Territory, thereby saving homesteaders an estimated $15,000,000.

Squabbling over the location of the territorial capital occupied much of the territorial era. Frank Greer, publisher of the *Oklahoma State Capital* in Guthrie, was an outspoken Republican and a harsh critic of Democratic policies and politicians. Partly to escape his scathing editorials, Democratic politicians often advocated moving the territorial capital from Guthrie, where it temporarily had been located by the Organic Act. In 1890, the territorial legislature voted to move the capital to Oklahoma City, but Territorial Governor George Steele vetoed the act. Partly to repay local Republican supporters, in 1891, Congress enacted legislation to locate the capital permanently in Guthrie, but prohibited the construction of permanent buildings. Guthrie thus remained the territorial capital, but the issue would rise again.

During this period, federal officials began to strip the tribes of Indian Territory of their self-governing status and to force the Indians to accept the individual allotment of tribal lands. Although the Choctaws, Chickasaws, Creeks, Seminoles, and Cherokees had been exempted from the provisions of the Dawes Act of 1887, the Five Civilized Tribes Act of 1893 created the Dawes Commission, named for its chairman Henry L. Dawes, to negotiate allotment. Other members of the commission were A. S. McKennon and M. H. Kidd. In 1897, Tams Bixby was named to the commission, and under his direction the Dawes Commission completed its work in 1906.

Arriving in Indian Territory in February of 1894 to meet with representatives of the Five Tribes in Checotah, the proposals of the Dawes Commission were rejected out of hand by the Indians.

✧

Oklahoma's territorial governors: George W. Steele, 1890-1891; Abraham J. Seay, 1892-1893; William C. Renfrow, 1893-1897; Cassius M. Barnes, 1897-1901; William M. Jenkins, 1901; Thomas B. Ferguson, 1901-1906; and Frank Frantz, 1906-1907. In addition, two territorial secretaries, Robert Martin and William C. Grimes, served as territorial governors in 1891-1892 and 1901, respectively, while awaiting the appointment of a new territorial governor by the president.

COURTESY *THE DAILY OKLAHOMAN.*

✧

Top, left: The restored home of Oklahoma Territorial Governor Thomas B. Ferguson in Watonga, where he published the Watonga Republican. *Ferguson served as Territorial Governor from 1901 until 1906. It was during his administration that the territorial assembly voted along party lines to oppose joint statehood with Indian Territory. Republicans, who had controlled Oklahoma territorial politics, were opposed to joint statehood because they feared losing control in a state dominated by Democrats.*

COURTESY OKLAHOMA DEPARTMENT OF TOURISM AND RECREATION; PHOTOGRAPH BY FRED MARVEL.

Top, right: Established in 1897, Eufaula's name is taken from an older Creek settlement along the banks of the Chattahoochee River in Alabama called Yufala, which meant "they split up here and went to other places." In 1895, Eufaula was the site of the meeting of Choctaw, Chickasaw, Creek, Seminole, and Cherokee delegates who rejected the government's proposal of the allotment of tribal lands. Eufaula's Foley Building, constructed by C. E. Foley in 1900, dominates the community's historic downtown area.

COURTESY DAVID FITZGERALD.

Bottom: A map showing the state of Sequoyah.

Separate meetings with individual tribes also accomplished nothing. Deciding to apply pressure to the Indians to accept allotment, Congress in 1895 enlarged the number of federal courts in Indian Territory to three, gave the courts authority over non-Indians and major felonies involving death or long prison sentences, and provided that when the three judges convened at McAlester they constituted an appellate court for Indian Territory.

Any allotment of tribal lands required a survey to be made of Indian Territory, and, in March of 1895, Congress authorized the United States Geological Survey to map the region. Another meeting with delegates from the Five Tribes took place at Eufaula in June of 1895; however, the results were the same as the previous meeting—the Indians refused even to consider allotment. They correctly feared the negative impact allotment would have on tribal sovereignty and on many Indian families, who they feared would ultimately be cheated out of their land. Congress reacted on June 10, 1896, by authorizing the Dawes Commission to compile tribal rolls and declaring that federal officials should establish a government in Indian Territory that would rectify the inequalities existing there between Indians and non-Indians.

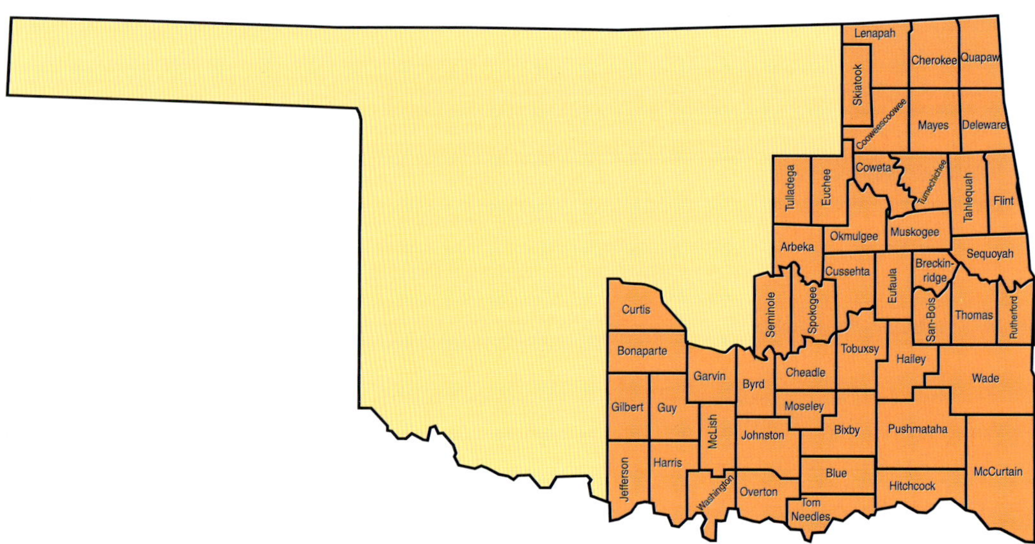

Faced with the inevitability of the government's actions, the ranks of the Five Tribes wavered. In April of 1897, the Choctaws and Chickasaws signed the Atoka Agreement, which provided for the survey of their lands in preparation for allotment, the reservation of mineral-bearing land for the tribe as a whole, and for the platting of towns and city lots. It also provided that their tribal governments would cease to exist as of March 4, 1906, and afterward the Indians would become United States citizens. However, the Choctaws and Chickasaws delayed its ratification until August of 1898. Meanwhile, the Seminoles had accepted a similar agreement, which was ratified by Congress on July 1, 1898. Thus, even though the Choctaws and Chickasaws first accepted allotment, it was first put into effect among the Seminoles.

In general, each tribal member was to receive 160 acres of land; however, if there was not sufficient land to be divided equally, the number of acres could be less than 160, as it was in the Cherokee Nation. In other circumstances, the Indians received larger allotments; for example, each member of the Osage tribe received approximately 500 acres. To make sure that the land was divided equally, it was separated into classes, and each member received a specified number of acres of each class of land. As a result, most allotments consisted of parcels of land that were not contiguous.

In the Creek and Seminole nations, freedmen also were allotted 160 acres. In the Cherokee Nation, they received the same amount as other tribal members. In the

Above: Prior to their removal to Oklahoma, the Seminoles welcomed runaway slaves into their tribe and went to war with the United States to protect the former slaves from being returned to their owners in the South. The government recognized the tribal membership of these ex-slaves following the Civil War, and, at the time of allotment, they were each granted 160 acres of land within the Seminole Nation.

COURTESY OKLAHOMA DEPARTMENT OF TOURISM AND RECREATION; PHOTOGRAPH BY FRED MARVEL.

Left: One of the first structures built in Ardmore in Pickens County of the Chickasaw Nation was this log cabin, which was located at the intersection of G and Second Streets Southeast. Although it has been added on to on the right side of the photograph, it is representative of the many log cabins used for housing throughout Indian Territory. The spaces between the hand-hewn walls have been filled in with cement. The gables on the end of the cabin were made of clapboard, and the roof was hand split wooden shingles. The small garden in the foreground provided extra food for the homeowner.

COURTESY THE DAILY OKLAHOMAN.

✧

Right: Much of the education of youth in Indian Territory was controlled by various religious sects. These are the students at the Catholic operated Quapaw Mission School in 1905-1906. Priests and nuns taught classes, while the children were required to wear uniforms.

COURTESY SOONER CATHOLIC MAGAZINE COLLECTION, WESTERN HISTORY COLLECTIONS, UNIVERSITY OF OKLAHOMA LIBRARIES.

Below: The iron-fronted Munzesheimer & Daube Store actually opened in 1888 although the date on the store front is 1889. Ardmore, one of the largest cities in Indian Territory, in 1906, was the focal point of a huge trade area in south-central Oklahoma and a large manufacturing center of asphalt-based paint. Ardmore's prosperity was due in part to the arrival of the Atchison, Topeka, and Santa Fe Railroad, which finished its main north-south line through the region in 1887.

COURTESY *THE DAILY OKLAHOMAN*.

Choctaw and Chickasaw nations, freedmen were allotted forty acres. In addition, special allotments were voted by Congress to several missionaries active among the Five Tribes.

Indian Territory was divided into twenty-six recording districts, with a town in each district designated as a recording center. These districts were not drawn according to tribal boundaries. Each allottee recorded the land they wished to be allotted at the nearest recording center. Land that was left over was declared surplus and opened to settlement.

The final blow to tribal governments occurred on June 18, 1898, with the passage of the Curtis Act, authored by Charles Curtis, a mixed-blood Kansa Indian. It provided that the payment of tribal funds be made directly to individual tribal members, abolished tribal courts, made all people in Indian Territory subject to the laws of the State of Arkansas, called for a survey of Indian Territory, and provided for the allotment of tribal lands based on rolls prepared by the Dawes Commission. In addition, it authorized the incorporation of towns in Indian Territory, the establishment of a school system open to all people, and the leasing of tribal mineral lands by the secretary of the interior. Finally, it abolished all tribal governments as of March 4, 1906.

Facing the inevitable fact that control of Indian Territory was being removed from tribal authorities, the Indians made one last attempt to preserve their authority. At Eufaula in 1902, representatives of the Five Tribes formed an executive committee to examine the alternatives available to the tribes in Indian Territory. Although nothing came of the first effort, in 1905 tribal leaders issued a call for a meeting of delegates to convene at Muskogee on August 21, 1905, as a constitutional convention for the proposed State of Sequoyah.

One hundred and eighty-two delegates were elected, seven from each of the twenty-six recording districts in Indian Territory and one delegate at large from each of the Five Tribes. Both qualified Indian and non-Indian voters participated in the election. Principal Chief of the Creeks Pleasant Porter was elected the convention's president, and one vice president from each the Five Tribes was selected—William H. "Alfalfa Bill" Murray of the Chickasaw Nation, Charles N. Haskell of the Creeks, W. C. Rogers of the Cherokees, Green McCurtain of the Choctaws, and John F. Brown of the Seminoles. Neither Murray nor Haskell were Indians. Alexander Posey, a Creek, was named secretary.

W. W. Hastings, a Cherokee, was chosen to chair the drafting committee charged with writing the proposed constitution. The delegates called for the establishment of the State of Sequoyah with forty-eight counties, a two-house legislature, a supreme court, and a judicial system. A bill of rights was included, and Fort Gibson was named the capital.

The Sequoyah Convention adjourned on September 8, 1905, and an election for the adoption of the constitution was set for November 7, 1905. It passed by a vote of 56,279 to 9,073. Nevertheless, when the constitution was forwarded to Congress, it found little support. Faced with the possibility of the addition of two Democratic senators from Indian Territory, Republicans in Congress favored combining the Twin Territories into one state.

Not all Indians readily accepted the end of tribal governments. The chief opposition came from conservative Creeks led by Chitto Harjo, also known as Wilson Jones or Crazy Snake. In 1900, Crazy Snake called upon Creek officials to restore ancient tribal laws and customs, but his plea was ignored. Undaunted, Crazy Snake's supporters gathered around the Hickory Ground near Henryetta. As his support continued to grow, federal troops, deputy United States marshals, and Indian police were called in to suppress the movement in 1901.

Left: A fire that swept the business district in April of 1896 devastated downtown Ardmore. Note the wall in the center of the photograph that has been propped up with poles to prevent its collapse. When the town was rebuilt, most of the original wooden structures were replaced with stone or brick buildings.

COURTESY THE DAILY OKLAHOMAN.

Below: Looking east down the Main Street of Okmulgee in the early twentieth century. The town square, where the Creek National Council House is located, is to the right of the photograph, surrounded by the low stone wall. As the capital of the Creek Nation, Okmulgee became a major trade center. Other important communities in the Creek Nation were Muskogee, Wagoner, Tulsa, Red Fork, Sapulpa, Checotah, Eufaula, and North Fork Town. North Fork Town was the intersection of the area's major north-south road, the Texas Road, and the Missouri, Kansas, and Texas Railroad with the east-west oriented California Road.

COURTESY THE DAILY OKLAHOMAN.

✧

Right: Restored to its Victorian elegance, Guthrie's Oklahoma Avenue is part of the largest contiguous urban National Register of Historic Places district in the United States. Guthrie, which served as the capital of Oklahoma Territory from 1890 until 1907 and of the State of Oklahoma from 1907 until 1910, was the social center of Oklahoma Territory. Dominated by Republican politics, Guthrie could not survive the Democrat-controlled state legislature, and, in 1910, after a statewide vote, the capital was moved to Oklahoma City.

COURTESY OKLAHOMA DEPARTMENT OF TOURISM AND RECREATION, PHOTOGRAPH BY FRED MARVEL.

Below: The Cherokee National Capitol in Tahlequah. The building, completed in 1869, served as the capitol of the Cherokee Nation until statehood, when it became the Cherokee County courthouse. The Cherokee Nation complex also included a nearby Supreme Court building and jail. Just across the street from the capitol was the National Hotel, built in 1848 to serve those attending sessions of the Cherokee National Council. It was built by a group of Mormons who operated the state's first brick plant nearby.

COURTESY OKLAHOMA DEPARTMENT OF TOURISM AND RECREATION; PHOTOGRAPH BY FRED MARVEL.

Nearly 100 of Crazy Snake's followers were arrested and taken before Federal Judge John R. Thomas in Muskogee. Thomas persuaded them to promise to end their resistance against enrollment and then released them. However, they continued to meet at Hickory Ground and year after year urged a return to the old ways.

By 1909, Crazy Snake and his followers were openly opposing the elected Creek government and both state and federal officials. Deciding that the movement had gone too far, Governor Charles N. Haskell ordered Colonel Roy V. Hoffman and 200 Oklahoma National Guard troops to Okmulgee County to arrest Crazy Snake. The guardsmen stayed in the field for almost two weeks with no success before being ordered out because they were costing the state $1,500 a day.

Haskell then commissioned former United States Deputy Marshal William Tilghman to capture Crazy Snake. He also was unsuccessful; however, in a shootout with lawmen, Crazy Snake had been mortally wounded. Fleeing to the Choctaw Nation, he died someplace in southeastern Oklahoma in 1911.

The continued factionalism among some of the tribes hindered the unification of Indian Territory. Thus, when the Sequoyah movement collapsed, any hope that Indian Territory would be admitted to the Union as a separate state was lost. With that option closed, the effort to combine the Twin Territories into a single state took on a new urgency.

The movement for Oklahoma statehood started as early as 1891, when a constitution convention in Oklahoma City forwarded a memorial to Congress for joint statehood for the Twin Territories. Although the measure was introduced in Congress in January of 1892, it quickly died. In the following decade, several plans for statehood were prepared, but all failed. In 1902, supporters of the movement introduced an Omnibus Statehood Bill for Oklahoma, New Mexico, and Arizona. It also failed. Similar bills in 1903 and 1904 also were defeated.

Left: *The Creek National Capitol is located in the town square of Okmulgee, which became the capital of the Creek Nation in 1869. The capitol housed the House of Kings, as the upper house of the Creek legislature was called, and the House of Warriors, the lower house. The square, two-story structure of brown stone topped by a cupola is a well preserved reminder of the community's heritage.*

COURTESY *THE DAILY OKLAHOMAN.*

In December of 1905, while Congress debated the proposed State of Sequoyah, five separate bills were introduced to admit Oklahoma Territory as a single state. None were successful. When statehood for Indian Territory was voted down, work began on the passage of an enabling act to join Oklahoma and Indian Territories into a single state. The Hamilton Statehood Bill, or Oklahoma Enabling Act, was approved by Congress on June 14, 1906, and signed by President Theodore Roosevelt two days later. The act required that the capital remain in Guthrie until 1913, that alcohol be excluded from what had been Indian Territory and the Osage Nation for twenty-one years, that a system of public education be established, that the Fifteenth Amendment be accepted, and that any constitution be submitted to the people for a vote of approval. Because there was no public land in Indian Territory to be set aside for education, Congress appropriated $5 million to help establish public schools.

A constitutional convention was called to convene in Guthrie on November 20, 1906. To provide equal representation for Indian and Oklahoma Territories, the Twin Territories were divided into 112 districts, with each having fifty-five districts. The remaining two districts were allotted to the Osage Nation. The district boundaries for Oklahoma Territory and one district in the Osage Nation were drawn by the territorial governor, chief justice, and secretary. The boundaries for Indian Territory and the other Osage Nation district were drawn by two United States judges and the commissioner to the Five Civilized Tribes. When the election of delegates took place, the greatest fears of the

Below: *The Creek Nation's Orphan Home was located just to the northeast of Okmulgee in the Okmulgee District of the Creek Nation. As independent-dependent nations within the United States, the Five Tribes—Creeks, Seminoles, Choctaws, Chickasaws, and Cherokees—maintained most of the same social and governmental agencies as the surrounding states and territories. The Creek Nation, for example, was divided into six districts—Okmulgee, Deep Fork, Wewoka, Eufaula, Muskogee, and Coweta. A judge plus a captain and four privates of lighthorsemen were elected from each district to provide law and order.*

COURTESY *THE DAILY OKLAHOMAN.*

Right: One of Indian Territory's best known outlaws was Belle Starr. Born Myra Belle Shirley in Missouri in 1848, Belle later moved to Texas and married Jim Reed. They had two children, Pearl and Ed Reed, who had become an outlaw, was murdered in 1875. Belle married Sam Starr in 1880 and became an intermarried citizen of the Cherokee Nation. Their home, called Younger's Bend, overlooked the Canadian River in the southwestern part of the Cherokee Nation and became a haven for outlaws. In 1882, Sam and Belle were convicted of horse stealing and sentenced to spend time at the Federal House of Corrections in Detroit, Michigan. They returned to Younger's Bend in 1886. That same year Sam was killed at a dance in nearby Whitfield. On February 2, 1889, Belle Starr was shot in the back and killed as she rode her horse in front of the cabin of neighbor Edgar Watson.

COURTESY THE DAILY OKLAHOMAN.

Below: The business district of Miami near the Quapaw Agency in northeastern Indian Territory in 1892. The town was established in 1890 when Jim Palmer opened a post office. It was named for his wife, a Miami Indian. The wooden, false-front businesses, with foundations built on stacks of stones, were typical of those that dotted Indian Territory in the late nineteenth century.

COURTESY THE DAILY OKLAHOMAN.

Republicans were fulfilled with Democrats winning 100 of the 112 seats.

Convening at 2:00 p.m. on November 20, 1906, the delegates chose William H. Murray as president and then adjourned for the Christmas holidays. Reconvening on January 3, 1907, the delegates created a two-house legislature; single four-year terms for most state officials, with a provision prohibiting reelection to the same office; a five member supreme court, that later was increased to nine members; and the popular election of practically every state official. In addition, a strong Corporation Commission was created to regulate business. Distrusting a powerful government, the delegates also included the initiative and referendum in the new constitution.

The questions of prohibition and segregation were not addressed in the constitution. A separate vote on prohibition was scheduled at the same time as the vote on the constitution. Prohibition was approved by a vote of 130,361 to 112,258. Segregation was delayed until the convening of the first state legislature, when Senate Bill Number 2 provided for "separate but equal" treatment of whites and blacks.

There was a powerful movement to grant the vote to women at the convention; however, much lobbying by the Oklahoma Woman Suffrage Association proved unsuccessful. Although Charles N. Haskell, the democratic floor leader, initially supported the effort, he was persuaded by his wife to change his mind.

Murray opposed the effort after counting the women voting in a Guthrie school board election and discovering that more black women voted than white. Wanting to limit the power of black voters, he helped defeat the measure on February 5, 1907, by a vote of fifty-four to thirty-seven to table, with twenty-one not voting.

Much of the convention's time was spent drawing county boundaries, and it was not until Murray forced several members of the committee on counties to resign and named Haskell as chairman of the committee that the work was completed. Seventy-five counties and their seats were established—forty in Indian Territory and thirty-five in Oklahoma Territory. As required by the Oklahoma Enabling Act, the Osage Reservation was organized as a single county, thereby becoming the only county in the United States in which the boundaries were drawn by Congress. Two more counties, Harmon and Cotton, were added in 1909 and 1914, respectively.

The convention adjourned on March 15, 1907, with the expectation of a popular election being called by Territorial Governor Frank Frantz; however, he delayed because

Murray refused to file an official copy of the proposed constitution. In the meantime, a minority constitution was prepared by disenchanted convention delegates that omitted many of the reform measures of the original document.

Adding to the confusion was the unfavorable reaction of President Roosevelt to the Oklahoma constitution and a lawsuit filed by citizens of Woods County who were dissatisfied with the division of their county. For a brief time, they persuaded a judge to issue an injunction to delay any vote on the proposed constitution until their complaint was heard. To silence criticism, Murray called the convention back into session in July of 1907 to make some changes suggested by President Roosevelt. That same month the Territorial Supreme Court voided the injunction against the election, and Murray filed an official copy of the constitution with territorial officials. Satisfied, Frantz set an election for September 17. The new constitution was approved by a vote of 180,333 to 73,059. New state officials were elected, and prohibition was approved. With the terms of the Enabling Act met, Oklahoma became the forty-sixth state of the Union on November 16, 1907.

Above: Wewoka, the capital of the Seminole Nation, was located on the border between the Seminole and Creek Nations. The boundary between the two tribes is one-half block east of Wewoka's Main Street. In Wewoka's town square was an old pecan tree that was used as the Seminole Whipping Post between 1899 and 1907. The floggings were administered by one of the tribe's twenty lighthorsemen, who also served as a national police force.

COURTESY *THE DAILY OKLAHOMAN.*

Left: A map of the Twin Territories.

Below: The Seminole Council House in Wewoka. The council was made up of the chiefs of the fourteen bands of Seminoles. The building burned in 1930.

COURTESY *THE DAILY OKLAHOMAN.*

JOE WILLIS

CHAPTER IX
THE FORTY-SIXTH STAR

Oklahoma's constitution was drafted during the "Progressive Era" in the United States. Outlining the state government in detail, the delegates crafted the second longest constitution in the Union. State government is divided into the legislative, executive, and judicial branches. The majority of state offices are elective, and the governor's power is diluted in comparison with many other states. Oklahoma's government also features an array of boards and commissions, most of which are structured to be somewhat independent of the governor. The legislature is the dominant branch of government, with the influence of various governors depending on their political skills and factors such as the balance of power between the parties in the legislature.

Candidates are selected in closed primary and runoff elections in which only voters registered as Democrats vote for Democrat candidates and only Republicans can vote for Republican candidates. Prior to 1944, the candidate receiving the largest number of votes was named that party's candidate. After 1944, if a candidate did not receive more than fifty percent of the votes, a runoff election was held between the two candidates with the greatest number of votes.

The legislative branch consists of a house of representatives and a senate, which are responsible for enacting laws. The house of representatives has 101 members, and the senate has forty-eight. House members are chosen for two-year terms, while senators are chosen for four-year terms, with one-half of them running for election or reelection every two years.

Members of the legislature are equally apportioned among state residents. At statehood a special census was taken to provide equal representation. Although the legislature was supposed to reapportion itself after every federal census, since 1907, the state house of representatives had reapportioned itself once, and the state senate had never. This resistance to reapportionment led to urban areas being under represented. By the 1960s, the state's urban population had grown significantly. However, rural legislators were unwilling to surrender their voting power. After several unsuccessful attempts to reapportion equally, federal courts intervened in 1964 to force reapportionment. When reapportionment was completed, one-third of the legislature came from Oklahoma and Tulsa Counties, the two most metropolitan areas of the state.

There are four types of legislation: (1) bills, which become law if passed by both houses and signed by the governor; (2) joint resolutions, which have the force of law if passed by both houses, but which may not become part of the state statutes; (3) concurrent resolutions, which express the will of both houses; and (4) simple resolutions, which express the will of the house in which they originate. Any member of the legislature may introduce legislation. Senate legislation is numbered consecutively, beginning with 1. House legislation is numbered consecutively beginning with 1001.

A bill passes through the legislature in a series of readings. The first reading takes place when the bill is introduced. It is then read aloud in the house of origin. The second reading takes place when the bill is assigned to a committee for study. If passed by the committee, the bill is printed with any changes made by the committee and then considered by the entire membership of its house of origin. This is called the third reading. If passed, the bill is reprinted to include any amendments and sent to the other house of the legislature, where it repeats the process of the first, second, and third readings. After being considered by the other house, it is returned to the house of origin with any changes. The house of origin then considers the changes, and, if they are accepted, the bill is printed in its final form and considered for its fourth reading, which is its final passage. If the two houses cannot agree on the changes, the bill is sent to a conference committee consisting of members of both houses to effect a compromise. Once the differences are reconciled, it is sent first to the house of origin for approval and then to the other house for approval.

Once a bill has been approved by both houses, it is sent to the governor. If the governor signs the bill it becomes law. If the governor vetoes the bill, the legislature may override his veto by a

✧

Democratic Oklahoma Governor-Elect Charles N. Haskell, Guthrie Mayor Leslie Niblack, and former Oklahoma Territorial Chief Justice Frank Dale making their way by carriage from the Royal Hotel in Guthrie to the Carnegie Library for Haskell's swearing in ceremony as the new state's first governor. So bitter had been the controversy between those advocating either separate or joint statehood for the Twin Territories, that Republican Territorial Governor Frank Frantz, who saw his party lose control of the new state legislature, rode to Haskell's inaugural in a separate carriage.

COURTESY THE DAILY OKLAHOMAN.

✧

Above: The Carnegie Library in Guthrie. When official word of Oklahoma's statehood was received shortly before noon on November 16, 1907, the secretary to Territorial Governor Frank Frantz, Dr. Hugh Scott, stepped from his office onto a gallery overlooking the street and shot his pistol into the air. Because of the controversy over the location of the territorial capital, there were no public buildings in Guthrie for territorial officials. Instead office space had been rented, usually from supporters of the Republican Party, inasmuch as Republican politicians dominated the territorial government. The front step of the Carnegie Library, therefore, was chosen as the site for Haskell to be sworn in as Oklahoma's first governor.

COURTESY DAVID FITZGERALD.

two-thirds vote in each house. If the override attempt fails in either house, the governor's veto stands and the bill does not become law.

The Oklahoma constitution reserved many rights to the people. The best examples of this are the initiative and referendum. The initiative allows the people to institute legislation. Once a sufficient number of signatures are obtained on an initiative petition and certified by the secretary of state, the governor places the initiative on the ballot for approval or rejection by the voters. If it passes it becomes law. The initiative frequently is used to pass controversial legislation, such as liquor by the drink or gambling. While enhancing the power of the state's citizens, the initiative petition also allows the legislature to avoid taking a stand on an issue, allowing it to go to a vote of the people.

The referendum is used to overturn a piece of legislation, and may be used against any item, section, or part of an act. Again, a petition is circulated. If sufficient signatures are acquired, it is submitted to the secretary of state for certification and placed on the ballot by the governor. If it is approved, the legislation is nullified, and such legislation cannot be proposed again for three years unless a petition bearing twenty-five percent of the state's legal voters is presented. The referendum usually is used against a controversial piece of legislation, such as House Bill 1017, which raised taxes to support education. Although opponents of the legislation were successful in getting a vote, the referendum failed, and House Bill 1017 remained the law; however, opponents of the

Right: The Oklahoma Constitutional Convention in session in Guthrie's City Hall. One hundred and twelve delegates were present: fifty five from Oklahoma Territory, fifty-five from Indian Territory, and two from the Osage Nation. In the election for delegates the worse fears of the Republican Party were realized. Democrats won 100 of the 112 seats and dominated the convention.

COURTESY OKLAHOMA HERITAGE ASSOCIATION.

measure successfully circulated an initiative limiting the power of the legislature to raise taxes without obtaining either the approval of the voters in a statewide election or that of three-fourths of the legislators.

The executive branch is headed by the governor and lieutenant governor. There is no term limitation for the lieutenant governor. George Nigh served in the office for seventeen years, 1959-1963 and 1967-1979. Initially, the governor was not allowed to succeed himself in office; however, in 1966 the constitution was amended to limit a governor to two consecutive terms.

The governor is the chief executive officer of the state and commander-in-chief of the state militia. He has the power to grant reprieves, commutations, paroles, and pardons for all offenses, except impeachment; grant state commissions; and to call the legislature into extraordinary session. The lieutenant governor assumes the governorship should the position be vacated by the governor and serves as president of the state senate. To facilitate the work of the executive branch, the governor appoints a number of cabinet members, including the secretaries of state, administration, agriculture, commerce, education, energy, environment, finance and revenue, health, personnel management and

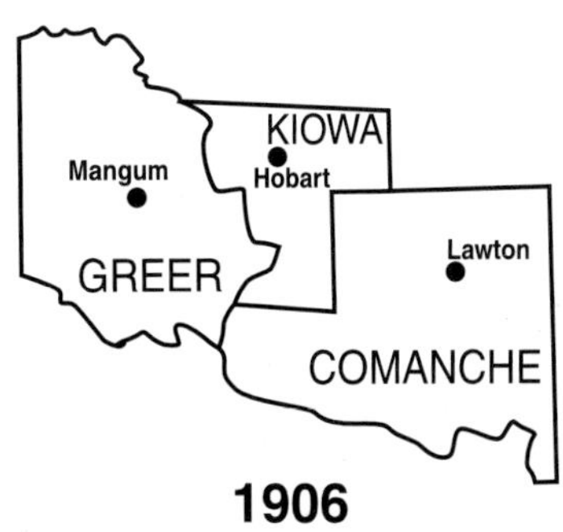

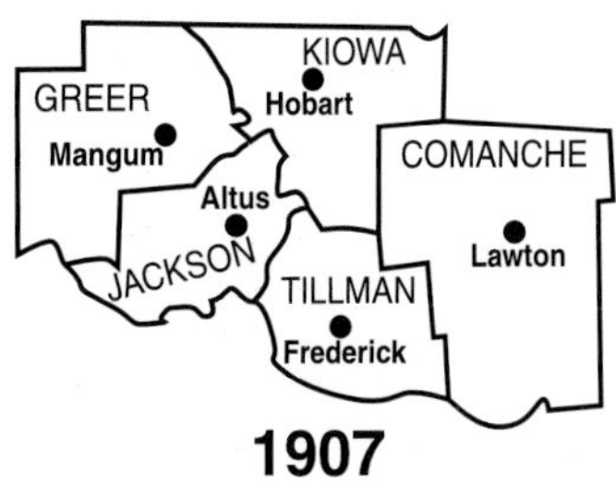

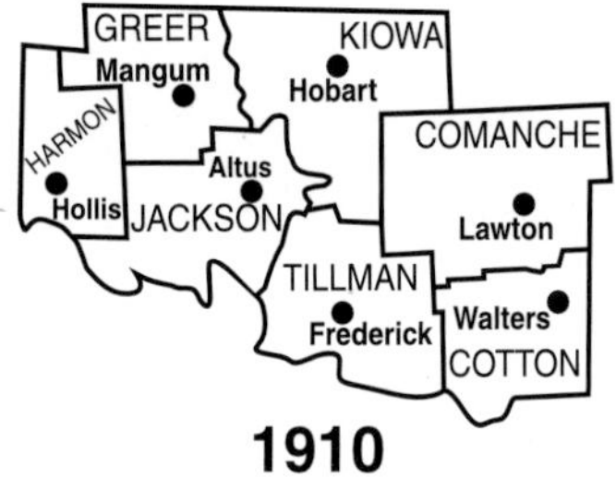

Maps showing county boundary changes between 1906 and 1910.

Above: In the general election of 1908, Albert Comstock Hamlin of Guthrie became the first black elected to the State Legislature—the first black man to hold such a position. In 1910, Oklahoma voters approved State Question 17, which required the passage of a literacy test for all voters except those whose ancestors could vote before 1866. It was not until 1964 that another black man was elected to the State Legislature.

COURTESY HELEN HOLMES COLLECTION, WESTERN HISTORY COLLECTIONS, UNIVERSITY OF OKLAHOMA LIBRARIES.

Top, right: Although many Native Americans opposed joint statehood, seeing it as the end of tribal government, most non-Indians supported the movement. Celebrations were held throughout the new state. In Hollis, in Greer County at the time of statehood, a hot air balloon highlighted the celebration. Hollis became the seat of Harmon County on May 22, 1909, when Old Greer County was divided to create Greer and Harmon Counties.

COURTESY JACK HALEY COLLECTION, WESTERN HISTORIES COLLECTION, UNIVERSITY OF OKLAHOMA LIBRARIES.

Right: Leo and Margaret Meyer. Meyer was a prominent Jewish leader and political figure in early Oklahoma Democratic politics. He was a member of the Constitutional Convention from Sayre. In 1910, he was elected State Auditor—the fourth highest official in state government.

COURTESY FRANK COLLECTION, WESTERN HISTORY COLLECTIONS, UNIVERSITY OF OKLAHOMA LIBRARIES.

human resources, safety and security, science and technology, tourism and recreation, transportation, and veterans affairs. There are several other elective members of the executive department, including the state auditor and inspector, state treasurer, attorney general, insurance commissioner, commissioner of labor, superintendent of public instruction, and three corporation commissioners. The offices of chief mine inspector and the commissioner of charities and corrections have been abolished.

Twice in state history, governors have been impeached and removed from office by the state legislature—Jack C. Walton in 1923 and Henry S. Johnston in 1929. However, by force of personality and political skill, some governors have exercised great power. The best example is William H. "Alfalfa Bill" Murray. When threatened by the legislature with impeachment, Murray replied "it'll be like a bunch of jack rabbits tryin' to get a wildcat out of a hole."

To enforce his will, Murray relied on his power as commander-in-chief of the National Guard, and resorted to martial law more than any other governor. When the price of oil plunged and oil men refused to reduce production voluntarily, Murray, arguing that he was protecting the future of Oklahoma's children by preventing the waste of a valuable natural resource, declared martial law in the summer of

Left: The Oklahoma State Supreme Court in 1932. Chief Justice E. F. Lester, Vice Chief Justice J. W. Clark and Justices Robert A. Hefner, Sr., Fletcher Riley, Thomas G. Andrews, Charles Swindall, James B. Cullison, Edwin R. McNeill, and W. H. Kornegay. The Oklahoma Supreme Court has appellate jurisdiction over civil matters. Criminal cases are appealed to the Court of Criminal Appeals.

COURTESY OKLAHOMA HERITAGE ASSOCIATION.

1931 and sent in guardsmen to enforce proration. The guardsmen remained in the fields sixty-five days, until the market stabilized and they were removed. In 1933, Murray ordered the guardsmen back into the Oklahoma City Field to shut down the wells. The field remained under martial law until the legislature passed a comprehensive oil code in March of 1933.

Murray also used the National Guard to eliminate toll bridges in the "Red River War" of 1931. For several years, the only means of crossing the Red River was by toll bridges; however, in July of 1931 the first of several state-built bridges were opened, offering free river crossings. When the free bridges were opened, owners of the toll bridges filed suit and a federal judge issued an injunction to block their use. Infuriated by what he believed was the usurpation of state authority by minor federal courts, Murray ordered the free bridges opened and declared martial law to enforce his decree.

State Highway Department workers quickly completed access roads to the bridges, and the guardsmen blocked the entrances to the toll bridges. Federal marshals attempted to serve court orders on Adjutant General Charles Barrett, but he refused to accept them. When the governor of Texas ordered the closing of the southern ends of the free bridges, Murray sent the guardsmen across the river to remove the barricades. Eventually, in June of 1932, a federal appeals court ruled in Murray's favor, an action later upheld by the United States Supreme Court.

Murray called out the National Guard on thirty-four occasions. Among the declarations of martial law was one that prevented a parade by workers in Henryetta's May Day; another stopped the sale of the 101 Ranch to satisfy creditors; one prevented blacks from using Hassman Park in the "white" side of Oklahoma City; and another to close down an Enid bank when its president ignored the bank moratorium of March 1931. Another use of martial law was to collect tickets at University of Oklahoma football games when irregularities in the athletic office were alleged.

The third area of state government is the judicial branch. The highest court in the state is the state senate, which sits as a court of impeachment from which there is no appeal. The two state courts of last resort are the state supreme court, which has appellate jurisdiction in civil matters, and the court of criminal appeals, which has appellate jurisdiction in criminal cases. There are nine members of the supreme court and five justices of the court of criminal appeals.

Below: The Constitution of the State of Oklahoma strips the governor of many powers normally assigned to a chief executive; however, strong state governors often used the National Guard to circumvent constitutional restrictions. Many governors have used this method, but William H. "Alfalfa Bill" Murray holds the record of declaring martial law on thirty-four occasions. During the height of the Great Depression, Murray sent the Oklahoma National Guard into the state's oil fields on two occasions in an effort to enforce pro-ration and drive up the price of crude. These guardsmen are overseeing production on a Champlin Oil Company lease in Oklahoma City.

COURTESY *THE DAILY OKLAHOMAN*.

Right: The Washita County Courthouse at Cordell was built in 1910. With statehood came the organization of county governments. Originally Oklahoma had seventy-five counties; however, in 1909 Harmon was created out of a portion of the original Greer County. In 1911, Cotton County was created from the southern part of Comanche County, with Walters named as the county seat. In 1911, there was an attempt to create Swanson County out of the southern half of Kiowa County and part of Comanche County. Swanson legally existed for 249 days until the Oklahoma Supreme Court refused to acknowledge its existence. Nonetheless, it was not until 1913 that Swanson County completely disappeared.

COURTESY DAVID FITZGERALD.

Below: A womens' rights parade in Bartlesville. The question of allowing women to vote long had been an issue in Oklahoma politics. The issue had been defeated at the Constitutional Convention. Governor William Murray's action resulted from his efforts to limit the black franchise after he viewed more black women voting in a Guthrie School Board election than white women.

COURTESY PHILLIPS PETROLEUM COMPANY.

There also is a court of civil appeals, with twelve justices in four judicial divisions. Final decisions of the court of civil appeals are only appealable to the supreme court if a majority of the supreme court justices allow it.

District courts are courts of general jurisdiction. The state is divided into twenty-six district court districts. Each district consists of an entire county or contiguous counties. Voters in each district elect a district judge and at least one associate district judge in a non-partisan election. District judges also may appoint special judges to serve at their pleasure. Decisions of district courts may be appealed to the state supreme court or the court of criminal appeals.

Judicial districts are administrated by a presiding judge chosen by the district judges within the district. There also is an assembly of presiding judges, subject to the rules, orders, and directives of the state supreme court or its chief justice. In cases of apparent conflict of interest, the assembly of presiding judges often assign justices to cases outside of their original jurisdiction.

Left: Jo Lynn Burger, Chief of the Cleveland Fire Department. Burger, who assumed her post in 1999, was one of only five female fire chiefs in the United States at that time.

COURTESY *THE CLEVELAND AMERICAN*; PHOTOGRAPH BY CECILIE HENNING.

The court on the judiciary, which has jurisdiction over judges, is divided into the trial and the appellate divisions. There are nine members of the trial division. Eight are appointed by the secretary of state and one by the Oklahoma Bar Association. There also are nine members of the appellate division. Five are appointed by the secretary of state, two by the supreme court, one by the court of criminal appeals, and one by the Oklahoma Bar Association. The council on judicial complaints is the investigatory body for the court on the judiciary. Its three members are appointed by the Oklahoma Bar Association, the speaker of the house of representatives, and the president pro tempore of the senate.

The worker's compensation court was created in 1951 and is responsible for adjudicating workmen's compensation claims. It has nine members, who serve six year terms. Whenever a vacancy occurs, the governor names a successor. Decisions of the worker's compensation court may be appealed to the state supreme court.

During the early and mid-1960s, Oklahoma's judicial system was rocked by scandal. Evidence gathered during the investigation of the Oklahoma Tax Commission case against Selected Investments revealed that for more than three decades some supreme court justices took bribes to influence the outcome of civil cases. Two supreme court justices, Earl Welch and Nelson S. Corn, were convicted in federal court and resigned from the bench. Justice N. B. Johnston was impeached and removed from the court by the state legislature. O. A. Cargill, Sr. was convicted of bribery, and Wayne W. Bayless, a supreme court justice between 1933 and 1948, resigned from the bar.

Below: United States District Judge Vicki Miles-LaGrange being sworn in as a federal judge for the Western District of Oklahoma in 1994. A graduate of Vassar College and the Howard University School of Law, Judge Miles-LaGrange was the first black female to be elected to the Oklahoma State Senate, the first black female to be appointed a federal judge in Oklahoma, and the first female to serve as a United States Attorney for the Western District of Oklahoma.

COURTESY *THE DAILY OKLAHOMAN*.

In response, a thirteen-member judicial nomination commission was established in 1967 to screen prospective judges before their appointment by the governor. Also a voter retention system was implemented. At the same time, justice of the peace courts were abolished, and replaced with two types of courts—municipal courts of record and municipal courts not of record. Their role is to administer town and city ordinances.

In an effort to ease the judicial case load, a dispute resolution advisory board was established in 1985. Proceedings are voluntary, confidential, and may not be used in court. Its mediators serve as neutral facilitators and offer fast and fair settlements of disputes.

Framers of the constitution also placed a great deal of power in the hands of independent agencies, boards, and commissions. There are hundreds of these bodies, controlling most aspects of government. Some, such as the members of the Corporation Commission, are elected statewide. Others, such as that of the Highway Commission, are appointed. Some boards, such as that of the Oklahoma Historical Society, have some directors who are appointed by the governor and other directors who are

✧

Top, left: At first the State of Oklahoma contracted with Kansas to imprison its criminals. Kansas in turn rented out Oklahoma prisoners as workers in mines. In 1910, Oklahoma officials began work on the Oklahoma State Prison in McAlester. Prisoners did much of the work of constructing the prison while living in tents on the prison grounds. This is the main guard tower and office of the prison while it was under construction. Prisoners in striped pants can be seen working on the right.

COURTESY *THE DAILY OKLAHOMAN*.

Top, right: The Frederick Fire Department responding to an alarm on North Eleventh Street in 1907. Oklahoma statehood also allowed the organization of additional city and town governments, which in turn provided better police and fire protection for local residents.

COURTESY JACK HALEY COLLECTION, MUSEUM OF THE GREAT PLAINS.

Bottom: The Oklahoma State Senate sitting as a Court of Impeachment against Governor Henry S. Johnston. The Chief Justice of the Oklahoma Supreme Court is presiding. When sitting as a Court of Impeachment, the Oklahoma State Senate is the highest court in the state. Johnston was convicted of "incompetency" and removed from office on March 20, 1929.

COURTESY *THE DAILY OKLAHOMAN*.

elected by the membership. Some commission members are appointed by other elected state officials. For example, members of the State Ethics Commission are appointed by the governor, the chief justice, the attorney general, the president pro tempore of the state senate, and the speaker of the house of representatives.

County government in Oklahoma is based on the commissioner system, in which voters elect nine officials. Each county is divided into three districts, and a commissioner is elected for each district. District boundaries are drawn by the commissioners after each federal census. If the commissioners refuse to reapportion after each census, that duty falls to the county excise board. The commissioners are responsible for supervising the administration of the county, budgeting county funds, letting county contracts and bids, approving claims against the county, incurring county indebtedness, overseeing county roads, coordinating federal funds, caring for the poor and indigent, and maintaining county equipment. County commissioners cannot remove other county officials from office, but they can implement ouster proceedings in the courts.

There are few checks and balances in the county commissioner system. The budgets of other county officials are dependent upon the commissioners; therefore anyone investigating irregularities in the commissioner's office might suddenly find their budget slashed. With no checks on their actions, the commissioner system is especially vulnerable to graft. For decades many of Oklahoma's county commissioners regularly took kickbacks from companies with which they did business. Parts that could be purchased by individuals for $8 in local stores cost as much as $80 from suppliers. During the early and mid-1980s, the state's commissioner system was investigated by federal officials. Eventually, more than 230 people, both commissioners and suppliers, were convicted of taking or giving kickbacks. Although this scandal prompted better oversight, the system remains virtually unchanged.

Other elected county officials are: county sheriff, who is the chief law officer; the court clerk, who maintains court records; the county clerk, who is the chief record keeper; the county treasurer, who handles finances; and

Above: The Municipal Building in downtown Muskogee. Muskogee, the location of the Union Agency for the Five Tribes, was a major settlement in Indian Territory prior to statehood; however, after 1907, when it became the county seat for Muskogee County, the community boomed.

COURTESY THE DAILY OKLAHOMAN.

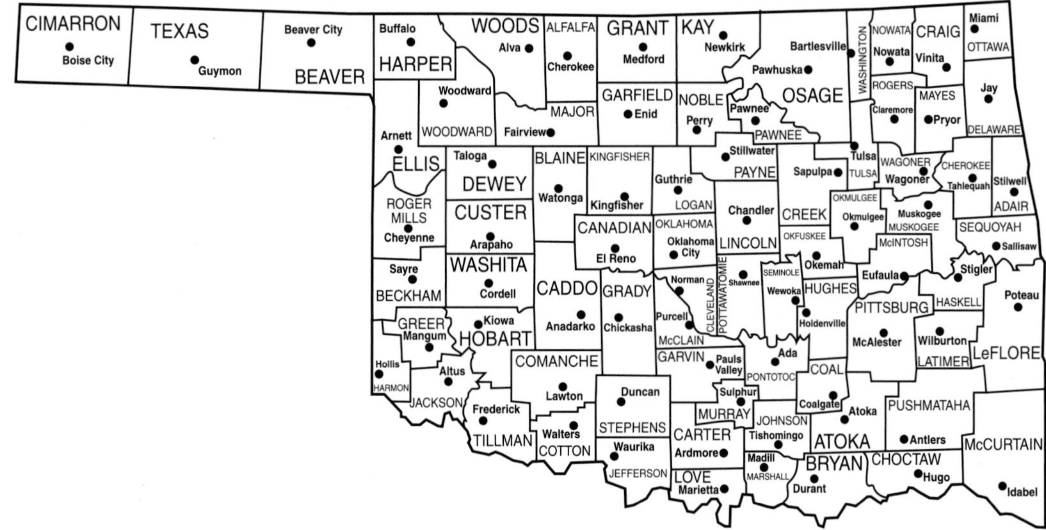

Bottom: A map of the counties and county seats of Oklahoma.

the county assessor, who assesses real and personal property, with the exception of railroad and public service company property. The ninth elected county official is the district attorney, whose jurisdiction corresponds with that of district courts and often overlaps two or more counties.

City and town government predates both territorial and state government. The earliest towns incorporated in Oklahoma were Fort Gibson and Vinita, which were incorporated in 1873; Webbers Falls, in 1885; and Chelsea, Chouteau, and Claremore, in 1889. They were incorporated under Cherokee Law. Mangum, in Old Greer County, was incorporated in 1886 under the laws of Texas. Between the opening of the Unassigned Lands in 1889 and the passage of the Organic Act of 1890, several communities, most notably Oklahoma City, Guthrie, El Reno, Stillwater, Kingfisher, and Norman, were organized. These governments were recognized in the 1890 legislation. Additional communities were organized under territorial law, and, at the beginning of the twentieth century, there were 147 cities or towns in Indian Territory and approximately 100 in Oklahoma Territory.

At statehood, the first Oklahoma legislature declared valid the cities and towns organized in the Twin Territories at the time of statehood so long as their ordinances did not conflict with state laws or the Oklahoma Constitution. Many of the existing territorial laws covering towns and cities were extended over the new state. It was not until 1977 that the state's Municipal Code was revised.

Cities and towns in Oklahoma have only those powers granted to them by the State of Oklahoma; however, unlike counties and school districts, they have legislative and judicial powers. Towns are governed by a board of trustees, composed of three or five trustees, depending on the number of wards into which the town is divided. One of the trustees serves as mayor.

For a town to become a city, it must have a population of at least 1,000 according to the last federal census. When this requirement is satisfied, a petition signed by thirty-five percent of the town's voters may request an election be held on the question, or the town board of trustees may call an election on the matter. The resolution must divide the city into either four or six wards and state what type of government the city will utilize. If the resolution passes, the county commissioners declare that the town is now a city and call an election for city officials.

Cities are governed by either a aldermanic, council-manager, or strong mayor-council form of government. Under the aldermanic form, a city is governed by a council composed of one or two councilmen elected from each ward. If the council wishes, it can elect a president who presides in the absence of the mayor. The mayor is the executive head of the city and is elected but votes only in case of a tie by the councilmen. The mayor can veto acts of the council, but the council can override the veto by a two-thirds vote.

Under a council-manager form of government, the council consists of one councilman from each ward and one councilman-at-large. A mayor is chosen from among the council

✧

The domeless Oklahoma Capitol Building in Oklahoma City. Completed in 1917, a shortage of building material resulted in the planned dome for the Capitol Building not being built. Although the Oklahoma Enabling Act prohibited the removal of the state capital from Guthrie before 1913, Governor Charles N. Haskell named Oklahoma City the state capital after a statewide election in 1910. When the courts ruled that Haskell's action was unlawful because of election irregularities, the governor called the State Legislature into special session and the solons quickly passed the Durant Bill, designating Oklahoma City the "permanent and immediate" capital.

COURTESY DAVID FITZGERALD.

members and presides over council meetings. A city manager is chosen by the council and serves as the executive head of the administrative branch of the city.

In a strong mayor-council form of city government, the mayor is elected at large and presides over council meetings. One councilman is chosen from each of the four to six wards into which the city is divided. All non-elected city officers are appointed by the mayor. The mayor supervises all city departments and is responsible for the enforcement of local ordinances and state laws.

School boards also are local governmental bodies. Each school district is governed by a school board elected by voters within the district. All teachers, administrators, and other school employees are hired by the board. It also is the highest appellate body within the district. The county superintendent of schools supervises dependent schools with a county. Independent schools are supervised by the state department of education.

Because of the progressive sympathies of the constitutional convention, state government in Oklahoma was designed to be firmly controlled by the people. The governor's office was limited in its power, and many administrative duties are performed by a multitude of governing boards, agencies, and commissions. In addition, many powers were relegated to the legislature and its leaders, particularly the speaker of the house of representatives and the president pro tempore of the senate. Although some governors have exercised more power than others simply by their assertive personalities and political acumen, historically, their role is subservient to the legislature. Framers of the constitution also stressed the powers of the people over the powers of politicians through the initiative and referendum. The fragmentation of power, however, has meant that responsibility for the successes and failures of state government is difficult to determine, with the governor often credited or blamed for events and policies that are beyond the control of that office.

✧

The World War I Memorial Mural at the Oklahoma State Capitol depicts the sacrifices made by state residents during the First World War. Oklahomans who served in the conflict usually were assigned to the Thirty-sixth or Ninetieth Infantry Divisions on the Western Front in France.

COURTESY OKLAHOMA DEPARTMENT OF TOURISM AND RECREATION; PHOTOGRAPH BY FRED MARVEL.

CHAPTER X

The Battle for Equality

With a stroke of his pen, President Abraham Lincoln took the first step to abolish slavery in America by signing the Emancipation Proclamation in 1863 during the Civil War. Within a few years, the Thirteenth, Fourteenth, and Fifteenth Amendments to the United States Constitution were ratified, giving full citizenship to blacks. But in reality, freedom for black citizens of Oklahoma existed only on paper at statehood in 1907.

Segregation was the law of the land after the United States Supreme Court declared in 1896, in the case of *Plessy v. Ferguson*, that separate but equal public facilities for blacks did not violate the Constitution's guarantee of equality and freedom for all Americans. Unfortunately, because whites controlled the early Oklahoma legislature, city councils, and school boards, black schools, parks, and other public facilities were never allocated sufficient funds to be "equal."

Oklahoma courts became the battleground for the struggle for civil rights, not just for blacks in Oklahoma, but for minorities all across the land. Lawyers, prodded by Oklahoma City black newspaper editor Roscoe Dunjee, forged a new day for blacks in the Sooner State, and brought about revolutionary change in the fight for equality.

During territorial days, blacks voted regularly and ran for office in some counties. The state constitution specifically prohibited the passage of any law that would hinder a citizen's right to vote based on race or color. However, the election of a black Republican, Albert Comstock Hamlin, to the Oklahoma House of Representatives from Logan County in 1908, frightened white leaders. Their answer was State Question 17, an overt move to follow other southern states to disenfranchise blacks.

In 1910, Oklahoma voters approved the question and amended the constitution to provide a literacy test for voters. The amendment required a voter to be able to read a section of the state constitution, but exempted any person whose ancestors could legally vote before 1866, the year blacks were granted the right to vote. The amendment, known as the "grandfather clause," was an open and obvious attempt to grandfather in white voters and to prevent blacks from exercising power at the ballot box.

In 1914, Dunjee took up the cause of suffrage for his people by publicizing the refusal of two Logan County Election Board officials to allow a black man to vote. The two men were indicted by a federal grand jury and convicted of violating the federal law guaranteeing the right of all citizens to vote. In June 1915, the United States Supreme Court, in *Guinn v. United States*, upheld the convictions of the two election board officials and threw out the "grandfather clause," branding it unconstitutional and declaring the state amendment an illegal attempt to abridge the right of a citizen to vote on the ground of ancestry. The *Guinn* case was the first national victory for a fledgling black organization known as the National Association for the Advancement of Colored People (NAACP), of which Dunjee became a state and national leader.

Oklahoma tried to sidestep the *Guinn* decision by passing a law that required all unregistered voters to register during a twelve-day period beginning April 30, 1916. The law did not specify where registration was to occur and provided no penalty for failure to register black voters. There were widespread reports of registrars refusing to register blacks by simply saying, "I don't have my registration book with me."

The legislature's move to eliminate blacks from the electoral process worked. The 1916 special session law was not successfully challenged until the United States Supreme Court ruled it unconstitutional in *Lane v. Wilson* in 1934, eighteen years later. The lack of black participation and the apportionment of legislative districts that favored rural Oklahoma prevented the election of another black to the state legislature until 1964, more than a half century after the election of Hamlin.

In 1952, Oklahoma City attorney A. B. McDonald, a candidate for the Democratic United States Senate nomination, challenged the state law that required the word "Negro" to be printed after the

✧

Prior to the adoption of peaceful sit-ins by Martin Luther King, Jr., and the Southern Christian Leadership Conference, Clara Luper, head of Oklahoma City's NAACP Youth Council, successfully used the tactic to win civil rights concessions in Oklahoma. On June 4, 1961, a group of black and white youths peacefully sat on the floor of the lobby of the Skirvin Hotel in downtown Oklahoma City to demand equal accommodations for all races.

COURTESY *THE DAILY OKLAHOMAN.*

✧

Top, left: Many buffalo soldiers served in Oklahoma, first as participants in the post-Civil War Indian wars and later to protect the Indian reservations from incursions by boomers. Henry O. Flipper, the first black graduate of the United States Military Academy at West Point, New York, was stationed at Fort Sill. A trained engineer, he designed and then oversaw the construction of what became known as Flipper's Ditch, which eliminated breeding grounds for malaria carrying mosquitoes.

COURTESY NATIONAL COWBOY HALL OF FAME & WESTERN HERITAGE CENTER, OKLAHOMA CITY.

Top, right: A map of the Territory of Lincoln adapted from Schönberg's Standard Atlas, *published by Schönberg and Company in New York City in 1867.*

name of black candidates on state election ballots. In July 1955, the United States Court of Appeals for the Tenth Circuit struck down the Oklahoma law.

Segregation in transportation, valiantly opposed by black leaders such as Roscoe Dunjee and Jimmy Stewart, a black office manager for Oklahoma Natural Gas Company, was an embarrassing reality from the time of statehood. The second bill introduced in the Oklahoma legislature after statehood was a Jim Crow law requiring railroads to provide separate cars for blacks and whites. The term "Jim Crow" came from a comedy act in the 1830s when a white comedian painted his face black and called the character "Jim Crow." Since that time, Jim Crow symbolized black or segregated, such as a Jim Crow hotel or train.

A month after statehood, the first legislature approved legislation requiring separate coaches on trains, street cars, and all forms of public transportation. The law mandated separate waiting rooms at railroad and street car stations and called for "conspicuous" signs in "plain letters" indicating the race for which it was set apart.

Right: J. W. Matthew's Pool Hall on Harrison Avenue in Guthrie. As the capital of Oklahoma Territory, Guthrie was a mecca for early-day black settlers. Local businesses such as Matthew's Pool Hall became social gathering places in which local men discussed politics and other community issues.

COURTESY GUTHRIE PUBLIC LIBRARY COLLECTION, WESTERN HISTORY COLLECTIONS, UNIVERSITY OF OKLAHOMA LIBRARIES.

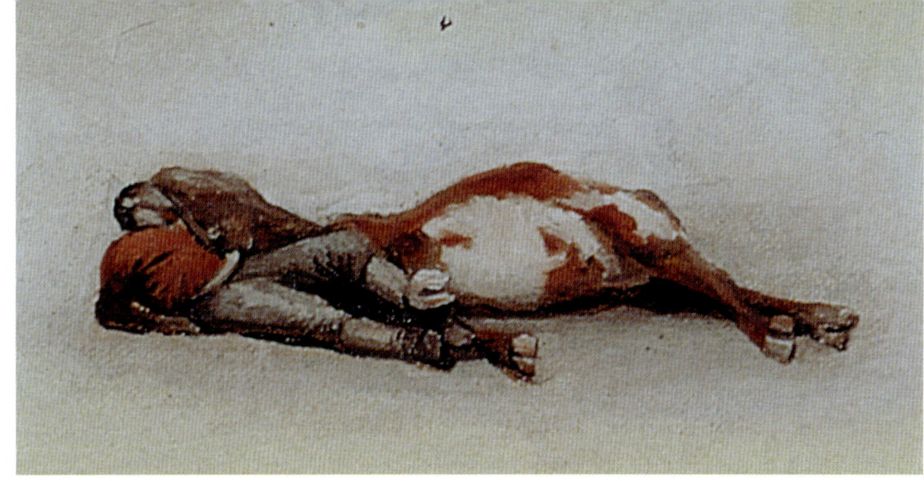

Oklahoma blacks began challenging the Jim Crow laws even before their effective date in February 1908. One of the first lawsuits was filed by E. P. McCabe, a prominent Guthrie black who had served as deputy treasurer of Oklahoma Territory, the first black man to hold public office west of the Mississippi River. McCabe lost his challenge as time and time again the Oklahoma and United States Supreme Courts upheld the Jim Crow laws. The Courts' theme continued to be that "separate, but equal accommodations for the races" was not repugnant to the Constitution. It took civil rights activists in Oklahoma almost fifty years to completely eliminate the discrimination caused by the Jim Crow laws.

In a scathing editorial in his newspaper, *The Black Dispatch*, in 1940, Dunjee explained why he so hated Jim Crow laws in public transportation:

> Why should a sick black woman have to ride in a filthy, stinking railroad toilet? Why should a bus driver tell black travelers to stand up while whites loll in seats which under the law belong to Negroes? Every time you suffer humiliating and unbearable treatment and remain silent, you are heaping coals on the fire of prejudice. Why feed the flames of race hate in this cowardly way?

In 1946, the United States Supreme Court outlawed segregation on railroad trains traveling interstate. A decade later, the high court ruled as unconstitutional all laws segregating passengers based on race. "Jim Crowism" was finally dead in Oklahoma only when Governor Henry Bellmon signed legislation in 1965 forever repealing the state's onerous Jim Crow laws.

Segregation in housing was widespread in early Oklahoma. Throughout the state, cities and towns passed ordinances assembling blacks in certain sections, apart from whites. The housing problem exploded in Oklahoma City in 1919, as blacks outgrew cramped sections of the city where they were allowed to live. The home of Beulah Maxwell, a black hairdresser who moved to a white neighborhood, was splintered by a bomb in 1919. A vigilante committee composed of fifteen black men hired a watchman for Maxwell, thus

Left: Black Oklahomans have a long tradition in the frontier spirit of the state. Bill Pickett, one of the West's best-known cowboys is credited with the invention of bulldogging as a rodeo sport. Pickett became world famous performing with Pawnee Bill Wild West Show. Pickett would gallop alongside a steer, leap onto the bovine's neck, and then bite the steer on the lip as he threw it to the ground. Pickett once performed the feat with a broken arm as the Pawnee Bill Wild West Show toured Great Britain.

FROM PAWNEE BILL MONTAGE,
COURTESY BRUMMETT ECHOHAWK.

Bottom: The soda fountain at Chamber's Ice Cream Parlor at 206 South Second Street in Guthrie in 1919. A large number of blacks settled in Oklahoma during the territorial period, fleeing the restrictive legislation of nearby Southern states. While some became tenant farmers, others migrated to the cities and became prosperous business owners.

COURTESY GUTHRIE PUBLIC LIBRARY COLLECTION,
WESTERN HISTORY COLLECTIONS,
UNIVERSITY OF OKLAHOMA LIBRARIES.

Left: Roscoe Dunjee, the father of the civil rights movement in Oklahoma. As editor of The Black Dispatch, *Dunjee was at the forefront in the equality movement in Oklahoma and was behind the Logan County case* Guinn v. United States, *which successfully overturned the "grandfather clause" nationwide.*

COURTESY *THE DAILY OKLAHOMAN.*

Right: Jimmy Stewart, shown here addressing the Oklahoma City City Council, was one of Oklahoma's most prominent civil rights leaders. Stewart had a passion for equality, and, as a national leader of the National Association for the Advancement of Colored People, he played a major role in developing local, state, and national civil rights policies.

COURTESY *THE DAILY OKLAHOMAN.*

ending the first terrorism attempt in the housing segregation fight.

The eyes of the nation were on Oklahoma in 1933 when Governor William H. "Alfalfa Bill" Murray urged the city council of Oklahoma City to pass a segregation ordinance that prevented blacks from living outside their designated areas. Before the ink was dry on the ordinance, Dunjee and other civil rights activists began a legal attack. Governor Murray, by executive order, declared martial law in a section of northeast Oklahoma City in a futile attempt to perpetuate the line of segregation. In 1935, in the case of *Onie Allen v. Oklahoma City*, the Oklahoma Supreme Court struck down the segregation ordinance. The opinion, written by Justice Fletcher Riley, was one of the first denunciations of segregation ordinances by a Southern court.

The Ku Klux Klan had limited influence in Oklahoma before 1921. However, as urban areas experienced phenomenal growth, law enforcement officers could not keep up with the crime wave. Vigilante groups were formed in Oklahoma City and Tulsa to punish lawbreakers. Where legal means failed to curb crime, illegal means were taken up. The methods used were brutal, direct, and effective. "Night-riders" in Tulsa went out and caught bootleggers, dope-peddlers, and gamblers, whipping them to within an inch of their lives. After a sweep of night-riding in Tulsa in 1922, most of the gangs were driven away and a solid Klan-influenced county government was elected.

The Klan attracted thousands of Oklahoma converts, many of whom were well-intentioned, not criminal, but young and hot-headed or fanatical social meddlers anxious to straighten out their neighbors with whips. Mississippi and Alabama have historically been ridiculed for atrocious Klan involvement, but Oklahoma holds the dubious distinction of enduring the greatest volume of Klan violence in the 1920s. Oklahoma City Klan No. 1 had a "whipping squad," charged with meting out justice. The squad was called the "San Hedrin," named after the Jewish body that tried and convicted Jesus.

The worst race riot in Oklahoma history occurred in Tulsa between May 31 and June 1, 1921. For twenty-four hours whites and blacks used bullets and fire to vent their rage before national guardsmen restored order.

The case of Jess Hollins was the basis for a crusade against all-white juries in Oklahoma in the 1930s. Hollins was accused of raping a white woman in Creek County, Oklahoma. A change of venue moved the trial to Okmulgee County, where the Oklahoma jury selection process was actually on trial. Even though more than seventeen percent of the citizens of Okmulgee County were black, blacks were excluded from the jury pool.

Twelve white jurors found Hollins guilty and sentenced him to die. The case was immediately appealed, eventually ending up on the docket of the highest court in the land, the United States Supreme Court. Oklahoma Attorney General Mac Q. Williamson represented the state in oral arguments before the Supreme Court. He opened the argument with an emotional account of rape at gunpoint. However, one justice leaned over the bench and told Williamson to stick to the legal points. The oral arguments took two days.

After lengthy deliberation, the Supreme Court, in a short unanimous decision written by Chief Justice Charles Evans Hughes, forever banished in America the system, still in use in Oklahoma and many states at that time, that excluded blacks from jury service. The Hollins case revolutionized court practices in Oklahoma. Attorney General Williamson simply announced that "hereafter Negroes will serve on Oklahoma juries."

Black leaders expressed strong opposition to the idea of separate schools for black children from the early days of Oklahoma. A complex school financing system perpetuated inferior schools for blacks for decades after statehood. Black schools were financed with a county-wide tax levy. White schools, however, received both county tax money and money from a school district property tax levy. Whites owned most of the property, and white schools received the great bulk of tax money earmarked for education. In some years, white schools received five times as much money as black schools. While many white schools were housed in acceptable, freshly-painted buildings, black children were relegated to dilapidated, worn-out schools.

Above: Known as North Tulsa, the Black Wall Street, or Little Africa, Tulsa's Greenwood District stretched from the Missouri, Kansas & Texas Railroad tracks north to Standpipe Hill and from Cincinnati Avenue east to Archer. A black cultural and entertainment center, Greenwood also was the scene of the infamous 1921 Tulsa Race Riot, one of the worse such riots in American history, which destroyed 1,000 homes, five hotels, thirty-one restaurants, four drug stores, eight physician offices, twenty-four grocery stores, a school, and a library. Today much of Greenwood has been restored to its former style.

COURTESY DAVID FITZGERALD.

Left: The Ku Klux Klan was a powerful influence in Oklahoma, the South, and the upper Midwest during the 1920s, attracting thousands of men, women, and children with its message of intolerance for blacks, Jews, Catholics, immigrants, gamblers, prostitutes, and others. By the 1970s, however, Oklahomans' views of the Klan had drastically changed as can be seen in this anti-Klan protest held in Durant in October of 1980 to protest the arrival of the Klan's Imperial Wizard in Idabel.

COURTESY THE DAILY OKLAHOMAN.

Above: Deep Deuce, Oklahoma City's Bourbon Street of jazz, was the musical birthplace of such musicians as Charlie Christian, Jimmy Rushing, and Buddy Anderson. Their music enlivened such establishments of Ruby's Grill, Slaughter Hall, Aldridge Theater, Rushing's Café, and Hallie Richardson Shoe Shine Parlor along Northeast Second Street. Thursday was the big evening along Deep Deuce as hundreds participated in The Walk when "they strutted their strut, showing off their clothes, their hairstyles...parading, socializing, stopping in the drugstores when they grew tired to eat an ice cream cone." It was an occasion for families to load up the car and go to Second Street.

COURTESY ANITA ARNOLD, BLAC, INC.

Another inequity was unequal pay for white and black school teachers. There was a substantial disparity between salaries for black and white teachers because of the interpretation of schools laws dividing tax money for support of separate schools.

In 1941, the Oklahoma legislature overhauled school laws that continued to be based on complete segregation. Blacks were prohibited from attending white schools, from elementary schools to the colleges and universities. The legislature made it a criminal misdemeanor for school administrators to admit blacks to white schools, for teachers to teach mixed-race classes, and for white students to attend them. School administrators faced fines of up to $500 for each day the law was violated.

By 1945, proponents of continued segregation pointed to Langston University as the place where blacks could obtain an equal higher education. However, black leaders countered the argument with facts. Langston's art department consisted of a one-room, cramped program, while the University of Oklahoma was bragging about a new $250,000 Oriental art collection. The stage was set for a legal battle that would pit a young black girl from Chickasha against the very institution of segregation in America, a battle that would be noticed nationwide.

Ada Lois Sipuel Fisher attempted to enroll in the University of Oklahoma Law School in January of 1946. University President George L. Cross, who personally abhorred the separate but equal education policies of the state but who was sworn to uphold state law, refused Fisher admission, handing her an honest and forthright letter that stated the only reason for denying admission was her race.

Thurgood Marshall, legal counsel for the NAACP in New York and later the first black to be appointed to the United States Supreme Court, was lead counsel in the bitter legal

Right: Eddie Christian and his band the Blue Devils, one of the most popular jazz bands in the nation, played in the Ritz Ballroom in Oklahoma City during the Roaring Twenties. Left to right: Eddie Christian on piano, Wesley Simmons on drums, Carl White on bass, Jim Dodson on guitar, Charles Young on trumpet, Cy Cannon on alto saxophone, and Leroy Parks on tenor saxophone.

COURTESY ANITA ARNOLD, BLAC, INC.

attack against the segregation policy of Oklahoma. The Oklahoma Supreme Court upheld the constitutionality of the Oklahoma law forbidding blacks to attend white schools. However, the United States Supreme Court reversed the Oklahoma high court and ordered the state to provide Fisher with a legal education equal to that received by white students.

Tragically, Oklahoma's leadership again balked at integration and set up a sham Langston University School of Law at the state capitol and appointed a three-man faculty. When the Langston law school was scheduled to close, officials at OU allowed Fisher to enroll. She completed her law school degree in 1951 and began a long and distinguished career as an educator and civil rights activist.

"Segregation is obvious discrimination," was the theme of another lawsuit against the University of Oklahoma on behalf of George W. McLaurin, a fifty-four-year-old teacher who applied for admission to the OU Graduate College in 1948. His case was selected as a test case by attorney Marshall from the cases of six blacks who were denied admission to OU.

A panel of three federal judges ruled that McLaurin must be admitted to OU or that the university must not offer the same graduate program for whites. However, the federal panel refused to declare Oklahoma's segregation laws unconstitutional. The OU Board of Regents ordered McLaurin admitted, but only on a segregated basis. McLaurin was forced to sit in an alcove of a classroom so that he could see the teacher but the white students could not see him. Separate toilet facilities and a separate desk in the library were provided.

Marshall called the treatment McLaurin received "stupid" and appealed the plan to the United States Supreme Court, which ruled in June of 1950 that the attempts to segregate McLaurin from the rest of the student body

✧

Above: Ada Lois Sipuel Fisher, right, discussing legal tactics with her attorneys, Amos T. Hall, of Tulsa, left, and Thurgood Marshall, during their fight to open higher education in Oklahoma to all races. Marshall, who later was appointed to the United States Supreme Court, was a frequent participant in civil rights actions in Oklahoma and often stayed with Roscoe Dunjee while in Oklahoma.

COURTESY *THE DAILY OKLAHOMAN.*

Left: Deep Deuce continued to be a center of black culture in Oklahoma and was the scene of several civil rights protests in the 1960s, including this march in 1965.

COURTESY *THE DAILY OKLAHOMAN.*

Right: Young protestors at the John A. Brown Department Store's lunch counter. Organized by Clara Luper, the youthful protestors would appear at the counter at lunch and politely ask "May we eat today?" Sometimes Luper would have the youths fasten white paper plates to their faces so they could ask to eat with "white faces." The publicity garnered by such peaceful protests helped breakdown the racial barriers of Jim Crowism in Oklahoma.

COURTESY *THE DAILY OKLAHOMAN.*

Below: Cavalry Baptist Church on North Walnut Avenue in northeast Oklahoma City was a center for the state's civil rights movement. Here protesters leave the church on their way to urge a boycott of businesses not open to all races.

COURTESY *THE DAILY OKLAHOMAN.*

violated his Fourteenth Amendment right to an equal education. The McLaurin and Fisher cases changed education forever in America.

Only four years later, in 1954, segregation in public elementary and secondary schools was outlawed by another case taken to the United States Supreme Court by Marshall. The case was *Brown v. Board of Education*. Even though *Brown* was a Kansas case, the ruling directly affected schools in Oklahoma and sixteen other states where segregation was mandated or allowed by state law. *Brown* sent a shock wave throughout American education, especially in the South. Newspapers throughout the world heralded the end of segregation in education. Jim Crow was finally dead, at least in the American classroom. Oklahoma, and its aggressive black leaders, played a major role in that death.

Oklahoma Governor Johnston Murray, and his successor, Raymond Gary, showed statesmanlike leadership in cautioning against overreaction to the *Brown* decision. Both men pledged to abide by the law as stated by the Supreme Court. The state legislature scrapped the old system of separate tax levies for black schools and submitted to the people a constitutional amendment revamping school finance laws. When opponents cried that passage of State Question 368 would spell the end to segregated education, Governor Gary strongly urged voters to approve the question. Voters listened and overwhelmingly passed the amendment by a vote of 231,097 to 73,021 on April 5, 1955.

Many of the landmark legal cases argued before the United States Supreme Court by Thurgood Marshall arose from discrimination cases in Oklahoma. Marshall enjoyed his time in Oklahoma, where he stayed with friends such as Jimmy and Mae Lois Stewart, lodging made necessary by the refusal of downtown Oklahoma City hotels to serve blacks.

Marshall loved riding around in a car and listening to rock and roll music. He also enjoyed Western movies. At the end of a hard day's legal wrangling, he often asked his Oklahoma host to "let me off at the movies." Marshall also preferred the taste of Oklahoma moonshine whiskey. Often, when bootleggers knew Marshall was coming to town, they delivered a case or two of "shine" for consumption of Marshall and his company of lawyers, secretaries, and admirers.

Marshall's first case in Oklahoma was the defense of W. D. Lyons, a black man accused of murdering a white man, his wife, and two children near Hugo and burning their home to hide the crime. When Marshall drove into Hugo, more than 1,500 whites and blacks surrounded the county courthouse, waiting for a chance to crowd into the tiny courtroom.

Marshall's life was threatened, and he was forced to sleep at a different well-guarded

home each night. The New York lawyer had the local crowd and jury spell-bound with his cross-examination of the state's witnesses. He forced local lawmen to admit they had stacked the bloody and charred bones of the victims on the defendant's body to procure the original confession. At the close of the trial, the jury did not heed the pleas of Marshall and convicted Lyons, sentencing him to life in prison.

Marshall appealed the Lyons case all the way to the United States Supreme Court, arguing that the trial judge erred by admitting into evidence Lyons' confession that was obtained after the defendant was beaten and held without food or water for almost twenty-four hours. The high court ignored Marshall's argument and upheld the conviction. It was Marshall's first defeat in a case before the Supreme Court and his first defeat in a major decision involving the rights of a black defendant.

By the mid-1950s, the cracks in the segregation wall in America were widening. The impact of the Supreme Court's ban on segregation in education spilled over into other areas of life. The Oklahoma State Fair, in September 1954, opened all its facilities to blacks. During the 1954 election season, state officials were called upon to pull down the signs on the doors of state capitol lavatories which read "White Gentleman" and "White Ladies." Roscoe Dunjee called the continued segregation in bathroom facilities "the most unbrotherly aspect of segregation to be found in Oklahoma."

It was difficult for blacks to dine in restaurants or lunch-counters in Oklahoma, even into the 1950s. Since before statehood, blacks

Hoping to draw attention to the segregation of most eating establishments in Oklahoma City, a group of civil rights demonstrators picketed the Anna Maude Cafeteria in downtown Oklahoma City. Here police wait on a patrol wagon to escort nine of the demonstrators to jail on charges of disorderly conduct.

COURTESY *THE DAILY OKLAHOMAN.*

Business owners would not budge, so Luper, heavily influenced by the non-violent teachings of Dr. Martin Luther King, Jr., led thirteen young black children to the Katz Drugstore food counter in downtown Oklahoma City in August 1958, for one of the first sit-in demonstrations in the South and border states after World War II.

Luper led hundreds of demonstrations in the late 1950s and 1960s, until the walls of segregation were broken in Oklahoma City eating establishments. An eleven-month economic boycott of downtown businesses helped break the spirit of lunch-counter owners. Luper and her Youth Council proved that change could be made without violence, unlike sit-in demonstrations that ended with riots and many arrests throughout the South.

In 1961, almost a decade since the United States Supreme Court officially struck down segregation in America's public schools, many schools in Oklahoma, particularly in the metropolitan areas, remained segregated because of housing patterns and the location of neighborhood schools. Dr. A. L. Dowell, a prominent black Oklahoma City dentist, filed a lawsuit against the Oklahoma City Board of Education on behalf of his son, who wanted to enroll in a high school where most of the students were white. The case was assigned to United States District Judge Luther L. Bohanon, an Arkansas native who grew up as the son of a tenant farmer near Kinta in eastern Oklahoma.

Bohanon took his assignment to the Dowell case seriously. For months he pored over stacks of charts, graphs, maps, and "future plans" of the Board of Education. Bohanon found staggering proof that public schools in Oklahoma City remained segregated with seven all-white and one black high school.

In March 1963, Bohanon handed down a thundering decision that found the Oklahoma City Board of Education guilty of enforcing a discriminatory student transfer policy that perpetuated segregation and of failing to have a sufficient plan for racial integration. Judge Bohanon ultimately imposed boundaries that forced the board of education to utilize busing of students across town to formerly

Prentice Gautt became the first black athlete to play in the Oklahoma All-Star Football game in 1956 and was the first black to make the University of Oklahoma's football team. Gautt's football field success, he became an All-American player, did much to ease the integration of Oklahoma's system of higher education.

COURTESY THE DAILY OKLAHOMAN.

had been prevented from eating with whites, not by law, but by tradition based on racial prejudice. With no integration laws on the books, restaurant owners used trespass laws to evict blacks from their premises.

Oklahoma City black leaders, including Clara Luper, a school teacher and advisor to the NAACP Youth Council, tried to negotiate with restaurant owners in Oklahoma City in 1957, hoping for an uneventful end to desegregation.

D. C. Minner and his wife, Shelby, owners of the Down Home Blues Club in Rentiesville, Oklahoma. A nationally renowned blues musician, Minner attracts nationwide crowds to his club where he maintains the traditional blues culture, which traces many of its roots to Oklahoma.

COURTESY DAVID FITZGERALD.

all-white or all-black schools to achieve racial integration in classrooms.

The very word "busing" caused instantaneous problems between blacks and whites in Oklahoma City. Demonstrations and counter-demonstrations marred the peaceful landscape of the capital city. On the first day of busing in August 1972, 3,500 busing opponents rallied at the state fairgrounds. Fights broke out at several schools. One student was killed. White flight occurred on an unprecedented scale. Private schools sprang up overnight, an obvious attempt to keep white children from being bused.

The final verdict on the success or failure of integration of Oklahoma's public schools may not come for decades. Some black leaders charged that "resegregation" of public schools was occurring after forced busing plans were discarded by local school boards. In 1997, twelve years after returning to a neighborhood school plan, 206 of the 209 students at Garden Oaks Elementary School in Oklahoma City were black. At the nearby Martin Luther King Jr. Elementary School, only six white students were in the student body of 303.

Black leaders in Oklahoma began to make inroads into areas of public service in the 1960s. Governor Dewey Bartlett appointed Charles Owens of Oklahoma City as the state's first black district judge in 1968. During the Bartlett administration, Ronnie Johnson became Oklahoma's first black state trooper. Hannah Atkins of Oklahoma City was the first black woman elected to the Oklahoma House of Representatives.

Later Vicki Miles-LaGrange of Oklahoma City established several firsts for black women in Oklahoma. She was elected to the Oklahoma State Senate and appointed as United States Attorney for the Western District of Oklahoma. In the 1990s, she became the first black federal judge in state history.

J. C. Watts was elected congressman from Oklahoma's Fourth District. A former football star at the University of Oklahoma, Watts was catapulted in the national spotlight as a young black Republican leader.

Oklahoma blacks never wavered in their passionate fight for equality. Their gains, both in the courtroom and in the streets, paved the way for more equal treatment of all minorities in the United States.

CHAPTER XI

THE WEALTH OF THE LAND

At statehood, the Twin Territories contained 1,414,177 people almost equally divided, with 733,062 in Oklahoma Territory and 681,115 in Indian Territory. Most of the people lived in rural areas. There were only five towns with populations of more than 10,000—Oklahoma City, Muskogee, Guthrie, Shawnee, and Enid—and only six with more than 5,000 inhabitants—Ardmore, McAlester, Chickasha, Tulsa, Lawton, and El Reno. There were important areas of mineral wealth, mostly in Indian Territory, including the coal mining region of southeastern Oklahoma, the Tri-State Mining District of northeastern Oklahoma, and an emerging oil and natural gas industry. In fact, in 1907, Oklahoma ranked third among the states in oil production. Nonetheless, most of the state's economy was based on agriculture. In 1907, Oklahoma ranked fifth among the states in cotton production, eighth in wheat production, and ninth in corn production.

Between 1899 and 1905, 16.75 million acres were opened to farmers in Oklahoma Territory. Cotton was king in the Twin Territories during this period. Okfuskee County boasted twenty-seven cotton gins, while McAlester and Ardmore in Indian Territory and Oklahoma City and Mangum in Oklahoma Territory were major cotton centers exporting to New England, France, Germany, and Japan. Cotton production peaked in 1926 at 1.77 million pounds.

If cotton was king, corn was queen. Corn provided not only a cash crop for sale, but food for families and fodder for animals. By 1909, corn was planted on 78.1 percent of state farms. Wheat replaced both corn and cotton as the major cash crop in the state after the introduction of the hardy winter variety of wheat—Turkey Red—by the Mennonites. Oklahoma constantly ranked third or fourth among the nation's wheat producing states.

As mechanization replaced horse and mule power on state farms in the early twentieth century, less manpower was needed to cultivate, plant, and harvest more acres. Tenant farms began to disappear and the number of farms dropped, as fewer people could farm more acres. The average size of an Oklahoma farm rose from 166.4 acres in 1920 to 478 acres in 1989. At the same time, the number of individual farms dropped from a peak of 204,000 in the 1930s to 69,000 in 1989.

Like farming, the lumber industry played a major role in the state's economic development. The heavily wooded terrain of southeastern Oklahoma encouraged an extensive lumbering industry, starting in 1868 when the state' first steam-powered sawmill began operations at Boggy Depot in the Choctaw Nation. Others quickly followed. Stringtown once contained twenty-two sawmills, and the Long-Bell Lumber Company mill at Antlers produced 150,000 board feet daily from timber fed to the mill by a ten-mile long tramway. Wright City, Broken Bow, and Hochatown also became lumber centers.

In 1888, the Choctaw Lumber and Coal Company began its timber operations and built a private railway to the region to carry its timber to market. In 1921, the Dierks Lumber Company acquired the Choctaw Lumber and Coal Company, and, in 1969, Dierks was purchased by the Weyerhaeuser Company. Eventually, Weyerhaeuser acquired title to almost one-half of the land in McCurtain County for its lumber operations. Weyerhaeuser's mill at Valliant is the largest paper mill in the United States.

The state's coal deposits were noted as early as 1719, when Bernard de la Harpe visited eastern Oklahoma. Commercial mining of coal started in 1872, when the Osage Coal and Mining Company opened a mine at Cross Roads, the junction of the California Trail and the Texas Road, hoping to supply coal to the Missouri, Kansas, and Texas Railroad. They soon were joined by the Choctaw Coal and Mining Company. McAlester quickly became the center of the region's coal mining activity and James J. McAlester the principal developer of the nearby mines. Other important coal towns were Hartshorne, Atoka, Savanna, Lehigh, Coalgate, Wilburton, and Henryetta.

Working in the mines was dangerous, and many experienced foreign miners were imported for the hard labor. The area around Krebs became well-known for its Italian heritage. During the coal strike of 1898-1902, a large number of blacks were imported from Alabama mines to replace strikers. Nine and

✧

Bob Stuchel, the driller on the discovery well of the Healdton Field in 1905, points to one of the numerous oil seeps that attracted oilmen to Carter County. Oklahoma and Indian Territories were well known during the late nineteenth century for their oil seeps. Some, such as Maytubby Springs in Bryan County, had been developed into health spas. However, until the allotment of tribal lands and the formation of the State of Oklahoma, it was difficult for oilmen to secure leases in the area and thus the opening of the state's huge oil fields was postponed.
COURTESY MAC MCGALLIARD COLLECTION, ARDMORE PUBLIC LIBRARY.

✧

Right: "Skyscrapers of the Plains" is the name commonly given to the huge grain elevators that rise above the rich wheat land of western Oklahoma. These are near the community of Orienta in Major County along the banks of the Cimarron River. Oklahoma is in the heart of America's breadbasket and its farmers constantly make it one of the top wheat producing regions in the nation.

COURTESY DAVID FITZGERALD.

Below: A typical broomcorn harvest crew in Oklahoma during the early years of the twentieth century. Broomcorn was once such an important crop to Oklahoma farmers that the world's price for broomcorn was set by the market at Lindsay in Garvin County, which proclaimed itself the "Broomcorn Capital of the World."

COURTESY CORN HISTORICAL SOCIETY,
WESTERN HISTORY COLLECTIONS,
UNIVERSITY OF OKLAHOMA LIBRARIES.

◆

Left: A train load of lumber being taken to market near Antlers in Pushmataha County. The home of the Long-Bell Lumber Company's mill, Antlers was at the center of the lumber industry in Oklahoma and produced more than 150,000 board feet daily. In addition to the railroad, the mill at Antlers was connected to the forest by a ten-mile long tramway that carried logs to the sawmills.

COURTESY PUSHMATAHA COLLECTION, WESTERN HISTORY COLLECTIONS, UNIVERSITY OF OKLAHOMA LIBRARIES.

Below: Loads of coal waiting shipment from the Dow Coal Mine Company in Savanna in Pittsburg County. The coal deposits were the remains of the huge shallow seas that once covered the region hundreds of millions of years ago. As the land sank the swamps and marshlands along their banks were buried, eventually creating the huge deposits of coal in southeastern Oklahoma.

COURTESY *THE DAILY OKLAHOMAN.*

a half hour days were common and most mining was done by hand. Safety measures were primitive and accidents frequent. The largest disaster occurred on January 7, 1892, at Mine No. 11 near Krebs, when approximately 100 men were killed and another 200 injured. Peter Hanraty began his career as a union organizer in the coal mines of eastern Oklahoma and increased the membership in the United Mine Workers of America from 400 to more than 16,000 between 1900 and 1908.

The importance of coal began to decline after 1910, as fuel oil began replacing coal in railroad engines. Production continued, however, peaking in 1920 at 4,840,225 tons, valued at $23,294,000. Serious decline followed the failed coal strike of 1924-1927. By the time the strike ended, sixty of the sixty-four banks in McAlester had closed, and the miners were disenchanted with the union leadership. Coal mining revived briefly during World War II, but never returned to the importance of the earlier years.

The Tri-State Mining District of northeastern Oklahoma, southeastern Kansas, and southwestern Missouri was one of the largest

◇

Top, left: One of the primitive gold mines sunk by some of the thousands of miners that rushed to the Wichita Mountains in the early twentieth century in what was the last gold rush in the forty-eight contiguous states. Attracted by the lore of lost mines and hidden treasures, an estimated 20,000 miners were busy in the Wichitas in 1901. Poverty Gulch, Sugar Tit Mountain, Craterville, and Rattlesnake Mountain all became common names among the miners that sunk thousands of shafts before the rush collapsed in 1904-1905.

COURTESY OKLAHOMA GEOLOGICAL SURVEY COLLECTION, WESTERN HISTORY COLLECTIONS, UNIVERSITY OF OKLAHOMA LIBRARIES.

Top, right: Kerr-McGee's Choctaw Mine in the coal fields of eastern Oklahoma was the deepest mine shaft in the Western Hemisphere in 1975. Total depth to the bottom of the shaft was 1,420 feet.

COURTESY *THE DAILY OKLAHOMAN.*

areas of lead and zinc production in the United States. La Harpe also noted the presence of lead during his 1719 tour of the region, and lead mines were licensed by the Cherokee National Council in the 1840s; however, serious development of the area did not start until later. Development in Ottawa County started around Peoria in the 1890s, and quickly spread to such mining communities as Cardin, Pitcher, Quapaw, Hockerville, Douthat, Century, and Commerce. By 1925, $10,463,040 worth of lead and $43,072,392 worth of zinc was being produced annually by miners in the Oklahoma Tri-State Mining area.

So rapid was the development that some of the mines penetrated into the nearby communities. The Turkey Fat Mine expanded beneath Commerce; however, the largest mining operation in the area was maintained by Eagle Pitcher Lead and Zinc Company, which dominated the region's mining activity. Many local residents grew rich from the deposits. John Quapaw was paid $105,000 for six acres by the Kansas Explorations Company in 1926. In 1919, the Oklahoma School of Mines was opened in Miami to train professional mining engineers.

One of the last gold rushes in the United States took place in the Wichita Mountains of southwestern Oklahoma. As early as 1657, Spanish miners were sinking shafts on Mount Scott. The ruins of a Spanish *arrastre*, a crude

Right: One of the early-day lead and zinc mines at Miami in Ottawa County. The primitive hand-powered windless was used to pull the ore from the crude shaft. Mining in the Tri-State Mining District, which covers northeastern Oklahoma, southwestern Missouri, and southeastern Kansas, started in the 1850s. By the 1920s Oklahoma's portion of the district was producing almost $20,000,000 worth of lead and zinc annually.

COURTESY *THE DAILY OKLAHOMAN.*

Left: Much of the lead and zinc production of northeastern Oklahoma was shipped to Bartlesville, where the Bartlesville Zinc Company maintained an extensive smeltering complex. Bartlesville had the advantage of being near both the lead and zinc mines and a plentiful supply of natural gas to power the smelters. Many of the workers at the smelters were Polish immigrants and their neighborhood near the smelter took on a definite ethnic personality. There was so much activity at the smelters that downtown Bartlesville often was covered with a blue haze.

COURTESY *THE DAILY OKLAHOMAN.*

mill used to separate gold from the host rock, still can be seen on the banks of Medicine Creek south of Meers. However, hostile Indians drove the early miners out of the region.

Mining in the area was revived by A. J. Meers, who began prospecting the Wichitas in 1885. He later founded the town of Meers, which, in 1901, became the center of the Meers Gold Mining District. Between its discovery and 1904, it was the richest gold producing area in the Wichitas, with some discoveries assaying $105 per ton.

In 1889, James Hale discovered the Golden Run Copper Mine northeast of Oreana, and, in 1892, some miners from Colorado located silver in Devil's Canyon. These discoveries touched off a rush to the Wichitas and the establishment of the Eureka Gold Mining District near Quartz Mountain in Greer County. By August of 1901, there were an estimated 20,000 miners in the Wichitas searching for gold.

Eventually, six additional gold mining districts were created before the boom busted

Below: A horse linked to a set of gears was used to raise and lower buckets of lead and zinc ore from this early mine near Miami. Many of the early mining operations in Ottawa County started as small operations that tapped the shallow veins of lead and zinc, which started at about 100 feet below the surface. Towns such as Cardin, Pitcher, Quapaw, Hockerville, Douthat, Century, Commerce, and Miami boomed during the heyday of the Tri-State Mining District.

COURTESY *THE DAILY OKLAHOMAN.*

Right: *A map showing the mineral resources located throughout Oklahoma.*

Bottom: *By the onset of the Roaring Twenties the early primitive forms of lead and zinc mining around Miami had been replaced by large corporate operations, such as this facility. Oklahoma's zinc production reached its height in 1920, with an output valued at $35,595,774. Lead production peaked in 1925, when Oklahoma's mines produced more than $13 million worth of the lead ore.*

COURTESY *THE DAILY OKLAHOMAN.*

in 1904. The Cache Gold Mining District in the Quanah Range of Comanche County reported mines producing $36 worth of gold per ton of ore. The remains of John Pearson's smelter can still be seen on the slope of Mount Sherman northeast of Cache. The Cooperton Gold Mining District was opened around the town of Cooperton, and the Mountain Park Gold Mining District was developed northwest of Mountain Park at Poverty Gulch. The Roosevelt Gold Mining District was one of the most thoroughly exploited regions of Kiowa County, and the Snyder Gold Mining District claimed the deepest mine in the Wichitas, the 220-feet deep Meek, Anderson, and Laughlin Mine. Just south of Nest Egg Mountain, the Wildman Gold Mining District was developed.

Although more than 2,500 shafts were sunk in the Wichitas, by 1904 the boom was over. Most miners abandoned the region, leaving their mines and equipment to decay. The remains of the massive Gold Bell Mining and Milling Company can still be seen nine miles west of Snyder. However, as late as 1917 prospectors were dredging placer gold from the creeks feeding the North Fork of the Red River and Deep Red Creek in Kiowa and Tillman Counties.

The Gypsum Hills of western Oklahoma provided raw material for plaster mills in the region. Several mills were located at Eldorado, Rush Springs, Watonga, Okeene, Bickford, Southard, Darrow, and Alva, and were producing $2,600,081 worth of gypsum annually by 1926. The huge natural gas production of the state resulted in several brick plants, and the plentiful supply of glass sand and natural gas made Tulsa a major glass producing center. The Great Salt Plains of northwestern

✧

Left: The rugged Wichita Mountains of southwestern Oklahoma long had attracted gold seekers. As early as 1657 Spanish miners penetrated the region searching for gold. The ruins of their arrastras still can be found along the banks of Medicine Creek near Meers; however, hostile Indians ended these early mining efforts.

COURTESY DAVID FITZGERALD.

Below: The Main Street of Healdton during the heyday of the Healdton oil boom. The twenty-fourth largest oil discovery of the first half of the twentieth century, Healdton produced 211 million barrels of crude between its discovery in 1913 and 1950.

COURTESY OKLAHOMA HERITAGE ASSOCIATION.

Oklahoma offered a plentiful supply of salt, as did the numerous salt water springs found in the state. One salt mine was operated by Texaco on its refinery in West Tulsa, where water was pumped into an underground salt dome. Brought to the surface, the brine was processed and the salt refined and marketed.

Oklahoma is one of the richest energy-producing regions in North America and is the location of several of the greatest oil discoveries ever made. It is the center of the huge Mid-Continent Oil and Gas Region stretching from Kansas, through Oklahoma, to Texas, and including parts of Arkansas and Louisiana. The region's oil deposits were well-known to Native Americans. New Spring Place, an oil spring near Oaks, was used by Indians for medicinal purposes. Western Carter and southern Stephens

✧

Above: The Rock Asphalt Paving Works of the Downard Asphalt Company in Ardmore. Southern Oklahoma, particularly Carter County, was the location of many asphalt seeps. Many of these seeps were mined and the asphalt taken to Ardmore, where it was used to make paving material or asphalt-based paint.

COURTESY OKLAHOMA GEOLOGICAL SURVEY COLLECTION, WESTERN HISTORY COLLECTIONS, UNIVERSITY OF OKLAHOMA LIBRARIES.

Below: The business district of Dropright in the Cushing-Drumright Field. Discovered by Tom Slick in 1912, the field was the tenth largest discovery in America prior to 1950 and produced an astounding 382,000,000 barrels of oil during the first half of the twentieth century. Thousands of people rushed to the Cushing-Drumright strike, giving rise to such towns as Dropright, Alright, Gasright, Damnright, Justright, and Drumright. Only Drumright survived.

COURTESY UNIVERSITY OF TULSA, MCFARLIN LIBRARY.

Counties also were well known for their natural oil seeps. The first oil well in the state was completed in 1859 by Lewis Ross while searching for saltwater at the Grand Saline in Mayes County. In 1887, Edward Byrd drilled eleven wells along Oil Branch Creek in Rogers County. However, drilling on Indian land was hindered by federal regulations, and it was not until 1897 that the state's first commercially successful oil well, the Nellie Johnstone No. 1, was completed by Michael Cudahay near Bartlesville.

Others quickly followed: the Red Fork Field across the Arkansas River from Tulsa in 1901 and the Cherokee Shallow Sand District in 1904. Red Fork was the first commercial field developed in Indian Territory and for a while the town of Red Fork rivaled Tulsa. The Cleveland Field, opened in 1904, was the first important field in Oklahoma Territory. One of its major developers was the Minnehoma Oil Company, owned by George F. Getty and his son, J. Paul Getty, who later became known as the "richest man in the world."

The discovery that launched the Oklahoma oil boom was made in 1905 on the Robert and Ida Glenn farm south of Tulsa. Attracted by nearby natural oil seeps, Robert Galbreath leased the farm for three cents per acre and completed the discovery well, the Ida Glenn No. 1, in October of 1905. The strike was so prolific that The Texas Company and Gulf Oil Company tied the region into their pipeline system, thereby giving Oklahoma oilmen their first major marketing outlet. In 1909, the

D. W. Franchot Company opened the first successful gas processing plant just east of Kiefer in the Glenn Pool Field. The Hogshooter Gas Field, opened in 1907 in Washington County, was the first dry gas field in the state.

With oil discoveries, Tulsa mushroomed overnight from a small Creek village called Tulsey Town into a major energy center known internationally as the "Oil Capital of the World." It was a mecca for such oilmen as Henry F. Sinclair, J. Paul Getty, William K. Skelly, Waite Phillips, and W. F. "Billy" Roesser. Roesser's income was as high as $3,000 daily until he went broke wildcatting. Starting over, he built a second fortune only to go broke again. In all, he made and lost $50 million. At one time, Tulsa contained six major refineries and was host to the International Petroleum Exposition and Congress, the largest gathering of oilmen in the world. It also is the home of *The Oil and Gas Journal*, considered to be the Bible of the energy industry.

North of Tulsa was the oil-rich Osage Reservation. Pioneer oilman Henry Foster, the founder of Cities Service Oil Company, once held the lease on the entire 2,286-square mile reservation. When the Osage lease was broken up, individual leases were offered for sale beneath the "million dollar elm" on the grounds of the Osage Agency in Pawhuska. Competition was so great that the Midland Oil Company once bid $1.9 million for a single 160-acre lease in the Burbank Field. It was in the Osage that the Phillips brothers, Frank and L. E., launched Phillips Petroleum Company, one of the world's largest energy concerns.

The Osage retained mineral rights to their reservation at the time of allotment and between 1901 and 1950 $300 million was divided between 2,229 Osage headrights. Known as the "richest Indians in the world," many of the Osages were cheated out of their headright payments. In the worst abuse, William K. Hale masterminded the Osage reign of terror in the 1920s, during which several rich Osages were murdered so that Hale could gain control of their headrights.

Production expanded to north-central Oklahoma when E. W. Marland completed the Willie Cries for War No. 1 in the Ponca City Oil Field. Marland went on to found Marland Oil Company, the forerunner of Conoco; was governor of Oklahoma; and was a major force behind the organization of the Interstate Oil Compact Commission. His mansion in Ponca City is a classic example of the extravagant wealth produced by the state's oil boom.

In 1912, Tom Slick uncovered the rich Cushing-Drumright Field, the tenth largest

✧

Below: A night scene in the Little River Field of Seminole County. The Seminole Oil Region covers almost 1,300 square miles in Seminole, Pottawatomie, Hughes, Okfuskee, and Pontotoc Counties and contains almost forty individual fields including five of the nation's giant oil discoveries—Earlsboro, St. Louis, Seminole City, Bowlegs, and Little River. The region first was opened to production in 1923 and within four years was America's premiere producer of high gravity crude.

COURTESY CITIES SERVICE OIL COMPANY.

✧

Top: A copper mine near Prague in Lincoln County in 1934. A. E. "Dynamite Ed" Perry, Walter Jarrett, and Fred Simpson worked the mine, which was owned by Leo Gravitt and Al Jeffers.

COURTESY *THE DAILY OKLAHOMAN.*

Middle: The interior of Woolaroc in the Osage Hills west of Bartlesville. It was the country estate of oilman Frank Phillips, who along with his brother, L.E. Phillips, founded Oklahoma-based Phillips Petroleum Company. Woolaroc in located on the famous Lot 185 where the Phillips brothers drilled their first successful oil well in the Osage and laid the foundation for Phillips Petroleum.

COURTESY DAVID FITZGERALD.

Below: Two gushers blowing wild in the Oklahoma City Field. Opened in 1928, the Oklahoma City Field was the last major find of Oklahoma's first oil boom. The pool was characterized by abundant, highly-pressurized concentrations of natural gas, which produced a multitude of "wild wells." The most famous of these was the Wild Mary Sudik, which threw crude so high into the air that it fell like rain in Edmond, twenty miles to the north, and Norman, an equal distance to the south.

COURTESY PHILLIPS PETROLEUM COMPANY.

oil field developed in America prior to 1950. Between 1912 and 1919, Cushing-Drumright produced three percent of all the oil produced in the world. Many of the Indians and freedmen who had received allotments in the region suddenly found themselves rich. Jackson Barnett's allotment produced $24 million worth of oil and Sarah Rector, the descendant of a slave, received $300,000 for hers.

The Healdton Field was developed at the same time as Cushing-Drumright. Although oilmen had been attracted by the region's numerous natural oil seeps as early as the 1880s, it was not until 1913 that the discovery well was drilled. Oil was found at such a shallow depth that it became known as the "poor man's field," because of the lower expense of drilling.

The Garber Field, located in 1917, and the Three Sands, or Tonkawa Field, discovered in 1921, continued to expand oil production in north-central Oklahoma. Oilmen at Three Sands found production at fourteen different oil-bearing zones. So great was its flow that twenty-six pipelines were built into the field.

The development of the Greater Seminole Field started in 1923 with the opening of the Wewoka Field. Before the close of the decade, five of the nation's largest pools were located in Seminole County—Earlsboro, Seminole City, Bowlegs, Searight, and Little River. Eventually, more than fifty pools were discovered in the field, and approximately $1,009,996,749 worth of oil was produced between 1926 and 1929.

The last great discovery of the early-day boom was the Oklahoma City Field, opened in 1928. It was at Oklahoma City that a young geologist named Dean A. McGee solved the riddle of its geology and proved the worth of geologists to oil companies. Production in the field was tremendous. One well, the McBeth No. 1, initially flowed 101,002 barrels of oil daily. The most famous well in the field was the Wild Mary Sudik, which blew wild from March 26 until April 4, 1926, throwing 20,000 barrels and 200 million cubic feet of gas daily into the air. So great was the flow of oil that two separate governors declared martial law in the Oklahoma City Field to control overproduction, drilling zoning, and drilling on the capitol grounds.

Oklahoma's first oil boom ended with the Great Depression, when the price of crude plunged. Ironically, the downfall of the economy was eased somewhat by continued drilling operations and construction projects financed by oil revenues.

World War II stimulated the search for crude, and in 1943 the first of the post-Depression fields, the West Edmond, was located. In 1949, there were more wells drilled in Oklahoma than in any other previous year. The West Short Junction Field was located in the early 1950s and the Sooner Trend in Logan, Kingfisher, and Garfield Counties in 1965. By 1975, Oklahoma had five oil fields ranked among the top 100 in the United States—Sho-Vel-Tum, the Sooner Trend, Golden Trend, Healdton, and the Postle Field in the Panhandle.

The Arab Oil Embargo of the 1970s, the deregulation of deep natural gas production, and the deregulation of oil prices generated another boom period. As the price of a barrel of oil passed $40, thousands of workers flocked to Oklahoma. Moreover, the price of deep natural gas escalated, and the Deep Anadarko Basin in western Oklahoma boomed. Unfortunately, the boom was short-lived. It collapsed in 1982 as the price of oil and natural gas plunged. However, along with agriculture, the energy industry remains one of the most important aspects of the state's economy. Oil and gas prices rose again in the early 1990s, only to fall dramatically again late in the decade, thereby continuing the industry's seemingly perpetual cycle of boom and bust.

Top: The palatial home of Oklahoma oilman and Governor E. W. Marland in Ponca City. Marland, the founder of Marland Oil Company, which became the basis of Conoco, opened north-central Oklahoma to production in 1911 when he completed the Willie Cries for War No. 1 on Ponca Indian land in Kay County. According to legend the lease was considered "sacred land" by Poncas, who at first refused to allow Marland to drill on the location; however, with the intervention of Joe, Zack, and George Miller, Ponca Chief White Eagle changed his mind. According to the legend, Marland was cursed for drilling on the sacred land, and later he lost his fortune.

COURTESY OKLAHOMA DEPARTMENT OF TOURISM AND RECREATION; PHOTOGRAPH BY FRED MARVEL.

Left: The Anne Howard No. 1 drilling rig, designed to push a drill bit below 20,000 feet, operating west of Elk City in Beckham County. Such depths were needed to tap the prolific Deep Anadarko Basin of western Oklahoma. This advancement in technology and deregulation of deep natural gas in the 1970s touched off the second Oklahoma oil boom. Elk City, Anadarko, Weatherford, and Clinton replaced the earlier boomtowns. Western Oklahoma's economy boomed until the energy bust of the early 1980s.

COURTESY DAVID FITZGERALD.

Oklahoma's oil boom era marked the true passing of the Wild West. Coming as it did at the end of the nineteenth and beginning of the twentieth centuries, it attracted many of the same characters as did the early gold, silver, and cattle booms. Outlaws, gamblers, and bootleggers flocked to the early oil boom towns, only to be tamed when more respectable citizens demanded law and order. It also produced an unbelievable amount of wealth. So great was the rush for black gold that the value of the oil produced by early-day Oklahoma oilmen was greater than the combined value of all the other mineral rushes to the American West. This huge influx of money helped launch Oklahoma into the modern era.

CHAPTER XII

THE TURBULENT DECADES

On November 16, 1907, Oklahoma's first governor, Charles N. Haskell, after being sworn in by Leslie Niblack and overseeing a statehood parade, hosted a barbecue dinner at Guthrie's Island Park. The jubilant mood was continued at the inaugural ball that night. At midnight, Oklahoma became a "dry" state, with liquor outlawed except for medicinal purposes. Most whiskey that remained unsold was shipped out of state. Some beer was poured into gutters as the saloons closed.

The new state inherited the debts of Oklahoma Territory and the territorial capital at Guthrie. Almost immediately, individuals began advocating moving the seat of government in spite of the fact that the Enabling Act required that it remain in Guthrie until 1913. Some proposed the creation of New Jerusalem in the geographic center as the new capital. Guthrie leaders, hoping to keep the capital, leased the Logan County Courthouse to state officials and made plans to build a new Convention Hall as a home for the state legislature. However, faced with the anti-Democratic editorials of the *Guthrie State Capital*, Democratic leaders were determined to move the capital.

Numerous communities made proposals—El Reno pledged 500 acres; Enid offered three sites; Granite proposed a forty-acre site in the nearby mountains; and Skiatook promised 500 acres and $80,000. To settle the issue, the Ledbetter Bill allowed any town that could present a petition with 5,000 signatures to be considered as the new location of the capital. Only Oklahoma City, Guthrie, and Shawnee met the requirement and were on the June 11, 1910 special election ballot. Oklahoma City won with 96,262 votes to Guthrie's 31,301 and Shawnee's 8,382.

Governor Haskell was in Tulsa when he learned the election results. Telegraphing his secretary, W. B. Anderson, to take the State Seal to Oklahoma City, Haskell chartered a train and hurried to meet his secretary. Arriving in time for breakfast on June 12, 1910, Haskell checked into the Lee-Huckins Hotel and personally lettered a sign saying "Governor's Office" for his room. "Under the law Oklahoma City is the state capital," he declared.

As most state officials rented office space in the new state capital, Guthrie leaders tried to block the move, and Judge John Burford prepared a suit challenging the election. Because of the uncertainty, the state supreme court remained in Guthrie, and other state officials signed documents in both cities. On November 14, 1910, the state supreme court ruled the special election void. Haskell then called the legislature into special session and the Durant Bill, declaring Oklahoma City the state capital, was passed. This too was challenged by Guthrie leaders; however, in a three to two verdict on February 11, 1911, the state supreme court upheld the action. This decision was sustained by the United States Supreme Court.

When Lee Cruce became governor in 1911, he brought with him a "righteous crusade." Personally, he was opposed to capital punishment and was a firm believer in "blue laws," which closed most businesses on Sundays. Failing in a bid to have the legislature abolish capital punishment, he commuted the sentences of twenty condemned men to life in prison. Fifteen others were lynched by mobs before the governor could act.

Cruce also enforced unpopular laws against horse racing, liquor, prizefights, and gambling. In March of 1914, he told the Panhandle and Southwestern Stockmen's Association, which planned a performance by a Chicago stripper named "Queenie," accompanied by a large supply of beer, that if it carried through on its convention plans he would use martial law to prevent its meeting in Tulsa. Likewise, when Tulsa promoters scheduled a horse race for April of 1914, Cruce ordered Adjutant General Frank M. Canton to stop the event. In spite of a state supreme court injunction against him taking any action to hinder the race, Canton sent two companies of national guardsmen to the Tulsa race track. When promoters ignored his declaration that the races were over, he had them fire two volleys over the heads of the horses at the starting line. Telling the startled crowd that the next volley would be to kill, the races quickly were canceled. Cruce also used the National Guard to prevent a Sunday roping contest in McAlester.

An unidentified black victim of the Tulsa Race Riot of 1921. No formal account of the number of people killed in the riot was ever established; however, estimates of as many as 300 blacks killed probably are accurate.

COURTESY ROYCE PETERSON.

Right: Sergeant John Hogan, Company C, 358th Infantry, from Shawnee in Pottawatomie County served in the Texas-Oklahoma Division or the Ninetieth Division in World War I. Note the T-O Division patch on his left shoulder. Most Oklahomans were assigned to the 179th Infantry Brigade within the division, with men from western Oklahoma serving in the 357th Infantry Regiment and men from eastern Oklahoma in the 378th Infantry Regiment.

COURTESY *THE DAILY OKLAHOMAN*.

Oklahoma's World War I governor was Robert L. Williams, who took office in 1915. During his administration the First Oklahoma Infantry was sent first to the Mexican Border and was combined with the Texas National Guard to form the Thirty-sixth Infantry Division, which served in France. Other guardsmen joined the Ninetieth, or T-O Division. To replace the First Oklahoma Infantry, state officials formed the Home Guard, which was the basis of the Second Oklahoma Infantry, the Third Oklahoma Infantry, and the First Separate Infantry Battalion. These state troops were used to quell labor disturbances in the state's coal fields.

To organize the state's war effort, Councils of Defenses were established. In addition, chapters of the Knights of Liberty and the American Protective League were formed to encourage citizens to purchase Liberty Bonds. Their anti-German rhetoric led to at least one riot in which a mob burned several businesses owned by German-speaking citizens in Muskogee. Instances of tarring and feathering of innocent citizens in the name of patriotism were common. Mennonites were especially singled out both because of their pacifism and German heritage. Several predominately Mennonite settlements changed their names to sound more patriotic. For example, Korn anglicized its name to Corn and Kiel became Loyal.

Not all Oklahomans supported the war effort. The Working Class Union, an offshoot of the International Workers of the World, or I.W.W., was the most vocal group opposed to United States participation in the war and was the organizer of several anti-draft riots. The group also was behind the Green Corn Rebellion, led by John Speer, in Seminole and Ponotoc Counties. Eventually three men were killed and eighty-six sentenced to prison for the anti-war effort.

In October of 1918, the state was swept by the Spanish Flu epidemic. More than 125,000 cases were reported before the disease ran its course. Nearly 7,000 Oklahomans died. To stop the epidemic, churches, schools, and movies were closed, and meetings of more than twelve people were banned.

The Oklahoma State Capitol was completed in 1917, during Williams' term. Original plans called for a dome, but the shortage of steel and other material created by the war caused architects to delay the construction of the dome. Although plans to add a dome have continued, the capitol remains domeless.

Below: Downtown Lexington in Cleveland County. Located on the banks of the Canadian River, Lexington was plagued by springtime floods; however, local businessmen refused to move to higher ground because the river was the boundary between wet Oklahoma Territory and dry Indian Territory to the south. Lexington was one of the region's most infamous liquor towns, with a host of saloons and liquor dealerships catering to Indians. Early saloons in Lexington included the Buckhorn Saloon, Two Brothers Saloon, Dutch Saloon, Commerce Saloon, J. H. Berry's Saloon, Fashion Saloon, French Saloon, and Thomas Farmer's Saloon; three years after its founding, however, Lexington still had no bank. With statehood, Oklahoma Territory also went dry, and at midnight on November 16, 1907, all saloons and wholesale liquor distributors, such as the one in the left of this photograph, were closed.

COURTESY CLEVELAND COUNTY HISTORICAL SOCIETY COLLECTION, WESTERN HISTORY COLLECTIONS, UNIVERSITY OF OKLAHOMA LIBRARIES.

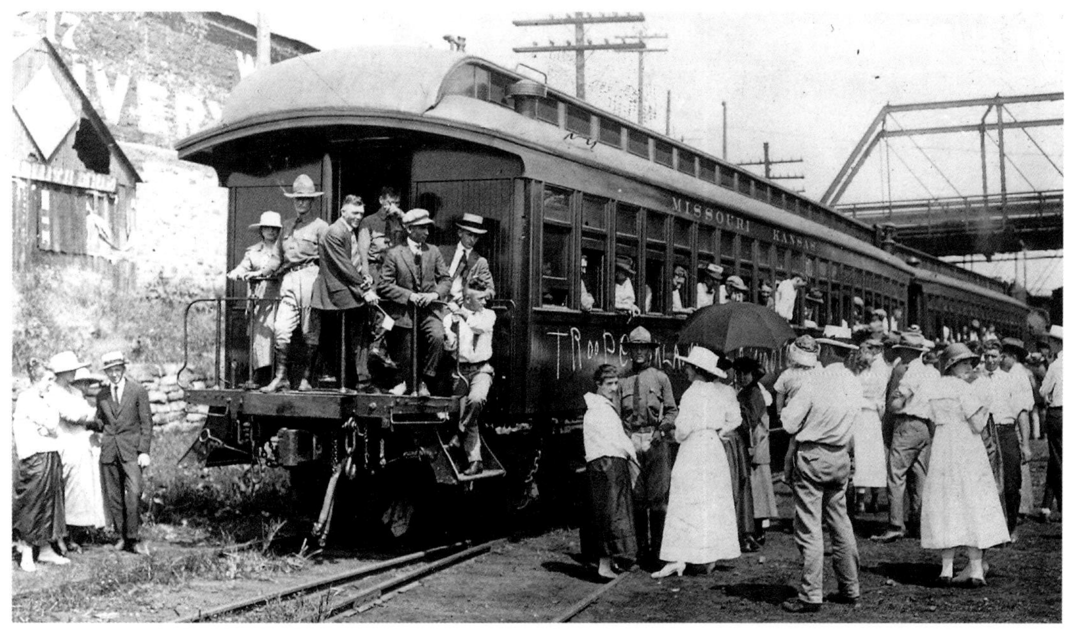

Left: *Oklahoma National Guardsmen of the 111th Ammunition Train boarding the Missouri, Kansas & Texas Railroad train in McAlester on their way to Fort Bowie, Texas, for service in World War I. The Oklahoma guardsmen and the Texas National Guard were combined to form the Thirty-sixth Infantry Division, which had more Native Americans among its troops than any other unit in the American Expeditionary Force.*

COURTESY *THE DAILY OKLAHOMAN*.

Labor troubles continued to plague Oklahoma in the post-war period. Governor J. B. A. Robertson used the National Guard to disperse I.W.W. telephone strikers at Drumright and striking coal miners in southeastern Oklahoma. The National Guard also was used to enforce Oklahoma's claim to the entire Red River during a dispute over oil well drilling rights. Texas claimed it had jurisdiction over the southern half of the river and oilmen claimed that the entire river was under federal regulation. In a series of cases in 1921, 1922, and 1923 federal courts supported Oklahoma's claim of ownership of the entire river bed.

National guardsmen were used to end the Tulsa Race Riot of 1921. The Tulsa incident was but one of several race riots nationwide during this period. Activity of the Ku Klux Klan was approaching its height, and Tulsa was sharply segregated. Most blacks were concentrated in the northern part of the community, known as "Little Africa," while whites lived south of the St. Louis and San Francisco Railroad tracks.

The riot was touched off when a nineteen-year old black delivery man, named Dick Rowland, entered an elevator in the Drexel Building in downtown Tulsa on May 30, 1921. Operating the elevator was seventeen-year old Sarah Page. Somehow, as Rowland got on the elevator, he apparently stepped on Page's foot. After that the stories differ. One account says that Rowland touched Page's arm as he apologized for stepping on her foot. Another says that Page slapped Rowland when he stepped on her foot, and then he grabbed her by the throat. Both accounts have her screaming. The screams were heard by a clerk in a nearby store who ran to see what was happening. Police were called but did nothing at first.

However, the version published in the Tulsa newspaper reported that Rowland, who the reporter called "Diamond Dick," attacked Page, tearing at her clothes and scratching her face. Eventually the story was distorted into the rape of a white woman by a black man, and talk of lynching began to spread. On May 31, Tulsa police took Rowland into protective custody and locked him in the county jail on

Below: A black nurse stares at the burned-out buildings of north Tulsa. A black hospital was one of the many buildings destroyed by the mob that invaded the Greenwood District at approximately 5:00 a.m. on June 1, 1921, after two days of building tension. Although the rioting was contained and brought under control by midnight, property losses to the black community were estimated at between $1.5 million and $4 million.

COURTESY ROYCE PETERSON.

✧

Top: A KKK public naturalization ceremony held by the Oklahoma Klan Number 1 of the Ku Klux Klan on the shore of Belle Isle Lake on July 10, 1923. The illuminated cross, American flag, KKK, and the word America were used to underline the Klan's policy of patriotism as applied to "America for Americans."

COURTESY *THE DAILY OKLAHOMAN.*

Middle: An open-air initiation ceremony of the Ku Klux Klan at Nowata on October 5, 1922. The new initiates are kneeling and taking their oath before an electrically illuminated cross while hooded and robed Klan members observe. Three "Ks" lighted by electric light bulbs illuminate the scene.

COURTESY BARTLESVILLE PUBLIC LIBRARY.

Below: A lone black man, in the center, stands among a group of whites as people began to gather in downtown Tulsa following the Tulsa Tribune's *editorial on the "assault" by Dick Rowland on Sarah Page, an elevator operator in the Drexel Building. The alleged attack took place on May 30, 1921, but police found no evidence of a crime. It was not until the following day, May 31, 1921, that Rowland was arrested after a store clerk had come forth the previous afternoon to report an attempted rape. On the afternoon of May 31, the* Tulsa Tribune's *editorial greatly agitated an already tense situation when it reportedly urged the lynching of Rowland.*

COURTESY ROYCE PETERSON.

the top floor of the Tulsa County Courthouse. Sheriff W. M. McCullough stationed six guards in the jail and disconnected the elevator to the top floor, leaving the only access to the jail through a stairway blocked by steel bars.

By 7:00 p.m. on May 31, a group of between 300 and 400 whites had gathered around the courthouse. When blacks learned of this, about thirty of them started for the court-house to protect Rowland. However, they were stopped

Left: After the appearance of the Tulsa Tribune's editorial, armed blacks hurried to the courthouse to protect Dick Rowland. Firing broke out between blacks and whites. As the blacks were forced back toward the Greenwood District, they managed to hold a line against the white mob along the Missouri, Kansas & Texas Railroad tracks. However, some whites managed to crawl across the tracks and set fire to the buildings in which the blacks had taken cover. Once black opposition had been overcome, the white mob surged through Greenwood, looting and burning more than 1,000 homes and businesses.

COURTESY ROYCE PETERSON.

by Sheriff McCullough and persuaded to return home. By late that evening the courthouse mob had grown to almost 2,000 whites. Two cars filled with blacks began circling the white mob as another group of armed blacks started marching once again on the courthouse. Other blacks began to gather in the streets of Little Africa.

The riot broke out about 10:00 p.m. when the two mobs clashed. A white man tried to disarm one of the blacks, a shot was fired, and the whites dispersed as they rushed to arm themselves. Pawn shops and sporting goods stores were looted for weapons, and one group of whites tried to storm the local National Guard armory, but were driven off by the guardsmen before they could seize any weapons. Gunfire became general as the whites rushed to put down the black "uprising." Police stationed along the St. Louis and San Francisco Railroad tracks tried to keep the two mobs separated, but were unsuccessful.

By midnight the white mob, by now outnumbering the blacks by two to one, pushed through the police line and invaded Little Africa. While 250 disarmed blacks were being held in the city jail and courtroom, few whites were arrested. In fact, 500 armed whites were given special police commissions. Another 1,500 blacks took shelter in the Tulsa Convention Hall for protection. Unable to control the situation, Tulsa officials appealed to Governor Robertson for help at 1:46 a.m. on April 1. Robertson dispatched Adjutant General Charles F. Barrett and National Guard units from Bartlesville, Muskogee, Oklahoma City, Vinita, and Wagoner to Tulsa by special train. They were commanded by Lieutenant Colonel L. J. F. Rooney.

Rooney posted the first guardsmen to arrive to protect banks, water works, electric plants, and downtown businesses. As more

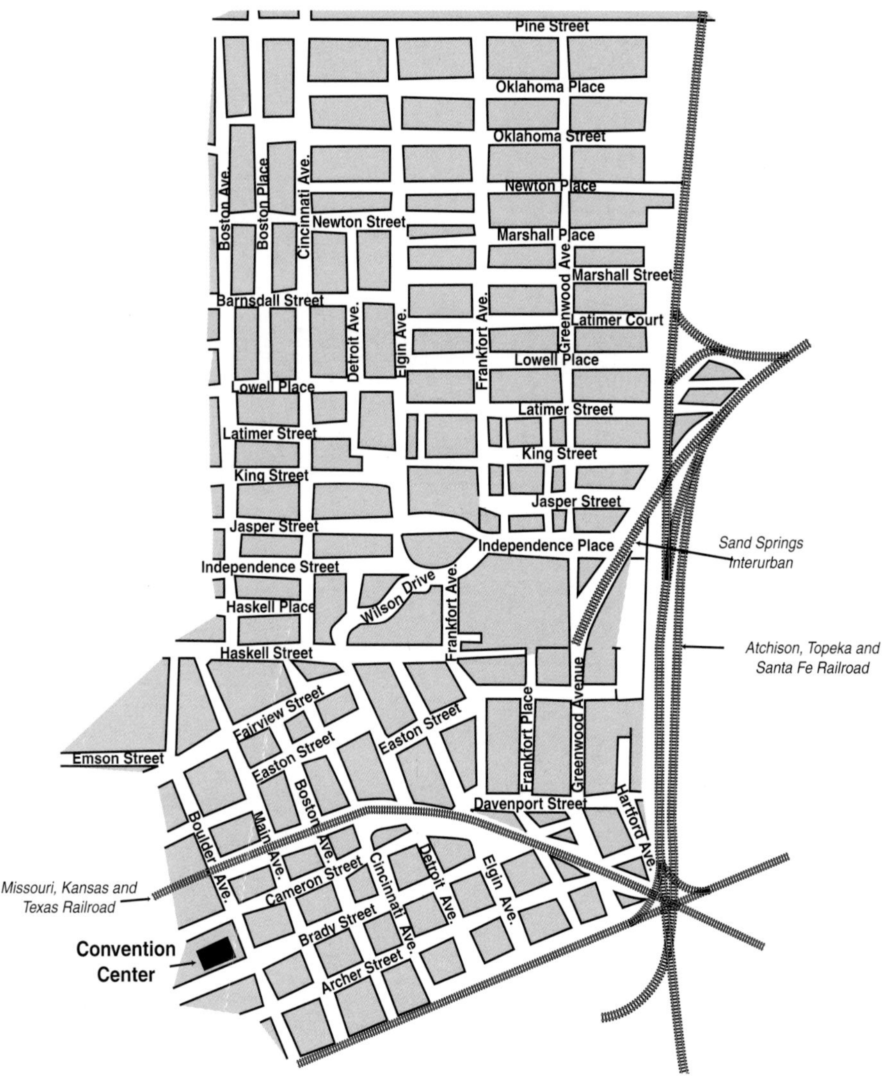

Below: The area of Tulsa in which the race riot of 1921 took place.

Right: Governor Jack C. Walton being sworn into office on January 8, 1923, by John Johnson, the Acting Chief Justice of the Oklahoma Supreme Court. After using his power of martial law to attempt to curb Klan violence and stifle political opposition, Walton was impeached by the State House of Representatives on October 23, 1923, convicted by the State Senate, and removed from office on November 9, 1923.
COURTESY THE DAILY OKLAHOMAN.

Middle: On November 1, 1924, the famous lawman Bill Tilghman was shot on the main street of Cromwell by Wiley Lynn, a federal prohibition agent. Tilghman was seventy years old when he was talked out of retirement to tame "Wicked Cromwell," one of the most infamous of Oklahoma's oil boomtowns.
COURTESY THE DAILY OKLAHOMAN.

Below: Oklahoma Governor Henry S. Johnston, seated third from the left at the center table, and his attorneys and advisors, during Johnston's impeachment trial in the Oklahoma State Senate in 1929. During the regular session of the legislature in January of 1929, thirteen charges of impeachment were presented to the State Senate by the House of Representatives. The senators acted on eleven of the charges, acquitted Johnston of ten, but convicted him of the eleventh, which was general incompetency.
COURTESY THE DAILY OKLAHOMAN.

troops arrived, they paraded through Tulsa to city hall. When Barrett appeared on the scene, he asked for martial law to be expanded to all of Tulsa County. Robertson complied.

As the guardsmen appeared on the streets, the rioting subsided; however, by then most of Little Africa was in flames. The majority of black residents fled, seeking refuge in the countryside. It was not until national guardsmen accompanied Tulsa firefighters into Little Africa that the flames were extinguished. Thirty-five city blocks in a two-mile long strip containing an estimated 1,000 residences were destroyed by fire. What was not burned was looted by white rioters. Property loss was reported at between $1.5 million and $4 million. An accurate death toll was never compiled, but the Red Cross reported almost 1,000 injured.

Most out-of-town guardsmen were sent home on June 3. That same day, martial law ended. Tulsa guardsmen remained on duty until June 4. Later, Sarah Page dropped the assault charge against Rowland.

Martial law played a major role in the impeachment of Robertson's successor Jack C. Walton. Walton had been the popular mayor of Oklahoma City who had won the governorship in 1922 with the support of the Oklahoma Farm Labor Reconstruction League, a radical socialist organization. Once in office, Walton filled many positions, including the presidency of Oklahoma A and M College, with his socialist supporters.

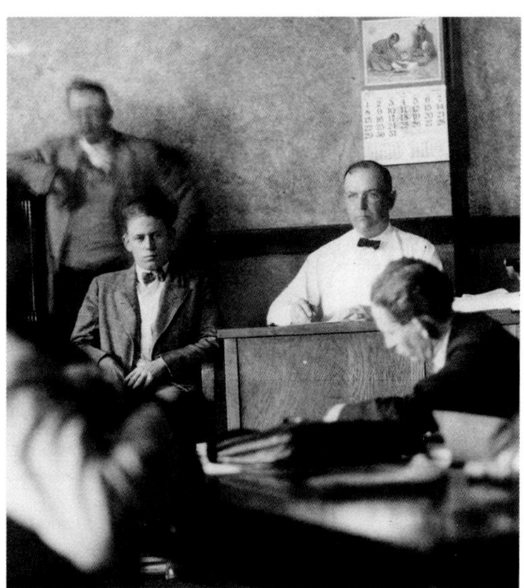

Top, left: A dance hall in Bishop's Alley in Seminole during the oil boom era of the 1920s. Bishop's Alley was separated from the more respectable portions of the community by a wide white line that Seminole Police Chief Jake Simms painted across Main Street. Bootleggers, prostitutes, gamblers, and other undesirables kept to the north side of the line, and "proper" residents remained south of the line. In the "dime-a-dance" dance halls such as the one pictured, the girls often danced with boots on because the floor was covered with mud tracked in by their customers.

COURTESY *THE DAILY OKLAHOMAN.*

Top, right: Matthew Kimes, on the left, and his accomplice Ray Doolin. Matthew and his brother George formed the Kimes Gang, which terrorized banks throughout the state in the 1920s. In August of 1926, the Kimes brothers robbed two banks in Covington in Grant County and headed for their hideout in Arkansas. They were cornered by lawmen near Sallisaw, where they killed Sequoyah County Deputy Sheriff Perry Chuculate and captured Sallisaw Police Chief J. C. Woll for a short period of time. Both Kimes brothers later were captured. George was sent to the prison in McAlester, but Matt was still in the Sequoyah County Jail when he escaped in November of 1926. He later was recaptured in Arizona and returned to prison in Oklahoma.

COURTESY *THE DAILY OKLAHOMAN.*

Middle: George Kimes on the witness stand in the murder trial of Luther Bishop in Oklahoma City in May of 1927. Luther Bishop was an Oklahoma State Crime Bureau agent who had been instrumental in the arrest of several Oklahoma outlaws in the 1920s. In 1926, he was brutally shot to death in the middle of the night at his Oklahoma City home.

COURTESY *THE DAILY OKLAHOMAN.*

Among the most vocal opponents of the Farm Labor Reconstruction League were members of the Ku Klux Klan. Often, the Klan's viewpoint was reinforced with whippings, and, when KKK activity in Okmulgee County reached new heights in June and July of 1923, Walton placed the county under martial law. When KKK activity spread, Walton placed portions of Tulsa County under martial law on August 13, 1923. He also suspended the writ of habeas corpus in Tulsa County. As opposition to Walton's socialist supporters and martial law proclamations increased, the governor placed the entire state under martial law on September 15, 1923, and Oklahoma County under "absolute martial law." National guardsmen also prevented an Oklahoma County grand jury from convening to investigate Walton's actions.

Such abuses prompted members of the Oklahoma House of Representatives to convene at the call of their leadership to look into the matter. When the lawmakers appeared at the capitol, they were prevented from meeting by national guardsmen, while Walton argued that the state legislature could not call itself into session. Opponents of the governor countered by circulating Initiative Petition Number 79, which authorized legislative leaders to call the legislature into special session. When the measure was approved by a vote of the people, legislative leaders called for a special session to convene on October 17, 1923. To outmaneuver the legislators, Walton called the legislature into special session on October 11, because, when called into special session by the governor, the legislature constitutionally could consider only those items proposed by the chief executive.

✧

Right: The police department in Wilson in Carter County. Left to right, Tom Griffin, chief; Ed Taylor, night chief; and Charles P. Jones, constable. On a Tuesday night in February of 1924, Taylor was summoned by the report of a disturbance at Park's Pool Hall. When he walked inside he was attacked and severely beaten about the head. Although his skull was fractured, Taylor managed to remain conscious, arrested Pick Couch, and took him to jail before rushing to Kilpatrick's Drug Store for medical aid. When the seriousness of his injury was discovered, he was rushed to the local hospital. Nonetheless, city officials expected him to be back at work the next Saturday night.

COURTESY MAC MCGALLIARD COLLECTION, ARDMORE PUBLIC LIBRARY.

Below: Jail at Ardmore used during the Carter County oil boom. Notice the primitive urinal underneath the stairs and the armed guard on top of the stone wall surrounding the jail yard.

COURTESY MAC MCGALLIARD COLLECTION, ARDMORE PUBLIC LIBRARY.

As called by the governor, the legislature convened on October 11, adjourned, and reconvened on October 17 under the provisions of Initiative Petition Number 79. Five days later, on October 23, 1923, the first two of an eventual twenty-two articles of impeachment were filed with the state senate. Among the charges were illegal collection of campaign funds, excessive and illegal expenditures in the primary election, padding the public payroll, the employment of his private chauffeur on the staff of the State Health Department, illegal issuance of deficiency warrants to employ unauthorized personnel, the prevention of a meeting of an Oklahoma County grand jury by the National Guard, the suspension of the writ of habeas corpus, the excessive use of the pardon power, and general incompetency. Walton was suspended from office, and Lieutenant Governor Martin E. Trapp became acting governor. On November 19, 1923, eleven of the twenty-two charges were sustained by the senate, and Walton was removed from office.

Trapp completed the more than three years remaining on Walton's term. The most important legislation during this period was an anti-mask law, which was used to curtail Ku Klux Klan activity, and the creation of a three-man highway commission, which administered the construction of roads in the state. The Ku Klux Klan opposition to Trapp and his anti-Klan activity led to an effort to impeach the governor and oust legislators opposed to the Klan. The effort failed.

Trapp wanted to run for reelection, but the state constitution prevented a governor from succeeding himself. Trapp argued that he was not "governor" but "acting governor" and therefore could run again. The Oklahoma County District Court upheld Trapp's argument, but the Oklahoma Supreme Court overturned the decision. Trapp was succeeded by Henry S. Johnston.

Almost as soon as he took office, Johnston persuaded the legislature to increase the highway commission from three members to five and packed it with his supporters. The new commissioners quickly found themselves at odds with powerful members of the legislature over road construction projects. Johnston also found himself embroiled in a controversy involving his personal secretary, Mrs. O. O. Hammonds. When Mrs. Hammonds banished some legislators from the governor's office, there were rumors of an improper relationship between the governor and his secretary.

Soon afterward, a group of legislators—led by Tom Knight, E. P. Hill, Tom Johnson, and Robert L. Graham—called for the legislature to convene on its own to investigate the highway department. However, Johnston persuaded the Oklahoma Supreme Court to declare Initiative Petition Number 79 void and used national guardsmen to block the gathering at the capitol. Unperturbed in what was called the "Ewe Lamb Rebellion," the solons convened at the Lee-Huckins Hotel in downtown Oklahoma City. Led by Hill, impeachment charges were prepared against Johnston in December of 1927; however, the state senate refused to consider the charges and adjourned.

When the next regular session of the legislature convened in January of 1929, anti-Johnston leaders forced the resignation of the pro-Johnston speaker of the house, Allen Street, within six hours and replaced him with James C. Nance. With the support of sixty members of the house of representatives who supported impeachment, the house voted thirteen charges against Johnston on January 21, 1929. Suspended from office, Johnston was tried by the senate and convicted on one of the thirteen charges—incompetency. On March 20, 1929, Johnston was removed from office and replaced by William J. Holloway. Afterward, an attempt was made to impeach two members of the Oklahoma Supreme Court, but the effort failed.

✧

Left: An oil field fire sweeping through the oil storage tanks surrounding Drumright during the Cushing-Drumright oil boom. Not only did the storage tanks often burn after being ignited by lightning, but also they provided a convenient site to dispose of unwanted bodies. One storage tank, behind the community's infamous Mad House Saloon, yielded seven bodies when it was drained.

COURTESY BARTLESVILLE PUBLIC LIBRARY.

Below: Carter County Sheriff Buck Garrett, seated, and his Chief Deputy Bud Ballew were two of Oklahoma's best known boom town lawmen in the early 1920s. When patrolling, Garrett would walk down one side of the street and Ballew the other, then when faced with trouble one of the lawmen would confront the offender while the other stood by, ready to shoot if necessary.

COURTESY MAC MCGALLIARD COLLECTION, ARDMORE PUBLIC LIBRARY.

CHAPTER XIII

Dust Bowl & Depression

Aside from adopting the run-off primary for elections, the most important event during the administration of Johnston's successor, William J. Holloway, was the onset of the Great Depression. Oklahoma was struck by the twin economic disasters of an extended drought and an international depression. The state's agricultural economy still was dominated by tenant farming, in which the landowner would divide the year's crops with a tenant who lived on the farm and did the work. As late as 1935, approximately sixty percent of the state's farmland was farmed by tenants. Thus, rural areas of the state were especially hard hit when crop prices plunged following the October 1929 stock market crash.

Cotton fell from twenty-eight cents per pound in 1923 to five cents per pound in 1931, and corn dropped from $1.39 per bushel in 1919 to 23 cents per bushel in 1932. Wheat sold for $1.46 per bushel in 1925 and thirty-two cents per bushel in 1932; oats brought forty-six cents per bushel in 1929 and fourteen cents per bushel in 1932. Likewise, the price of cattle dropped from $45.00 a head in 1929 to $11.10 in 1932, and hogs from $14.10 per head in 1928 to $2.75 per head in 1934. So great was the economic slump that by December of 1932, twenty-seven percent of Oklahomans were on relief.

At the same time, between 1932 and 1939, the state endured one of the driest periods in history. Record high temperatures were recorded. In July of 1936, the temperature reached 120 degrees in Alva, Altus, and Tishomingo. Much of the state's farmland had been cultivated during the push to feed the allies during World War I, and most of the natural cover had been destroyed. As the weather turned dry and hot, and the winds began to blow, a process known as saltation took place. Small particles of soil were dislodged by the wind and thrown into the air. When they fell to the ground, the particles dislodged other pieces until dust storms blotted out the sun.

As the west wind began to blow in the spring of 1934, huge dust storms built in the Texas Panhandle and eastern Colorado and raged across Oklahoma in what became known as the "dirty thirties." Looking out their windows, people saw nothing but a solid black wall of blown dust. Dinner guests were given wet towels to hold over their faces to keep out the dust while they ate. Native grasses disappeared, orchards were covered with dirt, and farmers walked over fences on piles of dust. It was not unusual for people to become lost during the dust storms and to be forced to wait out their passage beside the road. One of the worst storms blew across the entire United States to deposit its windblown soil in the Atlantic Ocean.

The value of farmland fell to as low as $5 per acre in some parts of the state. Many people in Oklahoma and surrounding states fled the region and headed west along US-66. So many residents left the Oklahoma Panhandle that enrollment at Panhandle Agriculture and Mechanical College at Goodwell dropped to ninety-two students. People continued to flee eastern Oklahoma as the Great Depression, dust, and desperation drove tenant farmers from their land. Along with residents of surrounding states, they were collectively known as "Okies," and they joined others who sought work in California, the "land of milk and honey." But California was suffering from the Great Depression, and the new arrivals were treated with scorn. Their plight was dramatically recorded in John Steinbeck's book *The Grapes of Wrath*. Okemah native Woody Guthrie told of the plight of those suffering from the economic downturn in his depression-era songs such as *Bound for Glory* and *This Land is Your Land*.

As a result of the Dust Bowl, Oklahoma took the lead in land conservation. Oklahoma's legislature enacted the nation's first soil conservation district law in 1937. In 1935, a shelterbelt project was implemented to plant trees in the western part of Oklahoma to abate much of the damage caused by wind erosion. Eventually, a strip was planted from Woodward County south through Tillman County. The Washita River in western Oklahoma was America's first river system to be developed with watershed flood control lakes, and the nation's first upstream flood control dam

Alexandre Hogue's Crucified Land. *In this 1939 painting, he graphically illustrated the plight of farmers during the Great Depression and Dust Bowl. Poor farming techniques, such as plowing up and down hillsides and improper corn and cotton dry-land practices, resulted in some portions of the state losing as much as seventy-five percent of the topsoil. Lincoln County often was referred to as the most eroded county in America.*

COURTESY GILCREASE MUSEUM.

Top, left: A dust storm approaching Hooker in the Oklahoma Panhandle on June 4, 1937. Although only a relatively small part of Oklahoma actually was in the Dust Bowl—those westernmost counties bordering the 100th Meridian and the Panhandle—many of the state's farmers were driven from their tenant farms by the increased mechanization of farm work. Tenant farming, which had been the backbone of Oklahoma's corn and cotton agriculture, collapsed when modern farm machinery made it possible for one farmer to do the work of several. This development, coupled with depressed agricultural prices, caused many landowners to evict tenant farmers.

COURTESY CORN HISTORICAL COLLECTION, WESTERN HISTORY COLLECTIONS, UNIVERSITY OF OKLAHOMA LIBRARIES.

Top, right: The Wild Mary Sudik in the Oklahoma City Oil Field. Oklahoma City was spared the worst of the Great Depression with the opening of the Oklahoma City Field in the late 1920s. The tremendous production of the field and the building boom that it spurred in Oklahoma City provided employment for thousands. The Wild Mary was completed near daybreak on March 26, 1930, just south of I-240, one mile west of its junction with OK-77. An Indian Territory Illuminating Oil Company well, the Wild Mary threw oil so high into the air that it fell to the ground twenty miles away. It was not until April 4, 1930, that workers were able to bring the runaway well under control.

COURTESY CITIES SERVICE OIL COMPANY

Right: Downtown Oklahoma City on March 16, 1935, when a massive dust storm swept in from the west.

COURTESY *THE DAILY OKLAHOMAN.*

was completed on Cloud Creek, north of Mountain View in Kiowa County, in 1948. In the mid-1950s, the Sand Stone Creek system near Cheyenne in Roger Mills County was the first fully completed watershed flood control system in the nation.

At the height of the Great Depression, William H. "Alfalfa Bill" Murray was elected governor. When he assumed office in January of 1931, the state was on the verge of bankruptcy, and many banks would not honor state warrants. Murray immediately cut expenditures and increased taxes to balance the budget. He also pushed the legislature to create the Oklahoma Tax Commission to collect state revenue. Some legislators grumbled about his tactics, but nothing was done. When challenged, Murray often resorted to martial law to enforce his orders.

During his administration, Oklahoma became the first state to appropriate money, $300,000, for relief. In the fall of 1931, Murray sent unemployed workers into rural areas to help with the harvest. They were paid by a share of the crops. He also ordered the release of out-of-work men when they were jailed for vagrancy. In 1932, money from the Reconstruction Finance Corporation began to reach Oklahoma, and Murray used part of it for free school books for the children of relief

✧

Left: Jack Riley of Boise City in the Panhandle's Cimarron County looking at what once was a flourishing orchard in April of 1935. The dust blowing across the region has almost reached the top of the 16-foot tall apple trees in the orchard.

COURTESY *THE DAILY OKLAHOMAN.*

Below: LaQuinta, the Spanish style home of H. V. Foster in Bartlesville. A pioneer oilman, Foster played a prominent role in the development of the Osage Nation, Greater Seminole, and Oklahoma City Fields. Built on fifty-two acres during the 1930s, the $500,000 mansion contained thirty-two large rooms and fourteen bathrooms. During its construction, Foster insisted that only married men, with families to support, be employed in the work so that their wages could be used to offset the effects of the Great Depression.

COURTESY DAVID FITZGERALD.

recipients, to build farm to market roads, and to finance "make-work" projects such as dams and lakes.

By the time E. W. Marland became governor in January of 1935, the efforts to combat the Great Depression under Franklin D. Roosevelt's New Deal were well under way, with numerous Civilian Conservation Corps and Works Progress Administration projects in progress. However, state-funded relief projects were chronically underfunded by the legislature. In an effort to provide relief, Marland ordered the distribution of National Guard rations to the hungry in Pittsburg County. In March of 1935, the legislature finally appropriated $600,000 to ease the plight of the poor, and by the end of Marland's administration, $2.5 million had been allocated for relief.

Neither Roosevelt's nor Marland's actions ended the effects of the Great Depression and Dust Bowl. Nature ended the Dust Bowl when the rains returned in the spring of 1939. This, coupled with new markets created by the rearmament of the world prior to the outbreak of World War II, brought the

Oklahoma's legendary aviator, Wiley Post, and his most famous airplane, the Winnie Mae. *Because of his record-setting distance and altitude flights, Post was one of the most recognized figures of the 1930s. Post, shown here with a patch over his left eye, lost sight in the eye during an oil field accident. Although he had a glass eye, Post seldom wore it during flights. As he explained, the glass eye usually became cold at higher altitudes and therefore gave him a headache, so he simply stopped wearing it. This portrait by Mike Wimmer was commissioned by the Wiley Post Centennial Committee in 1998 to celebrate the centennial of Post's birth. The portrait is permanently displayed on the fourth floor of the State Capitol.*

COURTESY OKLAHOMA DEPARTMENT OF TOURISM AND RECREATION; PHOTOGRAPH BY FRED MARVEL.

✧

Will Rogers, Oklahoma's most famous writer, philosopher, actor, and newspaperman of the 1920s and 1930s. Rogers was an early aviation enthusiast. He and Wiley Post were killed in an airplane crash near Point Barrow, Alaska in 1935. This portrait is one of four works by Charles Banks Wilson in the rotunda of the fourth floor of the State Capitol.

COURTESY OKLAHOMA DEPARTMENT OF TOURISM AND RECREATION; PHOTOGRAPH BY FRED MARVEL.

✧

Wiley Post, on the left, and Billy Parker, two of America's best known aviators during the 1930s standing beside a Lockheed Orion aircraft. Oklahoma-based Phillips Petroleum Company became heavily involved in the development of aviation fuel during the 1930s, which it marketed under the trademark Phillips 77. Parker was the head of aviation for Phillips Petroleum, and in 1934 he convinced Post to become a Phillips Petroleum pilot. Financed by Phillips Petroleum, Post flew the Winnie Mae *to new heights. On December 3, 1934, he took off from Bartlesville and is credited with discovering the Jet Stream at 50,000 feet in a pressure suit that he had designed. Caught in the high winds, Post was blown eighty miles to the southwest and landed at Hat Box Field in Muskogee.*

COURTESY PHILLIPS PETROLEUM COMPANY.

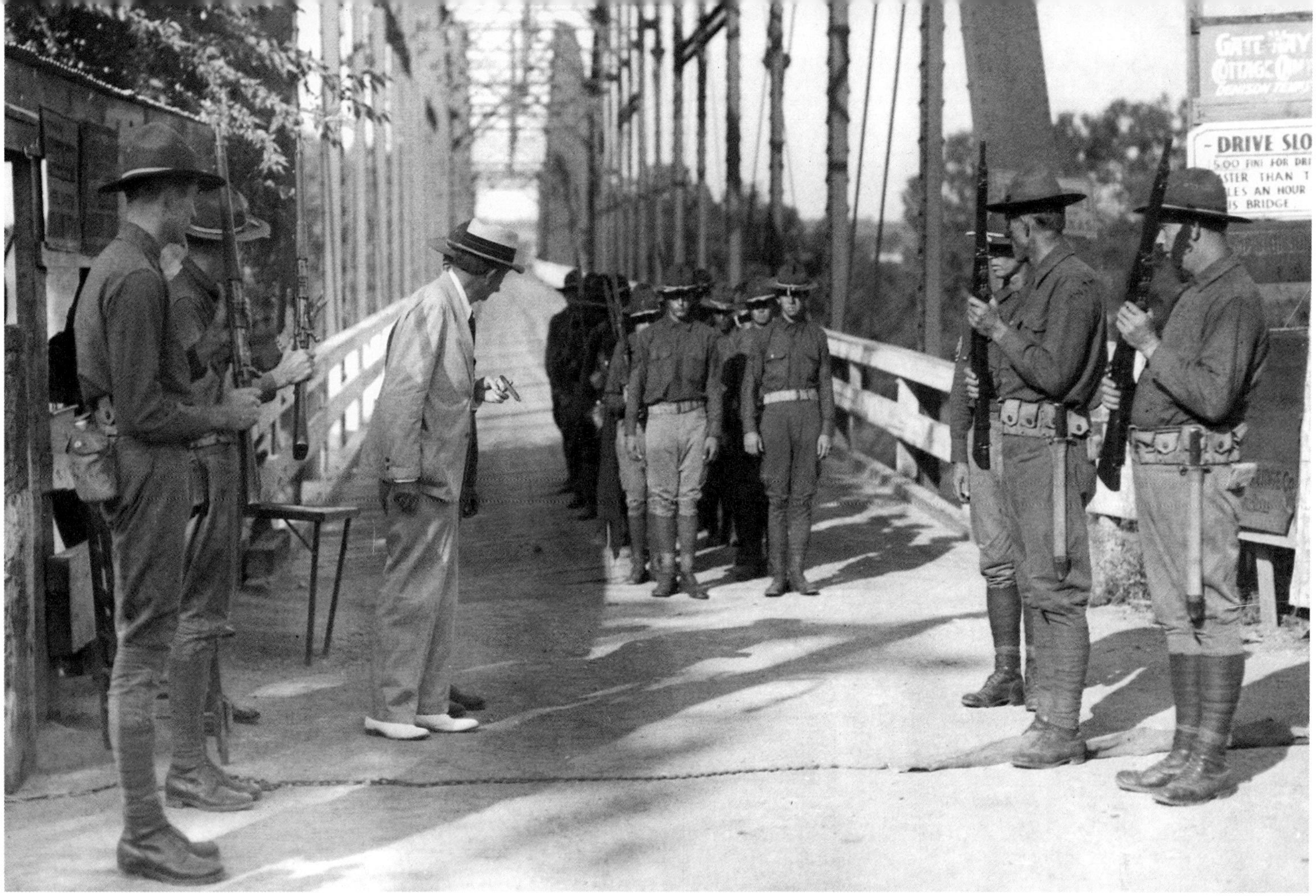

Top: Oklahoma Governor William H. "Alfalfa Bill" Murray observing a changing of the guard ceremony at the Red River bridge between Durant, Oklahoma, and Dennison, Texas, in 1931. Prior to the construction of free bridges across the river by the State of Oklahoma, the only means of crossing the river was by toll bridge. Just as the free bridges were about to open, the owners of the toll bridges went to federal court and obtained an order preventing the opening of the free bridges. Outraged by what he thought was an intrusion of federal officials into a state matter, Murray ignored the order, called out the Oklahoma National Guard, declared martial law over the bridges, and used the guardsmen to close down the toll bridges. Note the chain in the foreground that was used to block access to the bridge. When the Governor of Texas intervened on the side of the toll bridge owners, Murray declared martial law over the southern approaches to the bridges and sent Oklahoma guardsmen into Texas to open the approaches to the free bridges.

COURTESY *THE DAILY OKLAHOMAN.*

Above: The Civilian Conservation Corps (CCC) camp at Yukon in the spring of 1941. Organized along military lines and employing young men between the ages of eighteen and twenty-five, the CCC completed hundreds of public works projects in Oklahoma in addition to providing jobs for youthful workers. Most of the workers, who were provided food and shelter, were paid approximately $25 per month. Of this they were allowed to retain $5 spending money. The remainder was sent home to their families to ease financial hardships. The building on the far left is the camp's library.

COURTESY *THE DAILY OKLAHOMAN.*

✧

Above: Established in 1933, Weber's Root Beer stand on South Peoria Avenue in Tulsa has been one of the city's culinary landmarks for more than six decades.

COURTESY OKLAHOMA HERITAGE ASSOCIATION; PHOTOGRAPH BY JUDY DAWSON.

Below, left: Clyde Barrow of the infamous Bonnie and Clyde gang. Barrow is holding two rifles he used during his robberies. Leaning against the front of the automobile is a sawed-off, 12-gauge, pump shotgun. One of the most famous outlaw-lawmen shootouts of the 1930s took place at Stringtown on August 13, 1932 between Barrow and Ray Hamilton and Atoka County Sheriff Charles G. Maxwell and Deputy Sheriff Gene Moore. When the shooting was over Moore was dead and Maxwell badly wounded. Although Barrow escaped through Antlers to Texas, he later was killed by lawmen in northern Louisiana. Hamilton eventually was captured and executed at the Texas State Prison in Huntsville.

COURTESY *THE DAILY OKLAHOMAN.*

Far right: Charles "Pretty Boy" Floyd, center, was perhaps the most notorious Oklahoma outlaw of the 1930s. Floyd, whose family was from eastern Oklahoma, was viewed by many as the "Robin Hood of the Dirty Thirties." Bank foreclosures had made many rural residents resentful of banks during the Great Depression and Floyd's bank robberies often were perceived as a fit reward for bankers. However, to state lawmen, Floyd was a dangerous criminal. In January of 1932, Floyd and his gang robbed two banks in a single day—one in Paden and the other in Castle. In April of that year he killed lawman Erv Kelley near Bixby. Floyd finally was shot and killed in Ohio in 1934.

COURTESY *THE DAILY OKLAHOMAN.*

return of prosperity to Oklahoma farmers. With the outbreak of fighting, the state's economy rebounded with the huge demand for petroleum products, food to feed the expanding military, and the conversion of the state's economy to a wartime footing.

Leon C. Phillips assumed the chief executive's post just as America began to rearm, and, although he considered his main accomplishment a balanced budget amendment, his time primarily was spent on the war effort. Oklahoma's National Guard division, the Forty-fifth Infantry, or Thunderbird Division, including the 125th Observation Squadron, the forerunner of the state's Air National Guard, had been created by the National Defense Act of 1920 and participated in the famous Louisiana Maneuvers of 1940. Just as the exercise ended, the division was mobilized for federal service for a year in September of 1940.

Plagued by a shortage of modern equipment, the guardsmen gathered at Camp Barkley, Texas; however, as their one year active duty term neared an end, the War Department extended their service for the duration of the national emergency. At the same time, the division was modernized as it was reduced from four to three regiments. Guardsmen who were spun off fought in the Pacific as the 158th Regimental Combat Team, the 176th Engineers, and the 145th Quartermaster Company, where they participated in defense of Alaska, the invasion of Okinawa, and the construction of the Burma Road. The remainder of the Forty-fifth Division completed its training at Fort Devens, Massachusetts; Pine Camp, New York; and Camp Patrick Henry, Virginia, before participating in the battle for Sicily, the landing at Anzio, the Italian Campaign, the invasion of Southern France, and the battle for Germany.

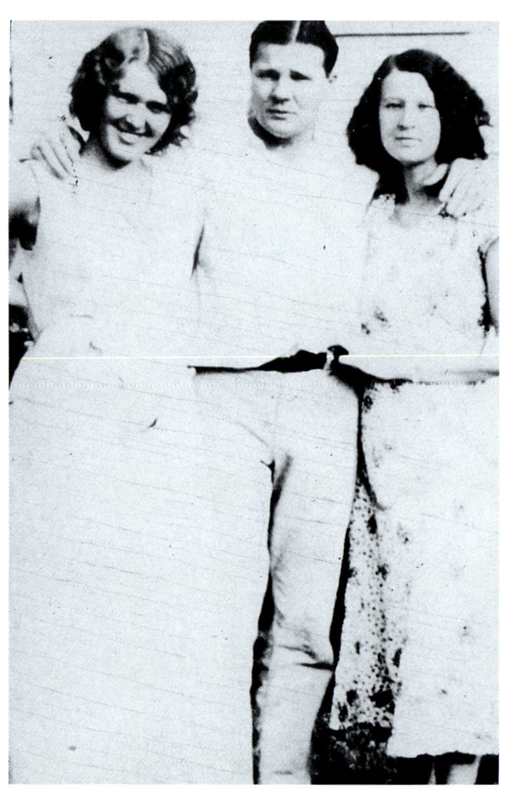

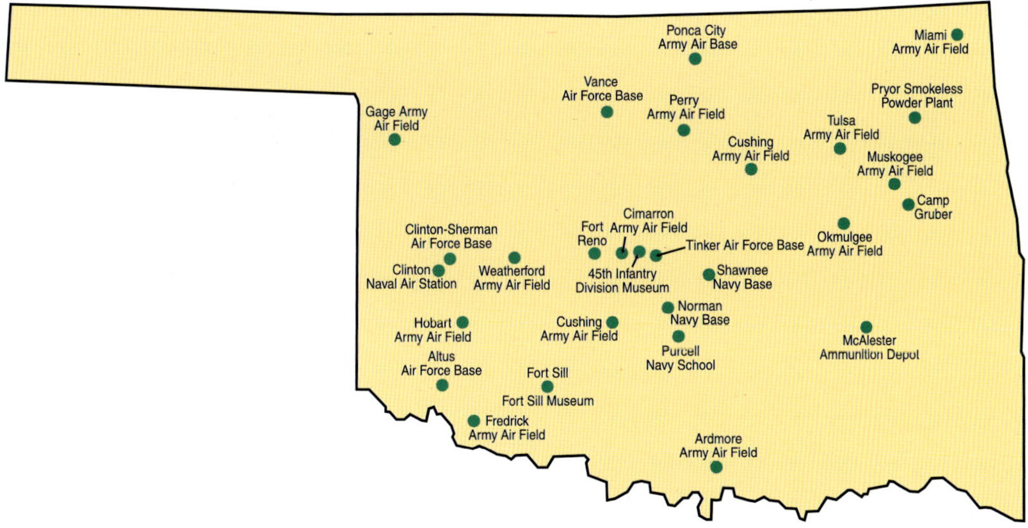

Nearly 200,000 men and women from Oklahoma served in the military during World War II. Tens of thousands of others worked in the many defense plants constructed in the state. The Douglas Aircraft Company's plant at Tinker Field built thousands of cargo aircraft during the war and became the base for the Oklahoma City Air Material Area. Army Air Corps training bases were opened at Will Rogers Field in Oklahoma City and Cimarron Field near Yukon, and a glider training center was maintained at Okmulgee. Other flight training centers were opened at Enid, Frederick, Altus, and Ardmore, and additional Army Air Corps training facilities were operated at Chickasha, Cushing, Gage, Hobart, Muskogee, Perry, Tulsa, and Weatherford. The Royal Air Force and the Royal Canadian Air Force trained pilots at Ponca City and Miami, and many Polish pilots were trained at Enid.

Navy training bases were opened on the University of Oklahoma campus. A naval flight school also was located on North Base in Norman and a major Navy medical facility was built there as well. Purcell was the site of a Navy gunnery school, and naval air stations were built at Clinton and Shawnee. McAlester was the site of a huge Navy ammunition depot. A womens' naval training facility was opened at Oklahoma A and M College in Stillwater.

Major Army training centers were opened at Fort Sill, Fort Reno, and Camp Gruber. Oklahoma also was the location for numerous prisoner of war camps. More than 40,000 German and Italian prisoners were held in

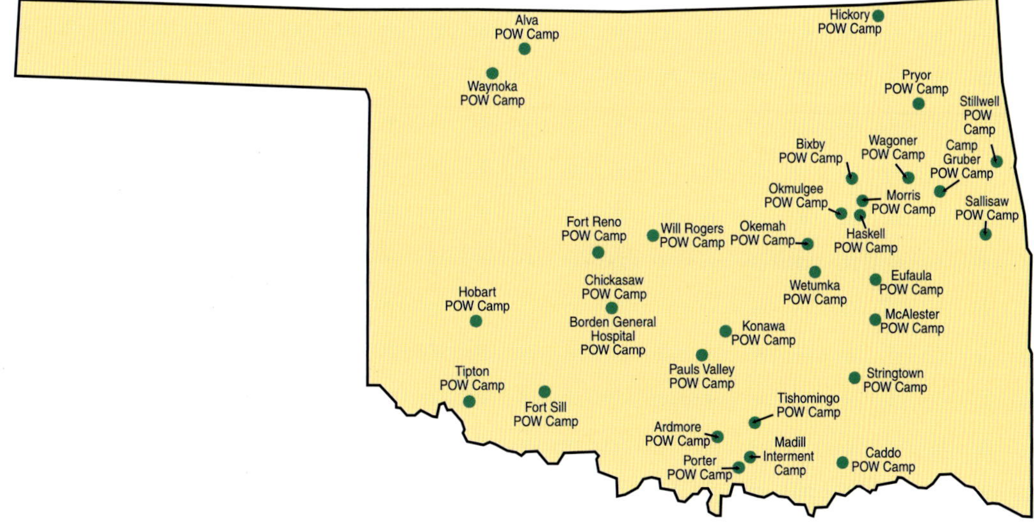

✧

Top: A map detailing the locations of military installations within Oklahoma.

Bottom: A map showing the location of the thirty prisoner interment camps set up in Oklahoma during World War II.

◇

Above: Customers of the First National Bank of Oklahoma City exchanging their Cash Relief Trust script for United States currency in March of 1933 after the end of the national bank holiday declared by President Roosevelt. When the president closed the banks to reorganize the nation's finances, many Oklahoma City businesses could not meet payrolls from cash they had on hand. To overcome the problem, the First National Bank of Oklahoma City issued special script, which could be used as money until the banks were reopened.

COURTESY *THE DAILY OKLAHOMAN.*

Right: A member of the Oklahoma National Guard on duty in front of the State Capitol in April of 1936. When Oklahoma City officials attempted to control drilling on the grounds of the State Capitol, Governor E. W. Marland, an oilman, declared martial law and ordered the guardsmen to prevent interference. Note the emblem on the right shoulder of the guardsmen. It is a Native American symbol for good fortune and was the one worn by the Oklahoma National Guard at the time of the outbreak of World War II. Unfortunately, it resembled the swastika of Nazi Germany, and to avoid confusion when the Oklahoma guardsmen were ordered overseas it was changed to the familiar Thunderbird of the Forty-fifth Infantry Division.

COURTESY *THE DAILY OKLAHOMAN.*

nineteen prisoner of war camps in the state. Interment camps for German and Italian nationals were opened at McAlester and Stringtown. Hardened Nazi prisoners were held at Alva and at Tonkawa. One German prisoner, Johannes Kunze, was tried and executed for treason by a group of German prisoners. Afterward, five of the Nazi leaders were hanged for the murder of Kunze.

Prisoners willing to work were paid eighty cents per day and often were used by local farmers to replace labor absorbed by the

war effort. Civilians were charged about $1.50 per day for prisoners. Eighty escape attempts were made, but none were successful.

Robert S. Kerr, who was elected governor in 1942 and took office in 1943, saw the state through the last of the war years and into the post-war era. Kerr was the first native-born Oklahoman to be chosen chief executive. A co-founder, with Dean A. McGee, of Kerr-McGee Oil Company, Kerr went on to become one of the nation's most powerful United States senators. His administration marked the transition of the state from a primarily rural population and agricultural economy to a modern state with urban centers and a diversified economic basis.

Left: Brigadier General Raymond McClain, seated in the jeep with no helmet, the commanding general of the Ninetieth Infantry Division, and Captain R. J. Kunkel, his aide, in the Fallaise pocket of France during World War II. McClain, who joined the Oklahoma National Guard in 1912, saw service in World War I and then returned to Oklahoma to help organize the Forty-fifth Infantry Division in 1923. Called to active duty with the Oklahoma National Guard in World War II, McClain eventually rose to the rank of Lieutenant General and was appointed the first Comptroller of the United States Army in 1949.

COURTESY OKLAHOMA HERITAGE ASSOCIATION.

Middle: The tremendous production of the Oklahoma City and East Texas fields drove the price of oil below $1.00 a barrel. In response, Governor William H. Murray issued an ultimatum on July 28, 1939, that the big oil companies raise the price to a minimum of $1.00 per barrel or he would take action. When nothing happened by August 4, Murray declared martial law within a fifty-foot radius of every oil well in the state and shut the wells down until the price rose to the minimum level. The troops stayed in the field until October when the price reached eighty-five cents a barrel and Murray relented. However, the end of martial law was only temporary, for in June of 1932 the guardsmen again were ordered to close the wells. It was not until the passage of a comprehensive Oil Code by the State Legislature that the troops were withdrawn in April of 1932. This is the headquarters of Colonel Cicero Murray who oversaw the closing of the Oklahoma City wells.

COURTESY *THE DAILY OKLAHOMAN.*

Bottom: World War II prisoner of war camp for Germans at Fort Reno in Canadian County. There were thirty-four main camps and numerous work camps housing approximately 40,000 German and Italian prisoners in the state during World War II.

COURTESY *THE DAILY OKLAHOMAN*

ARROWS TO ATOMS · 1957
50TH
ANNIVERSARY
AHOMA
EHOOD
NITED S
POSTAGE

CHAPTER XIV

ARROWS TO ATOMS

The rural to urban population shift that started during the war, when thousands of Oklahomans flocked to the war industries located in Oklahoma City, Tulsa, and other metropolitan areas, continued in the post-war era. Likewise, the state's economy continued to diversify as energy and agriculture combined with new manufacturing centers to form a new economic base. Roy J. Turner, who became governor in 1947, faced the rapid expansion of the state's system of higher education, as thousands of Oklahomans returned home from military service and enrolled in college under the GI Bill. The tremendous growth in higher education was matched by the burgeoning "baby boom" generation as it reached the state's primary and secondary schools.

Almost five years after being deactivated in November of 1945, the Forty-fifth Division was reactivated on September 1, 1950, as a result of the Korean Conflict. Mobilized at Fort Polk, Louisiana, the guardsmen sailed for Japan in May of 1951, where they were stationed in and around Hokkaido. In November of 1951, the division began to replace the 1st Infantry Division in Korea.

By this time, the Korean Conflict stalemated into a war of attrition. The Thunderbirds participated in Operation Snatch, skirmishes around Pork Chop Hill, and the Battle for Outpost Eerie, where Second Lieutenant Omar Manley, of Edmond, won the Congressional Medal of Honor. Oklahoma guardsmen began leaving Korea in March of 1952, and by June the division once again was in Oklahoma.

The Oklahoma Air National Guard also was called into federal service during the Korean Conflict; however, it was done so piecemeal. The Oklahoma City-based 137th Fighter Group began to enter active service in the fall of 1950 and served with the Tactical Air Command in France. Tulsa's 125th Fighter Squadron was called to active duty in April of 1951, and its pilots and P-51 fighters were shipped to Korea, where the flyers shifted to jet aircraft.

When Johnston Murray, the son of William H. Murray, was inaugurated governor in 1951, he formed part of the only father-son administrations in state history, and during his son's administration, Alfalfa Bill frequently could be seen wandering the halls of the state capitol. Murray's administration marked the beginning of change in state politics, as his Joint Committee on State Government sought to modernize the state's administration. In addition to placing almost 20,000 state employees under the merit system, Murray oversaw the amending of the state's constitution to allow women to serve on juries.

Raymond Gary, governor from 1955 until 1959, continued the reform effort. He successfully oversaw the integration of the state's public school system and established the Oklahoma Department of Commerce and Industrial Development to aid the effort to balance the state's economy between agriculture, manufacturing, and energy. However, it was his successor, J. Howard Edmondson, who most impacted the reform movement with the repeal of prohibition and expansion of the state's merit system.

To ensure repeal of prohibition, Edmondson ordered the commissioner of public safety, Joseph R. "Cannon Ball Joe" Cannon to dry up the state. Under Cannon's direction, the highway patrol raided private clubs, road houses, and other establishments that violated the state's liquor laws. Once the bootleggers were shut down and Oklahomans no longer were able to get "liquor by the wink," the state voted to repeal prohibition in 1959 by an 80,000 vote margin.

Edmondson also pushed the establishment of a central purchasing system to allow competitive bidding for lower prices for state supplies. The result was the creation of the State Board of Public Affairs to oversee a single purchasing division. Edmondson expanded the State Merit System and established the Oklahoma Personnel Board, which hired state employees on merit. It also limited the political activity of merit system workers.

When United States Senator Robert S. Kerr suddenly died on January 1, 1963, Edmondson resigned the governorship, allowing Lieutenant Governor George Nigh to assume the post. Nigh then appointed

✧

Left to right: Stanley Draper, managing secretary of the Oklahoma City Chamber of Commerce; Oklahoma Governor Raymond Gary; and Oklahoma City Postmaster Fred Shaw posing before a poster of the United States Post Office's stamp commemorating the semicentennial celebration of Oklahoma's statehood in 1959. The theme of the celebration was "Arrows to Atoms" to illustrate the transformation of the state from America's last frontier to a major player in a modern society.

COURTESY *THE DAILY OKLAHOMAN.*

◆

Right: One thing that pushed Oklahoma into the national spotlight in the post-World War II era was the success of the University of Oklahoma's football team under the direction of Charles "Bud" Wilkinson, shown here with quarterback Bobby Boyd, left, and center David Baker. The Oklahoma Sooners won back-to-back national championships in 1955 and 1956, set a record of thirty-one straight wins in 1948-1950, and then broke that record and set a new one with forty-seven consecutive wins from 1953 to 1957.

COURTESY *THE DAILY OKLAHOMAN.*

Below: During the administration of Governor J. Howard Edmondson, Oklahoma voters decided to end more than half a century of prohibition. Edmondson, who supported the measure, ordered his staff to "dry up the state" and put an end to "liquor by the wink" so that voters would have a clear choice-vote repeal of prohibition or have a truly dry state. In the weeks before the election, local lawmen did their best to close down the illegal liquor traffic. Here Tulsa vice-squad detective Bruce Baldwin, who is being held by Tulsa Police Captain Louis Skinner, kicks in the door of a Tulsa-based bootlegging operation. Observing is Oklahoma State Commissioner of Public Safety Joe Cannon, who became known as "Cannon Ball Joe" because of his effort to end bootlegging in the state.

COURTESY *THE DAILY OKLAHOMAN.*

✧

Left: In 1962, Henry Bellmon became the first Republican elected governor of Oklahoma. During his administration, the state legislature was forced to reapportion the state under the "one man, one vote" concept, which shifted political power from rural to urban Oklahoma. Here Bellmon is turning over the reins of state government to Dewey Bartlett, who followed Bellmon as the state's second elected Republican governor. Both went on to serve the state in the United States Senate.

COURTESY *THE DAILY OKLAHOMAN.*

Below: Governor David Hall and his wife leaving the State Capitol. In November of 1970, Hall defeated Dewey Bartlett in his bid for re-election by 2,181 votes, the closest gubernatorial election in state history. Unfortunately, Hall's administration was plagued by controversy. Shortly after leaving office in January of 1975, Hall was indicted by a federal grand jury. Convicted of bribery, he was sentenced to three years in a federal prison.

COURTESY *THE DAILY OKLAHOMAN.*

Top, left: The rocky shoreline of Lake Eufaula covers more than 600 miles and surrounds 102,200 surface acres of water, making it one of the largest man-made lakes in the world. Developed in the post-World War II era, Lake Eufaula has become one of the region's most popular water recreation areas.

COURTESY DAVID FITZGERALD.

Top, right: A portrait of Oklahoma's United States Senator Robert S. Kerr by Charles Banks Wilson. Kerr was the first native of Oklahoma to be elected governor of the state and later was elected to the United States Senate. Kerr was a major supporter of the $1.3 billion Arkansas River Navigation Project, which allows barge traffic as far upstream as the Port of Catoosa, just east of Tulsa.

COURTESY OKLAHOMA DEPARTMENT OF TOURISM AND RECREATION; PHOTOGRAPH BY FRED MARVEL.

Edmondson to complete Kerr's unexpired term. It was the first of four times that Nigh would serve as Governor of Oklahoma. In 1979, Governor David Boren resigned after being elected to the United States Senate so he could enter that body early and thereby acquire seniority. Nigh again assumed the governorship. Nigh became the first governor to succeed himself after the state Constitution was amended to allow two consecutive four-year terms, when he was elected to the office in 1978 and again in 1982.

In the 1962 election, the state Democratic party was split in a bitter primary election pitting former governor Raymond Gary against W. P. "Bill" Atkinson. This allowed Henry Bellmon to become the state's first Republican governor. Once in office, Bellmon continued to push reform.

Primary on his list was legislative reapportionment, which was accomplished after the intervention of federal courts in 1964. The shift of power from rural legislators to urban lawmakers was dramatic, with more than one-third of the solons chosen from metropolitan areas after reapportionment.

Although the Oklahoma Supreme Court bribery scandal was uncovered during Bellmon's term, it was during the term of his successor, Dewey F. Bartlett, the state's second Republican governor, that the judicial system was reformed, with the creation of a judicial nomination commission and a voter retention system. Also, to ease the case load of the supreme court, additional appellate courts were created, and an administrative director for the courts was named.

Oklahoma received a tremendous economic boost during Bartlett's administration with the completion of the McClellan-Kerr Arkansas River Navigation Project. The 445-mile long, $1.3 billion project connected the ports of Catoosa and Muskogee in Oklahoma to the Mississippi River and the world through the Port of New Orleans. Five of the system's seventeen locks and dams are located in Oklahoma.

Bartlett was the first governor in Oklahoma's history constitutionally able to succeed himself; however, in the closest gubernatorial race ever, he lost to David Hall in the November

1970 election. Hall won by only 2,181 votes. Hall's administration was mired in controversy. Two state grand juries, one in Tulsa and the other in Oklahoma City, looked into accusations of wrongdoing, but returned no indictments. In April of 1974, Oklahoma's attorney general, Larry Derryberry, asked the state legislature to impeach Hall, but the solons declined after conducting their own investigation.

Federal officials began investigating charges of bribery and extortion against Hall. In one instance, all public telephones within several blocks of the capitol were tapped by federal officials, and capitol policemen conducted sweeps of the capitol building and governor's mansion searching for listening devices. To keep his conversations secret, Hall met people in the capitol bathrooms and passed written messages on toilet paper. The messages then were burned and flushed down the toilet.

Hall's term expired on January 13, 1975. Three days later, he was indicted by a federal grand jury. Convicted of bribery in March, Hall was sentenced to three years in prison.

David Boren was chosen to succeed Hall after campaigning on a platform of reform. During his term, several state agencies were abolished or combined to streamline government. In addition, the Oklahoma state prison system was modernized. Much of it had been destroyed during a riot at the Oklahoma State Prison in McAlester during Hall's administration.

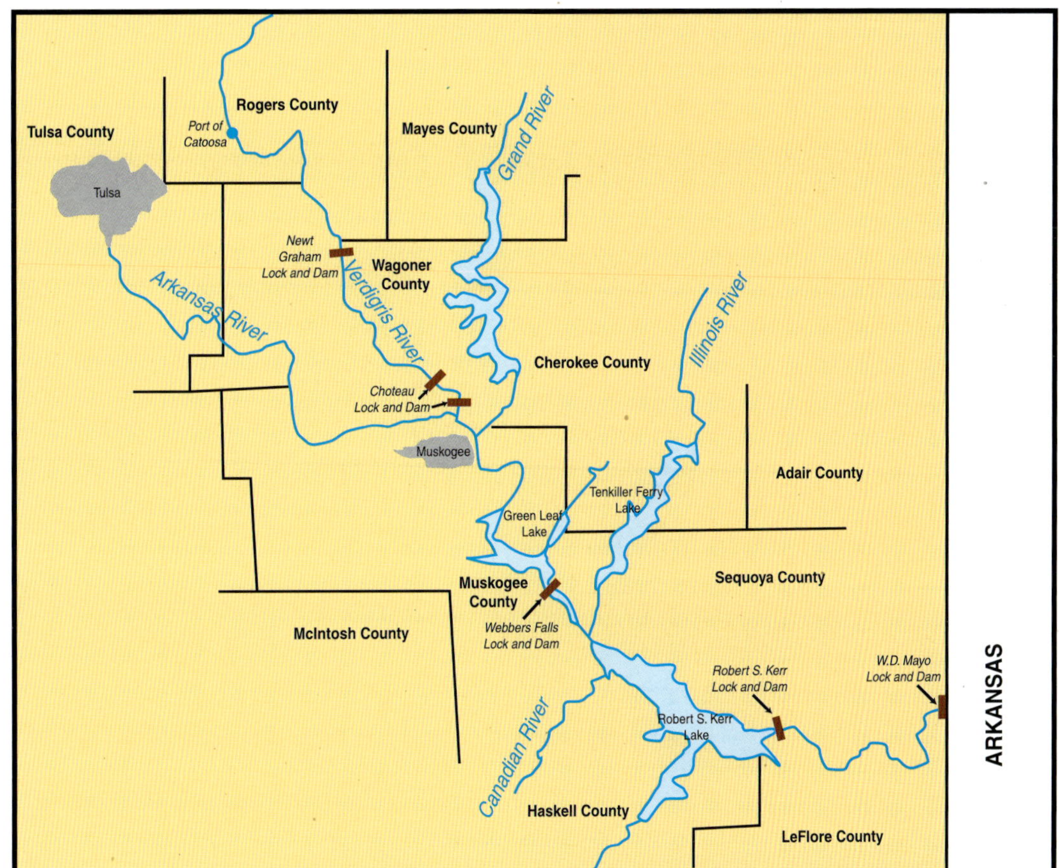

Above: An overlook on Lake Tenkiller State Park near Cookson in southeastern Cherokee County. Oklahoma, which boasts of more miles of shoreline than the East and Gulf coasts combined, began the development of its bountiful water resources in the post-depression era. Lake Tenkiller, which covers 12,500 acres of clear water supplied by the Illinois River, is deep within the Cookson Hills, making it one of the state's favorite vacation spots.

COURTESY DAVID FITZGERALD.

Left: A map showing the extent of the McClellan-Kerr Arkansas River Navigation System in Oklahoma.

Right: *An anti-Vietnam War protest on the campus at the University of Oklahoma in 1970. Although not to the extent as the rest of the country, by the early 1970s the anti-war movement had reached the Sooner State.*

COURTESY *THE DAILY OKLAHOMAN.*

Below: *The oil boom of the late 1970s and early 1980s went bust with the decline of natural gas prices and the collapse of Penn Square Bank in Oklahoma City in July of 1982. When the bank, which had underwritten much of the oil development in western Oklahoma, was closed by federal regulators, the economic chaos quickly spread to the oil fields. Within months the boom was over as oil dropped from near $40 per barrel to around $12 to $15 per barrel and even lower.*

COURTESY *THE DAILY OKLAHOMAN.*

Afterward, Federal District Judge Luther Bohanon ordered a reduction of inmates at the state penitentiary at McAlester and the state reformatory at Granite. Boren and legislative leaders pushed for funding for additional and more modern facilities to satisfy the federal court requirements. As a result, space for an additional 2,070 inmates was built.

George Nigh was elected governor in November of 1978, but assumed the office early, when Boren resigned to take a seat in the United States Senate. Nigh first was

elected lieutenant governor in 1958 and served until 1962. He again was elected lieutenant governor in 1966 and served until Boren's resignation.

Nigh's administration was marked by an era of tremendous economic growth fueled by the Deep Anadarko natural gas boom, as well as prosperity throughout the "oil patch." When he ran for reelection in 1982, Nigh carried every one of the state's seventy-seven counties, the only governor ever to do so, thereby also becoming the first governor to succeed himself.

During Nigh's second administration, Oklahoma was plagued by a county commissioner scandal in which more than 230 people, including commissioners and suppliers, were convicted of taking or giving kickbacks for the purchase of county equipment or supplies. However, no official ever appointed by Nigh was touched by the scandal. Also during Nigh's administration, Oklahomans chose to allow pari-mutuel betting on horse races in 1983 and, the following year, authorized liquor by the drink on a county-option basis.

In 1986, Oklahoma voters returned Henry Bellmon to the governor's office. First elected governor in 1962, Bellmon later served as a longtime United States Senator before returning to Oklahoma to be chosen governor again. It was during his second administration that secondary education in Oklahoma received an important financial boost by the passage of House Bill 1017, which raised taxes to fund educational needs. Challenged by a referendum petition that put the issue to a vote of the people, the measure was upheld. However, as a backlash, anti-tax leaders pushed through a initiative petition that required a seventy-five percent vote by the legislature or a vote of the people to raise taxes in the state in the future.

Left: Federal Judge Luther Bohanon was hung in effigy at the intersection of Grand Boulevard and North Western Avenue on August 1, 1969. Bohanon's ruling in the case of Dr. A. L. Dowell to allow his son, Robert, to attend previously all-white schools in Oklahoma City desegregated the state's largest school system. Most of Oklahoma's public school districts already had been integrated during the administration of Governor Raymond Gary. Bohanon's ruling was not popular, and as a result of white flight Oklahoma City school enrollment fell from 75,000 in 1967 to 36,500 in 1991.

COURTESY *THE DAILY OKLAHOMAN.*

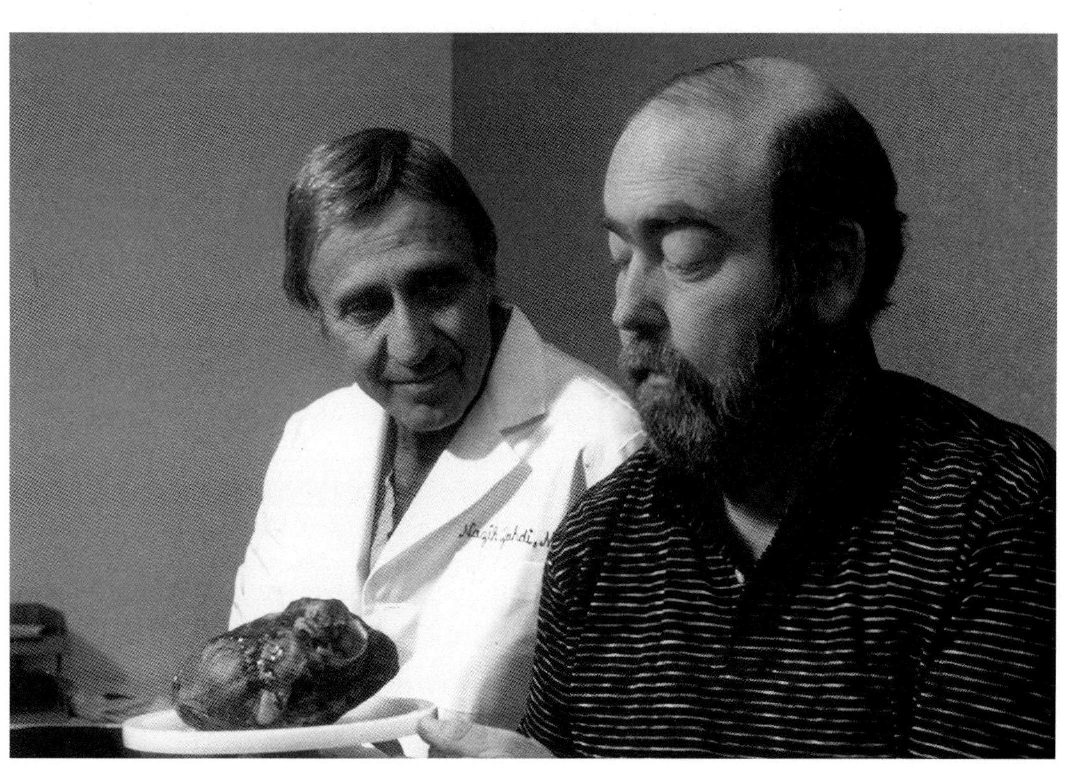

Below: Dr. Nazih Zuhdi showing Al Ruble his diseased heart which Zuhdi had replaced in a heart transplant operation. An internationally recognized pioneer in open heart surgery and transplantation methodology, Zuhdi established one of the major transplantation centers in the nation at Baptist Medical Center in Oklahoma City. Upon his retirement in 1999, the facility was named Nazih Zuhdi Transplant Center.

COURTESY NAZIH ZUHDI, M. D.

Right: Oklahoma City's Myriad Gardens was part of an ongoing effort to revitalize the downtown area. On the right is the Crystal Bridge, which houses an internationally renowned botanical display.

COURTESY DAVID FITZGERALD.

Below: Dr. Shannon W. Lucid shown onboard the Space Shuttle monitoring a satellite payload in the shuttle's cargo bay. Although born in Shanghai, China, Dr. Lucid considers Bethany her hometown. She has flown on all three space shuttles—the Atlantis, *the* Columbia, *and the* Discovery. *Lucid also spent time aboard the Russian space station* Mir.

COURTESY NATIONAL AERONAUTICS AND SPACE ADMINISTRATION.

As Oklahoma celebrated the centennial of the formation of Oklahoma Territory, the state had matured into a modern diversified political unit. A two-party political system in which Republicans and Democrats shared political power had developed. A thriving economy combining agriculture, energy, services, and manufacturing had been established. Oklahoma had become a leader in higher education and medical research, and a diverse population had been blended together to form a unique culture and heritage.

Left: Downtown Bartlesville. Once a small trading community serving surrounding farmers, Bartlesville mushroomed into a modern energy center because it became the headquarters of both Cities Service Oil Company and Phillips Petroleum Company as well as numerous other independent oil corporations and energy service companies. Its downtown is a blending of its boom town beginnings, such as the restored railroad depot in the center, its energy heritage, the square structure on the right is the Phillips Tower, and the modern headquarters of Phillips Petroleum Company in the background.

COURTESY DAVID FITZGERALD.

Bottom, left: A native of Weatherford, Oklahoma, Thomas P. Stafford was among the second group of American astronauts and flew four missions in space including serving as commander of Apollo X in May of 1969, the first flight of the lunar module to the moon. He also served in later Apollo and Skylab projects and commanded the American crew during the Apollo-Soyuz flight, a joint effort American Astronauts and Soviet Cosmonauts.

COURTESY NATIONAL AERONAUTICS AND SPACE ADMINISTRATION.

Bottom, right: Charles Banks Wilson's portrait of Carl Albert, the "Little Giant From Little Dixie," who rose from rural Oklahoma to serve as Speaker of the United States House of Representatives. At one point in his career, after the resignation of Vice President Spiro Agnew, he was first in line to become President of the United States in the event of the death or resignation of President Richard Nixon.

COURTESY OKLAHOMA DEPARTMENT OF TOURISM AND RECREATION; PHOTOGRAPH BY FRED MARVEL.

CHAPTER XV

OKLAHOMA'S DIVERSE CULTURAL HERITAGE

By 1996, Oklahoma ranked twenty-second among the states in population, with a total of approximately 3,300,900 people. By this time, Oklahoma's population was predominately urban. Fifty-one percent, or 1,162,100 people, lived in Oklahoma and Tulsa Counties, a dramatic shift from the time of statehood, when only five towns had more than 10,000 residents. Although eight of every ten Oklahomans were white in 1996, there were large Native American, black, and Hispanic minorities. The population diversity resulted from the combining of Indian Territory and Oklahoma Territory to form the State of Oklahoma and the cultural ties of the state to the Southwest.

The removal of the Eastern Indians to Indian Territory, the establishment of Plains Indians Reservations in western Oklahoma, and the concentration of a myriad of small tribes in the region in the post-Civil War era made Oklahoma the home to 146 different bands, tribes, clans, and confederations of Native Americans—the largest concentration of different tribes in the world. Oklahoma's Native American heritage is maintained by a number of powwows and dance festivals, including the Red Moon Memorial Day Powwow at Hammon, the Tulsa Powwow, the O-Ho-Mah Celebration at Anadarko, the Kaw Nation Powwow, and the Great New Moon Festival at Tahlonteeskee. Indian City, USA, near Anadarko, is host to the American Indian Hall of Fame, and Oklahoma City's Red Earth Festival is one of the largest gathering of Native American dancers in the world.

In addition to traditional tribal culture, Oklahoma's Native American tribes have produced five world renowned ballerinas—Yvonne Chouteau Terekhov, Moscelyn Larkin Jasinski, Rosella Hightower, Maria Tallchief Paschen, and Marjorie Tallchief Skibine. Alexander Posey and John Stink, Creek and Osage, respectively, are nationally known for their poetry. Admiral William Crowe, United States ambassador to Great Britain; Admiral J. J. "Jocko" Clark; and Major General Clarence Tinker are other internationally known Native Americans from Oklahoma. Will Rogers, a Cherokee, was known worldwide for his humor and wit.

Native American place names are found throughout Oklahoma. Many of the state's towns are named for Indian leaders: Battiest for Choctaw jurist Byington Battiest, Bigheart for Osage Chief James Bigheart, Bowlegs for the Seminole Headman Billy Bowlegs, Bushyhead for Cherokee Chief Dennis W. Bushyhead, Checotah for Creek Chief Samuel Checote, Eschita for a Comanche medicine man, Geronimo for the Apache Chief, Gray Horse for an Osage medicine man, Sequoyah for the originator of the Cherokee syllabary, Left Hand Spring for Arapaho Chief Left Hand, Littlerobe for Cheyenne Chief Little Robe, Lone Wolf for a Kiowa Chief, McCurtain for Choctaw Chief Green McCurtain, and Pawhuska for Osage Chief White Hair or Paw-Hiu-Skah. Some tribes gave their names to local communities, including Cheyenne, Arapaho, Shawnee, Kaw, Miami, Peoria, and Kickapoo. Of course Seminole, Cherokee, Creek, Pottawatomie, Caddo, Comanche, Muskogee, Choctaw, Ottawa, Delaware, Pawnee, and Kiowa Counties derived their names from Native American tribes. Broken Arrow, in the old Creek Nation, got its name from a ceremony in which an arrow was broken to symbolize the reunion of the pro-northern and pro-southern factions of the tribe after the Civil War.

Republican-controlled Oklahoma Territory was a mecca for blacks in the post-Civil War era. Encouraged by the Oklahoma Immigration Association and such leaders as Edward P. McCabe, many blacks fled to the area to avoid the "Jim Crowism" of surrounding states. In fact, there was a brief movement to make Oklahoma an all-black territory named Lincoln in which all officials were to have been black. One of the most prominent black communities in the territorial period was Langston, which was founded by McCabe. In Indian Territory during the post-Civil War period, the Five Tribes incorporated their freedmen into tribal society.

Eventually there were thirty named and two unnamed all-black communities established in Oklahoma. Among them was Boley, once the largest all-black community in the nation. It was the location of the state's

Oklahoma was a mixing ground for races. This gentleman, identified only as Mr. Dillihunter, had both black and Native American heritage. He was a watchmaker in Guthrie. His dress clearly reflects his Indian heritage.

COURTESY GUTHRIE PUBLIC LIBRARY COLLECTION, WESTERN HISTORY COLLECTIONS, UNIVERSITY OF OKLAHOMA LIBRARIES.

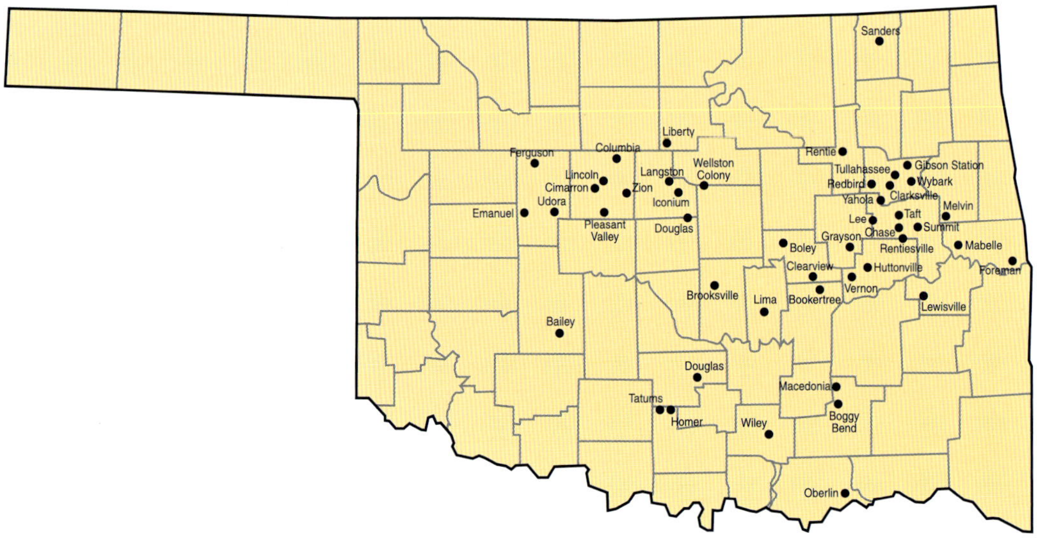

Top: A portion of the 400 landscaped acres that surround Tulsa's Gilcrease Museum. Established by oilman Thomas Gilcrease, the museum maintains extensive collections on the Western legacy of Oklahoma. Internationally recognized for its collection of Native American art, the museum, which is located at 1400 Gilcrease Museum Road, just off US-412 in west Tulsa, is open to the public seven days a week and is the site of numerous special events annually.

COURTESY DAVID FITZGERALD.

black grand Masonic Temple and the Creek-Seminole Colored College.

There are at least two other communities in Oklahoma named for prominent black settlers. Earlsboro was named after James Earls, a local black businessman, and Mabelle in Sequoyah County was named for Mabelle Mitchell, the daughter of Ed Mitchell, a well-known black resident.

Boley also boasted the Boley Wonders of the Oklahoma Negro Baseball League. The community was the birthplace of two major league baseball players—George Leo "Jeff" Jefferson, who played in the Negro Leagues between 1937 and 1949, and Cardell "Card" Camper, who played with the Cleveland Indians. Clearview was the home of Willie "Bill" Jefferson, who played in the Negro Leagues between 1928 and 1946. Boley also is the site of the largest all-black rodeo in the nation. Bulldogging is a rodeo event created and made famous by Bill Pickett, a black cowboy who

Right: A map showing many historically black towns in Oklahoma.

✧

Left: Flight of Sprit *by Mike Larsen portrays the tradition of Indian dance and its impact on Oklahoma's five premier Native American ballerinas—Moscelyn Larkin Jasinski, Yvonne Chouteau Terekhov, Maria Tallchief Paschen, Marjorie Tallchief, and Rosella Hightower.*

COURTESY OKLAHOMA DEPARTMENT OF TOURISM AND RECREATION; PHOTOGRAPH BY FRED MARVEL.

Below: Two examples of the intricate beadwork and designs that made early Native American dress so colorful. On the left is a woman's skirt and silver belt and necklace. On the right is a man's shirt, vest, and belt.

COURTESY BRIAN L. SMITH, MUSEUM OF THE GREAT PLAINS.

performed in the 101 Ranch Wild West Show. John Hope Franklin, who became known as the pre-eminent historian of the black experience in the United States, was born in Rentiesville, as was D. C. Minner, known worldwide for his contribution to blues music. The D. C. Minner Down Home Blues Club attracts tens of thousands of visitors annually. Lincoln Perry, a black actor whose character Step'n Fetchit was tremendously popular in the 1930s, is from Gowen in Latimer County.

Oklahoma City's Second Street, known as Deep Deuce, was another major center of jazz music. Black musicians such as Jimmy Rushing, Charlie Christian, and Buddy Anderson and bands such as the Oklahoma City Blue Devils were well-known performers at Ruby's Grill, Slaughter Hall, the Aldridge Theater, and Rushing's Cafe. The annual Deep Deuce Jazz Festival brings the glory days of jazz back to life, as does Tulsa's Greenwood Heritage Festival.

The opening of Oklahoma to settlement coincided with the height of European immigration to the United States. With most public lands elsewhere already taken, a number of German, English, Celtic, Italian, Spanish, Czechs, Polish, French, and Swedish homesteaders settled in Oklahoma, giving the state a diversity of culture and traditions. Many of the European immigrants who settled in Oklahoma tended to concentrate in ethnic enclaves.

✧

Top, left: Spirit Talk *by Woodrow Wilson Crumbo. In Crumbo's work a lone brave stands on a snowy cliff waiting for the spirits to reveal themselves. The spiritual heritage of Native Americans in Oklahoma is an important aspect of the state's cultural diversity.*

COURTESY MINISA CRUMBO HALSEY.

Top, right: Native American sculptor Willard Stone and some of his many works. Internationally famous for his creations, Stone is holding one of his favorite sculptures of his young daughter wearing traditional tribal dress and trying to put on white-mans boots. As Stone explained, the piece illustrates the problem of many Native Americans trying to adapt to a non-Indian world.

COURTESY OKLAHOMA HERITAGE ASSOCIATION.

Bottom: Spencer Asah was one of the famous Kiowa Five who received formal art training from Oscar B. Jacobson at the University of Oklahoma, and who founded one of the earliest and most recognized schools of Native American art. In addition to his fame as an artist, Asah was an accomplished Indian dancer.

COURTESY SAM DEVENNEY COLLECTION, MUSEUM OF THE GREAT PLAINS.

Large numbers of Germans homesteaded in Canadian, Garfield, and Kingfisher Counties. Many of them were Germans who had migrated first to Russia and then to Oklahoma. Kremlin in Garfield County is named after the Kremlin in Moscow, which gave its name to the community of Moscow in Woodward County. Berlin and Hamburg in Roger Mills County were named after cities in Germany. Okarche in Canadian County once boasted two German language newspapers.

Among the Germans from Russia were a large number of Mennonites. Mennonite colonies were found clustered around their churches in Kay, Grant, Noble, Garfield, Major, Blaine, Caddo, Washita, and Custer Counties. Meno was named for the founder of the Mennonite movement Menno Simons. Hartshorne is the home of the state's only Russian Orthodox Church, which served Russian immigrants, who were attracted to the area by the coal mining industry.

Jewish immigrants also settled in early-day Oklahoma. Large numbers of Jews, mostly from Germany and Austria, made their homes in Chickasha, Lawton, McAlester, Muskogee, Oklahoma City, and Tulsa, where they played prominent roles in the economic development of the area. Many of the early Jews who settled in Tulsa were from Latvia. Following the Russian Revolution of 1917, many Russian Jews fled to Tulsa. Among them were Sam Zarrow and his sons Henry and Jack, who became prominent oilmen and philanthropists. Most Jewish immigrants were attracted to the urban environment, few became farmers. Exceptions included Max Westheimer, Sam Daube, and Jake Bodovitz, who were cattle ranchers and merchants in Carter County. Westheimer and Daube also were prominent in the oil development of southern Oklahoma.

Top, left: Ralph Ellison wrote *The Invisible Man*, one of the nation's milestones in literature, in which he examines the plight of blacks in America. A native Oklahoman, Ellison drew heavily on his early life for his writings.

COURTESY ANITA ARNOLD, BLAC, INC.

Top, right: Oklahoma was a mecca for tens of thousands of European immigrants flocking to America in the last decades of the nineteenth and early twentieth century. Some of them became prosperous businessmen catering to concentrations of their fellow countrymen in towns and cities. This is the interior of a Czech-owned butcher shop. Numerous Czechs settled in the area near Prague, Yukon, and in rural Canadian and Kingfisher Counties. Both Prague and Yukon host annual Kolache Festivals in honor of their ethnic heritage.

COURTESY HELEN DEEDS COLLECTION, WESTERN HISTORY COLLECTIONS, UNIVERSITY OF OKLAHOMA LIBRARIES.

Many Jewish merchants, such as Simon Levine, who operated a store at Coalgate, and Ben Byers, who owned a dry goods store in Lehigh, were attracted to the coal mining regions of eastern Oklahoma.

Many Polish immigrants were attracted to the coal mines in the area around McAlester and Wilburton. Other Polish communities were in Oklahoma City and Harrah. Lithuanians and Ukrainians also worked in the coal mines of eastern Oklahoma. Large numbers of them settled in Pittsburg and Latimer Counties. Many Polish workers were attracted to the lead and zinc smelters in Washington County. West Bartlesville boasted a predominately Polish population that gave the area a distinct ethnic identity. St. Teresa of Avila Catholic Church in Harrah is the only Polish parish church in Oklahoma. Some Poles, such as Stanley Kolowski, fled to Oklahoma after enduring the horrors of the Dachau, Germany, death camp in World War II. Oklahoma Supreme Court Justice Marian P. Opala was born in Ludz, Poland.

Large numbers of Italian immigrants took work in the coal mines of eastern Oklahoma. McAlester, Wilburton, Coalgate, Lehigh,

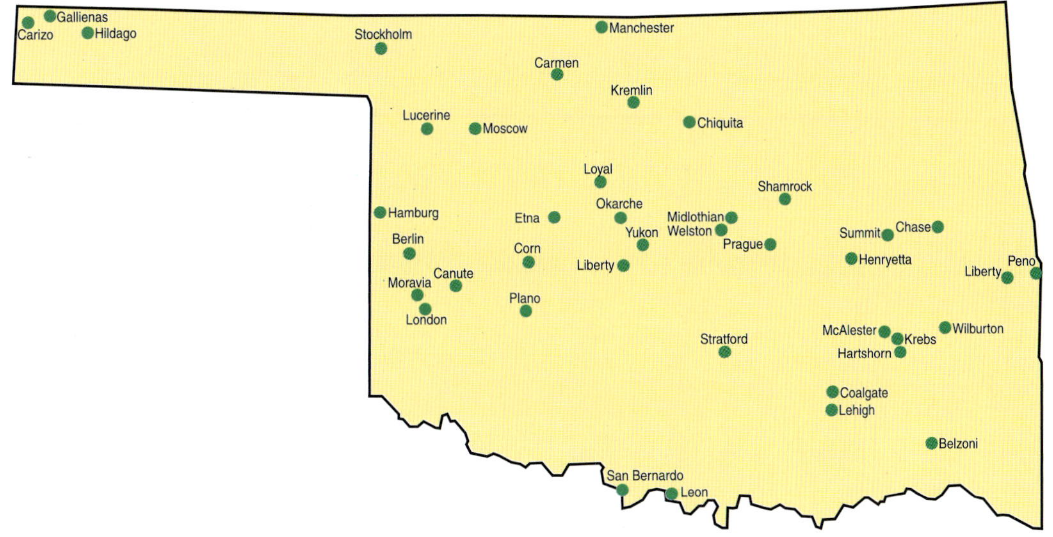

Bottom: A map showing some of the towns in Oklahoma with ethnic names.

✧

Above: Frank V. Zamudio and his hot tamale cart were a familiar site along the streets of Ada in Pontotoc County. Numerous Hispanics settled in Oklahoma, especially during the heyday of railroad construction as many worked on the construction crews.

COURTESY ADA PUBLIC LIBRARY COLLECTION, WESTERN HISTORY COLLECTIONS, UNIVERSITY OF OKLAHOMA LIBRARIES.

Right: The St. Cyril Orthodox Church at Hartshorne in eastern Pittsburg County. The community was in the center of the state's coal mining region and was the home to numerous European immigrants who worked in the mines. St. Cyril served ethnic Russians who lived in the community.

COURTESY DAVID FITZGERALD.

Bottom: The interior of Jake Klimkowski's restaurant in Harrah. Harrah, in eastern Oklahoma County, boasted a large concentration of Polish residents. Another enclave of Polish immigrants was found in Bartlesville, where many found work in the nearby zinc smelters.

COURTESY ELENORA WYSKUP COLLECTION, WESTERN HISTORY COLLECTIONS, UNIVERSITY OF OKLAHOMA LIBRARIES.

Left: *The Main Street of Shamrock in Creek County at the height of the Cushing-Drumright oil boom. Shamrock boasted a number of Irish residents who cherished their cultural heritage. The community had its own newspaper, called* The Brogue; *a blarney stone imported from Ireland; painted the stripes in its street green instead of white; and held a huge St. Patrick's Day celebration.*

COURTESY THE OKLAHOMA HERITAGE ASSOCIATION.

Henryetta, and Krebs boasted large Italian populations. Krebs was the site of the state's Christopher Columbus Society and the home of several famous Italian restaurants. The town of Belzoni in Pushmataha County was named for the Italian explorer and archaeologist G. B. Belzoni, and Etna in Blaine County derived its name from Mount Aetna in Italy.

One of the largest ethnic groups in Oklahoma are people of Czech descent. Most became farmers in the north-central part of the state. Their traditional culture is remembered in annual *kolache* festivals held in Prague and Yukon. The Shrine of the Infant Jesus Roman Catholic Church also is a legacy of early Czech settlers. Several communities, such as Moravia in Beckham County, which was named for a region of Czechoslovakia, and Prague in Lincoln County, named for the capital of Czechoslovakia, also have a Czech legacy. Matthew Anton Swatek, who was born in Prague, Czechoslovakia, was a prominent Oklahoma City builder who constructed many of the city's early public buildings and built the first concrete road in the state.

Swedish, English, and Scottish immigrants made many of the land openings. Annual Scottish Heritage Festivals are held in Tulsa and Midwest City. Midlothian in Lincoln County was named for a Scottish county. Many Welsh miners worked in the coal mines of eastern Oklahoma. London in Beckham County, Manchester in Grant County, Reydon in Roger Mills County, and Stratford in Garvin County were named for English cities. Lucerne in Woods County was named for Lucerne, Switzerland; Stockholm in Harper County for Stockholm, Sweden; and Canute in Washita County was named for the King of Denmark.

Irish workers were so predominant in the Cushing-Drumright Oil Field that the town of Shamrock practically was an extension of the old country. The local newspaper was called the *Shamrock Brogue*. Most streets were named after Irish towns, and street lines were

Below: A convention of the Mennonite Brethren Church at Corn, Oklahoma, in 1898. Although German, the Mennonites migrated first to Russia and then to Oklahoma in the nineteenth century. Many Mennonite colonies are found in Kay, Grant, Noble, Garfield, Major, Blaine, Caddo, Washita, and Custer Counties. The Mennonites brought Turkey Red Wheat to Oklahoma and revolutionized agriculture by providing a crop that thrived on the Great Plains.

COURTESY CORN HISTORICAL SOCIETY COLLECTION, WESTERN HISTORY COLLECTIONS, UNIVERSITY OF OKLAHOMA LIBRARIES.

Left: Downtown Boley in Okfuskee County. Established in 1903, Boley, the largest all-black community in America, prospered as a center for black businessmen who supplied merchandise to the numerous black farmers and ranchers in the area. Built along the Fort Smith and Western Railroad, it was the home of the Creek-Seminole Colored College and the location of the black Grand Masonic Lodge. The annual Boley Rodeo is still billed as the largest all-black rodeo in the nation and attracts thousands each year.

COURTESY OKLAHOMA DEPARTMENT OF TOURISM AND RECREATION; PHOTOGRAPH BY FRED MARVEL.

Right: A performer at the annual Juneteenth Jazz Festival and Heritage Celebration held in the Greenwood District of Tulsa. Greenwood, often referred to as the Black Wall Street, was the professional and business center of Tulsa's black citizens. Although the area was destroyed in the Tulsa Race Riot of 1921, it recently has been revitalized as one of the state's major black cultural centers.

COURTESY OKLAHOMA DEPARTMENT OF TOURISM AND RECREATION; PHOTOGRAPH BY FRED MARVEL.

Below: The Korn Concert Band. Corn in northeastern Washita County originally was spelled Korn, the German form of the word, because of the large number of German immigrants who settled in the region. However, in September of 1918, at the height of American involvement in World War I, the spelling was changed to Corn to reflect the patriotism of the local residents. Corn is but one of several communities in western Oklahoma boasting a traditional German heritage.

COURTESY CORN HISTORICAL SOCIETY COLLECTION, WESTERN HISTORY COLLECTIONS, UNIVERSITY OF OKLAHOMA LIBRARIES.

painted green. The community even boasted its own Blarney Stone.

Hispanic heritage in Oklahoma stemmed from the region's earliest recorded history. Spanish conquistadors were the first to penetrate the region, and Spanish miners in the Wichita Mountains were among the first to settle in Oklahoma. There are many Hispanic place names in the state. Carmen in Alfalfa County was named for Carmen Díaz, the wife of the President of Mexico; Carrizo in Cimarron County is the Spanish word for the water grass growing along the Beaver River; Chiquita in Noble County is the Spanish word for little girl; the Cimarron River and Cimarron County names are derived from *Río de los Carneros Cimarrón*, which is Spanish for River of the Wild Sheep; Gallienas in Cimarron County takes its name from the Spanish word referring to prairie chickens; Palo Duro Creek is in Texas County; Hidalgo, Spanish for lesser nobility, is a community in Cimarron County; the town of Leon in Love County is named after the Spanish word for lion. The town of Peno, in Leflore County, was named for a local Hispanic settler named Penocho, and the community of Plano in Washita County gets its name from the Spanish word of level or smooth. San Bernardo in Jefferson

County was named after Spanish governor Bernardo de Gálvez.

Many Hispanics immigrated to Oklahoma following the series of revolutions that swept Mexico during the early twentieth century. Gregorio Martines, who fought with Pancho Villa, fled to Oklahoma in 1917 and worked for the Atchison, Topeka, and Santa Fe and M-K-T railroads. Many of the early Hispanic immigrants followed his pattern of finding employment on railroads during the heyday of railroad construction in the state.

Large concentrations of Hispanics could be found in Blackwell, Edmond, Purcell, Pauls Valley, Ardmore, Medford, Enid, El Reno, Chickasha, Duncan, Waurika, Oklahoma City, Tulsa, and Sapulpa, where they worked for railroad section gangs. Railroads in Oklahoma paid higher wages than surrounding states to keep their Mexican workers. Even so, the average pay for Mexican labor was only $1.50 per day in 1907. By the 1920s, their pay had risen to $2.80 per day. Other Mexicans worked in the coal mines of eastern Oklahoma, where twenty-nine were killed in December of 1929 in a mine disaster at McAlester. Seasonal work was obtained during the annual *pizca*, or cotton harvest.

Much of Oklahoma's Western heritage is Hispanic in origin. The dress of early-day cowboys was influenced greatly by the Mexican cattle industry. Cowboys wore broad-brimmed *sombreros*, and leather chaps adopted from Mexican cowboys. The lariat was a direct lineage of the Spanish Southwest, as was the rodeo. José Barrera, of Pawnee, known as "Mexican Joe," was a world champion trick roper who performed with the Pawnee Bill Wild West Show worldwide. Little Flower Catholic Church near downtown Oklahoma City has a distinct Hispanic flavor and celebrates many traditional festivals.

In the more modern era, a large number of Asian-Americans settled in Oklahoma. Many of them were clustered in Oklahoma City, Norman, Stillwater, and Tulsa. A number of Chinese settled in Oklahoma Territory; many lived in the area just west of the railroad tracks in downtown Oklahoma City, where they were employed in numerous laundries. Some Chinese lived in basements beneath the laundries. Several tunnels were dug to connect the basements and, for decades these tunnels gave rise to the story of an "underground" Chinese city. One of the few Asian place names in Oklahoma is Ceylon in Lincoln County, named for the island nation.

From the "Land of the Redman," Oklahoma has matured into a multi-cultured state that represents a wealth of different heritages and tradition. The state hosts a multitude of traditional cultural events annually, as Oklahomans of all races and nationalities celebrate their lineages. This blending of many cultures has given the state a unique identity.

Miguel Covarrubias' Tehuana *from the collections of Gilcrease Museum in Tulsa. Gilcrease's huge collection of artwork offers a cross section of the state's diverse cultural heritage and provides visitors a graphic demonstration of Oklahoma's varied cultures.*

COURTESY GILCREASE MUSEUM.

BOk
AMOCO
BERNSEN

CHAPTER XVI

MODERN OKLAHOMA

As Oklahoma's cultural heritage diversified, so did the state's economy. By the end of the twentieth century, Oklahoma's economy included large segments of sales, service companies, and manufacturing concerns, as well as the traditional energy and agriculture industries. Nearly seven of every ten Oklahoma workers in 1994 were employed in service, retail businesses, or manufacturing. The remaining worked in agricultural services, mining, construction, transportation, public utilities, wholesale trade, retail trade, finance, insurance, real estate, and other small businesses. In the metropolitan area of Oklahoma City, with its concentration of federal and state facilities, nineteen percent of the work force is employed by local, state, and federal government. In 1994, Oklahoma's 80,519 business establishments employed 1,024,904 workers, who generated an annual payroll of $22,032,298,000.

In comparison, the energy industry produced $5,535,355,000 worth of crude oil, condensate oil, casinghead gas, and natural gas. Carter County was the state's major source of crude oil, producing 11,068,893 barrels in 1996. Custer County, with a 1996 output of 864,318 barrels, was first in condensate oil production. Top natural gas production was in Roger Mills County in 1996, with total production of 166,602,729 mcf. Garvin County led in casinghead gas production in 1996, with an output of 31,793,949 mcf.

The third factor in the state's economy remained agriculture. In 1995, Oklahoma's 71,000 farms produced cash receipts totaling $3,704,737,000—$1,133,469,000 for crops and $2,571,268,000 for livestock or livestock products. Winter wheat was the major crop, with the 1995 crop valued at $458,438,000. Corn, grain sorghum, cotton, hay, soybeans, and peanuts also were important cash crops. With 6,988,000 acres of forest land, lumbering remained a major aspect of the state's economy.

David Walters' years as Oklahoma's chief executive, 1991-1995, were plagued by campaign contribution scandals, which saw him plead no contest to the accusations. As an indication of the breaking of the Democratic hold on state offices, Republican Frank Keating was elected governor in 1994. The 1998 governor's campaign saw Laura Boyd, only the second woman to run for the governor's office; however, Keating easily won reelection. The most memorable event of Keating's first administration was the bombing of the Alfred P. Murrah Federal Building in Oklahoma City at 9:02 a.m. on April 19, 1995.

In the most deadly example of domestic terrorism in America in the twentieth century, Timothy McVeigh ignited a bomb the equivalent of 4,000 pounds of TNT hidden in a rented truck parked in front of the Murrah Building, killing at least 168 people. The exact count may never be known because the force of the explosion ripped victims apart, making the identification of some body parts impossible. When the bomb exploded it struck the building with a force of thirty-seven tons, sufficient to vaporize one victim standing near the entrance. The entire south face of the building collapsed into a huge pile of rubble. The blast was so powerful that it was heard throughout the city and its smoke plume could be seen for twenty miles.

As the dust and smoke of the explosion cleared, dazed survivors stumbled into the street. Damage was not limited to the Murrah Building; office workers in nearby structures, such as the *Journal Record* Building and Federal Courthouse, also were killed or injured as glass and other debris ripped through the air. Buildings throughout much of the downtown area were damaged beyond repair. As the first rescue workers rushed to the scene, they were greeted with sights of horror as the injured and dead filled Fifth Street in front of the Murrah Building. Most were covered with blood; many had their clothing shredded by flying glass.

Close to the truck bomb in the Murrah Building was a day care center. Many of the infants were in cribs along the north wall, which was made of glass. Only six of the twenty-two children in the day care survived. Three other children who were visiting the Murrah Building at the time of

Tulsa's modern skyline along Boston Avenue. On the left is the Cities Service Building, in the center is the Bank of Oklahoma Building, and the one on the right is the Mid-Continent Building. In the foreground in front of the Mid-Continent Building is the Amoco Building. Tulsa officials went to great pains to preserve the unique historic flavor of the city's downtown area, which features parks and pedestrian walkways.

COURTESY OKLAHOMA HERITAGE ASSOCIATION; PHOTOGRAPH BY JUDY DAWSON.

the explosion also were killed, making a total of nineteen.

As the magnitude of the act became clear, the reaction of the citizenry was quick. The Red Cross and other blood centers were swamped as Oklahomans rushed to donate blood for the injured. Emergency units from throughout Oklahoma City and surrounding communities hurried to the site to aid the early rescue efforts. Local fire, police, emergency medical personnel, and volunteers quickly brought order to the chaos as terrified family members searched for loved ones. Nearby hospitals called in all personnel to handle the emergency.

While the injured who had escaped the blast site were being cared for, the search for survivors still inside the Murrah Building began. Undaunted by the danger of falling debris, searchers rushed inside the Murrah Building. Some were found, but the destruction from the gas cloud was so great—it struck the building at a speed of 8,000 feet

Above: The lone Survivor Tree growing beside the Journal Record Building near the site of the Alfred P. Murrah Building bombing in downtown Oklahoma City. Following the April 19, 1995 blast, many of the injured who staggered out of the Murrah and other nearby buildings gathered near the tree, which became known as the Survivor Tree.

COURTESY OKLAHOMA DEPARTMENT OF TOURISM AND RECREATION; PHOTOGRAPH BY FRED MARVEL.

Right: The Fence which surrounded the rubble left by the Oklahoma City bombing became a focal point at the site, as tens of thousands of messages and keepsakes were left hanging on the fence. The site now contains the Oklahoma City National Memorial, dedicated to the victims of the most deadly act of domestic terrorism in American history.

COURTESY OKLAHOMA DEPARTMENT OF TOURISM AND RECREATION; PHOTOGRAPH BY FRED MARVEL.

Far right: Edmond native Shannon Miller being welcomed home after the 1992 Olympic Games in Barcelona, Spain. At the turn of the twenty-first century, she was the most decorated American gymnast in Olympic history.

COURTESY THE DAILY OKLAHOMAN.

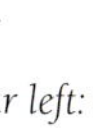

Far left: Guthrie's annual 89er Day Celebration attracts thousands of visitors to Oklahoma's former territorial capital, the state's first capital, and what is now one of the most significant historical preservation districts in the United States.

COURTESY OKLAHOMA DEPARTMENT OF TOURISM AND RECREATION; PHOTOGRAPH BY FRED MARVEL.

Left: Philbrook Museum of Art in Tulsa is the former home of Oklahoma oilman Waite Phillips, which he named Villa Philbrook. Restored to its original appearance with a new, architecturally compatible annex, the museum houses one of the state's leading art collections.

COURTESY OKLAHOMA DEPARTMENT OF TOURISM AND RECREATION; PHOTOGRAPH BY FRED MARVEL.

Above: Gilcrease Museum in Tulsa features the art collection of Tulsa oilman Thomas Gilcrease and spans the period from 10,000 BC to the present. Gilcrease was one of the first major collectors of Western American artworks, and his collection is often portrayed as "where the story of the American West unfolds." Located on a 400-acre site overlooking the scenic Osage Hills, the Gilcrease complex also includes historic theme gardens, natural meadows and woodlands, and Stuart Park. Gilcrease is open Tuesday through Saturday from 9:00 a.m. to 5:00 p.m.; Mondays from Memorial Day to Labor Day; and Sundays and Federal Holidays from 11:00 a.m to 5:00 p.m. In addition to the collections of art, Gilcrease has an extensive research library and Museum Shop, which offers unique selections of full-color prints of Gilcrease Museums paintings, reproduction of bronzes, books, jewelry, and other Native American items.

COURTESY GILCREASE MUSEUM.

✧

The statue of Ponca Chief Standing Bear by Oreland C. Joe in Standing Bear Park at Ponca City. Standing Bear's court challenge to the treatment of Native Americans forced the federal courts to rule that Indians had rights as people within the nation's legal system.

COURTESY OKLAHOMA DEPARTMENT OF TOURISM AND RECREATION; PHOTOGRAPH BY FRED MARVEL.

per second—it was difficult to believe anyone remaining inside could have survived. As word of the rescue effort spread, individuals and local restaurants dispatched food for the rescuers. Others donated clothing and other supplies; one sporting goods store in Stillwater sent boxes of knee pads for the rescue workers crawling through the debris.

As part of a nationwide disaster response network, rescue workers from around the

nation were called upon to assist the search for survivors. The first to arrive were from Phoenix, Arizona. Their efforts were hindered by worsening weather. High winds and rain made the Murrah Building more unstable. For a brief time during the afternoon on April 19, rescue efforts were halted because of the danger of the ruins collapsing.

That evening the workers returned, crawling through the rubble. Heavy equipment was brought in to give workers more access to the debris field. Great care had to be taken so that

Far left: Oklahoma baseball legend Mickey Mantle of Commerce was one of the most recognized sports figures of the twentieth century. The centerpiece of the revitalization of Bricktown was the construction of the Southwestern Bell Bricktown Ballpark, the highlight of which is a statue of Mantle standing before the third-base entrance. This portrait by Dr. Kenneth Wyatt hangs in the State Capitol.

COURTESY OKLAHOMA DEPARTMENT OF TOURISM AND RECREATION; PHOTOGRAPH BY FRED MARVEL.

Left: The Charles Banks Wilson portrait of Jim Thorpe, a Sac and Fox Indian from Lincoln County who was recognized as the "World's Greatest Athlete" following the 1912 Olympic Games. Unfortunately, Thorpe was stripped of his Olympic medals when it was discovered that he had briefly played professional sports. Later the medals were returned to the Thorpe family, which presented them for display in the State Capitol.

COURTESY OKLAHOMA DEPARTMENT OF TOURISM AND RECREATION; PHOTOGRAPH BY FRED MARVEL.

Below: Oklahoma City's major tourism projects at the close of the twentieth century was the revitalization of the historic Bricktown area, east of downtown. One of the most popular aspects of the effort was the construction of the Bricktown Canal, over which water taxies carry visitors to the area's numerous nightspots and other attractions.

COURTESY OKLAHOMA DEPARTMENT OF TOURISM AND RECREATION; PHOTOGRAPH BY FRED MARVEL.

✧

Right: The altar of Little Flower Catholic Church at 1125 South Walker is the center of much of the Hispanic heritage in Oklahoma City and the location of many traditional festivals and Holy Day Celebrations.

COURTESY OKLAHOMA HERITAGE ASSOCIATION; PHOTOGRAPH BY JUDY DAWSON.

Below: The Scottish marching band of bagpipes and drums performing at the annual Midwest City Scottish Festival. Other events include traditional Scottish games and entertainment.

COURTESY OKLAHOMA HERITAGE ASSOCIATION; PHOTOGRAPH BY JUDY DAWSON.

survivors would not be killed when the massive concrete blocks were lifted. The rescue workers were able to locate and extricate Priscilla Sayers that first day after she had laid in the rubble for more than five hours. Work continued throughout the night, aided by large floodlights illuminating the blast scene. Another survivor, Dana Bradley, was found. Before she could be freed from the debris, however, doctors were forced to remove one of her legs. One other victim was saved. Brandy Liggons became the last person to be pulled alive from the Murrah Building.

Immediately after the blast, officials launched a search for those responsible. The early effort was hindered by confusion.

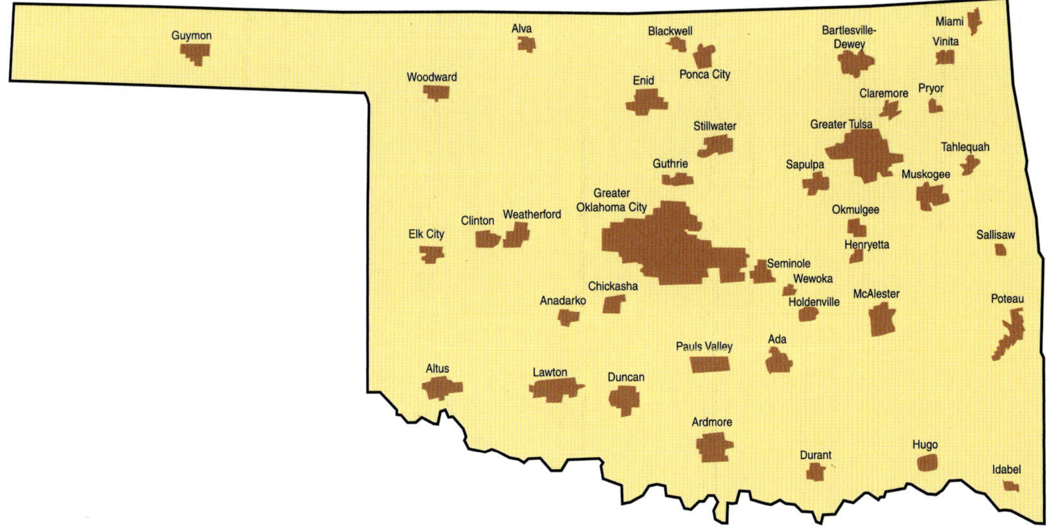

Top: Oklahoma's urban areas.

Bottom, left: The Greater Tulsa area.

Bottom, right: The Greater Oklahoma City area.

First reports hinted at a Middle Eastern tie. In fact, British officials detained one suspect of Middle East extraction. Turned over to American authorities, he was released after it was determined he had nothing to do with the bombing. Witnesses differed on how many were in the rented truck that held the bomb. Some said one. Others were sure there were two—a driver and a passenger. Initial reports alerted law officers to be on the lookout for John Doe Number 1 and John Doe Number 2. All this time FBI technicians combed the scene for clues.

However, it was a chance encounter with a Oklahoma Highway Patrol trooper that led to McVeigh's arrest. He was stopped on I-35 near Perry, Oklahoma, by trooper Charlie Hanger for not having a license plate on his yellow Mercury Marquis. While questioning McVeigh, Hanger noticed he was carrying a semiautomatic pistol beneath his jacket. A search found a five-inch knife. McVeigh was arrested for carrying concealed weapons and taken to the Noble County Jail in Perry, while authorities impounded and searched his automobile. The search turned up anti-government materials and a note indicating where he could purchase explosives.

In the meantime, the FBI had found the vehicle identification number from the truck containing the bomb and traced it to a Ryder rental office in Junction City, Kansas. The truck had been rented by McVeigh. Federal officials quickly arrested McVeigh, whose driver's license gave as his address the home of James Nichols. Further investigation revealed that McVeigh had served in Operation Desert Storm with James Nichols' brother Terry.

When the FBI searched Terry Nichols' rural home near Herington, Kansas, they found evidence of materials used to make the Oklahoma City bomb and a receipt for ammonium

nitrate, a key ingredient in the bomb. Nichols also was tied to the theft of explosives from a nearby quarry. As a result, Terry Nichols was arrested and charged with conspiracy in the bombing. Another friend of McVeigh, Michael Fortier, also was implicated.

Evidence against McVeigh continued to mount. He had served with distinction in the United States Army and received the Bronze Star for his service in Desert Storm but was given an early release by the military in 1991. Afterward, he became a harsh critic of the government and blamed federal officials for the tragedy at the Branch Dividian compound in Waco, Texas, and the shooting of innocent people by an FBI marksman at Ruby Ridge, Idaho. He was present at the assault at Waco where he passed out literature criticizing the government's action. He later moved to Arizona, where, along with Fortier, he built an ammonium nitrate bomb which they exploded in the desert.

At first Fortier denied any connection with the bombing, but he later cooperated with the investigation. He admitted that he was present when McVeigh planned the bombing and went with him to Oklahoma City to check the potential target in October of 1993. At that time, McVeigh told Fortier where he planned to hide his getaway vehicle. Searching the location, the FBI found the key to the Ryder truck.

Right: The Praying Hands *sculpture, located on the campus of Oral Roberts University in Tulsa, was created by Oklahoma City artist Leonard McMurry.*

COURTESY OKLAHOMA HERITAGE ASSOCIATION; PHOTOGRAPH BY JUDY DAWSON.

Below: The Southwestern Bell Bricktown Ballpark is home to the Oklahoma City RedHawks of the AAA Pacific Coast League and the major farm team of the Texas Rangers. The dramatic statue of Mickey Mantle is displayed at the third base entrance.

COURTESY OK EVENTS.

Likewise, Nichols' involvement became more clear to federal officials. According to Fortier, Nichols joined him and McVeigh to check out the Murrah Building again in early 1994. Additional investigation tied Nichols to the purchase of large amounts of ammonium nitrate in Kansas and racing fuel in Texas. The racing fuel was used to enhance the force of the bomb.

Initially, federal officials hoped to try McVeigh and Nichols in Oklahoma; however, it became apparent that an impartial jury could not be impounded, so a federal appeals court ordered the trial moved to Denver, Colorado. Enid, Oklahoma attorney Stephen Jones was appointed to represent McVeigh, and Texas attorney Michael Tiger represented Nichols. McVeigh was tried in the spring of 1997. Federal prosecutors successfully blocked Jones' effort to offer different theories on who was responsible for the bombing and tied McVeigh to the purchase of the ammonium nitrate used in the bombing by showing the jury his fingerprint on the receipt for the explosive. Fortier also testified about McVeigh's involvement. McVeigh was found guilty and sentenced to death. Nichols was tried in the fall of 1997 and also was found guilty; however, because he did not actually participate in the bombing, he was sentenced to life in prison.

The Oklahoma City bombing shocked the public. Oklahoma City was flooded with support worldwide. Money and other support poured in to help the victims survive. Rescue workers were impressed with the support they received from the local community. Food and other essentials freely were given as the community struggled to cope with the situation. The state's response to the tragedy and its aftermath became known among the rescue teams as the "Oklahoma Standard." Today, the site of the Murrah Building bombing is a national memorial, attracting tens of thousands of visitors annually. Surrounding the site is a chain link fence. Hundreds of thousands of expressions of support and sorrow have been left on the fence by fellow Americans and foreign visitors.

People worldwide were impressed with the bravery, compassion, and generosity displayed by Oklahomans in response to the bombing of the Murrah Building. Many were surprised by the fact that there was no looting. But those familiar with Oklahoma's heritage were not surprised. Frontier values remain strong in Oklahoma, and a major element of those values is a spirit of community, a willingness—indeed, an eagerness—to help their fellow citizens in times of need. Residents of the Twin Territories and, later, Oklahoma have endured severe difficulties periodically, but they have endured and then rebounded to build a better future. This proud heritage of optimism and determination will serve Oklahomans and the state well in the new millennium.

✧

Natural Falls State Park in far northeastern Oklahoma as of 1999 was the latest of a number of scenic and historic sites added to the state's parks system.

COURTESY OKLAHOMA HERITAGE ASSOCIATION; PHOTOGRAPH BY JUDY DAWSON.

Sharing the Heritage

historic profiles of businesses and organizations that have contributed to the development and economic base of Oklahoma

✧

Left to right: Rick Harding, of Bartlesville, Kelsey Arnold, of Oklahoma City, and Chris Back, of Fort Gibson. They are participating in the annual Christmas Season Candlelight Tour at Fort Gibson. Back is dressed in the uniform of a second lieutenant of the time, while Harding is wearing an ordinary enlisted man's uniform. They are portraying life at Fort Gibson during the 1840s.

COURTESY THE DAILY OKLAHOMAN.

✧

A geological phenomenon of the red beads, which can be found throughout much of Central Oklahoma, the Rose Rock is the official state rock of Oklahoma.

Quality of Life

healthcare companies,educational institutions, historical, and civic organizations contribute to Oklahomans' quality of life

Friends

Endodontic Associates, Oklahoma City

Chickasaw Nation

The national bell at the Chickasaw Capitol Building tolled promptly at 9 a.m. on November 17, 1998. Citizens of the Chickasaw Nation gathered on the capitol's lawn to commemorate the beautiful granite building's dedication in Tishomingo exactly 100 years earlier.

Governor Bill Anoatubby, in his third term of office, said, "This day is very important to us, because we are here to celebrate and cherish our past, take hold of the present and embrace the future."

No one at the ceremony that day had been alive to remember the dedication day. Written records preserve parts of what occurred, but personal versions have been preserved within families in the more traditional way of passing them down orally. This has been so from the beginning, from the time when the ancestors of present-day Chickasaw and Choctaws migrated to the Southeast, under the leadership of twin brothers, Chikasah and Chatah, who were navigating by a sacred leaning pole.

At one spot, the pole wobbled instead of leaning and this led to a disagreement between the brothers. Chatah and his much larger group of followers stayed put and became the Choctaw Nation. Chikasah and his followers continued east, eventually settling in northern Mississippi and becoming known as the Chickasaw Nation.

From that point, the small tribe, estimated at no more than 5,000, controlled additional land in a vertical strip in what became Kentucky, Tennessee, and Alabama. Like neighboring tribes, the Chickasaw spoke the Muskogean language, lived in single family wood framed houses and sustained themselves by hunting and agriculture, raising corn, beans, pumpkins, and squash.

The Chickasaws grouped their houses together to form at least seven villages on the Tombigbee Highlands. Each village had a log palisade fort, grounds for councils, ceremonies and ball games and a public building for religious and governmental functions. From these communities the Chickasaw ranged to the Atlantic Ocean, the Great Lakes, the Great Plains and the Gulf of Mexico. The most notable social characteristic of the early Chickasaws was their martial spirit; their enthusiasm for battle made them an unconquerable people.

In December 1540, the expedition of Hernando de Soto disrupted the tribe. The conquistadors demanded housing, food, and women. The Chickasaws acceded until their battle plan was set and its execution was optimally timed. When the Chickasaws attacked, the Spanish retreated to the Mississippi River. But this was only the first contact with European colonial powers that would battle for control of the lower Mississippi Valley.

In the seventeenth and early eighteenth centuries, England and France vied to make an alliance with the tribe. When the French failed, they armed the nearby Choctaws and battled the English-supported Chickasaws for forty years for control of the lower Mississippi Valley. At the battle of Akia in 1736 (in present-day Tupelo, Mississippi), the Chickasaws established their military preeminence. The French were never again a real threat to the Chickasaw domain, and their foothold in the lower Mississippi was broken; some historians believe that the Chickasaws should be given the most credit for why English and not French is spoken in the United States today.

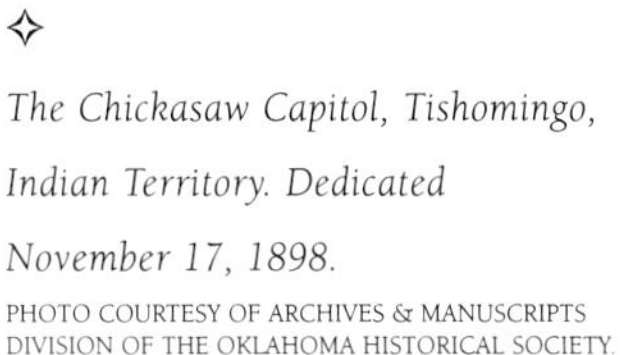

The Chickasaw Capitol, Tishomingo, Indian Territory. Dedicated November 17, 1898.

PHOTO COURTESY OF ARCHIVES & MANUSCRIPTS DIVISION OF THE OKLAHOMA HISTORICAL SOCIETY

✧ *Bill Anoatubby, thirtieth governor of the Chickasaw Nation.*

The Chickasaws remained England's allies throughout the American Revolution and felt betrayed when the English recognized the American independence. Once an independent people, the Chickasaws were now dependent on the colonial trade goods. They entered into debt and were introduced to rum and brandy by traders and adventurers, many of whom began settling among the Indians, intermarried and produced large mixed-blood families.

The colonial powers having withdrawn by the 19th century, the United States was free to expand. By 1818, the U.S. had concluded four treaties with the Chickasaws, which reduced the Chickasaw domain to northeastern Mississippi. These land cessions basically resulted from non-Chickasaw settlers' demand for more land. This necessitated abandoning the hunt and taking up agriculture. The full blood contingent was generally not receptive.

Though Americans continued to stream into the Indian nations in the Southeast, the tribes resolved to stay. Then, in 1830, President Andrew Jackson pushed through Congress the Indian Removal Act. Furthermore, the states of Mississippi and Alabama, with federal support, acted to abolish tribal governments and declared Indians subject to state laws. The Chickasaws would either lose their independence as a people or submit to removal.

In the Treaty of Pontotoc in 1832, the Chickasaw Nation ceded its 6.4 million-acre homeland in return for the proceeds from the land sale and provided acceptable lands could be found west of the Mississippi. Not wanting to be cheated by the government, the tribe agreed to pay for the cost of its removal. Finally in early 1837, Chickasaw leaders signed the Treaty of Doaksville, agreeing to pay the Choctaws, who had removed earlier, $530,000 for the right to live in the western part of the Choctaw Nation.

In the summer of 1837, the first 450 Chickasaws set off on the federally superintended migration to Indian Territory. This was out of a total population of 4,914 Chickasaws. During the next year, federal officials or vendors with federal contracts removed the bulk of the tribal members. Despite some painful personal losses, the removal was relatively orderly. Yet it was corrupted by massive scandals. Of the $1.5 million removal cost paid by the Chickasaws, $900,000 was paid for spoiled food or rations that were never delivered.

In their new home in the Choctaw Nation, the Chickasaws began reconstructing Chickasaw society over the next decade.

The first school, the Chickasaw Manual Labor Academy, opened in the district in 1851. Several more academies and a system of free elementary schools were also developed in the 1850s. During these years, the Chickasaw leadership determined to organize a government that would function separately from the Choctaws. Agitation on the part of the leadership with Washington led to the Treaty of Washington in 1855 that among other things empowered the tribe to create an independent and sovereign nation with boundaries identical to those of the old Chickasaw District.

In August 1856, the Chickasaws met at Good Spring (in Tishomingo) to draft a constitution providing for a governor, bicameral legislature, and judiciary department. The nation was divided into four counties with the capital being at Tishomingo City. Cyrus Harris was elected governor.

In 1861, the Chickasaws signed a treaty with the Confederacy. Even though the

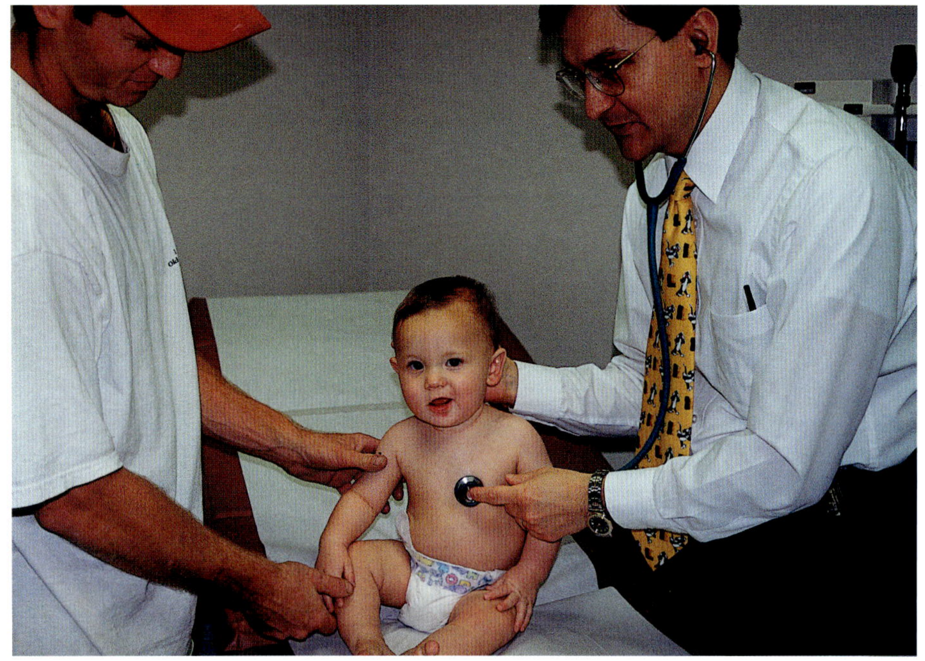

✧

Above: The Chickasaw Nation Health System renovated its hospital and clinics to accommodate more physicians and nurses to serve more patients, including the younger patients in pediatrics.

Below: Chickasaw Nation Head Start youth attend a tribal function as part of their ongoing cultural education program.

Chickasaws played only a minor role in the Civil War, it had a huge impact on the tribe. Though the U.S. restored the Chickasaw trust funds and resumed making annuity payments, the Treaty of 1866, signed with the Choctaws and U.S., authorized two railroad rights-of-way and established a U.S. court with limited jurisdiction in Indian Territory. These two measures facilitated the rising tide of intruders that would inundate the Chickasaw Nation by the end of the century.

Nevertheless, a new constitution was drafted. The tribe reopened and expanded its school system and by 1880, the literacy rate was 50 percent.

But by the early 1890s, the ability of the Chickasaw Nation to maintain its independence was severely hampered by Congress, which created the Dawes Commission to force tribes to terminate their governments and allot their domains in individual tracts to members of the tribes. In 1897, the Chickasaws and Choctaws ratified the Atoka Agreement with the federal government. It provided for the dissolution of tribal governments by 1906 and set in motion the development of tribal rolls for the land allotment process.

The final tribal roll of the Dawes Commission included approximately 1,500 full bloods, 4,100 mixed bloods, 635 intermarried whites, and 4,700 blacks. Once tribal government was terminated and most of the tribal estate was allotted, the Chickasaws became citizens of the new state of Oklahoma on November 16, 1907.

Most of the three decades following were devoted to disposition of the assets of the Chickasaws and Choctaws (which held their allotted lands in common) including timber land and mineral land. The federal government finally purchased the coal and asphalt lands for $8.5 million in 1948, nearly a half century after it agreed to do so. The sum was distributed per capita in 1949.

The Chickasaw governors in the first half of the twentieth century were appointed by the U.S. president to close out tribal business. Douglas H. Johnston served from 1904 until his death in 1939. Floyd E. Maytubby served from 1939 until his death in 1963. But by the time the Chickasaws had almost no tangible assets left, a grassroots democratic movement spread across the Chickasaw Nation. Overton James, appointed in 1963, became the first tribally elected governor since Oklahoma statehood, when he was elected in 1971. A new constitution, providing for a legislature and judicial branch, was drafted and ratified in 1983.

Chickasaw voters elect a governor and lieutenant governor team to four-year terms and thirteen-member tribal legislature and three tribal judges to three-year terms of office. There are over 38,000 registered Chickasaw citizens with about half at voting age of eighteen years old or older.

Today, Governor Bill Anoatubby, who succeeded Governor James in 1987, is the thirtieth governor to preside over the Chickasaw Nation. The governor, as chief executive, is responsible for running the day-to-day operations of the tribal government, which includes managing tribal assets and funding for operations of programs and services.

The Anoatubby administration set new policy standards for tribal self-determination and in twelve years rebuilt the government making it a nation with assets worth $95 million and an annual funding budget of $180 million. The nation brings in $49 million in gross revenues from nineteen businesses that help fund programs and employ over 1,700 people in south central Oklahoma. With governmental and business operations in place, the Chickasaw people have more opportunities than ever before in education, healthcare, housing, employment, and the chance to involve themselves in social and cultural activities that foster the preservation of Chickasaw language and customs.

The Chickasaw Nation has many great sons and daughters who have called Oklahoma their home, such as eighty-two-year-old Pearl Carter Scott, who learned to fly under the direction of Wiley Post and was inducted into the Oklahoma Aviation and Space Hall of Fame in 1995. Astronaut John Bennett Harrington, Lt. Commander, USAF, from Wetumka, who awaits his first shuttle mission assignment by NASA, is the first Native American and Chickasaw accepted into the space program. On the big screen, Chickasaw child actor Miko Hughes made his debut in a popular Stephen King film "Pet Sematary." Other Chickasaws chose a life of public office as did Oklahoma State Senator Helen Cole, her son Tom Cole who served as Oklahoma Governor Frank Keating's secretary of state, and Neal McCaleb, the secretary of transportation. And as they walked the halls of the state capitol building, ballerinas grace the rotunda in a mural painted by another famous Chickasaw, artist Mike Larson, one of many Chickasaw artisans around the country.

Known worldwide is Chickasaw storyteller Te Ata Fisher, born in Indian Territory in 1895. She performed before U.S. presidents, dignitaries, and the King and Queen of Great Britain. She was inducted into the Oklahoma Hall of Fame in 1957, and became Oklahoma's official state treasure in 1987.

From the theater to the state house and beyond, Chickasaws past and present shine through as they set the standards for generations to come, as the Chickasaw Nation continues to build a better tomorrow for a people of unconquerable spirit and ingenuity.

✧

Chickasaw John Bennett Harrington is the first Native American astronaut selected by NASA.

Choctaw Nation of Oklahoma

The honored history of the Choctaw Nation originally began with their occupation of western Alabama and central and southern Mississippi. The Choctaw established two principal cities, one located south of New Orleans, Louisiana and the other, near Mobile, Alabama. Their first contact with white settlers came under the arrival of explorer Hernando DeSoto in 1539 near the shores of present-day Tampa Bay, Florida. As DeSoto marched and fought through Florida into Georgia, Tennessee, Alabama, Mississippi, Arkansas, and Louisiana, the Choctaw met his men in a noble battle near Mobile. According to Spanish reports, the Choctaw lost several hundred warriors. They would remain undisturbed by Europeans for 160 years.

In 1698, the French came from Canada, established settlements and, along with the English, began peacefully trading with the Indians. The Choctaw were soon introduced to new materials and customs that proved useful, but with the English came war. Choctaw land became the site of the French and Indian War, a power struggle among France, England, Spain, and eventually the United States. A tribal civil war began as a result of a struggle erupting when England and France each tried to make an alliance with the Choctaws. By 1750, the French defeated the English faction leaving the Choctaws allied with the French and the final struggle for supremacy between England and France ended in 1760 with the French defeated. The French gave up claims to land west of the Mississippi, including the Choctaw Nation and less than twenty years later, the colonies won their independence from England, and the Choctaws came under the jurisdiction of the United States.

This new situation brought its own special problems. The Choctaw tribe had approximately 40,000 square miles of land with only 20,000 Indians residing in the area and because they were not farmers, the largest portion of their land was being used for hunting grounds. At the insistence of white settlers between 1801-1820, the United States government negotiated treaties with the Choctaws, which took more than half of their original land holdings.

When Mississippi joined the Union in 1817, it was strongly advised that the Choctaws concede their lands and move to a

Top: An 1866 Choctaw treaty delegation. Left to right, Allen Wright, Campbell LeFlore, Julius O. Folsom and F. Battiste. The delegation was given the heavy burden of making certain Choctaws were protected in dealings with the federal government.

PHOTO COURTESY OF OKLAHOMA HISTORICAL SOCIETY.

Right: The last Choctaw Council in 1905. Standing (left to right): J. P. Thompson, Tom Griggs, Ellis Bohannon, Peter Maytubby, Frank Folsom, and Peter Wilson. Seated (left to right): D. S. Noah, Joe Conser, George Choete, Jimmie Harkins, J. L. Ward, Wilson Shoney, C. H. Jones Morris Williams, Daniel Webster, and Amos Wilson.

PHOTO COURTESY OF E. R. "MONTE" MOSTELLER PHOTOGRAPHY.

territory west of the Mississippi that was to be a sovereign nation for the Indians and off limits to non-Indians. The Choctaws had two choices. They could take an individual land allotment and become a citizen of Mississippi or go to the new land and set up their own government. Because many Indian groups, especially the full bloods, believed that their property in the southeastern United States was a gift of the Great Spirit, it was impossible for the Indians to leave it.

They would eventually have no choice, however, as the event known as the "Trail of Tears" began to unfold.

The tears began as the mixed-bloods signed cession treaties accepted by the U.S. government as the will of the Indian Nations. The major treaties of the Choctaws were called the Treaty of Doak Stand, which occurred on October 18, 1820, and the Treaty of Dancing Rabbit Creek, which occurred on September 20, 1830. The treaty took effect in the fall of 1830 and established that the Choctaws would be removed to Indian Territory, into what are now the southeastern counties of Oklahoma, in return for their ten million acres in Mississippi.

The Choctaws were the first tribe to make the "Trail of Tears" on foot, by wagon, and the occasional steamboat. The move actually began in November of 1831 and didn't end until 1836. The trip was made difficult by unpredictable weather conditions, an outbreak of cholera, short food supplies and the subsequent health problems, and the insistence on the U. S. government's part to spare expenses. The first groups of the 17,000 Choctaws were all in their new land by early 1834. In 1836, another 4,000 of the 12,000 Choctaws in Mississippi found the white man's law too oppressive and joined their brothers in the west. So ended the Choctaw "Trail of Tears."

The Choctaw's trip to eastern Oklahoma was similar to all Indian removal trails. Old and new problems added to the difficulties of adjustment and internal differences had to be faced. The uniting of different tribes in one geographical area complicated adjustment even further. The Chickasaws and the Choctaws merged (1837-1855) and the Creeks and Seminoles united (1833-1856). There were many tribes that did not want to exist under another tribe's government and these problems were settled when the tribes were allowed to separate into five separate Indian land areas.

As in the other governments of the "Five Tribes," the Choctaws' basic law was democratic, with wide right to vote and lenient eligibility for holding office. The constitution provided sharp separation of legislature,

Left: The seat of government of the Choctaw Nation was at Tuskahoma from 1884-1907. The building has been preserved by the tribe as a reminder of the sacrifices made by early leaders to provide stable leadership for their people.

PHOTO COURTESY OF OKLAHOMA HISTORICAL SOCIETY.

✧

The Choctaw Tribal Complex in Durant.

executive, and judicial functions. The Bill of Rights included guarantees of trial by jury, religious liberty, and freedom of assembly. A constitution written in 1860 was written as a compromise and made use of the older constitution's organization with district chiefs and courts, but included from the new constitution a new national government with a two-house general council, a principal chief, and a supreme court.

The Choctaws in eastern Oklahoma were divided into the same districts they had in Mississippi, with each district governed by a chief elected every four years by the citizens of the district. The three chiefs met annually with members of the General Council (the legislative body) to make the laws and examine their relations with the United States. From 1837 to 1855, the Chickasaws merged and became a fourth district. After 1855, the area in the fourth district became the independent Chickasaw Nation.

Under the constitution, the principal chief, often referred to as the governor, was elected by the people for a two-year term and could serve no more than two terms successively. The candidate had to be a free, male citizen, thirty years old, a lineal descendant of the Choctaw or Chickasaw race, and a resident of the nation for at least five years preceding his election. The principal chief was entrusted with great power as he enforced the laws, commanded the militia, convened special sessions of the General Council, filled all vacancies in elective offices by temporary appointments that remained in force until the next general election, and held immense discretionary power in the administration of the contingent fund. The chief's original salary was $1,000 and increased to $2,000 in 1886. After the principal chief had served, he was commonly elected to the council where the prestige and experience he had acquired as chief made him a leading member and often sought election as principal chief for a third term as soon as the constitutional disability had expired.

The other executive officials of the Choctaw Nation were the national secretary, who was entrusted with the seal and the tribe's public documents; the treasurer, who had control of the disbursement of funds; the national auditor, who was originally intended to head the financial administration and to present financial plans and advise the General Council; and the national attorney, who was expected to give legal advice to the principal chief and other officers of the government.

After their arrival in Oklahoma, the first meeting of the Choctaw Tribal Council was held near Tuskahoma, where a spacious log council house was erected in 1839. The first capitol of the Choctaw Nation was named Nanih Waiya in memory of a sacred mount in Mississippi. In 1833, the General Council made an appropriation for the construction of a substantial brick building, the Tuskahoma

◆ Choctaw Nation Chief Gregory Pyle.

Capitol House, located about two miles northeast of the old Nanih Waiya Council House. The Choctaw Council House, and the 2,700 acres surrounding it, is the only Indian Council House still under the ownership of an Indian tribe. Since 1884, the old Choctaw Council House near Tuskahoma has been the scene of many events knit into the very fibers of the Choctaw people and serves as a symbol of their pride, their love for educating their children, and their desire for following an organized government for the general welfare of their nation.

During more recent years, the Choctaw Nation of Oklahoma has seen many changes that have resulted in many economic and social improvements. The leadership abilities of the Choctaw Nation's administration have resulted in profit-making business ventures that earn money for education, health and social programs, as well as enabling the tribe to develop economically.

Choctaw Bingo, which opened in December of 1987, has provided funds to purchase special medicines, helped supplement programs for Choctaws that provide energy assistance and eyeglasses, dentures and hearing aids, and have helped initiate economic development projects. The money from bingo has provided a scholarship fund for future teachers and for the young lady selected as Miss Choctaw Nation.

The Choctaw administration has also made education one of their highest priorities. At the youngest level, Head Start Centers throughout the tribal area supply small children with the opportunity to begin their education on the right foot. The higher education program received a supplement from tribal funds for college scholarships for Choctaws. The Tribal Council funded the adult Vocational Training Program, which allows Indian adults to earn their GED, because Congress had refused to fund the program. Jones Academy, which currently has 186 resident students, has built a spacious new dormitory and renovated the other buildings on campus. A storm shelter and new library are planned for the future.

The Choctaws have been proactive in working to make sure medical facilities are first-rate and under the Choctaw administration, the hospital at Talihina and three clinics at Broken Bow, Hugo, and McAlester were erected. A fourth outpatient clinic is in Poteau and is owned by the Tribe, and a fifth clinic is in Durant and is operated by a joint effort of the Choctaw and Chickasaw Nations. A new diabetes treatment center was opened in Antlers on November 7, 1997. In addition, the Hospitality House, a women's treatment center (Chi Hullo Li), and an alcohol recovery center are located near the Talihina Indian Hospital.

Twenty years ago, the Choctaw Nation had seventy-four employees. Today, that number has risen to more than 1,500. The Choctaw Nation has flourished as an Indian tribe, growing not only in membership (the third largest Indian tribe in the U.S.), but also financially (the tribe's net worth has grown to $98 million today). The Choctaw Nation has thirteen tribal community centers located throughout the ten and one-half counties of southeastern Oklahoma, as well as several tribally operated day care centers and family investment centers. Whether working with other tribes and governments, or working on an individual basis, the Choctaw Nation makes a conscious effort to seek more opportunities to help Choctaws prosper.

National Cowboy Hall of Fame & Western Heritage Center

The National Cowboy Hall of Fame and Western Heritage Center, located in Oklahoma City, began as the dream of Kansas City businessman, Chester A. Reynolds. He envisioned a monument to all men and women who helped shape the history of the American West. Reynolds died in 1958 before that vision could become a reality, but the many supporters he had recruited remained committed to the project. On June 26, 1965 the museum opened its doors to the public.

Today the museum is triple its original size and is served by a dedicated staff and strong volunteer force. Not only does the elegant, sprawling complex feature a superlative collection of classic and contemporary western art, including works by Charles M. Russell, Frederic Remington, Nicolai Fechin, Albert Bierstadt, Thomas Moran, and other noted masters, but it also is the keeper of thousands of rare artifacts and objects reflecting our western heritage.

As travelers approach the museum heading east on I-44, they glimpse an impressive scene of galloping horses across the museum's west exterior. Tom Ryan, a Midland, Texas artist, designed this 350-foot, three-dimensional "remuda". At the Hall's entrance, *Welcome Sundown*, a larger-than-life sculpture by Hollis Williford, depicts a weary cowboy at day's end. From the moment the doors swing open to the wide, deep foyer, the historic journey begins. "Breathtaking" is the frequent description of James Earle Fraser's majestic 18-foot sculpture, *End of the Trail*, which captures the essence and spirit of this national institution.

Standing guard at the permanent and temporary art galleries in the Edward L. Gaylord Exhibition Wing is the "Canyon Princess," a white marble cougar descending a mountainside. The eighteen-foot sculpture, which weighs 16,000 pounds, was donated to the museum in 1995 by famed Colorado sculptor Gerald Balciar.

One of the most intriguing elements in the museum's design is an early nineteenth century cattle town, Prosperity Junction. When visitors leave the glass and marble corridor to enter the dimly lit Livery Stable, they step into another era, where for some, a walk down Main Street recalls nostalgic memories of small town life. For others, it is an opportunity to see things used a hundred years ago, and experience a time gone by. Light streams from two-story buildings along the boardwalk. The raucous sound of a player piano spills out of the saloon, only to be countered by the soothing strains of organ music from the church at the other end of town. Authentically reproduced structures, filled with materials from the museum's collections, are open for browsing.

Across the hall, in the setting of a rough-hewn ranch building, The American Cowboy Gallery focuses on cowboy culture and ranching traditions. In the anteroom, an authentic chuck wagon from the Matador Ranch in

Top: End of the Trail *by James Earle Fraser.*

Below: Welcome Sundown *by Hollis Williford greets visitors at the entrance to the National Cowboy Hall of Fame.*

Channing, Texas, sits on a raised platform covered with prairie vegetation. An audio component narrates chuck wagon history and cowboy life on the range as life-like figures depicting a chuck wagon cook and two cowboys prepare the campsite.

In the gallery's cowboy culture section, a bunkhouse exhibit contains items common to the cowboy's life. Here, another audio-component allows visitors to push red checkers on a game table to activate a round of cowboy songs and tall tales. An impressive display of American stock saddles lines one wall. And perched on wide oak pedestals down the center of the room, life-size monochromatic mannequins feature cowboys from various ethnic backgrounds.

A special room, subtly lit and richly embellished, accentuates the Hall's exquisite rawhide collection by master braider Luis Ortega. A native Californian, Ortega's weaving of leather and horsehair into horse gear such as bridles, reins, headstalls, quirts, hackamores, and lead ropes became a rare art. In a pass-through to the ranching side of the gallery, exhibit cases display cowboy fashion from work clothes to Sunday best.

The story of ranching history in America begins with the Spanish vaquero. Love of elaborate design in clothing and equipment is reflected in the unique exhibit found in the ranching heritage room. Major cattle trails and famous ranch brands etch their way across the room on a 900-square-foot granite map. A touch-screen kiosk provides information on historic cattle trails. On the log-beamed ceiling high above hang two magnificent deer antler chandeliers.

A treatment of ranching traditions lines the south wall and includes Charro, early Texas, trail drives, open range, and the introduction of barbed wire, which significantly changed the ranching industry. More than 1,300 examples of the museum's 8,000-piece barbed wire collection are on display. A simple, but effective treatment of the branding iron also is addressed as paramount to the changes in cattle ranching at the turn-of-the-century.

The Western Entertainment Gallery is a colorful mixture of the evolution of the "western" from early motion pictures to the contemporary treatment of the genre. Among the cowboy heroes included in the Hall's prized collection of western performer memorabilia are Tom Mix, Gene Autry, Walter Brennan, Joel McCrea, Barbara Stanwyck, and Richard Farnsworth. John Wayne, the ultimate film cowboy, is duly honored in the exhibit. On display are firearms and bronzes donated to the museum by The Duke. Film clips from classic Wayne movies play in a small theater setting. Costumes and props from western television series and made for television movies are on exhibit. Both Barbara Stanwyck's petite black riding apparel worn in *Big Valley*, and the saddle used by Tom Selleck in the award-winning TNT production, *Last Stand at Saber River*, were donated by the actors.

✧

Top, left: An authentic chuck wagon from the Matador Ranch.

Top, right: The Main Street of Prosperity Junction.

Below: The American Cowboy Gallery focuses on cowboy culture and ranching traditions.

Plains; the role of trappers, traders and trailblazers in opening the West; the frontier experience of the U.S. Army; and the impact of hunting in the West. Other Grandee objects are exhibited in adjoining galleries and in the western town installation.

Access to the east wing can be had by retracing one's steps back to the main foyer, but in good weather most visitors prefer to make the trek across the outdoor spaces. Inside the Children's Cowboy Corral, a building separate from the museum proper, little buckaroos are encouraged to touch, see and hear cowboy life. The hands-on prairie day environment created around a twenty-foot artificial rock canyon invites children to experience the West as it was when cowboys and ranges were plentiful. Young children can dress up in boots and spurs, chaps and vests, climb on saddles, and slip into a cowboy tent.

Pretend pots of stew and an authentic chuck wagon let little ones make-believe they are "cookies," the nickname for chuck wagon chefs. A Texas longhorn steer creates photo opportunities that few parents can resist. Motion sensors trigger sounds of birds and howling coyotes that breathe a touch of wildlife into this educational retreat.

The charm of the Atherton Garden, and the graceful waterfall and natural vegetation in the Norma Sutherland Garden provide a peaceful transition to the quiet walkways and gentle streams that meander through the Freda Hambrick Garden.

Leonard McMurry's thirty-two-foot bronze of Buffalo Bill proudly overlooks Oklahoma City from Persimmon Hill. Nestled within this lush green landscape are interesting sculptures and historical tombstones. Here lies the famous bull, *Tornado*, conquered only once in his career by rodeo champion Freckles Brown. Famous bucking broncs *Midnight* and *Five Minutes to Midnight* also rest in the gardens, their graves marked by tombstones etched with poetic epitaphs.

The Western States Plaza, a connecting courtyard for the museum's two wings, offers a stunning view of James Earle Fraser's *End of the Trail*. At the south end of the plaza, a heroic-sized reproduction of Frederic Remington's bronze, *Coming Through The Rye*, accentuates

✧

The William S. and Ann Atherton Gallery. Emigrants Crossing the Plains *by Albert Bierstadt is featured on the exhibition wall.*

Inside The American Rodeo Gallery, visitors feel the excitement of a 1950s arena. The familiar voice of famous rodeo announcer Clem McSpadden invites one and all to experience rodeo in all its pageantry. From one chute, a determined cowboy hangs precariously onto a bucking bronc. And from another, a Brahma bull angrily awaits his escape.

Small monitors deliver actual film footage of six individual rodeo events and explain the scoring methods for each. Bleachers offer a spot to rest while taking in a brief video history of the pure American sport narrated by Reba McEntire and McSpadden. Display cases highlight the many facets of rodeo life—famous men and women in rodeo, rodeo clowns, trick roping and riding, Wild West Shows, and rodeo promoters. In a special section of the gallery, eight exhibit cases are dedicated to the history of women in rodeo. Costumes and trophies are spectacular under dramatic fiber optic lighting. Recent inductees into the Rodeo Hall of Fame also are honored, and touch-screen kiosks encourage visitors to explore rodeo's great champions through a long list of biographies and photographs.

The Joe Grandee Museum of the Frontier West is among the most extensive collections of western Americana held in a public institution. Noted artist, Joe Ruiz Grandee gathered more than 5,000 artifacts over some forty years, using many of the objects to translate authentic details to his narrative paintings. Four topical areas are interpreted in the Grandee Gallery: Native American life on the Great

the colorful row of flags that represent the seventeen western states. Glass walls in the full service restaurant, Dining on Persimmon Hill, allow a broad view of the plaza with its pool and bubbling fountains.

Also housed in the east wing of the building is the S. B. "Burk" Burnett Board Room, the Robert and Grace Eldridge Gallery, the administrative offices, and The Sam Noble Special Events Center. Named for its benefactor, Oklahoma oil man and philanthropist, Samuel Roberts Noble, the 16,000-square-foot room is considered by many to be Oklahoma City's crown jewel. On its walls hang the *Windows to the West*, five monumental landscape paintings. Each scene, divided into three panels and measuring eighteen feet high by forty-six feet wide, were created by the masterful strokes of Albuquerque, New Mexico artist Wilson Hurley.

Along the corridor that connects the east wing with the entrance to the museum is the Nona Jean Hulsey Rumsey Art Education Center and the Dub and Mozelle Richardson Theater. Within these spaces, children and adults are offered workshops and art classes. Beneath the public viewing area lies the Research Center, which serves as informational underpinning for the Hall's entire education and exhibition program. It also serves as a primary research facility for a variety of in-house publications, as well as for authors and publishers of western-related subjects from across the nation. Presently, the Research Center serves as the repository for 15,000 volumes of western Americana, 100,000 photographic images in various formats, 3,000 linear feet of manuscript material, and a variety of related ephemera.

Through special events, the Hall seeks to involve the local community and peoples from across the nation and the world. Each spring, during the Western Heritage Awards, the highly coveted bronze Wrangler Award is presented to outstanding works in literature, film, television, and music. Among the noted celebrities who have participated in the prestigious ceremonies are Tom Selleck, Robert Urich, Tommy Lee Jones, John Ritter, Jon Voight, John Wayne, Jane Russell, Richard Farnsworth, James Garner, Barry Corbin, Brad Johnson, Michael Martin Murphey, Don Edwards, Red Steagall, Vince Gill, and Reba McEntire.

In June, the Prix de West Invitational Exhibition and Sale provides buyers with an opportunity to purchase paintings and sculptures from America's finest contemporary western artists. The prestigious show remains on exhibit for three months for the enjoyment of visitors. Popular events with the local community are the Chuck Wagon Gathering and Children's Cowboy Festival, the Cowboy Poetry Gathering, and Michael Martin Murphey's Cowboy Christmas Ball.

Although this national memorial to the American cowboy is dedicated to preserving the rugged individualism and romantic spirit of the frontier, the National Cowboy Hall of Fame and Western Heritage Center covers a broad spectrum. The museum is committed to interpreting the heritage of the American West for the enrichment of the public through educational programs, outstanding exhibitions, *Persimmon Hill*, the museum's award-winning magazine, and through its popular annual events.

Above: Serving up golden biscuits at the annual Chuck Wagon Gathering.

PHOTO COURTESY OF JOE OWNBEY.

Below: The Wyoming Suite—The Lower Falls at Yellowstone *by Wilson Hurley.*

GILCREASE MUSEUM

✧

Top: Gilcrease Museum.

Below: Oil painting by Thomas Eakins— Frank Hamilton Cushing.

PHOTO COURTESY OF THE THOMAS GILCREASE INSTITUTE OF AMERICAN HISTORY AND ART, TULSA, OKLAHOMA.

Nestled in the Osage Hills, with a spectacular view of the wooded countryside in one direction and Tulsa's impressive skyline in another, Gilcrease Museum is home to the world's largest collection of art of the American West. This vast collection may be attributed to the vision of one man, Thomas Gilcrease.

Thomas Gilcrease was born on February 8, 1890 in Robeline, Louisiana, the eldest of fourteen children. Soon after his birth, the family moved to Indian Territory because his mother's Creek Indian ancestry enabled the family to live in the Creek Nation. At the turn of the century, when the federal government distributed the tribe's lands into private ownership, Gilcrease received 160 acres about twenty miles south of Tulsa. His allotment was in the Glenn Pool area, which, in 1905, became Oklahoma's first major oil field.

When he was sixteen, Thomas Gilcrease questioned his parents' judgment on his behalf and sued for his majority rights. He demonstrated his ability to take care of himself and by the age of twenty-one, having been a farmer, banker, storekeeper, and oil speculator, was a millionaire.

In 1914, Gilcrease purchased a native sandstone house and twenty-three acres northwest of downtown Tulsa. It became home for him and his first wife, Belle Harlow and their two sons, Thomas Jr. and Barton. The couple later moved to California and their marriage ended in divorce in 1926.

Primarily self-educated, Gilcrease was an avid reader and schooled himself in eight languages. In the 1920s and 1930s, he traveled extensively in Europe. Visiting the world's great museums, Gilcrease began an avocation, which led him to become a zealous collector.

Gilcrease returned to his Tulsa home in 1929 with his second wife, Norma Smallwood, Oklahoma's first Miss America. That year their daughter, Des Cygne L'Amour was born. His second marriage was brief and ended after lengthy litigation in 1939.

The Gilcrease Oil Company had been chartered in Oklahoma in 1922, but in 1937 it moved to San Antonio, Texas. By 1943, a portion of the Gilcrease collection was on public view at the oil company's offices.

The Thomas Gilcrease Foundation was also established in Texas during this time. Its purpose was to assist in the development of the art collection, which included the G. R. G. Conway compilation of Hispanic documents and the Philip G. Cole collection of Western Art consisting of works by Frederic Remington, Olaf Seltzer, and Charles Russell, among others.

In 1949, Gilcrease decided to move his collection back to Tulsa where it was displayed in a converted carriage house and garage next to his home. By then, he had acquired the majority of Alfred Jacob Miller's works, more than 2,500 of Thomas Moran's oils, watercolors, sketches, prints, and documents, and approximately sixty George Catlin paintings. The museum's collection of Catlins is second in size only to the Smithsonian's.

Gilcrease was a patron of American Indian artists and supported the careers of Acee Blue Eagle, Woody Crumbo, and Willard Stone. Interested in American Indian artifacts, Gilcrease accumulated more than 250,000 significant items.

A group of American documents from the Rosenbach Foundation was purchased in 1949. This group included the only known certified copy of the Declaration of Independence still in existence; one of nine originally produced and signed by Benjamin Franklin and Silas Deane. The original is in the National Archives in Washington, D.C. The Gilcrease collection houses more than 100,000 documents, manuscripts, rare books, and maps.

The Thomas Gilcrease Institute of American History and Art, better known as Gilcrease Museum, was deeded to the City of Tulsa in 1955 after Tulsans voted by a three to one margin to approve a $2.25 million bond issue. The bond money was used to pay off the debts incurred while Gilcrease was acquiring the art and artifacts in his collection. In return, he committed oil revenues to the City until the original bond amount was reimbursed. The funds were then to be used for maintenance. Over the years, these revenues far exceeded the original purchase price. In 1985, the Gilcrease Foundation made the final payment, reimbursing Tulsa for the 1954 bond issue. Thus, the collection became a gift from Thomas Gilcrease to the people of Tulsa.

Until his death on May 6, 1962, at the age of seventy-two, Gilcrease lived in the home next door to the collection and the museum he created and loved. He and his parents are interred in the mausoleum on the museum grounds.

The Thomas Gilcrease Museum Association was formed on October 24, 1956 and functions through an agreement with the City of Tulsa to promote and enhance Gilcrease Museum and its exhibitions, publications, special events, and educational and community outreach programs.

The facility and collection continue to expand. The building has grown from the original American Indian-style "long house" design to its present 127,786 square feet on 460 acres.

Outstanding examples of American fine arts at the museum include paintings by Winslow Homer, James McNeil Whistler, Thomas Eakins, William Merritt Chase, George De Forest Bruch, Benjamin West, John Singleton Copley, John Vanderlyn, and Thomas Sully. The art collection includes over 10,000 paintings, drawings, prints and sculptures by 400 artists from colonial times to the present.

Among the documents found in the Gilcrease collection is one of the earliest letters from America, written by Christopher Columbus' son, Diego Columbus, and dated January 12, 1512.

The oldest book in the museum was printed in 1494. The collection also includes an original manuscript of the Cherokee syllabary written by Sequoyah, the man who developed it.

There are more than 300,000 archaeological and ethnographical objects, historic and contemporary beadwork, ribbonwork, and clothing in the Gilcrease collection. With more than forty Native American communities represented, some of the largest Gilcrease holdings come from Arkansas, Oklahoma, Illinois, the Southwestern United States and Meso-America.

Today, just as in 1949, Thomas Gilcrease's legacy lives on. Gilcrease Museum, through its collections, is dedicated to bringing art, history, and people together to discover, enjoy, and understand the diverse heritage of the Americas.

✧

Above: Bronze statue by Frederick Remington—The Mountain Man 1903.

PHOTO COURTESY OF THE THOMAS GILCREASE INSTITUTE OF AMERICAN HISTORY AND ART, TULSA, OKLAHOMA.

Below: Oil painting by Joseph H. Sharp—Council Call of the Crows.

PHOTO COURTESY OF THE THOMAS GILCREASE INSTITUTE OF AMERICAN HISTORY AND ART, TULSA, OKLAHOMA.

Oklahoma Heritage Association

The Oklahoma Heritage Association is a non-profit organization dedicated to preserving Oklahoma's unique heritage and promoting enhanced pride in the state. Privately funded primarily by membership contributions, the Association has a statewide membership and a board of directors to establish policies and monitor operations.

The Association, which today pursues a wide range of activities, was founded in 1927 by Anna B. Korn of El Reno, who motivated a group of prominent citizens to meet on September 27, 1927, at the state capitol to create the Oklahoma Memorial Association and the Oklahoma Hall of Fame. The first Hall of Fame Banquet and Induction Ceremony took place on November 16, 1928, and thereafter the event has been held annually.

The Association obtained its first permanent home in 1970, when the family mansion of Judge and Mrs. Robert A. Hefner, Sr., and its contents, including priceless antiques and Judge Hefner's unique cane and bell collections, were donated. In 1971, the organization, led by full-time volunteer Stanley C. Draper, Sr., changed its name to the Oklahoma Heritage Association and expanded its membership, board of directors, and activities. Draper launched a successful building fund drive, which provided for the restoration of the home and establishment of the Anthony Oklahoma Heritage Gardens. The Oklahoma Heritage Center was opened to the public in 1972. In addition to the mansion, the facility now includes an Oklahoma Heritage Galleria, the Hefner Memorial Chapel, the Anthony Gardens, and offices for the staff. Draper added Association President Dr. Paul Lambert to the staff in 1973.

Top: The Oklahoma Hall of Fame Medallion is presented to the oustanding individuals who are inducted annually into the Oklahoma Hall of Fame.

Below: The Oklahoma Heritage Center, located at 201 Northwest 14th in Oklahoma City, is the headquarters of the Oklahoma Heritage Association.

By the time of his death in 1976, Draper, with the help of outstanding Oklahomans from throughout the state, had built a solid organization. Expansion of programs continued. For example, *The Judge: The Life of Robert A. Hefner,* was published in 1976, launching the Oklahoma Trackmaker Series of biographies. By 1999, the Association had published approximately sixty books in five different series.

The Association also established an awards program to recognize volunteers and local organizations statewide for their outstanding work in preserving Oklahoma's unique state and local heritage. A major education program was developed which involved the establishment of Oklahoma Heritage Week activities, with a poster competition for elementary students, essay competition for seventh, eighth, and ninth grade students, and a poster/ essay competition for high school students. In addition, the Association established the Fred Jones Oklahoma Heritage Scholarship competition to enable high school students to earn college scholarships based on demonstrated

knowledge of Oklahoma history. Moreover, the Nichols Oklahoma Heritage Scholarship, sponsored by John W. and Mary D. Nichols, annually provides $10,000 over four years to an outstanding student of Oklahoma History.

Other activities have included the creation of major awards for outstanding Oklahoma history teachers, the publication of *Oklahoma: Magazine of the Oklahoma Heritage Association*, and various social events and activities. The Association also sponsors special projects, such as the Oklahoma Heritage Map Series and the "Oklahoma" video, a fifty-seven-minute presentation on the dynamic heritage and geographic beauty of the state. The video has been shown throughout North America on The Nashville Network and on The History Channel as well as statewide on Oklahoma Educational Television Authority (OETA) and numerous commercial television stations within the state.

The original program of the Association, the Oklahoma Hall of Fame, has continued to grow in stature through the years. For a number of years, the black-tie event has been televised statewide by the OETA.

The current chairman of the board of the Association is Lee Allan Smith of Oklahoma City. Vice chairmen of the board are selected from each of the Association's membership zones, and directors are also elected from each of the membership zones. The Association functions with a small staff and a large number of volunteers. In addition to Lambert, full-time employees as of September 1999 include Gini Moore Campbell, Judy Dawson, Dr. Kenny A. Franks, Chandra Hastings, Pat Hensley, and June Wilson. Ron Hendricks, Anita Hood, and Sharon Shepler were part-time employees.

A time honored axiom states that "a society that forgets its past is doomed to repeat it." It is the mission of the Oklahoma Heritage Association to ensure that Oklahomans do not forget.

✧

Top: Governor Frank Keating posed with the winners of the Oklahoma Heritage Week competitions.

Below: A representative sampling of the Association's publications.

Oklahoma State System of Higher Education

✧

Number of Institutions:

1943-1944*: 18

11 senior colleges

7 junior colleges

1998-99: 25

2 comprehensive universities

11 four-year regional universities

12 two-year colleges

Enrollment:

1939-1940* total enrollment	27,000
1997-1998 total enrollment	209,371

Degrees Conferred:

1958-1959*	8,012
1997-1998	23,902

(Includes associate, bachelor's, master's, doctoral, and first professional degrees)

Total Budget:

1943-1944*	$6.3 million
1999-2000	$1.4 billion

(Includes state appropriations, tuition and fees, and gifts and grants)

** First year for which information is available.*

From the territorial days to the beginning of the new millennium, the Oklahoma State System of Higher Education has played a major role in the development of the Sooner state.

Oklahoma higher education began before Oklahoma became a state. The first territorial legislature created three institutions of higher learning in 1890. These institutions provided territorial residents with instruction in agriculture, mechanical arts, teacher training, liberal arts and the professions. Between 1890 and 1901, four institutions of higher learning were established in Oklahoma Territory. When the Oklahoma and Indian Territories combined to become a state in 1907, the first State Legislature duplicated Oklahoma Territory's higher education facilities in Indian Territory and spread access to public higher education throughout the new state.

From those early beginnings, Oklahoma's system of higher education has grown to include twenty-five public colleges and universities, ten constituent agencies and two higher education programs.

Throughout history, Oklahoma higher education has offered a broad range of programs and services enabling the state and its citizens to prosper. For example, state colleges and universities have improved Oklahomans' quality of life through lifelong learning opportunities, career preparation and research activities.

Through partnerships with business and industry, Oklahoma higher education has also greatly contributed to the state's development by attracting new businesses and developing specialized courses and programs to meet the changing needs of Oklahoma's work force. Serving as cultural centers for different regions of the state, many campuses also offer theater productions, art exhibits and speakers' forums for students and citizens in the communities they serve.

The Oklahoma State System of Higher Education is the state's legal structure for providing public collegiate-level programs and services. Established on March 11, 1941, the state system joins the areas of functions, programs of study, standards of education and finance among the campuses. Coordinating the system is the Oklahoma State Regents for Higher Education.

Comprised of nine members appointed by the governor and confirmed by the state Senate, the State Regents serve nine-year overlapping terms. The Regents set academic standards, determine functions and courses of study at state colleges and universities, grant degrees, recommend to the state Legislature budget allocations for each institution, and recommend proposed fees within limits set by the Legislature. Additionally, they manage twenty-three scholarships and several special programs.

In cooperation with the Office of State Finance, the State Regents also operate OneNet, the state's telecommunications and information network. They also oversee the Oklahoma Guaranteed Student Loan Program, which guarantees loans made to students by the private sector.

Serving as chancellor for the State Regents and chief executive officer for the State System is Dr. Hans Brisch, who assumed these positions in 1987. He follows a great heritage of leadership that includes Dr. M. A. Nash, 1943-1961; Dr. E. T. Dunlap, 1961-1981; Dr. Joe A. Leone, 1982-1987; and Dr. Dan S. Hobbs, 1987-1988.

In the last decade, under the leadership of Chancellor Brisch and the State Regents, Oklahoma higher education has undertaken several innovative and ambitious initiatives to build a nationally competitive higher education system and meet the state's diverse and changing needs. System accomplishments include higher standards for students and teachers, the creation of a world-renown state telecommunications network for education and government, and stronger partnerships with business and industry and other government agencies.

Most recently, the State Regents announced *Brain Gain 2010*, a long term plan to move Oklahoma from the bottom to the top one-third of all states for its educational and economic performance by increasing the proportion of Oklahoma's population with a college degree.

For more information on Oklahoma's System of Higher Education, please visit www.okhighered.org.

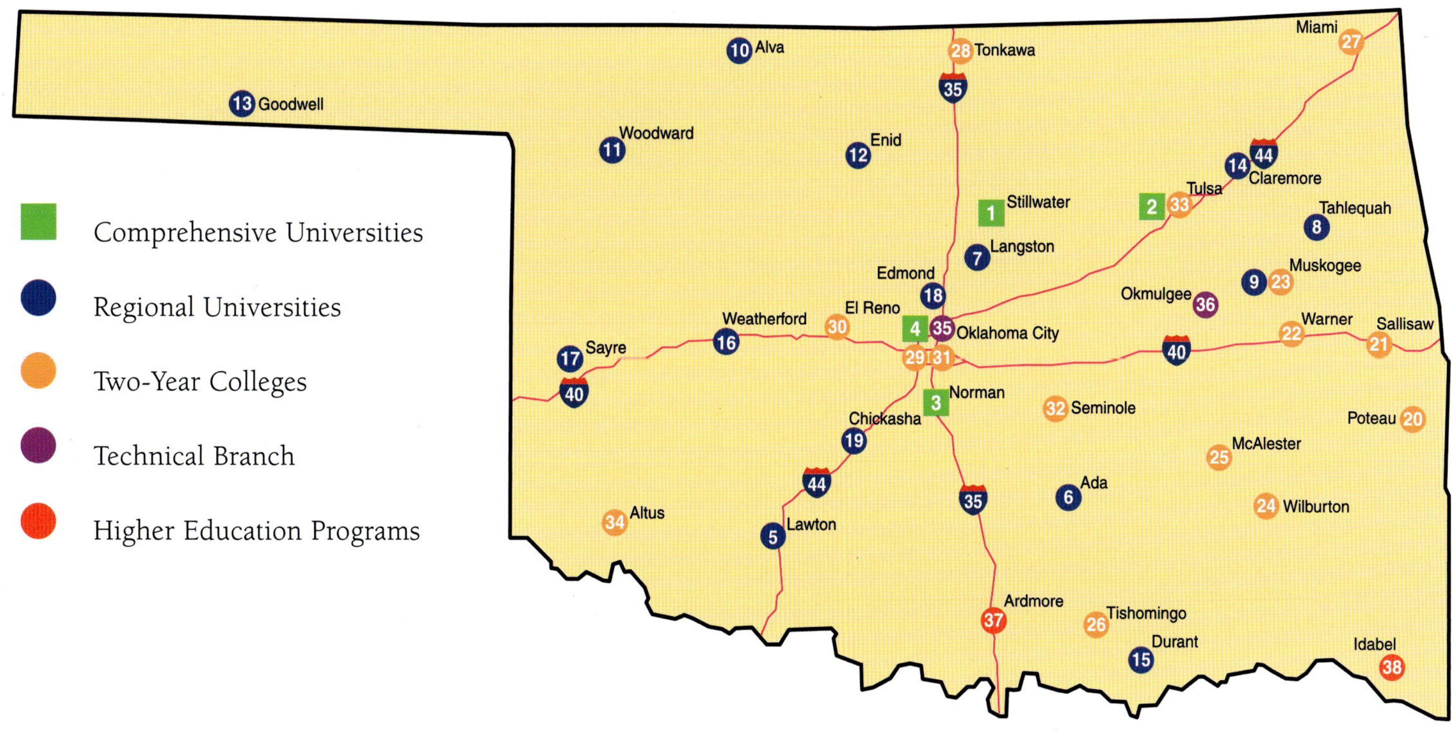

COMPREHENSIVE UNIVERSITIES

1. Oklahoma State University, Stillwater
    2. OSU-Tulsa
3. University of Oklahoma, Norman
    4. OU Health Sciences Center, Oklahoma City

REGIONAL UNIVERSITIES

5. Cameron University, Lawton
6. East Central University, Ada
7. Langston University, Langston
8. Northeastern State University, Tahlequah
    9. Northeastern State University, Muskogee
10. Northwestern Oklahoma State University, Alva
    11. Northwestern Oklahoma State University, Woodward
    12. Northwestern Oklahoma State University, Enid
13. Oklahoma Panhandle State University, Goodwell
14. Rogers State University, Claremore
15. Southeastern Oklahoma State University, Durant
16. Southwestern Oklahoma State University, Weatherford
    17. Southwestern Oklahoma State University, Sayre
18. University of Central Oklahoma, Edmond
19. University of Sciences & Arts of Oklahoma, Chickasha

TWO-YEAR COLLEGES

20. Carl Albert State College, Poteau
    21. Carl Albert State College, Sallisaw
22. Connors State College, Warner
    23. Connors State College, Muskogee
24. Eastern Oklahoma State College, Wilburton
    25. Eastern Oklahoma State College, McAlester
26. Murray State College, Tishomingo
27. Northeastern Oklahoma A&M College, Miami
28. Northern Oklahoma College, Tonkawa
29. Oklahoma City Community College, Oklahoma City
30. Redlands Community College, El Reno
31. Rose State College, Midwest City
32. Seminole State College, Seminole
33. Tulsa Community College, Tulsa
34. Western Oklahoma State College, Altus

TECHNICAL BRANCHES

35. Oklahoma State University Technical Branch-Oklahoma City
36. Oklahoma State University Technical Branch-Okmulgee

HIGHER EDUCATION PROGRAMS

37. Ardmore Higher Education Program, Ardmore
38. McCurtain County Higher Education Program, Idabel

Western Heights School District

The Western Heights School District originated with the consolidation of five rural elementary schools. The Council Grove, Camel Creek, Will Rogers, Wheatland, and New Hope schools were combined in 1959 to form the Council District. The name was changed to Western Heights because of the Western Electric Plant under construction in the district at the time of consolidation. Western Heights is now composed of four elementary schools (Pre-K-5), one middle school (grades 6-8), one high school (grades 9-12), and Western Heights Academy, an alternative school (grades 4-12). The district serves approximately 3,200 young people and employs 230 teachers. The goal of the district is to "educate every student for success."

Indeed, that is exactly what Western Heights' track record shows. In 1996, the District invested in a state-of-the-art fiber optic network and PCs for its high school, junior high school, and four elementary schools. Joe Kitchens, superintendent of Western Heights School District, stated "Technology is critical to our ability to deal with larger class sizes, busier teachers, and shrinking budgets." Western Heights has outfitted each of its 230 classrooms in the district with a Pentium processor-based PC, a color television for classroom computer viewing, ISDN phone connections, Internet access, Intel ProShare conferencing, and Linnaeus classroom management software. The District strives to provide teachers important tools for individualizing lesson plans, collaborating with one another and with outside experts, and staying in touch with busy parents. These classroom computers also give students access to unlimited outside resources and the ability to communicate with students around the world.

In April of 1998, Western Heights School District's Western Heights Public Schools' Student Computer Collaboration Project became part of the Smithsonian Institution's Permanent Research Collection on Information Technology Innovation at the National Museum of American History. At a point in our nation's history when thousands of schools will be able to become networked for the first time through new government technology initiatives and the discounts provided by the new "E-rate" program, Western Heights stands as a model school district in an underprivileged area that dared to dream big dreams—and then through passion and hard work managed to achieve them. The District has built community support for its technological revolution, broke through a maze of regulatory and legal hurdles, turned a staff that was computer illiterate into technological pros, forged closer relationships with local industry, and, most importantly, improved the learning experience for both students and teachers.

Testimonies of this student/teacher relationship through technology speak volumes regarding its importance in the District today. A Western Heights teacher, on leave while battling cancer, was able to continue communicating with her students via ISDN-based videoconferencing. She could stay in touch with the substitute teacher and assist with lesson planning or other instructional concerns. A Western Heights High School student was injured in a domestic shooting and was unable to attend school for four months. However, the

✧ *Above: Wyland Foundation/student mural.*

student was able to keep up with his classes through ISDN-based video-conferencing and progressed to the next grade level on schedule. Several Western Heights Elementary School students found a three-foot long prehistoric mammoth bone while playing near a local river. Using the Internet connection in their classroom, they were able to research and identify the source of the bone, learn more about prehistoric times, and use video-conferencing to share their discovery with students at other district schools—a far cry from the traditional classroom show-and-tell.

Western Heights School District is culturally diverse and serves an economically depressed area. Sixty-nine percent of the students who attend district schools have household incomes low enough to qualify them for the federal government's school lunch program. The video-conferencing and Internet access provide these students with learning experiences that their parents would not be able to provide them, such as trips to zoos, museums, parks in distant cities across the nation or around the globe.

So impressive is the implementation of this program that Bill Gates, the billionaire developer of Microsoft, devotes four pages of a chapter on creating "connected learning communities" in his newest release, *Business @ the Speed of Light*, to praising Western Heights. Gates calls it "perhaps the leading technology-driven curriculum in the country."

The beauty of the district is that it is small enough to know students and large enough to provide exciting opportunities for the staff and students. Western Heights provides accelerated classes, honors classes, remedial classes, inclusive special education environment, alternative school, school-to-work initiatives, ROTC, athletics, and a variety of clubs and after school activities. The district is known throughout the State of Oklahoma for its outstanding vocal and instrumental music programs, receiving national and state honors. Athletes compete annually on the state level with the 1998 baseball, softball, track, cross country, and wrestling teams advancing to the state playoffs.

Western Heights is at the forefront of today's ideas about providing a full-rounded educational experience for students. They're meeting their goal to "educate every student for success", and then some. Members of the Board include President Jann Davenport; Vice President Robert Everman; Members Reyna Helms, Lynda Howeth, and Eddie Wood. The Administration Staff consists of Superintendent Joe Kitchens; Assistant Superintendent Lisa McLaughlin; Director of Finance/Support Services Steve Freeman; Director of Personnel/Staff Development Rita Morgan; and Technology Coordinator Daryl McDaniel.

Metro Tech

Metro Tech is Education for Success in Oklahoma City.

Created by a vote of Oklahoma City citizens on June 26, 1979, Metro Tech Vocational Technical Centers serve students of the Oklahoma City and Crooked Oak Public Schools as well as adults at seven training sites throughout the metropolitan area. Metro Tech is one of twenty-nine area vo-techs in Oklahoma's nationally acclaimed vocational system.

Vocational classes, conducted in the high schools, have been available to Oklahoma City school children since the 1930s. The federal Vocational Education Act of 1963, however, allowed the State of Oklahoma to authorize "area vocational schools," an innovative approach to consolidating vocational training to provide high-tech equipment, modern facilities, low tuition, and small class sizes.

Area Vocational-Technical School District Number 22 was created to comprise the identical, 184-square mile territory of Oklahoma City School District I-89. In 1988, the name was changed to Metro Tech Vocational Technical Centers.

The main Springlake Campus, purchased in 1982, is a ninety-five-acre property located at 1900 Springlake Drive, the former site of Springlake Amusement Park. For sixty years the park was home to carnival entertainment, dancing, and roller coaster rides. Today, students substitute the "Thrills of Yesterday" for the "Skills for Tomorrow." With more than thirty-five full-time programs and over 200 short-term courses, Metro Tech provides career training and enhancement to some 20,000 students each year.

Full-time programs range from Aviation Maintenance Technology and Business and Computer Technology to Practical Nursing. High school juniors and seniors attend vocational classes for half a day at no cost and receive credit toward graduation as well as college credit for many programs. Adults may attend on a part-time or full-time basis at an extremely affordable tuition rate. Financial aid is available to qualified applicants. Career or academic tests offered through the Assessment Center help students make informed career decisions.

Short-term day, evening, and weekend classes focus on skills and interests that make an immediate difference in someone's life. These classes may range from two hours to over seventy hours.

In addition, customized training programs for business and industry can be tailored to specific company needs. Teleconferencing services, job profiling, and small business assistance are all available to Oklahoma City-area businesses. The Business Conference Center provides facilities for meetings and special events in a lovely, wooded setting.

Metro Tech is unique in its ability to provide quality education, training, and related services dedicated to preparing diverse populations for successful employment in a competitive, global economy.

✧

Top: Metro Tech students may choose from more than thirty-five full-time programs ranging from Aviation Maintenance Technology to Business and Computer Technology. The nationally acclaimed Aviation Career Center, located on the Will Rogers World Airport, offers a quality training experience for aviation-related careers.

Below: Full-time programs are available at no cost to high school juniors and seniors. Tuition for adults may be as low as $1 per hour with financial aid available to qualified applicants. College credit may be earned in many areas.

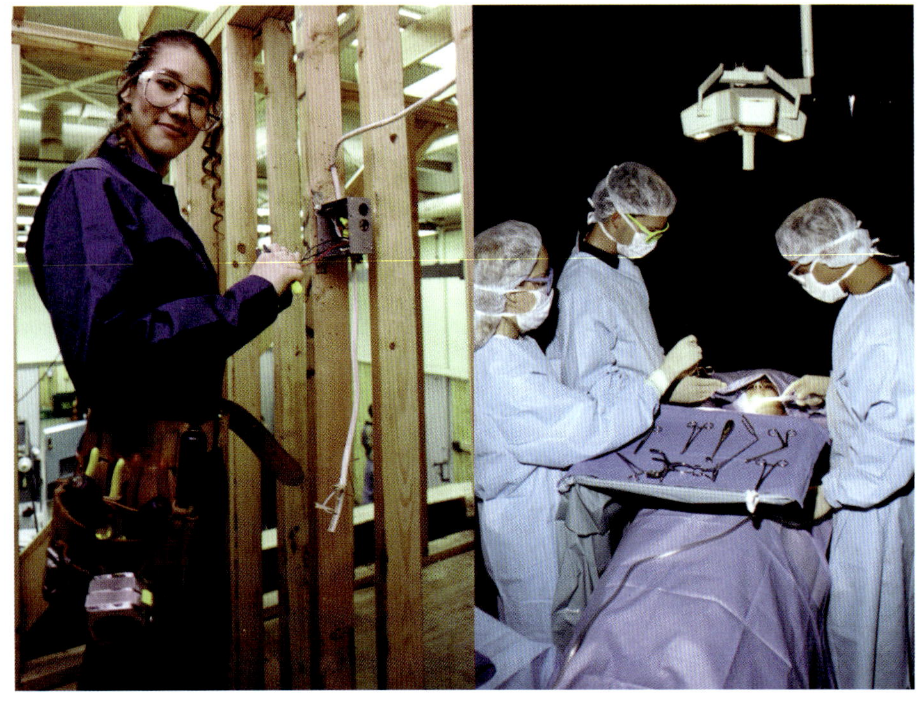

Oklahoma State University

On December 24, 1890, Oklahoma Territorial Governor George W. Steele signed legislation establishing the Territorial Agricultural and Mechanical College, present-day Oklahoma State University, at Stillwater, Oklahoma. It was a goal that local residents had sought ever since Oklahoma Territory had been created six months earlier, in May of 1890. Considered the choicest of the three territorial collegiate institutions because of its federally funded agricultural experiment station, Stillwater residents, on May 5, 1891, approved a $10,000 bond issue for construction of the school. The following month, after rejecting an alternate location in Perkins, a gubernatorial commission selected a 200-acre site for the school just to the north and west of downtown Stillwater.

Classes started on December 14, 1891, in Stillwater's Congregational Church and later were moved to the community's Presbyterian Church. Partitions on rollers were used to create classrooms. There were no buildings until four wood-frame structures for the experiment stations were completed in 1892. The first permanent structure, the College Building, better known as Old Central, was dedicated in June of 1894, and 144 students enrolled for classes.

From this modest beginning more than a century ago, Oklahoma State University has grown into an international institution covering more than 840 acres with 200 permanent buildings, offering classes to almost 21,000 students at its Stillwater campus. A far cry from its 1896 graduation class of six.

In addition to its Stillwater campus, the Oklahoma State University system maintains its OSU-Okmulgee campus, established in 1946; the OSU-Oklahoma City campus, opened in 1961; and the College of Osteopathic Medicine in Tulsa established in 1988. In 1999, the OSU-Tulsa campus was established. To further expand its service to Oklahomans, OSU has formed a number of business partnerships to offer graduate programs to professionals at Halliburton Services in Duncan, Phillips Petroleum in Bartlesville, Seagate Technology in Oklahoma City, and Conoco in Ponca City. Enrollment at the branch campuses and other programs pushes OSU total student involvement to almost 26,000.

A modern comprehensive land grant university serving the state, nation, and international communities, Oklahoma State University presents programs of the highest academic standards for candidates for bachelor, master, and doctoral degrees as well as degrees in Doctor of Osteopathy and Doctor of Veterinary Medicine and specialists in selected educational fields. OSU boasts a two million-volume library, modern research facilities, an active student lifestyle, and a nationally recognized athletic program. However, even with its international academic status, Oklahoma State University has not lost sight of personal student awareness and stresses the interests and needs of individual students. As a result, Oklahoma State University's graduation rate percentage for full-time, degree-seeking, undergraduate students is one of the highest in the nation.

Top: Old Central, the oldest building on campus. On the National Register of Historic Places, the interior of this campus showplace has been recreated to look as it did in 1894. Photographer: Andy Maxey.

Below: OSU, America's #1 Best Buy in Colleges and Universities is known for its academic and research excellence, its record 42 national athletic championships, and its friendliness.

NORTHERN OKLAHOMA COLLEGE

Northern Oklahoma College, with dual campuses in Tonkawa and in Enid, Oklahoma, is a prominent community college serving the educational, cultural and economic needs of the state and region. Its eight academic divisions offer thirty-nine programs leading to an associate of arts, associate of science or associate of applied science degree.

Created by the Oklahoma Territorial Legislature in 1901, Northern was founded in Tonkawa as University Preparatory School to ready young people in the north central region of the territory for entry into the University of Oklahoma at Norman. In 1920, Northern became one of the first junior colleges in the nation.

In June 1999, Northern purchased the buildings and grounds of the defunct historic and stately Phillips University campus in Enid, expanding its services to its Enid area students and providing for growth of its academic, student and community programs. Approximately 1,000 of Northern's more than 2,500 students are served at the Enid campus.

Under the direction of its eleventh president, Dr. Joe Kinzer, Jr., Northern employs approximately 150 full-time faculty and staff personnel. With an annual operating budget of more than $9 million, Northern makes a valuable economic contribution to the region.

Northern is a leading institution in Oklahoma for technology in the field of multimedia, computer and interactive television (ITV) courses. The college is making the commitment to reach students through the information highway by telecasting courses to several business/industrial and institutional off-campus sites.

Top: The historic Marshall Building dominates the Northern Oklahoma College Enid campus.

Below: Northern's Performing Arts Center on the Tonkawa campus is home to theatrical and musical productions throughout the year.

PHOTOS COURTESY OF DR. GLENN COPE.

Fully accredited by the North Central Association of Colleges and Schools, Northern is committed to the highest standards of performance in education programs, including academic transfer, career training and opportunities for lifelong enrichment. Northern became the first two-year college in Oklahoma to receive accreditation from the Association of Collegiate Business Schools and Programs, which recognizes Northern's Business program as one of the best in the state. In addition to the new Multi-Media and Digital Communications and Native American Leadership programs, Northern has added Process Technology, Music-Business, Athletic Training and Respiratory Care degree programs.

With emphases on small class sizes, quality faculty members, an extensive library and the latest in technological equipment, the educational experience exemplifies academic excellence. Numerous social and goal-oriented clubs and organizations furnish opportunities to develop the leadership and interpersonal skills essential for success in an increasingly technological world. Intercollegiate and intramural sports, fine arts programs and exhibitions, dramatic production, and outside scholars and speakers enrich the college experience.

Visitors will enjoy the exquisitely landscaped grounds of Northern's campuses, which are among only thirteen affiliate garden members of the Oklahoma Botanical Garden and Arboretum statewide system. The beautiful campuses provide a tranquil environment for the serious learning experience.

University of Science and Arts of Oklahoma

In 1996, USAO initiated the first consortium of its kind in Oklahoma to bring graduate programs to Chickasha and share USAO's unique offerings through interactive television. USAO serves southwest Oklahoma as a hub-site on the telecommunications network known as OneNet.

"USAO's faculty is credited with much of our success," says USAO President Roy Troutt. With 84 percent having earned the highest degree available in their field, USAO ranks well above average in faculty preparedness.

With record budgets that exceed $14 million, USAO serves as a significant player in the area's economy. It is one of the largest non-industrial employers in the area.

One of the few institutions with a statewide mission, USAO's student population comes from fifty-four counties across Oklahoma, thirteen other states, and twenty-two countries. Last year's freshman class was the largest ever. A $7.5 million Student Life Facilities Initiative is making dramatic changes in dormitories and the Student Center.

✧

Left: Nearly 500 students compete for fun and cash on the first Thursday each April in USAO's huge Montmartre Sidewalk Chalk Art Festival. Campus sidewalks become colorful murals during the all-day event with live music and academic competitions for high school students.

Chickasha is home to one of the most unique universities in the country—a school that ranks academically among the top liberal arts colleges in America, says *U.S. News and World Report's Best Colleges Guide*. The University of Science and Arts of Oklahoma has served as Oklahoma's public liberal arts college for more than ninety years.

From a list of nearly 1,800 schools surveyed, USAO has been named in "America's 100 Best College Buys" for quality and value—for the second year in a row.

Still another national publication calls USAO one of the friendliest to minority students. The *Winds of Change Annual College Guide for American Indians* recently profiled USAO in its national report.

One review says students at USAO find "a private college education at a public college price."

One of the reasons USAO has gained a national reputation in recent years is its progressive attitude about technology. A state-of-the-art computer network on campus links students and faculty to the Internet and to libraries around the world.

A decorated World War II Navy veteran, whose career in education spans six decades, Troutt has led USAO for twenty-five years. Under his tenure, the University's budget has quadrupled, its enrollment has doubled; and its liberal arts mission has become the point of unity that guides its future. During the Troutt years, USAO has gained a national recognition for its curriculum, called "a model for all other colleges in Oklahoma," by one former chancellor.

USAO has been accredited continuously since 1920—the third college in Oklahoma to earn accreditation—by the North Central Association. From statehood to a new millennium, USAO has served proudly.

Oklahoma School for the Deaf

Life for students on the campus of Oklahoma School for the Deaf in Sulphur, Oklahoma is one that every young person, deaf or hearing, should have the opportunity to experience as they strive to reach their educational goals. Located on thirty-seven acres, deaf or hard-of-hearing students from ages two to twenty-one have found a place to prepare for the demands of life through active, caring instructors and a number of social activities available throughout their stay.

✧

Above: Oklahoma School for the Deaf high school students perform "The Wizard of Oz."

Below: Oklahoma School for the Deaf, 1914.

The illustrious history of Oklahoma School for the Deaf actually had its beginnings in two Oklahoma towns established before statehood. Lura Rowland, a graduate of the Arkansas School for the Blind, established the International School for the Blind and Deaf at Fort Gibson, Indian Territory, in June of 1897. The school closed in 1907. Another facility, The Territorial School for the Deaf, was established by H. C. Beamer and Ellsworth Long in Guthrie in 1898 and remained there until 1908, when the school was relocated to Sulphur and renamed Oklahoma School for the Deaf. As buildings were constructed, the school continued to grow and the Industrial Arts Department printed the first edition of *The Deaf Oklahoman* in September, 1909.

Over a century later, Oklahoma School for the Deaf is accredited by the Oklahoma Department of Education and the Department of Vocational and Technical Education and offers psychological evaluations, audiological evaluations, distribution of captioned educational films and videotapes, parent education, vocational and career education, art festivals, and sign language instruction. A dedicated staff leads approximately 250 students at sites including Oklahoma School for the Deaf campus in Sulphur, the transitional living center in Oklahoma City, and a number of regional preschools across the state. In 1982, the school was legislatively designated as a statewide resource center for the needs of deaf children and school districts across the state. Today, Oklahoma School for the Deaf offers a low teacher-pupil ratio to maximize learning and is proud to have over ninety-five percent of its faculty holding master's degrees.

November of 1998 marked the centennial celebration of Oklahoma School for the Deaf and the publication of a history entitled *In Our Own Words*. Throughout the extensive work, which includes photos and detailed memories of many OSD alumni, it is apparent that this school is more than just an institute of education. Oklahoma School for the Deaf has chosen to not only educate but also to create a place in which students can flourish and work to fulfill their goals and dreams.

In commemoration of the school's centennial, the Oklahoma House of Representatives presented a citation that reads in part, "The Oklahoma School for the Deaf has served as an educational and cultural center which has enhanced the lives of countless deaf people throughout the state."

University of Oklahoma

Created by the Oklahoma Territorial Legislature in December of 1890 on forty acres and $10,000 in bonds voted upon by the citizens of Cleveland County, the University of Oklahoma would see its first building rise from the tall prairie grass just south of Norman in December of 1892. Under the leadership of President David Ross Boyd, three faculty members were hired to set a standard of academic excellence that would be at the core of one of the most impressive public universities of our time. Today, the university has eighteen colleges offering 134 bachelor's degrees, eighty-two master's degrees, fifty-one doctoral degrees, four graduate certificates, and one professional degree. Operating with a budget of approximately $797 million, the University of Oklahoma enrolls more than 27,000 students on campuses in Norman, Oklahoma City, and Tulsa and has approximately 1,830 full-time faculty members.

From the first commencement ceremonies of 1898, the University of Oklahoma has moved forward with the ambition to realize the dreams of its students and faculty. The School of Medicine was opened in 1910 and was later renamed the OU Health Sciences Center. From 1912 to 1923 construction of seven new buildings on the university campus were completed and enrollment climbed from 876 to 5,091, and faculty from 94 to 220.

University presidents such as William Bennett Bizzell, George Lynn Cross, and William S. Banowsky directed OU through amazing times of unprecedented growth, integration, political upheaval—momentous events that have allowed the university to carve an honorable place in the annals of Oklahoma history.

At the threshold of a new millennium, the University of Oklahoma stands ready to provide the best educational experience for students through excellence in teaching, research and creative activity, and service to the state and society. Under the leadership of David L. Boren, former governor and U.S. senator, OU is on its way to becoming a pacesetter for American higher education. The University of Oklahoma ranks in the top twenty public universities in the nation in private endowment. According to the Chronicle of Higher Education, OU became the first public university in Oklahoma history to rank in the top twenty.

The university has achieved a brilliant academic record among our nation's universities and has the highest number of Oklahoma Regents Scholars, National Merit and National Scholars per capita of any public university in the United States. They were named to the Fiske Guide to Colleges list among the nation's top 300 best higher education institutions.

OU is also one of only eight Division IA universities in the nation to receive the CHAMPS award for preparing student-athletes for life. The award is based on academic excellence, athletic excellence, personal development, community service and career development. The Sam Noble Oklahoma Museum of Natural History, scheduled to open in spring 2000, will be the largest university-based museum of natural history in the country with over five million natural history artifacts.

More information and video uplinks regarding the University of Oklahoma can be found on their Web site at www.ou.edu.

✧

Top: Multi-colored chrysanthemums grace OU's Pitman Parterre.

Below: The Peggy V. Helmerich Great Reading Room in Bizzell Memorial Library.

Northeastern State University

✧

Right: Stately Seminary Hall stands as the University's historic centerpiece, a reminder of the University's deeply rooted traditions and commitment to excellence in education.

Below: Northeastern's beautifully wooded 200-acre campus is a place like no other, where students have the chance to make lifelong friendships while pursuing a quality education.

In the spring of 1909 plans were underway for the final commencement ceremonies of the Cherokee National Female Seminary. It was a time of transition—on March 6, the Oklahoma legislature had passed an act that allowed the state to purchase the seminary from the Cherokee tribal government and create Northeastern State Normal School. For more than half a century, Cherokee female students had been educated in liberal arts at the institution that was founded as a free, compulsory public school system by tribal fathers. Under new ownership and direction, the institution would become coeducational and expand its horizons to include two branch campuses and classes at various satellite locations throughout northeastern Oklahoma—far beyond anything its founders could have envisioned.

Over the years Northeastern State University has developed from an institution that served 500 students during its first year of operation in 1909 to a comprehensive regional university that serves more than 8,000 students.

"Our success and growth are due in large part to a strong sense of traditionalism among those we serve and commitment among our faculty and staff to maintain the standards that originated with our roots almost 150 years ago," said NSU President Larry Williams.

The story of Northeastern actually began in 1851 when the first male and female seminaries opened at Park Hill. Except for a period between 1856 and 1871, the female seminary remained open until it burned to the ground on Easter Sunday, 1887. The Cherokee Council chose to rebuild on a forty-acre site north of Tahlequah.

Northeastern State Normal School's educational program consisted of four years of high school and two years of college-level study. In 1919, the institution became Northeastern State Teacher's College and began offering a four-year curriculum leading to a bachelor's degree. Twenty years later, the state legislature authorized changing the name to Northeastern State College and within two years the institution came under the governance of the Oklahoma State System of

Higher Education. In the 1950s, Northeastern emerged as a comprehensive state college, broadening curriculum to include liberal arts subjects and adding a master's level of study for elementary and secondary teachers. The 1970s expanded programs to include business and selected service areas. In 1974, the name was officially changed to Northeastern Oklahoma State University and later, in 1985, to Northeastern State University.

Experiencing phenomenal growth, NSU has since opened a branch campus in Broken Arrow and the Mike Synar Center for Technology in Muskogee, as well as renovated the College of Optometry, For Northeastern State University students this growth translates into more opportunities.

"We want people to be aware of the role Northeastern State University has played in the growth and development of this area," said President Williams. "This institution impacts the quality of life among citizens throughout northeastern Oklahoma, whether they choose to pursue a degree, participate in continuing education classes, or attend sporting events, cultural programs or entertainment shows that fill our calendar year-round.

"Without a doubt NSU is a living, breathing institution that plays a crucial role in many areas, both in the classroom and beyond."

Oklahoma City Public Schools

✧

Left: Although Oklahoma City Public Schools has a rich history, the district is always looking forward. The inception of magnet schools on the elementary level uses theme-based study enhanced by today's latest technology to ensure tomorrow's leaders recieve a quality education. Students apply to magnet schools in the district according to their preference of study.

Below: One of the city's first permanent school buildings, Emerson School, was built in 1894 and is still in use today.

Only six weeks after homesteaders rushed into Oklahoma Territory, schools were opened in Oklahoma City. A small metal tablet marks the site at 116 Park Avenue where the first school opened on June 1, 1889. At that time the schools operated as subscription, or private schools, at the cost of $1 per month for one child. Rates were cut to seventy-five cents for two or more children from the same family.

Men and women who had previous teaching experience conducted classes in tents such as the large structure donated by St. Luke's Methodist Church, or under the shade of large cottonwood trees. Needless to say, school enrollments increased so rapidly that provisions had to be made for more spacious accommodations.

The first school board was formed in February of 1891 under the direction of President Delos Walker and Secretary Major D. D. Leach. The 1891-92 school term, led by School Superintendent R. A. Sullins, was four months long and included an enrollment of 865 children of all ages.

In the fall of 1893, Oklahoma City's first high school was organized at the barracks of the military reservation at 4th and Walnut. The U.S. Government later granted the site to Oklahoma City Schools and Irving School was built at that location. From 1911 to 1916, the Irving School became the State Capitol when the capitol was moved from Guthrie. Two rooms were added for the Governor's office and the building was used until the present capitol complex was finished in 1916. In 1894, one of Oklahoma City's first permanent schools, Emerson School, was built at 7th and Walker. This building is still used by the district as an alternative school.

Today, the Oklahoma City Public Schools includes ninety sites and serves approximately 40,000 students from pre-kindergarten through twelfth grade. The District has 6,000 employees and serves a geographic area encompassing approximately 290,000 people in 184 square miles in two counties and six municipalities. Oklahoma City Public Schools has an annual operating budget of approximately $223 million.

With a mission to educate students for life-long learning and responsible living, Oklahoma City Public Schools plays an integral role in the community as a model urban school district. Students are self-confident and able to compete in a global society as they are led by highly motivated, professionally competent employees working with parents and the community to provide innovative and effective education programs.

Tulsa Community College

Tulsa Community College, originally Tulsa Junior College, opened its doors to a first class of 2,800 students in September, 1970. Now the largest two-year institution in the state, TCC has been nationally recognized as one of America's outstanding community colleges, ranking 26th out of more than 1,200 community colleges in number of annual graduates. With 111 degree programs, TCC serves approximately 30,000 students annually in college credit and continuing education programming on the Metro, Northeast, Southeast, and West campuses, a conference center, and a number of satellite and corporate training locations.

Since 1970, TCC has served more than 350,000 students, with classes scheduled days, nights, and weekends. For nearly thirty years, TCC's mission has been to provide a wide range of educational opportunities for its students. That commitment has earned the College national recognition.

The Carnegie Foundation for the Advancement of Teaching has recognized three Tulsa Community College faculty members as Oklahoma Professors of the Year: Ms. Kay Miller in 1994; Dr. Carla Thompson in 1995; and Ms. Sally Bright in 1998. The College was one of eleven community colleges in the nation to be recognized in 1999 by the National Science Foundation for "exemplary" K-12 teacher preparation.

TCC provides innovative learning opportunities. The College serves nearly 2,000 students per semester in distance learning classes, including on-line courses, interactive television, and telecourses. TCC's Fast Track accelerated degree program enables students to earn an associate's degree in approximately one year. Academic excellence includes three superior Phi Theta Kappa honor society chapters. In 1999, TCC's Northeast Campus Alpha Zeta Alpha Chapter was named No. 1 among all 1,400 international Phi Theta Kappa chapters, and Stephanie Wright, former Alpha Zeta Alpha president, was elected Phi Theta Kappa International President.

Ongoing academic excellence requires a commitment from both college and community. The advice and expertise of 562 representatives of local businesses, government, health, and public service agencies who serve on TCC advisory committees keep programs viable and graduates prepared. For example, TCC graduates in the Allied Health programs have an average ninety-eight percent pass rate on national licensure exams.

TCC supports Tulsa's economic development through corporate training that benefits Tulsa companies. Corporate training at TCC includes classes in business, communications, computer science, international language (TCC offers fourteen languages), international business, and other areas as needed by corporate clients.

TCC makes a dynamic impact on thousands of people's lives every day. The administration, faculty, and staff on each of TCC's four campuses remain dedicated to providing students the best of the College's teaching and talents.

Top: Newly elected Phi Theta Kappa International President Stephanie Wright and TCC Vice President Dr. Tom McKeon display some of Alpha Zeta Alpha Chapter's twelve awards won during the international convention.

Below: 1998 Oklahoma Professor of the Year Sally Bright (in red) is surrounded by some of the many students who benefit from her teaching abilities.

The Magnolia Oil Company baseball team at company's camp in the Healdton Oil Field in 1919. The team has just won the Oklahoma Petroleum Baseball League's 1919 championship. Among the team's members were: Rommie Davis, Colie Kimberlin, Bill Morgan, Lee Hudson, and Oscar Norvell.

COURTESY OKLAHOMA HERITAGE ASSOCIATION.

YMCA of Greater Oklahoma City

✧

Top: In the early 1900s, YMCA camping programs gave boys an opportunity to escape hot summers in the city and experience the woods and natural rivers and lakes.

Below: YMCAs were the place for teens to gather and socialize during the 1950s and early 1960s.

1889 was an amazing year for the people who would one day call themselves Oklahomans. Spring rains ushered in the first of five land runs that would open Oklahoma Territory to pioneers dreaming of a boundless future and a peaceful place to raise a family. Within a month, on May 14, 1889, the first of two meetings was held to organize the Young Men's Christian Association in the new territory. Approximately forty men assembled to elect officers at a second meeting held on June 2, 1889. By Christmas of 1889, the new organization had gathered 100 members.

One hundred and ten years and 17,000 members later, the YMCA of Greater Oklahoma City, a not-for-profit agency, remains one of the metro area's leading social service organizations, constantly striving to expand its horizons and discover new and better ways to meet the needs of the community. With outstanding programs and services implemented throughout nine area locations, the YMCA stands firmly upon a tradition of putting Christian principles into practice through programs that build a healthy spirit, mind, and body for all.

The history of the YMCA in Oklahoma City reflects the importance of strong leadership and the well-established and deeply committed service of volunteers. The first officers were elected in June 1889. For the next fifteen years, meetings were held in various temporary locations throughout the city such as the Overholser Opera House and the University of Oklahoma. The first permanent headquarters were established on the second floor of the newly constructed Baltimore Building in 1904. The rented space included several rooms and a gym. However, the noise of gymnasium activity created such a disturbance at the drug store on the first floor of the building that the gym had to be closed and the equipment stored.

In October 1916 a fund raising committee was established for construction of a permanent building and a $300,000 campaign was launched. A site was chosen at 125 Northwest 2nd Street and construction began in June 1917. The new facility was opened on

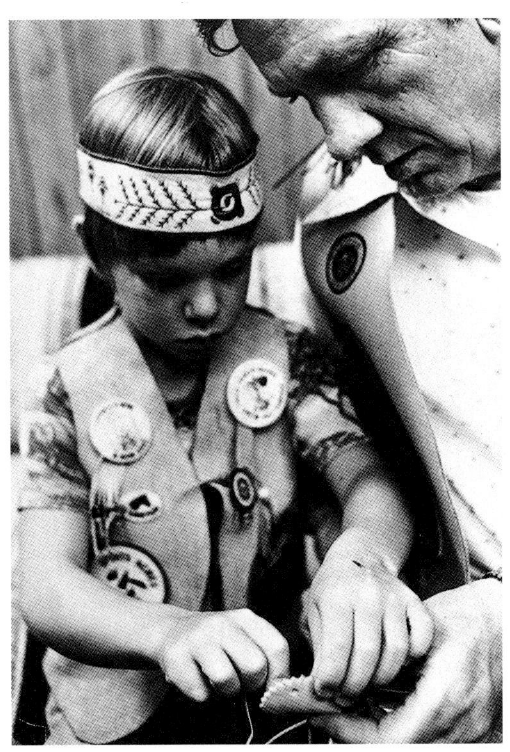

December 1, 1918. Incorporated in 1917, the first permanent board of directors was elected on January 2 of that year and included A. J. McMahan as president; E. K. Gaylord as vice-president; Charles W. Gunter, recording secretary; and Walter D. Caldwell, treasurer.

January 21, 1947 was the kickoff date established by such notable committee members as E. K. Gaylord, Robert S. Kerr, and C. R. Anthony for the Memorial Building Fund Campaign. This campaign would eventually raise $1,500,000 for construction of a new YMCA building at 5th and Robinson and an African-American branch at 4th and Stiles. *The Daily Oklahoman* ran front-page notices for months on end as money was raised for the project. With much support and a generous welcome from the community and businesses, construction of both YMCA buildings was completed in the Spring of 1952.

As the decade of the 1950s came to a close and the city's population began to grow and expand, the YMCA formed branch locations throughout the metro area and created a corporate board and staff to oversee the organization. Today the Association consists of eight branches located throughout the metropolitan area and Camp Classen, a 2,400-acre resident camp located in the Arbuckle Mountains near Davis, Oklahoma.

One of the most significant moments in the history of the YMCA of Greater Oklahoma City came on April 19, 1995 as the downtown building and corporate offices of the organization were destroyed along with many other buildings by what historians have labeled as the worst act of terrorism on U.S. soil in our nation's history. As the corporate board and staff came together to determine whether to rebuild or move to a new location, Mr. Edward L. Gaylord offered the historic Oklahoman building at 500 North Broadway and the property adjacent to it. His generous gift was accepted and work on a new downtown campus was completed in April, 1999.

Programs that provide for healthier lives in the community have been at the core of the YMCA since its creation by George Williams in London, England on June 6, 1844. Formed in response to unhealthy social conditions arising in the big cities at the end of the Industrial Revolution, the YMCA continues to set the standard for many community-based programs and services. Between 400 and 600 employees and over 1,000 volunteers oversee a wide variety of programs including youth sports, aquatics, camping, child care, and health and fitness that remain at the center of the YMCA of Greater Oklahoma City's goals for its 17,000 members and 30,000 program participants. More than fifty program sites operating in schools and churches throughout the metro area also provide a variety of programs including before and after school child care for more than 700 children between the ages of six and twelve. The YMCA of Greater Oklahoma City is the largest provider of this important program in the state.

The YMCA of Greater Oklahoma City carries today as its motto these words: "We build strong kids, strong families, strong communities." Serving as a vehicle to instill the values of caring, honesty, respect, and responsibility among its members and participants, the YMCA remains a beacon to the Oklahoma City community and its most dynamic community service organization. Surely those pioneer Oklahomans of 1889 would be honored to see over a century later what was born under that endless Oklahoma sky on a beautiful Sunday afternoon in June.

✧

Top: The Indian Guide program grew in the 1970s out of a desire to foster companionship between fathers and sons while learning about Indian lore.

Below: YMCA sports leagues have always emphasized positive personal growth, skill development, teamwork, participation, and fun!

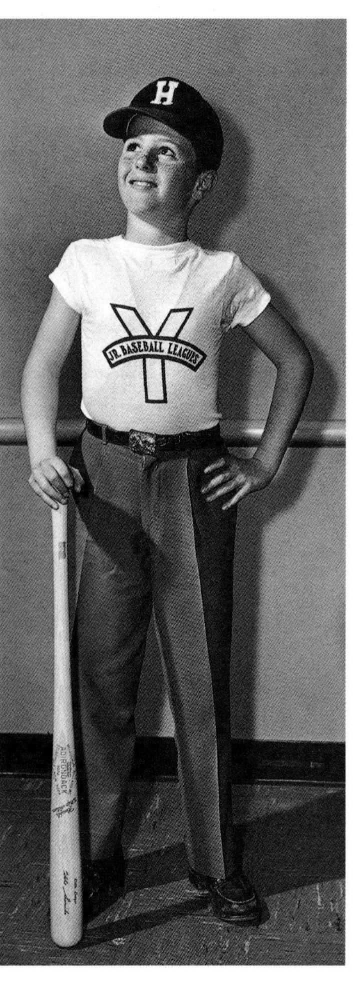

McCasland Foundation

The roots of the McCasland Foundation go back to the pioneer Oklahomans, J. C. McCasland and his wife, Olivia Atkins McCasland, who met and married in 1892 in Hope, Indian Territory. It was there that their three children, Hugh, Thomas Howard, and Naomi were born. J. C. worked in a post office and store, which he purchased after a few years. In 1898, the McCaslands moved into Duncan, Oklahoma Territory, where J. C. went into business partnership in another mercantile store. This was the type of business he pursued successfully during his entire career, which ended with his retirement in 1945. Both J. C. and Olivia had been school-teachers and they were vitally interested in the education of their children. J. C. served on the Duncan School Board and both he and Olivia were active in community and cultural affairs in Duncan throughout their lives.

Their son, Thomas Howard McCasland, founder of the McCasland Foundation, was the first young man from Duncan to attend the University of Oklahoma where he was an outstanding student and athlete. The year was 1912 and he was captain of the OU basketball team and played end on the football team, as well. He held scoring records in basketball and the record for catching the longest pass in football—all of which stood until the late 1940's. Upon graduation, he received the Silver Letzeiser Medal for outstanding academic achievement.

During World War I, Howard served in France with the Ninetieth Artillery Division. Upon his return in 1919, he planned to attend law school but became intrigued with the oil field activity connected with the Empire Field near Duncan. He began to buy and trade oil leases, which led to a long and profitable romance with the oil industry.

In 1926, Howard married Vivian Fullwood. They had two children, Mary Frances Maurer Michaelis, and Thomas Howard McCasland, Jr.

In 1946, Howard and a group of associates formed Mack Oil Company. The success of this business was to benefit the McCasland Foundation and, in turn, Duncan and the State of Oklahoma. In 1950, Howard and Vivian established the McCasland Foundation. This was only one of the many avenues Howard

Top: J. C. and Olivia Atkins McCasland, Oklahoma pioneers.

Bottom: Howard and Vivian Fullwood McCasland, Founders of the McCasland Foundation.

used to put into action the ideal, instilled by his parents, that you should give something back to the community where you live in return for the generous opportunities you have received. He has handed this creed down to his descendants.

He worked very hard for the benefit of Duncan and was an active leader in many worthwhile projects in Duncan for decades. In 1959, the Chamber of Commerce named him Duncan's Top Senior Citizen. He supported a number of organizations related to the oil industry and was named Outstanding Oil Man of the Year in 1972 by the Oklahoma Petroleum Council. Howard was also very interested in the University of Oklahoma, serving in numerous volunteer capacities. He was chairman of the board of the OU Foundation for eight years, and served on the board for thirty years, until his death in 1979. OU honored him with its highest award, the Distinguished Service Citation, in 1959. Howard was elected to the Oklahoma Hall of Fame in 1975. This honor climaxed a lifetime of public service and philanthropy that benefited Duncan and the State of Oklahoma.

The present trustees of the McCasland Foundation are all family members, with the one exception of a long time employee of Mr. McCasland's, who was the first executive director of the Foundation. The trustees of the McCasland Foundation have tried to carry on the ideals of Vivian and Howard McCasland. Their interests lie in the fields of education and health, the cultural life of the state, social services and the special interests of Oklahoma communities, especially in Western Oklahoma.

The McCasland Foundation sponsors a substantial scholarship program, is a patron of the Oklahoma Foundation for Excellence, and has supported major projects at most of the Oklahoma colleges and universities. The Foundation has placed endowed chairs or professorships at the University of Oklahoma, Oklahoma State University and Cameron University. Grants have been given to the University of Oklahoma for the Library, the School of Music, the Sarkeys Energy Center, and the Fred Jones Museum of Art. Other major grants have been given to the Oklahoma Museum of Natural History and the Oklahoma Summer Arts Institute.

Duncan projects hold a special interest for the trustees. In 1977, the Duncan Public Library was built through the McCasland Foundation. Both Duncan Regional Hospital and the Simmons Center (Duncan's Community Center) have received generous grants. The Foundation's most recent project in Duncan has been a larger than life-size bronze statue "On the Chisholm Trail" by native Oklahoma sculptor, Paul Moore, commemorating the American Cowboy and the Chisholm Trail. The adjoining visitors' center traces the history of the Chisholm Trail and the cowboys who rode it. It is free to the public and open every day.

The future of Oklahoma is vitally important to the trustees of the McCasland Foundation. They are looking ahead to further opportunities for serving the needs of Oklahoma in the new century.

✧

Left: On the Chisholm Trail by sculptor Paul Moore is located in Duncan.

Right: An artist's rendering of the Duncan Public Library built through the McCasland Foundation.

The Samuel Roberts Noble Foundation, Inc.

Located in Ardmore along Sam Noble Parkway, The Noble Foundation is one of the fifty largest private foundations in the United States, with an endowment of nearly $1 billion. Since its inception in 1945 through 1999, the Foundation has made $430 million in charitable expenditures. About half of that was spent in support of the various research and consulting operations performed internally, and about half has been in direct grants to educational and charitable organizations. Over 200 employees carry on the work of the Foundation.

It was the memory of broken land and broken people that spurred Lloyd Noble to create such a foundation. Noble had witnessed first-hand the best of times and the worst of times when it came to farming in Oklahoma. In the early part of the twentieth century, cotton was king. When the planting, growing, harvesting and, most of all, the weather were right, people prospered. It wasn't long before agriculture was an empire and Ardmore was its hub, one of the world's leading inland cotton-shipping centers. However, difficult weather conditions and wasteful farming practices left the land drained of agricultural potential. Hardware merchants Sam and Ed Noble, Lloyd Noble's father and uncle, became creditors to many destitute farmers.

Noble helped out in the family business, worked as the church janitor and he received his teaching certificate in 1914. After teaching in one-room schools for two years, he entered the University of Oklahoma as a pre-law student. During this time, oil was discovered on his mother's farm, and the oilfield proved an irresistible magnet. Persuading his mother, Hattie, to co-sign a note for $20,000 to finance a drilling company, Lloyd Noble began his lifetime oil career. He used his success from the oil business to help others in the name of his father—"the most charitable man I have ever known"—as he announced the creation of The Samuel Roberts Noble Foundation on September 19, 1945. Following his untimely death on February 13, 1950, at the age of fifty-three, the bulk of Lloyd Noble's estate was left to the Foundation.

Top: Noble Foundation founder Lloyd Noble.

Below: The Noble Foundation's Agriculture Division provides consulting services to more than 700 cooperators.

The primary focus of The Samuel Roberts Noble Foundation has always been agriculture. Today, the Foundation's two operating divisions—the Agriculture Division and the Plant Biology Division, carry out that focus.

The Agriculture Division uses an approach that includes a team of specialists in livestock, forages, soil fertility, agricultural economics, wildlife and fisheries, and horticulture to provide consulting services to "cooperators"—farmers and ranchers who have requested assistance in planning and implementing improved agriculture plans. The consultation is free to those who request it, and today the Foundation maintains records on over 700

active cooperators. The Division operates five farms with diverse soils and environmental conditions for demonstrating various management practices and conducting research field tests. The farms serve as field laboratories and classrooms, where new methods and techniques are observed and evaluated and where proven practices are demonstrated.

The Plant Biology Division was established in 1987 and is devoted to performing both fundamental and applied research on plant-microbe interactions and genetic modifications of plants for improved disease resistance and production potential. Collaborative efforts with the Agriculture Division provide an opportunity to see the fruits of cutting-edge molecular research reach the nation's farmers and ranchers. After more than ten years, the Plant Biology Division's programs on plant natural product biochemistry, disease resistant mechanisms, mychorrhizal interactions, and plant virus movement and evolution are well-established and leading to exciting new discoveries.

A new area of interest is Forage Biotechnology, which is dedicated to the development of a cool season perennial forage grass that is tolerant to Oklahoma's climate. The group also bridges and augments the basic science of the Plant Biology Division and the applied science of the Agriculture Division.

A Biomedical Division was established in the early 1950's with an early focus on cell nutrition and the basic metabolism of cancer cells. Several major areas of work were pursued in the Division's laboratories in Ardmore until 1992 when the Division was relocated to the Oklahoma Medical Research Foundation in Oklahoma City. The forty-year history of the Biomedical Division produced many important studies, including work on the cancer-fighters L-asparaginase and interleukin-1.

Today, the Foundation devotes about half its resources to the internal operating divisions, with the other half used for grants. The primary granting emphasis is on capital funding for higher education and basic health research. Most grants are made in Oklahoma, with the University of Oklahoma and Oklahoma State University being major recipients.

Noble had a vision of improving the quality of life for Oklahomans. More than a half century later this continues to be a driving force behind the innovative work and the charitable projects funded by The Noble Foundation.

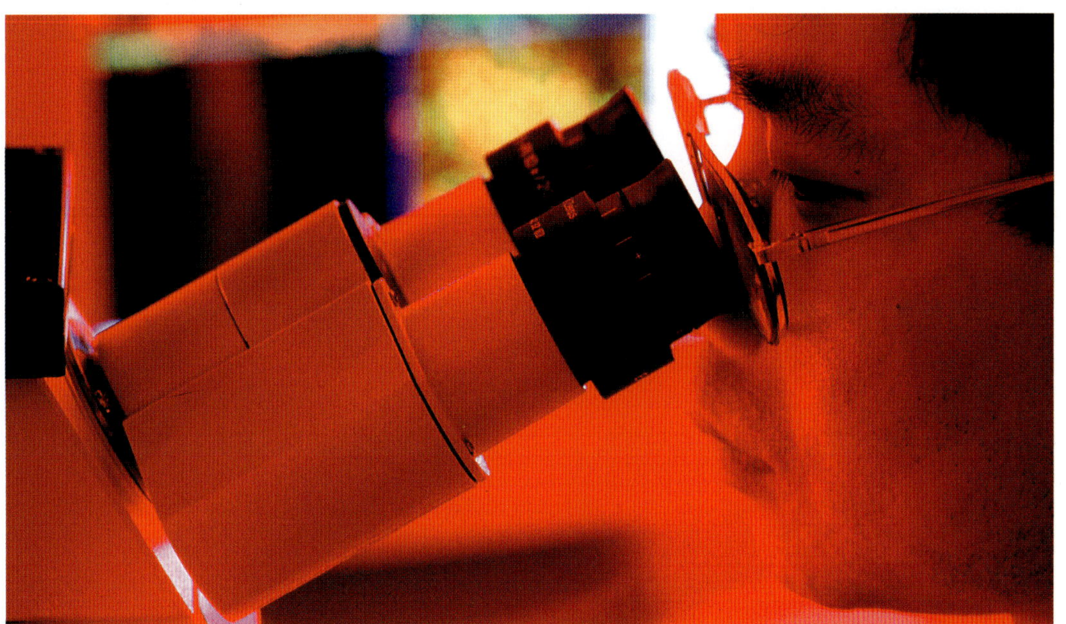

✧

Top: The Noble Foundation is composed of three major divisions: Administrative, Agriculture and Plant Biology, all of which are represented in this photo.

Left: A senior research associate in The Noble Foundation's Plant Biology Division operates a confocal laser-scanning microscope. The microscope allows NF scientists to obtain extremely clear images from living plant tissue.

Spring Creek Coalition

"The journey of a thousand miles begins with the first step." The Spring Creek Coalition (SCC) is a locally led grass roots organization formed in 1994 to preserve the most pristine large Ozark stream in Oklahoma. Spring Creek winds its way for thirty-four miles through the beautiful wooded hills of Mayes, Delaware, and Cherokee Counties. Threats to its water quality such as stream bank erosion, urbanization and illegal dumping have united concerned people. Together they are making a difference in the 124,000-acre watershed and blazing a trail for landowners in other watersheds.

The highest priority is to empower landowners with knowledge. The Coalition utilizes state agency services to teach about forestry, fertilization, wildlife habitat, waste management, groundwater, and other subjects affecting the integrity of Spring Creek. While landowner practices do affect the Creek, the Coalition is concerned about the impact of municipal and industrial operations. It is equally important that policy makers learn from landowners. The SCC board keeps the lines of communication open by maintaining a positive relationship with local, state, and federal governments.

The board does not assume the right to represent its members in controversial issues. Instead, they conduct public forums with balanced panels of experts, which enable landowners to make educated decisions. SCC volunteers monitor water quality, catalog fish, small invertebrates, and other plant and animal life along the Creek. Professional guidance and support for these activities are donated by a variety of state, university, tribal, and private individuals. One SCC goal is development of a GIS land use map for the watershed that will provide information for permitting, regulatory and conservation activities.

The organization solicits participation rather than financial support. "Talented and dedicated volunteers are our greatest resource," says Coalition President Jennifer Owen. "We have learned that every man, woman and child has something to contribute and it is always better than money could buy!" SCC volunteers host outdoor education, plant and wildlife tours, pick up trash and plant trees. They award children for 4H environmental projects, make school presentations and encourage student participation in SCC activities. "We play as well as educate and teach that you can't take without giving back. It means a lot to these kids to do something real," says board member (and teacher) Alicia Osborne. SCC members accomplish all this and more with an annual budget of less than a thousand dollars!

Spring Creek Coalition is making Oklahoma history by orchestrating hundreds of devoted people from all walks of life into a grassroots symphony of cooperation and achievement. "Never doubt that a small group of thoughtful, committed people can change the world. Indeed it's the only thing that ever has." - Margaret Mead

Top: Spring Creek, which begins in Delaware County near the town of Kansas, is the most pristine large Ozark Stream left in the state of Oklahoma.

Below: Volunteers, including students from local schools, help with litter clean up along Spring Creek. The Coalition advocates the rights and responsibilities of landowners and residents to protect their own natural resources.

Greater Oklahoma City Chamber of Commerce

✧

The Oklahoma City skyline.

Oklahoma City. A better living. A better life.

For more than a century these words have remained the central mission of the Greater Oklahoma City Chamber of Commerce. Begun in 1889 by a group of businessmen meeting in a small wooden structure at Broadway and Sheridan to organize the Board of Trade, the chamber stands today as one of the country's greatest sources for progressive, accomplished community design and economic development. With a dream to seek unity among business leadership and a vision to see common goals achieved, the chamber continues to create an irresistible quality of life for all residents of the region through seven areas: community improvement, creation of jobs, attraction of visitors, protection and enhancement of the business climate, providing valuable services to its members, effective management of all resources, and maintaining a highly motivated and professional staff.

The chamber most notably envisions Oklahoma City as a model community and internationally recognized destination for citizens, businesses, and visitors. Citizens are boosters of our community. With sixty-five employees and 4,000 members, the Chamber is the voice of business and the visionary organization in the community. The chamber is divided into eleven divisions including Economic Development, Small Business, Convention and Visitors Bureau, Metropolitan Events, Government Relations, Community Improvement/Education, Communications, Membership/Marketing, Finance/Information Technology/Personnel, and Executive areas.

The new millennium has brought several major objectives to the chamber as we continue to implement *Forward Oklahoma City—The New Agenda*, a $10 million, five-year economic development action plan. The promotion of special interest activities such as marketing Oklahoma City, passing Right-To-Work, enhancing business development, technology commercialization, international trade, private development, workforce development, and the enhancement of Tinker Air Force Base and Air Logistics Center remain a priority for the Chamber.

The *Wall Street Journal* ad campaign created by the chamber has been one of the most highly recognized avenues for promoting the "Best Kept Secrets" about Oklahoma City. From the ranking in *Places Rated Almanac* as one of the thirty-five best places to live in North America among 343 metro areas, to the city's ranking in *Fortune* magazine's Top 10 labor forces and labor-management relations among six U.S. cities for business, this campaign provides a great reminder to America that together, Oklahoma City and the Greater Oklahoma City Chamber of Commerce are truly setting the standard for a better living. A better life.

The Greater Oklahoma City Chamber of Commerce is located at 123 Park Avenue in Oklahoma City and on the Internet at www.okcchamber.com.

Roman Catholic Diocese of Tulsa

✧

Above: Most Reverend Edward J. Slattery, third Bishop of Tulsa.

Below: Holy Family Cathedral at Eighth and Boulder in downtown Tulsa.

History records a Catholic presence in what is now eastern Oklahoma in 1541, when eleven priests accompanied the expedition of Hernan de Soto some twenty miles along the Arkansas River west of what is now Fort Smith. The 1800s saw Catholic missionaries entering the region, and, in 1872, the first Catholic Church in Indian Territory was built at Atoka. However, it was not until February 1973 that the Tulsa Diocese actually came into being.

As early as 1928, Francis Clement Kelley, consecrated as second Bishop of Oklahoma in 1924, had planned to move his cathedral and chancery from Oklahoma City to Tulsa. The Depression, however, put paid to that plan. Bishop Kelley was a strong leader who was open to many of the reforms of the Second Vatican Council years before they became the trend of the universal Church. Kelley died in 1948, following a lengthy illness, and Bishop Eugene J. McGuinness, who had served as coadjutor since 1945, was named his successor.

Whereas Kelley's main interest had been in making converts to the Catholic faith, McGuinness was primarily concerned with providing priests to minister to them. During his tenure in Oklahoma, McGuinness dedicated 102 new church buildings, seventy rectories, forty-eight schools, thirty-eight convents, twelve parish halls, six new hospitals, and four hospital additions.

Feeling the weight of his heavy schedule, McGuinness petitioned the Pope for an auxiliary bishop and on December 5, 1957 Monsignor Victor Reed, rector of Holy Family co-cathedral in Tulsa, was appointed auxiliary to Bishop McGuinness. When McGuinness died of a heart attack later that same month, Reed was chosen to succeed him.

Plans for the Vatican Council were announced within a year of Reed's becoming a bishop, and its reforms provided the guiding principles for much of his episcopate. The early experiments he permitted were well received by many, but also brought angry complaints from others who felt their cherished traditions were being destroyed. From 1964 to 1975 nearly 100 Oklahoma diocesans and religious left the priesthood.

In 1970, the bishop and his consultors began a study of the problems connected with the long-awaited division of the diocese. While this was going on, the priests in the Tulsa deanery met independently in March 1971 and voted to formally request the division. Before much more could be accomplished, however, Bishop Reed died suddenly in September. His successor was Bishop John Raphael Quinn who was installed in January 1972.

Quinn cooperated with the process begun by Bishop Reed, and on December 19, 1972, it was announced that thirty-one counties in Eastern Oklahoma had been set aside as a new diocese, with Tulsa as its cathedral city. The diocese was formally erected on February 7, 1973, and Bernard J. Ganter, chancellor of the Galveston-Houston diocese, was ordained as the first bishop. He was succeeded by Bishop Eusebius J. Beltran (1978-1992), who subsequently was promoted to the post of archbishop of Oklahoma City, and by Bishop Edward J. Slattery (1994-present).

The Diocese of Tulsa, with its 80 parishes, has continued to serve the Oklahoma community in a number of ways, one of which is Catholic Charities of Tulsa. Now under the direction of Hazel Leitch, Catholic Charities has an extensive range of programs. Some of these include St. Elizabeth Lodge, which provides apartments for homeless families; Madonna House, for women with problem pregnancies; St. Joseph Residence, the first Oklahoma hospice for AIDS patients; and services directed toward Asian and Hispanic newcomers to the United States.

Another important function of the Tulsa diocese is the operation of several schools, most notably Bishop Kelley High School and a number of parochial schools. Other Catholic schools, such as Cascia Hall and Monte Cassino, as well as St. John Medical Center and Saint Francis Hospital, are owned and operated by religious orders and private foundations, although they share in the same Christian mission as the diocese.

Feed The Children

The mission of Feed The Children as a nonprofit Christian charitable organization is to provide physical, spiritual, educational, vocational/technical, psychological, economic, medical assistance, and other necessary aid to children, families, and persons in need in the United States and around the world. Created in Oklahoma City in 1979 by its founder, Larry Jones, a native of Kentucky and graduate of Oklahoma City University, the organization maintains its primary focus upon the needs of children and has distributed food and assistance to all fifty states and the District of Columbia, as well as numerous foreign countries.

The statistics regarding hunger in America today are staggering; one in four children are at risk or struggling with hunger sometime during the month. Nearly fifteen million boys and girls in the United States face the issue of hunger on a daily basis. Physicians, nurses, and dentists volunteer time and expertise as Feed The Children brings relief to communities everywhere. Emergency relief efforts have been at the forefront of this vital organization for many years, from hurricanes in South Carolina, to floods and tornadoes in the Midwest, to needy families in Kosovo, Central America, and around the globe. The dedicated staff and volunteers of Feed The Children have been there—willing and able to lend a helping hand in times of crisis.

In response to so many needs across the country and in many parts of the world, Larry Jones created the hunger relief organization and works with the "working poor." Statistics reflect that in strong economy, a record high number of poor children are in working families. In 1998 alone, Feed The Children helped supplement over 590,000 meals each and every day. Families and individuals also receive assistance through agencies, such as food pantries and church distribution centers located throughout the United States, working closely with Feed The Children.

Opportunities for volunteer service abound at the organization and provide elementary-age students to senior citizens the ability to work hand-in-hand in supplying others with much-needed assistance. These volunteers, through Feed The Children, are able to reach families truly in need, thus reflecting the idea that "one person can make a difference."

This page has been donated to Feed The Children on behalf of the tornado victims of 1999 from The Oklahoma Heritage Association and Historical Publishing Network with Eric Dabney donating his time to write this story.

✧

Top: Larry Jones provides baby food and other necessities to underprivileged families living on the Jicarilla Apache Indian Reservation in New Mexico.

Below: Dallas Cowboys join Feed The Children to give out family food boxes to Dallas area needy.

INTEGRIS
HEALTH INC.

✧

Top: INTEGRIS Baptist Medical Center: The flagship of the INTEGRIS Health system and a center of high-tech medicine.

Below: The hospital on the hill: open prairie and some residential development surrounded Baptist Memorial when it opened in 1959. Photo circa 1960.

INTEGRIS Health has a proud heritage in Oklahoma, with roots in faith-based service going back four decades.

INTEGRIS has grown to become the state's largest Oklahoma-owned health system with about 9,000 employees statewide. The company operates hospitals, rehabilitation centers, physician clinics, mental health facilities, fitness centers, independent living centers, and home health agencies across Oklahoma. Its headquarters are located on the campus of INTEGRIS Baptist Medical Center in Oklahoma City.

A not-for-profit corporation, INTEGRIS is managed by president and chief executive officer Stanley F. Hupfeld, FACHE, with the assistance of senior staff in the areas of physician services, facility operations, strategic services, and finance.

Founded in 1995, INTEGRIS evolved from the merger that same year between Oklahoma Health System and Southwest Medical Center in Oklahoma City. The INTEGRIS name signifies the integration of services, facilities, and operational philosophy that the organization provides to Oklahoma.

INTEGRIS Health through its affiliates, operates a system of fourteen hospitals, led in the Oklahoma City area by INTEGRIS Baptist Medical Center and INTEGRIS Southwest Medical Center. Collectively, the entities within the INTEGRIS Health system maintain more than 1,700 licensed beds and have medical staffs that number more than 1,200 physicians.

INTEGRIS Baptist Medical Center in Oklahoma City was first known as "the hospital on the hill" when it opened in 1959 as Baptist Memorial Hospital, surrounded by open prairie and a few homes. It was the vision of leaders of the Baptist General Convention of Oklahoma at that time to bring a Baptist hospital to the state's capital city. T. B. Lackey, head of the convention during this period, was a key driver in the construction of the hospital. Civic leader and Baptist layman Raymond A. Young also played a role in hospital leadership for three decades. W. P. Atkinson, a prominent local builder and developer of Midwest City, served as the general campaign chairman of the fund-raising effort to build the facility.

Henry G. Bennett, M.D., served as first chief of medical staff until the mid-1980s. James L. Henry was appointed as the administrator of the hospital in 1960 (he later became the chief executive officer of Oklahoma Healthcare Corporation).

Renamed Baptist Medical Center in 1972 and transferred from the Baptist General Convention to the newly organized Oklahoma Healthcare Corporation in 1978, today the facility is a center of cutting-edge medicine. INTEGRIS Baptist is home to a leading transplant program, a regional burn center, a heart center, a cancer center, a fertility institute, and a women's center. A special care unit emphasizes a health and humor approach. And the

entire INTEGRIS system was named one of only two health systems in Oklahoma among the 100 "most wired" techno-savvy healthcare systems in the nation by Hospital and Health Networks magazine in February 1999.

The Nazih Zuhdi Transplantation Institute (NZTI), founded by Nazih Zuhdi, M.D., has performed more than 1,000 transplants on patients ranging from six months to seventy-one years of age. Survival rates rank among the nation's best, and operations are performed on every major organ system, including the heart, lungs, liver, abdominal area, pancreas, and kidneys.

The neonatal intensive care unit (NICU) at INTEGRIS Baptist is considered one of the country's most innovative. The Iowa clinicians who cared for the famous McCaughey septuplets toured the NICU in 1998 to use it as a model for updating their own unit.

Meanwhile, clinicians guided by Paul Silverstein, M.D., founder and medical director of the INTEGRIS Baptist Burn Center, work toward advancing new treatments in the care of burn wounds. Alongside the burn center is a high-tech hyperbaric and wound care center, which includes the state's largest hyperbaric oxygen chamber.

INTEGRIS Southwest Medical Center, an acute-care hospital in southwest Oklahoma City, has also advanced dramatically from its opening in 1965. Under the leadership of president and CEO Dan Tipton, and the first chief of medical staff, Scott Hendren, M.D., the three-story building with seventy-three beds was first called South Community Hospital. Changing names to Southwest Medical Center in 1992, the facility now has more than 320 beds. It houses a cancer center and the only fully accredited sleep disorders center in the state. Also on the INTEGRIS Southwest campus stands one of the nation's top rehabilitation centers: the INTEGRIS Jim Thorpe Rehabilitation Hospital, the choice of the National Football League's Players' Association.

INTEGRIS' mental heath treatment network recently launched the James L. Hall Jr. Center for Mind, Body and Spirit, a program emphasizing holistic health.

INTEGRIS is extending its caring reach worldwide. In 1998, the company announced a telemedicine agreement with Cairo University in Egypt. The company also operates a regional telemedicine program for remote communities in Oklahoma.

Finally, INTEGRIS spends millions of dollars annually on the community and children. Programs include a project geared toward teaching former gang members entrepreneurial skills and "Camp Funnybone," a five-day camp that nurtures self-worth by teaching children the healing art of laughter. In the fall of 1999, INTEGRIS begins operating an existing elementary school, Western Village, in the Oklahoma City public school district as an enterprise school for at-risk students.

High-tech medicine, innovative ideas, and community programs. All of this to keep Oklahomans healthy—right from the beginning.

✧

Top: A father waits it out in Baptist Memorial's room for dads-to-be, circa 1960.

PHOTO COURTESY OF HILLERMAN.

Below: INTEGRIS Southwest Medical Center has grown from a community hospital to a medical center housing a cancer center, a sleep disorder center, and a top rehabilitation hospital.

Blue Cross and Blue Shield of Oklahoma

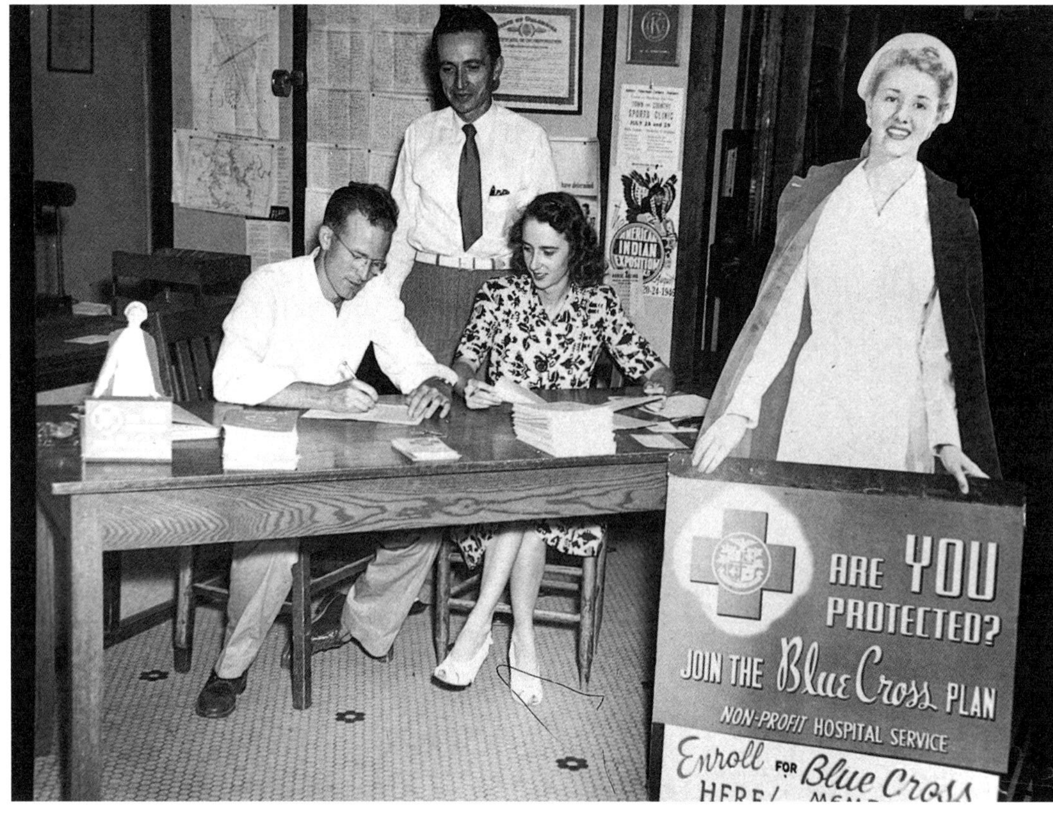

✧

Enrollment location for new Blue Cross members from the early years of the company.

It was one of the most exciting eras of the twentieth century. The Charleston. Flappers. Postwar euphoria. Lucky Lindy. Prohibition and bootlegging. The Teapot Dome Scandal. Warren Harding and Herbert Hoover. And with all these familiar developments of the 1920s, healthcare was also coming into its own.

Hospitals rapidly expanded their services during this period to serve a growing and more affluent middle class with new technology and an abundance of valuable new diagnostic tests. At the same time, a new concept in medicine was emerging and beginning to spread slowly across the country—prepaid medical insurance. In 1920, an official at Baylor University in Texas introduced to teachers in Dallas a plan to cover up to twenty-one days of hospital care for $6 a year.

A little over ten years later, this new idea found its way north of the Red River into Oklahoma. Civic and medical leaders visited the Baylor Plan and on their way back to Oklahoma decided to set up a similar program. They needed at least $10,000, and leaders in Tulsa and Oklahoma City challenged each other. The first community to raise $5,000 would be the headquarters of the new organization. The Tulsa contingent won and Group Health Services, the forerunner of Blue Cross and Blue Shield of Oklahoma, set up shop in Tulsa.

Nearly 10,000 Oklahomans signed up for Blue Cross coverage that first year. The plan's popularity grew each year, bringing more members and more insurance options to the people of Oklahoma. Today, approximately 450,000 Oklahomans are members of Blue Cross and Blue Shield of Oklahoma health insurance plans—nearly twenty percent of the state's population. The Tulsa headquarters, which began with a $5,000 bet, now employs more than 900 employees. Another 200 work in Oklahoma City and Lawton. Blue Cross and Blue Shield is proud to be a corporate leader in every Oklahoma community we serve.

In those early beginnings, health insurance simply protected members from unexpected health expenses. But the changing role of private health insurance has allowed Blue Cross and Blue Shield of Oklahoma to offer innovative programs and services for individuals, employee groups of all sizes, and seniors. Programs range from traditional coverage to preferred provider organization plans to BlueLincs Health Maintenance Organization.

Blue Cross and Blue Shield of Oklahoma is committed to the health and well-being of members through a number of creative programs, including:

Preventive Care—encouraging members to be proactive with their health by getting children immunized, having women's mammograms and other preventive measures.

Health and Wellness—programs educating members about the benefits of staying healthy through classes, newsletters and other helpful programs.

Health Management—early identification of chronic conditions like diabetes and asthma, along with comprehensive resources, encourage self-care and regular medical care to improve the quality of life for many members.

Blue Cross and Blue Shield's role has expanded dramatically over the years, but the uncompromising commitment to caring and personal service remains the same. As the plan encourages members to live healthier lives and actively participate in healthcare decisions, there has been a major increase in the opportunities to touch the lives of Oklahomans in the communities we serve. Added emphasis is placed on community outreach, including a number of exciting programs and services.

Blue Cross and Blue Shield of Oklahoma introduced the Caring Program for Children in 1995 to help families access quality healthcare for their children. The dynamic program benefits families of the working poor who earn too much to qualify for public assistance but not enough to afford health benefits for their families. Children in these families may see doctors for illnesses and receive regular check-ups and immunizations to stay healthy. Approximately 2,000 Oklahoma children have benefited from Caring Program for Children.

Screening for vision, high blood pressure, glaucoma, hearing and other possible health problems has become more convenient in Oklahoma thanks to the Mobile Health Screening Unit. This groundbreaking joint venture between Blue Cross and Blue Shield of Oklahoma and Oklahoma Lions Clubs travels the entire state screening Oklahomans of all ages. The thirty-foot mobile unit is colorfully decorated with scenes of Oklahoma history and is a popular attraction wherever it goes. Several thousand people receive screenings in the unit each year.

The Oklahoma Mobile Screening Unit, sponsored jointly by Blue Cross and Blue Shield of Oklahoma and Oklahoma Lions Clubs, is an important step toward improving the health of all Oklahomans.

Caring for the community is a hallmark of Blue Cross and Blue Shield. Giving back to the community is a point of pride, and nowhere is this more evident than the Plan's involvement with the United Way, in both Tulsa and Oklahoma City. Employees dedicate countless hours and pledge significant amounts of money to support the United Way's community-wide efforts.

Just as the Plan's health benefits role has evolved in the past sixty years, so too has the ability to offer broader solutions to individuals and group members. In addition to health insurance programs, Blue Cross and Blue Shield of Oklahoma (with its subsidiary companies, Member Service Life Insurance, BlueLincs HMO and GHS Property and Casualty) can offer individuals and companies of all sizes disability and life insurance, Section 125 administration, workers' compensation programs, and auto, home and personal property and casualty insurance.

More than sixty years ago, Oklahomans with a goal of providing cost-effective health insurance joined together to found Blue Cross and Blue Shield of Oklahoma. Their mission and commitment to caring is evident in the company's expanded role today. Blue Cross and Blue Shield of Oklahoma is proud to be an important part of the lives of thousands of members, in Tulsa and across this great state, for sixty years and counting.

Sylvan N. Goldman Center Oklahoma Blood Institute

"An Oklahoma response to an Oklahoma need." These words were spoken early in 1999 as Ronald O. Gilcher, M.D., F.A.C.P., president and chief executive officer of the Oklahoma Blood Institute, rose to accept the OU College of Medicine Alumni Association Evening of Excellence award on behalf of the organization as a distinguished Oklahoma institution.

The need for a dependable blood supply program came into glaring reality in 1974. Dr. Ted Violett, a pathologist at St. Anthony Hospital, related to a group of visionary physicians led by Dr. Don Rhinehart, who currently serves as Chairman of the Board at OBI, and Dr. Irwin Brown, that there was not enough blood for the surgeries which were scheduled. The physicians responded with the creation of a Blood Bank Committee who worked diligently to complete a thorough investigation of the blood system and its inadequacies in meeting the community's blood related healthcare services. Additionally, the physicians and civic leaders recognized that education and research projects in hematology and blood component therapy were needed to enhance patient care. In April 1976, these efforts culminated through the Oklahoma County Medical Society's incorporation of the Oklahoma Blood Institute, a 501(c)(3), not-for-profit, regional blood center.

On January 1, 1977, OBI began operations with a strong commitment to the people of Oklahoma to maintain the safety, quality, and availability of the blood supply; to provide specialized medical services that the medical community could not provide; to educate the medical and lay communities; and to pioneer applied research in blood-related issues. Two locations, the main facility and laboratory in Oklahoma City and a donor center in Lawton, were staffed with seventeen employees serving thirty hospitals in nine counties, with a projected blood need of 22,000 units in that year alone. A sub-center was soon opened in Enid and the first mobile donor station was acquired to make it more convenient for people to give blood.

In 1979, Gilcher was recruited from Central Blood Bank of Pittsburgh and the University of Pittsburgh School of Medicine. With an outstanding background in transfusion medicine and a specialty in hematology, Gilcher immediately provided a scientific expertise in blood-related issues and served as a consultant to hospital pathologists in the community. The need quickly arose to centralize the organization's work into a single facility that was closer to the Health Sciences community. Donations from Sylvan N. Goldman (famous for his invention of the shopping cart), the Noble Foundation, the Junior League of Oklahoma City, and several individuals soon enabled OBI to grow even more by providing funds for construction of a new building begun in January of 1982, and now the current headquarters located at 10th and Lincoln Boulevard in Oklahoma City.

Gilcher has continued the transformation of OBI as it stands as one of the most highly rec-

✧

Top: Dr. Ronald O. Gilcher, president and chief executive officer of OBI, with blood recipient Railee Creech.

Below: The Sylvan N. Goldman Center Oklahoma Blood Institute in Oklahoma City.

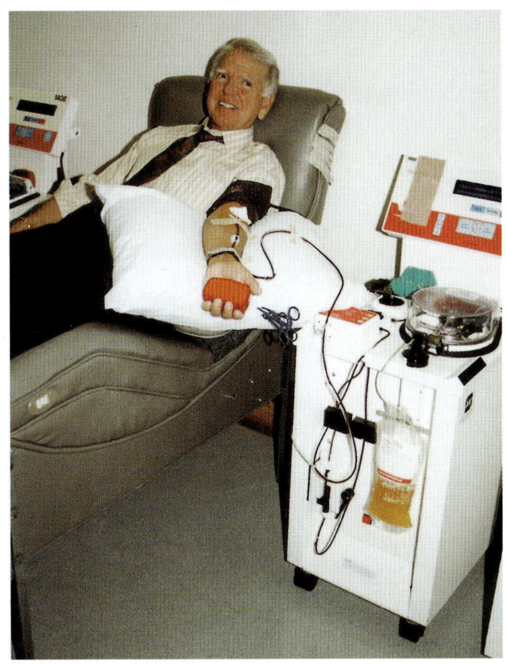

ognized regional blood centers in America today. A well-established commitment to provide preventive healthcare back to the community has led the organization into a new era of service in Oklahoma and throughout the nation. In 1986, OBI was the first blood center in the country to perform free cholesterol testing as a donor benefit, and in 1995, became the first to offer prostate-specific antigen (PSA) blood testing to men for prostate cancer screening. The Institute was also the first blood center to provide hepatitis B antibody testing to police officers, fire fighters and healthcare workers to determine whether the hepatitis B vaccine is providing adequate protection. In addition to health benefits, since 1978, OBI offers donors a plan that provides reimbursement for blood processing fees not covered by insurance, should a donor or their tax dependents need blood.

In 1991, the Blood Institute became the first blood center to use the HIV Antigen test on every blood donation as a FDA-approved research project. In October 1995, Gilcher testified before the U.S. House of Representatives' Committee on Government Reform and Oversight hearing on issues concerning the safety of the national blood supply. The focus of Gilcher's testimony was closing the window of opportunity of transfusion transmitted disease through the development and use of this HIV-1 antigen test at OBI. Largely due to OBI's research, the HIV antigen test was officially licensed by the FDA in March 1996 and is now performed on every blood donation in the nation. In 1997, Gilcher was appointed by the United States Department of Health and Human Services to serve on the advisory committee to the Blood Safety Council and was one of only three transfusion medicine experts in the nation to be selected for the committee.

While HIV and other viruses continued to pose new challenges to blood banks throughout the nation, never had OBI faced a challenge like the bombing of the Alfred P. Murrah Federal Building on April 19, 1995. The Oklahoma Blood Institute's first priority that morning was to meet immediate blood needs. Blood donated previously at drives and OBI centers across the state enabled the Blood Institute to deliver an additional 900 blood products to hospitals before victims arrived. After emergency needs were met, Oklahomans responded to the tragedy by donating blood to replenish the blood supply. OBI staff accommodated more than 7,000 donors in the first seventy-two hours following the bombing. Thanks to faithful Oklahoma donors, OBI was able to meet the blood needs of bombing victims, and remains well prepared for any crisis.

The Institute contributes its continued success to the high quality donor base in the state, with Oklahomans donating blood at a rate of twice the national average, and has not had to import blood into the state since 1981. With annual revenues of $28 million, this labor-intensive organization currently employs more than 450 Oklahomans in eleven locations and serves over seventy hospitals in the state, remains the largest blood center in Oklahoma and one of the largest in the nation. In addition to the main location in Oklahoma City, OBI maintains four donor centers in the Oklahoma City area and sub-centers in Lawton, Enid, Ardmore, Ada, Ponca City, and Tulsa.

The Oklahoma Blood Institute continues to be the critical link between blood donors and patients, steadfast in its philosophy of remaining a high quality medical organization first and a business second. "An Oklahoma response to an Oklahoma need" echoes a brilliant tribute to the past, present and future of this vitally important institution.

✧

Former Oklahoma Governor George Nigh donating plasma at the Oklahoma Blood Institute.

Valley View Regional Hospital, Ada, Oklahoma

Someone once said, "Whatever the mind can conceive and believe, the mind can achieve." And, so it is with people of vision, those who dream of great things then set out alone or in concert with others to achieve them.

In the mid-1930s, one man's vision inspired a community to build a hospital. Today, that healthcare institution is one of Oklahoma's finest rural referral centers, serving more than 175,000 residents of ten or more counties in south central Oklahoma.

At a small gathering of friends in Memphis, Tennessee in 1935, Ada physician, Dr. Earnest A. Canada, met a nurse from a small town in Kentucky. As they talked throughout the evening, he was particularly interested in the funding method her hometown used to build a hospital. Upon returning to Ada, Canada wrote to the organization that funded the hospital in rural Kentucky. The Commonwealth Foundation of New York replied, agreeing to provide a grant of $200,000 if the community of Ada would raise $40,000 to $60,000.

Dr. C. C. Morris, a local minister, joined in, and P. A. Norris, a prominent banker, gave life to the community's dream of building a new hospital when he donated land. A fund drive was launched that raised $138,000 in less than six months, which was quite a sum in the Depression era. And, what a mind had conceived at a party in Tennessee just three years earlier, had indeed been achieved because an entire community believed it could be done.

When Valley View Hospital opened its doors for the first time on July 24, 1938, an *Ada Evening News* reporter covering the event that day wrote: "The visitor stood on the roof garden of Valley View Hospital, marveling at the things he had seen and looking far to the east where green valleys stretched for miles, breathed half a question and half a prayer . . . 'Can all of this be real?'" Visitors to the current facility are likely to express similar thoughts. For truly, Valley View Regional Hospital is unique as healthcare institutions in rural communities go. Few small town hospitals are as well-equipped, and fewer still are as diverse in the services offered.

When changes in federal fire and life safety codes threatened accreditation in the early 1980s, the people of Ada came together again—this time in support of a one-cent city sales tax to help finance a new $33 million facility. A countywide fund drive the following year, in 1984, raised a record $2.5 million. On October 1, 1986, a new 200-bed, acute care, not-for-profit hospital opened on thirty-one beautifully landscaped acres, not far from the original site. So, from its modest, humble beginnings in the 1930s, Valley View Regional Hospital had emerged as a major healthcare provider in rural Oklahoma.

The changes in Medicare reimbursement of the '80s, and the financial uncertainties of the '90s, seemed to have little effect on VVRH. The hospital grew and prospered when hundreds of rural hospitals nationwide were closing their doors or being purchased by larger healthcare institutions and for-profit corporations. While success did not come easily, there was nothing magical about the formula used to attain it.

Top: Valley View Regional Hospital is located on thirty-one acres on Ada's eastside. The people of Pontotoc and surrounding counties have relied on the hospital for many years to meet their medical needs, and for leadership in the development of a healthier lifestyle.

Below: The original hospital, 1938. The structure on top of the building was a roof garden that was used by recovering patients, as well as hospital employees. In the early days, the building on the left served as living quarters for the hospital's nurses. It would be used later to expand services.

✧

Left: Background (left to right): Shaun Davison Kingery, great granddaughter of P. A. Norris; Susan Cason, daughter of P. A. Norris; Denver N. Davison, grandson of P. A. Norris. Foreground (left to right): Bryan Davison Kingery, great-great grandson of P. A. Norris; Chloe Kingery, great-great granddaughter of P. A. Norris; Trigg Cason Yerby, granddaughter of P. A. Norris; William N. Peterson, grandson of P. A. Norris; Brown Hoover, grandson of C. C. Morris; and Danny Joe Hoover, grandson of C. C. Morris.

Below: Left to right: Edwin R. Anderson, a member of the board of directors who donated the sign for the new hospital; Kenneth R. Johnson, chairman of the board of directors in 1986 when the new hospital opened; and Philip H. Fisher, president and CEO, who joined the hospital in 1977.

Winston Churchill once said, "To improve is to change, to be perfect is to change often." Valley View's management team and twelve-member, voluntary Board of Directors, all successful business and civic leaders in their own right, recognized long before diversification and modification were mandates for rural hospitals, that change is indeed necessary if small town hospitals are to survive. Through sound leadership, VVRH prospered at a time when others struggled to keep their doors open.

Valley View Regional Hospital has enjoyed many successes. Oklahoma's first hospital-based volunteer service was formed there in 1947. In 1973, VVRH opened one of the state's first hospital-based home care services. An outpatient surgery center was created in 1978 to shorten patient stays and to reduce costs. In 1982, Valley View's aggressive approach to services influenced it to become the state's smallest hospital with a stationary, full-body CT scan. Today, the hospital's radiology department is simply one of the state's best equipped, particularly in a rural community, with diagnostic capabilities in nuclear medicine, ultrasound, CT scan, magnetic resonance imaging, mammography, bone densitometry and cardiac catheterization. When the hospital purchased a Targis Microwave System in 1999, only two other hospitals in Oklahoma offered this state-of-the-art method for treating benign prostatic hyperplasia, commonly known as an enlarged prostate.

Patients throughout south central Oklahoma depend on VVRH for kidney dialysis, cancer treatment, physical rehabilitation, skilled nursing, obstetrical care and many of the latest surgical techniques. The hospital also operates the county's emergency medical service, a licensed paramedic life support system.

Although many changes have taken place during Valley View Regional Hospital's growth and development, its commitment to excellence and its dedication to patients have never changed. As the hospital faces the challenges of the new millenium, one has to believe they will be met with the same devotion to people, and with no less confidence for success.

Norman Regional Hospital

✧

Top: Norman Regional is poised to take technology into the new millennium for the communities it serves.

Below: From our earliest days, Norman Regional Hospital has been a a leader in healthcare for the residents of south central Oklahoma.

As the twenty-first century quickly approaches, Norman Regional Hospital remains focused on the health of the communities it serves. Over the past fifty-three years, Norman Regional has been committed to providing the most comprehensive healthcare services for the citizens of south central Oklahoma. This commitment has been our mission ever since the last brick was laid in the foundation on June 2, 1946. Our history is interwoven with the proud heritage of the communities we serve.

Dr. John L. Day, an early Norman physician, realized the need for a local hospital after World War I, and worked with the American Legion to establish a hospital. The Legion secured the Whitwell property at Johnson and North Ponca Streets as a location and raised funds for the two-story brick structure. Due to a personnel shortage during World War II, the hospital closed its doors in 1942 after eighteen years of operation. During the years Norman was without a hospital, the twenty-five miles to an Oklahoma City hospital was a hardship for families. Local reporters recounted numerous tragedies of families whose loved ones were seriously ill or injured and did not survive the trip.

The community received welcome relief when Norman Municipal Hospital reopened on June 2, 1946 thanks to the efforts of local physicians, citizens, and the chamber of commerce. The sixty-one-bed hospital was a source of great pride for those dedicated physicians and citizens responsible for its existence.

The hospital opened with a staff of twenty-nine employees and resumed serving the healthcare needs of the community with the most state-of-the-art technology of the day.

Norman Municipal changed its name to Norman Regional in 1984 to better reflect the many communities it serves. This regional focus marked the beginning of an era of unprecedented technological growth and specialization.

Today, Norman Regional Hospital is on the cutting edge of an ever-changing healthcare industry—promoting health and wellness through our many Centers of Excellence.

Lifestyle Center of America

One of the best kept secrets in Oklahoma sits atop a mountain just east of I-35 near Davis on Highway 110. The Lifestyle Center of America is led by a unique team of Christian healthcare professionals who believe that a healthful lifestyle can play a major role in preventing and reversing a number of today's chronic diseases, such as diabetes, hypertension, and heart disease. Smoking addiction and obesity also respond well to lifestyle intervention.

The Lifestyle Center of America owes its proud heritage and exciting future to the dreams of Roy Johnson, a beloved Ardmore pioneer and newsman whose initiative led to the discovery of the Healdton Oil Fields in 1911 with his son, Dr. Otey Johnson. Dr. Johnson and a team sought out consultants and visited healthcare facilities throughout the country with the plan to establish a lifestyle medicine center devoted to reversing chronic diseases. William V. Wiist was chairman of the board of trustees of Dr. Johnson's Ardmore Institute of Health. Wiist and board members chose the present site and began construction on a healthcare facility in 1993. Board members were Layton Sutton, M.D.; George Carlson, M.D.; Velda Lewis; Ruth Martin; and Bonnie Kendall. The 100,000-square-foot, $12 million Lifestyle Center of America opened its doors in July of 1996. Dennis Blum, Ph.D., was selected as the first president in January 1996.

With a specific focus upon lifestyle medicine, the Lifestyle Center of America continues with the vision of its founders, making significant inroads to diabetic care and other chronic diseases. Their research is being presented in major peer review conferences throughout the United States.

The Lifestyle Center of America offers nineteen, twelve, or seven-day lifestyle programs and a one-day get acquainted visit. The facility includes a restaurant, physician-supervised medical clinic, lecture auditorium, hands-on cooking lab, fitness center, and massage/hydrotherapy treatment area. For detailed information regarding the lifestyle center, its programs and services you may call 800-213-8955 or visit them on the Internet at www.lifestylecenter.org. If you are in the Sulphur area, the restaurant is open to the public by reservation. Tours are also available Monday through Friday at 2:00 p.m.

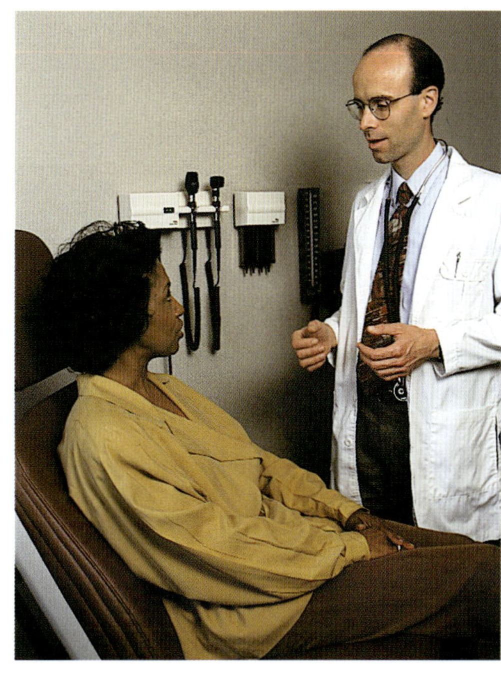

McBride Clinic, Inc. & Bone & Joint Hospital

Bone and Joint Hospital and McBride Clinic, Inc. specialize in the diagnosis and treatment of patients with arthritic and orthopedic conditions and those needing medical rehabilitation and occupational health services. This not-for-profit, 102-licensed bed hospital provides excellence in all aspects of care, through caring people, enhancing the quality of life of patients and others in the communities they serve.

Earl D. McBride, M.D. began his Oklahoma City orthopedic practice in 1920 with four rooms and an office in his residential home. Here he could keep patients overnight and have a neighbor prepare food for them. McBride Clinic and the Reconstruction Hospital expanded into a brick building located at 717 North Robinson in 1925 and added the Arthritis Department in 1927. The clinic continued to grow and was moved again in 1939 to a new 30-bed facility at Northwest 10th and Dewey and was renamed McBride Clinic and Bone & Joint Hospital. By 1947, the X-ray Department was making twenty-six films per day, there were eighty beds, a children's ward, dining room, and medical library. The clinic and hospital were treating 30,000 annually. In 1950, laboratory facilities were added along with the purchase of a two-story building just west of the clinic to be used for convalescing male patients. Expansion began again in 1956 with the addition of more beds, more lab space, and research facilities.

In 1957, Dr. McBride sold his interest in the hospital to three staff doctors—William K. Ishmael, M.D.; Elias Margo, M.D.; and Howard Shorbe, M.D. Hospital Administrator James A. Hyde, received approval in 1976 for financing to build a new hospital. With $7.7 million to finance a new facility, ground was broken in June of 1977 at 1111 North Dewey. The new structure would have 102 beds and five large operating suites. In 1979, B&J Parking Garage, Ltd., was formed and a parking garage was added for patients and employees.

Named to *U.S. News and World Report's* "America's Best Hospitals" 1995 list of forty quality hospitals performing orthopedic procedures, the complex has expanded to include the twenty-nine-bed Bone and Joint Rehabilitation Center, B&J Ambulatory Surgery Center, Osteoporosis Center, Emergency Room, McBride Sports Medicine Center and McBride Occupational Health Center. McBride Arthritis Clinics are located in Edmond, Norman and Oklahoma City. Bone and Joint Hospital merged with SSM of Oklahoma in May of 1995 and the new McBride Clinic office building and the B&J Ambulatory Surgery Center opened in March of 1998.

Involvement in charitable activities remains a vital part of this medical community through their work with United Way, The Arthritis Foundation, and Healthy U.

Collaborative efforts with the area wide Aging Agency and other agencies bring educational opportunities to Oklahomans every year.

Top: The McBride Clinic Orthopedic and Arthritis Center and the Bone and Joint Ambulatory Surgery Center building is the newest addition to the campus, which includes Bone and Joint Hospital and Bone and Joint Rehabilitation Clinic.

Right: Exceptional, caring professionals are part of the reason Bone and Joint Hospital was named to the U.S. News and World *Report's "America's Best Hospitals" list of hospitals performing orthopedic procedures.*

Saint Francis Health System

It all began with a young man's dream and a desire to help others. Through the past four decades, W. K. Warren's dream has evolved into what is known today as Saint Francis Health System. The system, which is comprised of approximately 7,000 employees, consists of Saint Francis Hospital, Laureate Psychiatric Clinic and Hospital, Warren Clinic, and Saint Francis Hospital at Broken Arrow. Together, they provide the Tulsa area and northeast Oklahoma with the most up-to-date treatment available in an atmosphere of caring compassion.

Saint Francis Hospital is a 935-bed facility and is known as one of the top hospitals in the nation. *U.S. News & World Report* recently included Saint Francis Hospital among its list of "America's Best Hospitals." The signature pink marble building has become a familiar landmark within Tulsa and the surrounding community. Services such as the Heart Center, The Children's Hospital and the Natalie Warren Bryant Cancer Center have had a significant impact on the healthcare of people throughout northeastern Oklahoma by providing specialized services unavailable elsewhere in the area.

The Warren family felt quality mental health services should be available to the community and founded Laureate Psychiatric Clinic and Hospital in 1988. From the start, the staff's goal has remained unchanged—helping each patient regain his or her footing and maintain their place in society.

In addition to a full spectrum of psychiatric treatment, Laureate is also involved in continuing research and education for the professional community and general public. Services are provided for children, adolescents, adults, and seniors through intensive programs for those with chemical dependency, eating disorders, and mood disorders with new specialty programs constantly being developed.

Through the years, it became apparent that as the healthcare industry began to shift towards a managed care environment, Saint Francis would need to broaden its primary care physician base in order to continue as a premier healthcare provider.

In response to these needs, Warren Clinic was established with its first location in Stillwater, Oklahoma, in January 1987. Since that time, the clinic has grown from three internal medicine specialists in Stillwater, to more than 150 doctors in practice throughout eastern Oklahoma. Today, Warren Clinic consists of physician offices in ten northeastern Oklahoma cities, including twenty-nine practice locations in Tulsa. Each clinic offers patients a wide spectrum of primary care medical services, from disease prevention to the management of patients with chronic medical conditions.

The newest addition of the Saint Francis Health System is Saint Francis Hospital at Broken Arrow, which is a full service hospital with a total of seventy-one beds. It is widely known for its outstanding inpatient and outpatient rehabilitation services. The hospital also provides services ranging from minor emergency to intensive care.

Through the years, Saint Francis Health System's mission as a Catholic healthcare facility has provided a blueprint for its patient-center and service-oriented care. Amazing strides in medical technology have occurred through the years in Saint Francis facilities, but the core ideals and integrity upon which Saint Francis Health System was built, have remained untouched by time. The foresight and generosity of Mr. and Mrs. W. K. Warren, and of their son, Bill, Jr., and grandson, John-Kelly Warren in the ensuing years, have established the cornerstone of healthcare that is Saint Francis Health System today. With a vision of excellence in medicine, the Warrens have successfully turned a vision into a place people know they can trust with their lives and those of their loved ones.

✧

Above: Tulsa's Laureate Psychiatric Clinic and Hospital is nestled in a beautiful setting of rolling lawns, ponds, and trees.

Below: Saint Francis Hospital's signature pink marble building has become a familiar landmark in Tulsa and the surrounding community.

COLEMAN

Building a Greater Oklahoma

Oklahoma's construction, communications,
and energy industries shape tomorrow's skyline,
providing working and living space for
Oklahomans and fuel for the nation

✧

The historic Coleman Theater dominates downtown Miami. Its unique architecture is a major tourist attraction to the restored business district. Miami originally was known as Jimtown, and was so called because the only residents were four farmers with the first name of Jim.

COURTESY DAVID FITZGERALD.

LIPPERT BROS., INC.

Quality, diversity, and commitment have been at the hallmark of Lippert Bros., Inc. since their beginning as general contractors in 1920. The founders, Erick W. and Walter H. Lippert, began as brick masons and as the projects grew, added two brothers as masons and another brother, a carpenter. From early residential projects in Boone, Iowa, they soon were remodeling commercial buildings. A contract to build the Boone High School launched the company on projects of greater scale.

Following the outbreak of World War II, the company completed a sewage-treatment plant at Camp McCoy, Wisconsin. This project set into motion a series of successful bids for the construction of numerous military training command projects throughout the southwest, including an important move to Oklahoma to build the water and sewage treatment systems at the new Tinker Air Force Base near Oklahoma City, and at Fort Sill, Altus, Frederick, Ardmore, and Childress, Texas.

Family Medicine Clinic, Oklahoma University Health Sciences Center, Oklahoma City, Oklahoma.

At war's end, the company built many projects for colleges and universities to accommodate the increasing number of returning veterans. Growing communities needed new church and commercial buildings. Lippert Bros., Inc. was ready with experienced staff to meet the challenge.

Erick Lippert was soon joined by his sons, Donald and Robert, who had completed their college education after returning from service in the Navy. Now that the Oklahoma City office was permanent, the company was incorporated in Oklahoma in 1947, becoming a distinct entity from the partnership in Iowa.

The company soon set a new standard of dedication and professionalism in high-profile construction projects throughout the area such as the Gold Star Memorial Library at Oklahoma City University, Saint Benedict's Abbey in Atchison, Kansas, the high school and a hotel in Parsons, Kansas, a manufacturing plant in Rogers, Arkansas, the high school in Phillips, Texas, John Brown University Chapel in Siloam Springs, Arkansas, a four hundred car parking garage in Denver, Colorado, the Glass House Restaurant over the Will Rogers Turnpike at Vinita, Oklahoma, and numerous Oklahoma churches.

Upon the death of Erick Lippert in 1964, his son, Donald E. Lippert, became president and continued building such landmark projects as the Citizens' Bank Tower, First Presbyterian Church, the original National Cowboy Hall of Fame and Western Heritage Center, Myriad Gardens Crystal Bridge, and the award-winning renovation of Central High School into One Bell Central for Southwestern Bell.

Lippert Bros., Inc. specialized in public works projects while continuing in general building construction. Water treatment projects include the plants at Arcadia Lake, Midwest City, Antlers, Draper Lake, and the thirty million-gallon-per-day addition to the Lake Hefner plant. Wastewater treatment plants include those at Lawton, Mustang, Del City, Ada, and the Cow Creek plant in Oklahoma City.

Other notable projects in Oklahoma City include the aquatics facility at Oklahoma City Community College featuring a fifty-meter Olympic lap pool with a separate diving tank, the *Wall Street Journal* printing facility, the Oklahoma County Juvenile Center, and the Remington Park grandstand superstructure which consisted of 19,000 cubic yards of concrete. Lippert Bros., Inc. was honored to have been selected to build the Oklahoma City National Memorial.

The company's proven excellence continues with a third generation of Lippert Brothers and an unparalleled work force completing between $20 million and $40 million in projects annually.

Donald E. Lippert, chief executive officer, is semi-retired and his son, D.E. "Rick" Lippert, is president. Key officers include Bruce Barta, vice president; Thomas M. Lippert, vice president; Gale Waldron, secretary-treasurer; Tolleson Payne, assistant secretary-treasurer; and Joel J. Lippert, estimator and project manager. John A. Lippert is president of Globe Construction, a subsidiary company.

Lippert Bros., Inc. has built many healthcare facilities over the years, including major buildings on the campus of the Oklahoma Health Science Center—the State Department of Health Building, Oklahoma University Bio-Medical Science Building, and the Family Medicine Building—McBride Bone and Joint Hospital in Oklahoma City, Edmond Hospital and a hospital in Arkansas City, Kansas. There were also a number of hospital renovations and additions completed.

Other healthcare facilities completed in recent years are the Canterbury Retirement Community, the Psychiatric Facility at Hillcrest Health Center, the Donald W. Reynolds Children's Center, and the Neuroscience Institute at Mercy Health Center.

The LBI mark of excellence has also been left on Oklahoma City's broadcasting community through the specialized construction of KAUT-TV, KOCO-TV, KWTV, and KFOR-TV, as well as a TV station in Austin, Texas.

The firm has completed educational facilities throughout the area including Oklahoma City University, Oklahoma State University, University of Oklahoma, University of Central Oklahoma, Oklahoma Christian University, Rose State College, Oklahoma Education Association, Oklahoma City Public Schools, Norman Public Schools, and Moore Public Schools.

Renovations requiring detailed and specialized workmanship include the Cathedral of Our Lady of Perpetual Help, First Baptist Church, Messiah Lutheran Church, the Federal Reserve Bank of Kansas City at the Oklahoma City Branch, and various retail establishments.

Entertainment facilities are also a specialty. Major theater projects are the Omnidome Theater at the Kirkpatrick Science and Air Space Museum at the Omniplex, the Cinemark Tinseltown twenty-screen theater in Oklahoma City, and the Tinseltown sixteen-screen theater with IMAX in Tulsa. Lippert Bros, Inc. completed the expansion and improvements to the Norick Arena at Oklahoma State Fair Park, part of the Metropolitan Area Projects, known as MAPS, in Oklahoma City.

The Lippert's work on the Norick Arena project received the American Institute of Architects' Keystone award and the Association General Contractors of America's Merit. The Central Oklahoma Chapter of the American Institute of Architects also presented the firm the Outstanding Contractor award. Prestigious safety awards have been received from the Oklahoma Municipal Contractors and the Associated General Contractors of America.

A visitor to the offices of Lippert Bros., Inc. sees a display of the company's logos spanning seventy-five years. The current red, black, and white logo seen boldly on signs at construction sites throughout the state symbolizes a quality contracting and utilities firm that takes pride in its work and heritage. Its third generation strongly believes in building the best for Oklahoma. Their dedication to providing professional construction services responsive to the needs of commercial, industrial, and government markets and unique projects utilizing quality materials and craftsmanship affirms the successful evolution of a company that started eight decades ago with the skill, diversity, and commitment to bring to reality the dreams of others.

✧

Above: Noble Research Center, Oklahoma State University, Stillwater, Oklahoma.

Below: Myriad Gardens, Crystal Bridge, Oklahoma City, Oklahoma.

PHOTO COURTESY OF GREG HURLSEY, PHOTOGRAPHER.

Southwestern Bell

✧

Below: The call of duty: Dorothy Burris, a wireless service representative in Oklahoma City assists a Southwestern Bell Wireless customer.

Above: At your service. Terry Stevens, a customer services technician in Oklahoma City, leaves his pager number with customers in case they have follow-up questions regarding service or repairs.

Southwestern Bell's legacy of service in Oklahoma goes back more than a century, and as we enter the new millennium, the company's connections to the state continue to grow. Today, Southwestern Bell offers a wide range of telecommunications services to customers in Oklahoma, Missouri, Arkansas, Kansas and Texas, including local telephone service, wireless communications, data communications, paging, Internet access, and messaging, as well as telecommunications equipment, and directory advertising and publishing. As a subsidiary of SBC Communications, Inc., named several times by *Fortune* magazine as the world's most admired telecommunications company, Southwestern Bell answers the call for residential and business customers of the fifteen million access lines the company serves in its five-state service region.

Southwestern Bell Today

With more than 4,000 employees in Oklahoma, Southwestern Bell has a significant impact at the local and statewide levels. The company continues to spark economic growth and development throughout the Sooner State. For example, this year the company opened a state-of-the-art Corporate Call Center in Oklahoma Center, investing more than $5 million in renovations and technology enhancements. The company also plans to expand the work force at the center this year with 75 new employees.

Each year in Oklahoma, Southwestern Bell's 4,180 employees generate more than $179 million in payroll and more than 4,270 retirees draw more than $47 million in pension resulting in a total impact of more than $100 million on the Oklahoma economy—based on goods and services purchased.

Southwestern Bell also continues to serve its customers with the highest level of customer service. Every business day, the company handles more than 16.6 million calls and directory assistance responds to 150,000 requests for information.

In Oklahoma, the network infrastructure includes more than 1.6 million access lines, and equipment, buildings and property valued at $5 billion. Annually Southwestern Bell invests millions of dollars to maintain, enhance and expand the vast Oklahoma network, ensuring leading-edge capabilities and virtually 100 percent reliability for all telecommunications services.

Products and Services

Southwestern Bell continually develops products, services and applications to enhance the quality of life for its customers. Key residential services include Caller ID, CallNotes, Call Waiting, Call Waiting ID, Call Forwarding, and Internet access. Key business applications include telecommuting, PC faxing; desktop videoconferencing; healthcare applications such as telemedicine; and general applications, such as distance learning.

In addition, Southwestern Bell develops and provides many state-of-the-art telecommunications technologies, including Integrated Services Digital Network (ISDN) which enables high-speed, simultaneous transmission of voice, video and data on regular phone lines. Local Area Network (LAN), which links phones, computers and videoconferencing equipment in one or several locations; and Frame Relay, a high-speed data transport technology, which allows businesses to quickly move information "frames" or packets from various remote locations to a single collection point.

In the past two years, two mobile clinics have used telemedicine and distance learning equipment supplied by Southwestern Bell to provide convenient quality health services to rural areas of Southwestern Oklahoma. Additionally, Southwestern Bell made a commitment to award $200,000 over the next three years to establish an osteopathic professorship to teach telemedicine at Oklahoma State University.

Wireless and Internet Services

Southwestern Bell Wireless, together with SBC's other wireless affiliates, is a leading wireless provider, serving 5.8 million customers and seven of the top ten markets nationwide. Southwestern Bell has a major wireless presence across Oklahoma. Southwestern Bell

offers extended home calling areas and one-stop-shopping for all wireless services, including messaging and prepaid services.

Southwestern Bell's priority has always been meeting customers' needs for hassle-free access to people and information, anywhere, anytime, at a reasonable cost and high quality.

In addition, Southwestern Bell also offers Internet access to its customers throughout Oklahoma. Southwestern Bell Internet Services is the nation's 8th largest Internet service provider, offering a broad range of simple, affordable and reliable Internet access services to more than 340,000 business and residential customers. SBIS, which provides Web hosting and both dedicated and dial-up Internet access, also is among the top three Internet service providers in its respective region.

Community Focus

Southwestern Bell continues to emphasize community partnerships with the Southwestern Bell Pioneers, a diverse group of active employees and retirees who volunteer more than 360,000 hours of service annually throughout Oklahoma. The majority of Pioneer efforts are centered on education, including Operation SchoolNet where Pioneers have wired more than 120 elementary and secondary schools in Oklahoma for Internet access. Southwestern Bell employees also serve on many civic and charitable organizations, including local chambers of commerce, school boards, the United Way, Salvation Army, American Red Cross, Boy Scouts and Girl Scouts.

Southwestern Bell and the Southwestern Bell Foundation, the company's philanthropic entity, provide millions of dollars annually to support programs and projects that strengthen education, economic development, health and human service and cultural diversity. Southwestern Bell invested $2 million in nonprofit organizations last year, and paid nearly $125 million in local and state taxes to support school social service and public works in Oklahoma. Another eighty schools benefited from $690,000 in education projects provided by the company.

Kindergarten teachers and college educators are learning together to integrate telecommunications technology into their daily curriculum as a result of the Oklahoma Telecommunications Technology Training Fund. The fund is being used to provide statewide training in the most effective use of telecommunications and distance learning technology for the enhancement of education throughout Oklahoma.

The training involves more than teaching educators how to use a computer. The program will allow educators to integrate technologies, such as the Internet and other high-tech tools, into the daily education process. The fund was created during the 1997 legislative session as part of the Oklahoma Telecommunications Act.

In an ongoing educational campaign to help fight fraud, Southwestern Bell continues its efforts to stop slamming and cramming. The company introduced in 1998 a new tool to fight slamming. Customers are now automatically notified when their long-distance service provider is changed. Southwestern Bell also announced that it would no longer provide billing services for the worst slamming and cramming offenders.

As these activities and initiatives demonstrate, Southwestern Bell, with its more than eighty-year history in Oklahoma, remains committed to the communities where its employees live and work. When consumers do business with Southwestern Bell, Oklahoma's friendly, neighborhood, global communications company—they're supporting the local economy.

Left: Preserving our proud past: Bob and Betty McCoy (pictured here) teamed up with David and Gary McCann to open a Pioneer Museum in Oklahoma City at 7001 Northwest 23rd Street.

Below: Bethany's Children's Center resident Lionel Garcia and Southwestern Bell Pioneer Fred Brooks take a break after completing work on a 20-foot by 30-foot physical therapy outdoor play yard. A group of Pioneers volunteered their time to build the play area in the center's therapy courtyard to benefit nearly 100 children.

Oklahoma Cattlemen's Association

Oklahoma is cattle country. Producers and cattle feeders, large and small, have been major contributors to the economy and life of this land for many years now. Though an abundance of wild livestock roamed the plains of Oklahoma after their introduction into the area by Spanish explorers and missionaries in the 1500s, today's cattle ranching was first introduced into the region by Indians of the Five Civilized Tribes. As the livestock industry began to take shape and grow in Oklahoma, modern ranches sprang up around the state and were producing thousands of quality calves each year. Shortly after 1900 several attempts were made to create a statewide association. By 1947, about thirty-six livestock organizations dotted the state. Cattlemen began to realize the importance of a large, unified state association as threats of declining prices and possible governmental intervention swept across the country.

On March 6, 1950 a group of Seminole cattlemen contributed $5 each to pay for a charter and incorporate the organization of the Oklahoma Cattlemen's Association. The first meeting of the group, with 500 members and $3500 in the treasury, was held on March 29, 1951 in Oklahoma City.

The Oklahoma Cattlemen's Association, headquartered in the historic Oklahoma National Stockyards, provides a voice for over 70,000 farms and ranches in Oklahoma, making the OCA the official spokesman of the beef cattle industry, the number one agricultural industry in the state. Oklahoma's beef cattle industry accounts for 5.6 percent of the gross state product, $3.52 billion in total economy-wide activity and $2.12 billion in total cash receipts, and provides the state with over 88,000 jobs in rural and urban areas. Oklahoma cattlemen produce approximately 5.4 million head cattle and calves each year through 62,000 producers, with 400,000 head of cattle in Oklahoma feed lots today. Oklahoma Cattlemen's Association members represent 4.6 percent of the nation's cattle and calves.

OCA makes available many important services. They include a theft reward program, youth awards, educational scholarships, beef and leadership education workshops, sponsorship of OCA Range Round-Up, OCA Fall Cattle Drive, Oklahoma CattleWomen, Inc., Oklahoma Junior Cattlemen's Association, and the OCJA Preview Show. The OCA is also the official state Brand Registrar with over 14,000 ranch brands registered. *The Oklahoma Cowman* is produced and published by the OCA. This monthly publication is the source of membership communication. *The Cowman* is Oklahoma's most respected livestock publication. Bound volumes dating to 1963 preserve Oklahoma's beef cattle history.

The OCA proudly supports it county organizations. Our Association is guided and funded by its member producers. Organization leaders are selected by their fellow producers and represent six districts throughout the state. With a voice in each area of the state, a diversity of Oklahoma's beef industry is represented.

A progressive industry held strong by its historic roots in the traditions of Oklahoma farmers and ranchers, the Oklahoma Cattlemen's Association continues to work closely in cooperation with the Oklahoma State University College of Agriculture Services and Natural Resources and the College of Veterinary Medicine, and the Oklahoma Beef Industry Council and others as they move forward propelling the industry along its successful course.

✧

Top: OCA Class V Young Cattlemen's Leadership Conference members visit the Oklahoma State Capitol.

Below: President John F. Kennedy attends Oklahoma Angus Field Day at the Kermac Angus Ranch, Poteau, Oklahoma, October 29, 1961. Pictured from the left: U.S. Senator Bob Kerr; Kennedy; Longtime OCA member Dr. Paul Keesee; U.S. Congressman Tom Steed; Mrs. Kerr; and American Angus Association Executive Vice-President Glen Bratcher.

Oklahoma Beef Checkoff Program Administered by the Oklahoma Beef Industry Council

The beef checkoff began in Oklahoma in January 1983, when the Oklahoma legislature authorized a checkoff of twenty-five cents-per-head each time a beef animal was sold. This legislation created the forerunner of the Oklahoma Beef Industry Council, the Oklahoma Beef Commission, as an agency of state government. The purpose of the checkoff was to generate money that could be used to fund beef promotion, research, and education.

At the same time, cattle producers were meeting to discuss the need for a nationwide beef checkoff that would be uniform and coordinated in all fifty states. Like Oklahoma's program, the purpose of the program was to provide funds for beef promotion, research, and education, as well as for international marketing programs. In December 1985, President Ronald Reagan signed the Farm Bill, which created the federal Beef Promotion Act and Order. The act gave cattle producers the authority to assess themselves $1-per-head each time a bovine was sold.

The beef checkoff program was initially set up as a pilot program so that beef producers would have an opportunity to vote on the beef checkoff program at a later date to indicate if they wanted it to continue. In May 1988, a national referendum was held and approximately eighty percent of those beef producers voting indicated they wanted to continue the program.

In 1990, Oklahoma beef producers requested that the Oklahoma legislature repeal the law that created the Oklahoma Beef Commission. On January 1, 1991, legislation became effective, and the Oklahoma Beef Industry Council was allowed to operate as a non-profit organization under the federal law. The council, which administers the checkoff program, is made up of nine voting directors who represent the Oklahoma Cattlemen's Association, the CattleWomen's Association, the Farm Bureau, the Farmers Union, Dairy Farmers of America, the Livestock Marketing Association, and the Senate and House Agricultural Committees.

A dynamic and profitable beef industry, which concentrates resources, consistently meets consumer needs, and increases beef demand is the vision of the Oklahoma beef checkoff program. The program exists because of beef producers' commitment to and investment in their industry. It is to the credit of all Oklahoma beef producers that the checkoff program operates in the spirit of self-help and cooperation.

Today, the beef checkoff program generates approximately $80 million a year, nationwide. Of the $1 per head that is collected in state, $.50 automatically goes to the Cattlemen's Beef Research and Promotion Board to support national beef promotion, research, and education across the United States.

The program has been successful in implementing advertising on national television, on radio and in magazines, which reaches millions of consumers each year, with campaigns like "Beef. Real Food For Real People" and the current, popular campaign "Beef. It's What's For Dinner." The checkoff has been instrumental in nutrition research and education that has measurably increased beef's image among healthcare professionals. It also reaches over 6.5 million students each year across the United States with valuable educational resources about the beef industry, nutrition and food safety.

The Oklahoma beef checkoff program continues to strengthen the beef industry's position in the market place by increasing demand for beef and maximizing beef producers' profits through promotion, research, education, and consumer information.

The Electric Cooperatives of Oklahoma

Founding fathers of rural-generated electricity in Oklahoma are shown on January 31, 1950 when they signed loan papers to build a generation and transmission system across the state to ensure the lowest-possible power would be available to rural consumers. The signing ceremony for the $12 million loan (which was repaid in record time) was attended by (left to right) Representative Victor Wickersham of Oklahoma; Representative Morgan Moulder of Missouri; Joseph M. Maddox, manager of Southwest Rural Electric Association, Inc., Tipton; Representative George Howard Wilson of Oklahoma; Billie Bryan, manager of Caddo Electric Cooperative, Binger; Jack Yokum, secretary to Representative Mike Monroney of Oklahoma; Howard G. Crocker, manager of Northwestern Electric Cooperative, Inc., Woodward; REA Administrator Claude R. Wickard (seated); Representative Toby Morris of Oklahoma; Representative George Christopher of Missouri; Clark McWhorter of Blair, Oklahoma, president of the National Rural Electric Cooperative Association; Representative Clare Magee of Missouri; Representative John Rankin of Mississippi (seated); Roy C. Boescher, manager of Cimarron Electric Cooperative, Kingfisher; SPA Administrator Douglas Wright; Cecil I. Neely, manager of Northfork Electric Cooperative, Inc., Sayre; and Don Dage, manager of Cotton Electric Cooperative, Walters.

The coming of age of electricity vastly changed daily life in rural Oklahoma. Cities and towns across the country had enjoyed electricity for years, but it was not economically feasible for rural Americans until the Rural Electric Administration was established under President Franklin Delano Roosevelt on May 11, 1935. Executive Order 7037, which created the REA, established it as a relief agency "to initiate, formulate, administer, and supervise a program of approved projects with respect to the generation, transmission, and distribution of electric energy in rural areas" and would set out to electrify farms across rural America. On May 21, 1936, President Roosevelt signed the Rural Electrification Act and transformed the REA into a full-status government agency. Through the outstanding technical and management skills of REA engineers, electricity became "do-able" for farmers and their co-ops across America. Farm wives were pushing their husbands to pay the $5 membership fee that would finally establish electricity in their homes.

The co-op idea seemed a natural way for farm families to bring the rural electrical enterprise into existence. Though it was met with skepticism, rural folks understood the principles of cooperation and soon realized the "dynamic force, which would carry rural America out of darkness."

Eventually, twenty-eight consumer-owned rural electric cooperatives were formed, providing state-of-the-art electrical distribution, on demand, in every corner of the state. Also, these co-ops formed large generation and transmission co-ops, Western Farmers and KAMO, to ensure affordable power would be available to distribute to consumers.

In their own words, many of the founders of these cooperatives share their stories—stories that echo a sense of purpose and Oklahoma pride.

Buddy Anderson, a member of the Choctaw Electric Co-op for fifty years, has served on the CEC's Board of Trustees for sixteen years. He is an Oklahoman through and through, living within two miles of his birthplace north of Valliant all his life. With a chuckle, he recalls growing up in the 1930s and having to carry milk to the spring in the morning to keep it cold, then carrying it back to the house for supper. When electricity finally arrived in the late 1940s, he and his wife rejoiced. The "roving Maytag salesman" was famous among members of the community. Though they used their entire savings for the down payment on an electric icebox, the salesman returned the next day to inquire if they would like to buy an electric washing machine on the same down payment. Oddly, he arrived just as Mrs. Anderson was stooped over her rub-board washing the clothes. "We got that washing machine. And life has just gone from better to best since then," says Buddy. "It was just a great experience and today, it remains the same. The co-op is always progressing, never standing still."

James Elms remembers paying the $5 membership fee and thinking to himself, "Okay, but it will never happen." Three or four years later, they were plugging in their Maytag washing machine. "It has been an overwhelming thing to see through the years...a real part of rural development." Elms has been on the board of Tri-County Electric Co-op for forty-five years. Today, the co-op represents to him an example of American progress and Oklahoma ingenuity.

The Red River Valley REA has provided the electricity in Harold Lester's home throughout his entire life. A board member since June of 1965, Lester remembers helping his father dig the hole for the electrical pole for lines to their home in 1938. He agrees that the co-op has always been progressive and has seen firsthand that "good members mean a good co-op."

J. Eugene Blackketter, a member of Western Farmers Electric Cooperative and a WFEC board member for twenty-eight years, says, "The real success story of generation cooperatives like Western Farmers is threefold—the quality and dedication of the people at the plant, a well-trained and totally dedicated management team, and a board with vision."

Cotton Electric Cooperative published a retrospective in 1994 of the role played by electric co-ops. "The year was 1937. People living in towns like Temple, Duncan, and Waurika were still without air conditioning. But thanks to electricity, they had running water, indoor plumbing, ceiling lights and lamps for youngsters to study. There were conveniences such as refrigerators, electric fans and the radio. Through the radio, they could keep up with the world, gathering around to laugh at *Amos and Andy*, or listen to the chilling speeches of Adolph Hitler in faraway Germany."

"But outside the towns, things were different. Unless the home had a 'Delco' generating system, rural families had no lights, no home appliances, no equipment to lighten the load of farm chores. Kids studied next to kerosene lamps; kitchens had wood stoves, hand pumps (or buckets), and everyone tramped out to the 'outhouse' when nature called."

The Cotton REC history continues, "Civic leaders began hearing about the new Rural Electrification Administration. They held meetings, drove rural roads, talking across fences to farmers in the fields, stopping on front porches and sitting in living rooms explaining how a $5 membership fee would make a big difference on the farm."

"Enough sign ups were made to have a state charter issued September 15, 1938, which states, 'Cotton Electric Cooperative, Inc....shall make electricity energy available to its shareholder-members at the lowest cost consistent with sound economy and good management.'"

As the formation of cooperatives rolled across Oklahoma, the availability of competitively priced electricity helped create the revolution in agriculture which now sees the world being fed by a relatively few farmers in America's breadbasket. Thanks to co-ops, the energy to support America's army and navy in World War II was never in doubt as lines were strung to drilling rigs and pump jacks across the oil belt.

Serving on the board of trustees of Northwestern Electric co-op for eleven years, Ray Smith looks to the future of the rural electric cooperatives with great anticipation. As deregulation appears on the horizon, Smith believes that today rural co-ops will benefit from a more aggressive, competitive stand in the marketplace.

The manager of the Association of Electric Cooperatives, Larry Watkins, shares this view. "The cooperative business model has proved to be the most efficient method of distributing electric energy. It continues to serve us well while enhancing the quality of life and improving productivity across Oklahoma. We are all prepared to continue that progress into the new millennium. It is still people that matter."

The Electric Cooperatives of Oklahoma—the power of human connections.

These pages are sponsored by the following cooperatives: Alfalfa Electric Cooperative, Caddo Electric Cooperative, Cimarron Electric Cooperative, Cotton Electric Cooperative, East Central Electric Cooperative, Kay Electric Cooperative, KAMO Power, Northeast Oklahoma Electric Cooperative, Oklahoma Electric Cooperative, Red River Valley Rural Electric Association, Rural Electric Cooperative, Southeastern Electric Cooperative, Southwest Rural Electric Association, Verdigris Valley Electric Cooperative, and Western Farmers Electric Cooperative.

✧

Above: Low-tech methods, like those used by KAMO Power and other cooperatives, built the 104,035 miles of powerlines across the state. In contrast, all the powerlines inside the towns of the state served by investor-owned utilities add up to less than 40,000 miles.

Below: The rural electric system has been pay as you go. Co-op systems that underpriced their product or failed to reinvest in plant and equipment were not eligible for loans. The result: a vital rural asset that does not require massive federal loans. Co-ops have been an example of combining public loans with private enterprise to achieve a national goal.

Lugert-Altus Irrigation District

The Lugert-Altus Irrigation District is responsible for operation of the system of canals and ditches that irrigate approximately 46,000 acres of privately owned land within Jackson and Greer Counties of southwestern Oklahoma, provide flood control on the North Fork of the Red River, act as an augmented municipal water supply for the City of Altus, fish and wildlife conservation benefits and, as a by-product later, recreational facilities were developed. Project features include the Altus Dam, Lake Lugert, the Main, Altus, West and Ozark Canals, a 221-mile distribution system, and twenty-six miles of drains.

Greer County was formed in 1886 by an act of the Texas Legislature. At that time, the State of Texas contended that the North Fork of the Red River was the boundary between Oklahoma and Texas but the U.S. Supreme Court decreed in 1896 that Greer County belonged to Oklahoma. The present counties of Jackson, Greer, and Harmon were formed later from the original Greer County. The area was largely homesteaded prior to 1890. Most of the project lands were dry-farmed for many years prior to the construction of the Altus Dam so crop yields were good in wet years and poor in dry years. Irrigation of small tracts by private interests after 1927 demonstrated the value of irrigation.

Engineering investigations to determine the feasibility of developing an irrigation project in the area began in 1902, and continued periodically until 1937. During 1937, renewed interest in irrigation by local civic leaders, such as W. C. Austin for whom the project was named, and the State of Oklahoma resulted in further investigations by several federal agencies. The efforts of these agencies were coordinated, and the Bureau of Reclamation conducted the remaining investigations and construction preliminaries. A project planning report issued in December of 1937 recorded the results of the investigation.

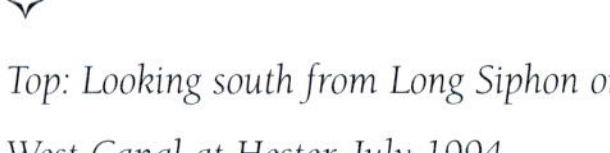

Top: Looking south from Long Siphon on West Canal at Hester, July 1994.

Below: The outlet from the W. C. Austin Dam to Main Canal at Lake Lugert.

Construction of the W. C. Austin Project was authorized by the Rivers and Harbors Act of June 28, 1938 and specifically by the President Franklin Roosevelt on February 13, 1941. Construction began on April 21, 1941 but was interrupted by World War II. Work resumed May 12, 1944 when the War Production Board lifted restrictions. The first section of canal lying within project lands was completed on April 30, 1946. First water deliveries to project lands were made on June 19, 1946. Construction of the distribution system was completed in 1949 and main drainage features were completed during 1953. The Lugert-Altus Irrigation District has constructed several additional miles of drains.

The district consists of six person board of directors elected by the shareholders for a term of three years. District staff consists of a district manager, secretary, treasurer, twelve ditch riders, superintendent/water master, equipment operators, and damtender. The district's total annual operating budget is $1.5 million. An usage information for 1993 to 1998 accounting for irrigated land planted showed an average of 73.3 percent was used for cotton; 8.2 percent wheat, milo, and other feed; 7.1 percent alfalfa; 1 percent peanuts; and 1 percent soybeans with the remaining 7.6 percent split amongst pecans, hay, pasture, and fallow fields.

It takes the farmers working with LAID to ensure smooth delivery. The farmers are pursuing water conservation at their end of the system while LAID is making great efforts to improve delivery efficiency, which is an indicator of how much water is lost in delivery due to seepage, spillage or a similar type of waste. Cooperative efforts with the Bureau of Reclamation have resulted in seepage studies, an evapotranspiration system, and flow meters. Mobile measuring equipment has also been acquired to ensure that farmers are receiving correct amounts of water. Projects undertaken by LAID follow an aggressive pattern towards increased water delivery efficiency with open canal laterals being replaced with pipe at a cost of $100,000 per year, and main canals being lined with clay, Teranap, and concrete.

One of Lugert-Altus Irrigation District's main goals is to educate farmers about farm conservation practices. The climate and the pricing structure associated with LAID influences farmers to be conscious of water usage and water wastage. Although no formal water conservation plan exists, many different water conservation measures are in use at LAID. Measures taken by some farmers include concrete head ditches, drip systems, center pivot systems, tailwater pits, and polypipe. Farmers that have not implemented equipment that increases irrigation efficiency recognized the cost benefits associated with the systems and monetary restrictions are the overwhelming cause of low conversion.

Goals for the future of Lugert Altus Irrigation District include reducing seepage and loss due to heavy weed growth, and develop and use evapotranspiration tools developed by the Bureau of Reclamation.

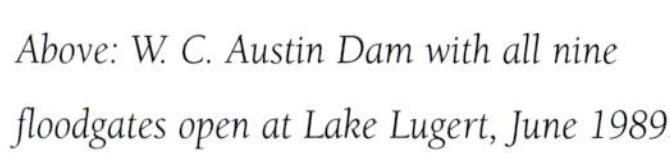

Above: W. C. Austin Dam with all nine floodgates open at Lake Lugert, June 1989.

Bottom: The District borrowed $1.2 million from Oklahoma Water Resources Board to finance this new concrete lining for Main Canal at Byrd Mountains, July 1997.

Esker (Formerly Teubner & Associates)

✧

Top: Russell W. Teubner, president, believes that computing and communication markets move like a pendulum. They swing from one approach, or technology, to another–and often return exactly where they began.

Below: The Stillwater offices of Esker (Teubner & Associates) are a tasteful combination of the old and new–preserving the historical essence of the building while incorporating the latest in technology to make an attractive, functional workplace.

Don't tell Russell W. (Russ) Teubner "it can't be done." That phrase only inspires him to find a solution and prove it CAN be done. Teubner and Associates was founded in 1983 to solve just such a problem.

Teubner, who graduated from Oklahoma State University's College of Business in 1978 with a bachelor's degree in management science and computer systems, was assistant director at OSU's computer center in Stillwater when the problem arose. The school had an IBM mainframe computer in place, and later purchased a mini-computer system from a different vendor. However, the systems were not compatible. Seeking a way to network the two systems, Teubner wrote a software program that allowed the computers to communicate with one another.

Figuring that other companies were encountering similar problems, Teubner asked OSU for permission to develop the software as a business. He was granted permission, but advised,"Don't quit your day job."

Teubner built his business on what he saw as a very simple principle. "Over time, computing and communication markets move like a pendulum. They swing from one approach, or technology, to another and often return exactly where they began. For example, in the mid-80s everyone said the mainframe was a dinosaur and began to install lots of mini-computer systems. Now, in the late '90s, the mainframe is back."

To exploit this principle, Teubner created a line of software products that help large organizations integrate existing and emerging technology or, as he says, "helping customers get from where they are to where they want to be." He adds, "And as long as the technology innovation rate exceeds the implementation rate, there is plenty of business opportunity."

Esker began in 1985 in Lyon, France as a software consulting company and became a European leader in connectivity software for the enterprise. Esker has subsidiary offices in the United Kingdom, France, Germany, Italy, Spain, and Australia, with an extensive network of distributors and resellers in forty-five countries.

As an European company that develops software products that integrate, and emerging technologies, Esker sought a strong United States presence and was attracted to Teubner by its common mission, as well as its solid reputation and products.

Thus, Esker S.A., a publicly held software company headquartered in Lyon, France and Teubner & Associates, Inc. a privately held software company in Stillwater, Oklahoma merged in June of 1998. The result was a more global company, giving it a stronger presence on both sides of the Atlantic.

Sixteen years after being told it can't be done, Teubner and Associates, has distinguished itself for three consecutive years as one of *Inc. Magazine*'s 500 fastest growing private companies in America. And, through its merger with Esker S.A., is now a $45 million public company, and the largest software company in Oklahoma.

Griffin Television, L.L.C. News 9 KWTV

Top: Stockholders of Oklahoma Television Corporation and owners of KWTV met on April 5, 1954 for groundbreaking ceremonies for the new tower. John Griffin wields the pick while Roy J. Turner prepares to scoop out the first shovel of earth. Others present are (left to right) Luther Dulaney, Edgar Bell, James Leake, and Henry Griffing.

Below: The Spirit of Oklahoma, *the KWTV news helicopter.*

The only locally owned and operated major television station in Oklahoma, KWTV began broadcast programming on December 20, 1953. On April 5, 1954, John T. Griffin, James Leake, and others broke ground on a 1,572-foot tower that would boost KWTV's signal to 316,000 watts. The September 20, 1954 issue of *LIFE* magazine would herald to the world that the tower would top the Empire State Building by 100 feet as the tallest man-made structure in the world. With such innovation and foresight, the late John T. Griffin, KWTV founder and a native Oklahoman, established a clear mission to focus resources upon the development of electronic information and a distinct excellence in local news journalism that is responsible to serving the needs of Oklahomans. It is little wonder that KWTV's motto "The Spirit of Oklahoma" leaves such an indelible impression upon the Oklahoma landscape.

In the early 1990s, the mantle of leadership passed from Martha Griffin-White to John and David Griffin. KWTV continues as a pioneer in the broadcast industry and has won the National Peabody Award and RTNDA (Radio Television News Directors Association) National Award for Overall Excellence.

In 1980, KWTV was the first commercial television station in the United States to install and operate Doppler radar—a technology that provides advance warning of impending severe weather. The station has continued to develop software and detection systems providing more accurate forecasting and presentation of weather warnings. This commitment to the safety of Oklahoma's families during severe weather was never more apparent than when the deadly F5 tornado of May 3, 1999 was detected nearly an hour before it moved into the southern sections of Oklahoma County.

KWTV's local ownership remains committed to its original principles of high journalistic standards as it embraces an active involvement with the communities of Oklahoma. The company is preparing for the future with projects such as Sooner Sports Properties, and NewsNow 53. In response to the needs of its viewers, 9Online has evolved as one of the most comprehensive Internet web sites in the broadcast industry. The ceaseless commitment to community involvement is reflected in the extensive calendar of community events undertaken by KWTV, and further underscored by the support and encouragement that the station gives to staff members as they participate in outside organizations and events that benefit the people of Oklahoma.

Dobson Communications Corporation

Dobson Communications Corporation began in the rural Oklahoma oil fields in 1936 as the Dobson family created the first telephone company in the local area. Today that same exchange remains in operation and stands as a testament to the heritage and determination that proudly follows the work of this nationally renowned communications corporation. A ceaseless commitment to the needs of rural customers continues today as the primary focus as Dobson Communications currently provides diversified telecommunications products and services to over 397,000 customers and employs nearly 1,700 people. The company provides wireless services to customers under the names Dobson Cellular Systems, Air Touch Cellular, Wilcom Cellular and Cellular One, and wireline services through Dobson Telephone, McLoud Telephone, Dobson Fiber and Logix Communications. Dobson currently has operations in ten states including Oklahoma, Arizona, California, Kansas, Maryland, Missouri, Pennsylvania, New York, Ohio, and Texas.

As three generations of the Dobson family successfully moved the company into the 1990s with the ownership of two small independent telephone companies and revenues of $9 million, the founder's grandson, Everett Dobson, looked toward to the future with a vision of taking the company to the next level in communications. Sensing the rural lifestyle and cellular service were made for each other, Dobson Cellular Systems was born. As president, chairman and CEO, Everett Dobson and a hand-picked team of communications experts applied the company's track record of success in rural cellular markets in Oklahoma and Texas and convinced capital investors to back the company's expansion plans. Through a series of acquisitions, Dobson now operates in ten states. The population base of all Dobson Cellular Systems markets is 5.8 million people.

In October of 1997, Dobson continued its tradition of innovative communications services when it launched Logix Communications, an integrated communications provider. Led by President Stephen Dobson and Chief Operating Officer William J. Hoffman, Logix provides integrated communications services in Oklahoma and Texas to small and mid-sized business customers. Its product line includes local and long distance, as well as Internet, data, and system integration solutions.

✧

Top: Everett Dobson, chairman and chief executive officer, Dobson Communications Corporation.

Bottom: Stephen Dobson, president, Logix Communications.

Everett Dobson also created the PRIDE (Promoting Individual Development and Education) Scholarship awards. PRIDE Scholarships were developed and introduced in 1996 to help young people in the Dobson service areas promote the strength and future of the company's rural service commitment. These scholarships are awarded for academic merit, extracurricular and leadership activities. Each recipient plans to utilize his or her higher education to promote community growth and development of the rural area in which they live.

From the Oklahoma oil fields of 1936 to the proud rural communities of the twenty-first century, Dobson Communications Corporation remains a vital figure in the ever-expanding needs of a new generation in communications.

OG&E

Pioneers in public service for nearly a century, Oklahoma Gas and Electric Company (OG&E) was formed in the Oklahoma Territory in February 1902. The electric power industry was still new—for it was only twenty-three years earlier, in 1879, that Thomas Edison had fashioned the concept of central power stations. Today, OG&E remains one of the oldest chartered corporations in Oklahoma and continues to provide "power at the speed of life."

OGE Energy Corp. is the parent company of Oklahoma Gas and Electric Company and Enogex Inc. Publicly traded on the New York Stock Exchange and Pacific Exchange under the ticker symbol "OGE," the company has about 39,000 registered shareowners and is headquartered in Oklahoma City. OGE Energy has about 2,800 employees.

OG&E is a regulated electric utility with about 696,000 retail customers in Oklahoma and western Arkansas, and a number of wholesale customers throughout the region. Its power comes from eight company-owned generating plants that are either coal- or natural gas-fired. OG&E delivers its electricity across an interconnected transmission and distribution system spanning 30,000-square miles.

The company stands by its dual responsibility of protecting the environment and providing safe, reliable, and reasonably priced power. Two of OG&E's largest power plants, Sooner and Muskogee, were recently recognized for the third consecutive year among the top twenty most efficient power plants in the country—without sacrificing any environmental or safety standards.

After nearly 100 years in business, OG&E has marked a number of notable milestones. In 1928, OG&E expanded into Arkansas by purchasing the Mississippi Valley Power Company. In 1949, OG&E was the first in the nation to use a gas/steam turbine combination to produce electricity. In 1963, OG&E built the world's largest combined-cycle generating unit. In 1976, OG&E's Muskogee Power Plant began using clean-burning, low-sulfur coal. In 1986, OG&E acquired its major gas supplier, Mustang Fuel, later renaming it Enogex. And in 1999, Enogex joined the nation's top ten largest gas pipeline companies with the acquisition of Transok, LLC.

While OG&E's electric rates are more than twenty percent below the national average, the company made history again in 1999 when OG&E filed a leading-edge rate plan with the Oklahoma Corporation Commission to lower rates by an additional $83 million and freeze them until 2002. And in 2002, Oklahomans will have a choice of who provides their electric energy when the electric industry deregulates. OG&E is preparing for the opportunity to be the energy provider of choice.

For more information visit OG&E on the Internet at www.oge.com.

✧

Below: Early statehood, OG&E meter men in a classic Model T utility truck.

Bottom: OG&E bucket truck hoists linemen to repair damage from the 1999 F5 Tornado in Oklahoma City.

PHOTO COURTESY OF OG&E.

Public Service Company of Oklahoma

Public Service Company of Oklahoma (PSO) originated during Oklahoma's pre-statehood days as the Vinita Electric Light and Power Company, which was chartered in 1889 to provide electric service in Indian Territory. On May 29, 1913, PSO was incorporated in Oklahoma, consisting of the original Vinita firm combined with electric companies at Atoka, Coalgate, Lehigh, Guthrie, and Tulsa. It was a humble beginning, but PSO officials soon revealed plans to provide electric service twenty-four hours a day.

Above: PSO powers the city of Tulsa and some 230 communities in eastern and southwestern Oklahoma. In foreground is Riverside Station, situated along the Arkansas River south of Tulsa, near Jenks.

Below: Louie the Lightning Bug is the company's popular safety "spokesbug," informing young children how to be safe around electricity. Louie conveys his safety messages through appearances in schools and parades as well as in television commercials.

During the prosperous '20s, PSO bounded ahead. Power lines were extended to communities without electric service. Small existing electric systems merged with PSO to form a single, integrated company allowing PSO to provide energy efficiently and at a lower price.

Expansion continued during the 1930s and 1940s. By 1947, PSO had established the 30,000-square-mile area it currently serves.

Today, PSO provides service to approximately one million people in eastern and southwestern Oklahoma. The company's capacity exceeds 3.7 million kilowatts, one-fourth provided by coal and three-fourths provided by natural gas. PSO is a wholly-owned subsidiary of the Central and South West (CSW) Corporation, a global energy services provider based in Dallas, Texas. Included in CSW's portfolio of energy-related businesses are four U.S. electric utility companies that operate in four states in the Southwest.

Today, PSO and the other CSW companies are preparing to operate in a restructured and highly competitive business environment. In Oklahoma, full retail competition commences July 1, 2002. Customers will be able to choose the provider of their electricity, but the delivery of that energy will remain the responsibility of local distribution companies.

PSO's formula for success in the marketplace is simple: continue to offer low prices (PSO's electric prices overall are forty percent below the national average) and excellent service, including highly reliable electric service and convenient around-the-clock access by customers whenever they need to contact PSO.

PSO is an important force for community growth and development. In 1998, PSO and other CSW electric utilities played roles in attracting 155 companies to build or expand facilities in their service areas, providing $561 million in investments and nearly 11,000 jobs.

PSO and the other CSW System electric companies have a long history of environmental stewardship including, in PSO's case, support for the Tallgrass Prairie Preserve, efforts to conserve and increase the population of threatened birds of prey, and promotion of non-polluting electric vehicles.

Another environmental initiative is to protect and improve the urban forest in the communities PSO serves. By properly pruning trees, planting appropriate species, and educating the public, PSO works to both beautify its communities and reduce interference of tree limbs with power lines. In 1998, PSO was honored for the sixth time with the Treeline USA designation presented by the National Arbor Foundation for its program.

The CSW System companies also are committed to using renewable and other forms of energy that have a minimal effect on the environment. In 1998, the companies announced plans to purchase 75,000 kilowatts of renewable energy from a wind generation facility in Texas. The companies also operate a seventy-five-acre renewable energy demonstration project in Texas that includes wind turbines, solar arrays, and rooftop photovoltaic systems.

PSO is headquartered in the building that housed Tulsa's Central High School for more than sixty years. This is appropriate, given the major role that PSO has played and continues to play in the economic history and development of Oklahoma.

Pioneer Telephone Cooperative, Inc.

As you drive through the beautiful town of Kingfisher, Oklahoma the historic edifice that has become the executive offices of Pioneer Telephone Cooperative, Inc. stands out not only as an architectural landmark in the heart of Kingfisher County, but also reflects an important tribute to the proud heritage of this "total communications company."

It was early in 1951 that Oklahoma State Senator Roy C. Boecher began hearing from rural residents hoping to obtain first-class telephone service for themselves. With no telephone cooperatives existing in Oklahoma and no laws regarding their establishment, the Senator took steps to create a telephone cooperative in the area. In 1953, Pioneer Telephone was created as a cooperative telephone company with four exchanges, four part time employees and an investment of $50,000.

Under the innovative leadership of Chief Executive Officer Johnnie R. Ruhl, the fourth employee hired by the company in 1953, and General Manager Richard Ruhl, Pioneer Telephone now employs over 600 people serving an area covering seventy-six exchanges, 10,900 square miles and over 50,000 member-families living in thirty Oklahoma counties. Pioneer Telephone has grown into a multimillion-dollar corporation, qualifying it as one of the largest telephone cooperatives in the United States. Diversification has allowed the company to achieve substantial growth in the past two decades. Creating a world of unlimited possibilities has been the cornerstone of the company as they provide the latest in telecommunication products and services.

The cooperative is governed by a thirteen-member board of trustees elected by fellow cooperative members in their districts. The Pioneer Board of Trustees are community leaders who are successful in their professions, and highly respected in their districts. Elected from individual districts, each member represents the entire cooperative membership and assures excellence in public relations for the company.

October of 1991 brought to Pioneer Telephone a historic opportunity when it began the restoration of the Anheuser-Busch Building constructed as a two-story rectangular brick veneer building in downtown Kingfisher between 1899 and 1900. In 1993, Pioneer Telephone Cooperative restored the building to its former Victorian beauty. For their dedication in restoring the building and the surrounding areas, the company received the Beautification and Landscaping Award presented by Keep Oklahoma Beautiful, Inc., at the Statewide Environmental Excellence Awards Banquet held in August of 1998. The Anheuser-Busch Building serves today as headquarters of Pioneer Telephone.

In 1996, the Board of Trustees, Management and Employees adopted the Strategic Plan, a tool to address the increasingly complex business environment in which Pioneer Telephone operates. One of the results of the Strategic Plan was the development of the company's mission statement for their future. That mission stands true today as the company moves into a new century of telecommunications services in Oklahoma, a century in which the possibilities and dedication to customers remains limitless for Pioneer Telephone Cooperative, Inc.

Mission Statement

The Pioneer Telephone Cooperative family of companies will provide high quality communications products and services as your total communications company. We are dedicated to our customers and employees while being partners in progress with our communities.

✧

Top: Front row (left to right): Johnnie Ruhl, Chief Executive Officer; Richard Ruhl, General Manager. Back row (left to right): Pete Peterman, Assistant General Manager; Harold Logsdon, Legal Counsel; Jim Eaton, Assistant General Manager.

Below: The warm glow of the streetlights in downtown Kingfisher illuminate the Pioneer Telephone Headquarters Building located on the corner of Highway 81 and Robberts Avenue. These nostalgic lamps stand invitingly on the hand-laid brick walk, reminiscent of early Kingfisher.

Manufacturing, Industry & Diversification

Oklahoma's manufacturers produce goods which contribute to economic growth and stability of the state

Friends

Johnson Oil Company,
Lawton

✧

Wayne Spears, better known as Pawnee Bill, and his horse Bear Paw, are familiar sites at parades throughout Oklahoma and other states. Spears, portraying Pawnee Bill who founded the famous Pawnee Bill Wild West Show, tours the nation promoting the Wild West heritage of the state.

COURTESY CINDY CARTMELL

HALLIBURTON COMPANY

✧

Top, left: Erle Halliburton, 1919 established New Method Oil Well Cementing Company in his one-room wood frame home in Wilson, Oklahoma.

Top, right: Erle Halliburton with his wife and partner, Vida, who once pawned her wedding ring when Erle's business was in need of immediate cash. Her investment paid off—and she did get the ring back.

Below: January 1920, Hewitt Field, Oklahoma. Erle Halliburton at far left in dark suit, directs his workmen, while Skelly Oil Company President William Skelly, center, looks on. Halliburton promised to bring the wild oil well under control or he would not charge a dime.

The Halliburton story begins in 1918 when Erle P. Halliburton joined the Perkins Oil Well Cementing Company as a truck driver. Erle, twenty-six years old, was married to Vida Halliburton, and had already worked at a long list of occupations. However, the job with Perkins would prove to be a springboard for the future for Halliburton and his family.

He only worked for Perkins for a year before he was fired for offering his boss too many suggestions, but that year seemed to deposit oil in Erle's blood. Years later, he would say, "The two best things that ever happened to me were being hired and then fired by the Perkins Oil Well Cementing Company."

Erle moved from California to Wichita Falls, Texas to take advantage of the gushing oil fields nearby. He went into business by making a deal with his neighbor. In exchange for the use of Erle's outdoor privy, the neighbor let Erle use his wagon and team of horses. Halliburton borrowed a pump, purchased some hoes, built a mixing box, and made it known to anyone that would listen that he was now in the business of cementing oil wells. He persuaded four friends to invest $250 to $1,000 each, for a collective fifty percent interest in his New Method Oil Well Cementing Company.

A scarcity of customers and the need to stay a step ahead of his creditors prompted Erle to move to Wilson, Oklahoma. His family now included Erle, Jr., age three, and Zola, age one. Erle found work at the new fields that were being drilled in Wilson, but there was no housing available, so they lived in an oil field shack for $50 a month. Later, Erle and a carpenter built a one-room house in three days. This tiny structure became home and office.

Each day, Erle worked in the fields and Vida tended to the house and handled business calls. In the evenings the couple did the

company's books. One evening, as they realized they would not have the funds to complete a job, the conversation turned to Halliburton's new idea: using a measuring line to continually measure the depth of the cement as it was pumped down a well. The next morning, Erle took Vida's suggestion and pawned her wedding ring to buy the materials for the measuring line. That was the beginning of Halliburton's real success.

The measuring line became a valuable tool for cementing oil and gas wells. Halliburton patented the idea. Things really started to move in January 1920, when Erle proved he could control gushing oil wells with his cementing process. With his reputation established, Halliburton bought his first cementing wagon and hired several full-time employees. Suddenly, Vida was very busy scheduling jobs and taking messages for her overjoyed husband.

Halliburton's success continued as his list of inventions grew with the Jet Mixer, which speedily mixed cement with water and pumped cement directly into the well pipe, and the Sack Cutter, which opened bags of cement and dumped them into the mixer.

In 1921, Halliburton moved to Duncan, Oklahoma, placing the company in the heart of the state's oil business. As word of Halliburton's services spread, Erle fitted five Army surplus trucks with cement pumps and used them in the oil fields within 500 miles of Duncan. By 1923, business was flourishing and Erle had a fleet of twenty cementing trucks.

In 1924, Erle proposed to seven large oil companies, his best customers, that they form a corporation. The oil companies needed Erle's patented services, so they agreed and formed Halliburton Oil Well Cementing Company (Howco).

It became Halliburton Company in 1960, after it had outgrown its original name. It had acquired Welex Jet Services, a wireline electric well service, and Otis Engineering, specializing in developing methods and manufacturing equipment for controlling pressures in oil and gas wells. Howco had grown well beyond oil well cementing, and now offered a wide range of energy services.

A major milestone occurred in 1962 when Halliburton acquired Brown & Root, a leading engineering and construction firm. Brown and Root had started in 1919 building roads in Texas, and had branched out to many kinds of engineering and construction work

✧

Top: In order to keep up with demand for his company's services, Erle Halliburton fitted Army surplus trucks with cement pumps.

Bottom: An illustration featuring the Halliburton Sack Cutter, which opened bags of cement and dumped them into a cement mixer, and the Halliburton Jet Mixer, which mixed cement with water and pumped cement directory into well pipe.

all over the world, including building the first commercial offshore oil platform in the Gulf of Mexico. The acquisition of Brown and Root gave Halliburton a whole new dimension. In addition to providing oil field services, the company now designed and built oil and gas pipelines, drilling platforms, and petrochemical plants.

Halliburton continued to grow and acquire companies that extended its ability to serve the energy industry. Then, in 1998, Halliburton merged with Dresser Industries, which nearly doubled its size to $17 billion in revenues and approximately 100,000 employees worldwide. Dresser's strengths in energy services, engineering, and energy equipment complemented Halliburton's existing capabilities, so that the combined company is now the world's leader in these three business segments.

Halliburton today has more than 300 working locations in over 120 countries. It is active in all phases of oil and gas exploration and development, from seismic interpretation to drilling and production, to construction of pipelines and processing plants. Halliburton also designs, builds, and/or provides project management for important structures all over the world, such as Houston's new baseball stadium and highways in developing countries. In addition, it provides crucial logistical services to the U.S. military in places like Haiti and the Balkans.

The vision and hard work of Erle and Vida Halliburton launched a company that is now one of the largest and most successful of its kind in the world. They would no doubt be pleased and proud to see all that has grown out of a borrowed wagon and team of horses.

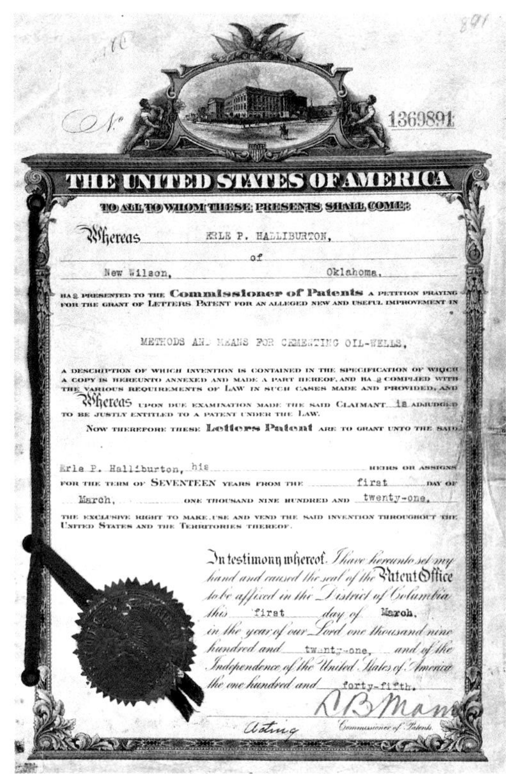

No. 1369891

THE UNITED STATES OF AMERICA

TO ALL TO WHOM THESE PRESENTS SHALL COME:

Whereas ERLE P. HALLIBURTON, of New Wilson, Oklahoma,

HAS PRESENTED TO THE Commissioner of Patents A PETITION PRAYING FOR THE GRANT OF LETTERS PATENT FOR AN ALLEGED NEW AND USEFUL IMPROVEMENT IN

METHODS AND MEANS FOR CEMENTING OIL-WELLS,

A DESCRIPTION OF WHICH INVENTION IS CONTAINED IN THE SPECIFICATION OF WHICH A COPY IS HEREUNTO ANNEXED AND MADE A PART HEREOF, AND HAS COMPLIED WITH THE VARIOUS REQUIREMENTS OF LAW IN SUCH CASES MADE AND PROVIDED, AND

Whereas UPON DUE EXAMINATION MADE THE SAID CLAIMANT is ADJUDGED TO BE JUSTLY ENTITLED TO A PATENT UNDER THE LAW.

NOW THEREFORE THESE Letters Patent ARE TO GRANT UNTO THE SAID Erle P. Halliburton, his HEIRS OR ASSIGNS FOR THE TERM OF SEVENTEEN YEARS FROM THE first DAY OF March, ONE THOUSAND NINE HUNDRED AND twenty-one, THE EXCLUSIVE RIGHT TO MAKE, USE AND VEND THE SAID INVENTION THROUGHOUT THE UNITED STATES AND THE TERRITORIES THEREOF.

In testimony whereof I have hereunto set my hand and caused the seal of the Patent Office to be affixed in the District of Columbia this first day of March, in the year of our Lord one thousand nine hundred and twenty-one, and of the Independence of the United States of America the one hundred and forty-fifth.

Acting Commissioner of Patents.

Top: A patent certificate for one of the many innovations Erle Halliburton brought to the oil and cement industries.

Right: A two-page advertisement for Halliburton Company from 1934. The advertisement shows different models of cement pumping vehicles from 1919 to 1934.

Phillips Petroleum Company

One of the world's largest energy concerns, Phillips Petroleum Company, traces its lineage to the beginning of the Oklahoma oil boom, when Frank and Lee Eldas Phillips, better known as L. E., incorporated Phillips on June 13, 1917. They were the sons of Lewis and Lucinda Phillips from Creston, Iowa. In 1903, a friend of the Phillips family, who was a Methodist missionary in Indian Territory, regaled them with stories of the Bartlesville oil boom.

Attracted by the business possibilities, Frank visited Bartlesville in June of 1903. He became excited over the prospects, returned to Creston, and convinced L. E. to join him to form the Anchor Oil and Gas Company. Frank then returned to Bartlesville and in 1904 began purchasing oil leases.

With more and more of his time being absorbed by his oil interests Frank persuaded L.E. to move to Bartlesville in 1905.

Frank and L. E. drilled several wells in the Bartlesville area. The first three were dry holes, but the Anna Anderson No. 1, drilled near the junction of the Big Caney and Little Caney Rivers was a producer. To handle the production, Frank, L. E., and another brother, Waite, incorporated the Lewcinda Oil Company in 1906. The name was derived from a combination of their parents' names, Lewis and Lucinda.

In 1914, Waite sold his shares of the oil investments to Frank and L. E. and moved to Tulsa. The following year, in December of 1915, Frank and L. E. sold all their oil properties, except those in the Osage. They used the money to expand the holdings of Lewcinda Oil Company in the Osage.

One of their leases was Lot 185, a 1,000 acre lease in the Osage on which they began an extensive drilling program. Their first six wells on the lease were dry, but the seventh, completed in February of 1917, was a 100-barrel per day producer. Encouraged, they started well No. 8 that blew in as a gusher and secured their future. By mid-1917, Lewcinda held twelve leases covering 15,500 acres in Kansas, Oklahoma, and Kentucky giving the company a total value in excess of $1,000,000. On June 13, 1917, Frank and L. E. incorporated Phillips Petroleum Company with a capital of $3,000,000 and within a few days transferred the holdings of Lewcinda Oil Company to the new corporation.

In 1951, Phillips' Research Division developed Marlex Plastic that revolutionized the manufacturing industry. In 1952, Phillips became the first American oil company to be approved by the United States Department of the Interior to undertake drilling operations in Alaska. In the 1960s, Phillips opened the Greater Ekofisk Fields in the North Sea 162 miles off the shore of Norway.

Still headquartered in Bartlesville, Phillips Petroleum Company enters the 21st century as one of the world's major energy concerns. Under the direction of J. J. Mulva, Phillips employs 16,000 people worldwide in all aspects of the energy industry. Phillips Petroleum Company ranks as the world's eighth largest energy company.

✧

Top: A portion of the Phillips Petroleum office complex as it appeared in 1991. In the foreground is Frank Phillips Park and Frank Phillips Tower Center. In the background are (left to right) the Phillips Petroleum Company's Plaza Office Building, Frank Phillips Tower, the Phillips Building, and the Adams Building.

PHOTO COURTESY OF THE PHILLIPS PETROLEUM COMPANY.

Bottom: The five Phillips brothers pictured in 1907. Left to right: Edd Raleigh (known as Ed) Waite, Fred, Frank, and Lee Eldas (known as L. E.).

PHOTO COURTESY OF THE OKLAHOMA HERITAGE ASSOCIATION.

Hickory Coal Company

Above: Frank J. (left) and Bill Podpechan in the Hickory office area in 1932.

PHOTO COURTESY OF LASSITER & SHORMAKER PHOTOGRAPHY.

Below: The coal office and Podpechan home until 1938 located approximately at 26th Street and Pittsbugh, Tulsa Oklahoma, 1932.

The importance of Oklahoma's coal was noted as early as 1719 when Bernard de la Harpe commented on the outcrops in the eastern part of the state. Commercial mining did not begin until 1872, by the time of statehood in 1907 it was an integral part of Oklahoma's economy. European miners, or their dependents, which were drawn to the coal deposits of eastern Oklahoma, undertook much of the early coal development.

Frank W. Podpechan is a third generation coal miner. His grandfather, John Podpechan, immigrated from Slovenia, Austria in the late nineteenth century, and settled as a coal miner in the area around Pittsburg, Kansas. Frank J. Podpechan was born in 1901 in Crawford County, Kansas. Frank W. Podpechan, his son, was also born in Crawford County, Kansas, on December 26, 1927. Two years later, in 1929, Frank W.'s father, Frank J., and mother, Mary, moved the family to Tulsa, Oklahoma, where, along with his brother, William R. Podpechan and a cousin, Sam Bregar, founded the first Hickory Coal Company. The location of the company was the intersection of 26th Street and South Harvard Avenue, and the underground coal mine was located at 26th Street and Pittsburg Avenue.

Hickory provided coal for the Sinclair Coal Company and fuel for the Public Service Company of Oklahoma. Approximately twenty miners were employed, hauling coal from the underground slope to the surface in mule drawn carts. However, with the onset of the Great Depression came a drop in demand for utility coal and Frank's father shifted emphasis to the domestic market supplying coal for heating and cooking for local residents and businesses. Hickory was closed down in 1941.

Frank and his sister, Rosemary, grew up in the area around the Hickory mine. Their brother, John, was born there in 1940. Frank attended Lanier Elementary School in Tulsa until the fifth grade when the family moved to Claremore, Oklahoma. While in high school and college Frank spent his summers working in his father's mining operation.

Frank's father, along with Paul Adamson, founded the Rogers County Coal Company in 1937, which he operated until 1950 before selling to Sinclair Coal Company, later to become a part of Peabody Coal Company. Afterward, he managed Peabody Coal Company's Oklahoma properties until he retired in 1968.

After graduation from Claremore High School in 1945, Frank W. Podpechan enrolled in Oklahoma State University in Stillwater and was a member of the Kappa Alpha fraternity. He also joined the 45th Infantry Division of the Oklahoma National Guard in 1948. Podpechan graduated with a Bachelor of Science degree in geology in 1950 just in time to be activated with the 45th Division for duty in the Korean War. After a two-year tour with the National Guard in Japan and Korea, Frank returned to the United States in May of 1952, and accepted a job with Stanolind Oil and Gas Company. To learn the job, he worked briefly as a roustabout and roughneck in West Texas and then was promoted to a junior geologist in Roswell, New Mexico. Soon afterward he was promoted to geologist and worked for Stanolind in Texas and New Mexico until 1957.

In that year, he joined a friend, Steve Helbing, who was a former landsman for Stanolind, to form Helbing and Podpechan, an independent oil and natural gas business in Albuquerque, New Mexico, which in 1959 moved to Roswell, New Mexico. In 1963, he was named exploration manager and vice president of Flag Oil Corporation and Redfern Development Corporation of Midland, Texas. Under the arrangement, Podpechan devoted one-half of his time to Flag Oil Company and Redfern while remaining free to pursue his own independent oil and natural gas interests.

He also acted as a consultant to Peabody Coal Corporation and purchased one-half interest in the Claremore Abstract Company.

In 1968, Podpechan joined Mesa Petroleum as vice president and Canadian manager and spent a year developing the company's oil interests around Calgary, Alberta, Canada. Later that same year, he formed Claremont Corporation with his four children. He resigned from Mesa in 1969 and returned to Claremore. At that time, he formed Sierra Resources, a Canadian oil and gas company, which later acquired Petroleum Reserve Corporation and became Skye Resources, Ltd.

However, Podpechan could never escape from the coal mining industry in which he was raised. In 1970, at the suggestion of his father, he organized Sierra Coal Corporation, which mined coal properties in Muskogee County, with a contract to supply the Tennessee Valley Authority.

Sierra Coal was merged with Petroleum Reserve Corporation and the company's offices were moved to Tulsa where Podpechan served as president of both Petroleum Reserve and Sierra Coal, later changed to Carbonex Coal Company and Sierra Resources Ltd. The companies went public in 1973 on the Toronto, Canada stock exchange and the name changed to Skye Resources, Ltd. Podpechan remained president of Skye Resources until 1981 when it merged with Campbell Resources, Inc., a Canadian corporation. In the same time frame (1976-1986) Podpechan also operated Sweetwater Coal Company in Rogers County, Oklahoma mining about 10,000 tons per month of metallurgical coal which was sold to Lone Star Steel.

After merging with Campbell, Podpechan moved Claremont's office to the Philtower Building in Tulsa, Oklahoma in March 1982 and established a new operation with his adult children, which continued until 1987, when Frank bought out his children and became 100 percent owner of Claremont.

In 1986, Podpechan and a group of investors formed a new Hickory Coal Corporation and purchased Carbonex's Oklahoma coal property strip mining company in northeastern Oklahoma. Podpechan became president and Russ Wienecke was named vice president and general manager. Eventually, Sweetwater Coal Corporation merged with Hickory, which then became one of the major coal producers in Oklahoma, mining as much as 350,000 tons per year of high grade metallurgical and steam coal. Coal sales lessened after the spring of 1992 and economic coal reserves were scarce, so, by the summer of 1993, it was evident that after a successful operation of seven years, profit margins were not now sufficient to continue mining. Hickory was shut down in October of 1993 and by December 1998 all of its reclamation obligations were fulfilled and it continues as an inactive corporation.

Although semi-retired, Podpechan remains active in the oil and natural gas industry and commercial real estate investments. He is the last of the family to pursue the coal business. He spends much of his time with his wife, four children, three stepchildren, four grandsons, and one granddaughter, and four step-granddaughters as well as numerous professional and civic organizations.

He was a founding contributor for a new Claremore Airport and the Heritage Hills Golf Course. Podpechan also is active in the American and Oklahoma Associations of Petroleum Geologists, the Oklahoma Heritage Association, Rogers College Foundation, Claremore Public Schools Foundation, Oklahoma Foundation for Excellence, the Indian Nations Council of the Boy Scouts of America, the Claremore Chamber of Commerce, the National Federation of Independent Business, the Aircraft Owners and Pilots Association, and numerous others.

Above: Frank W. Podpechan.

PHOTO COURTESY OF ORF PHOTOGRAPHY.

Below: A Hickory Coal strip mining operation located in Rogers County near Claremore, Oklahoma.

NOBLE AFFILIATES, INC.

Headquartered in Ardmore, Oklahoma, Noble Affiliates, Inc., through its subsidiary, Samedan Oil Corporation, has been engaged in exploration, production and marketing of oil and gas since 1932. With assets of over $1 billion, the 600 employee company is recognized as one of the nation's leading independent energy companies.

Above: Long recognized as one of the nation's leading independent energy companies, the company's Ardmore headquarters have evolved from the house pictured upper left to the building it currently occupies pictured above.

Right: For many years, Noble Affiliates had operations in Canada, most notably, the Meekwap field.

The pioneering spirit of Lloyd Noble, founder of the company, is at the heart of Noble Affiliates and its people. Noble was a law student at Oklahoma University when oil was discovered west of Ardmore on a tract of land owned by his mother and aunt. He persuaded his mother in 1921 to co-sign a note for $20,000 to finance the purchase of a drilling rig. Introduced by a friend at OU, Art Olson, a young driller from Big Muddy, Wyoming paired up with Noble and the partnership was named Noble Drilling of Oklahoma.

Noble and Olson acquired several more rigs and remained partners until 1930 when they made a joint decision to pursue the drilling business with separate companies. Noble formed several drilling companies that were eventually sold, merged, or combined to form the Noble Drilling Corporation that exists today. It was during these years that Noble began to expand its areas of operation.

Lloyd Noble and his men were major players in the early years as drilling contractors throughout the Western United States. Noble Drilling was the only American drilling company to be engaged by the D'Arcy Exploration Company, a subsidiary of Anglo-Iranian Oil Company, to drill 108 wells in Sherwood Forest for oil during World War II.

Samedan Oil Corporation had its beginnings in 1932 in Ardmore, Oklahoma. Due to low oil prices created by the boom in production from East Texas, many operators began a policy of paying Noble Drilling and other drilling contractors seventy-five percent of the well cost in cash, plus a bonus of another 150 percent out of production if the well was successful. Since Noble was assuming a large part of the risk, he formed his own exploration and production company and named it after his three children, Sam, Ed, and Ann (Samedan). Samedan's first production was located in the "Wildcat Jim" field in Carter County, Oklahoma, and was quickly followed by wells in East Texas, West Texas, New Mexico, and other fields in the United States. Canadian operations commenced in 1958. The company, through its subsidiary, Samedan Oil of Canada, Inc., conducted oil and gas operations in Canada until the properties were sold in 1997. The company experienced

tremendous growth during the 1970s. It was during this period of time that the company expanded its operations offshore in the Gulf of Mexico. Today, the company is recognized as one of the significant operators in the Gulf of Mexico and is expanding its holdings into water depths exceeding 6,000 feet.

Although Lloyd Noble spent much of his time in the oil fields, he also devoted a large part of his time to civic and charitable interests. In 1945, he created the Samuel Roberts Noble Foundation to assist in the alleviation of soil erosion and other problems through agricultural and medical research. Upon his untimely death at the age of fifty-three, Lloyd left the greatest part of his estate, which included most of the stock in Noble Drilling Corporation and Samedan Oil Corporation as well as all of his personal producing oil and gas properties, to the foundation.

The Tax Reform Act of 1969 required the foundation to sell eighty percent of its holding in each company, thus Noble Affiliates, Inc. was formed. In October of 1972, Noble Affiliates, Inc. became a publicly traded company with Noble Drilling Corporation, Samedan Oil Corporation and a sister company, B. F. Walker, Inc. as subsidiaries. In 1984, B. F. Walker was sold and in 1985 Noble Drilling was spun off to the shareholders leaving Samedan as the only subsidiary. Lloyd Noble's son, Sam, was chairman of Noble Affiliates until his death in 1992.

Today, Noble operates throughout the major basins of the U.S., as well as internationally in Argentina, China, Denmark, Ecuador, Equatorial Guinea, the Mediterranean Sea, the North Sea, and the United Kingdom. As of December 31, 1998, Noble had estimated proved reserves of 1.2 trillion cubic feet of gas and 116.6 million barrels of oil.

✧

Top: Noble Affiliates has been a strong presence in the Gulf of Mexico since the 1970s. Pictured is one of Samedan's many offshore platforms.

Left: Sam Noble on an Oklahoma property, was Chairman of Noble Affiliates until his death in 1992. He carried on the goals and ideals set forth by his father, Lloyd Noble.

Devon Energy Corporation

✧

Top, left: Devon Energy Corporation Co-founder John W. Nichols.

Top, right: Devon Energy Corporation Co-founder J. Larry Nichols.

Bottom: The Coleman Gas Plant in Alberta, Canada. The plant is owned by Devon Energy Corporation.

Devon Energy Corporation, headquartered in Oklahoma City, is an independent energy company engaged in oil and gas property acquisition, exploration and production. The company's properties are located primarily in New Mexico, Oklahoma, Texas, and Wyoming in the United States, and Alberta and British Columbia in Canada. Devon also has common stock that trades on both the American Stock Exchange and The Toronto Stock Exchange. Over the last twenty-eight years, Devon has enriched Oklahoma by being a leader in its industry, creating numerous jobs and giving back to the community.

John W. Nichols and his son, J. Larry Nichols, co-founded Devon and began operations as a very small company in 1971. Since that time, Devon has become one of the top fifteen public independent oil and gas companies in the United States and Canada. The company's reserves currently approach 300 million barrels of oil equivalent while total assets exceed $1.2 billion. Additionally, Devon has grown from a handful of employees to a workforce of over 800 people. Devon's growth through the years has been achieved by purchasing oil and gas properties and drilling for oil and gas reserves.

Since 1971, Devon has been very aggressive in the merger and acquisition arena by conducting thirty-five separate transactions with a total value approximating $2 billion. Devon's mergers and acquisitions have included a $250 million transaction with Kerr-McGee in 1996 and a $750 million merger with Canadian-based Northstar Energy in 1998. Besides acquisitions, exploration and development drilling for oil and gas has also played a significant role in Devon's growth. During the last ten years, the company has drilled over 1,600 wells with a ninety-four percent success rate. Thanks to successful drilling efforts and acquisitions, Devon's reserves and production have increased by factors of thirty-seven and thirty-three, respectively.

Devon Energy Corporation's Board of Directors includes John W. Nichols, chairman; J. Larry Nichols, president and chief executive officer; Thomas F. Ferguson, David M. Gavrin; Michael E. Gellert; John A. Hagg; Michael M. Kanovsky; and H. R. Sanders, Jr. Devon's executive officers are J. Michael Lacey, vice president, Operations and Exploration; Duke R. Ligon, vice president, General Counsel;

Darryl G. Smette, vice president, Marketing; H. Allen Turner, vice president, Corporate Development; William T. Vaughn, vice president, Finance; Donald A. Garner, president and chief operating officer of the Canadian Subsidiary; and John Richels, chief executive officer of the Canadian Subsidiary.

As Devon has grown in size, so has its continued commitment to the community. During the last twenty-eight years, the company and its employees have been involved in hundreds of charitable activities, providing both money and time to various organizations throughout Oklahoma and North America.

✧

Top: A Gilby oil well in southern Alberta, Canada. Four wells were completed in this area in 1998.

Bottom: Casing for use in a Panhandle Morrow exploratory well.

Duncan Equipment Co.

Duncan Equipment Co., under the leadership of President and Chief Executive Officer Gene Nelson until 1968, was founded in Duncan, Oklahoma in 1948 and is the supplier of choice for industrial products, innovative services, and technologically driven business solutions. Building customers' confidence by establishing high performance and integrity as a standard of excellence, the company continues to provide an atmosphere encouraging growth and achievement and the opportunity to make a difference at every level of industrial distribution.

Headquartered in Oklahoma City at 3450 South MacArthur, Duncan Equipment Co. (DECO) has prospered through many significant milestones along the way. The first such milestone came in 1956 when the Company built its first DECO Vacuum Unit. With the purchase of White Truck Company in 1965, a new corporation was formed, DECO Manufacturing Company, with J. H. Thornton serving as president from 1968 to 1980.

In 1971 DECO, purchased sixty-five percent interest in Stephens Industrial Supply Company in Oklahoma City, built a 20,000-square-foot building in Oklahoma City in 1975, and elected David Ragland president of Stephens Industrial Supply. In 1980, the board of directors elected David Ragland chairman and CEO of Duncan Equipment Co.

With DECO's rapid growth and strong reputation, several new endeavors were launched: offices in Tulsa, a fabrication shop for Chief-GMC Truck, and a new 20,000-square-foot facility in Duncan, Oklahoma. The remaining interest in Stephens Industrial Supply in Oklahoma City was purchased in 1981 and the name was changed to Duncan Equipment Co.

In 1984, a branch office was established in Wichita Falls, Texas and in 1987 a sales business unit for compressed and rotary air systems was added in Oklahoma. A sales branch in Joplin, Missouri was opened in 1991; a sales and warehouse facility in Sherman, Texas was built in 1994; and a fully automated warehouse "Pick-to-Light" system was installed in Oklahoma City in 1997.

Duncan Equipment Co. secured its first "customized in-plant" integrated supply contract with Smith Tool in Ponca City, Oklahoma in 1992. Judith Nelson-Ragland, DECO's largest shareholder and founder of the Resource Development Group, was elected chairperson of the board of directors in 1996. In 1997, DECO made a major commitment to become the leader in a technology driven industry.

Chief Executive Officer David Ragland continues to direct Duncan Equipment Co.'s 160 employees with sales reaching $70 million. Company locations include large warehouse, service, fabrication, and distribution centers in Tulsa, Oklahoma City, and Duncan, Oklahoma; and sales facilities in Dallas (established 1999), Wichita Falls, and Sherman, Texas, and Joplin, Missouri. The varied and highly productive sales and

Top: Gene Nelson founded Duncan Equipment Co. in 1948.

Below: In the mid-1950s, Duncan Equipment Co. became a GMC full line truck dealer.

services provided by Duncan Equipment Co. include:

- Industrial supply—industrial and mill supplies for industry.
- Integrated solutions—commodity management, integrated supply, Auto Crib, automated inventory control of tools and supplies without the hassle.
- Truck and fabrication—a franchised GMC and Volvo dealership.
- Safety products—decreasing the dangers of the industry.
- Supply chain management—lowering costs from acquisition to delivery.
- Resource development—the source for training and personnel development.
- Financial services—discover the power of leasing and financing.
- Pump equipment—including a complete stock of pumps, parts and service.
- Compressed air systems—emphasizing correct system design with complete rental, parts, service and "leased" air programs.
- Information technology—including EDI, bar-coding, customized Internet service, and more.

An extensive Website, www.deco.com, provides updated information and opportunities regarding the company's line of products and services. With its technological capabilities, Duncan Equipment is positioned to take full advantage of all the efficiencies gained through electronic commerce and assist its business partners in creating full technological interface.

Duncan Equipment Co. enjoys doing business with a large variety of regional, national and international customers such as Halliburton Energy Services, General Motors, Lucent Technologies, Autocraft, Charles Machine, American Airlines, and Fred Jones Remanufacturing. Many of these companies were founded in Oklahoma and have expanded into global markets.

Duncan Equipment Co. is affiliated with several organizations. idOne, a national sales, marketing, and purchasing organization of independent distributors, focuses on meeting needs of multi-unit regional and national companies with uniform quality products, exceptional services, and consistent pricing. iPower distribution group is an alliance of leading industrial suppliers who have combined resources to offer both domestic and international customers quality integrated supply solutions and reduced procurement costs. I.D.A., a national professional association, creates partnerships with customers and suppliers, achieving greater supply chain efficiencies.

Duncan Equipment Company plays an active role in community development and is a proud supporter of the Oklahoma Heritage Association, the United Way, and an Education Scholarship Fund. Gene Nelson, founder of the company, currently serves on the Board of Regents for Oklahoma Colleges. The promotion of the growth and well being of every aspect of life remains a hallmark of this family owned business begun in the heart of Oklahoma.

✧

Top: David Ragland, CEO of Duncan Equipment Co., is shown on the cover of the August 1999 issue of Industrial Distribution *magazine. Industrial distributors assisted in the cleanup and rebuilding after May's record-breaking tornadoes in Oklahoma City.*

COVER COURTESY OF INDUSTRIAL DISTRIBUTION; MARC BERLOW, PHOTOGRAPHER.

Below: Duncan Equipment moved into a new 50,000-square-foot central distribution facility in Oklahoma City in December 1999.

CHESAPEAKE ENERGY CORPORATION

Left: Aubrey K. McClendon, Chairman and CEO.

Right: Tom L. Ward, President and Chief Operating Officer.

Chesapeake Energy Corporation is an Oklahoma City-based, New York Stock Exchange-listed (NYSE: CHK) independent oil and natural gas producer. The company operates field offices in Lindsay, Waynoka, and Weatherford, Oklahoma in addition to other field offices in Kansas, Texas, Louisiana, and Canada. The company's operations are focused on developmental drilling and producing property acquisitions in three major onshore natural gas producing areas of the United States and Canada.

Chesapeake began operations in 1989 and now owns interests in 5,000 producing oil and gas wells concentrated in its three primary operating areas: the Mid-continent region consisting of Oklahoma, southwestern Kansas and the Texas Panhandle; the Gulf Coast region consisting primarily of the Austin Chalk Trend in Texas and the Tuscaloosa Trend in Louisiana; and the Helmet area of northeastern British Columbia. During 1998 the Company produced 130 billion cubic feet of gas equivalent, of which seventy-two percent was natural gas, making Chesapeake one of the top twenty public independent oil and gas companies in the United States as measured by annual production.

In late 1997 and early 1998, falling oil prices and significant geological and engineering challenges were addressed by Chesapeake's management through a strategic repositioning effort that prepared the company to benefit from the coming growth in natural gas demand. Rising electricity usage, decreasing nuclear power capability, and the significant environmental benefits of natural gas should make natural gas America's fuel of choice in the twenty-first century.

Chesapeake is well-positioned to capitalize on this strengthening natural gas market with 1.1 trillion cubic feet equivalent of proved natural gas reserves, an extensive land inventory, and the operational expertise generated by the drilling of almost 1,000 wells since its incorporation.

Importantly, Chesapeake is a homegrown Oklahoma company co-founded by two native Oklahomans, Aubrey K. McClendon and Tom L. Ward. Started in 1989 with a $50,000 investment and eight full-time employees, Chesapeake has grown to an enterprise value of $1.5 billion, is now the sixth largest oil company in Oklahoma, and currently employs 550 full-time, part-time, and contract employees.

Chesapeake's management, directors and employees own thirty percent of the company's outstanding common shares. This level of ownership, among the highest levels in the energy sector, keeps the Chesapeake team focused on the goal of continuing to build a first-class inventory of natural gas projects for the twenty-first century.

Kerr-McGee Corporation

In seventy years of operations, Kerr-McGee has grown from a small contract drilling firm with two steam rigs and big aspirations into a global energy and chemical company with assets of $5.6 billion. Kerr-McGee ranks among the largest United States-based independent exploration and production companies and conducts oil and gas activities in more than a dozen countries. Core operating areas are the Gulf of Mexico, including the Gulf's high-potential deep waters, and the North Sea.

In the chemical business, Kerr-McGee's most important product is titanium dioxide pigment, the world's preferred opacifier and whitener for paint, plastics and other products. Plants in the United States, Australia, Germany and Belgium supply pigment to customers in more than eighty countries. The company also produces electrolytic chemicals and railroad crossties.

Employees take pride in Kerr-McGee's tradition of corporate responsibility and in safety and environmental management programs that have earned national recognition for excellence. The company also has a long history of supporting important educational, health, civic, and cultural organizations serving needs in the communities where its employees live and work.

The story of Kerr-McGee begins in Ada, Oklahoma, in 1929, when Robert S. Kerr and a partner formed the Anderson & Kerr Drilling Company. The search for oil and gas called for a skilled geologist. Dean A. McGee, chief geologist for Phillips Petroleum Company, accepted the challenge in 1937 and joined the company that would change its name to Kerr-McGee in 1946.

With the business in capable hands, Kerr devoted his energy and extraordinary leadership talents to public service. He became Oklahoma's first native-born governor (1943-1947) and served his state and nation as a United States senator from 1948 until his death in 1963.

Kerr-McGee continued to grow. Exploration expanded into the Gulf of Mexico, where the company made history in 1947 by drilling the world's first commercial oil well out of sight and safety of land. The successful venture marks the beginning of the modern offshore industry and opened a vast new province to exploration and production. Over the next fifty years, Kerr-McGee contributed many other technological "firsts" to the offshore oil industry as operations expanded from the Gulf into the North Sea and other international areas.

The '50s and '60s were years of diversification. In 1967, Kerr-McGee entered the titanium dioxide business with an acquisition that included a plant at Hamilton, Mississippi. This plant would grow into one of the world's largest titanium dioxide operations.

In 1947, Kerr-McGee drilled the world's first successful well out of sight of land, using a small fixed platform and a converted war-surplus barge. The bold venture in the Gulf of Mexico marked the beginning of the modern offshore oil industry.

McGee, the innovator who dedicated his career to the energy industry and civic leadership, stepped down as chairman in 1983 after directing company operations for more than forty years. He was succeeded by Frank A. McPherson, whose vision guided Kerr-McGee through one of the worst depressions in oil industry history.

Luke R. Corbett became Kerr-McGee's fourth chairman in February 1997. Under his leadership, the company further strengthened and expanded its core businesses.

In February 1999, the company completed the largest transaction in its history, a merger with Oryx Energy Company. This transaction virtually doubled Kerr-McGee's oil and gas exploratory prospects, reserves, and production.

The high aspirations and optimism that launched a small drilling venture in 1929 remain alive throughout Kerr-McGee's worldwide operations. The company begins the new millennium determined to succeed in its two highly competitive industries by turning exciting exploration potential and solid growth opportunities into value for stockholders.

WARREN PETROLEUM COMPANY

✧

Top: Warren Building, January 27, 1961.

PHOTO COURTESY OF BOB MCCORMACK, PHOTOGRAPHER.

Below: W. K. Warren, Sr.

PHOTO COURTESY OF BLACKSTONE STUDIOS.

William Kelly Warren, an oil pioneer in Oklahoma, founded Warren Petroleum Company in 1922. A native of Tennessee, Warren was born in Nashville on December 3, 1897, the son of Thomas Hines and Amelia Elizabeth Cecil Warren. Educated in parochial schools, his first job was getting up at 3:30 a.m. to deliver the local newspaper before going to school. While delivering papers at St. Thomas Hospital, he became acquainted with Mrs. D. A. McDougal, from Sapulpa, Oklahoma, who advised him to "go west" and in February of 1916, he caught the train to Sapulpa where he was awed by the booming oil community.

Before leaving Nashville, William had met Natalie Overall. They were infatuated with one another and even though William had traveled to Oklahoma, they continued their relationship and were married on September 21, 1921. Their marriage brought forth seven children.

Warren's first job in Oklahoma was arranged by Mrs. McDougal with the railroad running from Depew to Shamrock. However, fascinated by the opportunities offered by the oil business he quit after five days. Wanting to learn all aspects of the oil industry, Warren then worked for Gypsy Oil Company, Gilliland Oil Company, Gulf Oil Corporation, Margay Oil Corporation, and McMan Oil and Gas Company in Oklahoma, Texas, and Louisiana. On March 15, 1922, with only $300 he opened his own office and incorporated the Warren Petroleum Company of Delaware. The new company had two employees—Warren and his wife, Natalie.

He concentrated on marketing natural gasoline and liquefied petroleum gases by purchasing the production of gasoline plants. The venture prospered and by May of 1925, the company owned the output of thirty-one gasoline plants in five states. Within four years, Warren's holdings had expanded to fifty gasoline plants. That same year 1929, he founded the Western Gasoline Company, which became the Warren Petroleum Company of Oklahoma in 1932. And in 1937, the Warren Petroleum Company of Oklahoma changed its name to Warren Petroleum Corporation.

By 1953, Warren Petroleum Corporation was one of the largest producers and marketers of natural gasoline and LPG with more than 2,000 employees. It maintained six terminal shipping operations in Texas, New Jersey, Florida, and Alabama; natural gas and LPG plants in Oklahoma, Texas, New Mexico, Illinois, and Indiana; and storage facilities in many states with a daily production of 595,000 gallons of natural gasoline and 672,000 gallons of LPG; and operated 4,700 railroad tank cars, the largest privately owned fleet in the world. Gulf Oil Corporation purchased the Tulsa-based Warren Petroleum Corporation on November 10, 1955, for more than $420 million, which set the milestone for the largest exchange of money in the energy industry up to that time.

After the sale, Warren organized the Transwestern Pipeline Company in 1959, however, most of his time was occupied with The William K. Warren Foundation which he chartered in 1945 and which received the legacy of Warren Petroleum Corporation. The Warren Foundation opened the doors of Saint Francis Hospital in 1960, without the use of tax dollars either at the federal or state level. Saint Francis Hospital is now part of Saint Francis Health System, and through the work of the System, the Warren Foundation continues to support the medical needs of the community.

Louis Dreyfus Natural Gas

To trace the history of Louis Dreyfus Natural Gas Corporation one must go back to 1979 and the founding of Bogert Oil Company of Oklahoma City. A successful independent natural gas and oil producer, Bogert was purchased and reorganized under its current name in July of 1990 by the French company Société Anonyme Louis Dreyfus et Cie, which itself is a historic (and highly successful) commodities trading company. The company immediately embarked upon an aggressive growth campaign that saw its original natural gas and crude oil reserves increase by more than 2.5 times in 1990 and nearly twenty-two times by the end of 1998.

Louis Dreyfus Natural Gas currently employs approximately 400 people throughout its entire organization, with half of those employees based at the headquarters in Oklahoma City. The company also maintains an office in Houston and field offices in Sonora, Corpus Christi and Kellerville, Texas; Kingfisher and Lindsay, Oklahoma; Carlsbad, New Mexico; and Syracuse and Lewisville, Arkansas.

Through the determined leadership of its executive management group and the knowledge and skills of a strong employee base, Louis Dreyfus Natural Gas has seen consistent, substantial growth in production, proved reserves, and cash flows throughout the decade. In 1998, total revenues for the company were $278.5 million, while daily production levels climbed to 333 million cubic feet equivalent per day, and proved reserves reached 1.3 trillion cubic feet equivalent. The company's success is directly attributable to its focus on four key points of business: 1.) building a large domestic natural gas reserve base; 2.) achieving superior results by focusing operations in core regions; 3.) growing production and reserves through balanced drilling programs and strategic acquisitions; and 4.) adding value through commodity price risk management.

Louis Dreyfus Natural Gas also remains committed to helping improve the lives of children in the local community. The company provides monetary donations and encourages employee volunteerism by allowing each employee up to four hours per month to work at one of the company's supported charities. Through its Community Relations Task Force, whose mission is to "positively impact children (birth to eighteen years) in the communities where we live and work," the company supports the following Oklahoma-based organizations: Infant Crisis Services, Hilldale Elementary School, The Christmas Connection, Fellowship of Christian Athletes, and the Pauline Mayer Shelter. The Community Relations Task Force also supports the Oklahoma Special Olympics, and sponsors a booth at "Haunt the Zoo" during the week of Halloween. The task force members share a strong desire to support the mission of this program through corporate resources including employee knowledge, skills, and time.

A true representation of the pioneering spirit, Louis Dreyfus Natural Gas is poised for a future without boundaries. With a strong work ethic based upon the values that have made our state what it is today, this visionary company moves into the twenty-first century committed in service and proud to call Oklahoma home.

✧

Left: Gas Well Drilling in Sonora, Texas.

PHOTO COURTESY OF DAN BRYANT.

Below: Louis Dreyfus Natural Gas has seen consistent, substantial growth in production, proved reserves, and cash flows throughout the 1990s.

PHOTO COURTESY OF CHRIS SHINN.

THE CHARLES MACHINE WORKS, INC.

✧

Top: The seed that grew to be The Charles Machine Works, Inc. was planted in 1902 when Carl Frederick Malzahn settled in Perry and established a blacksmith shop to serve the farm economy.

Below: As the economy of the early 1900s changed, the Malzahn family business changed to meet the times. The blacksmith shop became a machine shop operated by Charlie and Gus Malzahn. While the business still served area farmers, it also was actively involved in the growing Oklahoma oil industry.

In the summer of 1948, Ed Malzahn was standing by the rear door of Charlie's Machine Shop. Glancing toward a neighbor's yard he watched two men who worked for a local plumber as they labored with picks and shovels to hand-dig a shallow trench to replace a broken water line.

Looking away for a moment Malzahn noticed a large wheel-type-trenching machine sitting in an equipment yard. It was a huge machine used to open large ditches for pipelines. For two days Malzahn watched as the plumber's workers strived to complete a fifty-foot long, eighteen-inch deep ditch. Obviously, the large trencher could have done the work much quicker, but it was too large to get close to the house, and what plumber could afford such an expensive machine?

A thought occurred to Malzahn: "Why not develop a small, compact, low cost, easily maneuverable trenching machine for use in confined areas?" As he explained his plan to his father, Charlie Malzahn, they realized that the marketability of such a trenching machine was unlimited.

It was the birth of a Ditch Witch trencher. The Malzahn machine—a compact trencher, reasonably priced—became invaluable on construction sites, and is the innovation that launched a new industry.

The Malzahn family had long been involved in innovative projects. Carl Frederick Malzahn, a blacksmith by trade, and his wife, Anna, were German immigrants who settled first in Ohio, then Minnesota, and finally, with the 1893 opening of the Cherokee Outlet, in Perry, Oklahoma. The early-day blacksmith shop became the foundation for The Charles Machine Works, Inc. Carl and Anna had four daughters—Emaline, Irene, Marie, and Grace—and two sons. Their sons, Gustave (Gus), the eldest, and Charles (Charlie), worked in their father's shop, the Malzahn Blacksmith Shop, located just south of the Noble County Courthouse.

Carl died in 1913 from injuries suffered from an accident in the blacksmith shop, and the family business was taken over by Gus and Charlie. It was renamed the Malzahn Brothers' General Blacksmithing.

Anna died in 1918. That same year, Charlie entered the military for service in World War I. Just before leaving for duty in Maryland; he married Bertha Wolff of Orlando, Oklahoma. Like her husband, Bertha was a first generation German immigrant. Her father, George Wolff, and her mother, Mary Bertha Dorothea Pommerencki, came to America in 1892.

The newlyweds had a brief honeymoon in Maryland before Charlie sailed for France where he was assigned to Evacuation Hospital 16 of the American Expeditionary Force. They were reunited in August 1919 when Charlie returned home. Charlie and Bertha had two children. The eldest, a son, Edwin, better known as Ed, born in 1921, and a daughter, Virginia, born two years later.

In the post-war era the Malzahn Brothers' General Blacksmithing expanded into custom machining and welding. In 1926, a new brick shop was built on the site of the old wooden one. "Malzahn Brothers" was etched above the entrance. The building is still owned by the family today.

Gus died in 1928. Later, his wife, Helena, sold the business. Charlie planned to open his own business. However, his operational capital was in Perry's Farmers and Merchants Bank, which was closed down March 6, 1933, by the national bank holiday declared by President Franklin D. Roosevelt. It never reopened. Charlie spent a brief time working in Oswego, Kansas; however, his family remained in Perry. He rejoined them within a year and opened Charlie's Machine Shop. At first, Charlie was the company's only employee. A natural innovator, he made a portable electric welder—the area's first, and for years, its only portable welding machine.

The nearby Lucien Oil Field was discovered in 1932 on the farm of Bertha Malzahn's father. The resulting oil rush was a boom to Charlie's Machine Shop. Charlie quickly borrowed $10,000 from his father-in-law and used it to purchase a used lathe, a shaper, a drill press, and a milling machine. With the new equipment his workload soon outgrew the twenty-five by seventy-five-foot shop. Needing more space, Charlie twice moved to larger shops. The oil boom kept Charlie and his employees busy welding and doing custom machine work and in 1939 he expanded again, this time to a tract on Birch Street two blocks south of the Perry downtown square. Here he placed a sixty by 140-foot ex-compressor station that he had purchased from an operator in the nearby Three Sands Oil Field.

That same year Ed graduated from Perry High School and enrolled at Oklahoma State University from which he received a B.A. degree in mechanical engineering in 1943.

During his senior year at Oklahoma State University, Ed worked as an undergraduate instructor at the university's machine shop. One of his students, Mary Corneil from Nardin, Oklahoma, caught his eye. Although a gifted singer, Mary had taken a wartime job

✧

Above: An aerial shot of the modern manufacturing facilities of The Charles Machine Works, Inc. located in Perry, Oklahoma.

PHOTO COURTESY OF KEITH BALL, 1998.

Below: This 1953 photograph of the 12,000-square-foot Ditch Witch® production facility is a dramatic contrast to today's operation.

with the Douglas Aircraft Company and had been sent to Oklahoma State to train as a turret lathe operator. Ed later recalled, "I was smitten with her the first time I saw her in class." They were married in 1943 and moved to Midwest City, Oklahoma, where Ed worked for Douglas Aircraft as a machine shop and tooling specialist in the company's Tinker Army Air Corps Base plant.

As Charlie's Machine Shop expanded, Ed was asked by his father to return to the family business. Ed agreed and the newlyweds moved to Perry in January 1944 where his father made him an equal partner. Eventually, Ed and Mary had three children—Pamela, Don, and Leasa. In addition to working in the shop, Ed formed another partnership with Roy Uhl to lay pipelines and connect oil field tank batteries in the West Edmond Field. In 1945, Ed and Uhl, along with Dewey Moore, invented a portable telescoping drilling derrick, which was manufactured by Charlie's Machine Shop until the operation was sold to a division of United States Steel in 1948. Shortly afterward, Ed conceived the idea of the Ditch Witch trencher.

Following the summer of 1948, Charlie and Ed spent nearly two years developing their concept for a compact ditcher. Eventually, they designed a self-propelled ladder trencher. The ditching was done with small two-piece buckets each with sharp finger-like edges. The buckets were mounted on a vertical endless moving chain. As the chain revolved, the buckets gouged out chunks of dirt and deposited them on one side to produce a four-inch wide trench up to twenty-four inches in depth. The engine and power train were designed to operate in difficult ground conditions and very dusty environments. The trencher was mounted on a welded frame sitting on four small wheels with pneumatic tires. The trencher was very mobile and could be moved either forward or backward by an operator seated on a contoured metal seat operating simple lever controls. Named the Ditch Witch and costing $750 it was put on the market in February of 1950.

Top: In the late 1940s, Ed Malzahn (shown operating the equipment) developed the first service-line trencher, which launched an industry.

Below: More than half the world's trenchers carry the Ditch Witch brand. All are manufactured in Perry, Oklahoma and distributed through a worldwide dealer organization.

The Ditch Witch trencher was an immediate success with sales doubling every two years. By 1955, an improved marketing organization was centered around personnel trained as trenching machine specialists.

The Charles Machine Works, Inc. also manufactured the Geronimo Safety Slide, the Sky Witch, and the Hot Witch. The Geronimo Safety Slide was developed at the same time as the telescoping, portable drilling rig and was an inverted T-shaped safety device that allowed workers to slide from the top of a drilling rig to safety should an emergency occur. It was in production from 1947 until 1970 and then sold. The Sky Witch was developed in the 1950s as a portable hydraulic lift platform. The Hot Witch was a heated asphalt roller used to seal asphalt patches against moisture.

In 1957, seven years after the introduction of the Ditch Witch line, The Charles Machine

Works, Inc. doubled its 6,000-square-foot facility in downtown Perry to meet the demand for its trencher line. Two years later, another expansion was necessary and the company acquired 160 acres west of Perry and constructed a new 24,000-square-foot manufacturing plant, plus an 8,000-square-foot office complex.

In 1958, sales went international with the opening of an outlet in Australia, the Mole Engineering Pty, Ltd. That same year, The Charles Machine Works, Inc. was incorporated with Charlie and Ed Malzahn equal partners.

Charlie Malzahn died in October 1959, but Bertha continued to be actively involved in the company until her retirement. The Charles Machine Works, Inc. remains a family operation. Headed by Ed Malzahn, it is a privately held corporation with only members of the Malzahn family and company employees holding stock.

Its basic business philosophy remains unchanged for two generations—"pay as you go." It is a family value, which Ed learned as a youth. "When I was a kid," he recalled, "my dad sent me out to buy his daily supply of Beech Nut chewing tobacco. If he could shake a quarter out of his coin purse in the morning, he sent me off to the store. If nothing fell out of his purse, he sharpened a couple of plow shares, and then sent me to the store." The lesson was never forgotten.

From humble beginnings, the company has evolved into a dynamic organization responsible for technological advances that affect lives all over the world. It is a dramatic example of free enterprise at work. Ed Malzahn is personally responsible for many of the innovations introduced by his company, and he made others possible by creating an atmosphere where creativity and commitment to excellence flourish.

Ed Malzahn's contributions as an inventor, business owner, and manager have changed the way the world's utility infrastructure is constructed and maintained. Many segments of the rapidly expanding information highway are installed with Ditch Witch equipment.

With more than 1,400 employees, The Charles Machine Works, Inc. is the largest employer in Perry and Noble County and one of the largest employers in Northern Oklahoma. It has built and sold more than half the world's trenching machines, and the Ditch Witch trencher has twice been recognized by *Fortune Magazine* as one of the 100 best worldwide products built in America.

The company continues to set the standard for trenchers, horizontal directional drilling products, electronic locating, tracking, mapping/planning systems, vibratory plows, and related accessories.

Now, thanks to Ed's vision, as people drive through Perry and communities all across the globe, they often see Ditch Witch equipment being used to perform the same types of jobs Ed watched those two plumber's workers doing by hand years ago.

✧

Above: This compact but powerful Ditch Witch riding trencher is very popular both with contractors and rental customers.

Below: The Charles Machine Works, Inc. also offers a complete line of trenchless products. Its Jet Trac® directional drilling systems place utilities underground without disturbing the surface. An above ground Subsite® Electronics tracking unit monitors location and depth of the drilling tool working underground.

PHOTO COURTESY OF KEITH BALL, 1997.

ACME BRICK COMPANY

Top: Acme Brick has plants in Oklahoma City and Tulsa with a capacity exceeding 100 million bricks per year.

Below: The Acme Brick Company provides brick for commercial projects as well as for homes. One such project was the Bricktown Ball Park in Oklahoma City in 1998.

Acme Brick, a Texas-based pressed brick company founded in 1891 by George Ellis Bennett, has played a major role in the lives of Oklahomans since June of 1924. The company had recently purchased its first out-of-state brick company in Fort Smith, Arkansas and was negotiating to move north along the Arkansas River with the purchase of a well-known Oklahoma City company by the name of American Brick and Tile. American Brick and Tile was created in 1901 and produced approximately 20,000 bricks a day in its first several years of production. A merger was concluded in 1919 wherein American Brick and Tile acquired Cleveland Brick Company in Cleveland, Oklahoma, and subsequently added markets in northern Texas, Kansas, Arkansas, and western Tennessee.

Acme Brick was destined to make its mark upon Oklahoma as Acme's first branch office was opened in Oklahoma City in the summer of 1920. Leaders in the company soon realized just how good business was and acquired the properties of American Brick and Tile in 1924 and began construction on a "most modern brick plant" in Tulsa in 1925. As large shale planers harvested the rich red clay from the Oklahoma City plant, about 100,000 bricks were being produced each day. Acme added a plant in Clinton, Oklahoma in 1944.

Acme purchased the United Brick Division of Martin-Marietta Corporation in 1963 and took over plants in Missouri, Kansas, and Oklahoma with sites in Tulsa, Collinsville, and Oklahoma City. The plant at Collinsville was never put into operation, as it could not be run economically. In 1963, the company also opened plants in Edmond and a second site in Tulsa and, by December of 1965, employed 270 people statewide.

In 1970, a long-range goal of modernization was put into effect as the Oklahoma City plant, among others throughout the company, was improved and reopened in 1971. Minor improvements were made to other sites such as the Tulsa plant, as well. The Clinton plant

saw a new grinding system and new high-velocity burners between 1973 and 1975 as it was renovated to take the place of plants in Oklahoma City and Tulsa. With these changes in place, Acme Brick broadened its product line and increased output across the nation by thirty million bricks a year and saw sales increase to over $63 million a year by 1973.

Improvements continued through the 1970s as the Edmond plant increased production to twenty-six million bricks annually, and included the purchase of the Seminole Tile Plant in Seminole, Oklahoma. In addition, $5.5 million was spent on construction of a new Oklahoma City plant that opened in late 1979 with a design capacity of forty-six million bricks per year. By the mid-1980s, the Oklahoma City plant was producing fifty-five million bricks a year. A new plant in Tulsa was constructed in 1984 and went into a new computerized operation in October of 1985 with a design capacity of forty million bricks annually.

With the Acme purchase of American Tile and Supply in 1996, Acme has become one of the largest distributors of ceramic tile in the United States.

Sales offices are located in Tulsa and Oklahoma City with direct sales to contractors, home builders and individual home owners throughout the Sooner State

From only one common and one face brick of the late 1800s to the hundreds of brick shapes, styles, and textures, brick sculptures and building technology, the Acme Brick Company has remained a great influence through the industry. As a new century begins, Acme continues in its proud heritage of brick production and technology throughout Oklahoma and the Southwest.

✧

Acme Bricks are hard fired at temperatures that often exceed 2000° Fahrenheit.

CAMROSE TECHNOLOGIES, L.L.C.

Treating our customers as we would like to be treated. Maintaining and fostering positive mental attitudes. Acting consistently with dignity, trust, and integrity. Providing leadership to our employees while serving our customers.

Camrose Technologies, L.L.C., a member of the Oklahoma Minority Supplier Development Council, has maintained these characteristics as its mission statement since August 1997, when the company acquired assets of J. P. EMCO, Inc. and proceeded with its established growth plans in 1998. Camrose continues production of the existing business of injection-molded/painted fascias and bodyside components. In February 1999, the company entered into an agreement to acquire the assets of Door Handle Systems of Woodbridge, Ontario, Canada to include production of molding, casting, coating, painting, and assembly for General Motors, Ford, and Nissan customers across the country. In the third quarter of 1999, Camrose also began the assembly and sequencing of fascias to the General Motors assembly plant in Oklahoma City. In support of this substantial growth the company purchased two new Engel 3,500-ton injection molding machines and eleven smaller injection presses from 200 tons to 850 tons to support the new door handle business. Engineering studies are underway that will finalize plans to build a new 40,000-square-foot paint facility for bodyside parts. Camrose Technologies also signed on to the "Oklahoma Quality Jobs Program" in February 1999.

✧

Top: Camrose Technologies, L.L.C.'s Ada, Oklahoma headquarters.

Below: A 3,500-ton Engel injection molding machine used in the production of automobile fascias.

The main production building currently used by Camrose Technologies was first occupied by Kirkpatrick Brothers Manufacturing, who built furniture, in 1967. General Tire and Rubber Corporation acquired the building in 1973, at which time injection molding and painting of exterior automotive parts began. In September of 1983, General Tire sold the facility and operations to J. P. EMCO Company. In July of 1985, the name was changed to J. P. EMCO, Inc. A second production building was built in 1996 to accommodate the General

Motors P-90 program. It houses a state-of-the-art paint facility consisting of a five-stage wash system, dry-off oven, ten Fanuc articulated robots, final bake oven, mix room, sludge room, and a process (load and pack) area. The warehouse facilities were purchased from Thompson Building Company. Vindale, a well-known mobile home manufacturer in the early 1970s, owned the north warehouse. The south warehouse was owned by Clopay, a metal and wood garage door manufacturer in the mid-1970s.

Chief Executive Officers Dr. William F. Pickard of Regal Plastics Company and Ken Nichols of Ventra Group Inc. have led their companies in overseeing Camrose Technologies. Under their leadership, Camrose, which is headquartered in Ada on 46.5 acres, reached sales in excess of $47 million, secured 375 production employees, 100 salary employees, and a customer base that includes General Motors, Ford, Nissan, and Chrysler. Camrose operates over 11,000 square feet of offices, 228,000 square feet of manufacturing buildings, and 101,000 square feet of warehouse buildings. Pickard, a successful Detroit, Michigan businessman for more than twemty-five years as chairman of Regal Plastics Company and owner/operator of McDonald's Restaurants, has served on the Federal Home Loan Bank Board and the National Advisory Committee on Trade Policy Negotiations under the appointment of President George Bush. Nichols, ranked number one out of the top 100 entrepreneurs in Ontario, Canada in 1996, is the chairman and CEO of Ventra Group Inc. and currently chairs the Automotive Parts Manufacturers Association and co-chairs the Canada-Japan Business Committee, Automotive Sector.

Camrose Technologies Vice President and General Manager Joe Bacher and each valuable employee have not only ensured that the company continues to have a positive effect on the local community, both in taxes paid and in the creation of additional jobs for Oklahomans, but they also consider themselves role models in charitable activities. In 1998, the Ada Regional United Way fund-raising campaign was bolstered when Camrose employees, in only their first year as participants in the drive, contributed $10,000 to the organization. Camrose employees also take part in contributing to Relay for Life, a cancer fund raiser; Spirit of Christmas, to ensure that needy children receive Christmas gifts; Halloween Safe House; USWA Local 985 Family Picnic; Camrose Open House, with a charity dunk tank; Camrose Fishing Tournament; and Camrose Charity Golf Tournament, for the Pontotoc County Fund for Abused Children.

✧

Top, below: Camrose Technologies produces automobile fascias and door handles for clients like General Motors, Ford, Nissan, and Chrysler.

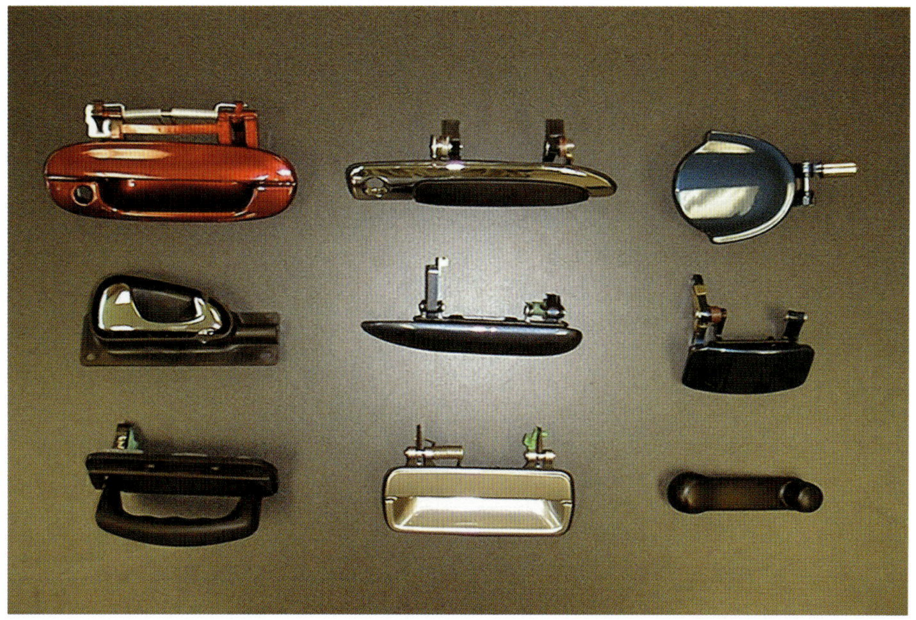

CMI CORPORATION

✧

Top: CMI's 1964 introduction of the AUTOGRADE® launched a revolution in highway or airport construction. High production assembly line principles were now being applied to road building.

Below: The ROTO-MILL® continued the CMI Revolution, this time in the field of pavement rehabilitation and regrading.

It all began in 1960 when the first interstate highway project contracted in Tulsa, Oklahoma revealed serious deficiencies in grade preparation which resulted in both base and pavement sections that did not meet job specifications. Similar problems were occurring throughout the U.S. In 1964, after four years researching every phase of the road construction industry and discussing the results with highly experienced industry personnel, Bill Swisher borrowed $500, filed corporation papers for a manufacturing company called Concrete Machinery Inc. (CMI), and began work on the engineering and construction of a revolutionary new machine called the AUTOGRADE®. This machine would be a combination dual-lane subgrader, material spreader, and finegrader and, more importantly, prove CMI's dedication to the philosophy that innovation must always be accompanied by quality. Thanks to this new machinery, federal engineers would later estimate savings of several billion dollars to American taxpayers.

Today, CMI Corporation is the worldwide leader in innovative roadbuilding technology. From the interstate construction boom of the early 1960s to federal laws appropriating money for their creation, the reality of the American highway system could not be fully implemented without the groundbreaking technology needed to meet close tolerance specifications and grading procedures along roads throughout the country. Bill Swisher and CMI immediately began engineering solutions to these problems. As AUTOGRADE® trimming and paving machines automated grade preparation and increased the productivity of grading contractors by over 500 percent and provided a quantum leap in finegrade accuracy, these same design principles were quickly applied to other paving processes. By the early 1970s, new CMI machines were successfully paving roads, highways, and airport surfaces from placement to surface texturing and curing throughout the world.

Innovations continued as CMI acquired asphalt hot mix production plants, bridge deck concrete finishing machines, and a complete line of trailers to serve the materials and heavy hauling requirements of road contractors and materials producers. In 1969, the company produced and tested the industry's first continuous mix, turbulent mass, and drum mix asphalt production plant. This led directly to the development of the modern parallel-flow drum mix plant.

In 1975, CMI introduced the ROTO-MILL® Pavement Profiler, bringing AUTO-GRADE® accuracy and productivity to the world of pavement maintenance and reconstruction. The costs of maintaining highway and airport surfaces, including profiling prior to the application of thinner, longer-lasting overlays, pavement mining for hot mix recycling and cold, in-place recycling were significantly reduced. The ROTO-MILL® now includes a family of machines ranging from 100 hp to 1200 hp, with cutting widths from as narrow as one foot to as wide as fifteen feet.

Innovative products have continued to appear over the years. In 1978, the industry's first hot mix asphalt plant capable of recycling old hot mix into new pavement without pollution and without sacrificing production capabilities for conventional mixes made from all new materials was introduced by CMI. In 1991, CMI and increased production by over 400 percent created the most significant new design in soil stabilizing/road reclaiming machinery. In 1992, CMI introduced a line of TRIPLE-DRUM™ hot mix asphalt production and recycling plants that are among the industry's most productive and cleanest operating. New products that remain true to quality and are able to extend productivity beyond the status quo have continued to be at the forefront of CMI throughout the decade.

With 1,900 employees and $250 million in revenues worldwide, the last several years have seen further acquisitions by CMI and include RexWorks Trashmaster products of Milwaukee, Wisconsin, Ross Company of Brownwood, Texas and C. S. Johnson Company of Champaign, Illinois, both manufacturers of concrete batching plants.

In September 1998, Swisher, founder and Chairman of the Board, welcomed Tom Engelsman as CMI's first new chief executive officer, who now leads Oklahoma City's 1,300 employees. Swisher stays busy promoting industry causes and is active on the board of Mercy Hospital, the board of Advisors to the OU Engineering School, United Way, Oklahoma State Fair Board, Oklahoma City Chamber of Commerce, is a past Area President of the Boy Scouts, and has served as Scoutmaster for the National Boy Scout Jamboree.

CMI's customer base is worldwide and has major contracts regarding the construction of airport runways, expressways, and interstate highways. The company moves into the next century expecting to expand into aggregate mining and production equipment to serve the total needs of the heavy construction industry, and continues to be the industry innovator providing lower cost/higher profit solutions to the world's paving needs.

Top: CMI's line of hot mix asphalt pavement production systems are sold worldwide. They are high production, highly efficient plants which operate to the highest ecological standards, minimizing air and noise polution.

Below: CMI's latest ROTO-MILL®, the PR-800-7/12, gives contractors increased options to pursue both local and city street work and highway jobs.

Fife Corporation

Irwin Fife founded Fife Corporation in 1939 in the garage of his Oklahoma City home. A World War I veteran who came to Oklahoma from Fayetteville, Georgia, and remained here until his death in 1971, Fife had been in the investment securities business. In 1938, a friend in the newspaper business happened to mention the need for a web guide to keep the paper in line on the high-speed newspaper printing presses. Fife immediately began to work on the problem and, in 1940, completed and installed his first working model.

Today, Fife Corporation is a $50 million a year company with 318 employees worldwide with world headquarters located in a 100,000-square-foot building at 222 West Memorial Road in Oklahoma City. The company has two wholly owned subsidiaries in Kelkheim, Germany, and Chiba City, Japan, along with sales and service offices throughout the world. Holding as its greatest asset a highly-skilled and dedicated work force with an average tenure of fourteen years, Fife Corporation has always been known in the market place for high-quality and progressive product research and development which produces the leading technology in the industry. Fife was a founding member of the Oklahoma State University Web Handling Research Center located in Stillwater, Oklahoma, and has been a sponsor since it was formed in 1986. The center performs fundamental research in web handling. Fife has also developed strong relationships with a true "blue chip" customer base including Johnson & Johnson, Kimberly-Clark, 3M, Du Pont, Firestone, Goodyear, Mobil Chemical, Eastman Kodak, and U.S. Steel.

✧

Top: Fife Corporation World Headquarters, Oklahoma City, Oklahoma, USA.

Below: One of Fife's earliest vacuum-operated steering guide systems, circa 1940.

Fife manufactures two basic products: automatic web guiding systems and web inspection systems. An automatic web guiding system is an industrial control used to laterally position a moving web. The term "web" is used to describe the continuous materials produced and processed, usually in rolled form, by a variety of industries, including: paper, paperboard, film, foil, textile, rubber, metal, plastic and composite industries. The guiding system serves to eliminate random lateral web motion by "guiding" the web to a desired fixed or constant position relative to the process machine. This form of control reduces trim and waste in the process and allows for increased line speed.

A web inspection system is a device that permits continuous monitoring of printing and coating processes at full-production speed. Quicker setup, less waste, faster production speeds, higher quality, and higher profits are possible because monitoring and adjusting are done without stopping the web. Fife has been awarded several patents over the past sixty years and recently filed for two patents for development of ultrasonic and laser-based sensor designs.

Maxcess International Corporation, with administrative offices located in Oklahoma City, serves as Fife's parent company and is a global holding company established in 1989 to acquire and operate companies serving the web accessory product segment of web processing industries. Maxcess' first acquisition in 1989 was Fife Corporation. In 1995, Maxcess International acquired another web accessory market leader: Tidland Corporation headquartered in Camas, Washington. Tidland produces high-quality web winding and slitting products. In 1996, Maxcess again expanded its portfolio by acquiring Magnetic Power Systems, Inc. (MAGPOWR®) headquartered in Fenton, Missouri. MAGPOWR is a leading manufacturer of magnetic particle and permanent magnetic clutches and brakes, controls, web tension systems and sensors. Maxcess also formed Talis International, L.L.C. in Millersville, Maryland, in 1996 to further enhance its electronic video web inspection technologies and to also serve as the Maxcess Technology Center.

By building on the strong base which Fife Corporation provided and by combining the strength and reputation of the finest names in the industry, Maxcess International is leading the consolidation of accessory companies serving the web processing industries. Maxcess International has a combined revenue of $100 million per year and operates facilities in seven countries around the world with 714 employees and has a compound annual revenue growth of twenty-four percent over the last five years.

Fife Corporation continues to hold at its core a valuable mission "to design, manufacture, market and service high-quality industrial process controls to improve the production efficiency of companies throughout the world, while creating leadership, value and success through customer focus and teamwork." Community and charitable involvement is reflective of this mission as the company supports organizations including United Way, Oklahoma Firefighters, Oklahoma Reserve Law Officers Association, American Legion, Junior Chamber of Commerce (Jaycee's), Oklahoma City Zoo, Omniplex, an annual blood drive for the Oklahoma Blood Institute, and a program called "Making the Grade"—a school-to-work transition program committed to encouraging high school students to finish school, pursue some form of post-secondary training and increase job readiness skills. Membership in local organizations includes the State Chamber of Commerce, the Oklahoma City Chamber of Commerce, and the Oklahoma Safety Council.

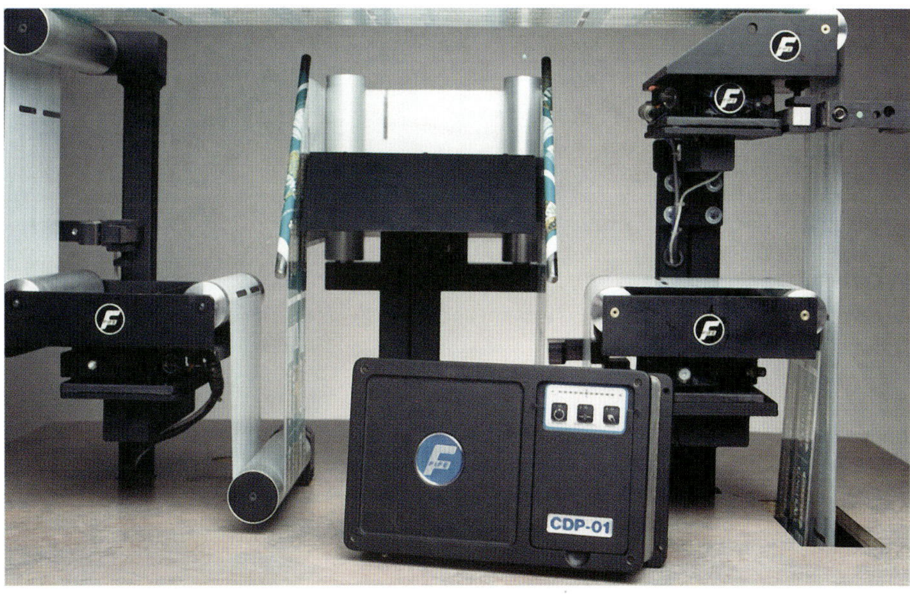

✧

Above: Fife's latest digital guiding technology.

Below: A display of Maxcess International's total web management capability.

GREAT PLAINS COCA-COLA BOTTLING COMPANY

Top: Plant located near Third and Broadway in 1920s. Inset (left to right): Virgil Browne and son, Henry W. Browne, Sr.

Below: Behind each case of Coca-Cola products shine the faces of more than 1,000 associates that make up the Great Plains Coca-Cola Bottling Company team.

Behind each can, twelve-pack, plastic bottle, or case of Coca-Cola products shine the faces of more than 1,000 associates that make up the Great Plains Coca-Cola Bottling Company team. This team reflects the company's grassroots organizational structure—organic, alive, and interdependent.

The collaboration and relationships among these associates, their other innovative techniques, and their progressive use of technology is the key to Coca-Cola's success in Oklahoma City. This commitment of knowledge and resources ensures there is "Always Coca-Cola."

The history of Coca-Cola and Oklahoma City is intertwined through generations of business leaders. In 1886, Dr. John S. Pemberton, a pharmacist in Atlanta, Georgia, invented Coca-Cola. Pemberton is the great-grandfather of Art Pemberton who owns and operates Oklahoma City's oldest grocery store, Crescent Market.

Company letterheads around the turn of the century stated that Coca-Cola is a beverage based on "the tonic properties of the wonderful Coca Plant and the famous Cola Nut." According to a booklet produced by The Coca-Cola Company in 1916, Coca-Cola is "pure water sterilized by boiling sugar-granulated—best quality, flavoring extracts and caramel. Caffeine—the active principal of tea, citric, and phosphoric acids."

In 1931, *Fortune* magazine claimed that Coca-Cola is ninety-nine percent sugar and water. The other one percent, it maintained, is caramel; fruit flavors; phosphoric acid; caffeine from tea, coffee, or chocolate; "Merchandise No. 5," three parts coca leaves (decocainized) and one-part cola nut; and a secret ingredient, "7X." Other ingredients that outsiders have claimed to find in Coca-Cola are cinnamon, nutmeg, vanilla and glycerin.

This original formula remained unchanged until 1985, when Great Plains Coca-Cola Bottling Company became the first bottler to introduce "New" Coke. It took just 90 days for the company to return to its roots. Today Coca-Cola Classic is the same "original formula" that Art Pemberton's great-grandfather concocted in 1886. The Coca-Cola Company maintains the secret formula for Coca-Cola, which it sells in concentrate form to franchised bottlers. Coca-Cola syrup is made from concentrate by bottlers in 5,000-gallon batches, with each batch containing 28,000 pounds of sweetener. Finally, Coca-Cola is one ounce of Coca-Cola syrup and 5.5 ounces of carbonated water mixed together and served chilled.

The Oklahoma City Coca-Cola franchise was incorporated in 1903 and purchased in 1922 by a group of business partners headed by Virgil Browne. At the age of forty-four, Browne moved to Oklahoma City from New Orleans for a short-term stint to establish the business.

This short-term business venture turned into much more than a lifetime. Virgil Browne is acknowledged as one of Oklahoma City's most prominent civic leaders, most notably recognized for his service as a director and officer of the Oklahoma City Chamber of Commerce for twenty-six consecutive years. Seventy-seven years later, Browne's descendants—Henry Browne, Sr., now chairman emeritus and his sons, Bob and Henry, Jr.—and an expert management team are in Oklahoma City carrying on the company and community leadership under the revised name, Great Plains Coca-Cola Bottling Company.

Just as history of the Browne family brings continuity and strength to this bottling company, the vitality or continuous improvement also positions the company for the next millennium.

The Just-In-Time mind set is the result of this continuous improvement path. Great Plains no longer stocks inventory in its sales centers. The product is produced and shipped direct ensuring freshness—the World's freshest according to audits and surveys. Great Plains is now the eighth largest Coca-Cola Bottler in the United States.

Through respect for people and the desire for progress, the internal organizational structure has become a Team Cell (sic) Network. This network serves to bond individual plant functions and associates into a seamless flow of development. The ideologies of respect, empowerment, teamwork, fact-based improvement, shared responsibility, trust, customer focus, flexibility, and cross-functional teams describe the components of this environment.

An educational video for the company explains: "Great Plains will always be a better place than the way it was just a few years ago. On our journey of continuous improvement, we listen, we learn, we share. As a result, our process becomes more precise. We become better."

The Great Plains Coca-Cola Bottling Company also continues to better the community by being a generous corporate citizen. The company is a major sponsor of the Oklahoma City Blazers hockey team, Redbud Classic, Lazy E Arena, Red Earth Native American Festival, Aerospace America, and the Children's Miracle Network, to mention just a few.

Coca-Cola has been a supporter of the Olympics since 1928. In 1996, the Great Plains franchise acted as a host for the torch relay run through the Oklahoma City area. This company is also the exclusive soft drink distributor for sporting events at both the University of Oklahoma and Oklahoma State University.

The spirit of Great Plains Coca-Cola Bottling Company can be seen in the faces of maintenance, sales, distribution, production, and service department workers. It is their commitment to learning and working together that guarantees it's "Always Coca-Cola." Thank you, Oklahoma!

Left: The Oklahoma City franchise was incorporated in 1903.

Below: Great Plains Coca-Cola Bottling Company located at 600 North May.

SAXON PUBLISHERS

The vision that would become Saxon Publishers was conceived early in the fall of 1970 as John Saxon became an instructor at Oscar Rose State College in Oklahoma City. Recently retired from a distinguished career of twenty-eight years in active duty for the Air Force, Saxon discovered that his students were neither comprehending nor retaining the algebra they were being taught. When several students suggested he write some problems for his class, Saxon decided to give it a try. The students were highly successful in learning algebra from his writings so he set out to write a college-level algebra book. Saxon soon realized the mission for this internationally recognized pacesetter in the educational field: We are dedicated to "turning around" education in America by publishing textbooks and instructional materials that have proven records of success in the classroom.

John H. Saxon, Jr. was born in Moultrie, Georgia in December of 1923, graduated from high school in Athens, Georgia, and attended the University of Georgia prior to enlisting in the Army. In 1943, he was appointed to the U.S. Military Academy at West Point and graduated in 1949 with a bachelor's degree in Engineering. He was soon stationed at Vance Air Force Base in Enid as a flight instructor. During the Korean War, Saxon flew fifty-five combat missions in a B-26 Night Intruder and flew five years as a test pilot for the Air Force. In 1961, he received his master's degree in electrical engineering from the University of Oklahoma and transferred to the Air Force Academy in Colorado, where he taught electrical engineering. He was assigned to Task Force ALPHA in Vietnam and again flew missions before his retirement as a Lieutenant Colonel in 1970.

Settling in Norman, Oklahoma after his retirement and working as a junior college instructor of college algebra, Saxon's material for struggling college algebra students was published by a major publisher in 1979. He then set out adapting his work for high school algebra students and enlisted several Oklahoma high school teachers to try his manuscripts with their students. With their success, he traveled to New York City with the new high school manuscripts only to find that publishers were not interested. Saxon, however, had two traits that would become the backbone for the success of his company: persistence and determination.

Mortgaging his home, borrowing from his children, and using his inheritance from his mother's estate, Saxon organized his own publishing company and in October 1981 published *Algebra 1*. He named his new company after his grandmother's farm and Grassdale Publishers was born.

For seven years, Saxon worked out of his home writing and publishing his books. By 1986, when he changed the company name to Saxon Publishers, Inc., he had published four

Top: John H. Saxon, Jr., founder of Saxon Publishers, Inc.

Below: John Saxon and some "Saxon" students.

books: *Algebra I*, *Algebra 2*, *Algebra 1/2*, and *Advanced Mathematics*. The popularity of the Saxon mathematics series led to the expansion of the mathematics series to cover grades K through 12. In addition, Saxon Phonics was launched in 1996. All the programs use the instructional method of incremental development and continuous review.

Today the company is owned by Saxon's four children, Dr. John H. Saxon III of Muskogee; Dr. Selby S. Harrison of Dallas; Dr. Bruce C. Saxon of Tulsa; and Sarah G. Perkins of Tulsa. Two of the Saxon siblings rotate serving on the board of directors along with the company president, Frank Y. H. Wang, Ph.D., and four outside board members who are accomplished business people.

Frank Wang was sixteen years old when he first responded in 1980 to an employment request from Saxon. Wang's various duties included "cutting and pasting," proofreading, checking problems, and editing. After graduating in 1982 from Norman High School, he left the company to enroll at Princeton University and received his B.A. in math in 1986. After receiving his doctorate degree in pure math from Massachusettes Institute of Technology in 1991, Wang forwent a career in academe and returned to Norman as the first vice-president of the publishing company. He has served as president of the company since 1994 and leads an executive management team of three vice presidents: Jill Gasaway, Operations/Finance and the longest serving full-time employee at the company; Fred Schilling, Marketing Sales and the first person recruited from the publishing industry to serve in the company; and Barbara Conteh Place, Product Development and the newest addition to the team in 1999.

In 1991, Saxon Publishers, Inc. relocated from a small suite of offices to a 20,000-square-foot building. A 100,000-square-foot distribution center was opened in 1997 in southeast Norman. Plans are underway for the building of a 60,000-square-foot office building, due for completion in 2000. The company now has over 200 employees and twenty-four educational representatives across the nation. School districts in all fifty states and several foreign countries use Saxon texts today.

At his death in October 1996, John Saxon was eulogized as having left an indelible impression on the face of education. Saxon Publishers is a tribute to his life's work and his vision.

Top: Saxon Publishers founder John Saxon and future President/CEO Frank Wang.

Below: Today, John Saxon's four children own Saxon Publishers, Inc. They are (left to right) Dr. Bruce Saxon, Mrs. Sarah Perkins, Dr. Selby Saxon Harrison, and Dr. John H. Saxon, III.

SMITHCO ENGINEERING, INC.

✧

Above: Orville L. Smith, owner and president of Smithco from 1952 to 1978.

Below: Smithco's corporate offices in Tulsa, Oklahoma.

Orville L. Smith, founder of Smithco Engineering, Inc., began working for General Electric Corporation in Schenectady, New York in 1941, as an electrical engineer. At that time, General Electric was developing the world's first atomic bomb and computer. They were also constructing generator sets for large transport ships used during World War II.

In 1943, Smith began work on a computer of his own on the floor behind the sofa in his home. In 1946, he left General Electric to work for the Happy Company in Tulsa as their Chief Engineer, conducting research on the uses for finned tubes.

Six years later, in 1952, with his wife, Sibyl, he started his own business and began manufacturing air-cooled heat exchangers. The family's Tulsa home became Smithco Engineering Inc.'s first office and Phillips Petroleum and TransContinental Pipeline became the company's initial customers. Their cash flow for materials was a combination of the money from Sibyl's private sugar bowl, which she was saving for a larger home for their growing family, and customer advances. The new Smithco Engineering, Inc. quickly outgrew the Smith's first home and the company was moved to a former chicken processing plant at 31st and Yale Avenue.

Orville's brother was an engineer for Stanolind (Standard) Oil Company, and with engineering talent running in the family, his son, Roy H. Smith, Jr., was studying petroleum engineering at the University of Tulsa. Orville hired his nephew Roy to provide drafting services. Clerical services were Sibyl's responsibility. During this early period of growth, the design and fabrication of the heat exchangers were done inside the new building and the final assembly of the units was done outside in the parking lot with rented trucks and cranes.

After only a year, the company moved to a larger facility at Second Street and Archer Avenue, then three years later, in 1956 moved to 500 North Trenton. At this point, Smithco began designing and manufacturing gas compression units in addition to air cooled heat exchangers and fabricated their own finned tubes. As the company expanded, Jim Lee joined the organization to handle purchasing and financial management. A decade and a half later, he became President of Smithco.

Roy H. Smith, Jr. graduated from the University of Tulsa in 1956 with a degree in Petroleum Engineering and became head of Smithco's sales division. He soon acquired the company's first international contract for delivery to Canada. A short time later, he took over the added responsibilities of plant management.

In 1958, Smithco built a new office and manufacturing plant in a former alfalfa field at West 41st Street and Jackson Avenue in West Tulsa and continued to expand its international presence. In the early 1960s, Smithco began developing highly technical computer software to support the engineering design process and in the 1970s Smithco International was formed to better serve the European and Middle Eastern markets. The sales office and two manufacturing plants were located Southwest of Paris, France.

When Orville retired in 1978 he sold Smithco to his nephew, Roy. Roy was instrumental in developing Smithco's custom software programs since the incorporation of the system in the 1960s, and, as the new owner of Smithco, he continued to purchase leading edge computer equipment and to develop innovative custom software to support all phases of the operation. This was a major focus of his time and resources and stemmed from the same philosophy that

had contributed to Smithco's initial growth and success.

Roy had the uncanny knack for predicting market cycles as well as pioneering major cost cutting ideas such as vendor partnering and putting experienced employees in business to become valued suppliers.

With the onset of the 1980s came the long spiraling downturn of the oil-related industries, which Roy had foreseen. Smithco, along with a devoted group of employees and suppliers, weathered the surprisingly lengthy oil crisis. During the downturn, he took the opportunity to significantly upgrade and improve computer systems further.

During this time, Roy's wife, Judy, came on board as accounting manager. When the market returned, Smithco was in a position to increase volume by 100 percent and to broaden its customer base significantly.

In 1986, Roy was diagnosed with cancer, and for the next twelve years he would continue to devote his life to the growth of Smithco and to the welfare of its employees. Smithco moved to its present location at 6211 and 6312 South 39th West Avenue in Tulsa in 1987.

As Roy and Judy took Smithco into the 1990s they established and acquired three additional companies, eventually increasing total volume by 700 percent. Judy established two of the companies and they purchased a third to broaden their manufacturing base. These companies were Metal Services, Inc., a steel fabrication corporation in Tulsa; Amercool Manufacturing, Inc., an air-cooled heat exchanger manufacturer in Tyler, Texas; and Transit Services, Inc. a flatbed, long and short haul trucking company in Tulsa. During this time, Judy was appointed CFO then CEO of Smithco. Even in the last six months of his extraordinary life, Roy and Judy established a fifth company, internationally. Smithco-Amercool Canada, Inc., is an air-cooled heat exchanger manufacturing facility located in Calgary, Canada.

By 1998, Roy had suffered several operations and he and Judy had traveled across the country regularly for specialized cancer treatments and protocols. Until his death in mid-1998, it was only for the last ninety days of his life that he was unable to make it to his office at Smithco and sit in front of his computer. At that point, Judy became, and is currently the owner, chairman and CEO of Smithco, and their other companies. She, along with Wayne Pyle, their good friend, business associate, president of Smithco and their other companies for the past several years, and former owner of Amercool, as well as with a group of loyal employees, has continued the direction set by Roy and Orville Smith. Smithco continues to grow and is currently a sixty-five percent international business.

Over the years, Smithco has supported many community efforts, civic projects, charitable events and educational organizations. Smithco will soon be celebrating its 50th anniversary in Tulsa. The combined companies employ more than 350 people.

✧

Top, left: Roy H. Smith, Jr., owner and president of Smithco, 1978 to 1998, and Judith A. Smith, owner and CEO of Smithco.

Above: Wayne Pyle, president of Smithco.

Below: Smithco's Air-cooled Heat Exchangers. Customer's Unit: British Petroleum, Installation Site: Toledo, 1991.

Tech Pack, Inc.

Since the first day of operation in 1985, founder and CEO of Tech Pack, Gary Clonts, has focused on good customer service as the root of the company's success. Operating as a manufacturer of custom corrugated boxes and a supplier of other specialized packaging materials, such as plastic bags, bubble wrap and tape, Tech Pack is prepared to service all types of industrial packaging needs throughout Oklahoma and neighboring states.

After operating for the first three years as a distributor of packaging materials, Tech Pack ventured into the manufacturing of corrugated boxes, which now comprises ninety-five percent of its gross sales. With this growth came the need for more production space to accommodate the growing number of flexographic printing presses and other manufacturing equipment. In 1996, Tech Pack moved into its current 113,000-square-foot facility in Oklahoma City. This multi-shift plant has state-of-the-art equipment that allows fast and accurate productivity of custom orders. In 1999, Tech Pack expanded its commitment with the acquisition of a 70,000-square-foot corrugated box plant in Tulsa, which had been in business for over thirty-six years. "This great expansion was part of a ten-year growth program designed to ensure that the company maintains its goal of increasing revenues by an additional $1 million per year. So far, that goal has been met," says Dan Meyer.

Top: An example of the modern flexographic printing presses at the Tech Pack facility in Oklahoma City.

Below: Tech Pack founder Gary Clonts (center) along with Tech Pack's management and sales teams. From left: J. R. Clonts, Dan Meyer, Joann Clonts, Gary Clonts, Randy Clonts, Chuck Friedlander, and Steve Maness.

In addition to the production growth, Tech Pack has also grown in employee numbers. From the original three, Gary Clonts, president and CEO, Meyer, who serves as vice president of marketing, and Randy Clonts, vice president of operations, the company has evolved into approximately ninety-four employees today. Gary's wife, Joann, serves as accounting manager and J. R. Clonts is vice president of purchasing. The attitude that everyone is family is an important one at Tech Pack, and it carries over into the day to day operations. The employees have been hand selected and average five years of service, and there are many that have achieved over ten years of service with Tech Pack. "We respect the job our employees do," says Gary, "and since my family has worked in every area of the business, we clearly understand the process. We operate on an open-door policy for the staff and assist with whatever needs to be done."

As with the staff, the development of strong, consistent relationships with customers is also a main goal at Tech Pack. The company strives to make the manufacturing and delivery process much easier for its customers. "We meet every packaging challenge," says Randy Clonts. "We have a wide range of machinery that can handle all corrugated requirements." Businesses in the Oklahoma City and Tulsa areas greatly appreciate Tech Pack's full service and technologically advanced approach. Working together, Tech

Pack's Tulsa facility coordinates with the Oklahoma City plant to maintain quality service to their customers. It is, indeed, Tech Pack's unique customer oriented philosophy that has allowed them to enjoy the steady growth in a highly competitive field.

Problem solving, Just-In-Time (JIT) delivery programs, and quality products are the standard at Tech Pack. The entire system is highly integrated between departments. Tech Pack has a consultative sales group, which brings customers' packaging challenges back to the design team for solutions. In turn, the design team, supported by a state-of-the-art CAD/CAM computer network, works side by side with the marketing department to support Tech Pack customers with an increase in their sales, and a decrease in damage claims through the design of attractive and durable packaging. Remaining aware of the market and customer needs, Tech Pack has a large commitment to its customers in warehousing and JIT delivery programs. This eliminates the need for customers to assemble or warehouse packaging items, which leaves more time and room for them to focus more of their efforts on their primary products. Tech Pack's own fleet of trucks makes daily deliveries each day to customers throughout Oklahoma and bordering states.

To further enhance customer relations, Tech Pack developed a website (www.techpack.com) to allow customers to tour its designing, manufacturing, and warehousing capabilities over the Internet. "Customers can always count on us to fulfill their packaging needs. We offer quality products and quality service to assure our customers operate more productively. We form an alliance between our company and theirs, and the result is a satisfied customer," says J. R. Clonts. The executive staff feels confident that this interdependent relationship is responsible for the company's continued growth.

The Oklahoma business community has not let Tech Pack's "customer first" approach go unnoticed. In 1990, the Oklahoma Private Enterprise Forum and the Oklahoma Venture Forum awarded Tech Pack for the company's outstanding contribution to Oklahoma's economic growth, productivity, and innovation. In 1992, the Greater Oklahoma City Chamber of Commerce awarded Tech Pack "The Best in Business." More recently, in 1997, the *Metro Journal* listed Tech Pack as one of the top fifty fastest growing companies in Oklahoma City.

Gary Clonts feels very positive about future business opportunities in Oklahoma. "The bright side of the story is what Oklahoma is doing. We are very excited about what is happening in the state and about the people who live and work here." Gary comments, "We thrive on solving our customers packaging problems. When we do, we not only gain a valued customer, but more importantly, a friend. To sum up our company, we are Tech Pack, The Packaging People—with a strong emphasis on people."

✧

Above: With more than 180,000 square feet of manufacturing and warehouse space throughout Oklahoma, Tech Pack offers an unique JIT delivery program to customers.

Below: Tech Pack's manufacturing facility located at 3801 Northwest 3rd in Oklahoma City. Prompt delivery is ensured by utilizing a fleet of company owned trucks.

The Williams Companies, Inc.

For more than nine decades, The Williams Companies, Inc. has been recognized as one of the world's pioneering pipeline and engineering concerns. Today, Williams' two primary businesses—energy and communications—position the company to take advantage of great opportunities in the next millennium.

Williams was founded in 1908 as the Williams Brothers Corporation by two brothers, David R. and S. Miller Williams. The company operated as the Williams Brothers Corporation from 1908 to 1949, the Williams Brothers Company from 1949 to 1971, and has been The Williams Companies, Inc. since 1971.

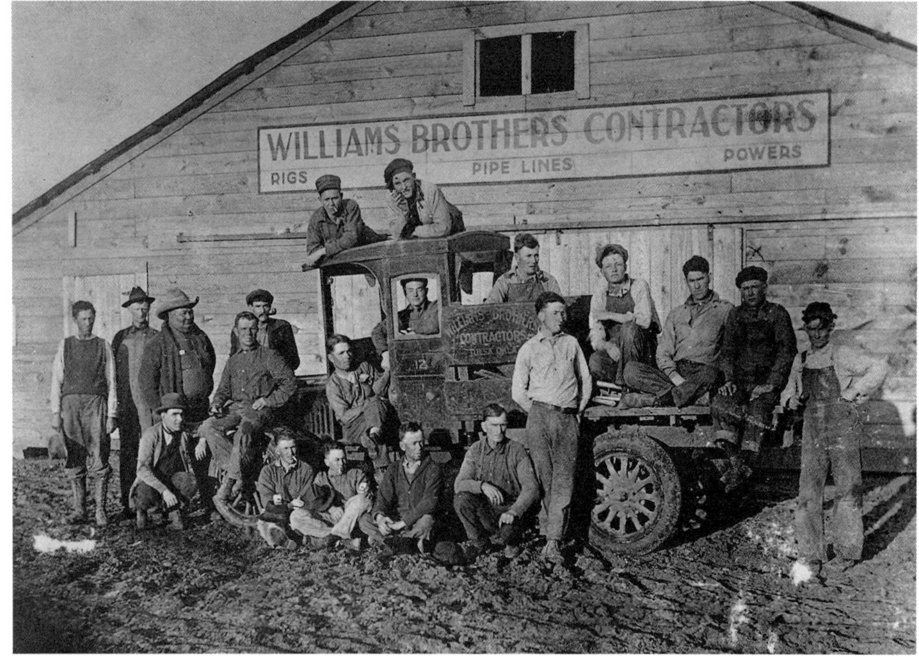

Below: An early Williams Brothers crew.

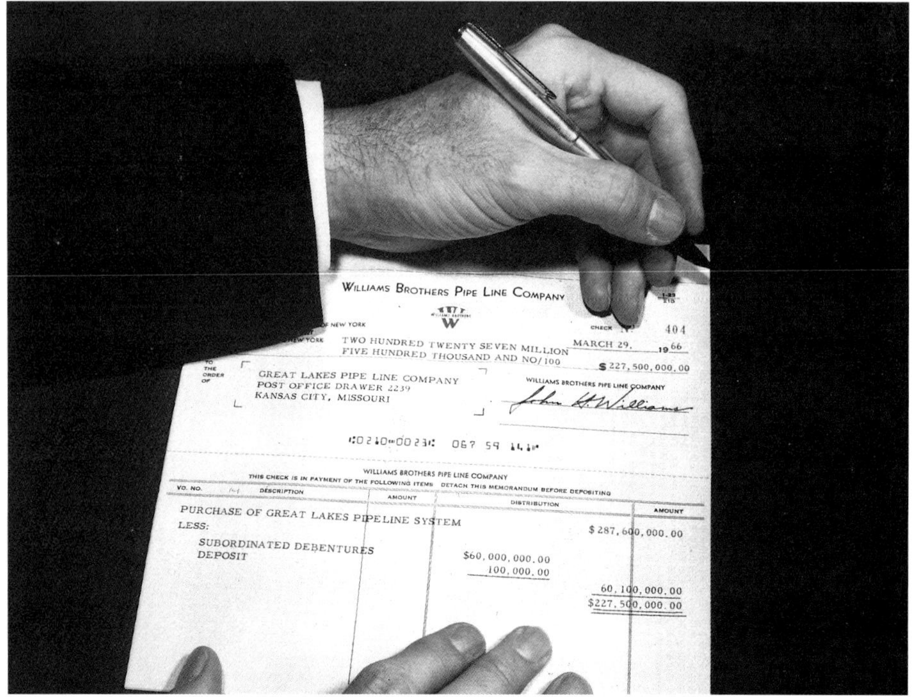

Bottom: John Williams signs the check for the purchase of Great Lakes Pipe Line.

When David and Miller Williams first came to Oklahoma from Fort Smith, Arkansas, in the early 1900s, they were involved in the building of railroad bridges, paving projects, and sewer and water pipeline construction in eastern Oklahoma and western Arkansas. Their experience with sewer and water pipelines made the Williams brothers two of the few contractors in the area familiar with pipeline construction. When the Oklahoma oil boom began in earnest, they quickly applied their expertise to the oil and natural gas industries. By 1915, pipeline construction had become the company's focal point. The brothers soon convinced most oil firms that they could build oil pipelines faster and cheaper than could the oil companies.

As Tulsa-based Williams climbed to the head of its profession during the 1920s and 1930s, the company was involved in such major pipeline projects as the Panhandle, Eastern Pipeline, Northern Natural, Colorado Interstate, Southern Natural, and Natural Gas Pipeline of America. With the onset of World War II, Williams played a major role in the completion of the Big Inch/Little Big Inch Pipeline linking the Mid-Continent and Gulf Coast oil regions to the East Coast. Among the company's major contributions to the pipeline industry was the adoption of modern equipment, such as backhoes, side-boom tractors, automatic wrapping and coating equipment, and ditching machines, which made Williams one of the most efficient pipeline construction operations and dramatically reduced the number of man-hours required in pipeline projects. Williams also pioneered many major across-water and offshore pipeline systems in the United States, South America, Africa, and the Middle East.

Williams built America's first commercial coal-slurry pipeline in 1956 and the world's first hydrogen-sulfide pipeline, which was constructed in Iran in 1967. When it completed MAPCO's LPG pipeline project in 1960, it revolutionized the pipeline industry by creating one of the first computer-controlled pipeline networks. Williams, incidentally, acquired MAPCO in 1998. In 1968, Williams completed the first major anhydrous ammonia pipeline in America.

Although primarily a pipeline design and construction company, in the mid-1960s Williams began to diversify. In 1966, Williams purchased Great Lakes Pipe Line Company's network of 6,228 miles of pipeline, seventeen refineries, and twenty terminals. In what was the largest cash-for-assets transaction in America at that time, Williams became the largest liquids pipeline in the nation.

Additional acquisitions helped Williams expand its pipeline design and construction focus. Williams began to produce and market nitrogen and phosphate fertilizers. It developed a nationwide natural gas transportation system, starting with the acquisition of two natural gas pipeline systems together providing more than 10,000 miles of pipeline; a natural gas and oil exploration and production company; and the nation's largest independently owned products pipeline system.

Another subsidiary, Williams Realty Corporation, was involved in commercial and real estate development, including the operation of the Williams Center in downtown Tulsa. Williams also controlled almost thirty-one percent of Peabody Holding Company, the largest producer of coal in America. Williams Exploration, Argico Chemical, Williams Realty, and Peabody Holding were divested in the mid-1980s.

In the 1980s, Williams converted some of its older pipelines into carriers for modern, secure, digital fiber-optic telecommunications.

After about ten years in the telecommunications business, Williams sold the long-distance portion of its telecommunications business in 1995; however, Williams reentered the network business as a major wholesale player in 1998.

Williams' commitment to community is widespread, with more than 23,000 employees worldwide at the end of 1999, and major offices in Tulsa, Houston, Salt Lake City and Owensboro, Kentucky. In 1998, the company was presented with the United Way of America's "Spirit of America" award, recognizing the nation's top company in all areas of corporate stewardship.

It all comes together in Williams' mission, which is encapsulated in a statement made by company Chairman Keith Bailey:

"Williams and its employees strive for leadership in all endeavors, business and charitable. Its current suite of growth projects should position Williams to continue to deliver superior value to shareholders and exceptional levels of support to the communities it serves."

✧

Above: Williams was the first to use decommissioned pipeline to house fiber-optic cable.

Below: Williams headquarters in downtown Tulsa.

American Trailers, Inc.

American Trailers is an Oklahoma Company founded in 1926 by Robert Randolph King. His innovations in trailer construction greatly contributed to the growth of the industry.

R. R. "Bob" King was born March 19, 1898 in Chickasha, Oklahoma, but soon moved with his family to Lockney, Texas. The oldest boy of nine children, Robert, at the age of seven began working in his father's blacksmith shop and helping on the family farm. He developed an early love of machinery and, as a teenager, left the farm and found work riveting and installing machinery on submarines in San Francisco, California. One of his favorite stories was to tell of surviving a major San Francisco earthquake while he was riveting on a docked submarine. King dedicated his evenings to mechanical engineering classes at Healds Engineering College.

As World War I was raging, King, fascinated with airplanes and flight enlisted as an aviator. He was to leave November 14, 1918 for flight training, but the war ended November 11. He remained interested in flying and later in life owned and piloted a series of airplanes.

When his money ran out, King left California and returned to Texas where he graduated from West Texas State College and went to work for Dallas Power and Light. In 1923, the American Body Company of Dallas, which built bodies for Model-T Ford trucks, hired him as an engineer. Within a year the company opened a small branch in Oklahoma City and transferred King to manage the new facility. The company's decision to sell it a few years later was the opportunity of a lifetime for Bob King. He purchased the Oklahoma City branch in 1926 for $500 cash and notes for the balance.

King named his new company American Body and Trailer Company and opened for business with five shop employees and a secretary. The company began by assembling Wayne school buses, but by 1928, American had manufactured its first trailer. During the Great Depression, American Trailers began to slowly expand its line and prosper. By 1935, a new plant was built at 1500 Exchange Avenue in Oklahoma City and American was manufacturing semi-trailers, flat bed trailers, livestock haulers, grain trailers and, beginning in the 1940s, oil field trailers. It was during this time King helped found the national Truck Trailer Manufacturers Association (TTMA). He later served as President of the association.

R. R. "Bob" King, founder of American Trailers, Inc.

When World War II erupted, industrial leaders, including King, were summoned to Washington and asked to help in the war effort. There was no way to transport fresh meat and produce to the front-line troops, which forced them to eat nothing but canned or dried foods, or simply live off the land. The Pentagon asked King to design a new type of trailer that could transport fresh foods to overseas troops.

King engineered the first refrigerated trailer by coupling a Briggs and Stratton gasoline engine with a refrigeration unit, lining the trailer with cork and sealing it with hot tar. It worked well, and was capable of maintaining below-zero temperatures. The first twelve refrigerated trailers were soon on their way across the Pacific Ocean. Unfortunately, a Japanese fighter plane sunk the ship and sent the trailers to the bottom of the ocean. Hundreds of refrigerated trailers were soon built and successfully transported to U.S. troops. Today, refrigerated trailers crisscross the nation with all types of perishable products.

Always the innovator, King later infused polyurethane foam in the wall cavities of

American's refrigerated trailers, thus making them lighter, more airtight, and allowing more payload.

At the close of World War II, American, Utility and Great Dane trailer companies joined forces and developed the first all-aluminum "stressed skin" trailers, built on the same principles used by the aircraft industry. The skin became a load-bearing part of the structure, resulting in stronger, lighter trailers that could carry even more payload and would not rust. The first aluminum vans came off the American's line in 1949. Aluminum trailers are now standard in the industry.

King renamed his expanding company American Trailers, Incorporated. They now manufacture a complete line of truck trailers, marketed throughout the southwest with branch plants in Tulsa, Oklahoma, Amarillo, Texas, and North Little Rock, Arkansas. Eventually there would be American distributors in twenty states.

The cattle industry was expanding in the 1950s, and railroads were the undisputed long-distance haulers for livestock. With the advent of better highways, King saw the need to engineer a multi-level trailer capable of carrying many more animals cross-country than the traditional flatbed trailer. In 1955, American Trailers developed a new "drop center" trailer with adjustable flooring that would make up to four decks, depending on the type of livestock to be hauled. It was an instant success. King nicknamed it the "Possum Belly" because of the unusual shape. The "Possum Belly" is on roads and highways today and is now built by numerous manufacturers.

American Trailers had outgrown the plant on Exchange Avenue and, in 1966, began plans to build a 100,000-square-foot facility on a forty-acre tract of land at 10th Street and Morgan Road in Oklahoma City. Most of the manufacturing was moved to the new facility within two years and the Exchange Avenue facility became a repair center. In 1969, The *Daily Oklahoman* listed American Trailers as one of the fastest growing companies in Oklahoma City and noted that it was the only trailer manufacturer in the state. By the time American merged with Fleming Foods in 1970, it employed more than 600 people. King remained as chairman of the board until his retirement at the age of seventy-two.

Though he died in 1995 at the age of ninety-seven, King is remembered today by his family as a quiet, unassuming man. His wife, LaReta Harlen-King, his children—Rita King-Moore, George A. King, and Jon R. King—and his four grandchildren revered him. He also lived to see four great-grandchildren.

During his long career, King was an enthusiastic supporter of Oklahoma. He was active in the Oklahoma City Chamber of Commerce and the downtown Kiwanis Club, and served as its president. He helped numerous civic and charitable organizations. It is notable; Mr. King saw to it that all of his siblings, that wanted one, received a college education.

R. R. "Bob" King continues to hold a special place in the hearts of many Oklahomans and, throughout the world, remains a pioneering leader in the transportation industry.

✧

Top: American's Refrigerated Trailer.

Above: The innovative "Possum Belly," an instant success.

W. B. JOHNSTON GRAIN COMPANY

The company that purchased the first load of wheat in Garfield County, nearly 106 years ago, is still thriving—buying and selling grain. W. B. Johnston Grain Company in Enid, Oklahoma was founded by the late Williston (Willis) Boyd Johnston who made the 1893 land run into Oklahoma Territory. His venture has since grown to become the largest independent grain company in Oklahoma.

W. B. Johnston was born in Newcastle, Pennsylvania. He was teaching in Kingman, Kansas when he decided to participate in the opening of the Cherokee Strip in 1893. While proving up his claim, Johnston worked as a stenographer at the Land Office in Enid then moved to a job with a Mr. Drennan, who handled products such as hay, grain, coal, salt, and flour to be sold to settlers. Later that year, Johnston bought out Drennan's business located on what is now the site of the Cherokee Strip Convention Center in downtown Enid. In the fall of 1897, Johnston moved the business to its present location at 411-415 West Chestnut, where the headquarters remain today. In 1910, Johnston built a 40,000-bushel elevator complete with corn shucking equipment and continued to operate the business until his death in 1937. In that year his son, Dale Johnston, took over as President and his son-in-law, Joe Meibergen, became vice president.

In 1939, the company-introduced mung beans into Oklahoma on strains of seed imported China. Johnston Seed Company was incorporated and is still located at 411 West Chestnut in Enid, with facilities on South Grand in Enid and in Crescent, Oklahoma. Johnston Seed Company is now involved in turf grass development and production. Its primary turf grasses are Guymon and Wrangler Bermuda grass and Cody, Tatanka and Bison Buffalo grass. The Company also produces and markets wildflowers.

In 1953 the grain company, in a joint venture with Johnston Seed Company and the Champlin family of Enid, built Johnston Terminal Elevator located at 30th and Willow Street in Enid, with a capacity of 4,.5 million bushels. In 1967, Johnston's purchased the Champlins' interest and it is operated today as a W. B. Johnston Grain Company facility.

In 1972, Johnston Enterprises was formed and is the non-operating holding company of W.B. Johnston Grain Company and Johnston Seed Company, Inc., as well as all of the other corporations that are subsidiaries of W. B. Johnston Grain Company and Johnston Seed Company. Joe Meibergen retired from active management in the company in 1972 and, in 1976; Joseph L. "Lew" Meibergen bought out the family's interest and continues to lead the company today.

Over the years, W. B. Johnston Grain Company has operated numerous country elevators, primarily located in northwestern Oklahoma and in the Texas panhandle. Though the company does not currently

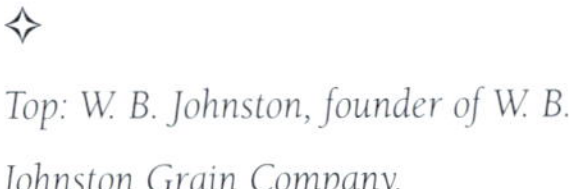

Top: W. B. Johnston, founder of W. B. Johnston Grain Company.

Below: Johnston's Port 33 at Inola, Oklahoma.

operate the elevators in the Texas panhandle, they have twenty-two Oklahoma country elevators and the terminal in Enid.

In 1980, Johnston's built a facility on the Verdigris River near Inola, Oklahoma on property leased from Verdigris Port 33. Later, the company purchased the thirty-five-acre port and renamed it Johnston's Port 33, Inc. It is operated as a wholly owned subsidiary of W. B. Johnston Grain Company. Johnston's Port 33 leases and manages the Port of Muskogee at Muskogee, Oklahoma and operates facilities at the Port of Chalmette and the Port of Gramercy in Louisiana, which are owned by Calciner Industries, Inc.

The Oklahoma ports handle bulk commodities and the Inola port has a grain facility. The Inola and Muskogee ports handle in excess of 1.5 million tons of product annually, including fertilizer, coke, steel, sand, bulk feed commodities, and numerous other products.

W. B. Johnston Grain Company has a total capacity exceeding 24 million bushels and handles primarily hard red winter wheat. Milo and soybeans were added with the passage of The Freedom to Farm Act of 1996. Johnston's also handles in excess of 300,000 tons of commercial fertilizer each year. In 1999, the company entered into a joint venture with six producers in northern Oklahoma and southern Kansas to build a cotton gin at Anthony, Kansas.

The Johnston companies employ approximately 300 people. Current officers of Johnston Enterprises, Inc. are Lew Meibergen, president, chairman, and CEO; J. L. "Butch" Meibergen II, vice president; Elizabeth A. Meibergen, vice president and assistant secretary-treasurer; Roger Henneke, vice president; Ed Polk, secretary-treasurer and chief financial officer. Officers of W. B. Johnston Grain Company are Lew Meibergen, chairman and vice president; J.L. "Butch" Meibergen II, president and CEO; Elizabeth A. Meibergen, vice president and assistant secretary-treasurer; Gene McVey, executive vice president; Roger Henneke, vice president; Dennis Craig, vice president; Ed Polk, secretary and chief financial officer. The officers of Johnston Seed Company are Lew Meibergen, chairman, vice president, and CEO; Leroy Mack, president and chief operating officer; J. L. "Butch" Meibergen II, vice president; Glenn Richards, Vice president; Joyce Hemphill, vice president; Ed Schovanec, vice president; Ed Polk, secretary-treasurer and chief financial officer.

In 1979, J. L. "Butch" Meibergen II joined Johnston's as the fourth generation to own and operate the company. In the summer of 1998, J. L. "Joey" Meibergen III began working part-time for the company and represents the fifth generation to be associated with Johnston Enterprises, Inc.

Johnston's takes pride in its 100-year plus service to producers in Oklahoma, Kansas and Texas and continues its mission to provide services in an efficient and modern fashion. In 1998, Johnston's handled nineteen percent of the Oklahoma wheat crop, sixty-two percent of the Oklahoma soybean crop, and forty-four percent of the Oklahoma milo crop. Johnston's will continue to serve its producer customers by providing handling and marketing facilities, crop insurance, risk management, and crop management services to its 10,000 customers.

✧

Top: Products of Johnston Seed Company.

Below: Johnston Terminal Elevator in Enid, Oklahoma.

Griffin Food Company

Since its beginnings on October 1, 1908, Griffin Food Company, founded by brothers J. T. and Charley Griffin, has manufactured and marketed quality food products and serviced their customers with integrity, courtesy and competitive pricing. Beginning with a few thousand dollars in sales the first month of business, a warehouse in McAlester, Oklahoma the size of a present-day convenience store and mule-drawn wagons, the operation has grown tremendously. Griffin Food now employs approximately 100 people requiring two city blocks in Muskogee for the current manufacturing plant, with deliveries made by company trucks and annual sales amounting to several million dollars. Today, the Griffin family name remains at the helm with President/CEO John W. Griffin, grandson of the founder.

It was, perhaps, the combination of Charley and J. T. and their selling and collecting abilities that was responsible for the company's quick growth in the beginning. But, it was their commitment to quality and staying up with technological advances that kept the company growing. The first proof of this happened in 1917 when J. T. followed his interest in the possibility of gleaning additional profits by manufacturing, as well as wholesaling, the items he handled. For his first step in this new direction he chose coffee. By early 1918, Griffin was marketing a high-grade coffee under his own label. J. T., on the other hand, recognized the need for a location nearer the center of his ever-expanding trade area. He constructed a three-story processing plant and administration headquarters in Muskogee in November of 1924.

Their visionary qualities extends into the company even today. With the celebration of its ninetieth Anniversary, Griffin Food Company announced a new expansion project. The new building will replace a portion of the old, adding an additional 16,000 square feet of new office area and 16,200 square feet of warehouse space. The existing building will also be remodeled with the projected completion date of December of 1999. Griffin takes pride in the creation of opportunities for the people in Muskogee and is active in contributing to local charities such as Salvation Army, United Way, Rotary, Meals on Wheels, Bedouin Shrine, CASA, and Little League baseball and softball.

Serving customers in a fifteen-state area, the Griffin product line consists of: mustards, syrups, vanilla, coconut, salad dressings, sandwich spread, jams, jelly, preserves, crystal white syrup and specialty mustards, bar-b-que sauce, Worcestershire sauce, soy sauce, picante sauce, molasses and peanut butter. Two of "Oklahoma's Favorite" products are Griffin Waffle Syrup and Griffin Strawberry Preserves. Before the Griffin name is placed on any of their products, the Quality Control Department makes sure the consumer will get the best quality available.

Below: Griffin Food Company in the early part of the twentieth century.

Bottom: History of some of the product lines of Griffin Food Company throughout the years.

The Unlaub Company, Inc.

Headquartered in Tulsa, The Unlaub Company, Inc., is Eastern Oklahoma's leader in industrial mechanical and electrical power transmission distribution since 1948. By providing bearings, synchronous and V-belt drives, conveyor and conveyor belting, industrial hose products, industrial electric motors and drives, and rock crushing, vibrating, and screening equipment, The Unlaub Company has served all markets from petrochemical to food processing; from furniture manufacturing to road construction.

Founded in Tulsa, in 1948 by Chuck Unlaub, the company quickly became a major supplier of industrial and mechanical power-transmission equipment components.

In 1953, B. J. Coulter returned to Tulsa after serving the United States in the Korean War and accepted a position at Unlaub. Years later, he was offered ownership and began his journey to acquiring controlling interest from the Unlaub heirs.

Under Coulter's management, Unlaub continued to grow, expanding throughout Tulsa, Eastern Oklahoma, and the adjoining states. With the upswing in the energy industry during the 1970s, branch offices were opened in Fort Smith, Arkansas; Oklahoma City, Oklahoma; and Houston, Texas. Coulter also expanded operations into the air-cooled heat exchanger industry so that Unlaub could better serve the oil and natural gas processing industries.

Unlaub became a Coulter family operation in August of 1979, when Coulter's wife, Billie, joined the company's management team and was named treasurer of the corporation. In November of that same year, their daughter, Karen Coulter-Hoff, joined the accounting division as a clerk and in 1981, son, Rod, went to work in Unlaub's warehouse division. In 1987, Rod Coulter moved to the company's outside sales division. In 1995, Karen and Rod began acquiring stock in Unlaub and, as a team, they began playing a more active role in management.

Today, under its president, Rod Coulter, Unlaub enjoys record sales from an ever-increasing base of loyal customers. He states this is solely due to the fact "we at Unlaub are an excellent team with a personal commitment to serve the customer. We have the undying belief that one leads by serving. Simply put, our mission is to serve."

The company's operations are overseen from its newly renovated offices at 1722 East King Place in Tulsa. Three warehouses with more than 20,000 square feet of stocking capability are maintained to ensure prompt delivery of Unlaub products.

Well aware of the importance of its role as a corporate citizen, Unlaub pledges that ten percent of its annual earnings have and will continue to be donated to local charities. As a proud partner with the Unlaub Company, The Tulsa Boys' Home has benefited greatly from this commitment. As Rod Coulter explained, it is vital that Unlaub return to the citizens of its sales area a portion of its profits so that both the company and the people of Oklahoma benefit from its success.

✧

Top: B. J. Coulter watches as Karen Coulter helps Rod Coulter learn to ride a bicycle, June 1971.

Below: Unlaub headquarters at 1722 East King Place, Tulsa, Oklahoma.

Oklahoma Steel & Wire

B. L. Moore and his brother-in-law, Robert Lockridge, founded Oklahoma Steel & Wire in 1979. The family-owned business has grown from five to 276 employees at the Madill, Oklahoma plant, eighty-five in the Centerville, Iowa plant, and 110 in a related plant in Norman, Oklahoma. Annual production of the three plants now exceeds 200,000 tons of steel each year and product distribution that serves the entire U.S. through a network of nationwide distributors and direct sales efforts.

The price of steel is actually what brought Moore to Oklahoma. He had originally considered Houston for the site of the company's manufacturing facility where access to the raw material for his product was a factor, but the lower cost of real estate in Madill quickly changed his mind. Today, the plant utilizes forty acres of land and 192,000 square feet of production space and operates twenty-four hours a day, seven days a week, fifty weeks a year. As this space has proven to be inadequate to keep up with the growing business the company has added 3,900 square feet for an administration facility.

When the company opened, there was one wire welder on staff, which kept the offering of products very limited to one market—agriculture. Oklahoma Steel & Wire's original product line consisted exclusively of livestock fence panels. Today, the line has expanded to include a wider variety of fence panels, barbed wire, woven wire, fence stays, and electric fence wire. The commercial product line is distributed primarily through home improvement stores and local lumber outlets and the industrial market is served by nine company sales representatives who work closely with customers assuring that their particular needs are met. The products they promote include straight and cut wire, highway reinforcement fabric, residential building fabric, and numerous other products for the prestressed concrete industry. The company also offers nearly 800 different designs of mesh. In addition, if what the customer needs is not among the selection, the firm will cut and bend mesh to a customer's design and specification.

The family commitment, to provide the highest quality product at the most competitive prices possible, started by the founders continues to this day as Moore's children—Max Moore, president and CEO; Craig Moore, internal operations manager; and Kathleen Moore, C.P.A. and chief financial officer—and granddaughter, Sarah Moore, database information specialist, and B. L.'s wife, Colleen, follow in this tradition.

The relationships between Oklahoma Steel & Wire and their customers speak volumes about the firm's dedication to quality products at competitive prices backed up by three generations of exceptional service.

T. H. Russell Co.

Headquartered in Tulsa, Oklahoma, T. H. Russell Co. is an engineering construction company engaged in the design, fabrication, and installation of gas and oil processing equipment.

Founded in 1972 by Thomas H. Russell, the company is a major player in the energy industry. Russell, who graduated from the University of Tulsa with a Bachelor of Science degree in chemical engineering in 1957, is a professional engineer, registered in four states. After graduation, he worked with Mobil Oil Company in natural gas production and plant operations, before joining Barnes & Click, Inc. in 1960, where he specialized in natural gas plant design and operations. He worked in various phases of the energy equipment industry until he started T. H. Russell Co. in 1972.

T. H. Russell Co. was originally organized as an engineering consulting firm, but within a year, the company constructed its first manufacturing shop. In 1974, the company also became involved in field construction. The company specializes in designing and building gas liquids recovery plants, gas and liquid treating units, liquid fractionating plants, and several types of refinery units.

Since 1974, the company has pioneered the construction of skid-mounted refrigeration plants. In 1976, T. H. Russell Co. completed its first cryogenic LPG recovery plant. Since then, it has completed thirty-two similar facilities and has become a recognized leader in the field.

In the last two decades, T. H. Russell Co. has designed and constructed more than 300 gas processing and oil refining plants. These projects include: gas dehydration; LPG fractionation; gas and liquid recovery plants; crude oil distillation and vacuum distillation units; catalytic reforming and hydrodesulfurization units; and gas compression facilities.

All of the units are designed and fabricated on the skid-mounted concept, which is highway transportable. All interconnecting piping is in place, complete with instrumentation and valving. Control wiring is installed and terminated in skid-edge junction boxes, and painting and insulation are completed to customer specifications. All units are hydrostatically tested prior to shipment. Larger units are assembled for water transportation from the Port of Catoosa Assembly Yard, which offers access to the Mississippi River and from there, worldwide delivery.

Overseas operations started in 1985 in Yemen. In 1989, T. H. Russell Co. built its first world-class gas treating plant. Since that date, it has built treating plants with a total gas capacity of over 1.2 billion cubic feet per day. In 1992, T. H. Russell Co. built a refinery on Sakhalin Island, which is the only producer of diesel fuel for the island.

The company has over 150 skilled employees in its Tulsa facility. In the 1980s, T. H. Russell Co. became an employee-owned company, as personnel were given the opportunity to buy shares through a stock option.

In 1998, the company merged with Applied Process Solutions, Inc. a worldwide supplier of process plants and equipment. APSI combines engineering talents and manufacturing capacities in the United Kingdom, Canada, and the United States in serving the worldwide energy industry.

✧

Above: A 350 million cubic feet-per-day Gas Treating Plant in northern Michigan.

Below: A 120 million cubic feet-per-day Cryogenic Gas Process Plant on the Ohio River.

SHAWNEE MILLING COMPANY

J. Lloyd Ford was a pioneer in Oklahoma manufacturing before statehood. Mr. Ford had grown up in Grand Rapids, Michigan and was attending the University of Michigan at Ann Arbor when he made a trip to his parents' homestead farm northwest of Shawnee, Oklahoma. Though at the time he aspired to become a surgeon, several more trips to the southwest would decide Ford's illustrious career. In May of 1901, he accepted a position selling flour for Acme Milling Company in Oklahoma City, and met Frances Sims and was married October 1903. He continued on the road until April 24, 1906, when he purchased the "Shawnee Roller Mills," incorporated the company and moved to Shawnee. This small flour mill that would eventually become the largest family owned mill in the southwest was built south of Shawnee, Oklahoma in 1897, where it operated as Shawnee Roller Mills. He later added branch mills, elevators, and warehouses in seventeen towns and cities among five states, with outlets for commodities in Oklahoma, Texas, Alabama, Georgia, Arkansas, Mississippi, Louisiana, Tennessee, Florida, and the Carolinas.

On October 22, 1946, the *Shawnee News Star* honored Shawnee Milling Company with a forty-year retrospect of the Company. Described in the article as a "colossal success" engineered through the courage and vision of the founder, J. Lloyd Ford, the Mill held "the unchallenged position as Shawnee's largest employer and Oklahoma's greatest producer of milled products."

Today, Shawnee Milling Company continues its century of growth in Oklahoma with an additional milling site in Okeene and grain receiving facilities in Kingfisher, Minco, Okarche, Roll, Arnett, and Gage. Shawnee Milling's 250 employees share in the sizable task of manufacturing flour, corn meal and animal feeds that are shipped into twenty-six states and several foreign countries. Shawnee Milling takes great pride in its continuous support of Shawnee schools, Oklahoma Baptist University, and St. Gregory's University as well as maintaining extensive involvement in service to the community.

Ford was thirty years old when he founded Shawnee Milling Company and would remain as President of the Mill until 1946, when his son, Leslie A. Ford, became president. Today the company continues its successful production under the leadership of Leslie's sons William Leslie Ford, president of Shawnee Milling, and Robert Lloyd Ford, manager of the Okeene plant and executive vice president of Shawnee Milling Company

Insistent upon creating quality products while maintaining dependable service and consistent value to customers across the nation, Shawnee Milling Company stands ready to prove their dedication to the traditions of J. Lloyd Ford started back in 1906 in Shawnee, Oklahoma.

✧

Top: J. Lloyd Ford, founder of Shawnee Milling Company.

Bottom: The predecessor of Shawnee Milling Company, circa 1906.

"I have a new job."

With those words in 1941 Joe Medley came home to announce to wife Fran and son Bill that a new beginning was on its way.

Coming out of the Depression and World War II looming on the horizon, the automobile salesman from Enid, Oklahoma was glad to find this new job. Automobiles would shortly be out of production due to the war effort and car salesmen would be obsolete, so selling industrial scales for Howe Scale Company was indeed a good opportunity.

Selling mostly motor truck scales to the agricultural industry in rural Oklahoma and West Texas would involve a lot of travel but Fran had a job as a secretary/bookkeeper and things were looking up.

Calling on grain elevators, cotton gins, and livestock sale barns in this mostly farm economy state, he was successful and, after a short while, decided to take the plunge and open up the Joe Medley Scale Company at 609 North Hudson in Oklahoma City. Joe was selling and servicing the equipment and Fran was doing the office work and bookkeeping.

Since most of the companies that were customers also used two wheel and four wheel hand trucks (to handle feed and seed) they took on a line of this type of equipment and entered into material handling equipment.

Today, this two person business has grown to Medley Material Handling Company employing over 150 people in three states—selling, renting, leasing, and servicing everything in the material handling field from the smallest casters to fifty-ton fork lift trucks.

Bill Medley's first job was pushing a two wheeler up and down North Hudson to sell it to the small business for handling products. After graduating from the University of Oklahoma in 1952, he entered the business full time as the third member of this still very small family business. Over the next few years, the material handling business potential became larger as Oklahoma changed to a more industrial economy. These post-war years also saw the fork lift industry become more and more important as companies began palletizing and stacking their products. In 1956, Joe Medley Scale Company became Medley Material Handling Company and took on the Yale Automatic Lift Truck line for Oklahoma, West Texas, and New Mexico.

Today, Medley is one of the oldest Yale dealers in the country. With steady growth expansion of branches began to emerge. The first was in Tulsa in 1958, which started with a sales representative working out of his home. In 1963, the Amarillo branch was opened with two employees. Today, each of these facilities employs over twenty people and has 10,000-square-foot facilities for sales service and rentals. The El Paso branch was opened in 1976 in an abandoned filling station and has today grown into a new ultra modern building that is known as "the finest material handling facility in the El Paso Juarez area." Service and sales branches were more recently opened in Albuquerque, New Mexico and Ponca City, Oklahoma.

Moving from Hudson Street in Oklahoma City to Northeast 26th in the late 1950s, the company built a 33,000-square-foot building at 4201 Will Rogers Parkway in 1980. This is indeed the best-equipped and most efficient material handling facility in the Southwest.

Mark Medley, grandson of the founder, joined the company in 1975 as a salesman and eventually became general manager. With Bill's retirement, Mark is now president of the company and has overseen additional growth in size and offices. Jerry Dyer serves as the general manager. Winning many awards for achievement over the years, the company was honored to have Bill Medley elected president of the international trade organization, Material Handling Equipment Distributors Association, in 1991.

As Medley Material Handling moves into another century as a thriving Oklahoma business, their mission remains the same. "Solving customer problems by providing unbeatable quality in sales parts service and rentals... Working to be the dominant supplier of new and used lift trucks and the best 'team' in their area.... To achieve a level of employee satisfaction unsurpassed by any of the competition... To be recognized as the premier industrial equipment organization by accomplishing 'Total Customer Satisfaction'... To be fair and profitable...To be the best!"

Medley Material Handling Company

✧

Above: First delivery truck at 609 North Hudson, circa 1942.

Below: Four generations of Medleys (left to right): Joe, Bill, Mark, and Ryan.

✧

Tribal Flag Plaza on the north side of the Oklahoma State Capitol, where many of the official flags of Oklahoma's Native Americans are flown.

COURTESY DAVID FITZGERALD.

Banking & Finance

investment banking and securities brokerage provide the financial foundation for a host of Oklahoma enterprises

Patrons

Dorcester Capital Company,
Oklahoma City

Friends

Bancfirst,
Oklahoma City

HCM Investments,
Oklahoma City

Norick Investment Co., LLC,
Oklahoma City

Raymond James
Financial Services,
Michael P. Mazzie, CFP,
Tulsa

Raymond James
Financial Services,
David Moore,
Financial Director,
Tulsa

First National Bank and Trust of McAlester

The year 1896 marked the end of one era and the beginning of another. In that year Congress passed legislation providing for the creation of tribal roles for the Choctaws in preparation of the elimination of their traditional tribal government and the individual allotment of land. That same year, on December 12, 1896, "Old Reliable"—the First National Bank of McAlester—opened for business as the First National Bank of South McAlester in a small frame building on Choctaw Avenue with a total capitalization of $50,000.

McAlester began much earlier. Originally know as Cross Roads, it was nothing but a dusty intersection of the California and Texas Roads until James J. McAlester opened a store there in 1869. Soon another merchant, Bill Pusley, and Judge Folsom, a blacksmith, joined him. In 1873, the settlement was granted its first post office.

Coal made McAlester a boom town after the Missouri, Kansas, and Texas Railroad built through the region in 1872, providing both a market for the coal to fire its engines and a means to ship it to other markets.

In 1885, Edwin Chadick, an eastern businessman, joined a wild turkey hunt to the area and noted the plentiful deposits of coal.

Top: First National Bank as it looked at about the time of statehood.

Right: The Pioneer Coal Miner Memorial was dedicated September 30, 1992, the Pioneer Coal Miner Memorial and the Wall of Memories in Chadick Park on 3rd Street is a tribute to the thousands of miners who labored in mines in the McAlester area, and especially to those who lost their lives in their work.

Opposite top, bottom: The First National Bank as it looked in the late 1950s and today.

After securing the necessary financial backing he planned to connect the coal mines to the St. Louis and San Francisco Railroad depot at Wister. When Chadick could not reach an agreement with McAlester, he purchased some property from Fritz Sittel a mile and a half south of McAlester's store.

By the fall of 1890, the Choctaw Coal and Railway Company had completed its line from Wister to the coal fields and a competing community, South McAlester, was established at the rail junction.

Soon South McAlester dominated its older cousin and in 1906 the two settlements were consolidated. That same year the First National Bank of South McAlester was renamed the First National Bank of McAlester.

As the first banking establishment in the community, the First National Bank of McAlester played a prominent role in the growth of the area and for a while was the only banking concern for local businessmen between Denison, Texas, and Oklahoma City. As the area prospered the First National constructed a new stone bank at 116 East Choctaw Avenue in 1897.

Ten years later, when the Panic of 1907 gripped the nation, it allowed the economy of McAlester to continue to grow by issuing Comptroller of the Currency approved clearinghouse certificates redeemable in cash at the bank.

In 1910, an extensive remodeling project was undertaken adding a second story to the

1897 structure. In 1914, the First National Bank of McAlester became a charter member of the Federal Reserve System, giving it the elasticity of a flexible currency system that allowed it to survive the extended coal strike of the early 1920s. When the strike was broken in 1927, only four of the sixty-five banks in the McAlester area survived the economic turmoil. Old Reliable was one, having paid out all withdrawals in full. So grateful were area merchants that they presented the bank's directors with a loving cup that adorned the directors' room for many years.

Black Tuesday, October 29, 1929, was the onset of the Great Depression. Before it was over, forty percent of America's banks would fail. Through it all Old Reliable kept its doors open, helping its customers cope with the financial disaster.

By February of 1933, the First National Bank of McAlester and a state bank were operating, when Governor William A. "Alfalfa Bill" Murray ordered Oklahoma's state banks to close. Although it was exempt from the governor's order the First National Bank complied. Shortly afterward, President Franklin D. Roosevelt ordered a fifteen-day bank holiday. When the depression began, Old Reliable had placed most of its funds with the Federal Reserve Bank System and thus maintained sufficient funds on hand to allow its depositors to meet their payrolls and other emergencies during the closing. When the Great Depression ended, Old Reliable was stronger than ever and continued to grow during the war years.

In 1955, a $300,000 remodeling project was completed along with a forty-two-foot mural, "The Homestead," which decorated the west wall and portrayed the region's Choctaw heritage. At the same time a drive-in window was added at the rear of the bank.

First National Bank presidents, past to present:

Charles C. Hemming	1896
Frank S. Genung	1897-1908
E. J. Fannin	1908-1909
James H. Gordon	1909
W. Perry Freeman	1910-1915
Robert P. Brewer	1915-1918
James H. Gordon	1918-1919
C. W. Crum	1919
Tom Hale	1920-1928
George A. Kilpatrick	1928-1929
James McClenahan	1929-1930
James H. Gordon	1930-1931
James McClenahan	1931
M. L. Stockton	1932-1940
Richard L. Crutcher	1940-1946
A. L. Fields	1946-1947
Richard L. Crutcher	1947
Oscar H. Kirk	1948-1963
Al Prucha	1963-1965
Clark Bass	1965-1984
chairman of the board	1984-1999
Ken Bass	1984-1996
R. Bruce Hall	1996-present
Wanda Bass, chairman of the board	1999

In 1966, seventy years after its founding, Clark Bass acquired the First National Bank of McAlester, which at the time had assets of approximately $15 million.

Born in Caddo in 1912, Bass was reared in nearby Durant, where his father was a cotton broker. After graduating from Durant High School, Clark attended Southeastern Oklahoma State University and then graduated from the University of Oklahoma. He returned to Durant and entered the consumer finance business before serving in the Army Air Corps in World War II.

Clark later recalled, "I knew when I was in junior high school that I was going to be a banker. I just knew it. I was just attracted to the industry, and I prepared myself for it when I was in college. I knew what I wanted to be."

When he returned to Durant in 1947, Clark Bass realized his dream when he purchased the Durant National Bank.

In 1951, Clark married Wanda Jones of Lufkin, Texas. To this union were born a daughter, Louise, and two sons, Carlton and Boyd.

In 1963, Clark and Wanda purchased control of the First National Bank and Trust of McAlester, with Clark being named the bank's president. As a partnership Clark and Wanda brought a unique blend of corporate citizenship and customer friendly banking with them.

As Wanda explained, "The major difference in banks today is the way people are treated. The First National Bank was built to accommodate our customers."

Building on such a philosophy, with Clark becoming chairman of the board in 1984, and Wanda as vice chairman, Old Reliable's total assets grew to near $50,000,000 and in 1999, assets were $425,000,000.

The First National Bank and Trust Company of McAlester went through a massive building campaign in 1970, constructing an edifice on East Choctaw Avenue that occupies an entire block.

Believing that a bank should be a leader in community development and put money back into the city it serves, Clark and Wanda took the lead in developing several projects in McAlester, including the McAlester Regional Health Center, the Fine Arts Center at McAlester High School, an assisted living center at the Health Center, the McAlester campus of Eastern Oklahoma State College, the Doctor's Building & Outpatient Surgery Center, the preservation of the Aldridge Hotel and a softball sports complex. They funded the Coal Miner Memorial and Coal Miner statue in McAlester and the Carl Albert Statue at the University of Oklahoma and at McAlester. They have also funded educational sporting facilities in McAlester and throughout Oklahoma.

Wanda and Clark Bass. Clark, chairman emeritus of the First National Bank and Trust Company, passed away June 14, 1999. Wanda, chairman of the board, continues to carry the torch she and her husband committed to many years ago.

Clark Bass was inducted into the Oklahoma Heritage Hall of Fame in 1995, followed by Wanda in 1998, as recognition of their outstanding civic and business leadership.

Clark Bass, chairman emeritus of the First National Bank and Trust Company, was in poor health for several months and passed away June 14, 1999. His legacy in the community of McAlester and Oklahoma will continue into the twenty-first century.

Wanda Bass, chairman of the board of the First National Bank and Trust Company, continues to carry the torch that she and her husband committed to many years ago.

The First National Bank and Trust Company of McAlester continues to grow and serve the people of McAlester and southeastern Oklahoma. It has truly lived up to its name, "Old Reliable," through the years.

Peoples National Bank

The Peoples National Bank of Checotah did not exist until 1911 but the heritage of its owners can be traced back to the seventeenth century when Anglo-Saxon settlers began marrying the Indians who lived in Georgia and Alabama. After the murder in 1825 of William McIntosh, chief of the Lower Creeks, the Stidhams and many other Creek mixed bloods, called Mestizos, began making plans to move to Indian Territory. The first Mestizos settled near Fort Gibson in 1828 and began to carve the Creek Nation from the lush wilderness.

A short thirty-three years after their arrival, the Creek Nation was again divided, this time by the Civil War. This was an especially difficult time for the Creek Indians, fighting many skirmishes, brother against brother; and in July 1863, they faced each other on the old Texas Road in the Battle of Honey Springs, just three and a half miles northeast of what was to become Checotah.

On February 13, 1872, Missouri-Kansas-Texas railroad workers, advancing through the Creek portion of Indian Territory toward Texas, established a railhead. It was called "Checote Switch" to honor the Creek Nation's progressive chief; and a town was born.

In 1911, the Peoples National Bank, owned by E. V. and Jo Keeney, was chartered and just three years later, in 1914, young George W. Stidham, III, was hired as a teller there. George was the grandson of G. W. Stidham, a Mestizo, who had arrived in Indian Territory in 1832. George was named president of the bank in 1937 and there has been a Stidham in a leadership role there ever since. In 1975, George named his elder son, Donal E. Stidham, president, while he continued as chairman of the board until his death, September 23, 1978. George Lee Stidham took over from his brother in 1985, and remained the chairman and CEO in 1999 when Donal S. (Mike) Stidham became the bank's president.

Helping lead the bank into the 21st century as president of the bank's holding company, Peoples National Bancshares, Inc., is Robert Jennings.

The Peoples National Bank has remained in the center of town since its founding. As the need for expansion arose, buildings next to the bank were purchased and incorporated into the operation, using original storefronts when possible.

After a devastating fire, which destroyed a city block in Checotah in 1992, the bank established a Community Development Corporation that made it possible to lend a local group of investors interest free money to rebuild the block. The bank's officers and employees have always taken a leading role in the Checotah Chamber of Commerce, Lions Club, Kiwanis Club, and other community organizations.

While strength in capital, growth in assets and the physical plant are important, the bank's place in history must be judged by the success of its customers. The variety of cultures in the Creek Nation has given Checotah's people the ease of the West, the hospitality of the Old South, and the energy of folks from above the Mason-Dixon Line.

From Diversity—Unity.

✧

Top: This life-size statue of a Mestizo was presented to the citizens of Checotah and the Creek Nation in the hope that future generations will take pride in their history.

Below: Peoples National Bank as it appeared in 1914.

Arkansas Valley State Bank

Arkansas Valley National Bank was founded in 1905—territorial days—two years before Oklahoma statehood in 1907! Ownership of Arkansas Valley State Bank, as it has been known since 1909, has not changed hands since its founding.

Threaded through the history of Broken Arrow, the bank was built on a dusty little street beside the railroad tracks, the lifeblood of the small community for years to come. The bank has grown and remodeled since its inception, but still occupies the property at 302 South Main Street in Broken Arrow where it originally occupied a fifty-foot storefront. Today, the bank occupies 25,500 square feet including a drive-in facility.

Owned by Arkansas Valley Bancshares, Inc., Arkansas Valley State Bank is a community bank that offers a wide variety of standard bank products from specific checking packages to diverse loan financing. Future branch locations are in planning with the first scheduled for completion in the year 2001.

Arkansas Valley State Bank has been a survivor, hunkering down during the hard times of the Depression, the Dust Bowl, and both World Wars. Following World War II, there was a period of steady progress before the bank and the community of Broken Arrow literally exploded with over two decades of exciting, unbelievable growth.

Top: The original fifty-foot storefront at 302 South Main Street in Broken Arrow, Oklahoma.

Below: Arkansas Valley State Bank executive officers are (left to right) Kelley Kimbrough-Rash, vice chairman of the board; Doug Kimbrough, chairman of the board/president; and Neely W. Kimbrough, senior executive officer, along with past bank officers G. A. Brown (top right corner) and Ivan Brown.

Even though times were good, the bank did not survive without struggles. There were times when other banks were going "belly-up" all over the state. Because of a prudent loan policy and careful attention to the needs of the people in the community, Arkansas Valley not only survived, but continued to prosper and grow with Broken Arrow. As the economy demanded, the bank has changed over the years by offering primarily agricultural loans in the beginning, to lending for housing and industry, to funding the newest business technologies today.

Through the years, Arkansas Valley State Bank has built its success and its future on the solid foundation of being a hometown bank willing to meet the needs of hometown families and businesses.

Founded with the help of investor and landowner, G. A. Brown, Arkansas Valley State Bank was named for the fertile farming area that surrounded it. Brown was the first of what is now four family generations at Arkansas Valley. He was father to Ian Brown, who was employed from 1961-1972 as president and CEO, and grandfather to Barbara Brown Kimbrough, who is currently on the board of directors; and great-grandfather of Doug Kimbrough, a twenty-year employee who now serves as president and CEO. Neely Kimbrough, senior executive officer, also served the bank as president and CEO. He is the father of Doug Kimbrough and Kelley Kimbrough-Rash, a twenty-five-year employee who serves the bank as vice chairman of the board.

Other longtime employees were President K. M. Rowe (1905-1961); "Murphy" Laws (retired 1957); W. E. "Earl" Laws (retired 1951); Roy Smith, cashier (1927-1967); Melvin Logsdon, cashier and loan officer (1951-1984); and Virginia W. Johnson (1957-1998), who worked in just about every position for the bank including that of president.

Neely Kimbrough joined Arkansas Valley State Bank as president in the early 1960s when the bank's total assets were $2 million. When told by a brother-in-law that the bank would one day be a $10 million bank, Kimbrough laughed. At the time, the statement seemed pretty funny.

Today, led by President and Chairman of the Board Doug Kimbrough, the bank has grown to over $170 million in assets, has seventy-five employees, and annual net earnings of nearly $1,700,000 in 1998 with 15,000 accounts.

Arkansas Valley State Bank strives to maintain a balance between maximizing profitability for the stockholders, providing fiduciary stability and innovative services for the community, and insuring a work environment for employees that encourages personal success through the achievement of corporate goals.

With an average growth of over five percent per year for the last ten years, Arkansas Valley State Bank has increased the ratio of loans to deposits and loans to assets while growing deposits and assets as well.

While continuing to do business based on customer service, the bank aims to become more available to customers and prospective customers through internet banking and planned branches as the future needs of Broken Arrow dictates.

Since inception in 1905, civic responsibility has been paramount with the bank and many community leaders have come from within its walls. The bank stands ready to fund worthwhile projects and provide manpower as Broken Arrow's growth continues. Arkansas Valley State Bank feels confident that the bank will remain profitable while playing a vital part of the community's future.

Through the leadership and involvement of the Brown-Kimbrough family, the bank has based its success on trust, stability, good old-fashioned hard work, and personal service to their valued customers.

Arkansas Valley State Bank. Your friends and neighbors since 1905.

✧

Top: Teller window of Arkansas Valley State Bank during the early 1900s.

Below: Arkansas Valley State Bank, still at 302 South Main Street, as it appeared in the 1990s.

The Central National Bank of Alva

The opening of the Cherokee Strip in 1893 brought a boom of numerous businesses and banks. One of the institutions that survived from that time is The Central National Bank of Alva, in Alva, Oklahoma owned and operated by the Myers Family since 1919.

Only after several mergers in the early years did the bank take the name it has today. The Alva National Bank was established in 1899. In June of 1907, Alva National had a capital stock of $40,000 and was fully equipped with the latest improved steel, fire and burglarproof safes and vaults. This equipment guaranteed depositors that their money would be absolutely safe and deposits amounted to $200,000. Officers of Alva National Bank in 1907 were George A. Harbaugh, president, and J. H. Schaefer, vice president.

During the years between 1907 and 1913, the Alva Security Bank purchased Alva National Bank with George A. Harbaugh as bank president. In September of 1913, G. A. Harbaugh, E. Anderson, T. F. Fennessey and H. E. Noble, owners of Alva Security, organized a new banking institution under the name of Central State Bank. The newly named bank continued to operate at the location of the former Alva Security. With new management and capital of $25,000, Central State Bank maintained the high standards set by Alva Security in Oklahoma banking circles. Since Central State Bank was considered a "state bank," the deposits were guaranteed by the Depositors Guaranty of the State of Oklahoma. This guarantee, in addition to the strong financial standing of the stockholders, made Central State Bank a successful institution. The capital of the original bank was $25,000, with deposits of about $200,000. The bank rapidly flourished and on October 31, 1917, Central State Bank absorbed the Woods County Union Bank. Harbaugh and George Meade had controlling stocks of the Union Bank at that time.

The situation remained much the same until January of 1919, when a young man by the name of W. D. Myers purchased a large interest in Central State Bank. By March 1922, Myers was president of Central State Bank and that same year the thriving institution was converted to a national bank. The Central National Bank of Alva (CNB) maintained steady growth in the early years and in 1926, saw the capital stock at $50,000 with surplus and profits amounting to $40,000. At the time, CNB was the largest bank in

✧

The Alva National Bank was established in 1899 and eventually became The Central National Bank of Alva.

The Central National Bank of Alva in 1999.

PHOTO COURTESY OF LYNN MARTIN.

Northwest Oklahoma and had resources of more than $1.3 million. The 1926 bank officers included Myers, president, and Edna Myers (W. D.'s wife), vice president. CNB continued to grow under Myers' direction and the acquisition of the Dacoma Bank took place on April 9, 1932.

Myers' wife, Edna Earle, served as one of the directors of the family owned bank until her death in 1959. The couple had five children, all of whom worked at the bank as young adults. The two surviving children are still affiliated with CNB—Gertrude, chairman of the board and CEO, and L. W., director. Gertrude learned a great deal about banking from her father and has made the prosperity of the bank her life-long career. She has continued in that tradition by sharing her knowledge and experience with her nieces and nephews who work in the bank today.

Upon his father's death in 1951, W. D. Myers, Jr., became president of the bank and served in that capacity until his own death in 1987. His wife, Lillie, served on the board and passed away in 1979. They had one daughter, Mary Margaret, currently vice president, trust officer, and a director of the bank.

L. W. Myers and his wife, Grace, had three children named Leo, Steve, and Marilyn. Grace Myers passed away in 1994. Leo and his wife, Colleen, have two children, Natalie and Phillip. Leo works in the bank's credit card department. His daughter, Natalie, works at the bank during the summer and on Saturdays. Steve, his wife, Suzie, and their three children live in Arizona. Marilyn and her husband, Tony Bouziden, have two children, Grace and George. Marilyn is a vice president of the bank and serves on the board of directors.

The Woodward Branches of Nation's Bank were acquired by CNB on March 13, 1998. The bank had gone through a series of purchases and mergers beginning with the sale of the Bank of Woodward to Bank Four in Wichita, Kansas on May 28, 1993. This purchase increased the total assets of CNB from $100 million to approximately $172 million. At that time, The Central National Bank of Alva reported total equity capital of $28,708,000 and resources of more than $172 million.

At the close of business in March of 1999, officers and directors of CNB included Gertrude Myers, chairman of the board/CEO; William R. Buckles, president; Orin R. Lancaster and Hugh R. Jones, senior vice presidents; Clint A. Elliott, senior vice president/operations; Mary Margaret Myers and Larry M. Jeffries, vice presidents & trust officers; Phil Hamilton, Marilyn Myers Bouziden, Patricia A. Headlee, Mark Brace, Ginger Boren, Brenda Evans, Kimberlee Schnoebelen, Joyce Gilbreath, vice presidents; Michael E. Fouts, vice president and cashier; J. Michael George and Jeffrey L. Klick, vice presidents and farm representatives; David Moore and Roger Wagner, assistant vice presidents.

First State Bank of Altus

Ninety years of quality banking—that is the crux of the story of First State Bank of Altus. From its beginning on October 14, 1909 in Martha, Oklahoma through the move in October 10, 1959 to Altus, Oklahoma, First State Bank of Altus has continued to maintain quality service to all customers despite radical changes in the banking industry throughout the century.

✧

Above: S.L. (Sanford) Doughty, President, stands in the foreground. Horace C. Doughty, Cashier, stands in the background. Approximately 1917.

Bottom: First State Bank of Altus in 1959, just after the move from Martha, Oklahoma.

In 1888, Henry Clay Doughty moved his family from Texas to a plot of land in Greer County, Unclaimed Territory. Within a few months Henry, Clint Maddox, and Thomas F. Medlin built a general store building. Medlin established a post office and named the town after his daughter, Martha, who was the first school teacher in the area. Before long, Henry bought out his partners in the mercantile store and established the first banking functions in Martha, Oklahoma. "Uncle" Henry possessed a large safe in the store and farmers and ranchers often asked him to keep their surplus money and valuables in his safe. The items were always available to them when they needed to reclaim their "deposits."

On October 10, 1909, Henry C. Doughty along with his sons, S. L., Horace C., son-in-law S. H. Starkey, farmer James Sheridan, and Altus residents J. A. Henry and B. M. Wooldridge chartered the Martha State Bank with a total capitalization of $10,000. The State of Oklahoma Banking Department issued its Certificate of Authority at Guthrie, Oklahoma on October 13, 1909 and listed J. A. Henry as president and B. M. Wooldridge as secretary. The building was erected at the main intersection in town. J. A. Henry soon sold out his interest to Henry C. Doughty's nephew, J. A. Doughty and Henry's second son, Forest. On January 1, 1914, Mr. Wooldridge resigned as secretary and cashier, and Earl S. Coots replaced him. Directors were now J. A. Doughty, F. M. Doughty, Clyde H. Doughty (F. M.'s son), S. L. Doughty, and Horace C. Doughty.

At "Uncle" Henry's death in 1925, the Martha State Bank had deposits of about $150,000 and was extending loans of about $50,000 to area people. Capital Stock and surplus totaled $10,000. Horace bought the ten shares of bank stocks owned by his father and became the cashier. S. L. continued to serve as president until 1941 when he resigned because of poor health. Horace became president and S. L.'s daughter; Eunice Rowsey became cashier.

The death of S. L. in 1943 led to the acquisition of all shares by Horace and his three sons. Horace remained as president, son

Nelson was named vice-president, son Harold was named cashier, and Eunice Rowsey was assistant cashier.

By the end of 1957, Harold and Nelson were both farming some of their father's land and had bought farms of their own. As farmers began consolidating land to remain efficient, it became necessary to finance greater amounts from year to year. As a small bank, Martha State Bank's capacity to make those larger loans due to capital structure began to become more and more inadequate. After the best cotton crop in history in 1957, Martha State Bank made application for permission to move the bank to Altus and change its name to First State Bank of Altus. On February 2, 1959, the board of directors of the bank approved submission of a proposed capitalization of the new bank for $100,000 of capital, $100,000 of surplus and $25,000 of undivided profits. The new building opened on October 10, 1959 at the corner of "Main" and "A" Street in Altus.

The bank added a remote express "drive-in" window in December of 1975. Bank personnel had grown from five in 1959 to twenty-six in 1976. Harold was Chief Executive Officer and Nelson was President. Horace was chairman of the board until his death October 19, 1982. In 1981, the bank made arrangements to buy neighboring property to build a remote drive-in facility and parking lots. A second floor meeting room was added to the main building. Further expansion continued in 1986, 1991, 1995, and 1996. A branch was added to the local Wal-Mart in 1995.

In 1999, First State Bank of Altus has $8 million in capital with a total of $76million in assets. Harold serves as chairman of the board of directors. President Paul Doughty has been instrumental in helping to secure a "Bar-S Foods" manufacturing-processing plant in Altus and has joined with other local businesses and the City of Altus to aid in the establishment and development of the "Luscomb Aircraft Manufacturing Plant." The bank continues their policy of contributing a sizeable portion of annual profits to local charitable and institutional organizations.

Perhaps First State Bank of Altus' greatest claim to fame, however, is its flexibility and willingness to adapt to the changing market of banking without compromising personal service. Striving to make the bank a "one-stop shop" for its customers, President Paul Doughty has added investment services, mortgage lending, and insurance to provide the community with opportunities that only a century of quality banking service can establish.

The very successful winning partnership of Harold and Nelson Doughty (which lasted over fifty years) abruptly ended with the sudden death of Nelson Doughty on June 28, 1999. During the two brother's partnership tenure, the bank grew from less than $1 million in assets to its current $76 million. It is only fitting that the new century welcomes a fourth generation of Doughtys to take over where the third generation left off. Nelson's two sons, Lee and Lynn along with Harold and his two sons, Steve and Paul, make up the board of directors as the twentieth century comes to a close.

For more information about First State Bank of Altus, you may contact the Museum of the Western Prairie in Altus for a copy of the Western Trails Historical Society's Summer, 2000 publication of the bank's history.

Top: First row: (left to right) Harold Doughty, chairman, and Nelson Doughty, vice chairman. Second row: Paul Doughty, president and CEO, and Nelson Lee Doughty, executive vice president.

Below: First State Bank of Altus, 1999.

First National Bank & Trust Company of Ardmore

The year was 1889, just two years after the City of Ardmore was founded. The institution was a private bank owned by J. F. Anderson and his son, Charles, which eventually held the honor of being the first nationally chartered bank established in Indian Territory. Though banking was a tough business at the time, J. F. Anderson wanted his sons to be bankers, and when he properly evaluated Ardmore as having a successful future, he provided the money for the new venture. The following year, a national charter was granted, and on August 13, 1890, the bank began operating under the name of the First National Bank of Ardmore.

It is presupposed that this charter was granted about the same time the bank moved into its first permanent headquarters. It was a two-story structure and the first brick building in Ardmore. Located at the northeast corner of Caddo and Main Streets between the Post Office and the Apollos Funeral Parlor, businesses began building around the bank and in 1890, the Federal Court House was opened.

This fast growing town, with its uneven wooden sidewalks and unpainted, speedily-built stores and homes was not prepared for the first of two major disasters that would challenge the endurance of those who had chosen to make Ardmore their home. In April of 1895, an early-morning fire swept through the business section and took several residences, as well. The only building spared was the Post Office, which had miraculously escaped as the winds pushed the flames west and south. The exact date of the move from the East Main location to the northeast corner of Washington and Main is not known, but the bank had been rebuilt at that location by 1903.

The bank was again rebuilt after an explosion occurred in September of 1915. A tank car of casing-head gas near the depot exploded and killed 42 people, injured hundreds, and left more than half the business section in smoldering ruins. Yet again the town pulled itself from the rubble to rebuild, this time through the assistance of volunteer payments of $1 million from the Santa Fe Railroad Company.

By 1919, First National Bank, along with many other businesses in the town, had rebuilt. The people of Ardmore and those associated with the bank felt the new building was one of the most striking architectural structures they had ever seen. Inside, the beauty of gold leaf murals and the stained glass skylight topping the thirty-five-foot ceiling brought sightseers from near and far.

The reorganization of the bank in December of 1923 brought one of Ardmore's early-day lawyers, E. A. Walker into the picture. A wealthy Iowa farmer and banker, John C. Voorhees, brought Walker to the Healdton area to handle his land and oil lease investments. Walker and Leon Voorhees, son of John C. Voorhees, soon bought the controlling interest at First National. These were prosperous years for the bank—years that would be hard to remember as the Great Depression took a strangle hold upon the country.

Described simply as "hard times" by most, the Great Depression was catastrophic for the banking industry. Following the stock market crash in 1929, on March 6, 1933, the newly inaugurated President Franklin D. Roosevelt, closed the First National along with every other bank in the nation. On April 19, a little over a month after closing, the bank received its third charter, and opened under the name of The First National Bank of Ardmore. Walker served as president. With the establishment of the Federal Deposit Insurance Corporation guarding against bank failures, public confidence in banking was restored.

The present day facility of First National Bank of Ardmore is located at 405 West Main, and was built in 1975. The bank was originally located at the northwest corner of Main and Washington. In 1946, eighty-five-year-old Walker, who was looking to liquidate his financial empire, bumped into Lloyd Judd, an Oklahoma City insurance executive and real estate broker, who was seeking a new venture to enter. The two men made the agreement and Judd became very active in civic affairs. Sadly, about a year after the Judds moved to Ardmore, the active banker experienced a heart attack, which was followed by a fatal stroke in May of 1949.

Judd's death did not slow the innovative changes taking place at First National. His son, John, was to carry on his father's concepts. Staying involved in his community, John was able to lead the bank in the expansion of services and support of existing industries while attracting new industries. The Trust Company was organized in 1964 and the First Data Bank Computer Center in 1968. In 1965, plans were formulated for a new bank building to be located at Main and D Street.

Today, the two-story main banking structure is located on the corner of Main Street, D Street and Broadway, with seven branches located in Marietta, Lone Grove, Ringling, and Airpark, and many ATM locations are available. Jim Patton is chairman of the board and Chris Tompkins is president and CEO. First National Bank directors include Bob Bramlett, Joe Brown, Curtis Davidson, Bob Drake, Tom Dunlap, John Kriet, Lovell McMillin, Jim Patton, Creede Speake, Jr., Chris Tompkins, Keith Walker, Wayman Woodley, and Henry Roberts.

✧

Opposite, top: An early location of the First National Bank of Ardmore at the northwest corner of Main and Washington Streets.

Opposite, bottom: The interior of First National Bank at Main and Washington.

Top: The interior of First National Bank at the northwest corner of Main and Washington.

Below: Today, First National Bank of Ardmore's main bank is located at 405 West Main. Customers always refer to the bank as "The Bank with the Fountain."

STOCKMANS BANK OF GOULD & ALTUS FORMERLY THE FIRST STATE BANK OFGOULD

Top: Interior of the Bookkeeping Department of First State Bank of Gould, 1910. A. R. Reeves (left) is the younger brother of First State Bank of Gould founder Herman H. Reeves (right).

Below: Herman Reeves used this 1908 Overland as he traveled to Eldorado, Oklahoma to return the $1,000 cash investment used to open First State Bank of Gould in 1910.

Today, as assistant chairman of the board, Georgia Crow is inspired as she tells the history of the bank. Stockmans Bank of Gould and Altus, formerly the First State Bank of Gould, has served the community and furnished the working capital for many farmers and ranchers in the area for over ninety years

It all began in 1910 as Herman H. Reeves, Georgia's father, sold his only asset, a team of mules, for $350. He then borrowed $650 and, together with the proceeds from the sale of the mules, he and Dr. J. P. Lee, L. O. Reeves, and C. H. Sharp founded the First State Bank of Gould on March 23, 1910. The first officers of the bank were Dr. Lee, president; L. O. Reeves, vice president; Herman Reeves, cashier; and Sharp as assistant cashier.

Organized with two employees and a capital stock of $10,000, the bank opened for business in a small corner of the local general store. Nearly a century later and only a short walk from that general store, Stockmans Bank has total assets of $54 million and twenty-two employees.

The bank has had five presidents in its history. Herman Reeves became the bank's second president in 1920, succeeding Dr. Lee. Upon the death of Herman Reeves in 1959, Emory S. Crow was elected president and held the office until 1978. Crow was then elected chairman of the board, with Charles H. Hill, Jr. filling the post of president. Rick Holder succeeded Hill and became president in 1986.

In 1920, Russell Reeves succeeded L. O. Reeves as executive vice president of the First State Bank of Gould, a position he held until entering the Army in 1942. A. V. Hendrick held the office until 1947, when Robert S. Carmack assumed the vice-presidency. In 1954, Emory Crow became the Executive Vice president and held the office until 1959, when he was elected president. Alton M. Coppage, who joined the staff in 1958, was elected vice president and cashier and filled those offices until his retirement in 1977.

Only five people have served as chairman of the Board. Herman Reeves served until 1959; Edna M. Reeves served from 1959 to 1971; Georgia Reeves Crow served from 1971 to 1978; and Emory Crow served from 1978 to 1988. Rick Holder has served as chairman of the board since 1988. Mark Holder serves as vice-president and chief executive officer of the bank's newest facility in Altus. With this new branch came the name change to Stockmans Bank.

The building presently occupied by the bank in Gould also served the community and the State of Oklahoma in a number of capacities. Herman Reeves was very active in civic affairs, serving as president of the Hollis Rotary Club and the Harmon County Chamber of Commerce. He also served as a member of the Oklahoma State Banking Board for twenty years, commissioned for that job by five different governors. Emory Crow was also very active in civic affairs throughout the community and served on the Oklahoma State Banking Board. Rick Holder, a graduate of Oklahoma State University, is currently active in several youth academic programs, sports organizations, 4-H, and is currently a board member of the Salvation Army, and the Western Oklahoma State College Foundation.

Stockmans Bank is also proud to sponsor the Oklahoma History Scholarship awarded by the Oklahoma Heritage Association. This prestigious award is given each year in the amount of $1,000 to a student of Hollis High School.

Stockmans Bank is extremely proud of the bank's growth and the accomplishments of its employees. However, not one event or achievement would be possible without their most valuable asset: the customers. The people of Stockmans Bank have always striven to provide friends and neighbors with the best banking service available, while honorably serving the community of Harmon County. A pledge to continue that same community-oriented, person to person approach to banking is at the heart of Stockmans Bank, just as it has been for nearly a century.

Above: Stockmans Bank offices in Gould.

Bottom: Stockmans new bank facility in Altus on North Main, opened in 1999.

The Trust Company of Oklahoma

✧

Left: Chairman Paul H. Mindeman.

Right: President Thomas W. Wilkins.

PHOTO COURTESY OF MCCORMACK PHOTOGRAPHY.

In an age when change is the dominant factor in the financial world, The Trust Company of Oklahoma is a stable, secure, and dependable entity. Oklahoma owned and managed, The Trust Company is committed to Oklahoma families and their financial future.

The Trust Company of Oklahoma is a unique financial institution. Totally independent from any other financial organization, it has no obligation to banks, brokerage houses, or other entities that could influence decisions about investments. The Trust Company's trust professionals make investment decisions based solely on each client's best interests.

Paul H. Mindeman, a highly respected trust officer in Tulsa, founded the firm in 1981, gathering together a group of the top trust officers from Oklahoma banks. Today, The Trust Company has grown to more than sixty trust professionals with extensive experience and a broad base of knowledge. Offices are located in Oklahoma City, Stillwater, and Muskogee, as well as two locations in Tulsa. Mindeman, who remains active in the company, is chairman and Thomas W. Wilkins is president.

The Trust Company's dedication to a personal relationship with each client is a major factor that distinguishes it from other financial institutions. Each client's individual level of risk tolerance is considered in every decision. The Trust Company manages its clients' assets with a combination of careful management and energetic innovation. Assets in personal accounts are never pooled, but are handled individually. Clients include corporations and organizations as well as individuals. Prompt, thorough reporting is a standard, and services are tailored to the level of the client's needs.

The firm provides a range of asset management services that include investment management; trustee for trusts; personal representative; guardian or conservator of estates; cash management for corporations, trustees and non-profit entities; management of corporate employee benefits programs; and trustee or custodian for individual retirement accounts. Often, The Trust Company is named agent and has investment management duties while the individual remains trustee with full authority over his or her trust.

In general, The Trust Company of Oklahoma's approach is one of careful analysis of future trends, constant reassessment of the factors affecting securities, and an attitude of healthy skepticism. The company's efforts and resources are concentrated on providing high quality investment and management services to individuals, corporations, and organizations. Its focus is on service, performance, independence, safety, and confidentiality.

The company's solid relationships with its clients and the results it produces for them have brought steady growth through the years, resulting in $1.8 billion under administration in 1999, larger than many mutual funds. However, personal service is and always will be the bottom line.

The First National Bank of Pawnee

Located in the heart of the Pawnee Indian Nation, The First National Bank of Pawnee has been a pacesetter for Pawnee County for more than 100 years. Founded in 1894, just a few months after the 1893 Land Run, the bank was the city's first financial institution and is one of the sixteen oldest banks in the state, and is the county's oldest continually operating business.

George M. Berry, one of FNB's founders, obtained a lot diagonally opposite the southwest corner of the Courthouse Square upon which was located a native sandstone building, home of the bank.

Because of the town's proximity to the Osage, Nez Pierce, Poncas, Otoe-Missouria, Cherokee, Creek, Sauk and Fox, and Iowa Nations, the bank's lobby was often filled with members of the various tribes. Communication was difficult at best and was compounded by the fact the main portion of the county was occupied by the Pawnee Nation, comprised of four bands, each with a separate dialect. The challenge of communication was solved when The First National Bank of Pawnee hired Tom Morgan "Sun Chief" as interpreter and bank guard; and, to this date, one of the bank's major goals is to maintain good communication with its customers.

Beginning business at the opening of a new country, The First National Bank of Pawnee has experienced war, droughts, depressions, and panics, but through cotton, cattle, wheat, oil, the fine school system, super rail transportation, and the designation of U.S. Highway 64, it has emerged stronger than ever.

It has continued to grow, outgrowing its original quarters. The old sandstone building was razed and a new building was erected in 1969 in its original location on the corner of Sixth and Harrison Streets. In 1984, a new four-lane drive-up bank was opened on the corner of Seventh and Illinois Streets. The facility is tied directly to the main bank through a sophisticated computer network. As Pawnee continued to grow, so did The First National Bank, and on July 4, 1991, a 7,000-square-foot addition to the main bank was opened.

With the generous support of the people of Pawnee County the bank has taken the lead in the economic growth of the region. Working with local businessmen and tribal leaders to bolster the area's economy and tap into the tourist potential offered by the natural beauty of the landscape and the rich cultural heritage.

The success of The First National Bank of Pawnee is closely tied to the success of the city. Pawnee is famous for Chester Gould and Dick Tracy, Pawnee Bill and his Wild West Show, it's rail and highway access, and the fact that over fifty percent of Oklahoma's population lives within one hundred miles.

✧

Top: A painting of Sun Chief (Tom Morgan), the bank's interpreter, hangs in the lobby of The First National Bank of Pawnee. The painting is by Brummett Echohawk.

Below: The First National Bank of Pawnee building, on an overlay of the 100-mile radius around the city of Pawnee.

PHOTOS COURTESY OF WILLIAM HOWELL AND DIGITAL COMPOSITION BY JUSTIN BRYANT.

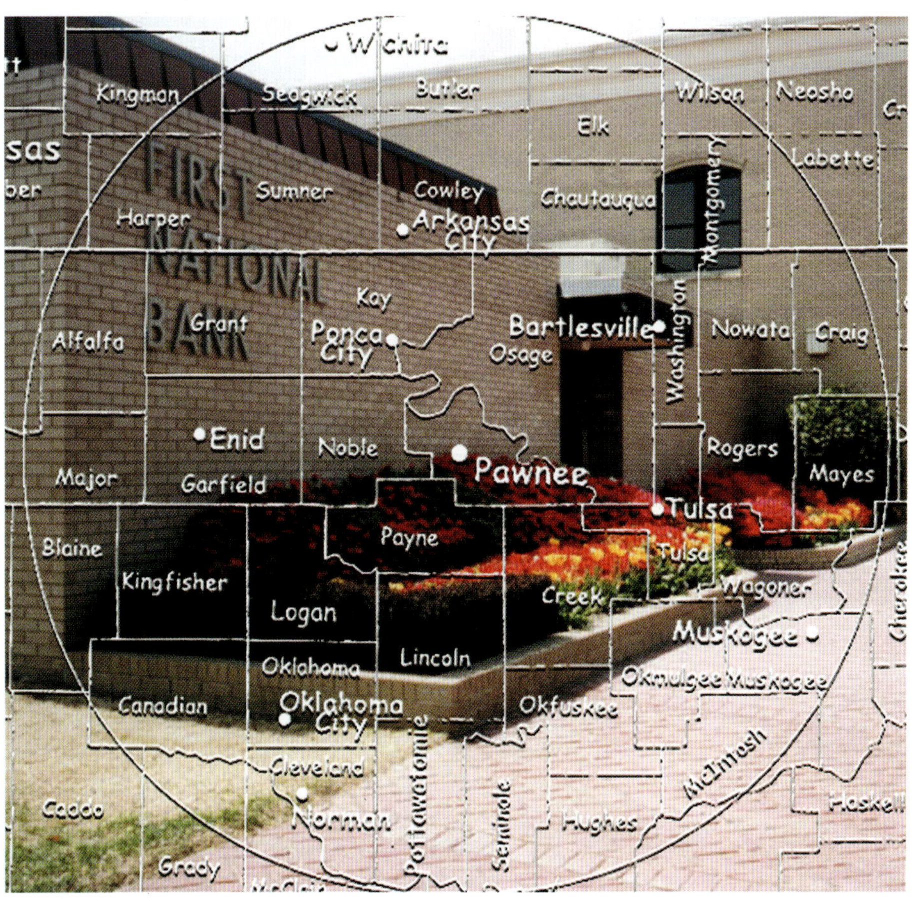

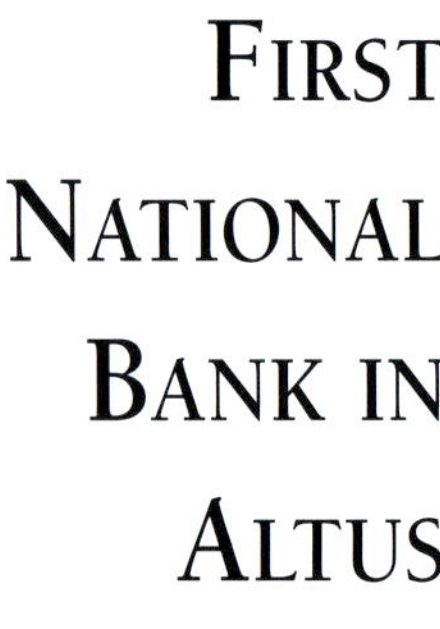

First National Bank in Altus

In 1887, Mr. and Mrs. J. R. McMahan were on a prospecting trip in a covered wagon with their four oldest children. Due to the death of a mule, McMahan stopped at Frazer to try to trade for another mule. While talking mule trade, McMahan learned the community had $200 which was to be paid for a term of school and he was successful in obtaining the position as instructor, remaining to teach four terms and permanently designating southwest Oklahoma as his home.

Fifteen years later, J. R. McMahan founded Altus National Bank and served as the president until 1937. Prior to entering the banking field, J. R. served as postmaster of Frazer, Greer County, Indian Territory. He was instrumental in getting the area designated as a county, in marking the boundary of the county, and in the naming of Altus as the county seat. J. R.'s son, Boyd, served as the second president from 1938 to 1953. It was during Boyd's presidency that the bank changed its name to the First National Bank in Altus. Boyd's son, John Boyd McMahan, is currently a member of the board of directors. J. R.'s youngest son, Hatton McMahan, Sr., was a member of the bank staff for nearly thirty years and served as president from 1953 to 1955. His term was cut short by a fatal illness.

H. B. Bellenger, the only non-relative to ever serve as president, did so from 1955 to 1960. He was executive vice president for many years and a bank employee for fifty years.

Top: J. R. McMahan, founder of the First National Bank in Altus served as president from 1902-1937. The bank is now under the leadership of Philip McMahan, the fourth generation of the McMahan Family to serve as president.

Below: The main branch of First National Bank in Altus is at the intersection of Main and Broadway in Altus, Oklahoma. The bank located here shortly after being organized in 1902.

Hatton McMahan, Jr. was the third generation of McMahan's to serve as president. His term began in January 1960 and ended March 1999. He continues to serve as chairman of the board. The fourth generation of McMahan's have also taken their place in the bank's history, with Philip McMahan, oldest son of Hatton, Jr., beginning tenure as president in 1999 after previously serving as executive vice president.

First National Bank in Altus has a mission to provide the highest quality financial services to the people of Southwest Oklahoma in a profitable manner. FNB-Altus was the first to open a drive-through facility and ATM machine in Altus. They currently have six offices serving Jackson, Kiowa, and Tillman Counties in Southwest Oklahoma. Although FNB-Altus has grown to a $150 million asset bank with $20 million in equity capital, they have kept the founder's idea of serving the community in the forefront. FNB-Altus sponsors the annual 4-H Banquet, Junior Livestock Show, school activities, local area youth activities, Little League baseball, basketball, and soccer as well as school sports. They provide educational materials such as "How To Do Your Banking" to area classrooms and open the bank for educational tours. The directors and staff serve on a variety of local boards and are involved in many civic organizations.

✧

A Redbud tree in full bloom. The Redbud is the official state tree of Oklahoma.

COURTESY DAVID FITZGERALD.

✧

Members of the Ninetieth or Texas-Oklahoma Division, sometimes called "Tough 'Ombres," about to depart the S. S. Leviathan *at Brest, France, on May 30, 1918. The division's 179th Infantry Brigade was known as the Oklahoma Brigade and was commanded by Brigadier General J. P. "Patsy" O'Neil.*

COURTESY *THE DAILY OKLAHOMAN.*

The Marketplace

Oklahoma's retail establishments, service industries, and leisure/convention facilities offer an impressive variety of choices for Oklahomans and visitors alike

Patrons

Oklahoma Lighting Sales,
Oklahoma City

Friends

Globe Life & Accident
Insurance Company,
Oklahoma City

Harold's of Norman,
Norman

Howard Johnson Hotel &
Convention Center,
Lawton

Stipe Law Firm,
McAlester

Irwin Auto Companies

The history of Irwin Auto Companies and the Irwin family, who have made Oklahoma their home since the 1890s, is foremost a story of vision and hard work. The success of the family continues today and is a clear reminder of the proud heritage that has led them throughout the twentieth century.

The family's first glimpse of Oklahoma began as Grant Chambers Irwin left his home in Pennsylvania at the age of twenty-two in a Conestoga wagon bound for Vancouver, Washington. Grant joined his sister, Martha Jane Irwin Fogle, and her husband, Adam Fogle, in May of 1887 on the 3,000-mile journey along the Ozark Trail. The trail took them through the tall prairie grass of present day Lincoln County, Oklahoma, where Grant would later buy a farm in 1894.

Upon their arrival in Washington State, Adam Fogle acquired a sawmill. Grant Irwin worked alongside Fogle in the sawmill until it was damaged by fire and the men were forced out of business. Having encountered such bad luck in Washington, Fogle and his wife had recently heard of the upcoming land run in Oklahoma and immediately set out for the event. Fogle was a Sooner among Sooners. He homesteaded a pre-selected site four miles east and one mile south of the present site of Meeker.

Grant Irwin remained in the Northwest, investing all of his earnings in the purchase of cattle. He traveled with his herd in a rail car to the Chicago Stockyards. While in Chicago he attended the 1893 World's Fair. After the World's Fair, he headed for the Oklahoma Territory to visit his sister. He had his life savings; the proceeds from the cattle sale, in gold coins safely packed away in his money belt. The visit was fortuitous as Irwin met the young lady whose family had homesteaded one mile north of the Fogles. In 1894, Irwin married Cecile Elnora Augustine and purchased the patent rights to the 160 acres across the section line from her parents.

Irwin never cared much for farming, yet took a great interest in machinery and the processing of products created by the farmers, thus beginning an entrepreneurial and extremely business-minded legacy that remains a strong force among family members to this day. Irwin had learned much about the sawmill business in Washington, and so acquired a sawmill that provided much of the lumber for the houses and barns built around what would become Meeker. He also acquired a cotton gin, which was later moved along with the sawmill to present-day Meeker.

During cotton season, Irwin walked three miles into Meeker every day. He arrived three hours early so he could fire the boiler to have steam pressure for the machinery when the ginning crew arrived at 7 a.m. At the time,

Top: Grant Chambers Irwin, born July 12, 1864, pictured in 1893 while attending the Chicago World's Fair.

Below: Grant Chambers Irwin, Cecile Elnora Augustine Irwin, and their first child, Arlie, pictured in 1895 or 1896, in front of Irwin's cotton gin and sawmill located on their farm southeast of present day Meeker, Oklahoma.

wood was still being used to generate steam to operate both the cotton gin and the sawmill. He worked twelve hours each day and walked home every night. The cotton gin prospered until about 1921 when the price of lint cotton dropped from around forty cents per pound to five cents per pound.

Grant and Cecile Irwin had eleven children. The seventh son, Ernest Leslie, was nicknamed "Cotton" for his white hair. Cotton married Bertie Evelyn Neer and they had four children—Herbert Grant, Richard L., S. Patrick, and H. Susan Irwin.

Cotton stayed in Meeker and continued the Irwin entrepreneurial tradition established by his father. With only $600 and a $1,000 guaranty from their mother, Cotton and his brother, Marion, acquired the Meeker Chevrolet dealership in 1938, creating a legacy that continues today. In 1942, WWII brought the cessation of all automobile manufacturing. With no new automobile sales, the dealership survived by patching up the aging local vehicles used by many area residents going to and from Tinker Field.

Shortly after WWII, Cotton entered the road construction industry after being awarded several contracts for dirt work and bridge construction on the Turner Turnpike. An economic downturn in the 1950s forced the closure and liquidation of all of Cotton's business interests. One of which, by that time, involved an ill-fated Edsel dealership. Ultimately, Cotton and his son, Richard, established a successful Meeker-based operation that primarily served the road construction industry. Independent Industries, Inc. has grown over the years to include not only bridge construction and heavy equipment sales, but, with Richard's guidance, has expanded to include the sale of steel, pipe, and timber acquired through demolition of railroads, pipelines, and bridges.

Cotton's oldest son, Grant, having grown up in the automobile business, was undeterred by the failure of his father's automobile ventures. He left Meeker and his father's employ for Western Oklahoma and the hope of owning his own dealership. Irwin negotiated a transaction to buy the Hydro Chevrolet franchise. Chevrolet questioned the future viability of a franchise in a community the size of Hydro and recommended another opportunity in Okeene, Oklahoma. Okeene had twice the population of Hydro, as well as a larger trade area. Chevrolet required a $60,000 capital investment for a franchise of this size. Grant, only twenty-nine years old, had managed to save $2,000. With the financial participation of several area investors, Irwin Chevrolet Company officially opened its doors on January 1, 1966.

The dealership prospered. With the help of one of the original investors, Albert Conley of Kingfisher, Grant gradually acquired ownership of the company. 1972 brought a

✧

Left: A national advertisement for the 1939 Chevrolet, one of the first models sold by the Irwin Motor Company.

Above: Cotton Irwin and Bertie Neer Irwin looking over one of the new automobiles.

Below: Grant and Richard Irwin excited about a ride in the new 1946 Ford convertible.

Above: Irwin Chevrolet Company after its relocation to Woodward in 1975.

Bottom: Grant Irwin (center) leads the 1982 ribbon-cutting ceremonies at his new Chevrolet showroom and service center on U.S. Highway 270. Irwin is flanked by Chevrolet Zone Manager R. X. Sarvis, Assistant Manager Wally Albers, and Woodward Chamber of Commerce officials Dana Heltzen, Sandi Bell, Bob Outhier, Dow Dozier, Carl Bogdahn, Jack Stout, Dwight Terry, and David Houston.

rare occurrence: high market prices for grain coupled with a bumper wheat crop in the Okeene area. In anticipation of this agricultural boom, Grant rigged over one hundred medium duty trucks for the upcoming harvest. Demand for these units was so great that Grant launched a new company to customize and equip these units. These conditions prevailed throughout 1973 as Irwin Chevrolet became a regional truck center for the High Plains Region including Kansas, Colorado, Texas, Nebraska, and the Dakotas. The dealership became widely respected as a resource for dealers without medium duty truck inventory and expertise.

Realizing that the Okeene dealership had reached the pinnacle of its growth, Grant sold the Okeene franchise in 1975 and upon Chevrolet's recommendation, moved his dealership operations to Woodward, Oklahoma. Grant would later become the largest medium duty truck dealer in the United States, with annual volume of over 600 units.

The failure of Penn Square Bank in Oklahoma City began a sequence of events that brought an end to the largest oil and gas boom Western Oklahoma had ever experienced. This was the first major setback Grant had experienced since leaving Midland, Texas and the family's failed Edsel dealership in a blowing dust storm a quarter century earlier. The timing of the "oil bust" could not have been worse for Grant. At Chevrolet's insistence, and based on a sales rate established during the "boom" years, Grant had just completed construction of a million-dollar facility in Woodward. Consumer demand for automobiles decreased in Oklahoma as unemployment rates increased and interest rates soared to record highs. The company was in a precarious cash position as it was forced to assume financial responsibility for a record number of vehicle repossessions.

As the economic crisis continued to escalate in Western Oklahoma, automobile dealership closures and foreclosures became as commonplace as bank failures. Many of the automobile dealerships in the smaller communities surrounding Woodward went out of business. With the help of a lot of loyal employees and customers, the dealership survived this extremely weak economic climate.

Today, Woodward is the trade center for area vehicle buyers. Following national trends, Irwin has added additional franchises over the years, helping to support the tremendous size of the company's facilities. In 1984, the Oldsmobile and Cadillac franchises were acquired and several years later the Chrysler, Plymouth, Dodge, and Jeep franchises were added. Irwin Auto Company has just completed its twenty-fifth year of operation in Woodward and Grant Irwin will begin his thirty-fifth year in business in Western Oklahoma with the addition of Buick, Pontiac, and GMC franchises.

The future of the company appears secure as the third generation of Irwins has entered the automobile business. In 1991, Grant Irwin, Jr., at age twenty-seven, became General Motor's youngest multiple dealer operator with the acquisition of his second automobile dealership which is located in Perryton, Texas. Grant and Grant, Jr. have formed an alliance to operate their dealership holdings. Grant's daughter, Tamara Irwin Cain, is an attorney and serves as general counsel to the family businesses. Grant's other daughter, Melinda Jane Irwin, is a certified public accountant who operates Dealer Services, L.L.C., an accounts receivable outsourcing service for the family dealerships. To date, Irwin Auto Companies operates thirty-two dealership franchises from eight sales locations in Western Oklahoma and the Texas Panhandle. The franchises employ over 100 persons.

With his family involved in the day-to-day operations of the automobile dealerships, Grant Irwin, Sr. has had additional time to devote to his manufacturing interests. While buying hoists to equip medium duty trucks, Irwin became acquainted with Dan Hill. In 1982, Hill and Irwin formed Dan Hill and Associates, Inc. and acquired the assets of a Norman trailer manufacturer with only eight employees. The company later acquired Mabar, Inc. a Fairview manufacturer originally formed in 1966 to build grain beds for agricultural trucks. Dan Hill successfully managed the company until his death in 1987. Since that time the company has been managed by Hill's son, Terry Hill, David Griffis, and Vickie Hill. The company manufactures a horizontal discharge trailer designed to transport and discharge road-building materials, primarily hot-mix asphalt. The company now employs 104 persons. In 1990, Irwin and other investors bought the assets of a bankrupt Marlow, Oklahoma machine shop and established Central Tank of Oklahoma, Inc. Central Tank successfully operates a coded shop with twenty-three employees.

Grant is quite modest about his entrepreneurial success and prefers to give all of the credit to the hundreds of Oklahomans who have been directly employed by his businesses over the past thirty-five years. In recent decades many young people have been forced to leave Western Oklahoma for employment in urban areas. Grant considers one of his greatest accomplishments to be the jobs his companies provide, thereby allowing over 300 families the opportunity to remain in Western Oklahoma and enjoy the quality of life that living in a rural setting brings. The Irwins continue to be motivated by a vision for business and a great love for rural Oklahoma—a land in which the Irwin entrepreneurial spirit was planted in the tall prairie grasslands over a century ago.

✧

Below: Flow Boy CB-4000 eight-axle semi-trailer with 32 tires capable of carrying 50 tons of hot asphalt.

Bottom: Flow Boy CB-4000 horizontal discharge trailer designed to transport and discharge road-building materials.

The Waterford Marriott Hotel

✧

Right: The Waterford Marriott Hotel, the crown jewel of Oklahoma City.

Below: Furnished with beautifully carved wood, bookshelves and glass cases, the Board Room is perfect for CEO board meetings.

Three stars and four diamonds make up the crown jewel known as The Waterford Marriott Hotel in Oklahoma City. With this distinct designation, The Waterford Marriott has become known as a mark of excellence. There are so many ways to enjoy this hotel that it might be difficult to fit it all in with just one visit. From the overnight accommodations, to the grand weddings and social affairs coordinated by the hotel, or the everyday business luncheon, The Waterford Marriott can address your need in style. With a full-time florist on staff and the large swimming pool flanked by four lion fountains, each experience reflects a style and service singular to this facility.

The Waterford Marriott Hotel features 197 guestrooms, including thirty-two suites. Located on the ninth floor, The Top Floor suites include first-class amenities and concierge services.

Long is the list of guests that have stayed since its opening. The 1,600-square-foot Presidential Suite has hosted dignitaries ranging from presidents to prime ministers. The list includes George Bush, Dan Quayle, and Al Gore; actors Dustin Hoffman, Tom Cruise, Helen Hunt, Bill Paxton, and *Twister* director, Jan DeBont; music entertainers the Eagles, Neil Diamond, John Tesh, Reba McEntire, Vince Gill, Elton John, the Rolling Stones, and 'NSync.

Oklahoma City companies also take advantage of the hotel's grand accommodations and image when recruiting or entertaining out-of-town business clients and partners. The management is proud of the fact that the hotel property reflects Oklahoma City as a cosmopolitan destination and helps to break down any stereotypical images. Those utilizing the 8,000 square feet of function space set-aside for community meetings and events can also enjoy the excellence served to guests.

The Board Room, which is adorned with wood paneling, bookshelves, and a marble fireplace, is complemented by the view of the garden and terrace. It can easily accommodate up to fifty guests. The Chapter Room is available for medium-sized conferences and meetings.

The elegant choice for weddings, receptions, large conferences, and other special

events is The Waterford Ballroom, complete with unique wrought iron and crystal chandeliers. A more intimate choice for private dinner parties for twelve, small meetings, and special celebrations is the Crystal Room.

Hotel Chef, Don Thiery, is on hand to make sure the dining experiences at The Waterford Marriott are as enjoyable as the rest of your visit. Casual, but elegant, The Veranda Restaurant offers room for 110 people in a light, airy white wicker setting with poolside views. The menu offers a variety of sandwiches, soups, salads, and lunch plates. Best known for its Sunday Jazz Brunch, The Veranda Restaurant features live jazz along with an elaborate brunch buffet.

An evening of fine dining in The Waterford Dining Room offers contemporary cuisine in a nineteenth century English country setting. The menu includes regional and continental gourmet specialties, including a smoked salmon appetizer to a "from-the-grill" dinner of a T-bone steak with grilled onions. No matter what your preference, The Waterford Marriott dining offers a special culinary experience for a variety of tastes.

The beauty of the building's interior and exterior structure has been maintained through attention to hotel aesthetics. A four-month, $3.3 million renovation was completed in March of 1996, which included a new front desk and lobby area, redesigned guest rooms, corridors, ballrooms, café, meeting rooms, and health spa. The addition of a porte-cochere and an enclosed terrace rounded out the renovation. Along with

Top: The Veranda Restaurant, open for breakfast and lunch, hosts an ever-popular Sunday Brunch in an open-air atmosphere.

Bottom: The Waterford Marriott offers over 8,000 square feet of banquet and meeting rooms including the Ball Room, which has comfortable banquet style seating for 250 or classroom seating for 200 people.

engineering and structural improvements made that are not really apparent, guests can enjoy a state-of-the-art phone system equipped with guest voice mail and in-room dataports. Current renovations include enlarging the concierge area and remodeling the Presidential Suite.

Despite the major physical restoration and improvements, The Waterford Marriott Hotel's service and tie to the community extends beyond the hotel walls. Some of the local recipients of the hotel's time and resources are the Greater Oklahoma City Chamber of Commerce, literacy programs, Feed the Children, and other charitable and nonprofit organizations.

The popular Sunset Serenade from the 1980s was brought back by the hotel and continues each spring for five Thursday nights. This event has raised funds for the Oklahoma City bombing relief fund and 1999 tornado victims. The hotel has also provided a generous number of hours of service and thousands of dollars of food products to specific events. In addition, the hotel has donated individual gift certificates to assist with fund-raising efforts and volunteer motivation programs.

One unique aspect of The Waterford Marriott Hotel is its proximity within a multi-use complex. Along with the hotel, Waterford Properties oversees more than 155,000 square feet of rented footage in several office buildings that surround the outer north portion of the complex. In addition, the Homeowners' Association manages the Waterford Condominium Complex.

There are several common areas for the complex, which include the boulevard, parking lot, and the pond, which is home to families of ducks and elegant swans. Artist Norma Penchansky Glasser is creator of the beautiful statue that sits at the point of the pond area. The large statue is titled "The Three Madonnas" and was dedicated in 1984.

The Waterford Complex ties its entities by name, but they are independently owned and managed. In 1997, The Waterford Marriott Hotel became an affiliate of Host Marriott, Washington, D.C. This new partnership offers guest conveniences such as Marriott's

Opposite, top: The Waterford Marriott Hotel features 197 guestrooms, thirty-two suites, and one Presidential Suite.

Opposite, bottom: Sunday Brunch in the Veranda Restaurant is one of the many specialties offered by The Waterford Marriott Hotel.

Left: Renowned chefs provide culinary delights in the elegance of the Waterford Dining Room.

Below: Begin your day with a workout at the Waterford Athletic Club and end the day relaxing poolside.

Rewards program, the best frequent traveler program in the industry, and an extensive central worldwide reservation system.

Interstate Hotels, an international hotel management firm, was selected to supervise the renovation and market and manage the property. Interstate has been ranked for the last four years in a row as the largest management company by both *Hotel Business* magazine and *Hotel/Motel Management* magazine. Interstate operates hotels in virtually every major market in the U.S. Waterford Marriott is sister to other luxury independent hotels such as the Roosevelt in New York City; The Charles Hotel in Cambridge, Massachusetts; and the Don DeSar Hotel in St. Petersburg, Florida. The Waterford Marriott Hotel in Oklahoma City has earned the honor of being part of this elite group.

General Manager Jeff Erwin, leads the hotel's 140 staff members in providing the very best safety, security, and comfort to each guest. In their quest to provide top-notch service, the Total Quality Management (TQM) process is being implemented over a five-year time frame, which guarantees the hotel's commitment to unparalleled service into the future.

Three stars and four diamonds cast a brilliant hue on The Waterford Marriott Hotel.

Atherton & Murphy Investment Company

Atherton and Murphy Investment Company is more than a business, it also represents a friendship that has spanned more than forty years. From oil and gas, cattle, restaurants, and real estate, the course of Bill Atherton and Pat Murphy's business relationship covers a wide range of projects.

The two Oklahoma State University graduates met in the oil fields of Trinidad, West Indies in 1960 while working for Core Laboratories, Inc. of Dallas, Texas. Pat Murphy, a geologist, and Bill Atherton, a petroleum engineer, soon discovered how well they worked together. They completed many significant engineering jobs for Shell, Texaco, British Petroleum, and Dominion Oil particularly in the new offshore fields of Trinidad.

When the oil field work slacked off, Murphy returned to the States, where he discovered there was little demand for geologists. He decided to get out of the oil business. In the meantime, Atherton continued working in Trinidad and South America.

When an acquaintance decided to start a doughnut shop in Wichita, Kansas, Murphy, who was looking for a new business venture, pitched in to help, hoping to gain sufficient experience to put in his own shop. However, before his doughnut shop could become a reality he met Dan and Frank Carney, the founders of Pizza Hut, Inc.

Pizza was beginning to grow in popularity and Murphy was intrigued by the possibilities. Abandoning his original plan for a doughnut shop in favor of a Pizza Hut, he opened his first franchise in 1960 in Bartlesville. It was the first franchised Pizza Hut in Oklahoma. "They conned me into taking a Pizza Hut franchise instead of opening the doughnut shop," Murphy later jokingly recalled.

Two years later Murphy contacted his friend, Atherton, who was still working in Trinidad, and invited him to become partners in another Pizza Hut in Stillwater. Atherton agreed, despite the fact that when he asked Murphy if he was making money, he told him "no." Unperturbed and convinced of the future of the Pizza Hut franchise, Atherton pooled his money with Murphy to raise $5,000 in 1962 to form their partnership, and the North Monroe Pizza Hut was opened in an old Quonset hut near the campus.

Atherton, who by now had formed his own reservoir engineering company in Trinidad, sold it to Cline and Gaffney Engineering in 1964 and returned to the United States. Atherton realized that his partner had pioneered the college market and they quickly decided to expand to the University of Arkansas in Fayetteville, where they proceeded to build the largest Pizza Hut in the United States at the time. This restaurant was the first Pizza Hut to have the distinctive red roof that became Pizza Hut's logo, and soon became the highest volume Pizza Hut in the system.

Originally intended as a sideline, the Pizza Huts became profitable, and in 1973 the partners incorporated as A&M Food Services, Inc.

Wanting to be involved in the entire process from construction through operations, A&M Contractors was created by Atherton and Murphy in 1973 to handle most of their new construction and remodeling as an effective cost-control program. A strong emphasis was placed on innovative restaurant design and construction.

By 1983 A&M Food Services was the largest Pizza Hut franchise-holder in the United States with more than 200 Pizza Huts spread over Arkansas, Oklahoma, Minnesota, Wisconsin, Iowa, Missouri, Texas, and Louisiana. The company became publicly held on September 20, 1983. A&M Food Services, Inc. was merged into Pepsico, Inc. on July 9, 1986 and became a wholly owned subsidiary of Pepsico.

Pizza was not Atherton and Murphy's only restaurant venture during this time. In 1977, the oil men-turned-restaurateurs opened a series of family-oriented restaurants called "Applegate's Landing." The name "Applegate" belonged to a friend in Wichita and "Landing" was added because Atherton thought it "sounded friendly." Within a short time, Applegate's Landing restaurants appeared in Tulsa, Bartlesville, Norman, and Springdale, Arkansas. The businessmen were also the founders of Taco Hut, Inc. which they subsequently sold in 1983.

The partners continue to be active in the oil business. According to Atherton, who jokingly remarked, "The oil fields brought us together and we are still drilling dry holes, sorry to say."

However, the primary business of Atherton and Murphy Investment Company is real estate, an interest that began through their restaurant franchises. From this beginning it has continued to evolve and grow.

Their current project is a strategically located 4,000-acre development twenty minutes from downtown Dallas, Texas and thirty minutes from downtown Fort Worth, the hub of the southwest economy. The property, with commercial and residential zoning, is just east of the 7,400-acre Joe Pool Lake, which is highlighted by more than two miles of Austin Chalk escarpment that rises approximately 300 feet above the lake. This combination of high bluffs and water offers potential residents a panoramic view of the area and quick access to the DFW Metroplex.

The closeness of the partners is reflected in the intimate friendship of the two families. In fact, Murphy is responsible for introducing Atherton to his wife of many years, Ann. The Athertons have two sons, Dirk Atherton of Ft. Myers, Florida, and Tom Atherton of Tulsa, and a daughter, Jessica Faubert of Tulsa. Murphy and his wife, Jetta Sue, have one son and one daughter, Brett Murphy of Tulsa and Julie Farr of Dallas, Texas. There is now a second-generation Atherton and Murphy partnership, with Tom and Brett forming Atherton & Murphy Enterprises, in the hotel business.

Atherton and Murphy's business philosophy can be expressed through G. Harvey's oil painting on the wall of their Tulsa office, in which a cowboy in a rain slicker is riding his horse down a muddy street with automobiles lining both sides. The award-winning painting is entitled, "With No Intention of Changing," and why should they?

✧

W. S. "Bill" Atherton and Pat Murphy, owners of Atherton & Murphy Investment Company, have been friends and business partners for more than forty years.

PHOTO COURTESY OF BJARNE HOLM PORTRAITS.

UNITED SUPERMARKETS OF OKLAHOMA, INC.

Henry Dewitt Snell was born in Clay County, Texas in 1892 and raised in Delhi, a small rural town near Sayre, Oklahoma. Though he had hoped to become a doctor, financial constraints held his dream at bay. In 1912, at the age of twenty, Snell went to work at Sayre Wholesale Grocery and later enrolled in a business course in Thomas, Oklahoma. The future of United Supermarkets of Oklahoma, Inc. and young Henry Snell was soon born.

Ross Dugger, owner of the Sayre Wholesale Grocery, remembers a story told by his father, E. B. Dugger. "Dad was needing additional help and one day he noticed Dewitt with his two-bit delivery wagon driven by mules. Dad yelled out, 'Hey young man, would you like to work for me?'" According to Dugger, Snell asked when he would start and then inquired about a salary. He was immediately hired.

Four years later, with $100 of his own money, a horse and buggy, and $800 borrowed from Dugger, "H. D. Snell's United Cash Grocery" was founded. Snell's motto was "We sell for Cash. Spot Cash." His grocery advertisements explained his method. "We buy for Cash and sell for Cash, which is a good reason why we sell for Less. Give us your patronage on the thought of our making prices in Sayre and saving you from the high credit store prices."

Soon the name changed to "United Cash." Personal service was the hallmark and groceries were "put up" by a friendly clerk via the phone and delivered to the kitchen door. As milk was still locally bottled, empty bottles were collected and returned for two cents credit. The early day logo incorporated the links of a chain with the saying inside, "Where Price and Quality Meet." Soon a meat market was added featuring fresh fryers and hens and, often, rabbits and squirrels.

✧

Top: H. D. Snell, founder of United Supermarkets of Oklahoma, Inc.

Above: First United Supermarket, Sayre, Oklahoma, 1916.

Right: Current United Store, Enid West.

✧

United Supermarkets of Oklahoma corporate headquarters, Altus, Oklahoma.

After World War I other United Cash stores were opened in Erick, Oklahoma, Shamrock and Wellington, Texas. In 1918, a store opened in Cordell and soon became the headquarters. The Elk City store opened in 1924 and was followed by openings in Sentinel, Carnegie, Altus, Mangum, Frederick and Snyder.

Snell had five children—Beatrice, Jack, Margaret, Jimmy, and Perry—who were all involved in the chain of stores at one time or another. Perry served as president of the Oklahoma stores until his retirement. Jack served as president of the Texas stores until his death in 1976. Perry's son Jay is now the president of the Oklahoma stores and Jack's son Robert is the president of the Texas stores.

Community and charitable activities include Quails Unlimited, United Way, Children's Miracle Network, Boy Scouts, Special Olympics and involvement in schools and churches throughout the state.

The growth of the United Stores has continued for over eighty-three years with the Oklahoma corporation now operating twenty-five stores and the Texas group operating forty-one stores. The Oklahoma stores employ approximately 1,400 men and women and have headquarters in Altus, with store locations currently in Sayre, Cordell, Hobart, Mangum, Frederick, Hollis, Clinton, Elk City, Altus, Walters, Cherokee, Enid, Woodward, Guymon, Kingfisher, Blackwell, Purcell, Weatherford, Bartlesville, Ponca City, and Lawton. Two stores are operated in Altus and Woodward, and three United stores are located in Enid.

Today, United continues to grow and expand to meet the needs of its customers. Bakery and deli departments have been added to stores in Elk City, Altus, Enid, Guymon, Woodward, Ponca City and Lawton. New Point of Sale equipment is currently being added to each of its twenty-five locations enabling United to offer its customers the finest in modern technology. Gasoline pumps are currently being added to the Elk city location. These additions are steps in adding such services to other locations across the state so United can better service its customers.

As nice as these modern conveniences are, the number one priority at United is still the customer. H. D. Snell said "If you are satisfied tell others, if you are not tell us." That same attitude is true today at United and can be seen prominently displayed throughout its stores. As has been the case for over eighty-three years, each United employee is taught from day one the importance of customer service. This service is described by United employees as delivering the "Personal Touch." United has always prided itself in having clean stores with low everyday prices and the best employees offering the best in customer service.

DUB RICHARDSON FORD

✧

Left: Dub Richardson was a recipient of the Time Magazine *Quality Dealer Award for 1976 at the National Automobile Dealers Association convention.*

Right: Rock Richardson.

One of the largest and oldest franchised dealerships in Oklahoma, Dub Richardson Ford has been a fixture of the Oklahoma City skyline since 1958. The dealership is a respected and well-known force in the business community. W. T. (Dub) Richardson was a visionary who bought Jerry Cravens Ford and moved it from Sixth and Robinson to its current location between 36th and 39th Streets on North May Avenue in Oklahoma City. At that time, people suggested that he had lost his mind moving so far north. It turned out that he was indeed very correct in thinking that Oklahoma City would move in that direction. Dub Richardson employs 180 outstanding and loyal people and today houses one of the largest automobile parts departments in the United States.

Dub and his wife, Mozelle Groner, were married in 1939 and have four children, fifteen grandchildren and five great-grandchildren. Both of their sons, W. T., Jr., (Jerry) and Rock joined the dealership. Jerry came to the dealership in 1965 and Rock several years later. Jerry received his business degree from the University of Oklahoma and his MLA from Oklahoma City University. He spent a two-year tour of duty as gunnery officer aboard the ammunition ship, U.S.S. Ranier, during the Vietnam War. Rock graduated from the University of Northern Arizona before joining his father in business. He later moved to Gulf Breeze, Florida where he publishes a weekly newspaper. Daughters Judy Markley and Susan Richardson are both devoted grandmothers. Susan is a freelance writer, student, and frequent traveler. She lives in Santa Fe, New Mexico. Judy is the development director of the Oklahoma School of Science and Mathematics in Oklahoma City. She continues her passion for helping humanitarian, educational, and economic development projects in Nicaragua.

Dub Richardson died May 17, 1990. With pride he could say that he was one of the founding fathers of the Cowboy Hall of Fame. His cowboy hat is enshrined at the Hall with others who bequeathed a legacy of the early West. His likeness, sculpted by Leonard McMurry, is in the foyer of the Hall's orientation theatre named in honor of Dub and Mozelle.

Dub Richardson Ford was left in the capable hands of Jerry, who then brought his son, Brad, into the dealership. Brad received his undergraduate degree from SMU and his MBA from the University of Texas in Dallas. He joined the dealership as general manager in 1998.

In midlife, Dub discovered a talent for metal sculpting. Working with Keating Donahoe, a local artist, he became an expert with a torch

turning old Ford fenders and scraps of copper and bronze into Western masterpieces. He never sold any of his work, but gave it to friends and organizations for charity auctions and was always amazed when the sale of his work brought hundreds of dollars.

While Dub was selling cars and molding magnificent metal sculptures, Mozelle was busy writing murder mysteries and travel books. In 1973, she was awarded the University of Oklahoma Writing Award and has been listed in *Who's Who in American Women*, and for twenty-five years has been listed in *Who's Who in the South and Southwest*.

With their spouses, children, grandchildren, and great-grandchildren, the Richardsons have left an indelible imprint on Oklahoma City and their state. The Dub Richardson family is one of diversified talents and they continue to share those talents with their communities. They pass that fine legacy to future generations.

Top: The Dub Richardson Family (left to right): Joy Richardson, Jerry Richardson, Judy Markley, Susan Richardson, and Mozelle Richardson at the unveiling of the Dub and Mozelle Richardson Theatre in the Cowboy Hall of Fame and Western Heritage Museum in Oklahoma City and a bust of Dub Richardson.

Left: An oil painting of Dub Richardson Ford presented to Dub Richardson by his family one Christmas. The painting is by Oklahoma City artist Greg Burns.

A-1 Freeman Moving & Storage, Inc.

Top: Jim Freeman, founder and chief executive officer of A-1 Freeman Moving Group.

PHOTO COURTESY OF ELSON-ALEXANDRE.

Bottom: Norma Freeman, vice-president of the A-1 Freeman Moving Group and president of the San Antonio agency.

PHOTO COURTESY OF ELSON-ALEXANDRE.

Providence is a word that often rises to the surface during a conversation with Jim Freeman, founder and chief executive officer of A-1 Freeman Moving Group. As Jim thought back over the course of his transportation career, from a dock worker at Lee Way to the professional turning point in his life when his wife and a friend talked him into trying a career in sales in the household goods moving business in 1964, he is pleased with the success that followed.

This year the Freeman Group celebrates twenty-five years in business. In 1974, after eleven years of sales in this industry and with the help of lifelong friend Tom Rogers, he borrowed $50,000 and North American Van Lines offered Freeman the opportunity to become an agent for the Oklahoma City branch of this worldwide company.

After three years the company purchased its first warehouse and entered into an agreement with Southwestern Bell for a new warehouse distribution project. Pleased with the warehouse, Southwestern Bell approached Freeman about leasing the building for ten years. The wheels were set in motion and Jim began construction on his present location at 11517 North Broadway Extension. With this beginning, the Freeman Group has been successful in owning its real estate in all operating locations.

Jim has had much help in building this family business. First to join him in 1978 was his son-in-law, Dennis Lovett. Dennis worked one summer from his teaching and coaching job and became interested in the business and soon joined the company. Dennis' expertise has been utilized in the corporate, operational, and management sides of the business including the Human Resource and Accounting divisions. Dennis serves as co-president along with Larry Vinzant.

The second family member to join the Freeman Group was Jim's wife, Norma, who worked in the medical field and was coaxed into the business by Jim. She excelled in sales, sales management and training. She serves as vice-president of the Group and is the president of their San Antonio agency.

Next to join the company was son-in-law, Larry Vinzant, who approached Jim in 1980 and, with his talent as a successful real estate broker, was a welcome addition to the family business. Larry is the General Manager of the Houston agency, the company's largest agency, along with corporate-wide sales, marketing responsibilities, and advertising.

Family strength and leadership coupled with a dedicated office and moving staff has made it possible to employ the very best in the industry to lead the expanding network

agency. Strength comes from the employees throughout the organization who continue to be the enabler for expansion. Beginning in 1985, the company moved into Austin, Texas and has since settled in Tulsa, Oklahoma; Fort Worth, Dallas, Houston, and San Antonio, Texas; and Atlanta, Georgia.

The Freeman Group is presently the largest agent in the western U.S. and the second largest North American Van Lines agent out of 830 agents providing worldwide household goods moving and storage, domestic and international. Other product lines include warehouse distribution, complete logistic provider, and specialized high value products transportation.

The Freeman Group takes pride in its top ranked hauling and award-winning driver fleet. Businesses such as State Farm Insurance, Halliburton, Lucent Technologies, Dillards, Hertz Corporation and Underwriters Laboratories have come to rely on these important aspects of the company and have looked to the Freeman Group for state of the art household goods moving and specialty services.

With ethics stressing service as a first priority and a good, strong employee base Freeman Moving Group has been ranked by The *Journal Record*'s 1999 *Book of Lists* as the largest moving company in the Oklahoma City area with revenues totaling $34 million in 1998. Superior financial stability and a strong commitment to growth in hauling fleet and competitive pricing has allowed the business to focus on providing quality service and, more importantly, given them time to spend thinking about the needs of employees and customers.

The operating creed and mission commitment established by the A-1 Freeman Moving Group best describes this market-focused worldwide transportation service company. Statements of strong integrity, innovative programs, and a character in business that strives to exceed expectations among customers and employees alike highlight this company's pledge to the community. Built upon the talents of motivated people who work together in order to exceed customer expectations and an innovative, personal commitment to total quality performance, the company continues to earn lasting customer relationships, a sustainable competitive advantage, market share leadership, and above average returns.

Top, left: Dennis Lovett, co-president, joined the company in 1978.

Top, right: Larry Vinzant, co-president, joined the company in 1980.

PHOTO COURTESY OF LEE RODRIGUEZ PHOTOGRAPHERS.

Below: A-1 Freeman Moving & Storage is the second largest North American Van Lines in the world.

Scott Rice

The year was 1920. Women voted in a national election for the first time. The Prohibition Amendment took effect. Of the three million miles of rural roads, ninety percent were for horse travel. Two-thirds of the world's oil originated in the United States.

H. J. Scott and Sidney E. Rice, who were married to sisters, borrowed $700 from their mother-in-law, Dorothy Pitcher, to start The Tulsa Rubber Stamp Company, which would later become Scott Rice.

Seventy-nine years later Scott Rice is one of the largest office furniture dealers in the nation. Continually evolving to meet the needs of its customers, Scott Rice has journeyed from a rubber stamp company, printing concern, and office supply firm to a company of people with the purpose of changing office space into workspace solutions.

The personal relationship between Scott and Rice may have begun with their marriage to sisters, but extended to a successful lifelong business relationship. Scott was President of the company and Rice, who was a quiet person and kept a low profile, was the salesman and innovator.

✧

Below: Scott Rice employees at 617 South Main, Tulsa, Oklahoma in 1934.

Bottom: Architects rendering of new Scott Rice office furniture showroom 610 South Main, Tulsa, Oklahoma during the 1950s.

The company began on the second floor of the Woolworth Building at 320½ South Main Street in Tulsa with just five employees. Two years later, in 1922, Tulsa Rubber Stamp consolidated with the Sterling Stamp Company. With the acquisition, Scott Rice obtained the services of Taft Welch, who later led the firm in its most ambitious expansion phase. The company incorporated in 1928 with a capital of $10,000 and expanded into printing and office supplies.

When World War II ended Scott Rice acquired an office furniture business, Terrell Cabinet Company, and quickly captured eighty-five percent of Oklahoma's office supply and furniture market.

Welch's influence continued to drive the company and in 1964 he pioneered the selling of the complete design package. "You don't sell a desk or a chair," he said. "You sell a concept." The company's first office interiors project was the Petroleum Club in Tulsa. Welch became president in 1965 and served through 1969. His son, William J. "Bill" Welch, succeeded him in 1969.

Scott Rice's first branch opened in Oklahoma City in 1967, and in 1969 the Livingston Oil Company (LVO) of Tulsa purchased the company. As a subsidiary of LVO, Scott Rice's business expanded throughout the Midwest with branch offices opened in Denver, Kansas City, Wichita, Dallas, and St. Louis.

In 1974, Ladd Petroleum, which began to divest itself of subsidiaries not related to the petroleum industry, purchased LVO. Daniel F. Smith, then president of Scott Rice, and George A. Hanson, president of Ross-Martin Company, combined their resources to purchase their respective companies from LVO. As part of the restructuring, they formed SRM Business Services, Inc. and purchased the Tulsa, Denver, and Wichita branches. They acquired the Oklahoma City Scott Rice operation in 1977.

The following year, SRM became a subsidiary of Kidde, Inc., with Scott Rice and Ross-Martin operating as separate divisions. During the same year, Scott Rice purchased McQuiddy Office Designers Inc. and in 1981 acquired Continental Office Supply. In 1987, Scott Rice merged John Hudson Office Supply with the Oklahoma City branch. Scott

Rice became a subsidiary of Hanson Industries in 1989.

Daniel Smith, who was made president in 1972, led the way into the field of computerization. Smith headed the firm from 1972 to 1987. Taking the reins as president from 1987 until 1997 was Raymond G. Jones. Under Jones' direction, Scott Rice dominated the office products market. In 1994, Corporate Express purchased the office supply portion of Scott Rice while Steelcase, the world's largest manufacturer of office furniture, took over the office furniture business.

George Basore became majority owner and president in 1998, bringing with him nearly two decades of experience with Steelcase. Under Basore's leadership, the company has reinvented itself. He felt it imperative to make investments in the people and change the culture, processes, and tools of the business.

Basore believes effective office furnishings providers of the future will deliver integrated interior products which support the concept of community based planning. Simplicity and flexibility will be the by-words. Structure and furnishings will adapt to corporate movement and to worker needs, not the other way around. Integrated interior products and services must be almost infinitely modifiable to accommodate innovation. Scott Rice represents products/services to fulfill this vision because Scott Rice can deliver them now.

All Scott Rice associates are involved in developing the strategic direction of the company. Each year a planning process is completed that involves all associates segmented into teams. These teams develop business plans that are synthesized by Scott Rice leadership into an overall business plan for the next year. To reach this vision, Basore has implemented Operation Gain$hare to make the business fun by creating an environment in which people can continuously learn and grow while they apply their skills, abilities, and talents to make money.

"Winning at business has the greatest reward: constant improvement of people's lives and livelihoods," according to Basore. "The people of Scott Rice will achieve this reward by working together as a team while building a dynamic company. After all, we're all in this business together and we're all accountable to each other for making sure it succeeds."

In early 1999, Scott Rice relocated its Tulsa operation to a new 42,000-square-foot building near the Broken Arrow Expressway. In addition to their new Tulsa facility, Scott Rice has expanded its operations and services in Oklahoma City.

Scott Rice's new infrastructure includes a new "state-of-the-art" automation system with electronic linkages to customers, approximately 75,000 square feet of multi-racked asset storage facilities with a proprietary bar code system, and an upgraded vehicle fleet with expanded moving and relocation equipment. These provide the foundation for Scott Rice's core interior workspace products and interior facility services such as furniture, design, installation, furniture maintenance, relocation services, asset storage and furniture rental.

✧

Above: Workspace solutions for the 21st century. Scott Rice "Changing Office Space into WorkSpace Solutions."

Below: Scott Rice associates participate in yearly business planning meeting for 1999.

GABLE & GOTWALS

Gable & Gotwals is one of Oklahoma's leading law firms, with offices in Tulsa and Oklahoma City. The story of Gable & Gotwals is the story of two firms which merged in 1997 and whose attorneys have played an important part in Oklahoma's history.

G. Ellis Gable and Charles P. Gotwals, Jr. formed a law firm in 1944 that eventually became Gable & Gotwals. However, the roots of the firm reach much deeper into Oklahoma history. Ellis Gable graduated at the age of seventeen from Northeastern Oklahoma State University, where his father was the president of the university. In 1926, at the age of twenty-one, he began his law practice in Tulsa. After Charles Gotwals returned from active service in World War II, he joined the firm. Ellis Gable continued his legal career until 1983, a span of fifty-seven years, and he currently is *of counsel* to Gable & Gotwals. Charles Gotwals became *of counsel* to the firm in 1983.

Gable & Gotwals merged with Arrington, Kihle, Gaberino & Dunn in 1997. That firm traces its roots to R.C. Allen, a former district judge and National Attorney for the Creek Indian Nation who began his practice in Oklahoma in 1911.

During the course of Oklahoma's history, the attorneys at Gable & Gotwals have made lasting impressions in the State of Oklahoma and elsewhere. Ten of its attorneys are veterans. Two have been members of the Oklahoma State Regents for Higher Education. The firm also boasts a former dean of the University of Tulsa School of Law, Joseph W. Morris, who also has served as a United States District Judge, vice president and general counsel of Shell Oil Company, and general counsel of Amerada Hess Corporation. In addition, Ron Ricketts is a former Tulsa County District Court Judge.

Gable & Gotwals has long emphasized service to the legal profession and to the community. Four of its members have served as president of the Oklahoma Bar Association, and eight have served as president of either the Oklahoma County Bar Association or the Tulsa County Bar Association. The firm continuously represents indigent clients on a pro bono basis. Community, civic, and charitable organizations throughout the state have Gable & Gotwals attorneys on their board of directors and among their volunteers. Through the Gable & Gotwals Foundation, which was the first private foundation founded by a law firm in Oklahoma for the support of charitable causes, the firm continues to set a strong example of community and civic pride and leadership.

Gable & Gotwals started with an emphasis on real estate, banking and insurance matters. Over the years the firm has generated perhaps the state's most expansive library of title opinions on real estate formerly owned by members of the Five Civilized Tribes. As the firm grew during its first few decades, it expanded its scope of services to include virtually all areas of civil law practice, especially complex business litigation. The Arrington, Kihle firm emphasized representation of one of the state's largest public utilities, Oklahoma Natural Gas Company (now ONEOK, Inc.), starting in 1919. Through that representation, Gable & Gotwals now has expertise in public utility and regulated industry law, as well as mergers and acquisitions.

During almost the entire history of the State of Oklahoma, members of Gable & Gotwals have participated in extraordinary transactions and courtroom battles, creating new Oklahoma law in many subject areas—from mergers of Fortune 500 companies to fundamental inheritance issues. Oklahoma's legal history is sprinkled with important lawsuits and transactions involving Gable & Gotwals attorneys, some of which have had nationwide implications.

In the 1970s, the firm represented the insurance defendants in the *Mullendore* litigation, which resulted in what was then one of the largest insurance settlements of record. John L. Arrington represented the plaintiffs in that case, and he joined Gable & Gotwals as part of the merger with Arrington, Kihle, Gaberino & Dunn in 1997.

In 1982, the Federal Deposit Insurance Corporation retained Gable & Gotwals to handle litigation resulting from the Penn Square Bank and subsequent financial institution failures. Through that representation, the firm developed expertise in areas of law that had been untouched since the Great

✧

G. Ellis Gable (left) and Charles P. Gotwals, Jr.

Depression. Later in that decade, Gable & Gotwals assisted in the aftermath of the *Texaco/Pennzoil* litigation, which is one of the most significant business disputes in the history of the United States.

Gable & Gotwals represented major plaintiffs in antitrust cases of nationwide importance involving infant formula and brand name prescription drugs, both of which impacted thousands of people. In 1996, Gable & Gotwals obtained for Occidental Petroleum Corporation a $742 million judgment arising out of the failed merger of Gulf Oil Corporation and Cities Service Company. Also, attorneys from Gable & Gotwals have played major roles in virtually every major bankruptcy reorganization proceeding in the Northern District of Oklahoma.

Gable & Gotwals continues to serve clients in many areas, including business litigation, banking, mergers and acquisitions, energy and regulated industries, taxation, bankruptcy, health care, estate planning, class actions, and arbitration. The firm's broad client base ranges from international conglomerates requiring sophisticated legal representation in complex matters to investor groups, small businesses, and individuals with simple legal needs. The firm sets the highest possible standards for client service and legal expertise. Gable & Gotwals has achieved tremendous results for its clients in the courtroom, at the closing table, and all places in between.

Gable & Gotwals has been a part of Oklahoma's history since R. C. Allen's move to Oklahoma in 1911 and the start of Ellis Gable's practice in 1926. The firm's deep, strong roots, which have grown and spread since 1911, ensure that Gable & Gotwals will be an important part of the state's future as well.

CONNER & WINTERS, A PROFESSIONAL CORPORATION

Conner & Winters was founded in Tulsa in 1933 by Benjamin Conner, a highly regarded lawyer whose practice commenced before statehood, and John Winters, an eager young Michigan law school graduate. The First National Bank and Trust Company of Tulsa was their principal, if not only, client. On the day after the partnership was formed, President Franklin D. Roosevelt issued his famous "national bank holiday" order that closed all the banks in the country, including the firm's main client. Winters enjoyed describing the difficulties of practicing law when barter replaced checks as a means of paying debts. In the succeeding decades, Conner & Winters has become one of the region's largest and most respected law firms, with offices in Oklahoma City, Northwest Arkansas, and Washington, D.C., as well as Tulsa.

The end of World War II marked the beginning of solid, steady growth for the firm, largely by the addition of highly ranked new graduates from law schools throughout the nation. In 1991 Conner & Winters became a professional corporation and began a rapid expansion, acquiring a number of exceptionally well-qualified attorneys from other firms with expertise in many specialized fields of law. The Oklahoma City office was opened in 1994. In quick succession, the Northwest Arkansas office was opened in Fayetteville in 1995, and the Washington, D.C. office in 1996. Some of this expansion was effected by mergers and other acquisitions of well-established smaller firms.

Top: David R. Cordell prepares for trial under the watchful eye of John Winters.

Below: Receptionist Cathy Yingst greets clients.

An understanding of the firm's philosophy is essential to an understanding of its growth and its appreciation by clients. John Winters used to tell junior partners and associates, "Our job is to show the client *how* it can be done, rather than say it can't be done." This is as pertinent today as it was then. Similarly, Roger Randolph, long a guiding light of the firm, displayed on his office wall a framed maxim written by his client, Waite Phillips, a major benefactor of Tulsa: "The when is as important as the how." This maxim has always been a guiding principle of the firm's practice.

Another integral aspect of the Conner & Winters philosophy is that the legal services provided by the firm must be performed in a cost-effective manner, consistent with quality, with the object of furnishing services equivalent to or better than those provided by the top law firms in major cities in the nation at rates competitive with those charged locally.

Thus Conner & Winters has grown as a full-service, business-oriented law firm recognized for its specialties in banking, finance, corporate and securities law, tax, employee benefits, labor relations and employment law, oil and gas, real estate and environmental law, estate planning, probate and trust law, litigation, mediation, arbitration and other dispute resolution, bankruptcy and reorganization as well as immigration, healthcare, and other complex areas of the law.

Farm Fresh, Inc.

Farm Fresh, Inc. is an Oklahoma co-op formed in November of 1974 to provide fluid milk products to independent grocers. The company began operations with a fluid milk processing facility in Ponca City. In 1979, the company acquired an additional ice cream and cultured dairy product plant in Lawton along with a bakery plant. The bakery plant which Farm Fresh still operates today produces sandwich bread, buns, rolls, and some variety breads.

The sales growth of the company in the mid-1980s created the need to expand the dairy production capability. In 1985, construction began on a dairy plant located in Chandler, Oklahoma which would jettison Farm Fresh well into the future in terms of operating efficiencies and capabilities. Chandler was selected because the town qualified for an Urban Development Action Grant and was centrally located within the state. When the Chandler plant was built the Lawton plant and the Ponca City plant closed their operations and consolidated at the plant in Chandler. Production at the new plant commenced in December of 1987.

The dairy plant uses state-of-the-art technology throughout the 145,000-square-foot facility. Currently, production in the plant provides a full line of fluid products including milk, chocolate milk, orange juice, water, fruit drinks, as well as ice cream, frozen yogurt, and cultured products.

In 1993, Farm Fresh acquired the Townley Dairy Company. This business was a dairy distribution system that serviced the non-supermarket segment of the food industry that includes schools, military bases, restaurants, and hospitals. In July 1996, this operation was renamed Farm Fresh DSD Division and Farm Fresh products were introduced. Farm Fresh currently supplies most of the school business in Oklahoma along with other segments of the food industry.

Later in 1993, Farm Fresh acquired the Cook Dairy Plant in Bricktown. The plant produced a wide range of frozen novelty products including popsicles and ice cream sandwiches. In 1998, novelty production at that plant was shut down and moved to the dairy plant in Chandler. A few novelty items were out-sourced to other companies in this region.

Today, in 2000, Farm Fresh continues to operate a dairy plant in Chandler, the bakery plant in Lawton, the DSD Division with locations throughout Oklahoma as well as Executive Offices in Oklahoma City and Administrative Offices in Ponca City. Farm Fresh continues in the tradition of supplying quality dairy and bakery products to Oklahoma, Kansas, Arkansas, Missouri, and Texas.

✧

Top: The Farm Fresh Dairy.

Below: Farm Fresh, Inc., formed in 1974.

Hotel Phillips

In 1908, H. V. Foster of Foster Petroleum Company brought his wife, Marie, and daughter, Ruth, from Chicago to Bartlesville to live at 821 Johnstone Avenue. Colonel Matson built the house. The Fosters lived in the house until 1930 then sold it to Mr. Howe "H. C." Price with Price Pipeline. Phillips Petroleum Company purchased the house from Price in 1948, and dismantled it to make way for the Phillips Apartment Hotel.

In 1948, when the building plans were announced, Bartlesville, like many American cities, faced a serious housing shortage. World War II had ended and industry was growing. The company's fast growth and expansion brought more and more people into Bartlesville. Designed especially to meet the large demand for apartments for married couples without children and single employees, the apartment hotel was to supplement the company's extensive family-type housing project under construction in southwest Bartlesville, the Jane Phillips Addition.

The Hotel Phillips was opened as the Phillips Apartment Hotel on June 1, 1950. It had twenty-eight five-room efficiency apartments, eighty-four large four-room efficiency apartments, sixty-four smaller four-room efficiencies, and twenty-eight hotel rooms. Fourteen color schemes were carried out in the drapes, carpeting, lamps, upholstery, and pictures. No adjoining rooms were alike in color schemes with duplication found only in opposite wings and on different floors.

Rigby Slight, who had thirty years of experience in the hotel business, was hired as the resident manager. Rent began at $75 a month or $6 a day. Phil Arnold, who became Vice President of R&D for Phillips, was the first occupant and rented a corner apartment on the seventh floor. He also put in his own furniture and installed the first private telephone in the building. Phillips employees were always given first consideration for apartments.

Innovations for the time were air conditioning in the summer months (especially nice since most Phillips offices at the time were NOT air-conditioned), a self-service laundry in the basement, self-service push-button elevators, streamlined kitchens, and a sun deck on top of the building. Also, each apartment was equipped with "forced draft ventilation" so cooking odors would not accumulate and cling to rooms after meals. Garbage was collected daily from an opening in the hall where groceries and other deliveries were made without entering the rooms. The lobby was considered a comfortable meeting place for residents.

In 1980, The Phillips Apartment Hotel was converted to a hotel called Hotel Phillips with 156 luxury guestrooms and suites. A few permanent residents remained, with the last to leave in 1991.

When Hotel Phillips opened as a hotel; each guest found a delicious apple in his or her room. The hotel still offers its guests apples and uses an apple tree as its logo.

Hotel Phillips strived for excellence in guest services and satisfaction, and was the first recipient in Oklahoma of American Automobile Association's four-diamond rating as "exceptional" in 1984-85.

Outstanding service and personal attention still make Hotel Phillips world class.

Top: Guestroom at Hotel Phillips, 1999.

Below: The entrance to Hotel Phillips, 1999.

Crowe & Dunlevy

Crowe & Dunlevy
ATTORNEYS AND COUNSELORS AT LAW

Crowe & Dunlevy, founded in 1902, is the largest and one of the oldest law firms in Oklahoma. The Firm is engaged in the general practice of law and has offices in Oklahoma City, Tulsa, and Norman. Crowe & Dunlevy is the Oklahoma member of *Lex Mundi*, an international association of over 150 independent law firms, which provides contacts and relationships with leading law firms throughout the world. As the Firm's 100th anniversary approaches, Crowe & Dunlevy is a part of the fabric and heritage of Oklahoma.

Crowe & Dunlevy has long been associated with charitable causes, as well as the arts and cultural enrichment programs in the state of Oklahoma and the communities it serves. The Firm's philosophy has traditionally been to support the needs of charitable organizations and activities in order to enhance the quality of life for all Oklahomans. This support is made possible through the work of the Crowe & Dunlevy Foundation, a private foundation organized by the shareholders of Crowe & Dunlevy to provide a vehicle for charitable contributions.

Most recently, the Firm helped initiate Oklahoma Lawyers for Children, a program that allows volunteers, on a *pro bono* basis, to assist the Public Defender's Office with cases involving deprived and neglected children. In addition, Crowe & Dunlevy established a Disaster Relief Committee and Guardian Angel Fund immediately following the bombing of the Alfred P. Murrah Federal Building in 1995. Since its inception, employees and others have generously donated their time, as well as financial contributions, to help further the mission of the Committee and Fund. Another significant program the Firm initiated is the Crowe & Dunlevy International Law Professorship at the University of Oklahoma College of Law whereby Harvard legal scholars from around the world serve as temporary faculty members.

The Firm is proud to recognize the leadership achievements of our members, both past and present, including: Presidents of the American, Oklahoma, Oklahoma County, Tulsa County, and Cleveland County Bar Associations; President of the National Health Lawyers Association; President of the American College of Trial Lawyers; President of the American College of Mortgage Attorneys; Trustee of the United States Supreme Court Historical Society; Chief Judge, United States Court of Appeals for the 10th Circuit; United States District Judge; Oklahoma Court of Appeals Judge; United States Tax Court Judge; United States Magistrate Judge; United States Attorneys; District Attorneys; United States Ambassador; Deputy Attorney General of the United States; former Lead and Associate Counsels of the Office of Independent Counsel; Chair of the Murrah Federal Building Memorial Task Force, the Oklahoma City National Memorial Foundation and the Board of Trustees of the Oklahoma City National Memorial Trust; White House Fellow; Deans of the University of Oklahoma College of Law; Mayors; Oklahoma State Representative; Oklahoma Corporation Commissioner; members of Boards of Regents for major state universities; as well as numerous listings in *Who's Who in America*, *Who's Who in American Law*, *Who's Who in the World*, and *The Best Lawyers in America*.

Crowe & Dunlevy is committed to the citizens and businesses of Oklahoma. We will continue our efforts to preserve and sustain the highest level of integrity that has served Crowe & Dunlevy so well throughout its existence—and lead us to new accomplishments in the years ahead.

BOYD CHEVROLET, INC.

At the age of eighteen and just out of high school, Charles R. Boyd, Sr. began his journey in the car business. He started by driving a parts delivery truck for five years in Pinebluff, Arkansas and later moved to Dallas, Texas where he was promoted to parts manager at the age of twenty-three. After serving for five years in that position, he was drafted into the Army. When his tour of duty was complete, Boyd returned to Texas and held the position of parts service manager in San Angelo. He later moved to Ft. Worth, Texas to work as a parts manager for Hudiburg Chevrolet. Boyd quickly climbed through the ranks to fixed operations manager and eventually became general manager.

In 1974, Boyd's life took a turn when he received a call from a dealer with an offer to buy a percentage of Cupp Chevrolet, located in downtown Oklahoma City. Boyd accepted the offer with the contingency that within five years he would be given the opportunity to be the sole owner. With the confidence that this would come to pass, he renamed the dealership Boyd Chevrolet. The dealership has thrived for most of its twenty-five years on Reno Avenue between Meridian and MacArthur with 145 employees and 1998 sales exceeding $58 million.

Though the company has been around for twenty-five years now, the car business has changed drastically during this time. Boyd recalls his early days in the car business when one piece of paper and a handshake bought you the car. Boyd was also among the first to keep late sales hours (10 p.m.) and is the only dealer to provide a service department open until midnight. This exceptional quality of service is completely in line with Boyd Chevrolet's mission to lead a team of dedicated professionals who are empowered to provide exceptional service and value and are continually striving to exceed all expectations. Customers know that Boyd Chevrolet is totally committed to excellence.

Boyd's forward thinking also made him realize that the car business was not just for men. In 1997, he promoted Jan Glenn, a woman who had been in his employment for fifteen years, to general manager. Glenn became the television and radio spokesperson for the dealership, which had to this point been primarily handled by Boyd himself. He felt that she had the ability and dedication to effectively handle the day-to-day operations as well as marketing and planning for the future. After all, keeping one step ahead of the competition is no easy task.

✧

Top: The 1974 groundbreaking ceremony for Boyd Chevrolet.

Middle: Boyd Chevrolet caused controversy in the 1980s by placing a Chevrolet truck hauling a Ford truck up a pile of rocks.

Bottom: New Vehicle Sales Manager Kevin Abbott and General Sales Manager Bobby Scott discuss a sales contract.

PHOTOS COURTESY OF THE YUKON REVIEW

The Oklahoma community also knows that Boyd Chevrolet is committed to them. The dealership supports many school projects and is involved in over seven different schools' FFA programs. Glenn states, "We support a lot of school programs or something related to education. After all, they are the future car buyers."

You might think all this success would go to a guy's head, but Boyd quickly lets you know that "the basis of success of this dealership is the people who work here, not me. I give them all the credit." Most people would say that humble attitude alone qualifies Charles R. Boyd, Sr. as a success in his own right.

Bill Gumerson & Associates

Bill Gumerson and Associates is a unique Design-Build firm focused upon residential and commercial projects, many of which have a historical basis and significance. Involved in renovation and historic preservation for over thirty years, Bill Gumerson attributes much of the success of his company to the foundation first laid by grandparents William and Lulu Dow-Gumerson, who arrived in Oklahoma prior to statehood, and his parents Dow and Jean Gumerson. William, a developer and builder, had passed his love for architecture on to his son, Dow, many years before. In the early 1970's Dow, a well-established architect in Oklahoma, invited Bill to become a consultant on several historic projects including the State Capitol Printing Company in Guthrie. Bill Gumerson and Associates was founded in 1975 and has seen continuous growth ever since.

Today, the firm has twelve to fifteen employees working on projects in Oklahoma, Colorado, Kansas and New Mexico. Among its noteworthy projects are such varied restoration works as the University of Oklahoma's Boyd House, home of President David and Molly Boren, the Hightower Building and residence, the Overholser Mansion, and the Oklahoma Governor's Mansion. C. R. Anthony and Company called upon the talents of the company when their building, only one block away from the Alfred P. Murrah Federal Building, was severely damaged by the April 19th bombing in downtown Oklahoma City. Bill Gumerson and Associates were able to restore the offices within seventy-two hours. Design-and-build projects have included the Oklahoma City Golf and Country Club, the Kappa Alpha Theta Sorority house in Norman, and the Nichols Hills Plaza Shopping Center.

Gumerson and his wife Mary Ellen have recently purchased their own renovation project in the form of an old airplane bungalow at 4019 North Classen in Oklahoma City. Saved from the wrecking ball, the Gumersons plan to turn the historic building into an office space and studio.

Gumerson continues to focus upon the needs of the community through memberships and leadership in historic preservation committees including Heritage Hills Historic Preservation, Inc., the State Capitol Preservation Commission, and the National Trust for Historic Preservation. He is a past member of the Oklahoma City Historical Preservation and Landmark Commission. He is also a board member of Friends of the Governor's Mansion and a recipient of the prestigious Overholser Mansion Award from the American Institute of Architects.

Bill Gumerson and Associates moves into the new millenium focused upon its great passion for the preservation of historic structures in Oklahoma. Proud of the family's Oklahoma roots and his home state's wonderful history, Gumerson claims six generations of Oklahomans to include his and Dianne's (1944-1996) children—Kristen, Will, and Katie—and stepchildren—Will and Lauren—and the latest edition to his family, grandchild Luther Andrew Bohanon.

✧

Top: The Boyd House, home of the President of the University of Oklahoma.

Below: A design-and-build project at 50 Penn Place, Oklahoma City.

The statue in front of the Oklahoma Territorial Museum by Oklahoma artist Fred Olds depicts the symbolic marriage of Mr. Oklahoma Territory and Miss Indian Territory representing the joining the Twin Territories into the State of Oklahoma on November 16, 1907.

COURTESY DAVID FITZGERALD.

Family Portraits

families and individuals whose legacies continue to shape the future of Oklahoma

Patrons

Rogers & Bell,
Tulsa

The Zink Family,
Tulsa

Friends

Charles and Marjean Cole,
Tulsa

Gordona Duca,
Tulsa

Mr. and Mrs. Ray M. League,
Enid

Herman and LaDonna Meinders,
Oklahoma City

THE HEFNER FAMILY

Robert A. Hefner, III, owner and managing partner of The GHK Company, an Oklahoma City-based natural gas exploration and production firm, is a third generation Oklahoma energy man, as well as a third generation politically active business executive. His grandfather, Robert A. Hefner, known to most longtime Oklahomans as simply "The Judge," was born in 1874, in a two-room shack in Hunt County, Texas. Like many other Texas families at the time, the Civil War and the rigors of Reconstruction had impoverished the Hefners. Hefner's childhood consisted of extremely hard work, including herding—at age thirteen—3,000 sheep in a frontier wilderness in West Texas. But it was while herding these sheep that he became inspired by the book he was reading—*John Halifax Gentleman*—to, in fact, become a gentleman himself. He attended North Texas Baptist College, graduated from the University of Texas in 1902 with a law degree and married Eva Maurine Johnson in 1906 at Jacksboro, Texas. (Eva was known affectionately in later years to the Hefner clan as "Mother Eva".) They had three children: Robert A. Hefner, Jr., Margaret Evelyn Hefner, and William Johnson Hefner.

Top: Judge Robert A. Hefner at his desk in Oklahoma City in 1947.

Below: The Hefner family on the front steps of the Hefner family home at 201 Northwest 14 in Oklahoma City (now the location of the Oklahoma Heritage House), circa 1940s. Left to right: Evelyn Hefner, Robert A. Hefner, Jr., William Hefner, Judge Robert A. Hefner, and his wife (Mother Eva).

Robert A. Hefner hung out his shingle in Beaumont, Texas, at about the same time the Spindletop oil field was discovered and his firm—Parker and Hefner—became division attorneys for the Southern Pacific Railroad. The family moved to Ardmore, Oklahoma, in 1909, where he was city attorney and legal counsel for several major oil companies. In 1927, the family moved to Oklahoma City. Hefner was Justice of the Supreme Court of Oklahoma from 1926 to 1933, then returned to private practice and was elected mayor of Oklahoma City, serving from 1939 to 1947. He was a key figure in mapping delicate details of the transaction that made it possible to gain Tinker Air Force Base for central Oklahoma and was instrumental in the development of the Bluff Creek Reservoir, whose name was changed and the lake dedicated as Lake Hefner in 1947. After his terms as mayor, he went into the oil business with both his sons. In 1949, Hefner was elected to the Oklahoma Hall of Fame. He died in 1971, at age ninety-six.

Robert A. Hefner III's father, Robert A. Hefner, Jr., was born in 1907. He graduated *cum laude* from Stanford University in 1928, attended Harvard Law for a year and returned to Oklahoma to receive his law degree from the University of Oklahoma in 1930. Following graduation, he spent a year traveling around the world. In 1931, he formed a law partnership with Charles W. Mason in Oklahoma City; in 1933, he formed a partnership with his father and in July of the same year was appointed assistant general counsel to General Counsel Stanley Reid of the Reconstruction Finance Corporation in

Washington, D.C. In September of 1933, he was appointed a captain, United States Army, in the Judge Advocate General's office.

Robert Hefner, Jr., returned to Oklahoma City in 1935 to practice law with his father. He sojourned to the Illinois Basin in 1936, where he practiced oil and gas law and, in 1937, opened a law office in Matoon, Illinois. He passed the bar exams in Illinois, Indiana and Kentucky and in 1938 moved his law offices to Evansville, Indiana. In 1946, he assumed leadership of The Hefner Company in Oklahoma City, a partnership comprised of his parents, his brother, William J. Hefner, and his sister, Mrs. Evelyn Hefner Combs. In 1952, Robert, Jr., formed The Hefner Production Company, also with family members. Under his direction, these companies drilled, produced and operated their own wells and owned a large mineral position in many oil and gas provinces.

Robert, Jr., was active in forming the Oklahoma Independent Petroleum Association and served on its board of directors; he was also named vice president of the Independent Petroleum Association of America. Robert, Jr., served as chairman of the board of the Oklahoma Heritage Association and was instrumental in arranging for the Hefner family home and furnishings, at 201 Northwest 14, to be donated to the Oklahoma Heritage Association in 1970. The building is now officially named the Oklahoma Heritage House. He was elected to the Oklahoma Hall of Fame in 1973 and received the Oklahoma Outstanding Oilman Award in 1976. He died in 1987, at age seventy-nine.

Robert A. Hefner III was born in 1935 in Washington, D.C. He graduated from the University of Oklahoma in 1957 and in 1959 formed the Glover-Hefner-Kennedy Company, which became known as The GHK Company and has focused the majority of its now forty-year history on the development of natural gas rather than oil.

Robert III, who is a geologist and geophysicist and was a founder in the 1980s of the University of Oklahoma Energy Center, is often referred to as the "Father of Deep Natural Gas" and is considered one of the world's premier natural gas wildcatters. In the 1950s and 1960s most experts thought there could be no commercial natural gas in the deep sector of the Anadarko Basin in western Oklahoma. Robert III defied that conventional wisdom and GHK's #1 Green well, completed in 1969 in Beckham County, Oklahoma, became the first well to establish the prolific gas producing capability of the Deep Anadarko Basin, thereby opening the province to billions of dollars of subsequent deep gas development. From the late 1960s to the early 1980s, Robert III drilled many of the world's deepest and highest pressure natural gas wells

Above: The Hefner family, 1965. From left to right: Robert A. Hefner, Jr., Evelyn Hefner Combs, Charles Hefner, Patricia Hefner, Drew Cunningham, Robert A. Hefner III, Judge Robert A. Hefner, Mrs. William Hefner, William Hefner, Elinor Hefner, Cathy Hefner, and Robert A. Hefner IV.

Below: Robert A. Hefner III in Oklahoma City, circa 1972, with geological maps of the Anadarko Basin.

and achieved major advancements in natural gas drilling, completion and production technology. In 1980, Robert III and GHK entered into the largest on-shore domestic joint venture in the history of the industry with Mobil Oil Corp., resulting in GHK/Mobil interests in over 224 deep wells in Oklahoma's Anadarko Basin and a total expenditure by all participants in excess of $1 billion.

Today, Robert III's GHK Company has domestic operations principally located in the Arkoma Basin in southeastern Oklahoma, where it has discovered a new, prolific gas field called The Potato Hills. The GHK Company has also had foreign operations in Russia and, additionally, in Colombia—where the firm began exploration in 1992, leading to the 1996 discovery of a world class oil field, possibly a giant, in the Magdalena River Basin northwest of Bogota. GHK subsequently consolidated its Colombian oil interests with Seven Seas Petroleum Inc., a Houston-based publicly traded oil and gas exploration and production company. In 1997, Robert III became chairman of the board, managing director and chief executive officer of Seven Seas. He is also chairman and one of the founders of English-American Import Export Company, the nation's principal supplier of vinyl packaging to the U.S. textile industry.

With the onset of the nation's energy crisis in the early 1970s, Robert III became a leading spokesman for the role of natural gas in an economically sound energy policy and testified eighteen times before Congressional committees in the 1970s and 1980s. He was one of the most influential individuals in the country in changing Federal policy relating to natural gas pricing and deregulation. Robert III was chairman of the Oklahoma Energy Advisory Council, and organized and was chairman of the Independent Gas Producers Committee. He has served as an ambassador-at-large for the State of Oklahoma.

Top: Robert A. Hefner III at the Gate of Heavenly Peace in the Forbidden City, Beijing, China, 1995. Hefner was in Beijing visiting with artists prior to his Through An Open Door Chinese art exhibition, book, and CD.

Below: The Robert A. Hefler IV family at the entrance to the Oklahoma Heritage House in 1998. Front row (left to right): Carol Hefner, Gabrielle Hefner, and Robert A. Hefner IV. Back row: Robert A. Hefner V, Alexis Yasmin Hefner, and Mary Iman Hefner.

Robert III has been an avid collector of items he feels representative of both the beauty and the spirit of enterprise in mankind's nature. As the Berlin Wall was coming down in 1989, he was able to purchase sixteen feet, which today stands in the Omniplex Science Museum in Oklahoma City. Additionally, he has a permanent collection of over 100 Chinese contemporary oil paintings which, outside of the museums of China, is believed to be the world's finest collection of the historic and artistically explosive period following the Cultural Revolution. An exhibition of these oil paintings was staged in 1997 at the Fred Jones, Jr., Museum of Art at the University of Oklahoma. Robert III has also recently published a full color book and a CD of these paintings entitled *Through An Open Door: Selections from the Robert A. Hefner III Collection of Contemporary Chinese Oil Paintings.*

Robert III is chairman emeritus of Ballet Oklahoma and, in 1981, won the *Forbes*

"Business in the Arts" award for long-term commitment and contributions to Ballet Oklahoma. He has served on the advisory board for the Guggenheim and is a founding director of The Bradshaw Foundation, organized to study and publish a book on the Bradshaw rock art of the Kimberley in Australia. He is also an honorary trustee of the Trust for African Rock Art.

In 1982, Robert III funded the publication of *Western Oklahoma*, a photographic essay book on the land and people of Western Oklahoma with full color photographs by the French photographer Daisy Decazes. He has been a member of numerous professional societies and organizations including the Advisory Council of the School of Advanced International Studies (SAIS) at Johns Hopkins University, on the Board of Directors of the Alliance to Save Energy, a Founding Director of the Business Council for Sustainable Energy and former Advisory Board member of the International Institute for Applied Systems Analysis in Austria.

Robert Hefner III has three children—Robert IV, Catherine Eva, and Charles Ray—and seven grandchildren, all Oklahomans!

Robert A. Hefner IV, born in 1955, attended the University of Miami in Florida and Occidental College in Los Angeles, then studied petroleum geology at the University of Oklahoma. After graduation from OU he was employed by Amoco International, then came home to work at The GHK Company. He is presently with Chesapeake Energy in Oklahoma City. He and his wife, the former Mary Carol Coury, have a son, Robert A. Hefner V, born in 1985, and three daughters: Mary Iman Hefner, born in 1987; Alexis Yasmin Hefner, born in 1990; and Gabrielle Hefner, born in 1995.

Catherine Eva Hefner Urice, born in 1956, graduated from Fleming College in Florence, Italy, with an Associate of Arts degree, then graduated from Colorado Women's College in Denver with both a Bachelor of Arts and a Bachelor of Fine Arts. She and her husband, Daniel Rex Urice, live in Nichols Hills. She represents her father's interests in the effort to develop African rock art. Rex is with the Oklahoma Medical Research Foundation. They have two daughters: Lily Louisa Urice, born in 1985; and Catherine Alexandra Urice, born in 1988.

Charles Ray Hefner, born in 1957, attended Pepperdine University in California, then graduated from the University of Oklahoma in 1982 with a Bachelor of Arts degree in business communications. He worked for his grandfather, Robert A. Hefner, Jr., overseeing the computer system, and in 1987 joined The GHK Company. He is presently Coordinator of Data Processing. Charles and his wife, the former Christine Jean Roots, live in Norman, where she is a librarian in the Norman public school system. They have one son, Steven Mclean Hefner, born in 1993.

✧

Top: The Charles Hefner family, 1998 (left to right): Steven Hefner, Christine Hefner, and Charles Hefner.

Above: The Urice family, 1999 (left to right): Lily Louisa Urice, Rex Urice, Alexandra Urice, and Catherine Hefner Urice.

Ed L. Calhoon, M.D.

✧

Above: Dr. Calhoon attributes a great portion of his achievements to the loyal and kind support of his wife, Felice.

Below: Dr. & Mrs. Calhoon are joined by their son, Scott (left) a general and vascular surgeon, and daughter, Lane (right), a political consultant.

Born December 9, 1922 in Beaver County, Oklahoma, Ed Latta Calhoon has vivid memories of family life on the farm, five brothers and a sister and an absorbing love of nature. His modest Christian upbringing valued honesty, integrity, and hard work. Those values have stayed with him throughout life and saturate his reputation as "the doctor who makes house calls," the "political activist for health," and "an unforgettable father, husband, and friend."

After graduating from high school as valedictorian, Calhoon enrolled at Northwestern State College in Alva in the fall of 1940. Interrupting college to join the Army following Pearl Harbor, Calhoon returned and pursued his medical aspirations. His disappointed mother had wanted all her sons to be ministers. Years later, after Calhoon and his two brothers, Jim and Harold, became physicians, their mother pursued higher education, entered the ministry, and was later ordained a deacon in the United Methodist Church. Currently, Calhoon sits on the Board of the United Methodist Foundation.

During his admission interview to the University of Oklahoma Medical School, Calhoon promised to return to a rural setting to practice. This decision has served his hometown and the surrounding areas well over the years, as he has served generations of the same families and truly earned the title "Family Doctor." After graduation in 1951, his plans for neurosurgery were shelved when community leaders asked him to fill the need for a doctor in Beaver. He had married Felice Warburton in 1949 and they had a son, Scott. Their daughter, Lane, was born after they moved to Beaver. Realizing the opportunity to walk right into full practice, Calhoon intended to stay only a couple of years. Forty years later, he still calls Beaver "home."

Ed Calhoon has been described as someone with "singleness of purpose," who is "tall (6'4"), lanky, has a great wit, down-to-earth understanding and razor-sharp intelligence." These characteristics drew additional patients to him from the states of Kansas and Texas, which neighbor the Oklahoma Panhandle. Calhoon was known to make house calls—some as far away as 100 miles. One particular set of house calls earned him national news attention. While attending a medical meeting in Oklahoma City in February of 1971, a blizzard paralyzed the Oklahoma Panhandle with snowdrifts twelve feet high. Concerned about people who might need medical care and unable to drive 220 miles home through deep snow, he called the governor's office and won permission to board a National Guard rescue helicopter to help victims.

✧

Left: Active in politics, Dr. Calhoon and other members of the Oklahoma State Regents for Higher Education are joined by President Bush. Calhoon chaired the Regents in 1995.

Below: Dr. Calhoon spearheaded efforts which resulted in realization of the Family Medicine Center.

Since 1954, Dr. Calhoon has run his medical practice without regularly scheduled appointments. He is known for being at his clinic from Monday through Friday and on Saturday mornings. Patients of all ages with every kind of need know that all they have to do is come in and Calhoon "will get to 'em when he can," in addition to his hospital and nursing home responsibilities.

Dr. Calhoon's interest in medical politics was born during his first year in medical school, when he waited tables at a political function in Oklahoma City. But it was not until 1965, after twelve years of practice and planning, that he ventured out beyond local community service leadership, which included Beaver School Board, Rotary, and many terms as Beaver County Republican Party Chairman. Calhoon's deep concern regarding adequate healthcare in rural areas and encroachment on the doctor-patient relationship led to his election as president of the Oklahoma State Medical Association in 1970. This was followed by over twenty-five years as a delegate to the American Medical Association (AMA) where he served with distinction. It was during his tenure as an AMA delegate that Calhoon was a member of its Rural Health Council and Council on Legislation and started to become more prominent in the Republican Party at the state and national levels. Following a prestigious appointment by President Reagan, he served for six years on the National Cancer Advisory Board to the National Institutes of Health and later on the Life Sciences Working Group Advisory Council to NASA. He believes these opportunities aided him in better serving Oklahomans and afforded future opportunities for furthering health issues and causes.

Governor Henry Bellmon appointed Calhoon to the Oklahoma State Regents for Higher Education in 1989 and he rose to its chairmanship in 1995. Organizing a lobbying effort, Calhoon was able to see the promotion of rural health needs win support and funding for construction of the first Family Medicine Building at the University of Oklahoma Health Sciences Center. The new training facility and the efforts it supports produce high quality primary care and rural practitioners.

Long is Calhoon's list of professional acclamations, awards and honors, culminating in his induction into the prestigious Oklahoma Hall of Fame in 1988. But even longer is the list of lives Calhoon has personally touched. His medical practice, political work, and love for the outdoors have offered many opportunities. Whether delivering a baby, mending a fence, or taking neighbors buckets of fresh sand-hill plums picked with grandsons Clay, Holt, and Reid, life on the shortgrass prairie has been good.

All in a day's work for this doctor in the country.

The Kroutil Family

✧

Top: Frank L. & Mary Kroutil, late 1920s.

Below: Yukon Mill & Grain Company, family owned since 1902.

The Kroutil Family, Frantisek, Sr. and Katerina, emigrated from Czechoslovakia to Nebraska in 1881, made the Land Run in Oklahoma on April 22, 1889, and settled in 1895 in the Shell Creek area west of Yukon. Today, driving past the area, you can see a water well hand pump out in the middle of a field that was probably used by the family. The migration to Oklahoma must have been extremely difficult for them. They had to travel in a wagon and care for their small baby, two small children, and three children between the ages of ten and twenty. Leaving their homeland and all they had ever known in Eastern Europe for the priceless dream of owning a piece of land, the couple must have had strong beliefs and firmly grounded religious principles in order to cope with life on the early Oklahoma frontier. They may have spent their first winter in the new territory sheltered in a sod house or dugout home, which were common in the Oklahoma Territory during the 1890s.

The older sons, John F. Kroutil and Frank L. Kroutil, along with A. F. Dobry, husband of their sister Mary and a brother-in-law, purchased the Yukon Mill and Grain Company on April 28, 1902. There were three other sons—Joseph, Thomas, and Robert. They sold coal, wheat, corn, wheat by-products, bran and shorts, and mixed feeds. A steam-powered electric generating plant was added in 1907, thus the Yukon Electric Company was formed. As a result, Yukon became one of the first small towns in Oklahoma to have electricity. The Mill also provided the electric lines out to Czech Hall, which remains the hub of many social events in the area today.

John Kroutil was the first of only two presidents of the Mill, and helped organize Yukon National Bank in 1912 along with Frank. John Kroutil supported Franklin Delano Roosevelt, serving as advisor to the President on farm problems. He also assisted in Wiley Post's efforts to raise money for a solo flight around the world. John passed away in 1954, Joseph died in 1901, and Frank passed away in 1932. Robert died in 1964. Raymond, son of Frank L. Kroutil, followed John as president in 1954

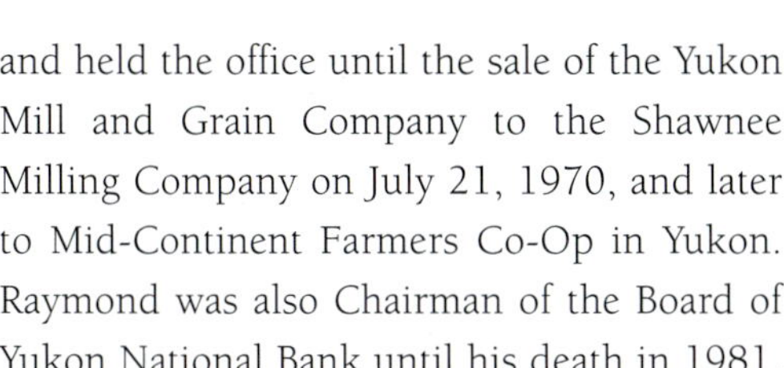

and held the office until the sale of the Yukon Mill and Grain Company to the Shawnee Milling Company on July 21, 1970, and later to Mid-Continent Farmers Co-Op in Yukon. Raymond was also Chairman of the Board of Yukon National Bank until his death in 1981.

During the 1920s, the Mill expanded quite rapidly, but disaster struck in 1921 when the Mill burned to the ground. The Company rebuilt the largest independent flour mill in the Southwest, using ten to 12,000 bushels of wheat a day, having a total capacity of 2,000 barrels a day, with storage of one million bushels of grain, as well as receiving stations for grain in Piedmont and Banner. In the late 1920s, the Mill shipped a solid trainload of flour to be delivered to Amsterdam, Holland. They have shipped flour to thirteen states in the Southeast and twenty countries overseas. During World War I, flour was shipped to Western Europe and, in World War II, the Mill ran around the clock sending flour to many countries including India and Indochina. After World War II, they ground yellow and white cornmeal, sent five and ten pound pancake and biscuit mixes to many institutions, and began exporting flour for companies such as Pillsbury and General Mills.

Yukon Mill and Grain Company was the first in the country to put out a cookbook. Flour sacks, in bright colors and prints, were often made into shirts, dresses, and pillowcases. For many years, the Yukon Mill furnished basketball and football uniforms for the Yukon High School athletes, hence the teams' name today, "The Yukon Millers." Norman Kroutil, son of Frank L. Kroutil, was a member of the Yukon School Board for many years and was Vice President of Yukon Mill and Grain Company.

Throughout their history, the Mill took great pride in its approximately 125 to 165 employees who had spent decades working in the mill. C. R. Wright, husband of Kathryn Kroutil Wright, joined Yukon Mill and Grain Company as their Executive Vice President in 1966. He is now Chairman of the Board and President of Yukon National Bank.

One of the outstanding landmarks in Oklahoma, the Yukon Mill sign, as it stands today, was created around 1949 after the first sign was blown away by strong winds. Ivan Lindell, a sheetmetalsmith living in Dibble, and Frank Bartodej of Yukon, made this sign. The sign has about 2,400 light bulbs and began blinking again in May of 1989, with the help in raising money for the project by John Knuppel and Joe Horn of the Yukon National Bank. The lights have always been easily recognized from a great distance and have provided many weary travelers the knowledge of being about halfway between the East Coast and the West Coast on famous Route 66.

For Oklahomans, the brilliant sign is a timeless reminder of an immigrant family's collective dreams spanning nearly a century—dreams that have been cultivated in Yukon, Oklahoma.

✧

Raymond and Gertrude Kroutil, parents of Kathryn Kroutil Wright. Photos circa 1965.

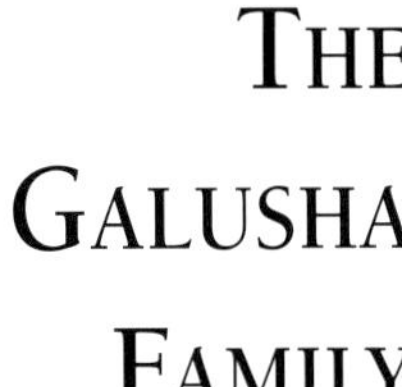

The Galusha Family

Jasper Jackson Galusha was born in Perkins, Oklahoma Territory, October 19, 1905. Jasper was the fourth child of four sons and five daughters born to Emma Mahala Dunlap Galusha and Perry Galusha.

Jasper's great-great-grandfather, Jacob, fled Slovakia to Great Britain with his parents following the Thirty Years War. In 1632, they settled in the Massachusetts Bay Colony. Daniel, one of Jacob's two children, settled in what became Vermont. In the westward sweep of the American Empire, Daniel moved to Ohio, Illinois, and Michigan. In Ohio, Lucien Edward Galusha was born in 1818. From Lucien came Perry (Illinois, 1861). Perry moved to Kansas in order to make The Run of 1889 into Oklahoma Territory. Perry and Emma Dunlap were married in Stillwater, and settled in Perkins. Throughout Jasper's school years, he worked to help support his parents' large family.

Jasper left home to attend high school in Ponca City, and graduated in 1927. While in school, he met Flora Van Winkle Steele. They were married in Oklahoma City, June 9, 1929.

Flora was born in White Eagle, Oklahoma Territory, October 7, 1907, the fifth child of Lucy Beckwith Steele and Guy Cooper Steele. Guy's brother, Dick, worked for the Department of Indian Affairs at the Ponca Indian Agency. Dick convinced Guy to bring his family and join him in purchasing the trading post, local post office, and 400 acres of farmland. Guy ordered a prefabricated farmhouse from Peter Van Winkle's sawmill. The milled and coded wood was shipped by rail from Arkansas to White Eagle.

The Beckwith family came from the Beckwiths of Jamestown (the first permanent English settlement in the New World, in 1609). Grandmother Mary Van Winkle lived with the Steeles when Flora was born, thus keeping Flora Van Winkle's name from being the fourth generation of Flora Minerva. Mary was a descendant of Jacob Waling, from Winkle, Holland, who immigrated to New Amsterdam in 1619. He changed their name to Van Winkle, and became a part of that original Dutch settlement on Manhattan Island. A few generations later, Peter Van Winkle developed the Van Winkle Saw Mill, near War Eagle, Arkansas, with over 400,000 acres of woodland. What remains of this estate serves as an Arkansas State Park, near Rogers.

The Steeles came to Arkansas from Tennessee. Captain John Bell Steele served in the First Arkansas Calvary during the Civil War. Guy Cooper Steele was born in Springdale, 1868, and graduated from the Rogers Academy in 1888.

When married, Jasper was a pressman for the *Ponca City News*. Though the depression years were in sight, he was well employed with an assured income. The pressman job was a six-day-a-week job of melting and pouring molten lead in an unvented basement.

Top: Flora and Jasper's wedding day, June 9, 1929, at the home of her brother, Milan Steele, in Oklahoma City. Dr. Joe Scroggs, Oklahoma University faculty member, officiated.

Below: Jasper and Flora seated on their rosewood sofa, made by Elijah Galusha of Troy, New York in 1840, on the evening of their Golden Wedding Anniversary.

In 1937, he was forced to give up his job due to advanced stages of severe lead poisoning. He was completely disabled and not expected to live. Faced with hospital bills and the care of four young children, Flora supplemented the $45 monthly disability check caring for mothers of newborn babies for one dollar a day; took in ironing; raised a large garden, chickens, a cow; and sold vegetables, eggs, and milk.

To help Jasper to regain his motor skills, Flora taught him to crochet. Crocheting became a lifelong hobby. When visiting other men in the hospital, he would teach them to crochet. His skill was such that his silk tablecloths were exchanged for the family's medical expenses.

For five years, Jasper slowly recuperated. During World War II, and not yet completely recovered, he felt compelled to serve his country. At the Ponca City Darr School, a British/Canadian flight training center, Jasper became a certified parachute rigger.

Following the war, Jasper again secured his union card as a pressman. He worked for the Oklahoma Publishing Company and retired from the *Dallas Morning News*. Flora worked as secretary to the superintendent of the Dallas School District.

In 1976, they retired to Bixby, Oklahoma. As avid gardeners, both spent their retirement years tending their award winning gardens. In 1983, Jasper was honored in being named a Paul Harris Fellow by Rotary International. After being married for sixty-six years, Jasper died on April 9, 1996.

Flora and Jasper have four sons: Jasper Harley, D.O.; John Richard; Joseph Allen, and David Eugene.

Harley and his late wife, Marlene, have three daughters: Cheryl, Laura, and Karen. In Tulsa, Harley founded Galusha Eye Associates, Inc., now specializing in cataract and laser surgery. Harley is one of the nation's pioneers in artificial lens implant and laser eye surgery. Marlene founded Oasis, an adult day care facility in Tulsa and was a well-known gerontologist specializing in aging and spirituality.

Richard (Dick) and wife, Letitia, were missionaries of the Christian Church, in the old Belgian Congo, for ten years. In 1969, Dick founded Youth Services of Tulsa, a delinquency prevention program and he managed Verdigris Valley Farms, a ranch and pecan orchard. Tish taught French and humanities at Wagoner High School. Their five children are Kimberly, D.O., Keith, Katy, Kelly, and Kris.

Joseph Allen and Paula's sons, John and Clarke, were born in New York City, where Joe, an industrial designer, designed and built the headquarters for Salomon Brothers and Revlon. He moved to Tulsa in 1981 to open JAG Corporation. Paula, a home economist, is a food writer for several journals.

David and Mary live in Ramona, California. They have a daughter, Marijane, and a son, Jeffrey. David is a retired Naval Captain, yet still works each day as a secondary educator in Julian, California. Mary, a schoolteacher, now counsels high school students in preparation for college.

Flora and Jasper, who witnessed first-hand the hardships of the Dust Bowl and Depression, were determined to provide the best possible future for their children. They managed to give their sons thirty-two years of higher education and taught them that along with privileges go responsibility, instilling the traits of hard work, gratitude and a deep respect for God.

✧

Above: Flora and Jasper being presented a chrome-plated crank and key to a 1930 Model A Ford, much like the one they owned the first twenty years of marriage.

Below: A family portrait on the Galushas' sixty-fifth wedding anniversary, June 9, 1994. Jasper and Flora are circled by their sons, (left to right) David, Joseph, Harley and Dick.

Paul H. Travis and Travis Ranch

In 1968 Paul H. Travis was invited by Melvin Hatley to attend a quarterhorse sale at his well-established quarterhorse ranch in Norman, Oklahoma. Travis had recently sold his group of five specialty mills developed to accommodate small items needed by the three large automotive companies in Michigan—General Motors, Ford, and Chrysler. Smaller equipment was needed to manufacture these items so, rather than set up such equipment in the large factories, the items were farmed out and produced by smaller manufacturing mills.

Having worked in the sales department of these small companies supplying items for the automotive giants, Travis soon realized he could manufacture these items as well as sell them. He bought a small mill in Rochester, Michigan off the auction block in 1942. This factory, with a modest beginning with only two or three items in production, became quite successful. By 1967, Travis, through the succeeding years, purchased and developed four more small mills that would primarily service the three automotive companies.

In 1967, a large conglomerate offered Travis a most enticing and satisfactory deal to buy his five specialty mills. Being an astute businessman he accepted the offer. With the offer came the requirement that he remain with the companies for two years to make a proper management transition. Anticipating that he would have less and less activity and responsibility in the mills as the two years passed, Travis looked about for another activity. Having acquired a few high-quality Appaloosa mares in Michigan, and having some success in racing them locally, he began to think seriously about raising horses as a retirement activity. News travels fast in the horse business in regards to new people with money coming into the arena. Thus, the invitation from Melvin Hatley to attend his quarterhorse sale in Norman.

Travis soon learned that quarterhorses had more money value in the horse arena than Appaloosas. So, before his two-year contract was up in Michigan, he sold his band of eleven Appaloosa mares early in 1965 and bought his first quarterhorse, Pana Bar, a AAA American Quarterhorse Association (AQHA) Champion. After two or three more trips to Norman, he purchased a 240-acre ranch. By 1970, his business in Michigan was concluded and he moved to the ranch in Norman. Subsequently, Travis purchased another 640 acres of land adjacent to his 240 acres, making a total of 880 acres and naming it Travis Ranch.

✧

Paul H. Travis.

PHOTO COURTESY OF NORMAN PHOTOGRAPHY.

Travis' interest in horses began as a small boy growing up in East Stroudsburg, Pennsylvania, in the heart of the Pocono Mountains. Driving his country doctor father's sleigh through the snowy Pennsylvania roads, Travis also enjoyed success in athletic activities and played basketball, ran track, and boxed while in high school.

After high school graduation, Travis attended Cornell University where he received "a couple of degrees in engineering," was named the Student Most Likely to Succeed in Business at his graduation and, when Kelvinator offered him a job in their factory, he moved to Michigan. Travis and his wife, Doris Eaton Travis, met just after she and her partner opened a branch studio of the famous Arthur Murray Dance Studios in the Statler Hotel in Detroit, Michigan. Doris was making calls to Arthur Murray customers when she first spoke to Travis—their courtship lasted for ten years. Born in Norfolk, Virginia, Doris had enjoyed a show business career on stages in Washington, D.C. and New York appearing for three years in the Ziegfield Follies, then in musical comedies and in early melodramatic talkies in Hollywood. Today she remains a vital part of Travis Ranch in its day-to-day operation.

With the original 240 acres, Paul Travis acquired what proved to be two outstanding quarterhorse stallions, *Three Chicks* and *Tiny Watch*. With his first quarterhorse stallion, *Pana Bar*, he now had three AAA AQHA champions as foundation stock for his breeding plans. Putting the same effort of learning into the horse business as he had in the automotive field, he studied pedigrees and set about to purchase the highest quality quarterhorse broodmares he could find. He was able to acquire such mares as *Fantasy*, *Gays Delight*, *Dimples Too*, *Three Deep*, and *Fantacia*.

His first quarter mare, *Miss Three Wars*, was the first to race at Ruidoso Downs. *Miss Three Wars* competed with the great stallion, *Easy Jet*, in the three main races of the season in 1969. *Easy Jet* won the Kansas Futurity and she beat him in the Rainbow Futurity. In the All American Futurity, on a day of heavy, continuous rains and a heavy, muddy track, *Easy Jet* inched her out of winning the final race of the contest. The little sorrel mare strove valiantly in mud above her ankles, but the larger stallion gradually took the lead, winning by a head.

In succeeding years, the Travis Ranch broodmares and stallions produced many outstanding racers. Not only were his own stallions *Three Chicks* and *Tiny Watch* top breeders for his mares, he sent several of them to other outstanding stallions such as *Easy Jet*, *Go Man Go*, and *Jet Deck*. He purchased shares in the thoroughbred stallion *What Luck* and this proved to be a most successful cross producing *Lucks Image Girl* and *Lucks Gay Chick* being prime examples.

In 1979, on an autumn afternoon, Travis enjoyed three stakes race victories. *Wranglers Chic Gay* and *Lucks Image Girl* won the All-American Congress Futurity and Derby at River Downs, while *Go Go Gay* took the winning trophy in the Shecky Greene Derby at the Commonwealth Ohio track.

The last stallion to race for Paul Travis was the Travis Ranch-bred *Lucks Gay Chick*, a stunning black horse who in his many races won a speed index of 104 and in 1982 was named Champion Aged Stallion of the Year by AQHA. The last outstanding filly to race for him was *Easy One Fine Day* who, in 1985, won the Oklahoma Futurity at Blue Ribbon Downs in Sallisaw, Oklahoma.

Three Chicks passed on his racing quality to the foals of other horsemen who brought their mares to Travis Ranch stallions. Two notable winners were *Chicks Deck* winning the Kansas Futurity in 1975 and *Chick Called Sue* winning the Rainbow Futurity, also in 1975.

Paul H. Travis leaves a legacy in Oklahoma of quality breeding and racing. Progeny from his stallions and mares still reveal the splendid bloodlines showing up in pedigrees of present winners and producers. Such an "outsider" as he will always be welcomed by native Oklahomans.

Top: Miss Three Wars, *Travis' first winner in the* Ruidoso Downs Rainbow Futurity.

Left: Easy One Fine Day *wins at the 1985* Blue Ribbon Downs in Sallisaw, Oklahoma.

Dr. J. Clyde Wheeler

✧

Above: Dr. Joseph Clyde Wheeler with Deborah Lee Whitten, October 1963.

Below: Dr. Joseph Clyde Wheeler and his wife, Dr. Ellen Jayne Maris Wheeler in their home in 1971.

For more than a half-century Dr. Joseph Clyde Wheeler was an important presence in his state, in his city, in the arts, in community service, and in his church, Oklahoma City's Crown Heights Christian Church (Disciples of Christ).

He was born in 1910 in rural Appalachian poverty, one of thirteen children of a coal miner and itinerant preacher. He worked his way through Berea College in Kentucky, where he was an outstanding student and athlete, graduating in 1934. He received his Bachelor of Divinity degree in 1937 from Lexington Theological Seminary.

After serving as statewide youth director of the Christian Church in Missouri, Wheeler came to Oklahoma City in 1945 to begin thirty-one years as pastor of Crown Heights Christian Church. He made an indelible mark. The membership, facilities, activities, and budget of the church expanded several times over, and its congregation provided leadership on state and national boards. Wheeler became a sought-after counselor and adviser to top community leaders and planners, and to several Oklahoma governors.

After retirement from Crown Heights, Wheeler served as interim minister of several churches in central Oklahoma. During his career he conducted more than 1,000 weddings and 1,000 funerals.

Himself the author of six books, Wheeler gave more than 100 book reviews each year and traveled extensively throughout the world. He was president of the Oklahoma City Ministerial Alliance, served on the Phillips University Board of Trustees and President's Council, and worked with the Oklahoma Council of Churches and the National Conference of Christians and Jews. As a director of the Oklahoma City Christian Church Coalition he helped organize thirteen Christian Churches in Oklahoma County.

While in the seminary Wheeler married his high school sweetheart, Gladys Whitt, and they were together for thirty-one years until her death. Their children were daughter Lucy Bo and son Joseph Clyde Wheeler, Jr. In 1969, he married Ellen Jayne Maris Miller and adopted her son, Don.

Wheeler was awarded an honorary Doctor of Divinity degree from Phillips University in 1960, an honorary Doctor of Human Letters degree from Findlay College in 1962, and an honorary Doctor of Letters degree from Oklahoma City University in 1968. He received the Distinguished Service Award from Berea College in 1974 and was made Honorary Alumnus of Southern Nazarene University in 1990.

He was an officer of the American Red Cross, Contact, Boy Scouts, American Cancer Society, and the Oklahoma State Mental Health Association. Wheeler worked tirelessly for the arts, helping support and build, among others, the Oklahoma City Symphony, Canterbury Choral Society, Shakespeare in the Park, and the Oklahoma City-County Library.

At Wheeler's funeral on February 6, 1998, grandson Derek Salyer expressed these words: "I miss him…I miss how he would take my grasped hand after a prayer and say, 'Shake the love around, shake the love around!' And the family circled in prayer would shake their hands like a mini football stadium wave."

Dr. J. Clyde Wheeler was a man who shook the love around, and he shook around inspiration, and the belief that worthy goals can always be accomplished. He was one of a kind.

Laban Samuel Records & Lester A. Maris

Dr. Ellen Jayne Maris Wheeler, professor of voice, opera history, and fine arts and human values at Oklahoma City University, loved hearing her mother's stories of high adventure on the Oklahoma frontier as a young girl. When she happened across her maternal grandfather's handwritten manuscripts, in which he recorded much of his life as an Oklahoma cowboy, she knew these stories must be told. With the support of her husband, Dr. J. Clyde Wheeler, she edited *Cherokee Outlet Cowboy* by Laban Samuel Records and published it through the University of Oklahoma Press in 1995.

Records was born at Milton, Switzerland County, Indiana on July 8, 1856. Growing up in Indiana and moving with his family to Peru, Kansas in 1870 as his father, a Methodist pastor, established congregations across the countryside, Records was a cowboy through and through. From his five foot four inch frame to his steely-blue eyes and beloved high-crowned Stetson hat, he rode the range from 1873 to 1887. A freighter along the Santa Fe Trail, a cowpuncher in the Dodge City stockyards, a cook for the Osage Agency at Pawhuska, and a line rider and foreman for the T-5 and Spade ranches in the Cherokee Outlet, Records finally settled on a homestead he claimed in the Cheyenne-Arapaho Land Run of 1892. He and his wife Dora raised three sons and two daughters and remained on the homestead for nearly fifty years. Laban Samuel Records died on August 17, 1940.

Lester Abram Maris, Ellen Jayne's paternal grandfather, decided as a boy on the family farm that he wanted to be a lawyer like his idol, Abraham Lincoln.

While studying law at Kansas University in Lawrence, Kansas, he met and fell in love with a beautiful young woman named Grace Miller, whom he married. From Lawrence, the family moved to Ponca City, Oklahoma Territory, living in a small frame home near downtown, with a barn out back for the cow.

Maris was a prominent attorney in Ponca City for forty years, serving his community in many ways. He was elected to the Second Oklahoma Legislature and earned attention as a leader of 1910 Republican efforts to force financial accountability from Governor C. N. Haskell.

He was a member of the Lions Club and the Masonic Lodge and worked as a volunteer with the Salvation Army. Not surprisingly for a man who kept a bronze bust of Lincoln in his downstairs library and a framed picture of Theodore Roosevelt in his bedroom, Maris served several terms as Republican county chairman. He sang bass in the choir at First Methodist Church, and never missed a Sunday except for annual fishing trips to Bemidji, Minnesota.

Lester A. Maris died in November 1942, at the age of sixty-four.

✧

Above: Left to right: Edith Lucinda Records Maris, Laban Samuel Records, Ralph Hayden Records, Dora Geneva Records Campbell, Earl Lester Records, Dora Belle Barker Records and Victor Laban Records. Circa 1904.

Below: Law office of Lester A. Maris, Ponca City, Oklahoma, circa 1920.

The Abernathy Family

✧

Left: Judge George Carl Abernathy, 1936.

Right: Jack H. Abernathy, 1996.

The Abernathy story in Oklahoma began with George Carl Abernathy and Carrie Howell. Both graduated from the University of Arkansas. George received his L.L.B. degree from the University of Pennsylvania and the couple moved to Shawnee, Oklahoma on July 2, 1904.

George and Carrie gave all their best energies to building and fostering the growth and progress of Shawnee. Elected alderman, George also held leadership roles in Rotary, Masonic Lodge, and was chairman of the County Council of Defense and the County Extension Board. He was active in the American, state, and the Pottawatomie County Bar Associations, the American Association of Insurance Councils, and was president of the Shawnee school board. He and his wife took an active role in the work of the First Presbyterian Church. Carrie was a charter member of the BB chapter of the PEO sisterhood, a Daughter of the American Revolution, and was the longest continuing member of the Hawthorne study club until her death in 1956.

In 1909, Governor Haskell appointed George as judge of the Superior Court, the first such appointment made in Pottawatomie County. In 1931, the General Assembly of the Presbyterian Church made him a member of their permanent judicial commission, the supreme judicial body of the fellowship in the United States.

They had four children, Kenneth, George Jr., Jack, and Ruth. Kenneth continued his father's law practice in Shawnee, George Jr. practiced law in Las Vegas, Nevada, and Ruth was a professor at UCLA.

Jack H. Abernathy married Mary Ann Staig of El Reno and continued the tradition of active participation begun by his parents. Jack served as production superintendent of Sunray Oil Company, president and chairman of Big Chief Drilling Company, president of Seneca Oil Company, vice chairman of the board of Entex, Inc., chairman and founder of Post Oak Oil Company, and was chairman of Southwestern Bank and Trust Company. He also was chairman of the National Petroleum Council, Mid-Continent Oil and Gas Association, Oklahoma State Registration for Professional Engineers, and a director of the American Petroleum Institute, International Association of Drilling Contractors, Benham Engineering Group, and Hinderliter Industries, and was a member of All-American Wildcatters. He was named to the Oklahoma Hall of Fame in 1971 and was awarded the Oklahoma Petroleum Council's "Oil Man of the Year" in 1979. He helped pioneer deep drilling and geothermal technologies. He was also active in oil and gas drilling in Bolivia, Australia, California, and Mississippi. For his role in the development of the Oklahoma City Oil Field, Jack Abernathy is memorialized by a park located east of the State Capitol.

Jack and Mary Ann had two children, Jack Jr. and Carri, and two grandchildren, Robert Stuart Abernathy, and Kelsey Ann Abernathy.

The Foreman Family

✧

Left: Major John A. Foreman. Major Foreman died in July 14, 1899 and is buried in El Reno Cemetery.

Right: Charles Stuart Staig and his wife, Gertrude Lee Foreman Staig.

Major John A. Foreman is considered the founding father of El Reno, Oklahoma. He acquired 160 acres of land in the run, filed his homestead, and then left for four days. When he returned, the Oklahoma Homestead and Town Company had jumped his claim. After much litigation he came to an agreement with the company and the town was officially chartered May 22, 1889. A heritage mural, located at the corner of Bickford and Woodson Streets in El Reno, portrays the history of the town, Canadian County, and western Oklahoma. This historic landmark represents many of the great events in the area including the painting of a man sitting near a sign that reads "U.S. Government Land Claim: Foreman, John and Mary."

John A. Foreman was born in New York in 1824. His father was English and his mother was Scottish. For a time he was a sailor on the Great Lakes. Around 1857, he became a farmer in Ottawa, Kansas. In 1861, Foreman joined the service as a Captain in the Kansas Infantry Volunteers and his activities during the Civil War are narrated in more than a score of documents in "The War of the Rebellion: A Compilation of the Official Records of the Union and Confederate Armies." He was wounded several times. He became a major in the Third Regiment of Indian Home Guards and was mustered out May 31, 1865.

Foreman became one of the early citizens of Muskogee, Oklahoma and had a fine reputation. He was the first president of the Indian International Fair Association. Foreman was permitted by the Creek Nation to operate a mill on the east side of town. He had the good of the country at heart, for he felt that it would reduce the price of bread. He erected a windmill and a steam engine for power. Later he added a cotton gin to the gristmill, the first cotton gin in that part of Indian Territory. The brand name of his flour was "Sunflower."

In 1892 in the present vicinity of El Reno, Foreman located cattle trails suitable to the interests of the Frisco Railroad. He temporarily moved to Wichita Falls, Texas, raised cattle and worked for the Rock Island Railway. He assisted the company in running a line from Kansas to El Reno.

Foreman had two families. His first wife was Amanda Oakley and they had two children, Mary Francis and Charles. Amanda died in 1869 and in 1885 John married Mary E. Randolph. They adopted a daughter, Gertrude Lee Foreman. They made their home at 100 North Macomb and continued to live there the rest of their lives. Gertrude Lee married Charles Stuart Staig, dispatcher for the Rock Island Railroad. They lived on Macomb just two doors north of Mary Foreman. Charles and Gertrude had five children; Mary Ann, Ellen Mae, Charles Stuart, Milton Stuart and Mertie Ann. Mary Ann remained in Oklahoma and married Jack H. Abernathy of Shawnee. They had two children, Jack, Jr. and Carri.

Luckinbill Inc.

Luckinbill Inc. began in Enid, Oklahoma as a plumbing and heating company in 1939 and was founded by Orville William Luckinbill. During Word War II, Orville was a controls technician at Champlin Refinery in Enid while still working on floor furnaces after hours. After the war, he returned to the business on a full-time basis. Since that time Luckinbill Inc. has become a statewide organization with the following specialties: plumbing, sheetmetal, air conditioning and refrigeration installation and service, water and sewer utility installation, digital controls, industrial painting, fire protection, and ASME welding. The company has offices in Enid, Oklahoma City, and Lawton and provides services in Woodward, Altus, and Tulsa, and has over 160 employees.

The Luckenbill family (original spelling) emigrated from southern Germany on the ship *Thistle* into Philadelphia on August 29, 1730. John Luckenbill moved west to Union County, Ohio in the 1800s where he died in 1855 at the age of sixty-seven. John's son, Peter, and his family moved with his mother, Margaret Kroninger Luckinbill, and his family to Guthrie Center, Iowa by 1856. Albert Luckinbill was born on May 16, 1856 in Johnson County, Iowa, the twelfth child of Peter and Mary Ann Dixon.

Albert Luckinbill and Catherine Ann "Kitty" Timmons, born in Indiana in July 1863, were married on September 14, 1885. They moved to Seward, Logan County, Oklahoma, eight miles south of Guthrie to escape the bitter Iowa winters. They arrived in Oklahoma City by train on March 20, 1892 and lived in a dugout south and east of the present Guthrie Liberty Lake, and eventually bought land and built a home in 1893.

Albert and Kitty had seven children. They were Frank, who married Ethel Maud Taylor; Hugh, who married Eva Husten; Edna Mildred, who married Allen J. Kellogg; Vance, who married Lucy Hawkins; Orville, who married Mary Schiehing; Ethel, who married Ralph Oran Oliver; and Ray, who died as an infant.

Orville, the second son of Hugh and Eva Luckinbill, was married to LaBeth Grant on November 7, 1937 in Enid. LaBeth was the daughter of Dennie Grant and Rosa Mae Richardson. Rosa Mae's grandfather, William Stenson Martin, was a medical doctor in the Chickasaw Indian Territory from the early 1880s until his death in 1890 near present-day Thackerville, Oklahoma. Orville and LaBeth had three children, Robert Frank, who died in infancy, Dennis Lee, and Anna Beth. Anna Beth married Vinson C. Smith and lives in Houston, Texas and has two children, Julianne Elizabeth Cantwell and Grant Edmund Smith.

Orville was chairman of the first Oklahoma Plumbing and Licensing Board in 1954, and president of the Oklahoma Association of Plumbing and Heating Contractors, as well as a board member of the national association. Orville and LaBeth were charter members of Emmanuel Baptist Church in 1961. Orville served as chairman of Enid Bass Hospital, the Oklahoma Baptist Rural Health Board, the Northwest Oklahoma Blood Institute, and the Enid YMCA. He was very active in the International Gideon Organization until his death on January 8, 1999.

LaBeth was a corporate officer in Luckinbill Inc. until 1990 when Anna Sue Luckinbill filled her position. LaBeth continued to work until a few months before her death on June 22, 1996. She handed her work over to her granddaughter, Susan Lee Luckinbill Miller.

Dennis Luckinbill joined the organization in 1972 after obtaining his B.S. and M.S. in mechanical engineering from Oklahoma State University and his Ph.D. in mechanical engineering from the University of Houston in 1968. He was an assistant professor of mechanical engineering at Tennessee Technological University for four years. Dennis served as chairman of the first Oklahoma Mechanical Licensing Board in 1987. He has served for over ten years on hospital boards including Enid Bass Hospital, Baptist Healthcare of Oklahoma, and as treasurer of the Integris Corporate Board. He is a registered professional engineer in Oklahoma and serves on the board of the Oklahoma Municipal Contractors Association, is a member of ASHRAE, and is a Gideon. He and his wife Anna Sue were married on May 30, 1964 and are active members of Emmanuel Baptist Church in Enid. They have four children—Deanna Lyn Gibson, Susan Lee Miller, Thad Robert Luckinbill, and Trent William Luckinbill.

✧

Orville & LaBeth Luckinbill, 1994.

Jesse Orien Hartsell & Family

Jesse Orien Hartsell was the first and only member of his immediate family to serve in the military since the Civil War, and his service was a decided contrast to theirs.

His maternal grandfather, Dr. John Edward Herndon, great-grandfather Reverend William James Herndon, and his paternal grandfather, Mathue Dennis Hartsell, natives of Missouri, Virginia, and Alabama, respectively, all served in the Confederacy. John Herndon served as a medic throughout the war and was a POW for a short time. William Herndon left the service after the Confederacy lost the Battle of Pea Ridge, went home, and freed his slaves. Mathue Hartsell went home early in the war to tend his crops and never returned.

So, what was the contrast between his ancestors' service and Jesse Hartsell's? Among several military honors including the Distinguished Flying Cross, Master Sergeant Hartsell began twenty-six years of honorable service to the military in 1940.

Hartsell was born to Aubrey and Nannie Hartsell in Sulphur, Oklahoma on August 27, 1921, graduated from Sulphur High School in 1940 and joined the Murray County National Guard. The group moved to Fort Sill near Lawton, Oklahoma then went to Abilene, Texas, where he transferred into the Air Force. Stationed in England during World War II, he flew seventy-two missions in a B-26 over Europe. One of his group's planes, affectionately known as "Flack Bait," was recently placed in the Smithsonian.

Hartsell married Sue Futch, a nurse, and accepted a teaching position at Shepherd Air Force Base, Wichita Falls, Texas. He returned to Europe with his wife and daughter, Jackie, during the Berlin Airlift. The conflicts in Korea and Vietnam sent Hartsell to Okinawa, Morocco, and Turkey.

Hartsell took advantage of the USAFI Program to attend college and, during his last year of military service, enrolled in the "Bootstrap Program" at the University of Nebraska and received a BS degree in history and political science. Following his retirement from the service, Hartsell settled with his family in Irving, Texas and worked as an electronics engineer, logistician, and technical writer. The last two years of Hartsell's life were spent in active service to his community and fellow man. Besides caring for his invalid wife, Hartsell taught a class in computers at the Senior Citizen's Center.

Jesse O. Hartsell died on November 13, 1998. Possessing a great love for reading, writing, poetry, and playing the French harp. He was also nearing completion of a documentary about his squadron, the 449th, during World War II in England. The soon-to-be-published book recalls the memory of his fellow servicemen and their wartime experiences.

Hartsell left a historic legacy of service to his family. His children include Jackie Briggs, husband Jay, and four children of Woodbridge, Virginia. JoAnne Young, husband Scott, and three children of Lincoln, Nebraska. Jesse's sister, Opal Hartsell Brown, remains active as a teacher, writer, and author near Sulphur, Oklahoma.

Top: Jesse Orien Hartsell, ready for a flight mission, in England, 1943.

Below: Jesse Hartsell and wife, Sue, enjoy a beautiful day at George Portman Park in Sulphur, Oklahoma.

THE PAULS OF PAULS VALLEY

The beauty of Pauls Valley and the adventurous spirit of its founder, Smith W. Paul, were detailed in a Christmas edition of *The Valley News* on December 22, 1898. The text relates how to this vale of untamed loveliness there came, in the year 1837, a man of Scotch birth, accompanied by his Chickasaw Indian wife Ela-Teecha. He saw the wonderful wealth of the soil—saw, and with characteristic Scottish thrift set to work. He built his cabin near the place where there is today a thriving little city, known as Pauls Valley in honor of this pioneer—Smith W. Paul. The city which immortalizes his name grew from a trading post to a village of three or four hundred inhabitants. On the gentle slope which leads to the hill where the Paul mansion still stands, a rugged landmark of the past, there is a simple monument of stone bearing the name of a pioneer, and beneath the name this inscription: "He was the First to Make This Valley Yield of Its Wealth."

The Santa Fe Railroad Station House, in Pauls Valley, was acquired to become a museum and now houses artifacts regarding the history of the community.

PHOTO COURTESY OF PETER JORDAN PHOTOGRAPHY, INC.

For nearly two centuries after the birth of Smith W. Paul in 1809, the Paul legacy continues as a reminder of this great Oklahoman's pioneering spirit. Paul's son, Sam Paul, became a prominent leader in the Senate of the Chickasaw Nation. William H. Paul, his grandson, remained a farmer and rancher in Pauls Valley throughout his life. Great-grandson, Homer Paul, held three terms in the state House of Representatives and four terms in the Senate, serving as president pro tem of the Senate in Oklahoma. Homer's wife, Helen Lafferty, a native of Claremore, resides in Oklahoma City and was honored as Oklahoma's Mother of the Year in the late 1970s. Haskell Paul, Homer's brother, was a well-respected lawyer and judge throughout his entire life in Pauls Valley. Homer and Haskell's sisters, Kaliteyo Paul Willingham and Winona Paul Gunning, reside in Oklahoma City. Haskell's widow, Carrie O'Hara Paul, resides in Paul Valley.

Homer's sons, who are Smith Paul's great-great grandsons, William G. and Homer, are both graduates of the University of Oklahoma College of Law and have continued in the family's endeavors to positively affect the State of Oklahoma.

William G. Paul has served as president of the Oklahoma Bar Association and now serves as president of the American Bar Association, the world's largest professional association. He has served as senior partner and chairman of the Executive Committee of Crowe and Dunlevy, was senior vice president and general counsel of Phillips Petroleum Company of Bartlesville from 1985 to 1996, after which he returned to Crowe and Dunlevy. William is married to Barbara Brite Paul, formerly of Norman. Their children include George Lynn Paul, Alison Paul Miller, Elaine Paul Seidel, and William Stephen Paul.

Homer Paul, Jr. is the chairman, president and chief executive officer of Citizens Security Bank and Trust Company in Bixby and served as president of the Oklahoma Bankers Association in 1980. He has served on the boards of the Oklahoma Bankers Association and the Oklahoma Finance Authorities and is active in the American Bankers Association. Citizens Security Bank has branches in Glenpool, Tulsa, and Bixby. Homer's wife, Ramona Ware Paul, is the assistant state superintendent of the Department of Education. Their children include Charles William Paul, Lela Paul Brown, twins Jennifer Jean Paul and Jamie Paul Simpson, twins Steven and Stuart Emmons, and Jerry Emmons.

At this writing, representing a seventh generation of Oklahoma Pauls are William's grandchildren Jack, Ingrid, Braden and Madelaine, and Homer's grandchildren Piper, Heidi, Emery, Hunter, and Casey.

Jimmie Baker

From T-Town to Tinseltown is an appropriate title for an upcoming biography of famed Oklahoma native television producer Jimmie Baker. However, Baker's storybook life had major stops at Muskogee, Oklahoma City, and Stillwater before he landed a job in a radio network mail room in Hollywood a half-century ago.

James Hollan Baker was born in Muskogee on March 16, 1920. However, the family moved to Tulsa when Baker was two years old. His mother paid fifty cents an hour twice weekly for after-school tap dancing lessons at Tulsa's Sidney Lanier Elementary School. Young Jimmie was a natural and soon teamed with two talented sisters, the act billed as "Little Jimmie Baker and the Wade twins."

While a student at Tulsa's Central High School, where one of his best friends was actor Tony Randall, Baker danced his way to an appearance on the Major Edward Bowes amateur hour on CBS Radio. Listeners had to have an imagination as they listened to Baker tap-dancing on the national radio show. Baker and a young crooner, Frank Sinatra, were winners and signed on with Bowe's summer road company for $25 per week.

During college days at Oklahoma A&M in Stillwater, Baker thrilled football fans as the drum major of the Cowboys marching band. In 1947, stepping so high that the top of his rabbit fur hat touched the ground, Baker tap danced during half-time shows on a mammoth bass drum that had been rigged with plywood. While in Stillwater, Baker founded a dance band called The Collegians, one of the most successful college big bands in the nation. Big Band music was popular and Baker's group played to audiences from coast to coast with top billing at Oklahoma City's largest hotel for several months.

Baker left Oklahoma for Hollywood in 1947. He began his radio career in the ABC mailroom. However, ABC executives soon saw talent potential in the friendly and fast-moving lad from Oklahoma. Within months Baker became an assistant radio producer. But when ABC moved into television in 1950, he became one of the new entertainment medium's pioneer producers.

Baker spent fifty years with Disney/ABC, producing thousands of television shows. He produced the original pilot for "Rowan & Martin's Laugh-In," and won five Emmy Awards and twelve Emmy nominations. He also won eleven Silver Angel and one Gold Angel Award for his television productions. The list of stars Baker has worked with in his career as a director and producer reads like a Hollywood Who's Who. In music, Baker worked alongside Johnny Mercer, Ella Fitzgerald, Sammy Davis, Jr., Frank Sinatra, and Harry James. From the film world, Baker has presented the talents of Marilyn Monroe, Charlton Heston, Bob Hope, Milton Berle, George Burns, James Stewart, Betty Grable, Lana Turner, and hundreds more.

A leader of charitable activities in Hollywood, Baker has for a quarter-century brought film and television stars for annual shows that have raised millions of dollars for children's clinics and schools. He also has produced programs to benefit Oklahoma State University, was a major contributor to OSU's centennial activities, and has produced the annual telecast of the Oklahoma Hall of Fame induction for many years.

Baker has never been far from his Oklahoma roots. In 1989, he was named to the Oklahoma State University Alumni Hall of Fame and was selected two years later for the group's highest award, the Henry G. Bennett Award. In 1993, he was elected to the Oklahoma Hall of Fame. In 1999, he regularly visited the Stillwater campus of his alma mater, where he was inducted into the OSU School of Education Hall of Fame, and was an active member of the Oklahoma Film Commission. In Hollywood, Baker continued with a production company, Jamie Productions, jointly owned with his son, James Carlton Baker.

✧

Top: Jimmie Baker (left) visits with bandleader Harry James during intermission of a 1947 dance at Gallagher Hall on the Stillwater campus of Oklahoma A&M.

Below: Jimmie fell in love with Sue Carlton, left, while his band played a yearlong engagement in the Silver Glade Room of the Skirvin Tower Hotel in Oklahoma City. They were married in 1948. In Hollywood, Sue became an established actress with many roles in movies, television dramas and television commercials.

The Sautbine-Brazelton Family

For more than a century the Sautbine-Brazelton family has been intertwined with the growth and development of the Sooner State. The matriarch of the Sautbine family was Nora B. (Grafton) Sautbine (1869-1957) who was born in Coalton, Ohio. Married to Laurentine David Sautbine, she had four children. The eldest, Charles David Sautbine (1888-1957) was born while the family lived near Bremer, Nebraska. The Sautbine family migrated to Iowa where Willis Grafton Sautbine (1890-1970) was born in Agency. Their third child, Lynden Richard (1899-1970) was born in Kremlin, Oklahoma Territory. Lela Dorothy (1902-1991) was born in Ottumwa, Iowa.

Charles became a sales executive with the Fred Jones Ford-Lincoln Motor Company in Oklahoma City and married Marjorie Whitlock. Willis became a major grain trader, but liquidated his financial holdings just prior to the crisis of 1929 and the Great Depression. Afterward, he reinvested in real estate, principally stripmalls in the Oklahoma City area. In the early 1950s, he married Gloria Gill. Lynden served in World War I and was once erroneously reported to have been killed in action. The two families were joined when Lela Sautbine married Arthur Davis Brazelton (1891-1971) of Houston, Texas, better known as Braz.

One of seven children, Braz was born in Belvadere, Tennessee, where the family had played a prominent role in that state's history as landholders and as members of both the state militia and the Tennessee legislature. When the family relocated to Houston, the Brazeltons became active in real estate and financial investments.

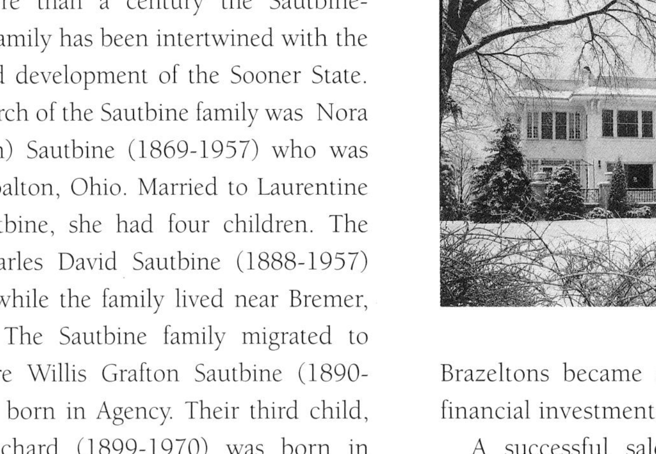

Top: The family home at 3615 North McKinley, Oklahoma City. Governor Robertson originally built the home. The Norwegian blue spruce to the left was a gift of the King of Norway.

Below: Beacon Club, First National Bank Building, Oklahoma City, about 1945. Left to right: Arthur D. (Braz) Brazelton; Mrs. C. D. (Marjorie) Sautbine; Lynden R. Sautbine; Willis G. Sautbine; Nora Belle Sautbine; Mrs. A. D. (Lela) Brazelton; W. Robert Brazelton; and Charles D. Sautbine.

A successful salesman for Cain's Coffee Company, Braz often played golf with another local celebrity—Howard Hughes. In 1924, Braz moved to Oklahoma City and he and Lela first occupied the large home, originally built by Oklahoma Governor J. B. A. Robertson, at 3615 North McKinley with Willis and Nora B. Sautbine. Later they moved to a home at 1801 Dorchester Drive in Nichols Hills.

Braz became involved in real estate and in wholesale dry cleaning and laundry and established several outlets in the shopping centers developed by Willis Sautbine. After the sale of the business, he worked for the State of Oklahoma overseeing the sale of surplus state property before retiring.

Lela Brazelton became a prominent figure in Oklahoma City, giving much of her time to charitable projects such as the McDowell Club, the Oklahoma City Art Center, and the Oklahoma City Symphony. Twice she was the leading fundraiser for the Oklahoma City Art Center. Braz was one of the original members of the Oklahoma City Golf and Country Club and a member of the Board of Directors of Crown Heights Methodist Church.

They had one son, W. Robert Brazelton, born in Oklahoma City in 1933. He received his Ph.D. in economics and taught at the University of Missouri-Kansas City. He has dealt successfully in the financial markets, especially in relation to the gold binge and the failure of the Soviet wheat harvests, which he correctly anticipated. He is the author of more than 40 articles and three major books. Upon retirement, he divides his time between Kansas City and Oklahoma City, where he works with academic and cultural institutions; and sets up personal trusts to benefit those organizations.

Lew Wentz

✧

Though he never married, Lew Wentz enjoyed the company of his grandnephews, Burke Healey and Baren Healey, pictured here with Lew, circa 1941.

Louis Haines Wentz, a legendary figure in Oklahoma, was one of its greatest oil men. He was a humble man who achieved great distinction in business, philanthropy, and politics. His interest in children led him to many avenues of stewardship. Also, he had a love of baseball, which he played and then coached for a number of years before moving to Oklahoma.

Wentz was born in Iowa in 1872 and made his way to Oklahoma from Pennsylvania in 1911. John G. McCaskey, a Pittsburgh businessman who made his fortune in the U.S. sauerkraut market, asked young Wentz to become his associate in a new oil company and protect his interests in several oil leases in Ponca City, Oklahoma. Wentz had only planned for a six-month stay in the state, but quickly fell in love with the area and made his permanent residence at The Arcade Hotel, a local boarding house and hotel at First and Grand in Ponca City. This remained his home until his death.

Wentz took great pride in his responsibility for the oil leases under his care and consistently found great success upon every lease he held. This personal philosophy of sound, ethical business in which Lew felt his handshake was as good, if not better, than any written contract was the product of his mother and father's influence. Lew would fondly remember his father's blacksmith shop in Iowa and the great care he took in the business. His staunch Methodist mother played a vital role as she taught her young son the virtues of character and discipline. His mother would be remembered every Mother's Day for many years in Ponca City as Lew bought a bouquet of flowers for the oldest mother attending each church in town.

Another Wentz custom was found in buying hundreds of gifts to be delivered at Christmas for less-fortunate children. In the beginning, he had to borrow money from the bank to pay for these gifts. Known only as "Daddy Longlegs," he continued this custom for nearly thirty years.

Wentz built a swimming pool and camp ground in Ponca City that is still in use today. He was instrumental in helping to establish and fund the Crippled Children's Society of Oklahoma that provided money for a crippled children's hospital, the forerunner of the Oklahoma Children's Memorial Hospital.

In 1927, Lew Wentz was ranked among the seven wealthiest men in the nation. Yet, never one to promote himself in any way, he would quietly perform these and many other gracious acts without publicity or praise. Wentz found that the word charity often rang hollow; he just wanted to "be of help." He often said, "I never consider what I have done for Oklahoma. I think only of what Oklahoma has done for me."

Elected National Committeeman to the Republican Party in 1940, Wentz was considered the "cornerstone" of the Party in Oklahoma and remained its undisputed leader until his death in 1949. Upon his death, Wentz continued his amazing legacy to the people of Oklahoma and his love for children. He left the majority of his estate to two of our universities, Oklahoma State University and University of Oklahoma, and the Masonic Lodge.

Yet, Wentz never needed the recognition that such great acts of kindness and charity often bring people. The family continues to learn of his many private contributions to his fellowman. He once said, "When a man tells you how important he is, the only person he is important to is himself." That is truly the legacy of one of Oklahoma's greatest citizens, Lew Wentz.

Roscoe Ernest (Rex) Walters, Sr. & Family

The next time you take a child by the hand and walk through a beautiful park filled with merry-go-rounds, slides, swings, and a number of other favorite playground equipment, you might want to remember the story of Rex Walters.

Rex and his wife Ella Brooks had met and married in El Reno in 1917. For the next twenty years Rex was a successful plant manager of E. A. Liebman Ice Company located in the Capitol Hill area and at 10th and May in Oklahoma City. When he was diagnosed with gallstones, the illness quickly became debilitating and recovery from the severe attacks often forced Rex to miss work and, eventually, he was fired. Little did anyone know that this would be the beginning of a whole new life for Rex, his family, and children everywhere.

Rex loved his family, especially the grandchildren. One evening, his oldest grandson, Mike, had come to visit. As they played, Rex realized that his new grandson needed a swing. When he finished his first swing made of thin planks of wood, and with the smile of his grandchild as the stamp of approval, Rex made a few more and was soon selling them from the front porch of his home. With this success and a patent he had been perfecting on an air purifier, he decided to open Rex Engineering & Sales Company on 10th Street near May Avenue in Oklahoma City in January of 1946. Eventually abandoning the air purifier invention and dealing entirely in playground equipment, the company name was changed to Rex Playground Equipment.

Rex's sons had grown up with a great love for engineering. Rex, Jr. received his general engineering degree and Jack received his degree in chemical engineering from the University of Oklahoma. Both set off for tours of duty in the Navy with Rex, Jr. returning to Oklahoma to work with his father. Jack worked in oil patches from Wyoming to Louisiana for over forty years and became a division drilling and production manager for Sohio Petroleum Company. Rex, Jr. became the director of the playground equipment company when his father died in 1967. In 1982, the Company stopped manufacturing their own equipment and began distributing for other companies that manufacture playground equipment.

Today, Rex, Jr.'s son, John, is the president of Rex Playground Equipment Company and recently added a store in Arkansas. These toys can be found in parks and backyards everywhere. Rex, Jr. and his wife, Maribeth, and Jack and his wife, Jean, live in Oklahoma City and enjoy reminiscing together among old photos and family memories—and still enjoy the smiles of helping a grandchild into one of those swings.

✧

Top: Rex and Ella Walters.

Below: Rex Engineering & Sales Company as it stood on Northwest 10th Street in Oklahoma City, circa 1950.

THE CHAPMAN-McFARLIN FAMILY

Perhaps the greatest legacy of Oklahoma's petroleum pioneers were their contributions to the quality of life in the Sooner state. Two leading philanthropists were Robert M. McFarlin and James A. Chapman, of the McMan Oil Company.

Born near Ovilla, Ellis County, Texas, on July 27, 1866, Robert M. McFarlin married Ida Mae Barnard in 1885. They had two daughters—Leta Mae and Pauline Caroline. A son, Robert Boger McFarlin, died as an infant. McFarlin moved to Norman, Oklahoma, in 1892, where he operated a dry goods store. After the Norman store failed in the depression of 1893, he began a ranching operation in the Creek Nation in what is now Hughes County, and settled in Holdenville, Indian Territory.

James A. Chapman was born in Ellis County, Texas, on April 3, 1881. His mother was Robert McFarlin's sister. In 1901, Chapman joined his uncle in Holdenville, and in January of 1908 he married Leta Mae McFarlin.

In 1903, McFarlin mortgaged his home in Holdenville and purchased a forty-acre tract of land in the Glenn Pool Oil Field. McFarlin, Chapman, Phillip A. Chapman (James' father), and H. B. Gooch formed the Holdenville Oil and Gas Company, which operated in the fledgling Oklahoma oil business.

In 1912, McFarlin joined the Chapmans and E. P. Harwell to form the McMan Oil Company, which quickly became the largest producer in the Mid-Continent Oil Region and the largest independent oil company in the United States involved solely in the production of oil. The McMan was the predominant independent in the Cushing and Healdton, Oklahoma fields and the Augusta, Kansas field. However, in 1916, McFarlin and Chapman decided to sell the McMan to Magnolia Petroleum Company of Dallas, for the princely sum of $38.7 million in cash and stock.

Afterwards McFarlin and Chapman organized the McMan Oil and Gas Company, which quickly became a major presence in the Yates field of the Permian Basin in Texas. The McMan Oil and Gas Company was sold to Standard Oil Company of Indiana for $20 million in 1930 to form the Stanoline Production Company. McFarlin and Chapman were also founding directors of Tulsa's Exchange National Bank. Chapman, with Harry Sinclair, recapitalized the Exchange Bank after the bank holiday of 1933 as the National Bank of Tulsa; today's Bank of Oklahoma, N.A. Chapman was also a partner in the famed Chapman-Barnard Ranch with Horace Barnard. It eventually controlled 100,000 acres of grazing land in Osage County, Oklahoma. McFarlin and Chapman owned six additional ranches in Oklahoma and New Mexico.

Following the sale of the first McMan Company, the McFarlins began the support of their community: funding a Methodist Church in Norman, an auditorium at Southern Methodist University and the McFarlin Library at the University of Tulsa.

James A. and Leta Chapman had a different concept of philanthropy and created their first charitable trust in 1949 for the benefit of Trinity University of San Antonio, Texas; John Brown University in Siloam Springs, Arkansas; Oklahoma Medical Research Foundation in Oklahoma City; and the University of Tulsa, St. John Medical Center Foundation, Hillcrest Medical Center Foundation and the Tulsa Area United Way, all in Tulsa.

From 1949 to 1980, the Chapmans, along with Leta's sister, Pauline McFarlin Walter, and a brother-in-law, Andrew G. Cowles, established a total of twelve trusts whose assets now total over $1.5 billion. Beyond the original seven, the beneficiaries also include Children's Medical Center, Holland Hall School, Tulsa Psychiatric Foundation, and St. Simeon's Episcopal Home, all in Tulsa; the Protestant Episcopal Church Foundation of the Diocese of Oklahoma in Oklahoma City; Presbyterian Children's Services of (Waxahachie) Texas; Southern Methodist University of Dallas; and Southwest Foundation for Biomedical Research and St. Mary's School, of San Antonio.

The Chapman-McFarlin family vision of philanthropy provided financial stability for these beneficiaries. The on-going support of the trusts provides a leadership edge. Now one of the largest grant-making organizations in the United States, the Chapman-Walter-Cowles trusts continue to create excellence in the southwest region where the family has its roots.

A rare photograph of Leta McFarlin Chapman and James A. Chapman, who, along with her sister, Pauline McFarlin and a brother-in-law, Andrew G Cowles, established a total of 12 trusts whose assets now total over $1.5 billion.

THE BERRY AND SEWELL FAMILIES

"Three Families United."

The opening of the Cherokee Strip in 1893 ushered many a dreamer into Oklahoma Territory. One of those visionary businessmen was Dan C. Bass, who made the Run with his wife, Sophia. John Russell Parker (J. R. P.) Sewell of Georgia, arrived in the Oklahoma Panhandle in 1899. Chandler livestock trader George M. Berry and his wife, Judith, had already arrived from Tennessee in the early 1890s with six children. His youngest son, Guy L. Berry, Sr., when married, would unite all three businesses for a century.

Guy L. Berry, Sr. graduated from Chandler High School and came to Sapulpa in 1915 as a bookkeeper at Oklahoma Natural Gas and after World War I, at American National Bank and Trust Company (ANB). His older brother, James D. Berry, began at ANB in 1907 remaining on the Board until his death in 1924. Guy, Sr. became cashier in 1925, vice-president in 1929, and president in 1939. He married Merle Knipe in 1922 and had two children, Guy, Jr. and Barbara. Guy, Jr. graduated from the University of Oklahoma and joined ANB in 1946; he became ANB president in 1956, and chairman in 1967 after his father's death. In 1946, Guy, Jr. married Dan Bass' granddaughter, Barbara Bass of Enid. Guy, Jr.'s sister, also named Barbara, married J. R. P. Sewell's grandson, Frank Asa Sewell, Jr. in 1947. Great grandsons of George Berry and D. C. Bass operate ANB.

In 1893, Dan Bass founded D. C. Bass and Sons Construction Company, which is now the oldest general contractor in the states of Oklahoma, Kansas, Texas, Colorado, and New Mexico. Dan's son, H. B., married Roberta Herring. His daughter, Geraldine, married Bill P. Jennings. In 1925, H. B. Bass assumed control of the company. In 1960, H. B. Bass and Bass Construction were inducted into the National Builders Hall of Fame at Pepperdine University. Some of the company's significant contributions include Great Lakes Pipeline, dormitories at the University of Missouri, several hospitals, and many "slipformed" grain elevators. The great grandson of George Berry and D. C. Bass owns the company today.

In 1899, J. R. P. Sewell started banks in Texhoma, Calvin, Allen, and Goodwell, Oklahoma; and Pampa and Alanreed, Texas. He would later found what is now Panhandle State University. His son, Frank Asa Sewell, Sr., assumed control upon his father's death in 1909. In February of 1936, Frank, Sr. and his wife, Leila Yates Sewell, moved to Clinton and bought First National Bank and Trust Company in Clinton (FNB). In the late 1940s and mid-1950s, he became president and then chairman of Liberty Bank in Oklahoma City. His daughter, Patience Sewell Latting, became mayor of Oklahoma City. His son, F. A. (Luke) Sewell, Jr. joined FNB in 1947 and became president in 1958. Presently, George Berry's and J. R. P. Sewell's great grandson is chairman of FNB.

The great grandchildren of pioneer businessmen George M. Berry, Dan C. Bass, and John Russell Parker Sewell continue to represent the family's business legacy by "growing" their respective communities through their Oklahoma companies.

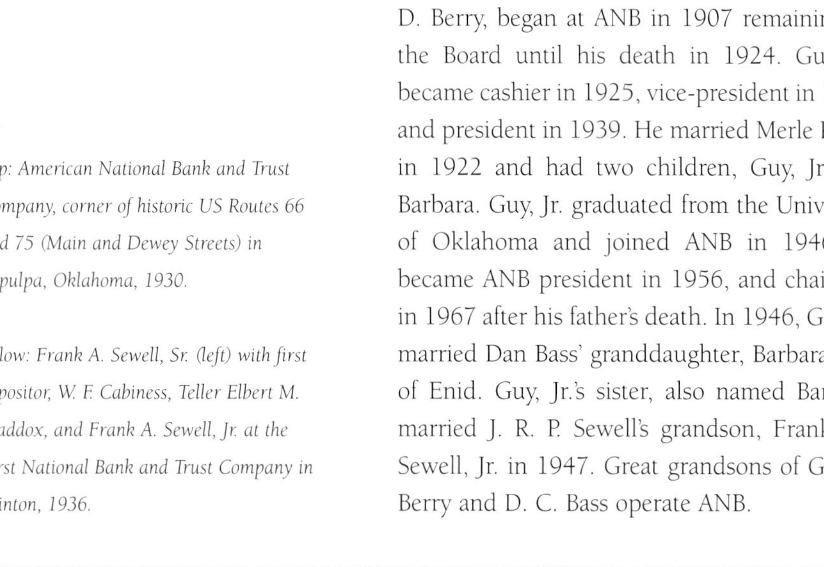

Top: American National Bank and Trust Company, corner of historic US Routes 66 and 75 (Main and Dewey Streets) in Sapulpa, Oklahoma, 1930.

Below: Frank A. Sewell, Sr. (left) with first depositor, W. F. Cabiness, Teller Elbert M. Maddox, and Frank A. Sewell, Jr. at the First National Bank and Trust Company in Clinton, 1936.

Ella Classen

Two decades before women in America won the right to vote, sprightly Ella Classen of Oklahoma City launched business ventures previously reserved for males.

Ella Lamb was born in Vermilion County, Illinois, in 1869. Her father dreamed of moving westward to take advantage of free government land in newly opened Oklahoma Territory. The Lambs settled near Edmond in Oklahoma County shortly after the Run of 1889. Ella's father died when she was twenty-one, leaving her to care for her mother, three younger brothers, and a sister, on the original Oklahoma homestead.

To supplement the meager income derived from farming, Ella took a job in the federal government's land office. There she met Anton Classen, an Illinois-born lawyer, who had built a fortune in land holdings during the first decade of Oklahoma Territory. By the time they were married in 1903, Ella had accumulated several pieces of property and had overseen the education of her younger siblings.

Together Ella and Anton added to their already substantial real estate holdings. She and her husband were original owners of the Oklahoma Railway Company that operated Oklahoma City's streetcar system. In 1908, the Classens built a power plant at Belle Isle Lake to generate electricity to run its streetcars. Up to four million people traveled on thirty-eight miles of "interurban" tracks with forty-eight cars and 150 employees. Belle Isle Lake was at the end of a stately north-south street appropriately named Classen Avenue. Later the school board in Oklahoma City honored the Classens by naming a new high school, Classen High School, for the pioneer developers.

In 1910, Ella developed a grassy hill near the Belle Isle Lake into a beautifully landscaped cemetery. Since Oklahoma law did not allow an individual to own a cemetery, Ella created, for 999 years, a state-sanctioned property trust called the Rose Hill Burial Park.

In 1917, Ella sold management rights of the cemetery to John J. Harden, a successful cemetery developer. Ella, ever the astute businesswoman, was specific in her instructions to Harden. The contract required Harden to "provide a suitable chapel or rest-house in and upon said grounds and an entrance gate...the same shall be suitable as a decent, modern, high grade, properly decorated, and first class burial park." Because of Ella's stringent requirements of Harden, Rose Hill became Oklahoma City's most popular cemetery.

Anton Classen died in 1922, leaving Ella to manage the vast real estate holdings the couple had acquired. Ella was equal to the task. She used profits from residential properties to finance investment in Oklahoma's infant oil and gas industry. She enjoyed the negotiations surrounding oil leases. Ella wrote her sister, Vinnie Leavitt, "I was tipped off by a friend who is a lease scout. They have been after me hot and heavy. At least twelve or fifteen have phoned me in the last weeks wanting to talk to me about leasing."

An astute negotiator, Ella began pooling lands for oil and gas leases in 1934, twenty-one years before Oklahoma enacted a pooling statute.

In her later years, Ella called upon her nephew, John Anton Leavitt, to manage the Classen holdings. Leavitt was educated at the University of Oklahoma and Columbia University in New York. He was a banking and finance professor and an economist with the Federal Reserve Bank.

Ella Classen died November 4, 1955, and was laid to rest at Rose Hill, the cemetery she had planned a half-century before.

Above: Ella Classen and her niece, Catherine, in one of Oklahoma City's first electric cars in 1911.

Below: In 1944, a citizens committee in Oklahoma City asked Ella Classen to represent Oklahoma at the launching of the U.S.S. Oklahoma City. Classen, a prohibitionist, took a bottle of Oklahoma City water with her to use in the christening of the ship. However, at the last minute, the water was switched with a bottle of champagne. Classen donated the silver service for the new ship. Admiring the gift are navy officials and Congressman Mike Monroney (right).

PHOTOS COURTESY OF ANN LANDRITH.

Oklahoma Heritage Association Board of Directors

chairman of the board:	Lee Allan Smith, Oklahoma City
vice chairmen:	Everett E. Berry, Stillwater
	James H. Boren, Tahlequah
	Edvin C. Boynton, Durant
	Ken Fergeson, Altus
	Becky J. Frank, Tulsa
	Tom J. McDaniel, Oklahoma City
	C. D. Northcutt, Ponca City
	Harold G. Powell, Norman
corporate secretary:	Sharon J. Bell, Tulsa
treasurer:	Ann Simmons Alspaugh, Oklahoma City
emeritus chairmen:	J. M. "Jack" Graves, Tulsa
	G. Lee Stidham, Checotah
directors:	Bill Armor, Laverne
	Pat Baldwin, Tulsa
	Wanda Bass, McAlester
	Clayton I. Bennett, Oklahoma City
	G. T. Blankenship, Oklahoma City
	L. D. Brittain, Lawton
	Ed L. Calhoon, Beaver
	Mike Cantrell, Ada
	Richard Chapman, Wright City
	Carol Crawford, Frederick
	William G. Creel, Bartlesville
	Herschal H. Crow, Jr., Altus
	Frederick Drummond, Pawhuska
	Vaughndean Fuller, Tulsa
	Jean G. Gumerson, Oklahoma City
	Fred C. Harlan, Okmulgee
	Skip Healey, Davis
	Hans Helmerich, Tulsa
	Gary Huckabay, Mustang
	David V. Hume, Enid
	Glen D. Johnson, Durant
	Larry E. Lee, Tulsa
	Roxana Lorton, Tulsa
	Karen Luke, Oklahoma City
	Tom H. McCasland, Jr., Duncan
	Herman Meinders, Oklahoma City
	Vicki Miles-LaGrange, Oklahoma City
	Melvin Moran, Seminole

John W. Nichols, Oklahoma City
Mary Jane Noble, Ardmore
Louise Painter, Oklahoma City
Wanda Sanders, Oologah
L. E. "Dean" Stringer, Oklahoma City
W. R. "Dick" Stubbs, Henryetta
Ben T. Walkingstick, Jr., Chandler
Martha Griffin White, Muskogee
J. Bryan Whitworth, Bartlesville
Mollie Williford, Tulsa
Ann D. Woolley, Ada
Joe Worley, Tulsa
Waldo Zerger, Jr., Tulsa
ex-officio: George Seminoff, Oklahoma City

Oklahoma Heritage Association Publications Committee

chairman: Everett E. Berry, Stillwater
vice chairman: W. R. "Dick" Stubbs, Henryetta
ex-officio: Lee Allan Smith, Oklahoma City
committee members: Sharon Bell, Tulsa
Mrs. Everett Berry, Stillwater
James H. Boren, Tahlequah
Edwin C. Boynton, Durant
Bob Burke, Oklahoma City
Don Ferrell, Chandler
LeRoy H. Fischer, Stillwater
Fred C. Harlan, Okmulgee
John Hefner, Oklahoma City
Virginia Kidd, Poteau
Vicki Miles-LaGrange, Oklahoma City
B. Chesley Montague, Lawton
Ann Woolley, Ada
Waldo Zerger, Tulsa

Index

D

E

F

G

H

Sponsors

Contributors

Authors

Kenny A. Franks, Ph.D., a native of Okemah, Paul F. Lambert, Ph.D., of Tishomingo, and Bob Burke, J.D., from Broken Bow, are all native Oklahomans. Together they have authored more than 100 books and articles on Oklahoma history.

Contributing Writers

Eric Dabney was raised in Kremlin, Oklahoma, and is a graduate of the University of Central Oklahoma. He has worked as a research assistant and editor on numerous projects, including biographies of Dewey Bartlett, Alfred P. Murrah, Wiley Post, and Abe Lemons.

Clyda Reeves Franks is a native of Cleveland, Oklahoma, and is the fomer editor of the *Cleveland American*. She is a freelance writer who has been published nationally, is executive secretary to the CEO of The First National Bank of Pawnee, and serves as public information director for the Pawnee Historical and Cultural Museum.

Editor

An Oklahoma City native, Gini Moore Campbell is managing editor of the Oklahoma Heritage Association. She has collaborated with the authors on more than forty projects during her ten years with the Association.

Photographers

Judy L. Dawson is the owner of Visuality Studio in Oklahoma City. She is a prolific freelance and studio photographer, having done work for local and statewide publications.

As owner of David G. Fitzgerald & Associates, Inc., in Oklahoma City, David G. Fitzgerald's photographs appear in commercial advertisement for national and international clients.

Fred W. Marvel has been a photographer with the Industrial Development & Park Department and the Tourism & Recreation Department since 1966.